# DIGITAL PRINCIPLES

# DIGITAL PRINCIPLES

## Foundation of Circuit Design and Application

**SECOND EDITION**

**Arun Kumar Singh**
*BTech., MTech., PhD (Pursuing)*
Professor & Dean
Goel Institute of Technology & Management
Lucknow (UP)

**Manish Tiwari**
*BE, ME, PhD*
Assistant Professor
Department of Electronics & Communication Engineering
MNNIT, Allahabad (UP)

Publishing Globally

**NEW AGE INTERNATIONAL (P) LIMITED, PUBLISHERS**
**LONDON • NEW DELHI • NAIROBI**
Bangalore • Chennai • Cochin • Guwahati • Hyderabad • Kolkata • Lucknow • Mumbai
Visit us at **www.newagepublishers.com**

Published by New Age International (P) Ltd., Publishers
First Edition: 2008
Second Edition: 2014
**Reprint: 2018**



## GLOBAL OFFICES

- **New Delhi** **NEW AGE INTERNATIONAL (P) LIMITED, PUBLISHERS**
  7/30 A, Daryaganj, New Delhi-110002, (INDIA)
  **Tel.:** (011) 23253771, 23253472, **Telefax:** 23267437, 43551305
  **E-mail: contactus@newagepublishers.com • Visit us at www.newagepublishers.com**
- **London** **NEW AGE INTERNATIONAL (UK) LTD.**
  27 Old Gloucester Street, London, WC1N 3AX, UK
  **E-mail: info@newacademicscience.co.uk • Visit us at www.newacademicscience.co.uk**
- **Nairobi** **NEW AGE GOLDEN (EAST AFRICA) LTD.**
  Ground Floor, Westlands Arcade, Chiromo Road (Next to Naivas Supermarket)
  Westlands, Nairobi, KENYA, **Tel.:** 00-254-713848772, 00-254-725700286
  **E-mail: kenya@newagepublishers.com**

## BRANCHES

- **Bangalore** 37/10, 8th Cross (Near Hanuman Temple), Azad Nagar, Chamarajpet, Bangalore- 560 018
  **Tel.:** (080) 26756823, **Telefax:** 26756820, **E-mail: bangalore@newagepublishers.com**
- **Chennai** 26, Damodaran Street, T. Nagar, Chennai-600 017, **Tel.:** (044) 24353401, **Telefax:** 24351463
  **E-mail: chennai@newagepublishers.com**
- **Cochin** CC-39/1016, Carrier Station Road, Ernakulam South, Cochin-682 016, **Tel.:** (0484) 2377303, **Telefax:** 4051304
  **E-mail: cochin@newagepublishers.com**
- **Guwahati** Hemsen Complex, Mohd. Shah Road, Paltan Bazar, Near Starline Hotel, Guwahati-781 008,
  **Tel.:** (0361) 2513881, **Telefax:** 2543669, **E-mail: guwahati@newagepublishers.com**
- **Hyderabad** 105, 1st Floor, Madhiray Kaveri Tower, 3-2-19, Azam Jahi Road, Near Kumar Theater, Nimboliadda Kachiguda, Hyderabad-500 027, **Tel.:** (040) 24652456, **Telefax:** 24652457
  **E-mail: hyderabad@newagepublishers.com**
- **Kolkata** RDB Chambers (Formerly Lotus Cinema) 106A, 1st Floor, S N Banerjee Road, Kolkata-700 014
  **Tel.:** (033) 22273773, **Telefax:** 22275247, **E-mail: kolkata@newagepublishers.com**
- **Lucknow** 16-A, Jopling Road, Lucknow-226 001, **Tel.:** (0522) 2209578, 4045297, **Telefax:** 2204098
  **E-mail: lucknow@newagepublishers.com**
- **Mumbai** 142C, Victor House, Ground Floor, N.M. Joshi Marg, Lower Parel, Mumbai-400 013
  **Tel.:** (022) 24927869, **Telefax:** 24915415, **E-mail: mumbai@newagepublishers.com**
- **New Delhi** 22, Golden House, Daryaganj, New Delhi-110 002, **Tel.:** (011) 23262368, 23262370, **Telefax:** 43551305
  **E-mail: sales@newagepublishers.com**

**ISBN: 978-81-224-3560-3**
**C-17-04-10344**

Printed in India at Nisha Enterprises, Delhi.
Typeset at Kalyani Computers, Delhi.

**NEW AGE INTERNATIONAL (P) LIMITED, PUBLISHERS**
7/30 A, Daryaganj, New Delhi-110002
Visit us at **www.newagepublishers.com**
**(CIN: U74899DL1966PTC004618)**

*This book is dedicated to*
*Our Parents*

# PREFACE TO THE SECOND EDITION

There are several improvement has been implemented in this edition on the basis of suggestions and comments received from various readers to fulfill the course requirement on digital elements.

Chapter 1, 5, and 9 are rewritten and also some additional articles and topics are added in chapter 2.

In this second edition authors incorporated most of the suggestions as received by different readers and user of this book.

We welcome constructive suggestions and comments from the readers for further improvement of this book at singh_a_k@rediffmail.com.

**A.K. SINGH**
**MANISH TIWARI**

# PREFACE TO THE FIRST EDITION

Digital Electronic is intended as a comprehensive text for the courses in digital electronic circuits. The objective of this book is to develop in the reader the ability to analyze and design the digital circuits. The increased uses of digital technology in objects used for day-to-day life necessitate an in-depth knowledge of the subject for the professionals and engineers.

There are lots of references available on Digital Circuit Design, which discusses various topics separately. But through this text our notion was to discover the topics rather than to cover them. This comprehensive text fulfills the course requirement on the subject of digital circuit design for B. Tech degree course in Electronics, Electronic & Communication, Electronic & Electrical, Electronic & Instrumentation, Electronic Instrumentation & Control, Instrumentation & Control Engineering of different technical Universities.

This text is also bound to serve as a useful reference book for various competitive examinations. Although there is no special pre-requisite before starting this book, but elementary knowledge of switching fundamentals like Boolean algebra, number systems, and logic gate would definitely help. Every chapter of the book starts with simple facts and concepts and traversing through the examples & figures, it uncovers the advanced topics. The book is divided into four parts, Part A, Part B, Part C, and Part D. Each part covers relevant topics in totality. Parts are organized in such a way that practicing engineers & students may go to the particular part directly.

***Part A* Digital Technology,** is composed of 4 chapters. Chapter 1 deals with the numbering systems and chapter 2 is a review tour to the switching fundamentals, canonical forms and basic digital devices. People who are familiar with these topics may skip these two chapter without the loss of generality. Chapter 3 deals with combinational logic design using MSI & LSI circuits are presented that includes multiplexers, demultiplexers and decoders. Chapter 4 introduces the sequential circuits. It starts with discussions on flip-flops, deals with registers its modes and finally concludes with the detailed counter design.

***Part B* Memory:** includes chapters 5 and 6. Chapter 5 deals with Programmable Logic Devices, ROM, PLAs, PALs, CPLDs and FPGA. Chapter 6 deals with the semiconductor memory devices to be used with computer system. It also includes memory system designs and introduces Magnetic and Optical memories also.

***Part C* Wave Shaping Circuits and Waveform Generators:** includes 3 chapters. Chapter 7 deals with wave shaping circuits. Various waveforms and examples along with qualitative description is given to clarify the concept. Chapter 8 includes various Multivibrators, Schmitt trigger, and application of popular IC-555. Chapter 9 deals with the Analog to Digital and Digital to Analog Converters. It details various parameters and characteristics of these devices with some consideration on practical aspects.

***Part D*** **Logic Families:** includes one chapter that go in depth of semiconductor switching devices and various logic families with detailed qualitative and quantitative descriptions. Circuits are simplified topologically and equivalent circuits are drawn separately to clarify the concepts.

The text also includes 3 rich appendices giving information about IC fabrication, BiCMOS circuits and GaAs based circuits.

All the topics are illustrated with clear diagram and simple language is used throughout the text to facilitate easy understanding of the concepts. The authors welcome constructive suggestions and comments from the readers for the improvement of this book at singh_a_k@rediffmail.com or at manishtiwari_me@rediffmail.com

**A.K. SINGH**
**MANISH TIWARI**

# ACKNOWLEDGEMENTS

This book is the result of the dedication and encouragement of many individuals. We are thankful to our Directors and all our colleagues at BBD Group of Educational Institutions.

We would like to thank our family members for their continuing support and our parents for their blessings.

We thankfully acknowledge the contributions of various authors, data manuals, journals, reference manuals etc. from where materials have been collected to enrich the contents of the book.

Finally, we would like to thank the people at New Age International (P) Limited, especially Mr. L.N. Mishra, who continues support and encourages writing and who made the book a reality. Thanks are also due to Mr. Saumya Gupta, M.D. New Age International (P) Limited for his involvement in the project.

In last but not the least by the blessing of almighty and good fortune we get such a supporting and cooperative people around us who in one way or other help us to complete this project in time.

**AUTHORS**

# CONTENTS

# PART B: MEMORIES

## PART C: WAVE SHAPING CIRCUITS AND WAVEFORM GENERATORS

# PART A

# DIGITAL TECHNOLOGY

**1**
**CHAPTER**

# NUMBERING SYSTEMS AND CODES

## 1.0 INTRODUCTION

Inside today's computers, data is represented as 1's and 0's. These 1's and 0's might be stored magnetically on a disk, or as a state in a transistor, core, or vacuum tube. To perform useful operations on these 1's and 0's one have to organize them together into patterns that make up codes. Modern digital systems do not represent numeric values using the decimal system. Instead, they typically use a binary or two's complement numbering system. To understand the digital system arithmetic, one must understand how digital systems represent numbers.

This chapter discusses several important concepts including the binary, octal and hexadecimal numbering systems, binary data organization (bits, nibbles, bytes, words, and double words), signed and unsigned numbering systems. If one is already familiar with these terms he should at least skim this material.

## 1.1 A REVIEW OF THE DECIMAL SYSTEM

People have been using the decimal (base 10) numbering system for so long that they probably take it for granted. When one sees a number like "123", he doesn't think about the value 123; rather, he generates a mental image of how many items this value represents. In reality, however, the number 123 represents:

$$1*10^2 + 2*10^1 + 3*10^0$$

or

$$100 + 20 + 3$$

Each digit appearing to the left of the decimal point represents a value between zero and nine times an increasing power of ten. Digits appearing to the right of the decimal point represent a value between zero and nine times an increasing negative power of ten. For example, the value 123.456 means:

$$1*10^2 + 2*10^1 + 3*10^0 + 4*10^{-1} + 5*10^{-2} + 6*10^{-3}$$

or

$$100 + 20 + 3 + 0.4 + 0.05 + 0.006$$

## 1.2 BINARY NUMBERING SYSTEM

Most modern digital systems operate using binary logic. The digital systems represent values using two voltage levels (usually 0v and +5v). With two such levels one can represent exactly two different values. These could be any two different values, but by convention we use the values 0 and 1. These two values, coincidentally, correspond to the two digits used by the binary numbering system.

### 1.2.1 Binary to Decimal Conversion

The binary numbering system works just like the decimal numbering system, with two exceptions: binary only allows the digits 0 and 1 (rather than 0–9), and binary uses powers of two rather than powers of ten. Therefore, it is very easy to convert a binary number to decimal. For each "1" in the binary string, add $2^n$ where "$n$" is the bit position in the binary string (0 to $n$–1 for $n$ bit binary string).

For example, the binary value $1010_2$ represents the decimal 10 which can be obtained through the procedure shown in the table 1.1:

**Table 1.1**

| Binary No. | 1 | 0 | 1 | 0 |
|---|---|---|---|---|
| Bit Position (n) | 3rd | 2nd | 1st | 0th |
| Weight Factor ($2^n$) | $2^3$ | $2^2$ | $2^1$ | $2^0$ |
| Bit * $2^n$ | $1*2^3$ | $0*2^2$ | $1*2^1$ | $0*2^0$ |
| Decimal Value | 8 | 0 | 2 | 0 |
| Decimal Number | 8 + 0 + 2 + 0 = 10 | | | |

All the steps in above procedure can be summarized in short as

$$1*2^3 + 0*2^2 + 1*2^1 + 0*2^0 = 8 + 0 + 2 + 0 = 10_{10}$$

*i.e.*,

1. Multiply each digit of the binary number by its positional weight and then add up the result.
2. If any digit is 0, its positional weight is not to be taken into account.

### 1.2.2 Decimal to Binary Conversion

The inverse problem would be to find out the binary equivalent of given decimal number, for instance, let us find out binary of $19_{10}$ (decimal 19)

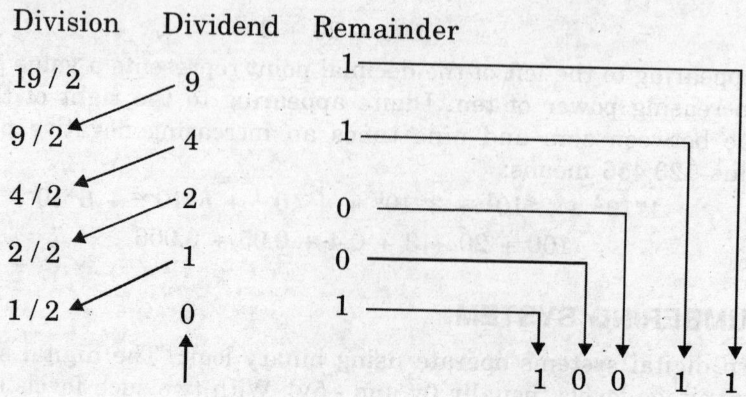


Dividend is 0, stop the procedure.

Our final number is $(10011)_2$.

*i.e.*,

1. Divide the decimal number by 2 producing a dividend and a remainder. This number is the LSB (least significant bit) of the desired binary number.
2. Again divide the dividend obtained above by 2. This produces another dividend and remainder. The remainder is the next digit of the binary number.
3. Continue this process of division until the dividend becomes 0. The remainder obtained in the final division is the MSB (most significant bit) of the binary number.

### 1.2.3 Binary Formats

In the purest sense, every binary number contains an infinite number of digits (or *bits* which is short for binary digits). Because any number of leading zero bits may precede the binary number without changing its value. For example, one can represent the number seven by:

111      00000111      ..0000000000111      000000000000111

Often several values are packed together into the same binary number. For convenience, a numeric value is assigned to each bit position. Each bit is numbered as follows:

1. The rightmost bit in a binary number is bit position zero.
2. Each bit to the left is given the next successive bit number.

An eight-bit binary value uses bits zero through seven:

$$X_7\ X_6\ X_5\ X_4\ X_3\ X_2\ X_1\ X_0$$

A 16-bit binary value uses bit positions zero through fifteen:

$$X_{15}\ X_{14}\ X_{13}\ X_{12}\ X_{11}\ X_{10}\ X_9\ X_8\ X_7\ X_6\ X_5\ X_4\ X_3\ X_2\ X_1\ X_0$$

Bit zero is usually referred to as the *low order* bit. The left-most bit is typically called the *high order* bit. The intermediate bits are referred by their respective bit numbers. The low order bit which is $X_0$ is called LEAST SIGNIFICANT BIT (LSB). The high order bit or left most bit. *i.e.,* $X_{15}$ is called MOST SIGNIFICANT BIT (MSB).

### 1.2.4 Data Organization

In pure mathematics, a value may take an arbitrary number of bits. Digital systems, on the other hand, generally work with some specific number of bits. Common collections are single bits, groups of four bits (called *nibbles*), groups of eight bits (called *bytes*), groups of 16 bits (called *words*), and more. The sizes are not arbitrary. There is a good reason for these particular values.

#### *Bits*

The smallest "unit" of data on a binary computer or digital system is a single *bit*. **Bit**, an abbreviation for Binary Digit, can hold either a 0 or a 1. A bit is the smallest unit of information a computer can understand. Since, a single bit is capable of representing only two different values (typically zero or one) one may get the impression that there are a very small number of items one can represent with a single bit. That's not true! There are an infinite number of items one can represent with a single bit.

With a single bit, one can represent any two distinct items. Examples include zero or one, true or false, on or off, male or female, and right or wrong. However, one are *not* limited to representing binary data types (that is, those objects which have only two distinct values). One could use a single bit to represent the numbers 321 and 1234. Or perhaps 6251 and 2. One could also use a single bit to represent the colors green and blue. One could even represent two unrelated objects with a single bit. For example, one could represent the color red and the number 3256 with a single bit. One can represent *any* two different values with a single bit. However, one can represent *only* two different values with a single bit.

To confuse things even more, different bits can represent different things. For example, one bit might be used to represent the values zero and one, while an adjacent bit might be used to represent the values true and false. How can one tell by looking at the bits? The answer, of course, is that one can't. But this illustrates the whole idea behind computer data structures: *data is what one define it to be*. If one uses a bit to represent a boolean (true/false) value then that bit (by definition) represents true or false. For the bit to have any true meaning, one must be consistent. That is, if one is using a bit to represent true or false at one point in his program, he shouldn't use the true/false value stored in that bit to represent green or blue later.

Since, most items one will be trying to model require more than two different values, single bit values aren't the most popular data type used. However, since everything else consists of groups of bits, bits will play an important role in programs. Of course, there are several data types that require two distinct values, so it would seem that bits are important by themselves. However, individual bits are difficult to manipulate, so other data types are often used to represent boolean values.

## Nibbles

A *nibble* is a collection of four bits. It wouldn't be a particularly interesting data structure except for two items: BCD (*binary coded decimal*) numbers and hexadecimal numbers. It takes four bits to represent a single BCD or hexadecimal digit. With a nibble, one can represent up to 16 distinct values. In the case of hexadecimal numbers, the values 0, 1, 2, 3, 4, 5, 6, 7, 8, 9, A, B, C, D, E, and F are represented with four bits (see "The Hexadecimal Numbering System"). BCD uses ten different digits (0, 1, 2, 3, 4, 5, 6, 7, 8, 9) and requires four bits. In fact, any sixteen distinct values can be represented with a nibble, but hexadecimal and BCD digits are the primary items we can represent with a single nibble.

## Bytes

Computer memory must be able to store letters, numbers, and symbols. A single bit by itself cannot be of much use. Bits are combined to represent some meaningful data. A group of eight bits is called a byte. It can represent a character and is the smallest addressable datum (data item) on the most of the digital systems (*e.g.,* 80 × 86 microprocessor). The most important data type is the byte. Main memory and input/output addresses on the 80 × 86 are all byte addresses. This means that the smallest item that can be individually accessed by an 80 × 86 program is an eight-bit value. To access anything smaller requires that you read the byte containing the data and mask out the unwanted bits. The bits in a byte are normally numbered from zero to seven using the convention in Fig. 1.1.

Bit 0 is the *low order bit* or *least significant bit*, bit 7 is the *high order bit* or *most significant bit* of the byte. All other bits are referred by their number.

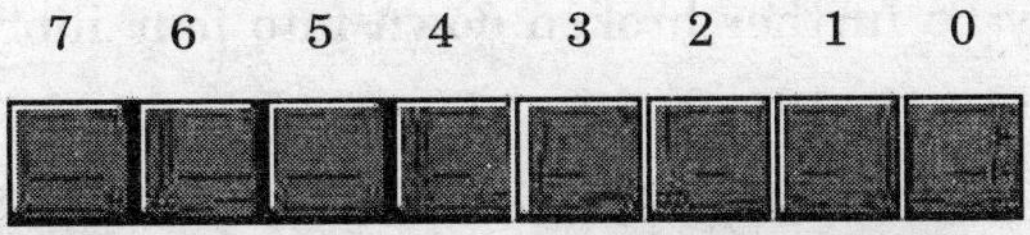


**Fig. 1.1** Bit numbering in a byte

**Note:** That a byte also contains exactly two nibbles (see Fig. 1.2).

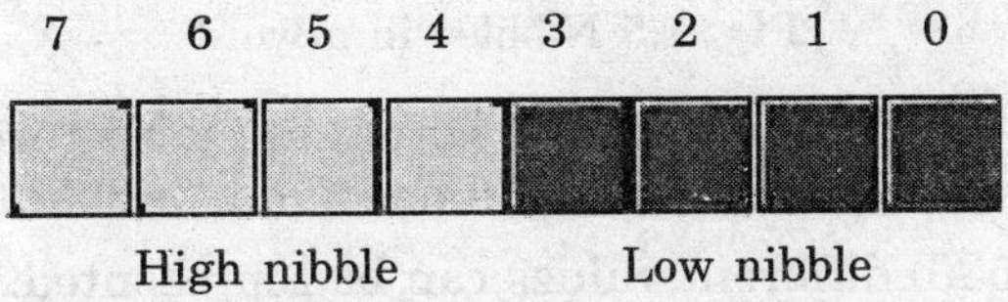


**Fig. 1.2** The two nibbles in a byte

Bits 0–3 comprise the *low order nibble*, bits 4–7 form the *high order nibble*. Since, a byte contains exactly two nibbles, byte values require two hexadecimal digits.

Since, a byte contains eight bits, it can represent $2^8$, or 256, different values. Generally, a byte is used to represent numeric values in the range 0.255, signed numbers in the range –128.. + 127 (refer "Signed binary representation"). Many data types have fewer than 256 items so eight bits is usually sufficient.

For a byte addressable machine, it turns out to be more efficient to manipulate a whole byte than an individual bit or nibble. For this reason, most programmers use a whole byte to represent data types that require no more than 256 items, even if fewer than eight bits would suffice. For example, we'll often represent the boolean values true and false by $00000001_2$ and $00000000_2$ (respectively).

Probably the most important use for a byte is holding a character code. Characters typed at the keyboard, displayed on the screen, and printed on the printer all have numeric values.

## *Words*

A word is a group of 16 bits. Bits in a word are numbered starting from zero on up to fifteen. The bit numbering appears in Fig. 1.3.

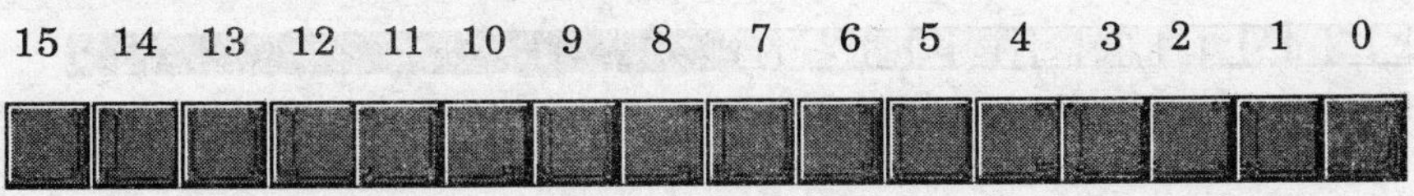


**Fig. 1.3** Bit numbers in a word

Like the byte, bit 0 is the low order bit and bit 15 is the high order bit. When referencing the other bits in a word use their bit position number.

Notice that a word contains exactly two bytes. Bits 0 through 7 form the low order byte, bits 8 through 15 form the high order byte (see Fig. 1.4).

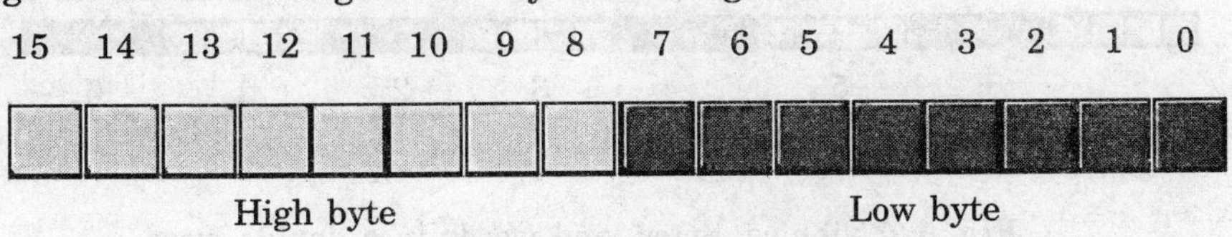


**Fig. 1.4** The two bytes in a word

Naturally, a word may be further broken down into four nibbles as shown in Fig. 1.5.

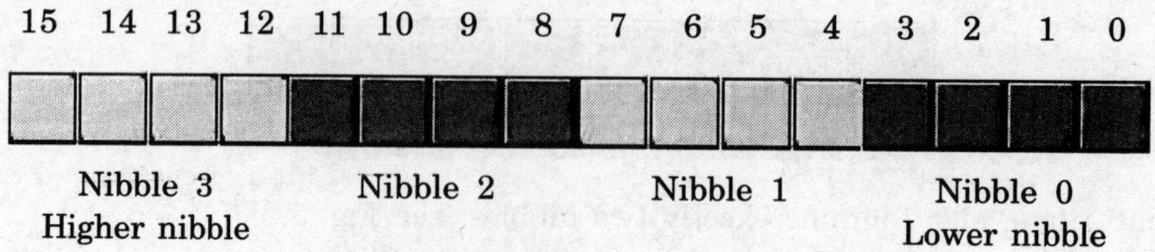


**Fig. 1.5** Nibbles in a word

Nibble zero is the low order nibble in the word and nibble three is the high order nibble of the word. The other two nibbles are "nibble one" and "nibble two".

With 16 bits, $2^{16}$ (65,536) different values can be represented. These could be the values in the range 0 to 65,535 (or –32,768 to +32,767) or any other data type with no more than 65,536 values.

Words can represent integer values in the range 0 to 65,535 or –32,768 to 32,767. Unsigned numeric values are represented by the binary value corresponding to the bits in the word. Signed numeric values use the two's complement form for numeric values (refer "Signed binary representation").

## *Double Words*

A double word is exactly what its name implies, a pair of words. Therefore, a double word quantity is 32 bits long as shown in Fig. 1.6.

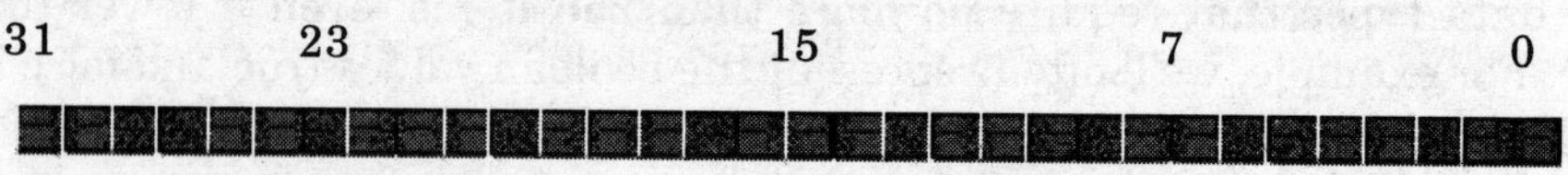


**Fig. 1.6** Bit numbers in a double word

This double word can be divided into a high order word and a low order word, or four different bytes, or eight different nibbles (see Fig. 1.7).

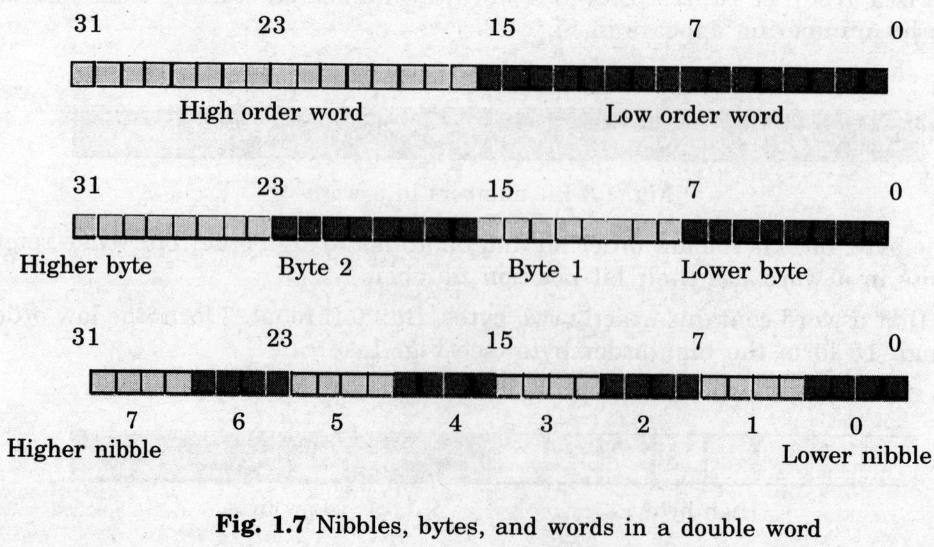


**Fig. 1.7** Nibbles, bytes, and words in a double word

## 1.3 OCTAL NUMBERING SYSTEM

The octal number system uses base 8 instead of base 10 or base 2. This is sometimes convenient since many computer operations are based on bytes (8 bits). In octal, we have 8 digits at our disposal, 0–7.

| Decimal | Octal |
|---|---|
| 0 | 0 |
| 1 | 1 |
| 2 | 2 |
| 3 | 3 |
| 4 | 4 |
| 5 | 5 |
| 6 | 6 |
| 7 | 7 |
| 8 | 10 |
| 9 | 11 |
| 10 | 12 |
| 11 | 13 |
| 12 | 14 |
| 13 | 15 |
| 14 | 16 |
| 15 | 17 |
| 16 | 20 |

### 1.3.1 Octal to Decimal, Decimal to Octal Conversion

Converting octal to decimal is just like converting binary to decimal, except instead of powers of 2, we use powers of 8. That is, the LSB is $8^0$, the next is $8^1$, then $8^2$, etc.

To convert 172 in octal to decimal:

$$\begin{array}{ccc} 1 & 7 & 2 \\ 8^2 & 8^1 & 8^0 \end{array}$$

$$\begin{aligned} \text{Weight} &= 1*8^2 + 7*8^1 + 2*8^0 \\ &= 1*64 + 7*8 + 2*1 \\ &= 122_{10} \end{aligned}$$

Converting decimal to octal is just like converting decimal to binary, except instead of dividing by 2, we divide by 8.

To convert 122 to octal:

$$\begin{aligned} 122/8 &= 15 \text{ remainder } 2 \\ 15/8 &= 1 \text{ remainder } 7 \\ 1/8 &= 0 \text{ remainder } 1 \\ &= 172_8 \end{aligned}$$

If using a calculator to perform the divisions, the result will include a decimal fraction instead of a remainder. The remainder can be obtained by multiplying the decimal fraction by 8. For example, 122/8 = 15.25. Then multiply 0.25 * 8 to get a remainder of 2.

### 1.3.2 Octal to Binary, Binary to Octal Conversion

Octal becomes very useful in converting to binary, because it is quite simple. The conversion can be done by looking at 3 bit combinations, and then concatenating them together. Here is the equivalent for each individual octal digit and binary representation:

| Octal | Binary |
|---|---|
| 1 | 001 |
| 2 | 010 |
| 3 | 011 |
| 4 | 100 |
| 5 | 101 |
| 6 | 110 |
| 7 | 111 |

To convert back and forth between octal and binary, simply substitute the proper pattern for each octal digit with the corresponding three binary digits.

For example, 372 in octal becomes 011 111 010 or 011111010 in binary.

777 in octal becomes 111 111 111 or 111111111 in binary.

The same applies in the other directions:

100111010 in binary becomes 100 111 010 or 472 in octal.

Since, it is so easy to convert back and forth between octal and binary, octal is sometimes used to represent binary codes. Octal is most useful if the binary code happens to be a multiple of 3 bits long. Sometimes, it is quicker to convert decimal to binary by first converting decimal to octal, and then octal to binary.

## 1.4 HEXADECIMAL NUMBERING SYSTEM

The hexadecimal numbering system is the most common system seen today in representing raw computer data. This is because it is very convenient to represent groups of 4 bits. Consequently, one byte (8 bits) can be represented by two groups of four bits easily in hexadecimal.

Hexadecimal uses a base 16 numbering system. This means that we have 16 symbols to use for digits. Consequently, we must invent new digits beyond 9. The digits used in hex are the letters A, B, C, D, E, and F. If we start counting, we get the table below:

| Decimal | Hexadecimal | Binary |
|---|---|---|
| 0 | 0 | 0000 |
| 1 | 1 | 0001 |
| 2 | 2 | 0010 |
| 3 | 3 | 0011 |
| 4 | 4 | 0100 |

....*Contd*

| | | |
|---|---|---|
| 5 | 5 | 0101 |
| 6 | 6 | 0110 |
| 7 | 7 | 0111 |
| 8 | 8 | 1000 |
| 9 | 9 | 1001 |
| 10 | A | 1010 |
| 11 | B | 1011 |
| 12 | C | 1100 |
| 13 | D | 1101 |
| 14 | E | 1110 |
| 15 | F | 1111 |
| 16 | 10 | 10000 |
| 17 | 11 | 10001 |
| 18 ... | | |

### 1.4.1 Hex to Decimal and Decimal to Hex Conversion

Converting hex to decimal is just like converting binary to decimal, except instead of powers of 2, we use powers of 16. That is, the LSB is $16^0$, the next is $16^1$, then $16^2$, etc.

To convert 15E in hex to decimal:

$$\begin{array}{ccc} 1 & 5 & E \\ 16^2 & 16^1 & 16^0 \end{array}$$

$$\begin{aligned} \text{Weight} &= 1*16^2 + 5*16^1 + 14*16^0 \\ &= 1*256 + 5*16 + 14*1 \\ &= 350_{10} \end{aligned}$$

Converting decimal to hex is just like converting decimal to binary, except instead of dividing by 2, we divide by 16.

To convert 350 to hex:

$$\begin{aligned} 350/16 &= 21 \text{ remainder } 14 = E \\ 21/16 &= 1 \text{ remainder } 5 \\ 1/16 &= 0 \text{ remainder } 1 \end{aligned}$$

So, we get 15E for 350.

Again, note that if a calculator is being used, you may multiple the fraction remainder by 16 to produce the remainder. 350/16 = 21.875. Then to get the remainder, 0.875 × 16 = 14.

### 1.4.2 Hex to Binary and Binary to Hex Conversion

Going from hex to binary is similar to the process of converting from octal to binary. One must simply look up or compute the binary pattern of 4 bits for each hex code, and concatenate the codes together.

To convert AE to binary:

$$\begin{aligned} A &= 1010 \\ E &= 1110 \end{aligned}$$

So, AE in binary is 1010 1110

The same process applies in reverse by grouping together 4 bits at a time and then look up the hex digit for each group.

Binary 11000100101 broken up into groups of 4:

0110 0010 0101 (note the 0 added as padding on the MSB to get up to 4 bits)

$$\begin{array}{ccc} 6 & 2 & 5 \end{array}$$

$$= 625_{16}$$

### 1.4.3 Hex to Octal and Octal to Hex Conversion

These conversions are done through the binary conversion. Recall that, a group of 4-bits represent a hexadecimal digit and a group of 3-bits represent an octal digit.

#### *Hex to Octal Conversion*

1. Convert the given hexadecimal number into binary.
2. Starting from right make groups of 3-bits and designate each group an octal digit.

**Example 1.1.** *Convert* $(1A3)_{16}$ *into octal.*

**Solution.**

1. Converting hex to binary

$$(1A3)_{16} = \underbrace{0001}_{1}\ \underbrace{1010}_{A}\ \underbrace{0011}_{3}$$

2. Grouping of 3-bits

$$(1A3)_{16} = \underset{\downarrow\atop 0}{\underline{000}}\ \underset{\downarrow\atop 6}{\underline{110}}\ \underset{\downarrow\atop 4}{\underline{100}}\ \underset{\downarrow\atop 3}{\underline{011}}$$

so, $$(1A3)_{16} = (0643)_8 \equiv (643)_8$$

#### *Octal to Hex Conversion*

1. Convert the given octal number into binary.
2. Starting from right make groups of 4-bits and designate each group as a Hexadecimal digit.

**Example 1.2.** *Convert* $(76)_8$ *into hexadecimal.*

**Solution.**

1. Converting octal to binary

$$(76)_8 = \underbrace{111}_{7}\ \underbrace{110}_{6}$$

2. Grouping of 4-bits

$$(76)_8 = \underset{\downarrow\atop 3}{\underline{11}}\ \underset{\downarrow\atop E}{\underline{1110}} \equiv \underset{\downarrow\atop 3}{\underline{0011}}\ \underset{\downarrow\atop E}{\underline{1110}}$$

so $$(76)_8 = (3E)_{16}$$

## 1.5 RANGE OF NUMBER REPRESENTATION

The range of numbers that can be represented is determined by the number of digits (or bits in binary) used to represent a number. Let us consider decimal number system to understand the idea.

Highest decimal number represented by 2 digits = 99

But $99 = 100 - 1 = 10^2 - 1.$

The power of 10 (in $10^2 - 1$) indicates that it is 2 digit representation.

So, highest 2-digit decimal number $= 10^2 - 1$

and lowest 2-digit decimal number = 00

Thus, range of 2-digit decimal number = 00 to $10^2 - 1$

It is evident that a total of 100 or $10^2$ numbers (00 to 99) can be represented by 2-digits.

So, we conclude that for $n$-digit representation

range of decimal numbers = 0 to $10^n - 1$

highest decimal number $= 10^n - 1$

total numbers that can be represented $= 10^n$

Note that highest $n$-digit decimal number can be represented by $n$ 9s (*i.e.*, 10 – 1) *e.g.*, highest 2 digit decimal number is represented by 2 9s which is 99.

The above discussion can be generalized by taking base-$r$ number system instead of base-10 (or decimal) number system. Thus, with $n$-digit representation–

> Total distinct numbers that can be represented $= r^n$
>
> Highest decimal Number $= r^{n-1}$
>
> Range of Numbers = 0 to $r^{n-1}$
>
> where, $r$ = base or radix of Number system
>
> $n$ = Number of digits used for representation

It is worth noting that highest decimal number can be represented by $n$ $(r - 1)$s in base-$r$ system.

Let us consider the base-2 or binary number system. Thus $2^n$ distinct quantities, in the range 0 to $2^n - 1$, can be represented with $n$-bit. If $n$ = 4-bits, total distinct quantities (*i.e.*, numbers) that can be represented

$$= N = 2^4 = 16$$

the range of numbers = 0 to $2^4 - 1$ = 0 to 15

and Highest decimal number $= 2^4 - 1 = 15$

The highest decimal number 15, is represented by four 1s *i.e.*, 1111. The range 0 to 15 corresponds to 0000 to 1111 in binary.

If we want to represent a decimal number M using n-bits, then the number M should lie in the range 0 to $2^n$–1 *i.e.*,

$$0 \le M \le 2^n - 1$$

or

$$2^n - 1 \ge M$$

or $$2^n \geq M + 1$$

or $$n \geq \log_2 (M + 1)$$

where M and $n$ are integers.

In the similar way, if we want to represent N distinct quantities in binary then N should not exceed $2^n$.

$$2^n \geq N$$

or $$n \geq \log_2 N$$ Both $n$ and N are integers

**Example 1.3.** *How many bits are required to represent*

*(i) 16-distinct levels*

*(ii) 10 distinct levels*

*(iii) 32 distinct levels*

**Solution.** (*i*) We have, $2^n \geq N$

or $2^n \geq 16 \Rightarrow 2^n \geq 2^4$

or $n \geq 4 \Rightarrow n = 4$

Thus, at least 4-bits are required to represent 16 distinct levels, ranging from 0 to 15.

(*ii*) We have, $n \geq \log_2 N$

or $n \geq \log_2 10 \Rightarrow n \geq 3.32$

but $n$ should be integer, so take next higher integer value

*i.e.*, $n = 4$ bits

So, minimum 4-bits are required to represent 10 distinct levels, ranging from 0 to 9.

(*iii*) $n \geq \log_2 N$

or $n \geq \log_2 32 \Rightarrow n \geq \log_2 2^5$

or $n \geq 5 \Rightarrow n = 5$

So, minimum 5-bits are required to represent 32 levels, ranging from 0 to 31.

**Example 1.4.** *Calculate the minimum no. of bits required to represent decimal numbers*

*(i) 16* *(ii) 63*

**Solution.** (*i*) We have, $n \geq \log_2(M + 1)$ where M = given number

so $n \geq \log_2(16 + 1) \Rightarrow n \geq \log_2(17)$

or $n \geq 4.09$

taking next higher integer *i.e.*, $n = 5$ bits.

Thus, at least 5-bits are required to represent decimal number 16.

(*ii*) $n \geq \log_2 (M + 1)$

$n \geq \log_2 (63 + 1) \Rightarrow n \geq \log_2 64$

or $n \geq \log_2 2^6$ or $n \geq 6$ bits

So, minimum 6-bits are needed to represent decimal 63.

**Example 1.5.** *In a base-5 number system, 3 digit representation is used. Find out*

*(i) Number of distinct quantities that can be represented.*

*(ii) Representation of highest decimal number in base-5.*

**Solution.** Given radix of number system $r = 5$

digits of representation $n = 3$

digits in base-5 would be – 0, 1, 2, 3, 4

(*i*) we have relation

$$\text{no. of distinct quantities} = r^n$$
$$= 5^3 = 125$$

So, 125 distinct levels (quantities) can be represented.

(*ii*) Highest decimal number can be represented by $n(r - 1)$s *i.e.*, by three 4s.

So, highest decimal number = 444

## 1.6 BINARY ARITHMETIC

The binary arithmetic operations such as addition, subtraction, multiplication and division are similar to the decimal number system. Binary arithmetics are simpler than decimal because they involve only two digits (bits) 1 and 0.

### Binary Addition

Rules for binary addition are summarized in the table shown in Fig. 1.8.

| *Augend* | *Addend* | *Sum* | *Carry* | *Result* |
|---|---|---|---|---|
| 0 | 0 | 0 | 0 | 0 |
| 0 | 1 | 1 | 0 | 1 |
| 1 | 0 | 1 | 0 | 1 |
| 1 | 1 | 0 | 1 | 10 |

**Fig. 1.8** Rules for binary addition

As shown in 4th row adding 1 to 1 gives 9 carry which, is given to next binary position, similar to decimal system. This is explained in examples below:

**Example 1.6.** (*i*) *Add 1010 and 0011* (*ii*) *Add 0101 and 1111*

**Solution.**

$$\begin{array}{rl} 1\ \ \ \ \ \ & \leftarrow \text{Carry} \\ 1\,0\,1\,0 & \\ +\ 0\,0\,1\,1 & \\ \hline 1\,1\,0\,1 & \end{array} \qquad \begin{array}{rl} 1\,1\,1\ \ & \leftarrow \text{Carry} \\ 0\,1\,0\,1 & \\ +\ 1\,1\,1\,1 & \\ \hline 1\ 0\,1\,0\,0 & \\ \uparrow\ \ \ \ \ \ \ \ & \\ \text{Carry}\ \ \ \ \ & \end{array}$$

### Binary Subtraction

The rules for binary subtraction is summarized in the table shown in Fig. 1.9.

| *Minuend* | *Subtrahend* | *Difference* | *Borrow* |
|---|---|---|---|
| 0 | 0 | 0 | 0 |
| 0 | 1 | 1 | 1 |
| 1 | 0 | 1 | 0 |
| 1 | 1 | 0 | 0 |

**Fig. 1.9** Rules for binary subtraction

The process of subtraction is very similar to decimal system in which if a borrow is needed it is taken from next higher binary position, as shown in row 2.

**Example 1.7.** *Subtract 0100 from 1011*

**Solution.**

| | | | | |
|---|---|---|---|---|
| 1 | | | | ←Borrow |
| 1 | 0 | 1 | 1 | ←Minuend |
| –0 | 1 | 0 | 0 | ←Subtrahend |
| 0 | 1 | 1 | 1 | ←Difference |
| ↑ | ↑ | ↑ | ↑ | |
| $C_3$ | $C_2$ | $C_1$ | $C_0$ | |

There is no problem in column $C_0$ and $C_1$. In column $C_2$ we made 0 –1, so result = 1 and borrow = 1. Then this borrow = 1 is marked in column $C_3$. So result in column $C_2$ is 1. Then in column $C_3$ we first made 1 – 0 to get result = 1 and then we subtracted borrow from result, thus we get 0 in column $C_3$.

"Thus in subtraction, first subtract the subtrahend bit from minuend and then subtract borrow from the result."

Watch out the next example to further clarify the concept.

**Example 1.8.** *Subtract 0110 from 1001*

**Solution.**

| | | | | |
|---|---|---|---|---|
| 1 | 1 | | | ←Borrow |
| 1 | 0 | 0 | 1 | ←Minuend |
| –0 | 1 | 1 | 0 | ←Subtrahend |
| 0 | 0 | 1 | 1 | ←Difference |
| ↑ | ↑ | ↑ | ↑ | |
| $C_3$ | $C_2$ | $C_1$ | $C_0$ | |

Here, in column $C_1$ we get difference = 1 and borrow = 1. This borrow is marked in column $C_2$, and difference = 1 is shown in the column $C_1$. We now come to column $C_2$. Here by 0–1 we get difference = 1 and borrow = 1. Now this borrow is marked in column $C_3$. But in column $C_2$ already we have 9 borrow so this borrow = 1 is subtracted from difference = 1 which results in 0. Thus, the difference = 0 is marked in column $C_2$.

In the similar way we process column $C_3$ and we get difference = 0 in column $C_3$.

## Binary Multiplication

Binary multiplication is also similar to decimal multiplication. In binary multiplication, if multiplier bit is 0 then partial product is all 0 and if multiplier bit is 1 then partial product is 1. The same is illustrated in example below:

**Example 1.9.**

```
     1 0 0 1 ←— Multiplicand
       1 0 1 ←— Multiplier
     -------
     1 0 0 1 ←— Partial product when multiplier bit = 1
   0 0 0 0 × ←— Partial product when multiplier bit = 0
 1 0 0 1 × ×
 -----------
 1 0 1 1 0 1 ←— Final product
```

### Binary Division

Binary division is also similar to decimal division as illustrated in example below:

```
                     1 0 1
Divisor → 1 0 0 1 ) 1 0 1 1 0 1  ← Dividend
                     1 0 0 1
                     × × 1 0 0 1
                         1 0 0 1
                         × × × ×
```

## 1.7 NEGATIVE NUMBERS AND THEIR ARITHMETIC

So far, we have discussed straightforward number representation which are nothing but positive number. The negative numbers have got two representation

(*i*) complement representation.

(*ii*) sign magnitude representation.

We will discuss both the representation in following subsections.

### 1.7.1 1's and 2's Complement

These are the complements used for binary numbers. Their representation are very important as digital systems work on binary numbers only.

#### *1's Complement*

1's complement of a binary number is obtained simply by replacing each 1 by 0 and each 0 by 1. Alternately, 1's complement of a binary can be obtained by subtracting each bit from 1.

**Example 1.10.** *Find 1's complement of (i) 011001 (ii) 00100111*

**Solution.** (*i*) Replace each 1 by 0 and each 0 by 1

```
0 1 1 0 0 1
↓ ↓ ↓ ↓ ↓ ↓
1 0 0 1 1 0
```

So, 1's complement of 011001 is 100110.

(*ii*) Subtract each binary bit from 1.

```
  1 1 1 1 1 1 1 1
 −0 0 1 0 0 1 1 1
  1 1 0 1 1 0 0 0  ← 1's complement
```

one can see that both the method gives same result.

#### *2's Complement*

2's complement of a binary number can be obtained by adding 1 to its 1's complement.

**Example 1.11.** *Find 2's complement of (i) 011001 (ii) 0101100*

**Solution.** (*i*)

| | | |
|---|---|---|
| | 0 1 1 0 0 1 | ← Number |
| | 1 0 0 1 1 0 | ← 1's complement |
| | + 1 | ← Add 1 to 1's complement |
| | 1 0 0 1 1 1 | ← 2's complement |

(*ii*)

| | | |
|---|---|---|
| | 0 1 0 1 1 0 0 | ← Number |
| | 1 0 1 0 0 1 1 | ← 1's complement |
| | + 1 | ← Add 1 to 1's complement |
| | 1 0 1 0 1 0 0 | ← 2's complement |

There is an efficient method to find 2's complement based upon the observation made on the above 2 examples. Consider the number and its 2's complement of example (*ii*) as shown below:

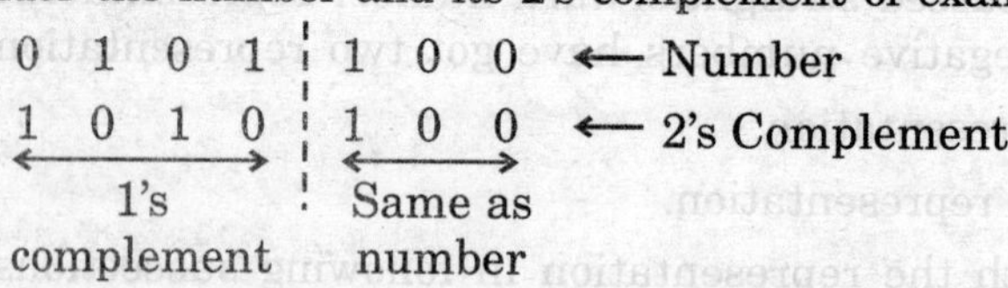


**Fig. 1.10** Number and its 2's complement

The above figure clearly shows that to find 2's complement of a binary number start from right towards left till the first 1 appears in the number. Take these bits (including first 1) as it is and take 1's complement of rest of the bits. Workout below examples to enhance your understanding.

**Example 1.12.** *Find 2's complement of (i) 101100 (ii) 10010 (iii) 01001*

**Solution.** (*i*) Number = 101100

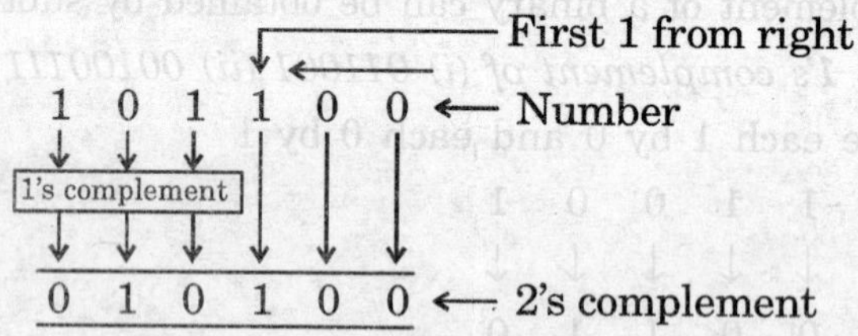


(*ii*) Number = 10010

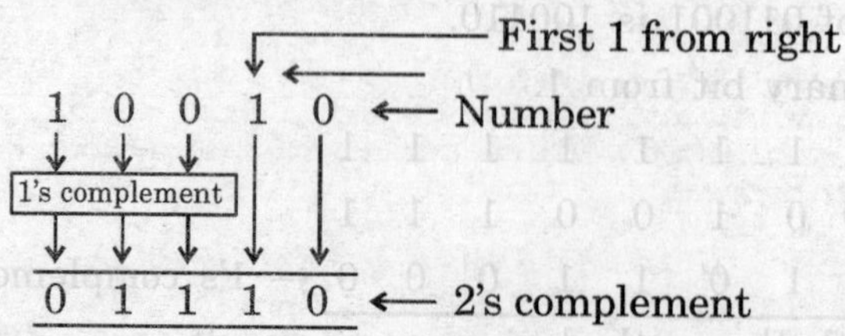


(*iii*) Number = 01001

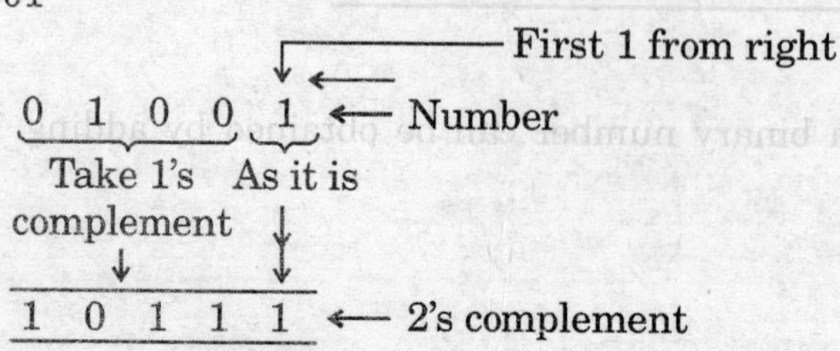

It is interesting to note that taking complement twice leaves the number as it is. This is illustrated below in Fig. 1.11.

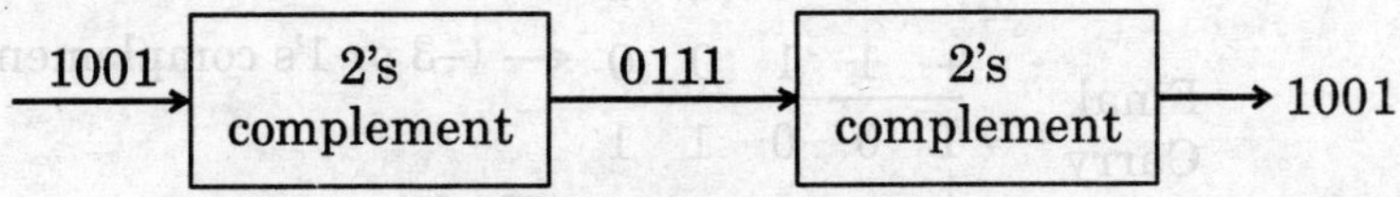


**Fig. 1.11** Effect of taking complement twice

To represent a negative number using complements the process involves two steps.

(1) obtain the binary representation of equivalent positive number for given negative number. *e.g.*, if given number is –2 then obtain binary representation of +2.

(2) Take the appropriate complement of representation obtained in step 1.

**Example 1.13.** *Obtain 1's and 2's complement representation of –5 and –7.*

**Solution.** (*i*) –5

1. binary of +5 = $(0101)_2$
2. 1's complement of $(0101)_2$ = $(1010)_2$ ← Represents $(-5)_{10}$
   2's complement of $(0101)_2$ = $(1011)_2$ ← Represents $(-5)_{10}$

(*ii*) –7

1. binary of +7 = $(0111)_2$
2. 1's complement of $(0111)_2$ = $(1000)_2$ Represents $(-7)_{10}$
   2's complement of $(0111)_2$ = $(1001)_2$ Represents $(-7)_{10}$

Note that in above two examples, for positive numbers we obtained such a binary representation in which MSB is 0. *e.g.*, for +7 we obtained $(0111)_2$ not just $(111)_2$. It is because for all positive numbers MSB must be 0 and for negative numbers MSB should be 1. This will be more clear in subsection 1.7.3.

### 1.7.2 Subtraction Using 1's and 2's Complement

Before using any complement method for subtraction equate the length of both minuend and subtrahend by introducing leading zeros.

1's complement subtraction following are the rules for subtraction using 1's complement.

1. Take 1's complement of subtrahend.
2. Add 1's complement of subtrahend to minuend.
3. If a carry is produced by addition then add this carry to the LSB of result. This is called as end around carry (EAC).
4. If carry is generated from MSB in step 2 then result is positive. If no carry generated result is negative, and is in 1's complement form.

**Example 1.14.** *Perform following subtraction using 1's complement.*

(*i*) 7 – 3 (*ii*) 3 – 7

**Solution.** (*i*) 7 – 3: binary of 7 = $(0111)_2$
binary of 3 = $(0011)_2$ both numbers have equal length.

**Step 1.** 1's complement of $(0011)_2$ = $(1100)_2$

**Step 2.** Perform addition of minuend and 1's complement of subtrahend

$$\begin{array}{lrrrrl} & 0 & 1 & 1 & 1 & \leftarrow (7) \\ & + \ 1 & 1 & 0 & 0 & \leftarrow (-3 \text{ or 1's complement of } +3) \\ \hline \text{Final Carry} \rightarrow & 1 \ \ 0 & 0 & 1 & 1 & \\ & & & + & 1 & (\text{EAC}) \\ \hline & 0 & 1 & 0 & 0 & \end{array}$$

**Step 3.** EAC

**Step 4.** Since, carry is generated in step 2 the result is positive.

since $(0100)_2 = (4)_{10}$

so, result = +4 which is correct answer

(*ii*) 3 – 7:

binary of 3 = 0011

binary of 7 = 0111

**Step 1.** 1's complement of 0111 = 1000

**Step 2.** Perform addition of minuend and 1's complement of subtrahend

$$\begin{array}{lrrrrl} & 0 & 0 & 1 & 1 & \leftarrow (3) \\ & 1 & 0 & 0 & 0 & \leftarrow (-7 \text{ or 1's complement of } +7) \\ \hline \text{Result} = & 1 & 0 & 1 & 1 & \\ \hline \end{array}$$

**Step 3.** No carry produced so no EAC operation.

**Step 4.** Since, no carry produced in step 2, result is negative and is in complemented form. So, we must take 1's complement of result to find correct magnitude of result.

1's complement of result $(1011)_2 = (0100)_2$

so, final result $= -(0100)_2$ or $-(4)_{10}$

Note that when (in example (*ii*) the result was negative (step 2), MSB of the result was 1. When (in example (*i*)) the result was positive the MSB was 0. The same can be observed in 2's complement subtraction.

**2's complement Subtraction** Method of 2's complement is similar to 1's complement subtraction except the end around carry (EAC). The rules are listed below:

1. Take 2's complement of subtrahend.
2. Add 2's complement of subtrahend to minuend.
3. If a carry is produced, then discard the carry and the result is positive. If no carry is produced result is negative and is in 2's complement form.

**Example 1.15.** *Perform following subtraction using 2's complement.*

(*i*) 7 – 5 (*ii*) 5 – 7

**Solution.** (*i*) 7 – 5: binary of 7 = $(0111)_2$, binary of 5 = $(0101)_2$ — both the numbers should have equal length.

**Step 1.** 2's complement of subtrahend $(=0101)_2 = (1011)_2$

**Step 2.** Perform addition of minuend and 2's complement of subtrahend

```
                 0 1 1 1 ← (7)
               + 1 0 1 1 ← (–5 or 2's complement of +5)
Final
Carry ——→      1 0 0 1 0
               ↑
               Discard the final carry
```

**Step 3.** Since, a final carry is produced in step 2 (which is discarded) the result is positive. So,

$$\text{result} = (0010)_2 = (2)_{10}$$

(*ii*) 5 – 7:

$$\text{binary of } 5 = (0101)_2$$

$$\text{binary of } 7 = (0111)_2$$

**Step 1.** 2's complement of subtrahend (= 0111) = 1001

**Step 2.** Addition of minuend and 2's complement of subtrahend

```
  0 1 0 1 ← 5
  1 0 0 1 ← (–7 or 2's complement of +7)
  1 1 1 0 ← Result
↑
No final carry
```

**Step 3.** Since, final carry is not generated in step 2, the result is negative and is in 2's complement form. So, we must take 2's complement of result obtained in step 2 to find correct magnitude of result.

$$\text{2's complement of result } (1110)_2 = (0010)_2$$

$$\text{so, final result} = -(0010)_2 = -(2)_{10}$$

### 1.7.3 Signed Binary Representation

Until now we have discussed representation of unsigned (or positive) numbers, except one or two places. In computer systems, sign (+ve or –ve) of a number should also be represented by binary bits.

The accepted convention is to use 1 for negative sign and 0 for positive sign. In signed representation MSB of the given binary string represents the sign of the number, in all types of representation. We have two types of signed representation:

1. Signed Magnitude Representation
2. Signed Complement Representation

In a **signed-magnitude** representation, the MSB represents the sign and rest of the bits represent the magnitude. *e.g.*,

```
+5 = (0  1 0 1)₂          –5 = (1  1 0 1)₂
      ↑    ↑                    ↑    ↑
      |  Magnitude              |  Magnitude
      |                         |
    + sign                    – sign
```

Note that positive number is represented similar to unsigned number. From the example, it is also evident that out of 4-bits, only 3-bits are used to represent the magnitude. Thus, in general, $n - 1$ bits are used to denote the magnitude. So, the range of signed representation becomes $-(2^{n-1} - 1)$ to $(2^{n-1} - 1)$.

In a **signed-complement** representation the positive numbers are represented in true binary form with MSB as 0. Whereas the negative numbers are represented by taking appropriate complement of equivalent positive number, including the sign bit. Both 1's and 2's complements can be used for this purpose *e.g.*,

$$+5 = (0101)_2$$
$$-5 = (1010)_2 \leftarrow \text{in 1's complement}$$
$$= (1011)_2 \leftarrow \text{in 2's complement}$$

Note that in signed complement representation the fact remains same that $n - 1$ bits are used for magnitude. The range of numbers

| | | |
|---|---|---|
| In 1's complement | 0 to $(2^{n-1} - 1)$ | Positive Numbers |
| | $-$ 0 to $-(2^{n-1} - 1)$ | Negative Numbers |
| In 2's complement | 0 to $(2^{n-1} - 1)$ | Positive Numbers |
| | $-$ 1 to $-2^{n-1}$ | Negative Numbers |

To illustrate the effect of these 3 representations, we consider 4-bit binary representation and draw the below table. Carefully observe the differences in three methods.

| *Decimal* | *Signed Magnitude* | *1's Complement* | *2's Complement* |
|---|---|---|---|
| +0 | 0 0 0 0 | 0 0 0 0 | 0 0 0 0 |
| +1 | 0 0 0 1 | 0 0 0 1 | 0 0 0 1 |
| +2 | 0 0 1 0 | 0 0 1 0 | 0 0 1 0 |
| +3 | 0 0 1 1 | 0 0 1 1 | 0 0 1 1 |
| +4 | 0 1 0 0 | 0 1 0 0 | 0 1 0 0 |
| +5 | 0 1 0 1 | 0 1 0 1 | 0 1 0 1 |
| +6 | 0 1 1 0 | 0 1 1 0 | 0 1 1 0 |
| +7 | 0 1 1 1 | 0 1 1 1 | 0 1 1 1 |
| –8 | — | — | 1 0 0 0 |
| –7 | 1 1 1 1 | 1 0 0 0 | 1 0 0 1 |
| –6 | 1 1 1 0 | 1 0 0 1 | 1 0 1 0 |
| –5 | 1 1 0 1 | 1 0 1 0 | 1 0 1 1 |
| –4 | 1 1 0 0 | 1 0 1 1 | 1 1 0 0 |
| –3 | 1 0 1 1 | 1 1 0 0 | 1 1 0 1 |
| –2 | 1 0 1 0 | 1 1 0 1 | 1 1 1 0 |
| –1 | 1 0 0 1 | 1 1 1 0 | 1 1 1 1 |
| –0 | 1 0 0 0 | 1 1 1 1 | — |

**Fig. 1.12** Different signed representation

From the table, it is evident that both signed magnitude and 1's complement methods introduce two zeros +0 and – 0 which is awkward. This is not the case with 2's complement. This is one among the reasons that why all the modern digital systems use 2's complement method for the purpose of signed representation. From the above table, it is also evident that in signed representation $\frac{2^n}{2}$ positive numbers and $\frac{2^n}{2}$ negative numbers can be represented with $n$-bits. Out of $2^n$ combinations of $n$-bits, first $\frac{2^n}{2}$ combinations are used to denote the positive numbers and next $\frac{2^n}{2}$ combinations represent the negative numbers.

**Example 1.16.** *In a signed representation given binary string is $(11101)_2$. What will be the sign and magnitude of the number represented by this string in signed magnitude, 1's complement and 2's complement representation.*

**Solution.**

$$\text{The number N} = (11101)_2$$

$$\text{since MSB} = 1 \text{ the given number is negative.}$$

(*i*) In signed magnitude, MSB denotes sign and rest of the bits represent magnitude. So,

$$(1\ \ 1\ \ 1\ \ 0\ \ 1)_2 = -13$$

Magnitude

sign

(*ii*) In 1's complement if number is negative (*i.e.*, MSB = 1) then the magnitude is obtained by taking 1's complement of given number.

$$\text{1's complement of } (11101)_2 = (00010)_2$$

so, $$(11101)_2 = -2 \text{ in 1's complement.}$$

(*iii*) In 2's complement if number is negative (*i.e.*, MSB = 1) then magnitude is obtained by taking 2's complement of given number.

$$\text{2's complement of } (11101)_2 = (00011)_2$$
$$= 3$$

so, $$(11101)_2 = -3 \text{ in 2's complement.}$$

**Example 1.17.** *Obtain an 8-bit representation of –9 in signed magnitude, 1's complement and 2's complement representation.*

**Solution.** We first find binary of 9 *i.e.*, $(9)_{10} = (1001)_2$

Next we represent 9 using 8-bits. So, $N = (00001001)_2$

$$= (9)_{10}$$

(*i*) In signed magnitude, MSB shows sign and rest of the bits shows true magnitude. So,

$$(-9)_{10} = (10001001)_2$$

(*ii*) In 1's complement, negative number is represented by taking 1's complement of positive number. So,

$$(-9)_{10} = \text{1's complement of } (00001001)_2$$
$$= (11110110)_2$$

(*iii*) In 2's complement

$$(-9)_{10} = \text{2's complement of } (00001001)_2$$
$$= (11110111)_2$$

### 1.7.4 Arithmetic Overflow

When the result of an arithmetic operation requires $n+1$ bits, upon operating on $n$-bits number, an overflow occurs. Alternately, if result exceeds the range 0 to $2^n - 1$, an overflow occurs.

Let us consider the addition of two 4-bit numbers

|  |  |
|---|---|
| 9 ⟶ | 1 0 0 1 |
| +8 ⟶ | 1 0 0 0 |
| 17 ⟶ | 1 0 0 0 1 |

Thus, addition of two 4-bits numbers requires 5-bits ($n$+1 bits) to represent the sum. Alternately, the result of addition of 4-bits, falls outside the range 0 to 15 (*i.e.*, 0 to $2^4$–1). Thus, overflow has occured.

In case of **signed arithmetic** the overflow causes the sign bit of the answer to change. In this case, an overflow occurs if the result does not lie in the range $-2^{n-1}$ to $2^{n-1} - 1$. In signed arithmetic overflow can occur only when two positive numbers or two negative numbers are added.

Let us consider 4-bit signed 2's complement representation.

1. Addition of two positive numbers +6 and +5

|  |  |
|---|---|
| +6 ⟶ | 0 1 1 0 |
| + +5 ⟶ | 0 1 0 1 |
| +11 | 1 0 1 1 |

Since, MSB of result is 1, if reflects a negative result which is incorrect. It happened because overflow has changed the sign of result.

2. Addition of two negative numbers –6 and –5

|  |  |  |
|---|---|---|
| –6 ⟶ | 1 0 1 0 | ⟵ 2's complement of 6 |
| –5 ⟶ | 1 0 1 1 | ⟵ 2's complement of 5 |
| –11 | 1 0 1 0 1 |  |

↑ Carry (the leading 1)

In 2's complement if a carry is generated after the addition then carry is discarded and result is declared positive. Thus, result = $(0101)_2$ = +5 which is wrong, because addition of two negative numbers should give a negative result. This happened due to overflow.

Note that overflow is a problem that occurs when result of an operation exceeds the capacity of storage device. In a computer system, the programmer must check the overflow after each arithmetic operation.

### 1.7.5 9's and 10's Complement

9's and 10's complements are the methods used for the representation of decimal numbers. They are identical to the 1's and 2's complements used for binary numbers.

***9's complement:*** 9's complement of a decimal number is defined as $(10^n - 1) - N$, where $n$ is no. of digits and N is given decimal numbers. Alternately, 9's complement of a decimal number can be obtained by subtracting each digit from 9.

$$\boxed{\textbf{9's complement of } N = (10^n - 1) - N.}$$

**Example 1.18.** *Find out the 9's complement of following decimal numbers.*

*(i) 459* *(ii) 36* *(iii) 1697*

**Solution.** *(i)* By using $(10^n - 1) - N$; But, $n = 3$ in this case

So, $(10^n - 1) - N = (10^3 - 1) - 459 = 540$

Thus, 9's complement of 459 = 540

*(ii)* By subtracting each digit from 9

$$\begin{array}{r} 9\ 9 \\ -3\ 6 \\ \hline 6\ 3 \\ \hline \end{array}$$

So, 9's complement of 36 is 63.

*(iii)* We have $N = 1697$, so $n = 4$

Thus, $10^n - 1 = 10^4 - 1 = 9999$

So, $(10^n - 1) - N = (10^4 - 1) - 1697 = 9999 - 1697$

$= 8302$

Thus, 9's complement of 1697 = 8302

**10's complement:** 10's complement of a decimal number is defined as $10^n - N$.

$$\boxed{\textbf{10's complement of } N = 10^n - N}$$

but $10^n - N = (10^n - 1) - N + 1$

$= \text{9's complement of } N + 1$

Thus, 10's complement of a decimal number can also be obtained by adding 1 to its 9's complement.

**Example 1.19.** *Find out the 10's complement of following decimal numbers. (i) 459 (ii) 36.*

**Solution.** *(i)* By using $10^n - N$; We have $N = 459$ so $n = 3$

So, $10^n - N = 10^3 - 459 = 541$

**So, 10's is complement of 459 = 541**

*(ii)* By adding 1 to 9's complement

9's complement of 36 = 99 – 36

= 63

Hence, 10's complement of 36 = 63 + 1

= 64

### 1.7.6 r's Complement and (r – 1)'s Complement

The *r*'s and (*r* – 1)'s complements are generalized representation of the complements, we have studied in previous subsections. *r* stands for radix or base of the number system, thus *r*'s complement is referred as *radix complement* and (*r* – 1)'s complement is referred as *diminished radix complement*. Examples of *r*'s complements are 2's complement and 10's complement. Examples of (*r* – 1)'s complement are 1's complement and 9's complement.

In a base-$r$ system, the $r$'s and $(r - 1)$'s complement of the number N having $n$ digits, can be defined as:

$$(r - 1)\text{'s complement of } N = (r^n - 1) - N$$

and

$$r\text{'s complement of } N = r^n - N = (r - 1)\text{'s complement of } N + 1$$

The $(r - 1)$'s complement can also be obtained by subtracting each digit of N from $r-1$. Using the above methodology, we can also define the 7's and 8's complement for octal system and 15's and 16's complement for hexadecimal system.

### 1.7.7 Rules for Subtraction using (r–1)'s Complement

Let M (minuend) and S (subtrahend) be the two numbers to be used to evaluate the difference D = M – S by $(r - 1)$'s complement and either or both the numbers may be signed or unsigned.

Until and unless specified the given rules are equally applied for both signed and unsigned arithmetic. For the clarity of process, let us assume that two data sets are:

Unsigned data— $M_u = 1025$, $S_u = 50$ and $D_u = M_u - S_u$

Signed data— $M_s = -370$, $S_s = 4312$ and $D_s = M_s - S_s$

***Step 1. Equate the Length***

Find out the length of both the numbers (no. of digit) and see if both are equal. If not, then make the both the numbers equal by placing leading zeros.

$M_u = 1025$, $S_u = 50 \rightarrow S_u = 0050$

$M_s = -370$, $S_s = 4312 \rightarrow M_s = -0370$

***Step 2. Represent Negative Operands (for Negative Numbers only)***

If either or both of operands are negative then take the $(r - 1)$'s complement of the number as obtained in step 1.

$M_s = -370$ $(r - 1)$'s of $M_s = 9999 - 0370 = 9629$

$S_s = 4312$

***Step 3. Complement the Subtrahend***

In order to evaluate difference take the $(r - 1)$'s complement of the representation obtained for the subtrahend $S_u$ in step 1 and $S_s$ in step 2.

$S_u = 0050$, $(r - 1)$'s of $S_u = 9999 - 0050 = 9949$ and $M_u = 1025$

$S_s = 4312$, $(r - 1)$'s of $S_s = 9999 - 4312 = 5687$ and $M_s = 9629$

***Step 4. Addition and the Carry (CY)***

Add the two numbers in the step 3 and check whether or not carry generated from MSB due to addition.

$$M_u = 1025,\ S_u = 9949 \rightarrow D_u = M_u - S_u = \underset{\substack{\downarrow \\ CY}}{1}0974$$

$$M_s = 9629,\ S_s = 5687 \rightarrow D_s = M_s - S_s = \underset{\substack{\downarrow \\ CY}}{1}5316$$

### Step 5. Process the Carry (CY)

In step 4, we obtained result as CY, D. The CY from MSB contains some useful information especially in some unsigned arithmetic. Processing of carry for $(r - 1)$'s complement is

- In this case, if a carry is generated from MSB in step 4, add this carry to the LSB of the result. In step 4, we got CY = 1, $D_u$ = 0974 also CY = 1, $D_s$ = 5316. After adding carry to the LSB (generated in step 4) we get, $D_u$ = 0974 + 1 → 0975 and $D_s$ = 5316 + 1 → 5317. The carry in this case is called "end-around carry".

### Step 6. Result Manipulation

The way result is manipulated is different for signed and unsigned arithmetic.

(*a*) UNSIGNED

1. If a carry is generated in step 4 then the result is positive(+) and the digits in the result shows the correct magnitude of result.
2. If there is no carry from MSB in step 4 then the result is negative (–) and the digits in result is not showing the correct magnitude. So, we must go for a post processing of result (Step 7) to determine the correct magnitude of the result.

(*b*) SIGNED

1. If the MSB of result obtained in step 5 is lesser than the half radix (*i.e.*, MSB < $r/2$) then the result is +ve and representing the correct magnitude. Thus, no post processing is required.
2. If the MSB of result obtained in step 5 is not lesser than the half radix (*i.e.*, MSB ≥ $r/2$) then the result is –ve and correct magnitude of which must be obtained by post processing (Step 7).

### Step 7. Post Processing and Result Declaration

By the step 6(*a*) – 1 and the step 6(*b*) – 1 we know that if the result is positive (+ve) it represents the correct magnitude whether it is signed or unsigned arithmetic. However, the negative results are not showing correct magnitudes *so post processing in principle is needed for declaration of negative results.*

(*a*) Declare positive results. As per the rules, the result of the unsigned arithmetic is positive. Therefore,

$$D_u = +0975$$

(*b*) Process and declare negative results. As per the rules the result of signed arithmetic is negative and is in complemented form. Take the $(r - 1)$'s complement to find the complement and declare the result.

$$(r - 1)\text{'s of } D_s = 9999 - 5317 = -4682$$

Therefore, $$D_s = -4682$$

### 1.7.8 Rules for Subtraction using r's Complement

For better understanding and clarity, let us assume the same data sets of (*r* – 1)'s complement method:

Unsigned data— $M_u$ = 1025, $S_u$ = 50 and $D_u = M_u - S_u$

Signed data— $M_s$ = –370, $S_s$ = 4312 and $D_s = M_s - S_s$

***Step 1. Equate the Length***

Same as for (*r* – 1)'s complement *i.e.*

$M_u$ = 1025, $S_u$ = 50 → $S_u$ = 0050

$M_s$ = –370, $S_s$ = 4312 → $M_s$ = –0370

***Step 2. Represent Negative Operands***

Take the *r*'s complement of negative operands

$M_s$ = –370, *r*'s of $M_s$ = 9999 – 370 + 1 = 9630

$S_s$ = 4312

***Step 3. Complement the Subtrahend***

Take the *r*'s complement of the representation obtained for the subtrahend $S_u$ in step 1 and $S_s$ in step 2 to evaluate the difference

$S_u$ = 0050, *r*'s of $S_u$ = 10000 – 0050 = 9950 and $M_u$ = 1025

$S_s$ = 4312, *r*'s of $S_s$ = 10000 – 4312 = 5688 and $M_s$ = 9630

***Step 4. Addition and Carry (CY)***

Add the two numbers in the step 3 and check whether or not carry generated from MSB due to addition. (Same as (*r* – 1)'s complement).

$M_u$ = 1025, $S_u$ = 9950 → $D_u$= 10975
↓
CY

$M_s$ = 9630, $S_s$ = 5688 → $D_s$ = 15318
↓
CY

***Step 5. Process the Carry (CY)***

If there is carry from MSB in step 4 then simply discard it. In step 4, we got CY = 1, $D_u$ = 0975 also CY = 1, $D_s$ = 5318. After discarding the carry we get, $D_u$ = 0975 and $D_s$ = 5318.

***Step 6. Result Manipulation***

The way result is manipulated is different for signed and unsigned arithmetic.

(*a*) UNSIGNED

1. If a carry is generated in step 4 then the result is positive (+) and the digits in the result shows the correct magnitude of result.

2. If there is no carry from MSB in step 4 then the result is negative (–) and the digits in result is not showing the correct magnitude. So, we must go for a post processing of result (Step 7) to determine the correct magnitude of the result.

(*b*) SIGNED

1. If the MSB of result obtained in step 5 is lesser than the half radix (*i.e.*, MSB < $r/2$) then the result is +ve and representing the correct magnitude. Thus, no post processing is required.
2. If the MSB of result obtained in step 5 is not lesser than the half radix (*i.e.*, MSB $\geq r/2$) then the result is –ve and correct magnitude of which must be obtained by post processing (Step 7).

### Step 7. Post Processing and Result Declaration

(*a*) Declare positive results. As per the rules, the positive result shows the correct magnitude. Since, the result of the unsigned arithmetic is positive. Therefore,

$$D_u = +0975$$

(*b*) Process and declare negative results. As per the rule, the result obtained of signed arithmetic is negative and is in complemented form. Take the *r*'s complement to find the complement and declare the result.

$$r\text{'s of } D_s = 10000 - 5318 = 4682$$

Therefore, $$D_s = 4682$$

## 1.8 BINARY CODED DECIMAL (BCD) AND ITS ARITHMETIC

The BCD is a group of four binary bits that represent a decimal digit. In this representation, each digit of a decimal number is replaced by a 4-bit binary number (*i.e.*, a nibble). Since, a decimal digit is a number from 0 to 9, a nibble representing a number greater than 9 is invalid BCD. For example, $(1010)_2$ is invalid BCD as it represents a number greater than 9. The table shown in Fig. 1.13 lists the binary and BCD representation of decimal numbers 0 to 15. Carefully observe the difference between binary and BCD representation.

| *Decimal Number* | *Binary Representation* | *BCD Representation* |
|---|---|---|
| 0 | 0 0 0 0 | 0 0 0 0 |
| 1 | 0 0 0 1 | 0 0 0 1 |
| 2 | 0 0 1 0 | 0 0 1 0 |
| 3 | 0 0 1 1 | 0 0 1 1 |
| 4 | 0 1 0 0 | 0 1 0 0 |
| 5 | 0 1 0 1 | 0 1 0 1 |
| 6 | 0 1 1 0 | 0 1 1 0 |
| 7 | 0 1 1 1 | 0 1 1 1 |
| 8 | 1 0 0 0 | 1 0 0 0 |
| 9 | 1 0 0 1 | 1 0 0 1 |

Contd...

| 10 | 1 0 1 0 | 0 0 0 1   0 0 0 0 |
|---|---|---|
| 11 | 1 0 1 1 | 0 0 0 1   0 0 0 1 |
| 12 | 1 1 0 0 | 0 0 0 1   0 0 1 0 |
| 13 | 1 1 0 1 | 0 0 0 1   0 0 1 1 |
| 14 | 1 1 1 0 | 0 0 0 1   0 1 0 0 |
| 15 | 1 1 1 1 | 0 0 0 1   0 1 0 1 |

**Fig. 1.13** Binary and BCD representation of decimal numbers

**BCD Addition:** In many application it is required to add two BCD numbers. But the adder circuits used are simple binary adders, which does not take care of peculiarity of BCD representation. Thus, one must verify the result for valid BCD by using following rules:

1. If Nibble (*i.e.,* group of 4-bits) is less than or equal to 9, it is a valid BCD Number.
2. If Nibble is greater than 9, it is invalid. Add 6 (0110) to the nibble, to make it valid.

   OR

   If a carry was generated from the nibble during the addition, it is invalid. Add 6 (0110) to the nibble, to make it valid.
3. If a carry is generated when 6 is added, add this carry to next nibble.

**Example 1.20.** *Add the following BCD numbers. (i) 1000 and 0101 (ii) 00011001 and 00011000*

**Solution.** (*i*)

$$\begin{array}{rcr} 1\ 0\ 0\ 0 & \longrightarrow & 8 \\ +\ 0\ 1\ 0\ 1 & \longrightarrow & +\ 5 \\ \hline 1\ 1\ 0\ 1 & & 13 \end{array}$$

Since, $(1101)_2 > (9)_{10}$ add 6 (0110) to it

So,

$$\begin{array}{rr} & 1\ 1\ 0\ 1 \\ & 0\ 1\ 1\ 0 \\ \hline \underbrace{1} & \underbrace{0\ 0\ 1\ 1} \\ 1 & 3 \end{array}$$

So, result = 00010011

(*ii*)

$$\begin{array}{rrcr} & 1 & & \longleftarrow \text{Carry generated from nibble} \\ 0\ 0\ 0\ 1 & 1\ 0\ 0\ 1 & \longrightarrow & 19 \\ 0\ 0\ 0\ 1 & 1\ 0\ 0\ 0 & \longrightarrow & +18 \\ \hline 0\ 0\ 1\ 1 & 0\ 0\ 0\ 1 & & 37 \\ \hline \end{array}$$

Since, a carry is generated from right most nibble we must add 6 (0110) to it.

So,

$$\begin{array}{rrl} 0\ 0\ 1\ 1 & 0\ 0\ 0\ 1 & \\ & 0\ 1\ 1\ 0 & \\ \hline 0\ 0\ 1\ 1 & 0\ 1\ 1\ 1 & \longrightarrow (37)_{10} \\ \hline \end{array}$$

So, result = 00110111

**BCD Subtraction:** The best way to carry out the BCD subtraction is to use complements. The 9's and 10's complement, studied in subsection 1.7.5, are exclusively used for this purpose. Although any of the two complements can be used, we prefer 10's complement for subtraction. Following are the steps to be followed for BCD subtraction using 10's complement:

1. Add the 10's complement of subtrahend to minuend.
2. Apply the rules of BCD addition to verify that result of addition is valid BCD.
3. Apply the rules of 10's complement on the result obtained in step 2, to declare the final result *i.e.*, to declare the result of subtraction.

**Example 1.21.** *Subtract 61 from 68 using BCD.*

**Solution.** To illustrate the process first we perform the subtraction using 10's complement in decimal system. After that we go for BCD subtraction.

we have,
$$D = 68 - 61$$

So, 10's complement of 61 = 99 – 61 + 1 = 39

So,
$$\begin{array}{r} 68 \\ +39 \\ \hline 107 \end{array}$$
↑ Carry

In 10's complement if an end carry is produced then it is discarded and result is declared positive. So,

$$D = +07$$

by using BCD

1.
$$\begin{array}{lcl} & & \quad 1 \leftarrow \text{Carry generated from nibble} \\ \text{BCD of } 68 = & & 0\;1\;1\;0\;\;1\;0\;0\;0 \\ \text{BCD of } 39 = & + & 0\;0\;1\;1\;\;1\;0\;0\;1 \\ \hline & & 1\;0\;1\;0\;\;0\;0\;0\;1 \end{array}$$

2. Check for valid BCD– Since a carry is generated from right most nibble, we must add 6 (0110) to it. Since, the left most nibble is greater than 9, we must add 6(0110) to it.

Thus,
$$\begin{array}{rr} & 1\;0\;1\;0\;\;0\;0\;0\;1 \\ + & 0\;1\;1\;0\;\;0\;1\;1\;0 \\ \hline 1 & 0\;0\;0\;0\;\;0\;1\;1\;1 \end{array}$$
↑ Carry

3. Declaration of result – We got end carry is step 2. In 10's complement arithmetic, end carry is discarded and result is declared positive. Hence,

$$D = (00000111)_2 = (7)_{10}$$

## 1.9 CODES

Coding and encoding is the process of assigning a group of binary digits, commonly referred to as 'bits', to represent, identify, or relate to a multivalued items of information. By assigning each item of information a unique combination of bits (1's and 0's), we transform some given information into another form. In short, a code is a symbolic representation of an information transform. The bit combination are referred to as 'CODEWORDS'.

There are many different coding schemes, each having some particular advantages and characteristics. One of the main efforts in coding is to standardize a set of universal codes that can be used by all.

In a broad sense we can classify the codes into five groups:

(*i*) Weighted Binary codes

(*ii*) Non-weighted codes

(*iii*) Error–detecting codes

(*iv*) Error–correcting codes

(*v*) Alphanumeric codes.

### 1.9.1 Weighted Binary Codes

In weighted binary codes, each position of a number represents a specific weight. The bits are multiplied by the weights indicated; and the sum of these weighted bits gives the equivalent decimal digit. We have been familiar with the binary number system, so we shall start with straight binary codes.

(*a*) **Straight binary coding** is a method of representing a decimal number by its binary equivalent. A straight binary code representing decimal 0 through 7 is given in Table 2.

**Table 2**

| *Decimal* | *Three bit straight Binary Code* | *Weights MOI* $2^2$ | $2^1$ | $2^0$ | *Sum* |
|---|---|---|---|---|---|
| 0 | 000 | 0 | 0 | 0 | 0 |
| 1 | 001 | 0 | 0 | 1 | 1 |
| 2 | 010 | 0 | 2 | 0 | 2 |
| 3 | 011 | 0 | 2 | 1 | 3 |
| 4 | 100 | 4 | 0 | 0 | 4 |
| 5 | 101 | 4 | 0 | 1 | 5 |
| 6 | 110 | 4 | 2 | 0 | 6 |
| 7 | 111 | 4 | 2 | 1 | 7 |

In this particular example, we have used three bits to represent 8 distinct elements of information *i.e.*, 0 through 7 in decimal form.

Now, the question arises, if $n$ elements of information are to be coded with binary (two valued bits), then how many bits are required to assign each element of information a unique code word (bit combination). Unique is important, otherwise the code would be ambiguous.

The best approach is to evaluate how many code words can be derived from a combination of $n$ bits.

For example: Let $n$ = no. of bits in the codeword and $x$ = no. of unique words

Now, if $n = 1$, then $x = 2$ (0, 1)

$n = 2$, then $x = 4$ (00, 01, 10, 11)

$$n = 3, \text{ then } x = 8 \text{ (000, 001, ..., 111)}$$

and in general, $n = j$, then $x = 2^j$

that is, if we have available $j$ no. of bits in the code word, we can uniquely encode max $2^j$ distinct elements of information.

Inversely, if we are given $x$ elements of information to code into binary coded format, the following condition must hold:

$$x \leq 2^j$$

or $j \geq \log_2 x$

or $j \geq 3.32 \log_{10} x$

where $j$ = number of bits in code word.

**Example 1.22.** *How many bits would be required to code the 26 alphabetic characters plus the 10 decimal digits?*

**Solution.** Here, we have total 36 discrete elements of information.

*i.e.,* $x = 36$

Now $j \geq \log_2 x$

therefore, $j \geq \log_2 36$ or $j \geq 3.32 \log_{10} 36$

or $j \geq 5.16$ bits

Since, bits are not defined in fractional parts, we know $j \geq 6$.

In other words, a minimum of 6 bit code is required that leaves 28 unused code words out of the 64 which are possible ($2^6 = 64$ and $64 - 36 = 28$).

This system of straight binary coding has the disadvantage that the large numbers require a great deal of hardware to handle with. For example, if we have to convert decimal 2869594 to straight binary code a rigorous division of this number by 2 is required until we get remainder 0 or 1.

The above difficulty is overcomed by using another coding scheme called as BCD codes.

(*b*) **Binary codes decimal (BCD) codes:** In BCD codes, individual decimal digits are coded in binary notation and are operated upon singly. Thus, binary codes representing 0 to 9 decimal digits are allowed. Therefore, all BCD codes have at least four bits ($\because$ min. no. of bits required to encode to decimal digits = 4)

For example, decimal 364 in BCD

$$3 \rightarrow 0011$$
$$6 \rightarrow 0110$$
$$4 \rightarrow 0100$$
$$364 \rightarrow 0011\ 0110\ 0100$$

However, we should realize that with 4 bits, total 16 combinations are possible (0000, 0001, ..., 11 11) but only 10 are used (0 to 9). The remaining 6 combinations are unvalid and commonly referred to as 'UNUSED CODES'.

There are many binary coded decimal (BCD) codes all of which are used to represent decimal digits. Therefore, all BCD codes have at least 4 bits and at least 6 unassigned or unused code words shown in Table 3.

Some example of BCD codes are:

(*a*) 8421 BCD code, sometimes referred to as the natural binary coded decimal (NBCD) Code;

(*b*)* Excess-3 code (XS3);

(*c*)** 84 –2 –1 code (+8, +4, –2, –1);

(*d*) 2 4 2 1 code

**Example 1.23.** *Lowest $[643]_{10}$ into XS3 code*

| | | | |
|---|---|---|---|
| Decimal | 6 | 4 | 3 |
| Add 3 to each | 3 | 3 | 3 |
| Sum | 9 | 7 | 6 |

Converting the sum into BCD code we have

| 9 | 7 | 6 |
|---|---|---|
| ↓ | ↓ | ↓ |
| 1001 | 0111 | 0110 |

Hence, XS3 for $[643]_{10}$ = 1001 0111 0110

**Table 3. BCD codes**

| *Decimal Digit* | *8421 (NBCD)* | *Excess-3 Code (XS3)* | *84–2–1 Code* | *2421 Code* |
|---|---|---|---|---|
| 0 | 0000 | 0011 | 0000 | 0000 |
| 1 | 0001 | 0100 | 0111 | 0001 |
| 2 | 0010 | 0101 | 0110 | 0010 |
| 3 | 0011 | 0110 | 0101 | 0011 |
| 4 | 0100 | 0111 | 0100 | 0100 |
| 5 | 0101 | 1000 | 1011 | 1011 |
| 6 | 0110 | 1001 | 1010 | 1100 |
| 7 | 0111 | 1010 | 1001 | 1101 |
| 8 | 1000 | 1011 | 1000 | 1110 |
| 9 | 1001 | 1100 | 1111 | 1111 |

* XS3 is an example of nonweighted code but is a type of BCD code. It is obtained by adding 3 to a decimal number. For example, to encode the decimal number 7 into an excess 3 code. We must first add 3 to obtain 10. The 10 is then encoded in its equivalent 4 bit binary code 1010. Thus, as the name indicates, the XS3 represents a decimal number in binary form, as a number greater than 3.

** Dashes (–) are minus signs.

There are many BCD codes that one can develop by assigning each column or bit position in the code, some weighting factor in such a manner that all of the decimal digits can be coded by simply adding the assigned weights of the 1 bits in the code word.

For example: 7 is coded 0111 in NBCD, which is interpreted as

$$0 \times 8 + 1 \times 4 + 1 \times 2 + 1 \times 1 = 7$$

The NBCD code is most widely used code for the representation of decimal quantities in a binary coded format.

For example: (26.98) would be represented in NBCD as

$$\begin{array}{lcllll} & & 2 & 6 & 9 & 8 \\ (26.98)_{10} & = & (0010 & 0110. & 1001 & 1000)\text{ NBCD} \end{array}$$

It should be noted that on the per digit basis the NBCD code is the binary numeral equivalent of the decimal digit it represents.

### Self complementing BCD codes

The excess 3, 8 4–2–1 and 2421 BCD codes are also known as self complementing codes.

Self complementing property– 9's complement of the decimal number is easily obtained by changing 1'0 to 0's and 0's to 1's in corresponding codeword or the 9's complement of self complementing code word is the same as its logical complement.

When arithmetic is to be performed, often an arithmetic "complement" of the numbers will be used in the computations. So, these codes have a particular advantage in machines that use decimal arithmetic.

**Example 1.24.** *The decimal digit 3 in 8.4–2–1 code is coded as 0101. The 9's complement of 3 is 6. The decimal digit 6 is coded as 1010 that is 1's complement of the code for 3. This is termed as self complementing property.*

## 1.9.2 Non Weighted Codes

These codes are not positionally weighted. This means that each position within a binary number is not assigned a fixed value. Excess-3 codes and Gray codes are examples of non weighted codes.

We have already discussed XS3 code.

### *Gray code (Unit Distance code or Reflective code)*

There are applications in which it is desirable to represent numerical as well as other information with a code that changes in only one bit position from one code word to the next adjacent word. This class of code is called a unit distance code (UDC). These are sometimes also called as 'cyclic', 'reflective' or 'gray' code. These codes finds great applications in Boolean function minimization using Karnaugh map.

The gray code shown in Table 4 is both reflective and unit distance.

**Table 4. Gray codes***

| *Decimal Digit* | *Three bit Gray Code* | *Four bit Gray Code* |
|---|---|---|
| 0 | 0 0 0 | 0 0 0 0 |
| 1 | 0 0 1 | 0 0 0 1 |
| 2 | 0 1 1 | 0 0 1 1 |
| 3 | 0 1 0 | 0 0 1 0 |
| 4 | 1 1 0 | 0 1 1 0 |
| 5 | 1 1 1 | 0 1 1 1 |
| 6 | 1 0 1 | 0 1 0 1 |
| 7 | 1 0 0 | 0 1 0 0 |
| 8 | – | 1 1 0 0 |
| 9 | – | 1 1 0 1 |
| 10 | – | 1 1 1 1 |
| 11 | – | 1 1 1 0 |
| 12 | – | 1 0 1 0 |
| 13 | – | 1 0 1 1 |
| 14 | – | 1 0 0 1 |
| 15 | – | 1 0 0 0 |

## *Binary to Gray Conversion*

(1) Place a leading zero before the most significant bit (MSB) in the binary number.

(2) Exclusive-OR (EXOR) adjacent bits together starting from the left of this number will result in the Gray code equivalent of the binary number.

Exclusive–OR– If the two bits EX–OR'd are identical, the result is 0; if the two bits differ, the result is 1.

---

*Gray codes are formed by reflection. The technique is as follows:

In binary we have two digits 0 and 1.

**Step I.** Write 0 and 1 and put a mirror, we first see 1 and then 0. Place 0's above mirror and 1's below mirror.

We have got gray code for decimal digits 0 through 4.

**Step II.** Write these 4 codes and again put a mirror. The code will look in the order 10, 11, 01 and 00. Then place 0's above mirror and 1's below mirror.

Proceeding intactively in the same manner. We can form Gray code for any decimal digit.

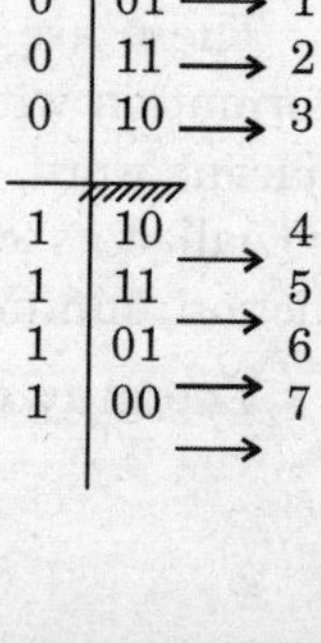

**Example 1.25.** *Convert binary 1010010 into Gray code word.*

$$\begin{array}{ccccccccccccccc} 0 & & 1 & & 0 & & 1 & & 0 & & 0 & & 1 & & 0 \\ & \diagdown\!\diagup & & \diagdown\!\diagup & & \diagdown\!\diagup & & \diagdown\!\diagup & & \diagdown\!\diagup & & \diagdown\!\diagup & & \diagdown\!\diagup & \\ & 1 & & 1 & & 1 & & 1 & & 0 & & 1 & & 1 & \end{array} \Rightarrow (1010010)_2 = (1111011)_{Gray}.$$

### *Gray to Binary Conversion*

Scan the gray code word from left to right. The first 1 encountered is copied exactly as it stands. From then on, 1's will be written until the next 1 is encountered, in which case a 0 is written. Then 0's are written until the next 1 is encountered, in which case a 1 is written, and so on.

**Example 1.26.** *Convert Gray code word 1111011 into binary.*

$$\begin{array}{ccccccc} 1 & 1 & 1 & 1 & 0 & 1 & 1 \\ \downarrow & \downarrow & \downarrow & \downarrow & \downarrow & \downarrow & \downarrow \\ 1 & 0 & 1 & 0 & 0 & 1 & 0 \end{array} \Rightarrow (1111011)_{Gray} = (1010010)_2.$$

**Example 1.27.** *Convert Gray code word 10001011 into binary.*

$$\begin{array}{cccccccc} 1 & 0 & 0 & 0 & 1 & 0 & 1 & 1 \\ \downarrow & \downarrow & \downarrow & \downarrow & \downarrow & \downarrow & \downarrow & \downarrow \\ 1 & 1 & 1 & 1 & 0 & 0 & 1 & 0 \end{array}$$

$$\Rightarrow \qquad (10001011)_{Gray} = (11110010)_2.$$

### 1.9.3 Error Detecting Codes

Binary information is transmitted from one device to another by electric wires or other communication medium. A system that cannot guarantee that the data received by one device are identical to the data transmitted by another device is essentially useless. Yet anytime data are transmitted from source to destination, they can become corrupted in passage. Many factors, including external noise, may change some of the bits from 0 to 1 or vice-versa. Reliable systems must have a mechanism for detecting and correcting such errors.

Binary information or data is transmitted in the form of electromagnetic signal over a channel whenever an electromagnetic signal flows from one point to another, it is subject to unpredictable interference from heat, magnetism, and other forms of electricity. This interference can change the shape or timing of signal. If the signal is carrying encoded binary data, such changes can alter the meaning of data.

In a single bit error, a 0 is changed to a 1 or a 1 is changed to a 0.

In a burst error, multiple (two or more) bits are changed.

The purpose of error detection code is to detect such bit reversal errors. Error detection uses the concept of **redundancy** which means adding extra bits for detecting errors at the destination.

Four types of redundancy checks are used: Parity check (vertical redundancy check) (VRC), longitudinal redundancy check (LRC), cyclic redundancy check (CRC), and checksum.

For a single bit error detection, the most common way to achieve error detection is by means of a **parity bit.**

A parity bit is an extra bit (redundant bit) included with a message to make the total number of 1's transmitted either odd or even.

Table 5 shows a message of three bits and its corresponding odd and even parity bits.

If an odd parity is adopted, P bit is chosen such that the total no. of 1's is odd in four bit that constitute message bits and P.

If an even parity is adopted, the P bit is chosen such that the total number of 1's is even.

**Table 5. Parity bit generation**

| *Message* | | | *Odd Parity (P) bit* | *Even Parity bit (P)* |
|---|---|---|---|---|
| *x* | *y* | *z* | | |
| 0 | 0 | 0 | 1 | 0 |
| 0 | 0 | 1 | 0 | 1 |
| 0 | 1 | 0 | 0 | 1 |
| 0 | 1 | 1 | 1 | 0 |
| 1 | 0 | 0 | 0 | 1 |
| 1 | 0 | 1 | 1 | 0 |
| 1 | 1 | 0 | 1 | 0 |
| 1 | 1 | 1 | 0 | 1 |

The message with the parity bit (either odd or even) is transmitted to its destination. The parity of the received data is checked at the receiving end. If the parity of the received data is changed (from that of transmitted parity), it means that at least one bit has changed their value during transmission. Though the parity code is meant for single error detection, it can detect any odd number of errors. However, in both the cases the original codeword cannot be found.

If there is even combination of errors (means some bits are changed but parity remains same) it remains undetected.

## *Longitudinal Redundancy Check (LRC)*

In LRC, a block of bits is organised in rows and columns (table). For example, a block of 16 bits can be organised in two rows and eight columns as shown in Fig. 1.14. We then calculate the parity bit (even parity/odd parity, here we are using even parity) for each column and create a new row of 8 bits, which are the parity bits for the whole block.

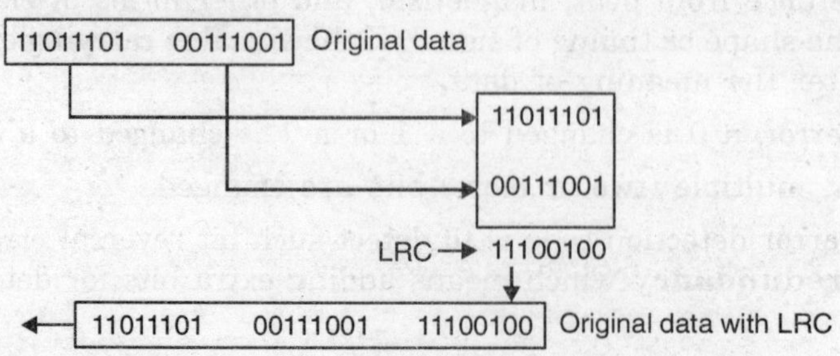


**Fig. 1.14**

## *Cyclic Redundancy Check*

CRC is most powerful of the redundancy checking techniques. Cyclic redundancy check is based on binary division. A sequence of redundant bits called CRC or CRC remainder is appended to the end of a data unit. After adding CRC remainder, the resulting data unit becomes exactly divisible by another predetermined binary number. At the destination, this data unit is divided by the same binary number. If there is no remainder, then there is no error. The question is how to obtain correct CRC? CRC is the remainder obtained by dividing the data unit by a predetermined divisor if it has exactly one bit less than divisor and by appending the CRC to the data string make it completely divisible by the divisor.

The CRC generator and CRC checker are shown in Fig. 1.15($a$) and Fig. 1.15($b$) respectively.

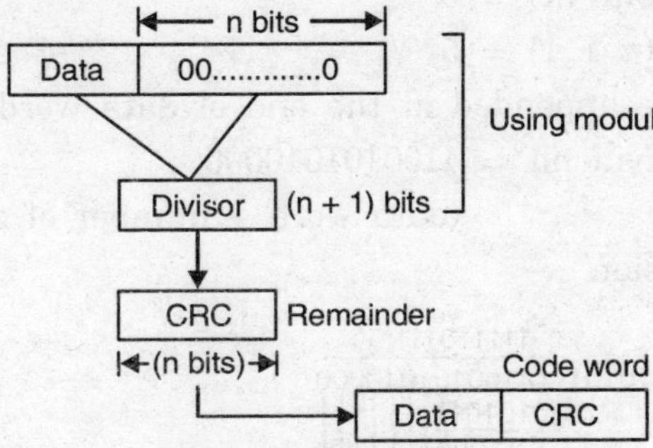


**Fig. 1.15(*a*)** CRC generator

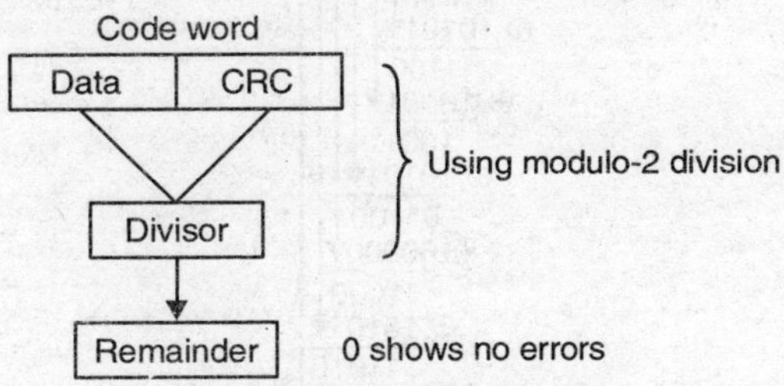


**Fig. 1.15(*b*)** CRC checker

**Example 1.28.** *For the divisor 10101, check whether there are errors in the received code-word 1100 1001 01011.*

**Solution.** As shown in Fig. 1.15($b$).

Code word: 1100 1001 01011.

Divisor : 10101

Using modulo-2 division, we obtain

```
                             111110001
         Divisor → 10101 ) 1100100101011 ← Received code word
     Modulo-2 sum ← ⊕ 10101
                          11000
                        ⊕ 10101
                           11010
                         ⊕ 10101
                            11111
                          ⊕ 10101
                             10100
                           ⊕ 10101
                              00011011
                           ⊕      10101
                                  1110 ← Remainder
```

Since, remainder is non-zero shows that there are errors in the received code word.

**Example 1.29.** *Generate the CRC code for the data word of 1100 10101. The divisor is 10101.*

**Solution.** As shown in Fig. 1.15($a$).

Data word: 1100 10101.

Divisor : 10101

The no. of data bits (k) = 9

The no. of bits in divisor ($n$ + 1) = 5

Therefore, no. of zeroes to be appended at the end of data word will be $n$ = 4

Hence, dividend = 1100101010000

(data word + number of zeroes)

Carry out the modulo-2 division

```
          111110111
  10101 ) 1100101010000
        ⊕ 10101
           11000
         ⊕ 10101
            11011
          ⊕ 10101
             11100
           ⊕ 10101
              10011
            ⊕ 10101
               01100
             ⊕ 00000
                11000
              ⊕ 10101
                 11010
               ⊕ 10101
                  11110
                ⊕ 10101
                   1011 → CRC
```

Therefore, the CRC will be 1011.

Hence, code word = Data + CRC

= 1100101011011

## *Checksums*

The checksums method is used to detect double errors in bits. Since, the double error will not change the parity of the bits, the checker will not indicate any error.

In the checksums method, initially a word A (let 11001010) is transmitted, next word B (let 00101101) is transmitted. The sum of these two words is retained in the transmitter. Then a word C is transmitted and added to the previous sum; and the new sum is retained. Similarly, each word is added to the previous sum; after transmission of all the words, the final sum called the checksum is also transmitted. The same operation is done at the receiving end and the final sum obtained here is checked against the transmitted checksum. If the two sums are equal there is no error.

## *Burst Error Detection*

So far, we have considered detecting or correcting errors that occur independently or randomly in digit positions. But disturbances can wipe out an entire block of digits. For example, a stroke of lightening or a human made electrical disturbance can affect several transmitted digits. Burst errors are those errors that wipe out some or all of a sequential set of digits.

A burst of length $b$ is defined as a sequence of digits in which the first digit and $b$th digit are in error, with the $b$-2 digits in between either in error or received correctly.

It can be shown that for detecting all burst errors of length $b$ or less; $b$ parity check bits are necessary and sufficient.

To construct such a code, lets group $k$ data digits into segment of $b$ digits in length as shown in Fig. 1.16:

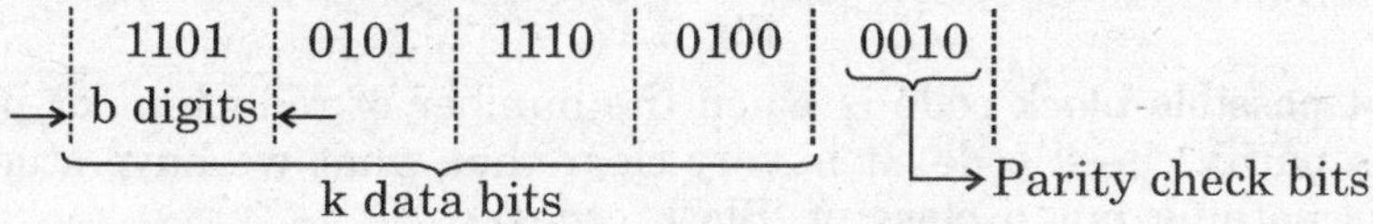


**Fig. 1.16** Burst error detection

To this we add a last segment of $b$ parity check digits, which are determined as follows:

"The modulo-2 sum* of the $i$th digit in each segment (including the parity check segment) must be zero."

It is easy to see that if a single sequence of length $b$ or less is in error, parity will be violated and the error will be detected and the reciever can request retransmission of code.

### 1.9.4 Error Correcting Codes

The mechanism that we have covered upto this point detect errors but do not correct them. Error correction can be handled in two ways. In one, when an error is encountered the receiver can request the sender to retransmit entire data unit. In the other, a receiver can use an error correcting code, which automatically corrects certain errors.

In theory, it is possible to correct any binary code errors automatically using error correcting codes, however, they require more reductant bits than error detecting codes. The number of bits required to correct a multiple-bit or burst error is so high that in most cases, it is inefficient to do so. For this reason, most error correction is limited to one, two, or three-bit errors. However, we shall confine our discussion to only single bit error correction.

As we saw earlier, single bit errors can be detected by the addition of a redundant (parity) bit to the data (information) unit. This provides sufficient base to introduce a very popular error detection as well correction codes, known as Block codes.

**Block codes:** [($n$, $k$) codes] In block codes, each block of $k$ message bits is encoded into a larger block of $n$ bits ($n > k$), as shown in Fig. 1.17. These are also known as ($n$, $k$) codes.

---

*Modulo–2 sum denoted by symbol $\oplus$ with the rules of addition as follows:

$$\left\{\begin{array}{l} 0 \oplus 0 = 0 \\ 0 \oplus 1 = 1 \\ 1 \oplus 0 = 1 \\ 1 \oplus 1 = 0 \end{array}\right\}$$

The reductant* (parity) bits '*r*' are derived from message bits '*k*' and are added to them. The '*n*' bit block of encoder output is called a codeword.

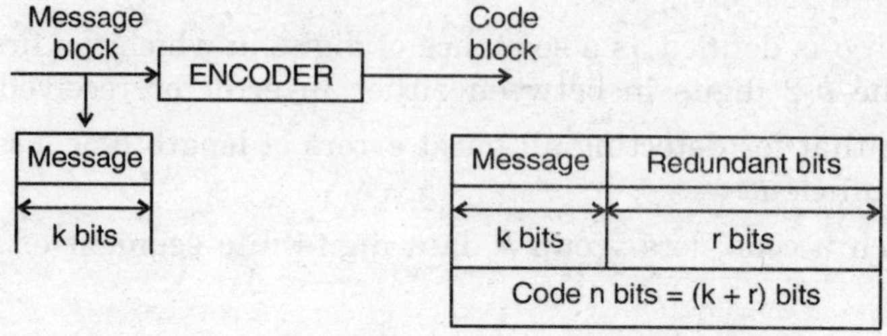


**Fig. 1.17**

The simplest possible block code is when the number of reductant or parity bits is one. This is known as parity check code. It is very clear that what we have studied in single bit error detection is nothing but a class of 'Block codes'.

R.W. Hamming developed a system that provides a methodical way to add one or more parity bit to data unit to detect and correct errors weight of a code.

### *Hamming Distance and Minimum Distance*

The weight of a code word is defined as the number of nonzero components in it. For example,

| *Code word* | *Weight* |
|---|---|
| 010110 | 3 |
| 101000 | 2 |
| 000000 | 0 |

The 'Hamming distance' between two code words is defined as the number of components in which they differ.

For example, Let U = 1010

V = 0111

W = 1001

Then, D (U, V) = distance between U and V = 3

Similarly, D (V, W) = 3

and D (U, W) = 2

The 'minimum distance' ($D_{min}$) of a block code is defined is the smallest distance between any pair of codewords in the code.

From Hamming's analysis of code distances, the following important properties have been derived. If $D_{min}$ is the minimum distance of a block code then

(*i*) '*t*' number of errors can be detected if

$$D_{min} = t + 1$$

(*ii*) '*t*' number of errors can be corrected if

$$D_{min} = 2t + 1$$

It means, we need a minimum distance ($D_{min}$) of at least 3 to correct single error and with this minimum distance we can detect upto 2 errors.

---

*The '*r*' bit are not necessarily appear after '*k*' bits. They may appear at the starting, end or in between '*k*' data bits.

Now coming to our main objective *i.e.*, error correction, we can say that an error occurs when the receiver reads 1 bit as a 0 or a 0 bit as a 1. To correct the error, the reciever simply reverses the value of the altered bit. To do so, however, it must know which bit is in error. The secret of error correction, therefore, is to locate the invalid bit or bits.

For example, to correct a single bit error in a seven bit data unit, the error correction code must determine, which of the seven data bits has changed. In the case we have to distinguish between eight different states: no error, error in position 1, error in position 2, and so on, upto error in position 7. To do so requires enough redundant bits to show all eight states.

At first glance, it appears that a 3-bit redundant code should be adequate because three bits can show eight different states (000 to 111) and can thus indicate the locations of eight different possibilities. But what if an error occurs in the redundant bits themselves. Seven bits of data plus three bits of redundancy equals 10 bits. Three bits, however, can identify only eight possibilities. Additional bits are necessary to cover all possible error locations.

### *Redundant Bits*

To calculate the number of redundant bits ($r$) required to correct a given no. of data bits ($k$), we must find a relationship between $k$ and $r$. Figure 1.18 shows $k$ bits of data with $r$ bits of redundancy added to them. The length of the resulting code is thus $n = k + r$.

If the total no. of bits in code is $k + r$, then $r$ must be able to indicate at least $k + r + 1$ different states. Of these, one state means no error and $k + r$ states indicate the location of an error in each of the $k + r$ positions.

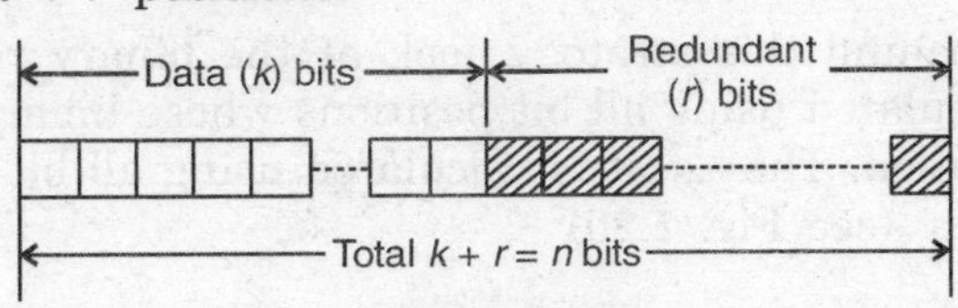


**Fig. 1.18**

Alternatively, we can say the $k + r + 1$ status must be discoverable by $r$ bits; and $r$ bits can indicate $2^r$ different states. Therefore, $2^r$ must be equal to or greater than $k + r + 1$:

$$2^r \geq k + r + 1$$

The value of $r$ can be determined by plugging in the value of $k$ (the length of data unit). For example, if the value of $k$ is 7 ($\Rightarrow$ seven bit data), the smallest $r$ value that can satisfy this equation is 4:

$$2^4 \geq 7 + 4 + 1$$

and

$$2^3 \ngeq 7 + 4 + 1$$

## 1.9.5 Hamming Code

So far, we have examined the number of bits required to cover all of the possible single bit error states in a transmission. But how do we manipulate those bits to discover which state has occured ? A technique developed by R.W. Hamming provides a practical solution, Hamming code is a class of block code ($n$, $k$) and we are going to discuss (11, 7) Hamming code.

### *Positioning the Redundant Bits*

The 'Hamming code' can be applied to data units of any length and uses the relationship between data and redundant bits as discussed above. As we have seen, a 7 bit data unit ($k = 7$) requires 4 redundant bits ($r = 4$) that can be added to the end of data unit (or interspersed with data bits). Such that a code word of length 11 bits ($n = 11$) is formed.

In Fig. 1.19, these bits are placed in positions 1, 2, 4 and 8 (the positions in an 11-bit sequence that are powers of 2). We refer these bits as $r_1$, $r_2$, $r_4$ and $r_8$.

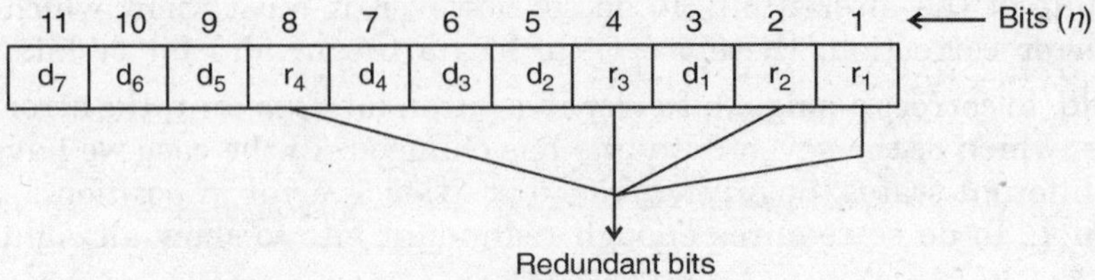


**Fig. 1.19**

In the Hamming code, each $r$ bit is the redundant bit for one combination* of data bits. The combinations (modulo-2 additions) used to calculate each of four $r$ values (viz, $r_1$, $r_2$, $r_4$ and $r_8$) for a 7 bit data sequence $d_1$ through $d_7$ are as follows:

$r_1$ : bits 1, 3, 5, 7, 9, 11

$r_2$ : bits 2, 3, 6, 7, 10, 11

$r_4$ : bits 4, 5, 6, 7

$r_8$ : bits 8, 9, 10, 11

Each data bit may be included in more than one redundant bit calculation. In the sequences above, for example, each of the original data bits is included in at least two sets, while the $r$ bits are included in only one.

To see the pattern behind this strategy, look at the binary representation of each bit position. The $r_1$ bit is calculated using all bit positions whose binary representation includes a 1 in the right most position. The $r_2$ bit is calculated using all bit positions with a 1 in the second position, and so on. (see Fig. 1.20)

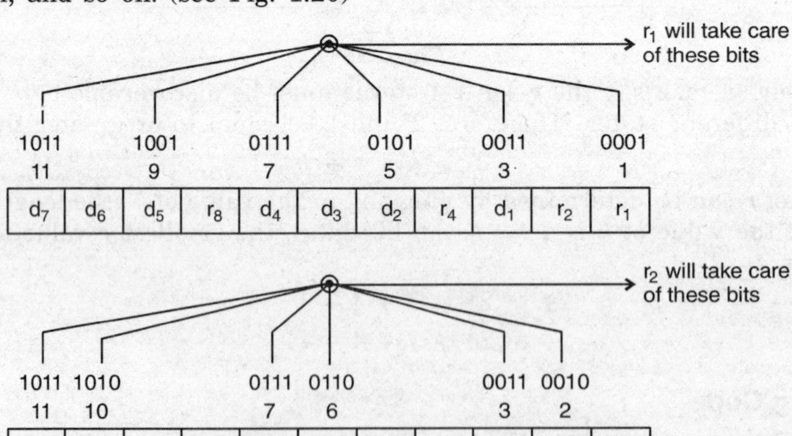


---

*In codes combination of bits means modulo 2 addition the data bits. Modulo-2 addition applies in binary field with following rules.

$$0 \oplus 0 = 0$$

Modulo 2 → ⊕

$$0 \oplus 1 = 1$$

$$1 \oplus 0 = 1$$

$$1 \oplus 1 = 0$$

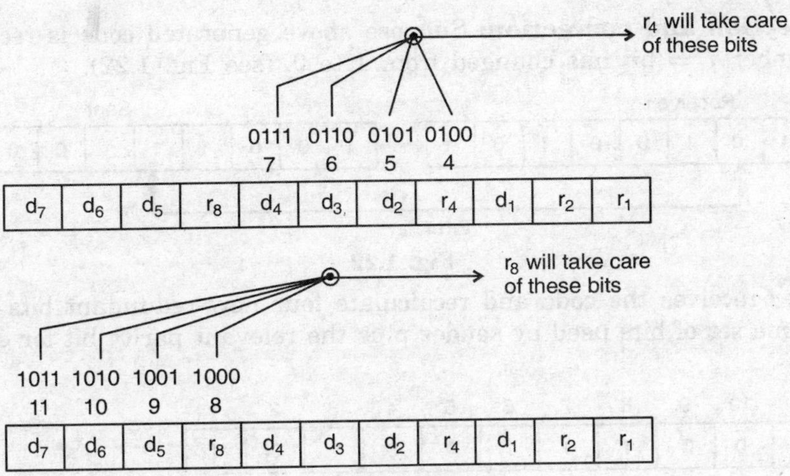


**Fig. 1.20**

### *Calculating the* r *values*

Figure 1.21 shows a Hamming code implementation for a 7 bit data unit. In the first step; we place each bit of original data unit in its appropriate position in the 11-bit unit. For example, let the data unit be 1001101.

In the subsequent steps; we calculate the **EVEN** parities for the various bit combinations. The even parity value for each combination is the value of corresponding $r$ bit. For example, the value of $r_1$ is calculated to provide even parity for a combination of bits 3, 5, 7, 9 and 11.

*i.e.,* 1011 1001 0111 0101 0011 0001

Here, the total no. of 1's are 13. Thus, to provide even parity $r_1 = 1$.

Similarly, the value of $r_2$ is calculated to provide even parity with bits 3, 6, 7, 10, 11, $r_4$ with bits 5, 6, 7 and $r_8$ with bits 9, 10, 11. The final 11-bit code is sent.

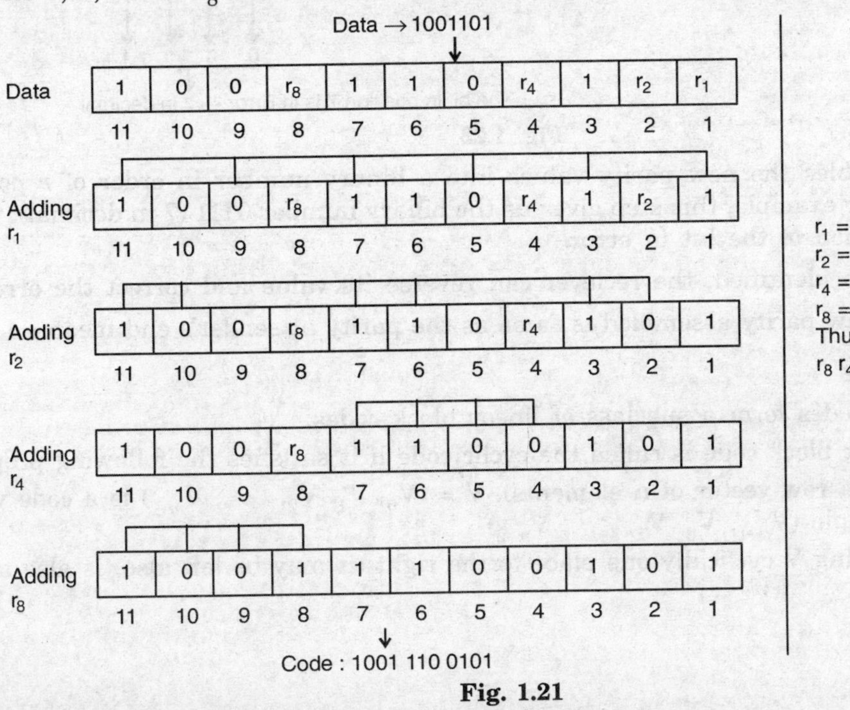


**Fig. 1.21**

**Error detection and correction:** Suppose above generated code is received with the error at bit number 7 ⇒ bit has changed from 1 to 0. (see Fig. 1.22).

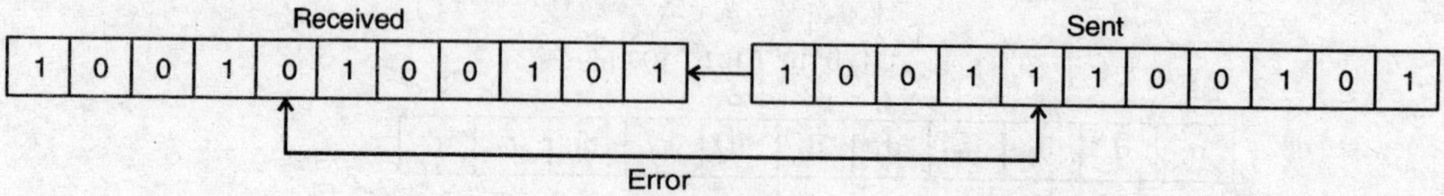


**Fig. 1.22**

The receiver receives the code and recalculate four new redundant bits ($r_1$, $r_2$, $r_4$ and $r_8$) using the same set of bits used by sender plus the relevant parity bit for each set shown in Fig. 1.23.

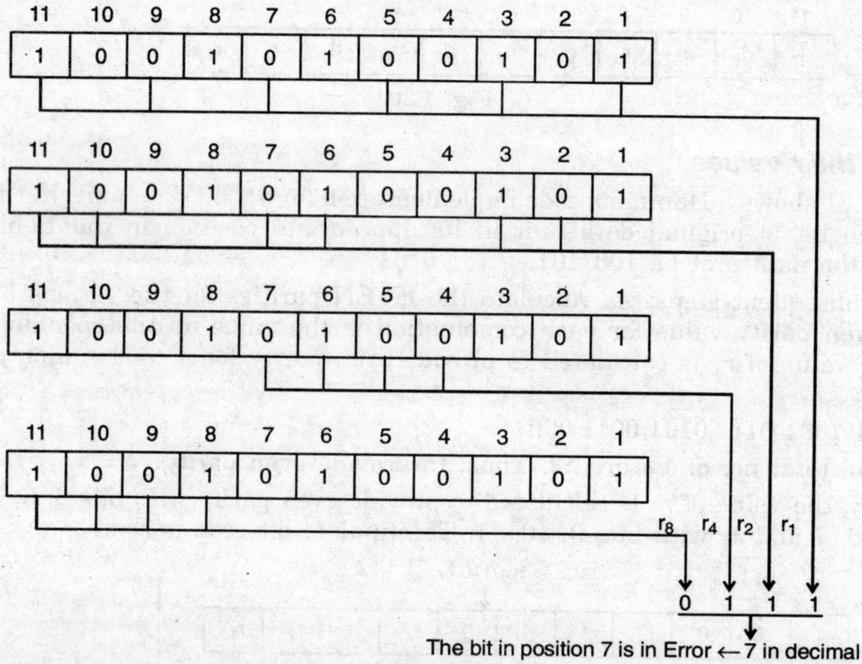


**Fig. 1.23**

Then it assembles the new parity values into a binary number in order of $r$ position ($r_8$, $r_4$, $r_2$, $r_1$). In our example, this step gives us the binary number 0111 (7 in decimal), which is the precise location of the bit in error.

Once the bit is identified, the reciever can reverse its value and correct the error.

**Note:** If the new parity assembled is same as the parity at sender's end mean no error.

## 1.9.6 Cyclic Codes

Binary cyclic codes form a subclass of linear block codes.

An $(n, k)$ linear block code is called the cyclic code if it satisfies the following property:

If an $n$ tuple (a row vector of $n$ elements), $V = (V_0, V_1, V_2, \ldots, V_{n-1})$ is a code vector or V, then the $n$ tuple $(V_{n-1}, V_0, V_1, \ldots, V_{n-2})$

is obtained by shifting V cyclically one place to the right (it may be left also) is also a code vector of V.

$V^1 = (V_{n-1}, V_0, V_1, \ldots, V_{n-2})$. From above definition it is clear that

$$V^{(i)} = (V_{n-i}, V_{n-i+1}, \ldots, V_0, V_1, \ldots V_{n-i-1}).$$

An example of cyclic code:

$$\begin{array}{cccc} 1 & 1 & 0 & 1 \\ 1 & 1 & 1 & 0 \\ 0 & 1 & 1 & 1 \\ 1 & 0 & 1 & 1 \\ \hline 1 & 1 & 0 & 1 \end{array}$$

It can be seen that 1101, 1110, 0111, 1011 are obtained by a cyclic shift of $n$-tuple 1101 ($n$ = 4). The code obtained by rearranging the four words is also a cyclic code. Thus, 1110, 0111, 1011 are also cyclic codes.

This property of cyclic code allows to treat the codewords as a polynomial form. A procedure for generating an $(n, k)$ cyclic code is as follows:

The bits of uncoded word (message), let $D = [d_0, d_1, d_2, \ldots, d_{k-1}]$ are written as the coefficients of polynomial of degree $k - 1$.

$$D(x) = d_0x^0 \oplus d_1x^1 \oplus d_2x^2 \oplus \ldots \oplus d_{k-1}\, x^{k-1}$$

Similarly, the coded word, let $V = [v_0, v_1, v_2, \ldots, v_{n-1}]$ are written as the coefficients of polynomial of degree $n - 1$.

$$V(x) = v_0x^0 \oplus v_1x^1 \oplus v_2x^2 \oplus \ldots \oplus v_{n-1}\, x^{n-1}$$

The coefficients of the polynomials are 0's and 1's and they belong to the binary field with the modulo-2 rules for addition as described in Hamming codes.

Now, we will state a theorem* which is used for cyclic code generation.

**Theorem.** If $g(x)$ is a polynomial of degree $(n-k)$ and is a factor of $x^n+1$, *then* $g(x)$ generates an $(n, k)$ cyclic code in which the code polynomial $V(x)$ for a data polynomial $D(x)$ is given by

$$V(x) = D(x).\, g(x)$$

where
$V(x)$ – Code word polynomial of degree $(n - 1)$
$D(x)$ – Data word polynomial of degree $(k - 1)$
$g(x)$ – Generator polynomial of degree $(n - k)$

**Example 1.30.** *Consider a (7, 4) cyclic code. The generator polynomial for this code is given as* $g(x) = 1 + x + x^3$. *Find all the code words of this code.*

**Solution.** It is a (7, 4) cyclic code

$$n = \text{No. of bits in coded word} = 7$$

and

$$k = \text{No. of bits in data word} = 4.$$

$$(n - k) = \text{No. of redundant bits in code word} = 3$$

It implies that, there are 16 different messages that are possible (0000, 0001, 0010 . . . 1110, 1111). Correspondingly, there will be 16 different codes (of 7 bits).

Now, according to above theorem, the generator polynomial $g(x)$ must be a factor of $(x^n + 1)$** and of degree $(n - k)$.

$$x^n + 1 = x^7 + 1$$

If we factorize this polynomial we get

$$x^7+1 = \underset{\text{I}}{(x + 1)}\ \underset{\text{II}}{(x^3 + x + 1)}\ \underset{\text{III}}{(x^3 + x^2 + 1)}$$

---

*Without giving proof that is beyond the scope of this book.

**+ means modulo-2 operation ⊕ in binary codes.

$$\text{I Factor} \rightarrow x + 1$$
$$\text{II Factor} \rightarrow x^3 + x + 1$$
$$\text{III Factor} \rightarrow x^3 + x^2 + 1$$

The I factor does not satisfy the requirement that it must be of degree $(n - k)$ but the II and III do satisfy.

Therefore, we can either choose II Factor or III Factor as generator polynomial $g(x)$. However, the set of codewords will naturally be different for these two polynomial.

In this example, we have taken $g(x)$ as $1 + x + x^3$.

*i.e.,* we have to encode the 16 messages using generator polynomial.

$$g(x) = 1 + x + x^3.$$

Consider, for example, a data word 1010.

$$D = (d_0, d_1, d_2, d_3) = (1010)$$

Because, the length is four, the data polynomial D($x$)

will be of the form $d_0 + d_1x + d_2x^2 + d_3x^3$

$$D(x) = 1 + 0.x + 1.x^2 + 0.x^3 = 1 + x^2$$

The code polynomial
$$V(x) = D(x) \,.\, g(x)$$
$$= (1 + x^2) \,.\, (1 + x + x^3)$$
$$= 1 + x + x^2 + \underbrace{x^3 + x^3}_{0} + x^5$$

*i.e.,*
$$V(x) = 1 + x + x^2 + x^5$$

Because, if $x = 1$ then $x^3 = 1$

or if $x = 0$ then $x^3 = 0$

$$0 \oplus 0 = 1 \oplus 1 = 0$$

Because, the length of codeword and ($n$) is 7.

So, the standard polynomial will be of the form.

$$V(x) = V_0 + V_1x + V_2x^2 + V_3x^3 + V_4x^4 + V_5x^5 + V_6x^6$$

Comparing this standard polynomial with above poly. for V($x$)

we get
$$V = [1110010]$$

In a similar way, all code vectors can be found out.

### 1.9.7 Alphanumeric Codes

For the inherently binary world of the computer, it is necessary to put all symbols, letters, numbers, etc. into binary form. The most commonly used alphanumeric code is the ASCII code, with other like the EBCDIC code being applied in some communication applications.

#### *ASCII Alphanumeric Code*

The American Standard Code for Information Interchange (ASCII) is the standard alphanumeric code for keyboards and a host of other data interchange tasks. Letters, numbers, and single keystroke commands are represented by a seven-bit word. Typically, a strobe bit or start bit is sent first, followed by the code with LSB first. Being a 7-bit code, it has 2^7 or 128 possible code groups.

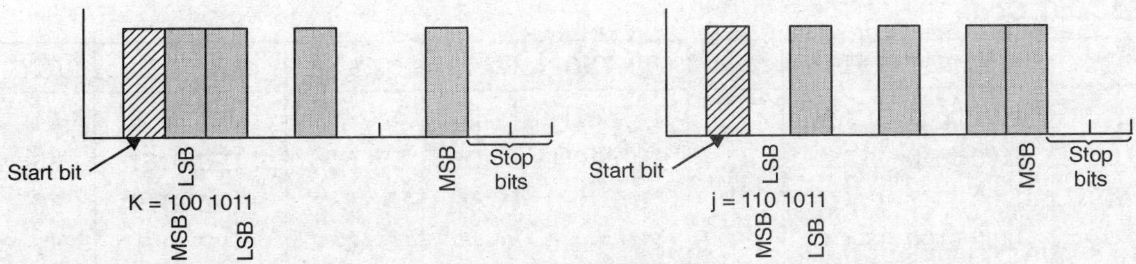


### ASCII Alphanumeric Code

| Char | 7 bit ASCII | HEX | Char | 7 bit ASCII | HEX | Char | 7 bit ASCII | HEX |
|---|---|---|---|---|---|---|---|---|
| A | 100 0001 | 41 | a | 1100001 | 61 | 0 | 0110000 | 30 |
| B | 100 0010 | 42 | b | 1100010 | 62 | 1 | 0110001 | 31 |
| C | 100 0011 | 43 | c | 1100011 | 63 | 2 | 0110010 | 32 |
| D | 100 0100 | 44 | d | 1100100 | 64 | 3 | 0110011 | 33 |
| E | 100 0101 | 45 | e | 1100101 | 65 | 4 | 0110100 | 34 |
| F | 100 0110 | 46 | f | 1100110 | 66 | 5 | 0110101 | 35 |
| G | 100 0111 | 47 | g | 1100111 | 67 | 6 | 0110110 | 36 |
| H | 100 1000 | 48 | h | 1101000 | 68 | 7 | 0110111 | 37 |
| I | 100 1001 | 49 | i | 1101001 | 69 | 8 | 011 1000 | 38 |
| J | 100 1010 | 4A | j | 1101010 | 6A | 9 | 011 1001 | 39 |
| K | 100 1011 | 4B | k | 1101011 | 6B | blank | 0100000 | 20 |
| L | 100 1100 | 4C | l | 110 1100 | 6C | . | 010 1110 | 2E |
| M | 100 1101 | 4D | m | 110 1101 | 6D | ( | 010 1000 | 28 |
| N | 100 1110 | 4E | n | 110 1110 | 6E | + | 010 1011 | 2B |
| O | 100 1111 | 4F | o | 110 1111 | 6F | $ | 010 0100 | 24 |
| P | 101 0000 | 50 | p | 111 0000 | 70 | * | 010 1010 | 2A |
| Q | 101 0001 | 51 | q | 111 0001 | 71 | ) | 010 1001 | 29 |
| R | 101 0010 | 52 | r | 111 0010 | 72 | - | 010 1101 | 2D |
| S | 101 0011 | 53 | s | 111 0011 | 73 | / | 010 1111 | 2F |
| T | 101 0100 | 54 | t | 111 0100 | 74 | , | 010 1100 | 2C |
| U | 101 0101 | 55 | u | 111 0101 | 75 | = | 011 1101 | 3D |
| V | 101 0110 | 56 | v | 111 0110 | 76 | RETURN | 000 1101 | 0D |
| W | 101 0111 | 57 | w | 111 0111 | 77 | LNFEED | 000 1010 | 0A |
| X | 101 1000 | 58 | x | 111 1000 | 78 | 0 | 011 0000 | 30 |
| Y | 101 1001 | 59 | y | 111 1001 | 79 | 0 | 011 0000 | 30 |
| Z | 101 1010 | 5A | z | 111 1010 | 7A | 0 | 011 0000 | 30 |

### EBCDIC Alphanumeric Code

The extended binary coded decimal interchange code (EBCDIC) is an 8-bit alphanumeric code which has been extensively used by IBM in its mainframe applications.

### EBCDIC Code

| *Char* | *EBCDIC* | *HEX* | *Char* | *EBCDIC* | *HEX* | *Char* | *EBCDIC* | *HEX* |
|---|---|---|---|---|---|---|---|---|
| A | 1100 0001 | C1 | P | 1101 0111 | D7 | 4 | 1111 0100 | F4 |
| B | 1100 0010 | C2 | Q | 1101 1000 | D8 | 5 | 1111 0101 | F5 |
| C | 1100 0011 | C3 | R | 1101 1001 | D9 | 6 | 1111 0110 | F6 |
| D | 1100 0100 | C4 | S | 1110 0010 | E2 | 7 | 1111 0111 | F7 |
| E | 1100 0101 | C5 | T | 1110 0011 | E3 | 8 | 1111 1000 | F8 |
| F | 1100 0110 | C6 | U | 1110 0100 | E4 | 9 | 1111 10001 | F9 |
| G | 1100 0111 | C7 | V | 1110 0101 | E5 | blank | ... | ... |
| H | 1100 1000 | C8 | W | 1110 0110 | E6 | . | ... | ... |
| I | 1100 1001 | C9 | X | 1110 0111 | E7 | ( | ... | ... |
| J | 1101 0001 | D1 | Y | 1110 1000 | E8 | + | ... | ... |
| K | 1101 0010 | D2 | Z | 1110 1001 | E9 | $ | ... | ... |
| L | 1101 0011 | D3 | 0 | 1111 0000 | F0 | * | ... | ... |
| M | 1101 0100 | D4 | 1 | 1111 0001 | F1 | ) | ... | ... |
| N | 1101 0101 | D5 | 2 | 1111 0010 | F2 | - | ... | ... |
| O | 1101 0110 | D6 | 3 | 1111 0011 | F3 | / | ... | ... |

## 1.10 SOLVED EXAMPLES

**Example 1.** *Convert each binary number to the decimal:*

(*a*) $(11)_2$
$(1011)_2$
$(10111)_2$
$(1111)_2$
$(11010111)_2$
$(1001)_2$

(*b*) $(.11)_2$
$(.111)_2$
$(.1011)_2$
$(.10101)_2$
$(.0101)_2$
$(.110)_2$

(*c*) $(11.11)_2$
$(1011.1011)_2$
$(1111.0101)_2$
$(11010111.110)_2$
$(1001.10101)_2$

**Solution.** (*a*)

$$(11)_2 = 1 \times 2^1 + 1 \times 2^0 = 2 + 1 = 3$$

$$(1011)_2 = 1 \times 2^3 + 0 \times 2^2 + 1 \times 2^1 + 1 \times 2^0 = 8 + 0 + 2 + 1 = 11$$

$$(10111)_2 = 1 \times 2^4 + 0 \times 2^3 + 1 \times 2^2 + 1 \times 2^1 + 1 \times 2^0 = 16 + 0 + 4 + 2 + 1 = 23$$

$$(1111)_2 = 1 \times 2^3 + 1 \times 2^2 + 1 \times 2^1 + 1 \times 2^0 = 8 + 4 + 2 + 1 = 15$$

$$(11010111)_2 = 1 \times 2^7 + 1 \times 2^6 + 0 \times 2^5 + 1 \times 2^4 + 0 \times 2^3 + 1 \times 2^2 + 1 \times 2^1 + 1 \times 2^0$$
$$= 128 + 64 + 0 + 16 + 0 + 4 + 2 + 1 = 215$$
$$(1001)_2 = 1 \times 2^3 + 0 \times 2^2 + 0 \times 2^1 + 1 \times 2^0$$
$$= 8 + 0 + 0 + 1 = 9$$

(*b*)
$$(.11)_2 = 1 \times 2^{-1} + 1 \times 2^{-2}$$
$$= .5 + .25 = (.75)_{10}$$
$$(.111)_2 = 1 \times 2^{-1} + 1 \times 2^{-2} + 1 \times 2^{-3}$$
$$= .5 + .25 + .125 = (.875)_{10}$$
$$(.1011)_2 = 1 \times 2^{-1} + 0 \times 2^{-2} + 1 \times 2^{-3} + 1 \times 2^{-4}$$
$$= .5 + 0 + .125 + .0625 = (.6875)_{10}$$
$$(.10101)_2 = 1 \times 2^{-1} + 0 \times 2^{-2} + 1 \times 2^{-3} + 0 \times 2^{-4} + 1 \times 2^{-5}$$
$$= .5 + 0 + .125 + 0 + .03125 = (.65625)_{10}$$
$$(.0101)_2 = 0 \times 2^{-1} + 1 \times 2^{-2} + 0 \times 2^{-3} + 1 \times 2^{-4}$$
$$= 0 + .25 + 0 + .0625 = (.3125)_{10}$$
$$(.110)_2 = 1 \times 2^{-1} + 1 \times 2^{-2} + 0 \times 2^{-3}$$
$$= .5 + .25 + 0 = (.75)_{10}$$

(*c*)
$$11.11 = ?$$

From part (*a*) and part (*b*), we see that

$$11 = 3$$
$$11 = .75$$

Therefore, $(11.11)_2 = (3.75)_{10}$

$$1011.1011 = ?$$
$$(1011)_2 = 11$$
$$(.1011)_2 = .6875$$

Therefore, $(1011.1011)_2 = (11.6875)_{10}$

$$1111.0101 = ?$$
$$(1111)_2 = 15$$
$$(.0101)_2 = .3125$$

Therefore, $(1111.0101)_2 = (15.3125)_{10}$

$$11010111.110 = ?$$
$$11010111 = 215$$
$$.110 = .75$$
$$(11010111.110)_2 = (215.75)_{10}$$
$$1001.10101 = ?$$
$$1001 = 9$$
$$.10101 = .65625$$
$$(1001.10101)_2 = (9.65625)_{10}$$

**Example 2.** *How many bits are required to represent the following decimal numbers, represent them in binary?*

*(I) $(17)_{10}$ (II) $(27)_{10}$ (III) $(81)_{10}$ (IV) $(112)_{10}$ (V) $(215)_{10}$*

**Solution.** (I) Let $n$ bits required

$n$ should be such that

$$2^n \geq \text{Given Number (N)}$$

Therefore, $\quad 2^n \geq 17$

*i.e.,* $\quad n \geq 5$

Therefore, minimum number of bits required = 5.

Remainder

$$\begin{array}{r|rl} 2 & 17 & 1 \quad \uparrow \text{LSB} \\ 2 & 8 & 0 \\ 2 & 4 & 0 \\ 2 & 2 & 0 \\ 2 & 1 & 1 \quad \text{MSB} \\ & 0 & \end{array}$$

$(17)_{10} = (10001)_2$

(II) $(27)_{10}$

The minimum number of bits required is given by

$$2^n \geq \text{N (given number)}$$

$$2^n \geq 27$$

*i.e.,* $\quad n \geq 5$

$$\begin{array}{r|rl} 2 & 27 & 1 \quad \uparrow \text{LSB} \\ 2 & 13 & 1 \\ 2 & 6 & 0 \\ 2 & 3 & 1 \\ 2 & 1 & 1 \quad \text{MSB} \\ & 0 & \end{array}$$

$(27)_{10} = (11011)_2$

(III) $(81)_{10}$

The minimum number of bits required is given by

$$2^n \geq \text{N}$$

$$2^n \geq 81$$

*i.e.,* $\quad n = 7$

Remainder

$$\begin{array}{r|rl} 2 & 81 & 1 \quad \uparrow \text{LSB} \\ 2 & 40 & 0 \\ 2 & 20 & 0 \\ 2 & 10 & 0 \\ 2 & 5 & 1 \\ 2 & 2 & 0 \\ 2 & 1 & 1 \quad \text{MSB} \\ & 0 & \end{array}$$

$(81)_{10} = (1010001)_2$

(IV) $(112)_{10}$

The minimum number of bits required is given by

$$2^n \geq \text{N}$$

$$2^n \geq 112$$

*i.e.,* $\quad n = 7$

$$\begin{array}{r|rl} 2 & 112 & 0 \quad \uparrow \text{LSB} \\ 2 & 56 & 0 \\ 2 & 28 & 0 \\ 2 & 14 & 0 \\ 2 & 7 & 1 \\ 2 & 3 & 1 \\ 2 & 1 & 1 \quad \text{MSB} \\ & 0 & \end{array}$$

$(112)_{10} = (1110000)_2$

(V) $(215)_{10}$

The minimum number of bits required is given by

$$2^n \geq 215$$

*i.e.,* $\quad n = 8$

$$\begin{array}{r|rl} 2 & 215 & 1 \quad \uparrow \text{LSB} \\ 2 & 107 & 1 \\ 2 & 53 & 1 \\ 2 & 26 & 0 \\ 2 & 13 & 1 \\ 2 & 6 & 0 \\ 2 & 3 & 1 \\ 2 & 1 & 1 \quad \text{MSB} \\ & 0 & \end{array}$$

$(215)_{10} = (11010111)_2$

**Example 3.** *Convert the following numbers as indicated:*

*(a) decimal 225.225 into binary, octal and hexadecimal.*

*(b) binary 11010111.110 into decimal, octal and hexadecimal.*

*(c) octal 623.77 into decimal, binary and hexadecimal.*

*(d) hexadecimal 2AC5.D into decimal, octal and binary.*

**Solution.** (*a*) 225.225 = $(?)_2$

| | | Remainder | |
|---|---|---|---|
| 2 | 225 | 1 | LSB ↑ |
| 2 | 112 | 0 | |
| 2 | 56 | 0 | |
| 2 | 28 | 0 | |
| 2 | 14 | 0 | |
| 2 | 7 | 1 | |
| 2 | 3 | 1 | |
| 2 | 1 | 1 | MSB |
| | 0 | | |

Integer part = 11100001

| $(.225)_{10}$ | = | $(?)_2$ | Carry |
|---|---|---|---|
| .225 × 2 | = | 0.450 | 0 |
| .450 × 2 | = | 0.900 | 0 |
| .900 × 2 | = | 1.800 | 1 |
| .800 × 2 | = | 1.600 | 1 |
| .600 × 2 | = | 1.200 | 1 |
| .200 × 2 | = | 0.400 | 0 |
| .400 × 2 | = | 0.800 | 0 |
| .800 × 2 | = | 1.600 | 1 |
| .600 × 2 | = | 1.200 | 1 ↓ |

Fraction part = 001110011

Therefore,

$$(225.225)_{10} = 11100001.001110011$$

$$(225.225)_{10} = (?)_8$$

From the previous step, we know the binary equivalent of decimal no. as 11100001.001110011.

For octal number, binary number is partitioned into group of three digit each starting from right to left and replacing decimal equivalent of each group.

| –11 | 100 | 001 | . | 001 | 110 | 011 |
|---|---|---|---|---|---|---|
| 011 | 100 | 001 | . | 001 | 110 | 011 |
| ↓ | ↓ | ↓ | | | | |
| 3 | 4 | 1 | | 1 | 6 | 3 |

$$(225.225)_{10} = (341.163)_8$$
$$(225.225)_{10} = (?)_{16}$$

For hexadecimal number, instead of three four digits are grouped.

$$\underbrace{1110}\ \underbrace{0001} . \underbrace{0011}\ \underbrace{1001}\ \underbrace{1\text{- - -}}$$
$$\underbrace{1110}_{14 \equiv E}\ \underbrace{0001}_{1} . \underbrace{0011}_{3}\ \underbrace{1001}_{9}\ \underbrace{1000}_{8}$$
$$(225.225)_{10} = \text{E1.398}$$

(*b*) $$(11010111.110)_2 = (?)_{10}$$

From example 1.6.1

$$(11010111.110)_2 = (215.75)_{10}$$
$$(11010111.110)_2 = (?)_8$$
$$\underbrace{-11}\ \underbrace{010}\ \underbrace{111}$$
$$\underbrace{011}_{3}\ \underbrace{010}_{2}\ \underbrace{111}_{7} = 327$$
$$\underbrace{.110}_{6} = 6$$
$$(11010111.110)_2 = (327.6)_8$$
$$(11010111.110)_2 = (?)_{16}$$
$$\underbrace{1101}_{13 \equiv D}\ \underbrace{0111}_{7} = \text{D7}$$
$$\underbrace{0.110\text{-}}_{1100} \;\; \underbrace{1100}_{12 = C} = \text{C}$$
$$(11010111.110)_2 = (\text{D7.C})_{16}$$

(*c*) $$(623.77)_8 = (?)_2$$

$$623 = 110010011$$
$$0.77 = 111111$$
$$(623.77)_8 = (110010011.111111)_2$$
$$(623.77)_8 = (?)_{16}$$
$$\underbrace{\text{- - -}1}\ \underbrace{1001}\ \underbrace{0011}$$
$$\underbrace{0001}_{1}\ \underbrace{1001}_{9}\ \underbrace{0011}_{3} = 193$$
$$\underbrace{1111}\ \ \underbrace{11\text{ - -}}$$
$$\underbrace{1111}_{15 \equiv F}\ \ \underbrace{1100}_{12 = C} = \text{FC}$$
$$(623.77)_8 = (193.\text{FC})_{16}$$

$$(623.77)_8 = (?)_{10}$$

$$623 = 6 \times 8^2 + 2 \times 8^1 + 3 \times 8^0$$

$$= 384 + 16 + 3$$

$$= 403$$

$$0.77 = 7 \times 8^{-1} + 7 \times 8^{-2}$$

$$= 7 \times 0.125 + 7 \times 0.015625$$

$$= 0.875 + 0.109375$$

$$= 0.9843$$

$$(623.77)_8 = (403.9843)_{10}$$

(*d*) $(2AC5.D)_{16} = (?)_2$

$$2AC5 = 0010101011000101$$

$$D = 1101$$

$$(2AC5.D)_{16} = (10101011000101.1101)_2$$

$$(2AC5.D)_{16} = (?)_8$$

| -10 | 101 | 011 | 000 | 101 | . | 110 | 1 - - |
|---|---|---|---|---|---|---|---|
| 010 | 101 | 011 | 000 | 101 | . | 110 | 100 |
| 2 | 5 | 3 | 0 | 5 | | 6 | 4 |

$$(2AC5.D)_{16} = (25305.64)_8$$

$$(2AC5.D)_{16} = (?)_{10}$$

$$2AC5 = 2 \times 16^3 + 10 \times 16^2 + 12 \times 16^1 + 5 \times 16^0$$

$$= 2 \times 4096 + 10 \times 256 + 12 \times 16 + 5 \times 1$$

$$= 8192 + 2560 + 192 + 5$$

$$= 10949$$

$$D = 13 \times 16^{-1}$$

$$= 13 \times .0625$$

$$= 0.8125$$

$$(2AC5.D)_{16} = (10949.8125)_{10}$$

**Example 4.** *Obtain the 9's and 10's complement of the following decimal numbers: (i) 10000, (ii) 00000, (iii) 13469, (iv) 90099, (v) 09900*

**Solution.** 9's complement

| (*i*) | (*ii*) | (*iii*) | (*iv*) | (*v*) |
|---|---|---|---|---|
| 99999 | 99999 | 99999 | 99999 | 99999 |
| 10000 | 00000 | 13469 | 90099 | 09900 |
| 89999 | 99999 | 86530 | 09900 | 90099 |

10's complement = 9's complement + 1 (LSB)

| (*i*) | (*ii*) | (*iii*) | (*iv*) | (*v*) |
|---|---|---|---|---|
| 89999 | 99999 | 86530 | 09900 | 90099 |
| + 1 | + 1 | + 1 | + 1 | + 1 |
| 90000 | 100000 | 86531 | 09901 | 90100 |

**Example 5.** *Perform the subtraction with the decimal numbers given using*
*(1) 10's complement.*
*(2) 9's complement.*
*Check the answer by straight subtraction*
*(a) 5249 – 320 (b) 3571 – 2101.*

**Solution.** (*a*) **Using 10's complement.** 10's complement of 320

```
 9999
–0320
-----
 9679
   +1
-----
 9680
```

Therefore, 5249 – 320 = 5249 + 9680

```
        5249
       +9680
CY → (1)4929
discarded
```

Result = 4929

**Using 9's complement.** 9's complement of 320

```
 9999
–0320
-----
 9679
```

Therefore, 5249 – 320 = 5249 + 9679

```
        5249
      + 9679
CY → (1)4928
         └──→1
        4929
```

Result = 4929

**By straight subtraction**

```
 5249
– 320
-----
 4929
```

Hence, results are same by each method.

(*b*) **Using 10's complement**

10's complement of 2101 =

```
 9999
–2101
-----
 7898
   +1
-----
 7899
```

Therefore, 3571 – 2101 = 3571 + 7899

```
        3571
       +7899
CY → (1)0470
discarded
```

Result = 470

**Using 9's complement**

9's complement of 2101 = 7898

Therefore, 3571 – 2101 = 3571

```
                    3571
                   +7898
            ------------
       CY → (1)0469
             └──→1
            ------------
                     470
```

**By straight subtraction**

```
   3571
  –2101
  -----
    470
```

Hence, results are same by each method.

**Example 6.** *Obtain the 1's and 2's complement of the following binary numbers (I) 11100101 (II) 0111000 (III) 1010101 (IV) 10000 (V) 00000.*

**Solution.**

(*I*) 1's complement = 00011010

2's complement = 1's complement + 1 = 00011011

(*II*) 1's complement = 1000111

2's complement = 1000111

```
  1000111
        1
  -------
  1001000
```

(*III*) 1's complement = 0101010

2's complement = 0101011

(*IV*) 1's complement = 01111

2's complement = 10000

(*V*) 1's complement = 11111

2's complement = 00000

## 1.11 EXERCISE

**1.** Write 9's and 10's complement of the following numbers:

+9090

–3578

+136.8

–136.28

**2.** (*a*) Convert the decimal integer's +21 and –21 into 10's complement and 9's complement.

(*b*) Convert the above two numbers into binary and express them in six bit (total) signed magnitude and 2's complement.

**3.** (*a*) Find the decimal equivalent of the following binary numbers assuming signed magnitude representation of the binary number:

(*I*) 001000 (*II*) 1111

(*b*) Write the procedure for the subtraction of two numbers with $(r - 1)$'s complement.

(*c*) Perform the subtraction with the following binary numbers using 2's complement and 1's complement respectively.

(*I*) 11010 – 1101 (*II*) 10010 – 10011

(*d*) Perform the subtraction with following decimal numbers using 10's complement and 9's complement respectively.

(*I*) 5294 – 749 (*II*) 27 – 289

**4.** Convert:

(*I*) $(225.225)_{12}$ into Hexadecimal number.

(*II*) $(2AC5.15)_{16}$ into Octal number.

**5.** Perform the following using 6's complement:

(*I*) $(126)_7 + (42)_7$

(*II*) $(126)_7 - (42)_7$

**6.** Represent the following decimal numbers in two's complement format:

(*I*) +5 (*II*) +25 (*III*) –5 (*IV*) –25 (*V*) –9

**7.** Represent the decimal numbers of question 6 in ones complement format.

**8.** Find the decimal equivalent of each of the following numbers assuming them to be in two's complement format.

(*a*) 1000 (*b*) 0110 (*c*) 10010 (*d*) 00110111

**9.** Convert the following octal numbers into equivalent decimal numbers:

(*a*) 237 (*b*) 0.75 (*c*) 237.75

**10.** Represent the following decimal numbers in sign-magnitude format:

(*a*) –11 (*b*) –7 (*c*) +12 (*d*) +25

2
CHAPTER

# REVIEW OF THE DIGITAL FUNDAMENTALS

## 2.0 DIGITAL (BINARY) SIGNAL REPRESENTATION

### Positive and Negative Logic

The binary signals (except during transition) have two discrete values at the input or output of any gate. One signal value represents logic-0 (LOW) and the other, logic-1 (HIGH). The two different representations of the digital signals are shown in Fig. 2.0*a* and Fig. 2.0*b*.

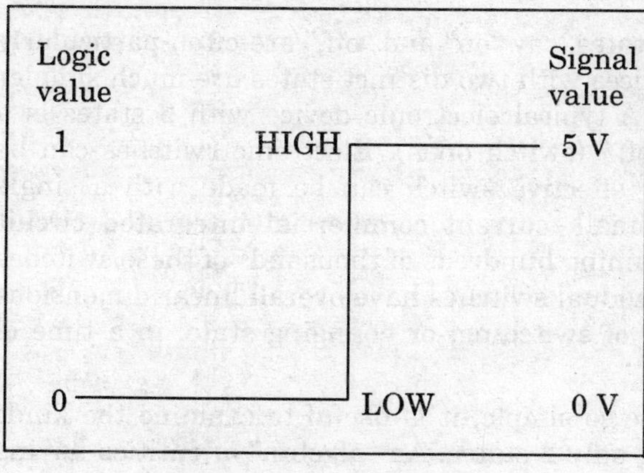


**Fig. 2.0*a*** Positive Logic

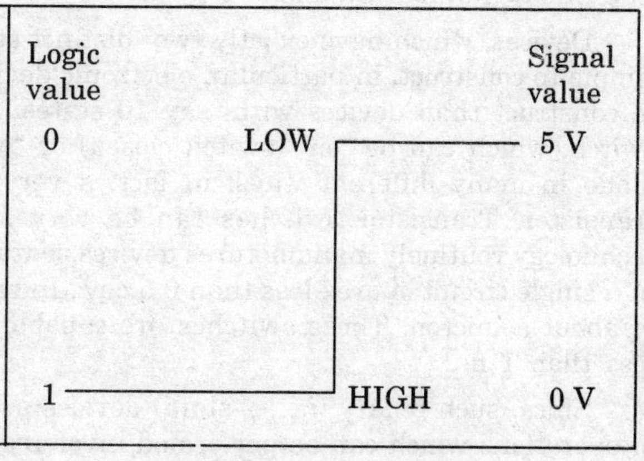


**Fig. 2.0*b*** Negative Logic

In Fig. 2.0*a* higher of two levels has been designated as HIGH level and the lower of the two levels has been designated as LOW level. This representation of binary (digital) signal is known as positive logic representation. In contrast to this, in Fig. 2.0*b* the lower of the two levels has been designated as HIGH level and the higher as LOW level. This representation of binary (digital) signal is known as negative logic representation.

Practically, voltage corresponding to a given level is not fixed; instead voltages in a limited range are designated as a level. As long as the voltage belongs to a particular level it will be taken as that level and the exact value of the voltage is irrelevant.

For example, any voltage in the range 4 to 5 V will be considered as LOW in the negative logic system and HIGH level in the positive logic system. In the same way, any voltage in the range 0 to 1V will be considered as HIGH in the negative logic system and LOW level in the positive logic system. The actual ranges of voltages for individual level are not same for all types of circuits but are different for different logic families (see Chapter 10).

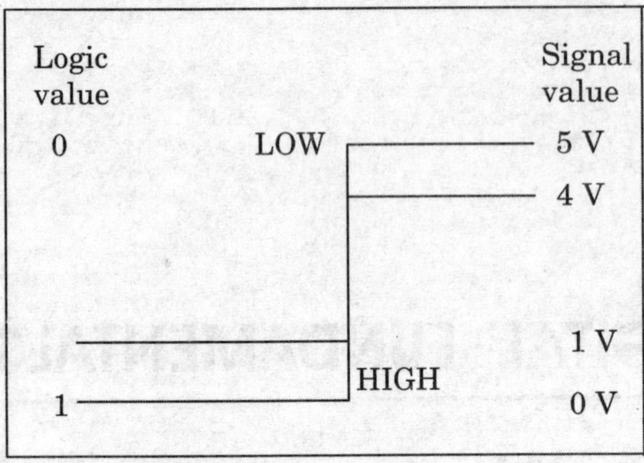


**Fig. 2.0*c*** Negative Logic

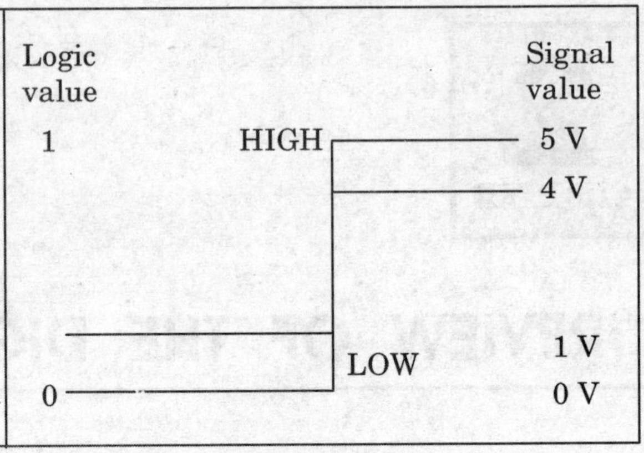


**Fig. 2.0*d*** Positive Logic

## 2.1 SWITCHING FUNCTIONS – LOGIC

Many things can be described by two distinct **states**; for example, a light can be "on" or "off;" a door can be "open" or "closed;" a statement can be "true" or "false." Indeed, we can define a number system which has only two digits, 0 and 1, to represent any number we wish (the binary number system).

Devices, which have exactly two distinct states, say "on" and "off," are often particularly simple to construct; in particular, electronic devices with two distinct states are much simpler to construct than devices with, say 10 states. A typical electronic device with 2 states is a switch, which can be "on" (switch closed) or "off" (switch open). Electronic switches can be made in many different ways; in fact, a very effective switch can be made with a single transistor. Transistor switches can be very small; current commercial integrated circuit technology routinely manufactures devices containing hundreds of thousands of these switches in a single circuit of area less than 0.5 $cm^2$. Individual switches have overall linear dimensions of about a micron. These switches are capable of switching, or changing state, in a time of less than 1 ns.

Since, such binary (*i.e.*, 2-state) devices are so simple, it is useful to examine the kinds of operations which can be performed involving only 2 states. An "algebra" of entities having exactly two states ("true" and "false" or "1" and "0" was developed by the mathematician George Boole, and later called Boolean Algebra. This algebra was applied to electronic switching circuits by Shannon, as a "switching algebra." This algebra is extremely useful in that it can allow us to describe switching functions which perform many common operations, including binary arithmetic.

Switching algebra can be defined as an algebraic system consisting of the set {0,1}, two binary operations called OR (+) and AND (·) and one unary operation (–) called NOT, or complementation, or inversion.

These operations are defined as follows:

| OR (+) | AND (·) | NOT (–) |
|---|---|---|
| $0 + 0 = 0$ | $0 \cdot 0 = 0$ | $\overline{0} = 1$ |
| $0 + 1 = 1$ | $0 \cdot 1 = 0$ | $\overline{1} = 0$ |

$$1 + 0 = 1 \qquad 1 \cdot 0 = 0$$
$$1 + 1 = 1 \qquad 1 \cdot 1 = 1$$

This switching algebra has a number of properties which can be given as:

**Idempotency**

$$A + A = A; \qquad A \cdot A = A$$

**Commutativity**

$$A + B = B + A; \qquad A \cdot B = B \cdot A$$

**Associativity**

$$(A + B) + C = A + (B + C); \qquad (A \cdot B) \cdot C = A \cdot (B \cdot C)$$

**Distributivity**

$$A \cdot (B + C) = A \cdot B + A \cdot C; \qquad A + (B \cdot C) = (A + B) \cdot (A + C)$$

**Absorption**

$$A + (A \cdot B) = A; \qquad A \cdot (A + B) = A$$

**Consensus**

$$A \cdot B + \overline{A} \cdot C + B \cdot C = A \cdot B + \overline{A} \cdot C; \qquad (A+B) \cdot (\overline{A}+C) \cdot (B+C) = (A+B) \cdot (\overline{A}+C)$$

**Note:** In both cases, the term which is eliminated is called the *consensus* of the remaining two terms.

**de Morgans theorem**

$$\overline{A+B} = \overline{A} \cdot \overline{B}; \quad \overline{A \cdot B} = \overline{A} + \overline{B}$$

de Morgans theorem can be generalized to

$$\overline{F(A_1, A_2, \ldots, A_n, 0, 1, +, .)} = F(\overline{A_1}, \overline{A_2}, \ldots, \overline{A_n}, 1, 0, +, .)$$

That is, the complement of any expression can be obtained by replacing each variable and element with its complement, and at the same time interchanging the OR and AND operators.

Note that each of the preceding properties occur in pairs, and that one of the pairs can be obtained from the other simply by replacing the AND operator by the OR operator, and vice-versa. This property is called "duality", and the operators AND and OR are said to be "dual". This property comes about because if the 1's are changed to 0's and 0's are changed to 1's in the definition of the AND function, the function becomes the OR function; similarly, the OR function becomes the AND function. This property is general, and if one theorem is shown to be true, then its dual will also be true.

In electrical engineering and logic design, switching operations are performed with **logic gates**. These logic gates use voltages or currents to represent the logic values 0 and 1; typically, logic 0 is 0V, and logic 1 is 5V (positive logic). These logic gates are the components of an electric circuit, and special symbols are used to represent these circuit elements.

The NOT gate has the circuit symbol or logic symbol shown in Fig. 2.1 (*a*).

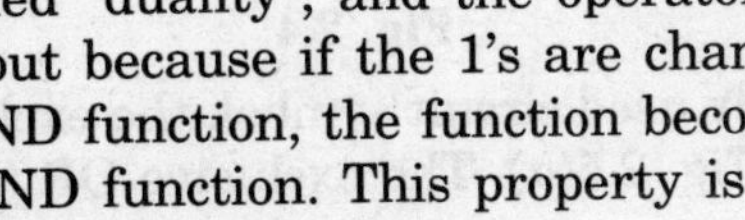


**Fig. 2.1**

The input (A) is on the left, and the output ($\overline{A}$) is on the right. Note that the little circle (O) denotes the NOT function, and the circuit symbol without the circle shown in Fig. 2.1 (*b*) performs no logic function, and is called a "buffer." The NOT gate is often called an "inverter."

**Note:** Although the "buffer" performs no logic function, it is commonly used to increase the output capability of other logic devices.

The AND and OR gates have the circuit symbols shown in Fig. 2.2(*a*) and 2.2(*b*), respectively.

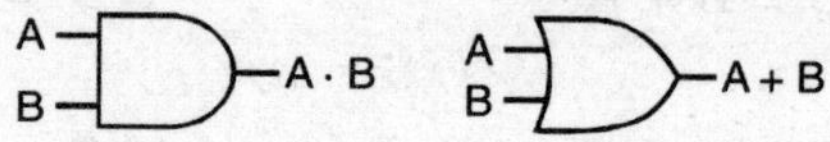


(*a*) (*b*)

**Fig. 2.2**

One can also use this notation to denote other switching functions; *e.g.*, the NAND function, AND followed by NOT is shown in Fig. 2.3 (*a*). The NOR function, OR followed by NOT, is shown in Fig. 2.3 (*b*).

(*a*) (*b*)

**Fig. 2.3**

One can also extend this notation to N-input logic gates; *e.g.*, for an N-input OR gate or an N-input AND gate, we have the symbols shown in Fig. 2.4 (*a*) and (*b*), respectively.

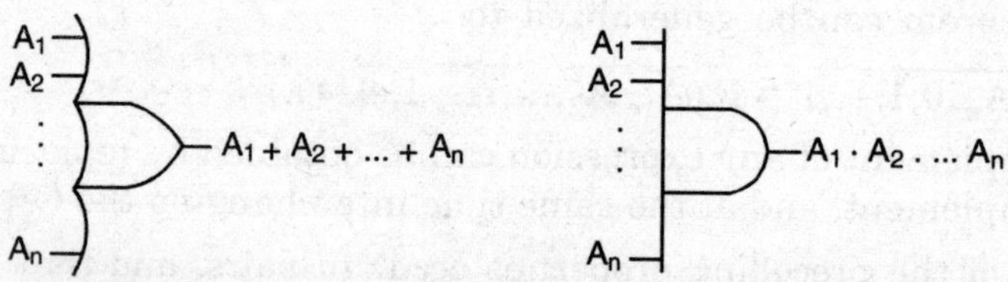


(*a*) (*b*)

**Fig. 2.4**

There is one other commonly used circuit symbol, the exclusive-OR function. This function has the logic symbol shown in Fig. 2.5(*a*). The exclusive-OR (XOR) function is denoted by the symbol ⊕ and has the truth table shown with the logic symbol in Fig. 2.5. The XOR function is useful for comparing two values for equality, and has obvious applications as an arithmetic function.

| A | B | A ⊕ B |
|---|---|---|
| 0 | 0 | 0 |
| 0 | 1 | 1 |
| 1 | 0 | 1 |
| 1 | 1 | 0 |

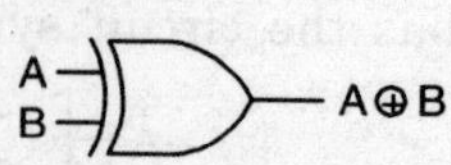


**Fig. 2.5**

Any of the three basic logic function AND, OR, NOT can be represented in –ve logic as well. This is explained for OR gate as follows:

+ve logic 'OR'

| A | B | Y |
|---|---|---|
| 0 | 0 | 0 |
| 0 | 1 | 1 |
| 1 | 0 | 1 |
| 1 | 1 | 1 |

–ve logic 'OR'

| A | B | Y |
|---|---|---|
| 1 | 1 | 1 |
| 1 | 0 | 0 |
| 0 | 1 | 0 |
| 0 | 0 | 0 |

**Fig. 2.5(*a*)**

As shown, replace every "1" by "0" and "0" by "1" in the truth table of the +ve logic to derive the corresponding –ve logic truth table. This means complementing each of the input and the O/P. The same is done by using bubbles at I/Ps and at O/P. The bubble stands for complementing. Using such a notation for complementing is called "ASSERTION LEVEL LOGIC". Note that the truth table of –ve OR is same as truth table of the AND. Thus, we can say –ve OR is equivalent to the AND. The reader is encouraged to derive similar equalities for other gates.

## 2.2 SWITCH IMPLEMENTATION OF SWITCHING FUNCTIONS

As the name suggests, switching functions can be implemented using simple switches. In fact, in digital electronic circuits, transistors are used as simple switches in circuits very similar those which follow. The functions NOT, AND and OR can be easily implemented with two simple switches, as shown in Fig. 2.6 (*a*), (*b*) and (*c*). Note that, the power supplied to the circuit is shown, (a battery in this example) and a device to detect the output (a lamp) is also shown. They are not part of the logic, but are required to make the switching logic useful.

In the case of the AND function, Fig. 2.6 (*b*), the two switches are in series with each other; in the case of the OR function, the two switches are connected in parallel. For the NOT function, the switch is connected in parallel with the output (the lamp). NAND and NOR gates can be constructed in a similar way.

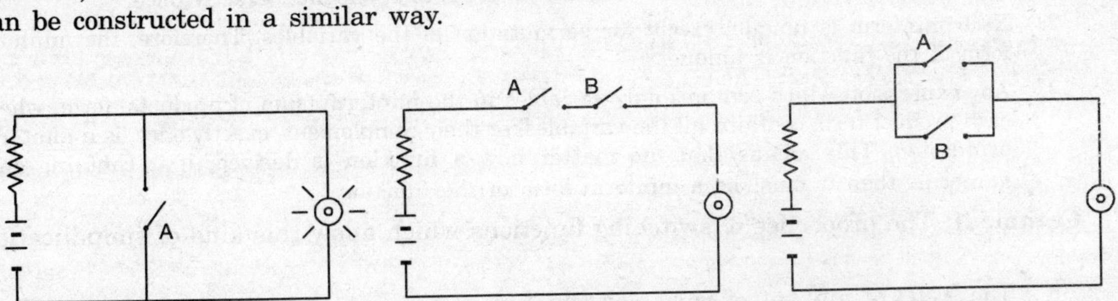


(a) NOT gate (b) AND gate (c) OR gate

**Fig. 2.6** Switch implementation of NOT, AND and OR

These circuits can be combined to form more complex switching functions. (If you have not seen it before, try to construct a simple switching circuit for the XOR function).

**Note:** The inputs for these simple switches are mechanical; *e.g.,* the press of a finger. For electronic switches such as transistors, the inputs can be the outputs of other logic functions, so very complex logic circuits can be designed which operate "automatically".

## 2.3 CANONICAL FORMS OF SWITCHING FUNCTIONS

It is possible to construct a truth table for any switching function (*i.e.*, any function of switching variables.) However, such a truth table does not aid us directly in constructing a set of logic gates which can be used to evaluate the function, or to design a logic circuit. The truth table is useful in that it does provide a complete, unique description of the switching function.

One can derive from the truth table certain unique expressions which defines the function exactly; in fact, the expression is exactly equivalent to the truth table and consequently shares the properties of the truth table. One such expression is called the **minterm form** of the expression, or, alternately, the **sum of products** (SOP) form.

*e.g.*, for the function $Y = A \oplus B$, the truth table is:

| A | B | $Y = A \oplus B$ |
|---|---|---|
| 0 | 0 | 0 |
| 0 | 1 | 1 |
| 1 | 0 | 1 |
| 1 | 1 | 0 |

This is equivalent to

$$Y = \bar{A} \cdot B + A \cdot \bar{B}$$

This is the minterm form, or sum of products form, of the function. It is obtained by ANDing together the variables, or their complements, which have a 1 in the function column. If the variable has value 1, the variable is taken; if not, its complement is taken. Each of these ANDs of all the variables, or their complements, is called a **minterm**. The minterms are then ORed together to give the function specified in the truth table.

**Note:**

1. Each minterm contains all the variables or their complements, exactly once.
2. Each minterm is unique, except for permutation of the variables. Therefore, the minterm form of the function is unique.
3. Any expression which contains only variables in the minterm (sum of products) form, where each product term contains all the variables, or their complement, exactly once, is a minterm expression. This means that, no matter how a function is derived, if it contains only minterms then it must be a minterm form of the function.

**Comment:** The properties of switching functions which allow this kind of simplification are:

1. The AND of any set of variables which results in a 1 is unique.
2. Any terms equal to 1 which are ORed together still equal 1. (*i.e.*, 1 + A = 1).

A dual form of the preceding, called a **maxterm form**, or **product of sums** (POS) form can also be written. The maxterm form of a function can be obtained from the truth table for a function by applying the principle of duality to the way described previously for deriving the minterm form of a function. Another way to find the maxterm form of a function is to write down the minterm expression for the complement of the function, $\overline{Y}$, and apply de Morgans theorem; *e.g.*,

| $A$ | $B$ | $Y = A \oplus B$ | $\overline{Y} = \overline{A \oplus B}$ |
|---|---|---|---|
| 0 | 0 | 0 | 1 |
| 0 | 1 | 1 | 0 |
| 1 | 0 | 1 | 0 |
| 1 | 1 | 0 | 1 |

In minterm form,

$$\overline{Y} = \overline{A}\cdot\overline{B} + A\cdot B$$

Complementing both sides,

$$\overline{\overline{Y}} = Y = \overline{\overline{A}\cdot\overline{B} + A\cdot B}$$

Applying de Morgans theorem,

$$Y = (\overline{\overline{A}+\overline{B}})\cdot(\overline{A\cdot B})$$

$$= (A+B)\cdot(\overline{A}+\overline{B})$$

This is the maxterm form of the switching function $Y = A \oplus B$. It can be obtained easily from the truth table by ORing together all the variables or their complements which give a zero for the function; if the variable has value 0 then it is ORed directly, if it has a value 1, it is complemented. Each term is called a **maxterm**, or a sum term. The expression is equal to the AND of all the maxterms, and is said to be the maxterm form of the function.

**Example:** *Find the minterm and maxterm expressions corresponding to the following truth table:*

| | $A$ | $B$ | $C$ | $Y$ | *Minterms* | *Maxterms* |
|---|---|---|---|---|---|---|
| 0 | 0 | 0 | 0 | 1 | $\overline{A}\cdot\overline{B}\cdot\overline{C}$ | |
| 1 | 0 | 0 | 1 | 0 | | $A + B + \overline{C}$ |
| 2 | 0 | 1 | 0 | 1 | $\overline{A}\cdot B\cdot\overline{C}$ | |
| 3 | 0 | 1 | 1 | 1 | $\overline{A}\cdot B\cdot C$ | |
| 4 | 1 | 0 | 0 | 0 | | $\overline{A} + B + C$ |
| 5 | 1 | 0 | 1 | 0 | | $\overline{A} + B + \overline{C}$ |
| 6 | 1 | 1 | 0 | 1 | $A\cdot B\cdot\overline{C}$ | |
| 7 | 1 | 1 | 1 | 1 | $A\cdot B\cdot C$ | |

**Solution.**
**Minterm form:**

$$Y = \overline{A}\cdot\overline{B}\cdot\overline{C} + \overline{A}\cdot B\cdot\overline{C} + \overline{A}\cdot B\cdot C + A\cdot B\cdot\overline{C} + A\cdot B\cdot C$$

(Note that as many minterms are used as the number of 1's in the truth table for Y.)

**Maxterm form:**

$$Y = (A+B+\overline{C})\cdot(\overline{A}+B+C)\cdot(\overline{A}+B+\overline{C})$$

(Note that as many maxterms are used as the number of 0's in the truth table for Y.)

Sometimes the minterm and maxterm expression are written in a kind of "shorthand," where the values (0 or 1) of the set of variables is used to form a binary number, the decimal equivalent of which designates the appropriate minterm or maxterm. *e.g.*, the minterm form of the above function is written as:

$$Y = \Sigma(0, 2, 3, 6, 7)$$

The maxterm form is written as:

$$Y = \pi(1, 4, 5)$$

**Note:** The order in which the variable are written down in the truth table is important, in this case. Also, note that the possible numbers have values from 0 to $2^n - 1$, where n is the number of variables, and that the numbers which appear in the minterm form do not appear in the maxterm form, and vice versa.

The minterm or maxterm form of the function is not usually the simplest or most concise; *e.g.*, the preceding function can be simplified as follows; from the minterm form:

$$Y = \overline{A}\cdot\overline{B}\cdot\overline{C} + \overline{A}\cdot B\cdot\overline{C} + \overline{A}\cdot B\cdot C + A\cdot B\cdot\overline{C} + A\cdot B\cdot C$$

$$= \overline{A}\cdot(\overline{B}\cdot\overline{C} + B\cdot\overline{C} + B\cdot C) + A\cdot(B\cdot C + B\cdot C)$$

but $B\cdot\overline{C}+B\cdot C = B\cdot(C+\overline{C}) = B$

so $Y = \overline{A}\cdot(\overline{B}\cdot\overline{C}+B) + A\cdot B$

$$= \overline{A}\cdot(B + \overline{C}) + A\cdot B$$

$$= \overline{A}\cdot B+\overline{A}\cdot\overline{C} + A\cdot B$$

$$= \overline{A}\cdot\overline{C}+(A+\overline{A})\cdot B$$

$$= \overline{A}\cdot\overline{C}+B$$

Systematic ways exist to reduce the complexity of minterm or maxterm forms of switching functions but we will not discuss them here. *For the same one can reference book–Digital Principles—by A. K. SINGH.* The problem is computationally complex for functions with a large number of variables (more than 20 variables is considered quite complex) but for a small number of variables (up to 6 or 8) interesting techniques are available.

The following is an algorithm for finding the minterm form of a switching function of $n$ variables $A_1, A_2, \ldots, A_n$:

1. Expand the expression fully, eliminating all parentheses. This should result in a set of AND terms, all of which are ORed together.
2. Examine each AND term; if it is a minterm (*i.e.*, if it contains each variables $A_1, \ldots A_n$ or its complement exactly once) retain it, and consider the next term.
3. In each AND expression which is not a minterm, for each variables which does not occur, AND the expression with $A_i + \overline{A}_i$.
4. Expand each expression and eliminate redundant terms.

**Example 2.** *We can find the minterm expression for* $Y = \bar{A}\cdot\bar{C}+B$, *the function we previously simplified, as follows:*

**Solution.**

$$Y = \bar{A}\cdot\bar{C}+B$$

$$Y = \bar{A}\cdot\bar{C}\cdot(B+\bar{B})+B\cdot(A+\bar{A})\cdot(C+\bar{C})$$

$$= \bar{A}\cdot\bar{C}\cdot B + \bar{A}\cdot\bar{C}\cdot\bar{B} + (B\cdot A + B\cdot\bar{A})\cdot(C + \bar{C})$$

$$= \bar{A}\cdot\bar{C}\cdot B + \bar{A}\cdot\bar{C}\cdot\bar{B} + B\cdot A\cdot C + B\cdot A\cdot\bar{C} + B\cdot\bar{A}\cdot C+B\cdot\bar{A}\cdot\bar{C}$$

$$= \bar{A}\cdot B\cdot\bar{C} + \bar{A}\cdot\bar{B}\cdot\bar{C} + A\cdot B\cdot C + A\cdot B\cdot\bar{C} + \bar{A}\cdot B\cdot C + \bar{A}\cdot B\cdot\bar{C}$$

$$= \bar{A}\cdot\bar{B}\cdot\bar{C} + \bar{A}\cdot B\cdot\bar{C} + \bar{A}\cdot B\cdot C + A\cdot B\cdot\bar{C} + A\cdot B\cdot C$$

as before.

In a similar way, we can write an algorithm to derive the maxterm form of a switching function. In this case, step (2) becomes:

Step (2) In each OR expression which is not a maxterm, for each variable $A_i$ which does not occur, OR the expression with $A_i\cdot\bar{A}_i$.

Step (3) will normally require the use of the distributivity theorem

$$A + B \cdot C = (A + B) \cdot (A + C)$$

$$Y = \bar{A}\cdot\bar{C} + B$$

**Example 3.** *Find the maxterm form of*

**Solution.**

$$Y = \bar{A}\cdot\bar{C} + B$$

$$= (\bar{A}+B)\cdot(\bar{C}+B)$$

$$= (\bar{A}+B+C\cdot\bar{C}).(\bar{C}+B+A\cdot\bar{A})$$

$$= (\bar{A}+B+C)\cdot(\bar{A}+B+\bar{C})\cdot(\bar{C}+B+A)\cdot(\bar{C}+B+\bar{A})$$

$$= (\bar{A}+B+C)\cdot(\bar{A}+B+\bar{C})\cdot(A+B+\bar{C})$$

as before.

## 2.4 KARNAUGH MAP SIMPLIFICATION

It is always desirable to simplify a given Boolean function (as either a Boolean expression or a Truth Table) so that the *logic gates* and the *inputs* to these gates necessary for representing the function are both minimized.

Deduction method could be used to apply various axioms and theorems to the given expression so that a simpler form can be derived. However, this is very heuristic and one need practice as well as skill to succeed.

The following section shows the construction of K-map (conversion of truth-table to K-map) using examples and rules to get the simplified Boolean expression for the corresponding truth-table.

**Two Variable K-Map**

| *A* | *B* | *Y* |
|---|---|---|
| 0 | 0 | 0 |
| 0 | 1 | 0 |
| 1 | 0 | 1 |
| 1 | 1 | 1 |

⇒

| | $\overline{B}$ | B |
|---|---|---|
| $\overline{A}$ | 0 | 0 |
| A | 1 | 1 |

**Three Variable K-Map**

| *A* | *B* | *C* | *Y* |
|---|---|---|---|
| 0 | 0 | 0 | 0 |
| 0 | 0 | 1 | 0 |
| 0 | 1 | 0 | 1 |
| 0 | 1 | 1 | 1 |
| 1 | 0 | 0 | 0 |
| 1 | 0 | 1 | 1 |
| 1 | 1 | 0 | 1 |
| 1 | 1 | 1 | 1 |

⇒

| | $\overline{C}$ | C |
|---|---|---|
| $\overline{A}\overline{B}$ | 0 | 0 |
| $\overline{A}B$ | 1 | 1 |
| AB | 1 | 1 |
| $A\overline{B}$ | 0 | 1 |

**Four Variable K-Map**

| *A* | *B* | *C* | *D* | *Y* |
|---|---|---|---|---|
| 0 | 0 | 0 | 0 | 0 |
| 0 | 0 | 0 | 1 | 0 |
| 0 | 0 | 1 | 0 | 0 |
| 0 | 0 | 1 | 1 | 1 |
| 0 | 1 | 0 | 0 | 0 |
| 0 | 1 | 0 | 1 | 1 |
| 0 | 1 | 1 | 0 | 1 |
| 0 | 1 | 1 | 1 | 1 |
| 1 | 0 | 0 | 0 | 0 |
| 1 | 0 | 0 | 1 | 0 |
| 1 | 0 | 1 | 0 | 0 |
| 1 | 0 | 1 | 1 | 1 |
| 1 | 1 | 0 | 0 | 0 |
| 1 | 1 | 0 | 1 | 1 |
| 1 | 1 | 1 | 0 | 1 |
| 1 | 1 | 1 | 1 | 1 |

| | $\overline{C}\overline{D}$ | $\overline{C}D$ | CD | $C\overline{D}$ |
|---|---|---|---|---|
| $\overline{A}\overline{B}$ | 0 | 0 | 1 | 0 |
| $\overline{A}B$ | 0 | 1 | 1 | 1 |
| AB | 0 | 1 | 1 | 1 |
| $A\overline{B}$ | 0 | 0 | 1 | 0 |

Once K-map is constructed one can apply the following rules to get the simplified Boolean expression for the corresponding truth-table. (as illustrated by examples)

## 1. Identifying Pairs, Quads and Octets

Consider following K-mass that are constructed for given truth-tables.

| | $\overline{C}\,\overline{D}$ | $\overline{C}D$ | $CD$ | $C\overline{D}$ |
|---|---|---|---|---|
| $\overline{A}\,\overline{B}$ | 0 | 1 | 1 | 0 |
| $\overline{A}B$ | 0 | 0 | 0 | 1 |
| $AB$ | 0 | 0 | 0 | 1 |
| $A\overline{B}$ | 0 | 0 | 0 | 0 |

Pairs : $y = \overline{A}\,\overline{B}D + BC\overline{D}$

| | $\overline{C}\,\overline{D}$ | $\overline{C}D$ | $CD$ | $C\overline{D}$ |
|---|---|---|---|---|
| $\overline{A}\,\overline{B}$ | 0 | 0 | 0 | 1 |
| $\overline{A}B$ | 1 | 1 | 0 | 1 |
| $AB$ | 1 | 1 | 0 | 1 |
| $A\overline{B}$ | 0 | 0 | 0 | 1 |

Quads: $y = B\overline{C} + C\overline{D}$

| | $\overline{C}\,\overline{D}$ | $\overline{C}D$ | $CD$ | $C\overline{D}$ |
|---|---|---|---|---|
| $\overline{A}\,\overline{B}$ | 1 | 1 | 0 | 0 |
| $\overline{A}B$ | 1 | 1 | 0 | 0 |
| $AB$ | 1 | 1 | 0 | 0 |
| $A\overline{B}$ | 1 | 1 | 0 | 0 |

Octet : $y = \overline{C}$

## 2. Overlapping Groups

One can use the same 1 more than once.

| | $\overline{C}\,\overline{D}$ | $\overline{C}D$ | $CD$ | $C\overline{D}$ |
|---|---|---|---|---|
| $\overline{A}\,\overline{B}$ | 1 | 1 | 0 | 0 |
| $\overline{A}B$ | 1 | 1 | 0 | 0 |
| $AB$ | 1 | 1 | 1 | 0 |
| $A\overline{B}$ | 1 | 1 | 0 | 0 |

$y = \overline{C} + ABD$

## 3. Rolling the Map

One can roll the map horizontally or vertically to get simpler expression.

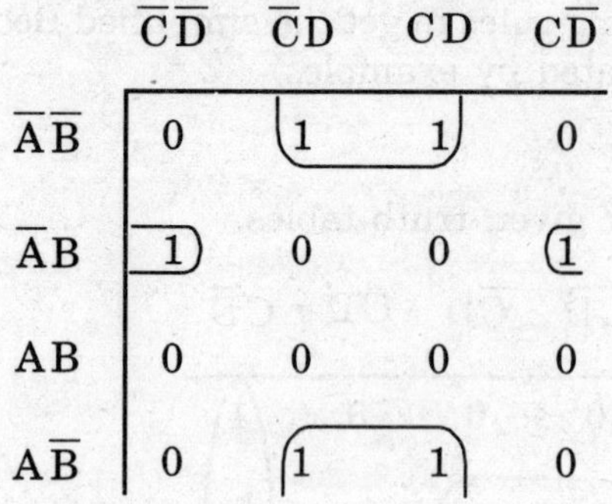


$y = \overline{B}D + \overline{A}B\overline{D}$

## 4. Eliminating Redundant Groups

A group whose all 1s are already used by other group is a redundant group and therefore can be eliminated.

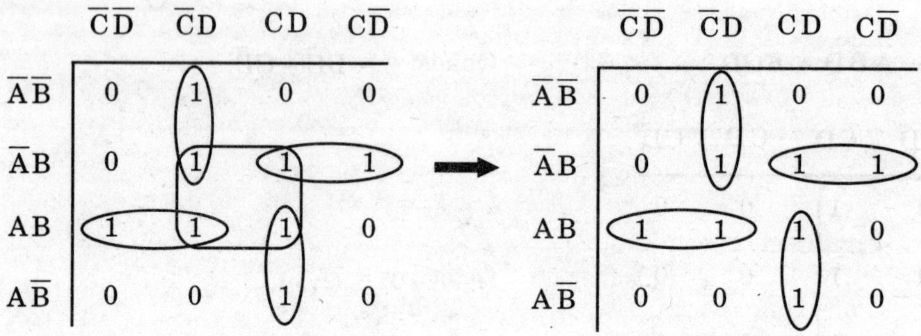


$y = \overline{AC} + \overline{A}B + CD + AB$

## 5. Don't Care Conditions

Sometimes certain input conditions never occur during normal operation and so the corresponding output never appears. Such outputs are entered as X in the truth-table. The X is called as *don't care condition*. This X can be taken either as 0 or as 1, whichever produces a simpler logic circuit.

| *A* | *B* | *C* | *Y* |
|---|---|---|---|
| 0 | 0 | 0 | 0 |
| 0 | 0 | 1 | 0 |
| 0 | 1 | 0 | 1 |
| 0 | 1 | 1 | 1 |
| 1 | 0 | 0 | 0 |
| 1 | 0 | 1 | 1 |
| 1 | 1 | 0 | X |
| 1 | 1 | 1 | X |

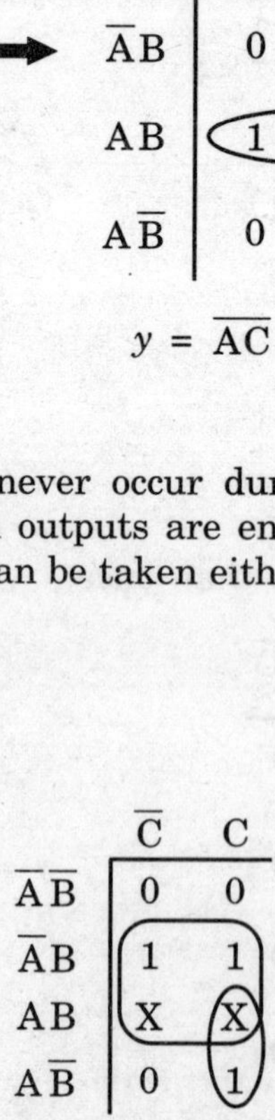


$y = B + AC$

## 2.5 MINIMIZATION USING QUINE-MCCLUSKEY (TABULAR) METHOD

The K-map method is suitable for simplification of Boolean functions up to 5 or 6 variables. As the number of variables increases beyond this, the visualization of adjacent squares is difficult as the geometry is more involved.

The 'Quine-McCluskey' or 'Tabular' method is employed in such cases. This is a systematic step by step procedure for minimizing a Boolean expression in standard form.

### Procedure for Finding the Minimal Expression

1. Arrange all minterms in groups, such that all terms in the same group have same number of 1's in their binary representation. Start with the least number of 1's and continue with grouping of increasing number of 1's, the number of 1's in each term is called the index of that term *i.e.,* all the minterms of same index are placed in a same group. The lowest value of index is zero. Separate each group by a thick line. This constitutes the I stage.
2. Compare every term of the lowest index (say *i*) group with each term in the successive group of index (say, $i + 1$). If two minterms differ in only one variable, that variable should be removed and a dash (–) is placed at the position, thus, a new term with one less literal is formed. If such a situation occurs, a check mark (✔) is placed next to both minterms. After all pairs of terms with indices *i* and $(i + 1)$ have been considered, a thick line is drawn under the last terms.

   When the above process has been repeated for all the groups of I stage, one stage of elimination have been completed. This constitutes the II stage.
3. The III stage of elimination should be repeated of the newly formed groups of second stage. In this stage, two terms can be compared only when they have dashes in same positions.

   The process continues to next higher stages until no further comparisons are possible. (*i.e.*, no further elimination of literals).
4. All terms which remain unchecked (No ✔ sign) during the process are considered to be prime implicants (PIs). Thus, a set of all PIs of the function is obtained.
5. From the set of all prime implicates, a set of essential prime implicants (EPIs) must be determined by preparing prime implicant chart as follows:
   (*a*) The PIs should be represented in rows and each minterm of the function in a column.
   (*b*) Crosses should be placed in each row corresponding to minterms that makes the PIs.
   (*c*) A complete PIs chart should be inspected for columns containing only a single cross. PIs that cover minterms with a single cross in their column are called EPIs.
6. The minterms which are not covered by the EPIs are taken into consideration and a minimum cover is obtained form the remaining PIs.

Now to clarify the above procedure, lets do an example step by step.

**Example 4.** *Simplify the given function using tabular method.*

$$F(A, B, C, D) = \Sigma(0, 2, 3, 6, 7, 8, 10, 12, 13)$$

**Solution.**

1. The minterms of the function are represented in binary form. The binary represented are grouped into a number of sections in terms of the number of 1's

index as shown in Table of Fig. 2.7.

| *Minterms* | *Binary ABCD* | *No. of 1's* | *Minterms Group* | *Index* | *Binary ABCD* |
|---|---|---|---|---|---|
| $m_0$ | 0000 | 0 | $m_0$ | 0 | 0000✔ |
| $m_2$ | 0010 | 1 | $m_2$ | 1 | 0010✔ |
| $m_3$ | 0011 | 2 | $m_8$ | | 1000✔ |
| $m_6$ | 0110 | 2 | $m_3$ | 2 | 0011✔ |
| $m_7$ | 0111 | 3 | $m_6$ | | 0110✔ |
| $m_8$ | 1000 | 1 | $m_{10}$ | | 1010✔ |
| $m_{10}$ | 1010 | 2 | $m_{12}$ | | 1100✔ |
| $m_{12}$ | 1100 | 2 | $m_7$ | 3 | 0111✔ |
| $m_{13}$ | 1101 | 3 | $m_{13}$ | | 1101✔ |

**Fig. 2.7**

2. Compare each binary term with every term in the adjacent next higher category. If they differ only by one position put a check mark and copy the term into the next column with (–) in the place where the variable is unmatched, which is shown in next Table of Fig. 2.8.

| *Minterm Group* | *A* | *B* | *C* | *D* | |
|---|---|---|---|---|---|
| 0, 2 | 0 | 0 | – | 0 | ✔ |
| 0, 8 | – | 0 | 0 | 0 | ✔ |
| 2, 3 | 0 | 0 | 1 | – | ✔ |
| 2, 6 | 0 | – | 1 | 0 | ✔ |
| 2, 10 | – | 0 | 1 | 0 | ✔ |
| 8, 10 | 1 | 0 | – | 0 | ✔ |
| 8, 12 | 1 | – | 0 | 0 | PI |
| 3, 7 | 0 | – | 1 | 1 | ✔ |
| 6, 7 | 0 | 1 | 1 | – | ✔ |
| 12, 13 | 1 | 1 | 0 | – | PI |

**Fig. 2.8**

| *Minterm Group* | *A* | *B* | *C* | *D* | |
|---|---|---|---|---|---|
| 0, 2, 8, 10 | – | 0 | – | 0 | PI |
| 0, 8, 2, 10 | – | 0 | – | 0 | PI eliminated |
| 2, 3, 6, 7 | 0 | – | 1 | – | PI |
| 2, 6, 3, 7 | 0 | – | 1 | – | PI eliminated. |

**Fig. 2.9**

3. Apply same process to the resultant column of Table of Fig. 2.8 and continue until no further elimination of literals. This is shown in Table of Fig. 2.9 above.
4. All terms which remain unchecked are the PIs. However, note that the minterms combination (0, 2) and (8, 10) form the same combination (0, 2, 8, 10) as the combination (0, 8) and (2, 10). The order in which these combinations are placed does not prove any effect. Moreover, as we know that $x + x = x$, thus, we can eliminate one of these combinations.

   The same occur with combination (2, 3) and (6, 7).
5. Now we prepare a PI chart to determine EPIs as follows shown in Table of Fig. 2.10.

| | | *Minterms* | | | | | | | | |
|---|---|---|---|---|---|---|---|---|---|---|
| *Prime Implicants* | | *0* | *2* | *3* | *6* | *7* | *8* | *10* | *12* | *13* |
| (8, 12) | | | | | | | × | | × | |
| (12, 13) | * | | | | | | | | × | × |
| (0, 2, 8, 10) | * | × | × | | | | × | × | | |
| (2, 3, 6, 7) | * | | × | × | × | × | | | | |
| | | ✔ | | ✔ | ✔ | ✔ | | ✔ | | ✔ |

**Fig. 2.10**

(*a*) All the PIs are represented in rows and each minterm of the function in a column.

(*b*) Crosses are placed in each row to show the composition of minterms that make PIs.

(*c*) The column that contains just a single cross, the PI corresponding to the row in which the cross appear is essential. Prime implicant. A tick mark is part against each column which has only one cross mark. A star (*) mark is placed against each. EPI.

6. All the minterms have been covered by EPIs.

Finally, the sum of all the EPIs gives the function in its minimal SOP form

| *EPIs* | *Binary Representation* | | | | *Variable Representation* |
|---|---|---|---|---|---|
| | *A* | *B* | *C* | *D* | |
| 12, 13 | 1 | 1 | 0 | – | ABC′ |
| 0, 2, 8, 10 | – | 0 | – | 0 | B′D′ |
| 2, 3, 6, 7 | 0 | – | 1 | – | A′C |

Therefore, $F = ABC' + B'D' + A'C$.

If don't care conditions are given, they are also used to find the prime implicating, but it is not compulsory to include them in the final simplified expression.

**Example 5.** *Simplify the given function using tabular method.*

$$F(A, B, C, D) = \Sigma(0, 2, 3, 6, 7)$$

$$d\ (5, 8, 10, 11, 15)$$

**Solution.** 1. Step 1 is shown in Table of Fig. 2.11. The don't care minterms are also included.

| *Minterms* | *Binary* A B C D | *No. of 1's* | *Minterms Group* | *Index* | *Binary ABCD* |
|---|---|---|---|---|---|
| $m_0$ | 0 0 0 0 | 0 | $m_0$ | 0 | 0 0 0 0✔ |
| $m_2$ | 0 0 1 0 | 1 | $m_2$ | 1 | 0 0 1 0✔ |
| $m_3$ | 0 0 1 1 | 2 | $m_8$ | | 1 0 0 0✔ |
| $m_5$ | 0 1 0 1 | 2 | $m_3$ | 2 | 0 0 1 1✔ |
| $m_6$ | 0 1 1 0 | 2 | $m_5$ | | 0 1 0 1✔ |
| $m_7$ | 0 1 1 1 | 3 | $m_6$ | | 0 1 1 0✔ |
| $m_8$ | 1 0 0 0 | 1 | $m_{10}$ | | 1 0 1 0✔ |
| $m_{10}$ | 1 0 1 0 | 2 | $m_7$ | 3 | 0 1 1 1✔ |
| $m_{11}$ | 1 0 1 1 | 3 | $m_{11}$ | | 1 0 1 1✔ |
| $m_{15}$ | 1 1 1 1 | 4 | $m_{15}$ | 4 | 1 1 1 1✔ |

**Fig. 2.11**

2. Step 2 is shown in Table of Fig. 2.12.
3. Step 3 is shown in Table of Fig. 2.13.

| *Minterm Group* | *Binary* A B C D |
|---|---|
| 0, 2 | 0 0 – 0 ✔ |
| 0, 8 | – 0 0 0 ✔ |
| 2, 3 | 0 0 1 – ✔ |
| 2, 6 | 0 – 1 0 ✔ |
| 2, 10 | – 0 1 0 ✔ |
| 8, 10 | 1 0 – 0 ✔ |
| 3, 7 | 0 – 1 1 ✔ |
| 3, 11 | – 0 1 1 ✔ |
| 5, 7 | 0 1 – 1 PI |
| 6, 7 | 0 1 1 – ✔ |
| 10, 11 | 1 0 1 – ✔ |
| 7, 15 | – 1 1 1 ✔ |
| 11, 15 | 1 – 1 1 ✔ |

**Fig. 2.12**

| *Minterm Group* | *Binary* A B C D | |
|---|---|---|
| 0, 2, 8, 10 | – 0 – 0 | PI |
| 0, 8, 2, 10 | – 0 – 0 | PI Eliminated |
| 2, 3, 6, 7 | 0 – 1 – | PI |
| 2, 3 10, 11 | – 0 1 – | PI |
| 2, 6, 3, 7 | 0 – 1 – | PI Eliminated |
| 2, 10, 3, 11 | – 0 1 – | PI Eliminated |
| 3, 7, 11, 15 | – – 1 1 | PI |
| 3, 11, 7, 15 | – – 1 1 | PI Eliminated |

**Fig. 2.13**

4. All the terms which remain unchecked are PIs. Moreover, one of two same combinations is eliminated.
5. Step 5 is to prepare a PI chart to determine EPIs as shown in Table of Fig. 2.14. Note, however, that don't care minterms will not be listed as column headings in the chart as they do not have to be covered by the minimal (simplified) expression.

| *Prime Implicants* | | *Minterms* | | | | |
|---|---|---|---|---|---|---|
| | | *0* | *2* | *3* | *6* | *7* |
| (5, 7) | | | | | | × |
| (0, 2, 8, 10) | * | × | × | | | |
| (2, 3, 6, 7) | * | | × | × | × | × |
| (2, 3, 10, 11) | | | × | × | | |
| (3, 7, 11, 15) | | | | × | | × |
| | | ✔ | | | ✔ | |

**Fig. 2.14**

6. All the minterms have been covered by EPIs.

Therefore $\boxed{F(A, B, C, D) = B'D' + A'C}$

**Example 6.** *Simplify the given function using tabular method:*

$$F(A, B, C, D, E, F, G) = \Sigma(20, 28, 38, 39, 52, 60, 102, 103, 127)$$

**Solution.** Step 1 is shown in Table of Fig. 2.15.

| *Minterms* | *Binary ABCDEFG* | *No. of 1's* | *Minterms Group* | *Index* | *Binary ABCDEFG* |
|---|---|---|---|---|---|
| $m_{20}$ | 0 0 1 0 1 0 0 | 2 | $m_{20}$ | 2 | 0 0 1 0 1 0 0✔ |
| $m_{28}$ | 0 0 1 1 1 0 0 | 3 | $m_{28}$ | | 0 0 1 1 1 0 0✔ |
| $m_{38}$ | 0 1 0 0 1 1 0 | 3 | $m_{38}$ | 3 | 0 1 0 0 1 1 0✔ |

*Contd.....*

| | | | | | |
|---|---|---|---|---|---|
| $m_{39}$ | 0100111 | 4 | $m_{52}$ | | 0110100✔ |
| $m_{52}$ | 0110100 | 3 | $m_{39}$ | 4 | 0100111✔ |
| $m_{60}$ | 0111100 | 4 | $m_{60}$ | | 0111100✔ |
| $m_{102}$ | 1100110 | 4 | $m_{102}$ | | 1100110✔ |
| $m_{103}$ | 1100111 | 5 | $m_{103}$ | 5 | 1100111✔ |
| $m_{127}$ | 1111111 | 7 | $m_{127}$ | 7 | 1111111PI |

**Fig. 2.15**

2. Step 2 is shown in Table (Fig. 2.16).
3. Step 3 is shown in Table (Fig. 2.17).

| *Minterms Group* | *A* | *B* | *C* | *D* | *E* | *F* | *G* | |
|---|---|---|---|---|---|---|---|---|
| 20, 28 | 0 | 0 | 1 | – | 1 | 0 | 0 | ✔ |
| 20, 52 | 0 | – | 1 | 0 | 1 | 0 | 0 | ✔ |
| 28, 60 | 0 | – | 1 | 1 | 1 | 0 | 0 | ✔ |
| 38, 39 | 0 | 1 | 0 | 0 | 1 | 1 | – | ✔ |
| 38, 102 | – | 1 | 0 | 0 | 1 | 1 | 0 | ✔ |
| 52, 60 | 0 | 1 | 1 | – | 1 | 0 | 0 | ✔ |
| 39, 103 | – | 1 | 0 | 0 | 1 | 1 | 1 | ✔ |
| 102, 103 | 1 | 1 | 0 | 0 | 1 | 1 | – | ✔ |

**Fig. 2.16**

| *Minterms Group* | *A* | *B* | *C* | *D* | *E* | *F* | *G* | |
|---|---|---|---|---|---|---|---|---|
| 20, 28, 52, 60 | 0 | – | 1 | – | 1 | 0 | 0 | PI |
| 20, 52, 28, 60 | 0 | – | 1 | – | 1 | 0 | 0 | PI Eliminated |
| 38, 39 102, 103 | – | 1 | 0 | 0 | 1 | 1 | – | PI |
| 38, 102, 39, 103 | – | 1 | 0 | 0 | 1 | 1 | – | PI Eliminated |

**Fig. 2.17**

4. All the terms which remain unchecked are PIs. Moreover, one of two same combinations is eliminated.
5. PI chart to determine EPIs is shown in Table Fig. 2.18.

| *Prime Implicants* | | 20 | 28 | 38 | 39 | 52 | 60 | 102 | 103 | 127 |
|---|---|---|---|---|---|---|---|---|---|---|
| 127 | * | | | | | | | | | × |
| (20, 28, 52, 60) | * | × | × | | | × | × | | | |
| (38, 39, 102, 103) | * | | | × | × | | | × | × | |
| | | ✔ | ✔ | ✔ | ✔ | ✔ | ✔ | ✔ | ✔ | ✔ |

**Fig. 2.18**

6. All the minterms have been covered by EPIs.

Therefore, F (A, B, C, D, E, F, G) = ABCDEFG + A′CEF′G′ + BC′D′EF

## 2.6 SOLVED EXAMPLES

### 2.6.1 Design of a Half Adder

A binary half adder is a switching circuit which will add together two binary digits (called binary bits), producing two output bits, a sum bit, S, and a carry bit, C. It has the following truth table:

| *A* | *B* | *S* | *C* |
|---|---|---|---|
| 0 | 0 | 0 | 0 |
| 0 | 1 | 1 | 0 |
| 1 | 0 | 1 | 0 |
| 1 | 1 | 0 | 1 |

It is immediately obvious from the truth table that the two functions S and C can be implemented as $S = A \oplus B$, and $C = A \cdot B$ as shown in Fig. 2.19 (*a*). Fig. 2.19 (*b*) shows a logic symbol for a half adder. (Logic symbols for devices more complex than the basic logic gates are usually just boxes with appropriately labeled inputs and outputs).

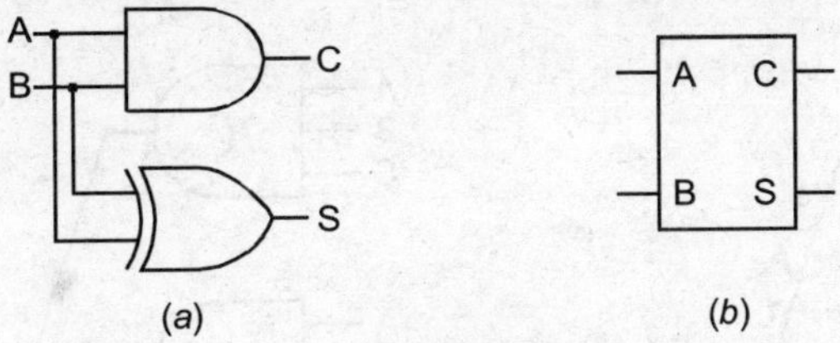


**Fig. 2.19**

### 2.6.2 Design of a Full Adder

A binary full adder is a switching circuit which will add together two binary digits (called binary bits), and a third bit called a carry bit which may have come from a previous full adder. It produces both a sum bit and a carry bit as output. The full adder, therefore, has 3 inputs A, B and C where C is the carry bit, and 2 outputs; the sum, S, and the carry C+. It is possible to connect N such full adders together to add two N bit numbers.

It should be immediately obvious that the sum bit for a full adder can be obtained using two half adders, one which adds digits A and B together producing, say, Z as the sum and the other adding Z and C together to form the sum of A, B and C. Clearly, a carry output should be produced when either of the half adders produces a carry, so the carry output for the full adder can be obtained by ORing together the Carry outputs of the full adders. Such an implementation of a full adder is shown in Fig. 2.20.

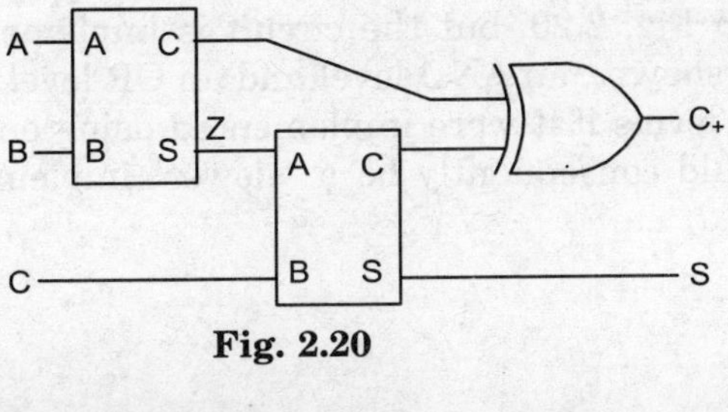


**Fig. 2.20**

We will also consider the design of a full adder starting from its description as a truth table. The truth table for a full adder is as follows:

| *A* | *B* | *C* | *S* | *C* |
|---|---|---|---|---|
| 0 | 0 | 0 | 0 | 0 |
| 0 | 0 | 1 | 1 | 0 |
| 0 | 1 | 0 | 1 | 0 |
| 0 | 1 | 1 | 0 | 1 |
| 1 | 0 | 0 | 1 | 0 |
| 1 | 0 | 1 | 0 | 1 |
| 1 | 1 | 0 | 0 | 1 |
| 1 | 1 | 1 | 1 | 1 |

We can write the outputs in minterm form as:

$$S = \overline{A}{\cdot}\overline{B}{\cdot}C + \overline{A}{\cdot}B{\cdot}\overline{C} + A{\cdot}\overline{B}{\cdot}\overline{C} + A{\cdot}B{\cdot}C$$

$$C+ = \overline{A}{\cdot}B{\cdot}C + A{\cdot}\overline{B}{\cdot}C + A{\cdot}B{\cdot}\overline{C} + A{\cdot}B{\cdot}C$$

These functions can be implemented directly as shown in Fig. 2.21.

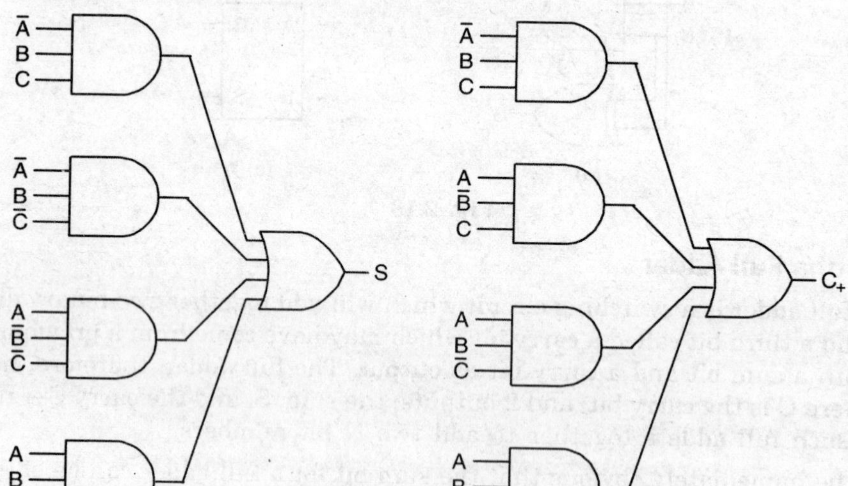


**Fig. 2.21** A full adder implemented directly from its minterm form

Note that this implementation of the full adder requires more logic gates than the implementation shown in Fig. 2.20, but the circuit is implemented using only three "levels" of logic; a NOT level (not shown), an AND level and an OR level. The previous implementation would require more logic levels if it were implemented using only AND-OR-NOT (AON) logic. This implementation would consequently be a "slower" implementation, due to the inherent delay in each logic gate.

The function S cannot be reduced any further using only "AON" logic, but C+ can be rewritten as:

$$C+ = \bar{A}{\cdot}B{\cdot}C + A{\cdot}B{\cdot}C + A{\cdot}\bar{B}{\cdot}C + A{\cdot}B{\cdot}C + A{\cdot}B{\cdot}\bar{C} + A{\cdot}B{\cdot}C$$

where the term A.B.C has been twice repeated.

Therefore,
$$C+ = (\bar{A}+A){\cdot}B{\cdot}C + A{\cdot}C\,(\bar{B}+B) + A{\cdot}B{\cdot}(\bar{C}+C)$$

$$= \bar{B}{\cdot}C + A{\cdot}C + A{\cdot}B$$

With a little manipulation of the switching functions, we can arrive at the implementation shown in Fig. 2.20:

$$S = \bar{A}{\cdot}\bar{B}{\cdot}C + \bar{A}{\cdot}B{\cdot}\bar{C} + A{\cdot}\bar{B}{\cdot}\bar{C} + A{\cdot}B{\cdot}C$$

$$= \bar{C}{\cdot}\,(\bar{A}{\cdot}B + A{\cdot}\bar{B}) + C{\cdot}\,(\bar{A}{\cdot}\bar{B} + A{\cdot}B)$$

Recognizing that $A \oplus B = \bar{A}{\cdot}B + A{\cdot}\bar{B}$ and $\overline{A \oplus B} = \bar{A}{\cdot}B + A{\cdot}\bar{B}$

We get
$$S = \bar{C}{\cdot}(A \oplus B) + C{\cdot}(\overline{A \oplus B})$$ or, letting $Z = A \oplus B$,

$$S = \bar{C}{\cdot}Z + C{\cdot}\bar{Z} = C \oplus Z$$

C+ can be written as

$$C+ = \bar{A}{\cdot}B{\cdot}C + A{\cdot}\bar{B}{\cdot}C + A{\cdot}B{\cdot}\bar{C} + A{\cdot}B{\cdot}C$$

$$= C{\cdot}(\bar{A}{\cdot}B + A{\cdot}\bar{B}) + A{\cdot}B{\cdot}(C + \bar{C})$$

$$= C{\cdot}(A \oplus B) + A{\cdot}B$$

$$= C{\cdot}Z + A{\cdot}B$$

The preceding expressions for S and C+ are effectively in the form implemented by Fig. 2.20. Using only AON logic, we can represent:

$$S = C{\cdot}Z + C{\cdot}\bar{Z} \quad \text{where} \quad Z = \bar{A}{\cdot}B + A{\cdot}\bar{B}$$

and
$$C+ = C{\cdot}Z + A{\cdot}B$$

Both the half adder and the full adder are useful functional blocks. In particular, the full adder is often used as the basic building block to construct larger adders which add many bits simultaneously. Figure 2.22 shows the implementation of a four bit adder, which adds together two four bit numbers ($A_3\ A_2\ A_1\ A_0$ and $B_3\ B_2\ B_1\ B_0$) and produces a 5 bit result ($S_4\ S_3\ S_2\ S_1\ S_0$), using four full adders. In general, *n* full adders are required to implement an adder for two *n*-bit words. The general expression for the sum and carry bits generated in the *i*th addition stage is

$$S_i = (A_i \oplus B_i) \oplus C_i$$

and
$$C_{i+1} = A_i{\cdot}B_i + (A_i + B_i){\cdot}C_i$$

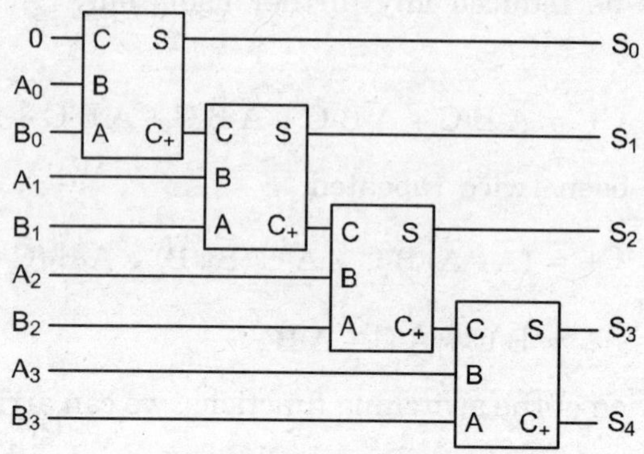


**Fig. 2.22** A four bit adder

Note that, for this type of adder, before the result of the add operation is correct, the carry result must be allowed to propagate through *all* of the full adders. Because of this, this implementation of a wide word adder is called **a *ripple carry*** adder.

It is possible, of course, to design an adder which has no such ripple at all, simply by creating a truth table for each bit of the $n$-bit adder and implementing each bit from, say, its minterm form. This becomes quite tedious, however, for large $n$ (specification of an 8-bit adder would require 9 truth tables, each with 256 lines). It is also possible to devise logic functions which generate only the $n$ carry bits for an add operation on two $n$ bit numbers. These functions are called **carry look-ahead functions**, and are commonly used in the construction of fast wide word adders. Such carry look-ahead adders are commonly used to implement the add operations on the fastest computers. As we will see, it is possible to connect the carry look-ahead units in a tree-like fashion to give reasonably fast carry generation in a much smaller time than required in the ripple carry adder.

Logic expressions for this "carry look-ahead" function can be derived from the logic functions for the full adder. Recall that, for 2 $n$-bit words $A = (A_{n-1}, A_{n-2}, \ldots, A_1, A_0)$ and $B = (B_{n-1}, B_{n-2}, \ldots, B_1, B_0)$ we saw earlier that the bit $S_i$ for the $i$th digit of the sum S was $S_i = (A_i \oplus B_i) \oplus C_i$.

and the carry $C_{i+1}$ was

$$C_{i+1} = A_i \cdot B_i + (A_i + B_i) \cdot C_i$$

The expression for the carry, $C_{i+1}$, can be rewritten as

$$C_{i+1} = G_{i+1} + P_{i+1} \cdot C_i$$

where $G_{i+1} = A_i \cdot B_i$ is the carry generation term

and $P_{i+1} = A_i + B_i$ is the carry propagation term

Note that $G_{i+1}$ and $P_{i+1}$ depend only on $A_i$ and $B_i$.

From this recurrence relation, we see that, if we have an initial carry in $C_0 = G_0$ then

$$C_1 = G_1 + P_1 \cdot G_0$$

$$C_2 = G_2 + P_2 \cdot (G_1 + P_1 \cdot G_0)$$

$$= G_2 + P_2 \cdot G_1 + P_2 \cdot P_1 \cdot G_0$$

$$C_3 = G_3 + P_3{\cdot}G_2 + P_3{\cdot}P_2{\cdot}G_1 + P_3{\cdot}P_2{\cdot}P_1{\cdot}G_0$$

$$\vdots$$

Note that the product terms for the $i$th carry bit correspond to AND gates with inputs numbering from 2 to $i$; consequently for large $i$th AND gates will require a large number of inputs. (They cannot be connected in series because this would reintroduce a ripple effect.) Fortunately, carry look-ahead units can be cascaded in a kind of tree fashion, as shown in Fig. 2.23.

The fact that this cascading is possible is apparent from the original relation, $C_{i+1} = G_{i+1} + P_{i+1}.C_i$. All that is necessary at any level, say, $l$, is to have the term $C_{l-1}$ available. This can come from a previous level of carry look-ahead units, and replaces the initial carry input, $C_0$. (Note that the adders used in with a carry look-ahead unit should have outputs for generate, G, and propagate, P rather than for the carry, $C_{out}$).

Figure 2.23 shows an implementation of part of a 16 bit adder, using 4-bit carry look-ahead functions.

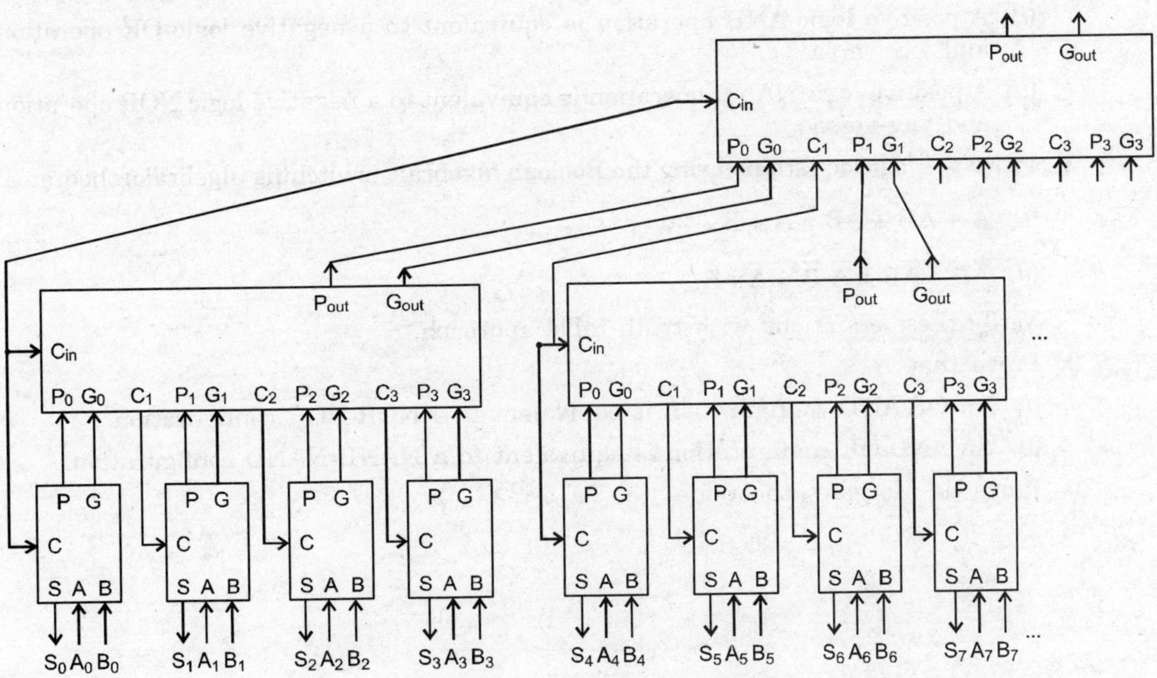


**Fig. 2.23** A carry look-ahead adder

## 2.7 EXERCISE

**1.** Obtain the following operations using only NOR gates.

(*a*) NOT (*b*) OR (*c*) AND

**2.** Obtain the following operations using only NAND gates.

(a) NOT (*b*) AND (*c*) OR

**3.** Find the operation performed for each of the gates shown in figure below, with the help of truth table.

**4.** Write the expression for EX-OR operation and obtain

(*i*) The truth table.

(*ii*) Realize this operation using AND, OR, NOT gates.

(*iii*) Realize this operation using only NOR gates.

**5.** Verify that the (*i*) NAND (*ii*) NOR operations are commutative but not associative.

**6.** Verify that the (*i*) AND (*ii*) OR (*iii*) EX-OR operations are commutative as well as associative.

**7.** Prove that

(*i*) A positive logic AND operation is equivalent to a negative logic OR operation and vice-versa.

(*ii*) A positive logic NAND operation is equivalent to a negative logic NOR operation and vice-versa.

**8.** Prove the logic equations using the Boolean algebraic (switching algebraic) theorems:

(*i*) $A + A\overline{B} + \overline{A}B = A + B$

(*ii*) $AB + \overline{A}B + \overline{A}\,\overline{B} = \overline{A} + B$

Verify these equations with truth table approach.

**9.** Prove that

(*i*) An OR-AND configuration is equivalent to a NOR-NOR configuration.

(*ii*) An AND-OR configuration is equivalent to a NAND-NAND configuration.

**10.** Prove de Morgan's theorems.

3

CHAPTER

# COMBINATIONAL LOGIC—USING MSI AND LSI CIRCUITS

## 3.0 INTRODUCTION

When designing logic circuits, the "discrete logic gates"; *i.e.*, individual AND, OR, NOT *etc.* gates, are often neither the simplest nor the most economical devices we could use. There are many standard MSI (medium scale integrated) and LSI (large scale integrated) circuits, or functions available, which can do many of the things commonly required in logic circuits. Often these MSI and LSI circuits do not fit our requirements exactly, and it is often necessary to use discrete logic to adapt these circuits for our application.

However, the number and type of these LSI and VLSI (very large scale integrated) circuits is steadily increasing, and it is difficult to always be aware of the best possible circuits available for a given problem. Also, systematic design methods are difficult to devise when the types of logic device available keeps increasing. **In general the "best" design procedure is to attempt to find a LSI device which can perform the required function, or which can be modified using other devices to perform the required function**. If nothing is available, then the function should be implemented with several MSI devices. Only as a last option should the entire function be implemented with discrete logic gates. In fact, with present technology, it is becoming increasingly cost-effective to implement a design as one or more dedicated VLSI devices.

When designing all but the simplest logic devices, a "top-down" approach should be adopted. The device should be specified in block form, and attempt to implement each block with a small number of LSI or MSI functions. Each block which cannot be implemented directly can be then broken into smaller blocks, and the process repeated, until each block is fully implemented.

Of course, **a good knowledge of what LSI and MSI functions are available in the appropriate technology makes this process simpler.**

## 3.1 THE DIGITAL MULTIPLEXER

One MSI function which has been available for a long time is the digital selector, or multiplexer. It is the digital equivalent of the rotary switch or selector switch (*e.g.*, the channel selector on a TV set). Its function is to accept a binary number as a "selector input," and present the logic level connected to that input line as output from the data selector.

A digital multiplexer (MUX) is a combinational circuits that selects one input out of several inputs and direct it to a single output. The particular input selection is controlled by a set of select inputs. Figure 3.1 shows block diagram of a digital multiplexer with $n$ inputs lines and single output line.

For selecting one out of $n$ input, a set of $m$ select inputs is required where

$$n = 2^m$$

On the basis of digital (binary) code applied at the select inputs, one output of $n$ data sources is selected. Usually, an enable (or strobe) input (E) is built-in for cascading purpose. Enable input is generally active-low, *i.e.,* it performs its intended operation when it is low (logic).

**Note:** 16:1 are the largest available ICs, therefor for larger input requirements there should be provision for expansion. This is achieved through enable/stroble input (multiplexer stacks or trees are designed).

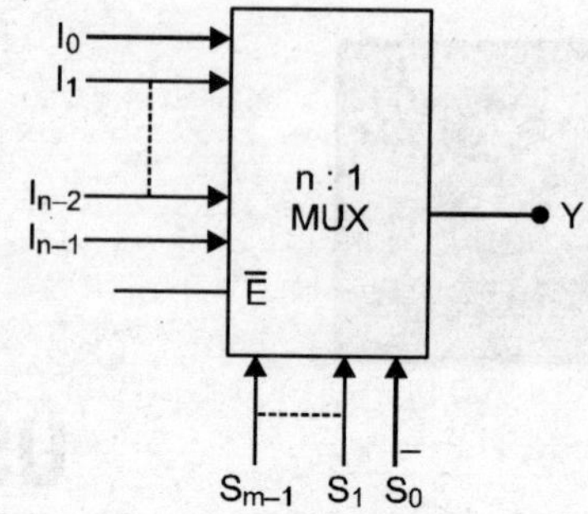


**Fig. 3.1** Block diagram of the digital multiplexer

A circuit diagram for a possible 4-line to 1-line data selector/multiplexer (abbreviated as MUX for multiplexer) is shown in Fig. 3.2. Here, the output Y is equal to the input $I_0$, $I_1$, $I_2$, $I_3$ depending on whether the select lines $S_1$ and $S_0$ have values 00, 01, 10, 11 for $S_1$ and $S_0$ respectively. That is, the output Y is *selected* to be equal to the input of the line given by the binary value of the select lines $S_1S_0$.

The logic equation for the circuit shown in Fig. 3.2 is:

$$Y = I_0 \cdot \overline{S}_1 \cdot \overline{S}_0 + I_1 \cdot \overline{S}_1 \cdot S_0 + I_2 \cdot S_1 \cdot \overline{S}_3 + I_4 \cdot S_1 \cdot S_0$$

This device can be used simply as a data selector/multiplexer, or it can be used to perform logic functions. Its simplest application is to implement a truth table directly; *e.g.,* with a 4 line to 1 line MUX, it is possible to implement any 2-variable function directly, simply by connecting $I_0$, $I_1$, $I_2$, $I_3$ to logic 1 in logic 0, as dictated by a truth table. In this way, a MUX can be used as a simple look-up table for switching functions. This facility makes the MUX a very general purpose logic device.

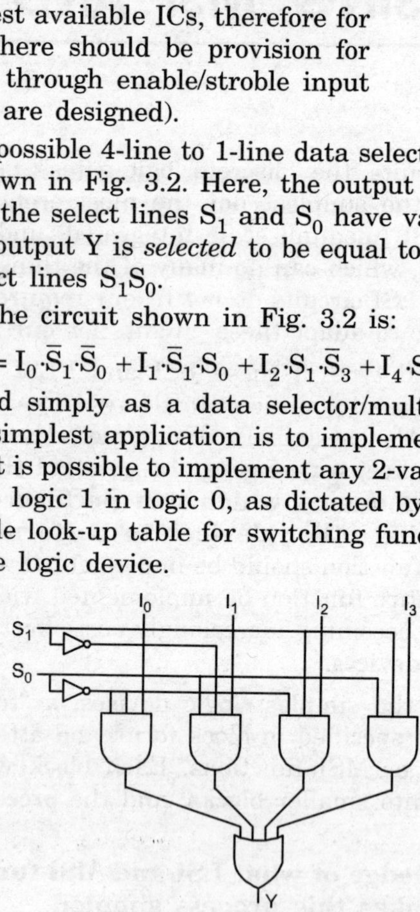


**Fig. 3.2** A four-line to 1-line multiplexer

**Example 1.** *Use a 4 line to 1 line MUX to implement the function shown in the following truth table* $(Y = \overline{A} \cdot \overline{B} + A \cdot B)$.

| A | B | Y | | |
|---|---|---|---|---|
| 0 | 0 | 1 | = | $I_0$ |
| 0 | 1 | 0 | = | $I_1$ |
| 1 | 0 | 0 | = | $I_2$ |
| 1 | 1 | 1 | = | $I_3$ |

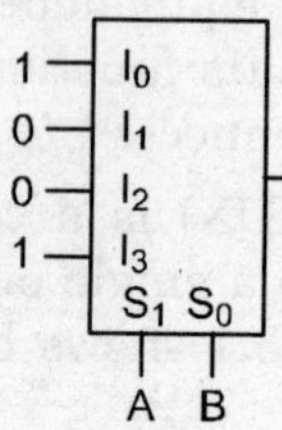


**Fig. 3.3** A 4-line to 1-line MUX implementation of a function of 2 variables

Simply connecting $I_0 = 1$, $I_1 = 0$, $I_2 = 0$, $I_3 = 1$, and the inputs A and B to the $S_1$ and $S_0$ selector inputs of the 4-line to 1-line MUX implement this truth table, as shown in Fig. 3.3.

The 4-line to 1-line MUX can also be used to implement any function of three logical variables, as well. To see this, we need not only that the only possible functions of one variable C, are C, $\overline{C}$, and the constants 0 or 1. (*i.e.*, C, $\overline{C}$, $C + \overline{C} = 1$, and 0). We need only connect the appropriate value, C, $\overline{C}$, 0 or 1, to $I_0$, $I_1$, $I_2$, $I_3$ to obtain a function of 3 variables. The MUX still behaves as a table look up device; it is now simply looking up values of another variable.

**Example 2.** *Implement the function*

$$Y(A, B, C) = \overline{A}{\cdot}\overline{B}{\cdot}C + \overline{A}{\cdot}B{\cdot}\overline{C} + A{\cdot}\overline{B}{\cdot}\overline{C} + A{\cdot}B{\cdot}C$$

*Using a 4-line to 1-line MUX.*

Here, again, we use the A and B variables as data select inputs. We can use the above equation to construct the table shown in Fig. 3.4. The residues are what is "left over" in each minterm when the "address" variables are taken away. To implement this circuit, we connect $I_0$ and $I_3$ to C, and $I_1$ and $I_2$ to $\overline{C}$, as shown in Fig. 3.4.

| *Input* | *"Address"* | *Other variables (residues)* |
|---|---|---|
| $I_0$ | $\overline{A} \cdot \overline{B}$ | C |
| $I_1$ | $\overline{A} \cdot B$ | $\overline{C}$ |
| $I_2$ | $A \cdot \overline{B}$ | $\overline{C}$ |
| $I_3$ | $A \cdot B$ | C |

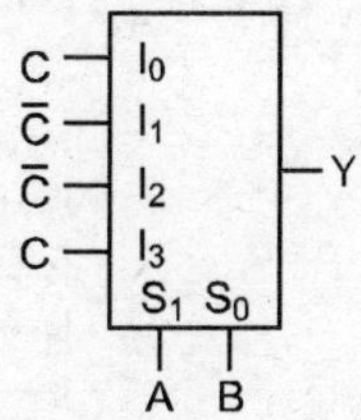


**Fig. 3.4** A 4-line to 1-line MUX implementation of a function of 3 variables

In general a 4 input MUX can give any function of 3 inputs, an 8 input MUX can give any functional of 4 variables, and a 16 input MUX, any function of 5 variables.

**Example 3.** *Use an 8 input MUX to implement the following equation:*

$$Y = \overline{A}{\cdot}\overline{B}{\cdot}\overline{C}{\cdot}\overline{D} + \overline{A}{\cdot}\overline{B}{\cdot}C{\cdot}D + \overline{A}{\cdot}B{\cdot}\overline{C}{\cdot}D + \overline{A}{\cdot}B{\cdot}\overline{C}{\cdot}\overline{D} + A{\cdot}\overline{B}{\cdot}\overline{C}{\cdot}D + A{\cdot}\overline{B}{\cdot}C{\cdot}\overline{D}$$
$$+ A{\cdot}B{\cdot}\overline{C}{\cdot}\overline{D} + A{\cdot}B{\cdot}\overline{C}{\cdot}D$$

Again, we will use A, B, C as data select inputs, or address inputs, connected to $S_2$, $S_1$ and $S_0$, respectively.

| *Input* | *"Address"* | *Residues* |
|---|---|---|
| $I_0$ | $\overline{A} \cdot \overline{B} \cdot \overline{C}$ | $\overline{D}$ |
| $I_1$ | $\overline{A} \cdot \overline{B} \cdot C$ | D |
| $I_2$ | $\overline{A} \cdot B \cdot \overline{C}$ | $D + \overline{D} = 1$ |
| $I_3$ | $\overline{A} \cdot B \cdot C$ | |
| $I_4$ | $A \cdot \overline{B} \cdot \overline{C}$ | D |
| $I_5$ | $A \cdot \overline{B} \cdot C$ | $\overline{D}$ |
| $I_6$ | $A \cdot B \cdot \overline{C}$ | $\overline{D} + D = 1$ |
| $I_7$ | $A \cdot B \cdot C$ | |

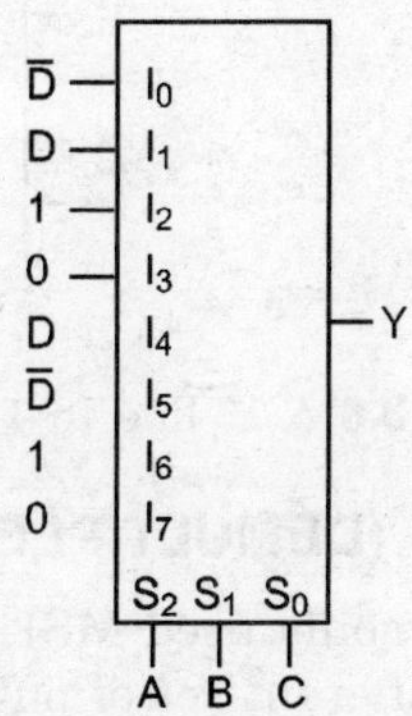


**Fig. 3.5** An 8-line to 1-line MUX implementation of a function of 4 variables

Values of the address set A, B, C with no residues corresponding to the address in the above table must have logic value 0 connected to the corresponding data input. The select variables A, B, C must be connected to $S_2$, $S_1$ and $S_0$ respectively. A circuit which implements this function is shown in Fig. 3.5.

This use of a MUX as a "table look up" device can be extended to functions of a larger number of variables; the MUX effectively removes the terms involving the variables assigned to its select inputs from the logic expression. This can sometimes be an effective way to reduce the complexity of implementation of a function. For complex functions, however, there are often better implementations, as we use PLDs (see chapter 5).

Although, it is obvious how the function shown in Fig. 3.2 can be extended a $2^n$ line to 1-line MUX, for any $n$, in practice, about the largest devices available are only to 16-line to 1-line functions. It is possible to use a "tree" of smaller MUX's to make arbitrarily large MUX's. Figure 3.6 shows an implementation of a 16-line to 1-line MUX using five 4-line to 1-line MUX's.

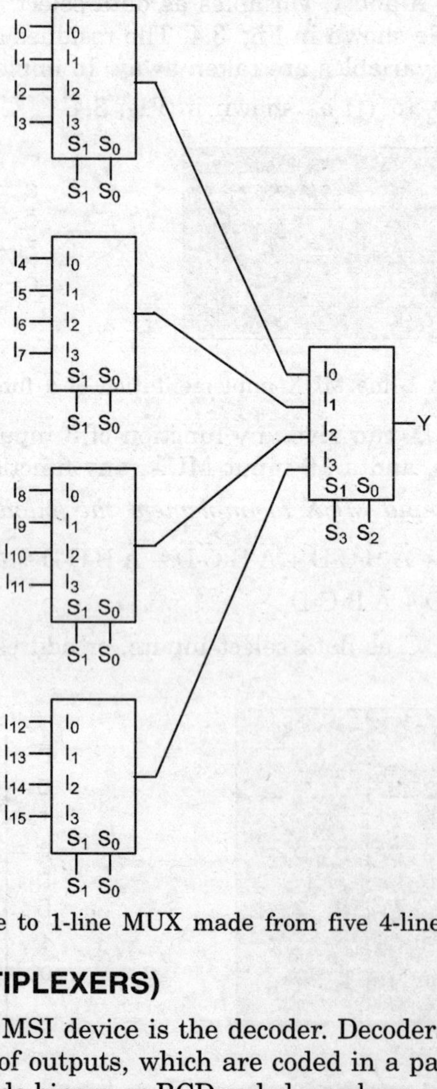


**Fig. 3.6** A 16-line to 1-line MUX made from five 4-line to 1-line MUX's

## 3.2 DECODERS (DEMULTIPLEXERS)

Another commonly used MSI device is the decoder. Decoders, in general, transform a set of inputs into a different set of outputs, which are coded in a particular manner; *e.g.*, certain decoders are designed to decode binary or BCD coded numbers and produce the correct output to display a digit on a 7 segment (calculator type) display. Decoders are also available to convert numbers from binary to BCD, from binary to hexadecimal, etc.

Normally, however, the term "decoder" implies a device which performs, in a sense, the inverse operation of a multiplexer. A decoder accepts an $n$ digit number as its $n$ "select" inputs and produces an output (usually a logic 0) at one of its $2^n$ possible outputs. Decoders are usually referred to as $n$ line to $2^n$ line decoders; *e.g.,* a 3-line to 8-line decoder. This type of decoder is really a binary to unary number system decoder. Most decoders have inverted outputs, so the selected output is set to logic 0, while all the other outputs remain at logic 1. As well, most decoders have an "enable" input $\overline{E}$, which "enables" the operation of the decoder—when the $\overline{E}$ input is set to 0, the device behaves as a decoder and selects the output determined by the select inputs; when the $\overline{E}$ input is set to 1, the outputs of the decoder are *all* set to 1. (The bar over the E indicates that it is an "active low" input; that is, a logic 0 enables the function).

The enable input also allows decoders to be connected together in a tree-like fashion, much as we saw for MUX's, so large decoders can be easily constructed from smaller devices. The enable input also allows the decoder to perform the inverse operation of a MUX; a MUX selects as output one of $2^n$ inputs, the decoder can be used to present an input to one of $2^n$ outputs, simply by connecting the input signal to the $\overline{E}$ input; the signal at the selected output will then be the same as the input at $\overline{E}$—this application is called "demultiplexing." The demultiplexer (DEMUX) performs the reverse operation of a multiplexer. A demultiplexer is a circuit that accepts single input and transmit it over several (one of $2^n$ possible) outputs.

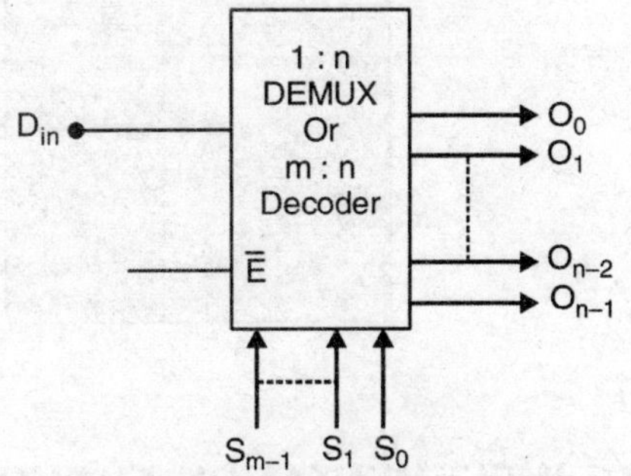


**Fig. 3.7** Block diagram of the demultiplexer/decoder

In the block diagram (Fig. 3.7) a demultiplexer, the number of output lines is $n$ and the number of select lines is $m$.

where $n = 2^m$

On the basis of select input code, to which output the data will be transmitted is determined. There is an active-low (low-logic) enable/data input. The output for these devices are also active-low.

**Note:** 4-line to 16-line decoders are the largest available circuits in ICs.

A typical 3-line to 8-line decoder with an enable input behaves according to the following truth table, and has a circuit symbol as shown in Fig. 3.8.

| $E$ | $S_2$ | $S_1$ | $S_0$ | $O_0$ | $O_1$ | $O_2$ | $O_3$ | $O_4$ | $O_5$ | $O_6$ | $O_7$ |
|---|---|---|---|---|---|---|---|---|---|---|---|
| 1 | x | x | x | 1 | 1 | 1 | 1 | 1 | 1 | 1 | 1 |
| 0 | 0 | 0 | 0 | 0 | 1 | 1 | 1 | 1 | 1 | 1 | 1 |
| 0 | 0 | 0 | 1 | 1 | 0 | 1 | 1 | 1 | 1 | 1 | 1 |
| 0 | 0 | 1 | 0 | 1 | 1 | 0 | 1 | 1 | 1 | 1 | 1 |
| 0 | 0 | 1 | 1 | 1 | 1 | 1 | 0 | 1 | 1 | 1 | 1 |
| 0 | 1 | 0 | 0 | 1 | 1 | 1 | 1 | 0 | 1 | 1 | 1 |
| 0 | 1 | 0 | 1 | 1 | 1 | 1 | 1 | 1 | 0 | 1 | 1 |
| 0 | 1 | 1 | 0 | 1 | 1 | 1 | 1 | 1 | 1 | 0 | 1 |
| 0 | 1 | 1 | 1 | 1 | 1 | 1 | 1 | 1 | 1 | 1 | 0 |

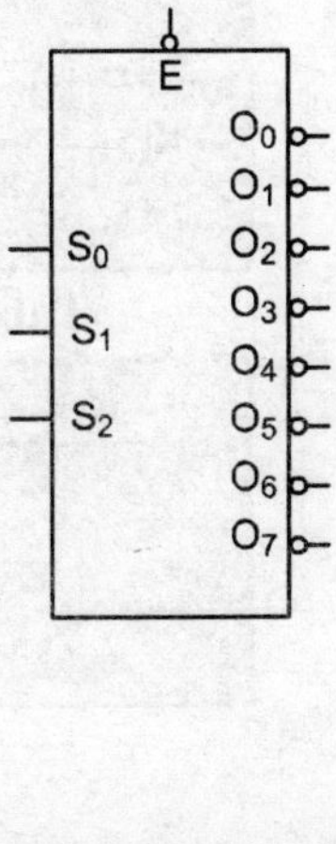


**Fig. 3.8** An 3-line to 8-line decoder

Note that, when the $\overline{E}$ input is enabled, an output of 0 is produced corresponding to each minterm of $S_2$, $S_1$, $S_0$. These minterm can be combined together using other logic gates to form any required logic function of the input variables. In fact, several functions can be produced at the same time. If the selected output was a logic 1, then the required minterms could simply be ORed together to implement a switching function directly from its minterm form. Using de Morgan's theorem, we can see that when the outputs are inverted, as is normally the case, then the minterm form of the function can be obtained by NANDing the required terms together.

**Example 4.** An implementation the functions defined by the following truth table using a decoder and NAND gates is shown in Fig. 3.9.

| A | B | C | $Y_1$ | $Y_2$ |
|---|---|---|---|---|
| 0 | 0 | 0 | 0 | 1 |
| 0 | 0 | 1 | 1 | 1 |
| 0 | 1 | 0 | 1 | 0 |
| 0 | 1 | 1 | 0 | 0 |
| 1 | 0 | 0 | 1 | 0 |
| 1 | 0 | 1 | 0 | 1 |
| 1 | 1 | 0 | 0 | 1 |
| 1 | 1 | 1 | 0 | 0 |

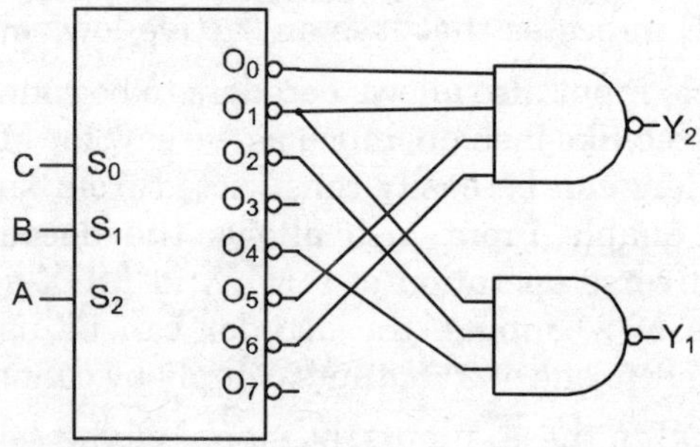


**Fig. 3.9**

## 3.3 IMPLEMENTATION EXAMPLES OF COMBINATIONAL LOGIC DESIGN USING MUX/DEMUX

We have already seen how to implement combinational circuits using MUX/DEMUX. The standard ICs available for multiplexers are 2:1, 4:1, 8:1 and 16:1. The different digital ICs are given in appendix B, but for sake of convenience some of the MUX/DEMUX ICs are given here in Table 3.1.

**Table 3.1A Standard multiplexer ICs**

| *IC No.* | *Description* | *Output* |
|---|---|---|
| 74157 | Quad. 2:1 Multiplexer | Same as input |
| 74158 | Quad 2:1 MUX | Inverted input |
| 74153 | Dual 4:1 MUX | Same as input |
| 74352 | Dual 4:1 MUX | Inverted input |
| 74151A | 8:1 MUX | Complementary outputs |
| 74152 | 8:1 MUX | Inverted input |
| 74150 | 16:1 MUX | Inverted input |

**Table 3.1B Standard demultiplexer/decoder ICs**

| *IC No.* | *Description* | *Output* |
|---|---|---|
| 74139 | Dual 1:4 Demultiplexer (2-line-to-4-line decoder) | Inverted input |
| 74155 | Dual 1:4 Demultiplexer (2-line-to-4-line decoder) | 1Y-Inverted I/P<br>2Y-Same as I/P |

Contd....

| 74138 | 1:8 Demultiplexer (3-line-to-8-line decoder) | Inverted I/P |
|---|---|---|
| 74154 | 1:16 Demultiplexer (4-line-to-16-line decoder) | Same as input |

When using the multiplexer as a logic element either the truth table or one of the standard forms of logic expression must be available. The design procedure for combinational circuits using MUX are as follows:

STEP 1: Identify the decimal number corresponding to each minterm in the expression. The input lines corresponding to these numbers are to be connected to logic 1 (high).

STEP 2: All other input lines except that used in step 1 are to be connected to logic 0 (low).

STEP 3: The control inputs are to be applied to select inputs.

**Example 5.** *Implement the following function with multiplexer.*

$$Y = F(A, B, C, D) = \Sigma m\,(0, 1, 3, 4, 8, 9, 15)$$

**Solution. STEP 1:** The input lines corresponding to each minterms (decimal number) are to be connected to logic 1.

Therefore, input lines 0, 1, 3, 4, 8, 9, 15 have to be connected to logic 1.

**STEP 2:** All other input lines except 0, 1, 3, 4, 8, 9, 15 are to be connected to logic 0.

**STEP 3:** The control inputs A, B, C, D are to be applied to select inputs.

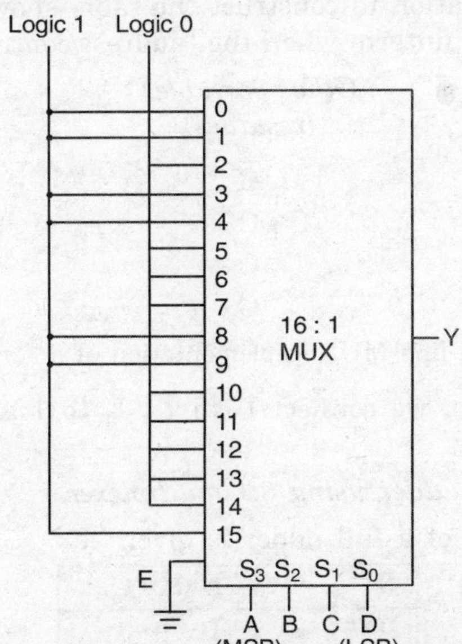


**Note:** Although, the given procedure is simple to implement but the 16 to 1 multiplexers are the largest available ICs, therefore, to meet the larger input needs there should be provision for expansion. This is achieved with the help of enable/stroke inputs and multiplexer stacks or trees are designed.

**Example 6.** *Implement the following function with a 4×1 multiplexer:*

$$Y = F(A, B, C) = \Sigma m\,(1, 3, 5, 6)$$

**Solution.** Given $Y = F(A, B, C) = \Sigma m\ (1, 3, 5, 6)$

$$= \bar{A}\bar{B}C + \bar{A}BC + A\bar{B}C + AB\bar{C}$$

We use the A and B variables as data select inputs. We can use the above equation to construct the table shown in Fig. 3.10. The residues are what is "left over" in each minterm when the "address" variables are taken away.

| *Input* | *"Address"* | *Other variables (residues)* |
|---|---|---|
| $I_0$ | $\bar{A}\bar{B}$ | C |
| $I_1$ | $\bar{A}B$ | C |
| $I_2$ | $A\bar{B}$ | C |
| $I_3$ | AB | $\bar{C}$ |

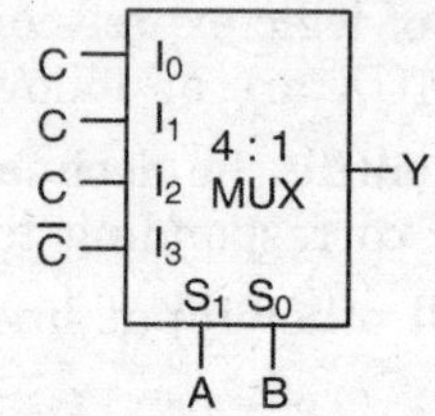


**Fig. 3.10** A 4-line to 1-line MUX implementation of a function of 3 variables.

To implement this circuit, we connect $I_0$, $I_1$ and $I_2$ to C and $I_3$ to $\bar{C}$ as shown in Fig. 3.10.

**Example 7.** *Using four-input multiplexer, implement the following function*

$$Y = F(A, B, C) = \Sigma m\ (0, 2, 3, 5, 7)$$

*Control variables A, B.*

**Solution.** Given $Y = F(A, B, C) = \Sigma m\ (0, 2, 3, 5, 7)$

$$= \bar{A}\bar{B}\bar{C} + \bar{A}B\bar{C} + \bar{A}BC + A\bar{B}C + ABC$$

We can use the above equation to construct the table shown in Fig. 3.11. The residues are what is "left over" in each minterm when the "address/control" variables are taken away.

| *Input* | *"Address"* | *Other variables (residues)* |
|---|---|---|
| $I_0$ | $\bar{A}\bar{B}$ | $\bar{C}$ |
| $I_1$ | $\bar{A}B$ | $C + \bar{C} = 1$ |
| $I_2$ | $A\bar{B}$ | C |
| $I_3$ | AB | C |

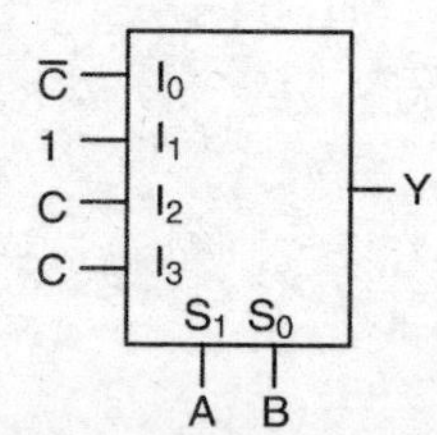


**Fig. 3.11** A 4-line to 1-line MUX implementation of a function of 3 variables

To implement this function, we connect $I_0$ to $\bar{C}$, $I_1$ to 1 and $I_2$ and $I_3$ to C, as shown in Fig. 3.11.

**Example 8.** *Design a full adder using 8:1 multiplexer.*

**Solution.** The truth table of a full adder is given as

| *A* | *B* | *C* | *S* | $C_F$ |
|---|---|---|---|---|
| 0 | 0 | 0 | 0 | 0 |
| 0 | 0 | 1 | 1 | 0 |
| 0 | 1 | 0 | 1 | 0 |
| 0 | 1 | 1 | 0 | 1 |
| 1 | 0 | 0 | 1 | 0 |
| 1 | 0 | 1 | 0 | 1 |
| 1 | 1 | 0 | 0 | 1 |
| 1 | 1 | 1 | 1 | 1 |

$$S\ (A, B, C) = \bar{A}\bar{B}C + \bar{A}B\bar{C} + A\bar{B}\bar{C} + ABC = \Sigma m\ (1, 2, 4, 7)$$

$$C_F\ (A, B, C) = \bar{A}BC + A\bar{B}C + AB\bar{C} + ABC = \Sigma m\ (3, 5, 6, 7)$$

The implementation for summation expression is

STEP 1: The input lines corresponding to 1, 2, 4, 7 are to be connected to logic 1.

STEP 2: Other input lines are to be connected to logic 0.

STEP 3: Control inputs A, B, C are to be applied to select inputs Fig. 3.12A.

Similarly for carry expression.

STEP 1: The input lines corresponding to 3, 5, 6, 7 are to be connected to logic 1.

STEP 2: Other input lines are to be connected to logic 0.

STEP 3: Control inputs A, B, C are to be applied to select inputs Fig. 3.12B.

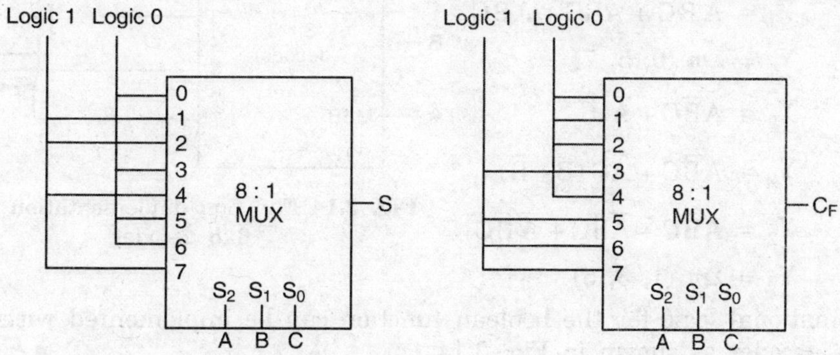


**Fig. 3.12** Full adder implementation using 8:1 Multiplexer.

**Example 9.** *Implement a full adder with a decoder and two OR-gates.*

**Solution.** From the previous example we note that expression for summation is given by

$$S\ (A, B, C) = \Sigma m\ (1, 2, 4, 7)$$

and expression for carry is given by

$$C_F\ (A, B, C) = \Sigma m\ (3, 5, 6, 7)$$

The combinational logic of full adder can be implemented with due help of 3-line to 8-line decoder/1:8 demultiplexer as shown in Fig. 3.13.

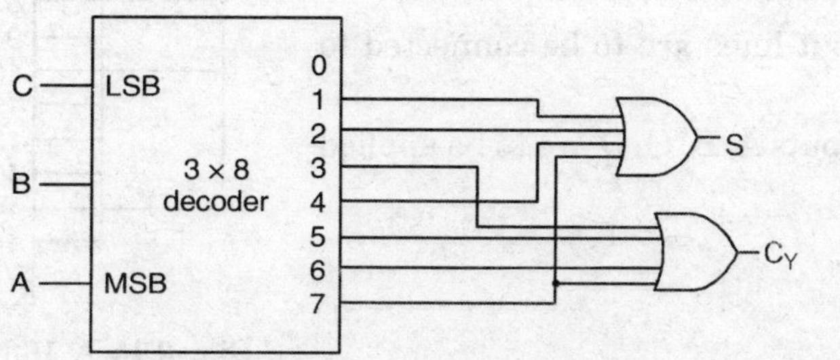


**Fig. 3.13** Full adder implementation using 3 × 8 decoder.

**Example 10.** *A combinational circuit is defined by the following Boolean functions. Design circuit with a decoder and external gates.*

**Solution.** $Y_1 = F_1(A, B, C) = \overline{A}\,\overline{B}\,\overline{C} + AC$

$Y_2 = F_2(A, B, C) = A\overline{B}C + \overline{A}C$

Given $Y_1 = \overline{A}\ \overline{B}\ \overline{C} + AC$

First we have to write the expression in minterms, if the expression is not in the form of minterms by using $(x + \overline{x} = 1)$

Therefore $Y_1 = \overline{A}\,\overline{B}\,\overline{C} + AC$

$Y_1 = \overline{A}\,\overline{B}\,\overline{C} + AC\,(B + \overline{B})$

$Y_1 = \overline{A}\,\overline{B}\,\overline{C} + ABC + A\overline{B}C$

$Y_1 = \Sigma m\ (0, 5, 7)$

$Y_2 = A\overline{B}C + \overline{A}C$

$Y_2 = A\overline{B}C + \overline{A}C\,(B + \overline{B})$

$Y_2 = A\overline{B}C + \overline{A}BC + \overline{A}\,\overline{B}C$

$Y_2 = \Sigma m\ (1, 3, 5)$

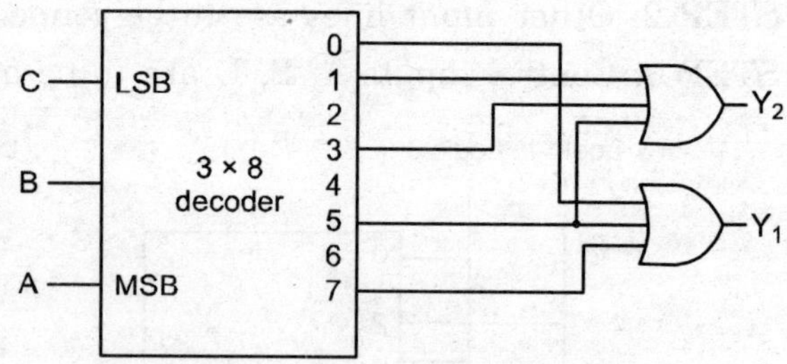


**Fig. 3.14** Function implementation using 3×8 decoder.

The combinational logic for the boolean function can be implemented with the help of 3-line to 8-line decoder as shown in Fig. 3.14.

**Example 11.** *Realise the given function using a multiplexer*

*Y(A, B, C, D) =* $\Sigma m$ *(0, 3, 5, 9, 11, 12, 13, 15)*

**Solution.** To implement the given function, first we have to express the function in terms of sum of product. *i.e.,*

Y (A, B, C, D) = $\Sigma m$ (1, 2, 4, 6, 7, 8, 10, 14)

Now the given function in this form can be realized as

**Step 1:** Input lines corresponding to 1, 2, 4, 6, 7, 8, 10, 14 are to be connected to logic 1.

**Step 2:** Other input lines are to be connected to logic 0.

**Step 3:** Control inputs A, B, C, D are to be applied to select inputs.

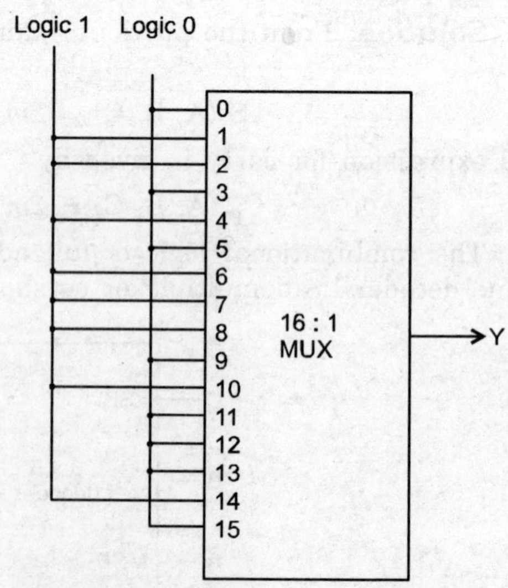


**Fig. 3.15** A 16-line to 1-line MUX implementation.

**Example 12.** *Realize the following boolean expression using 4:1 MUX(S) only.*

$$Z = \overline{A}\,\overline{B}\,\overline{C}\,\overline{D} + \overline{A}BC\overline{D} + A\overline{B}C\overline{D} + A\overline{B}C\overline{D} + A\overline{B}\,\overline{C}\,\overline{D} + ABCD$$

**Solution.** Given $Z = \Sigma m\ (0, 6, 8, 10, 11, 15)$

To implement the given boolean expression we must have 16 inputs and 4 selection inputs.

Since, 4:1 mux has 4 input lines and two selection lines. Therefore, we can use 4, 4:1 MUX with their select lines connected together. This is followed by a 4:1 MUX to select one of the four outputs. The select lines of the 4:1 MUX (final) are driven from inputs A, B. The complete circuit is shown in Fig. 3.16.

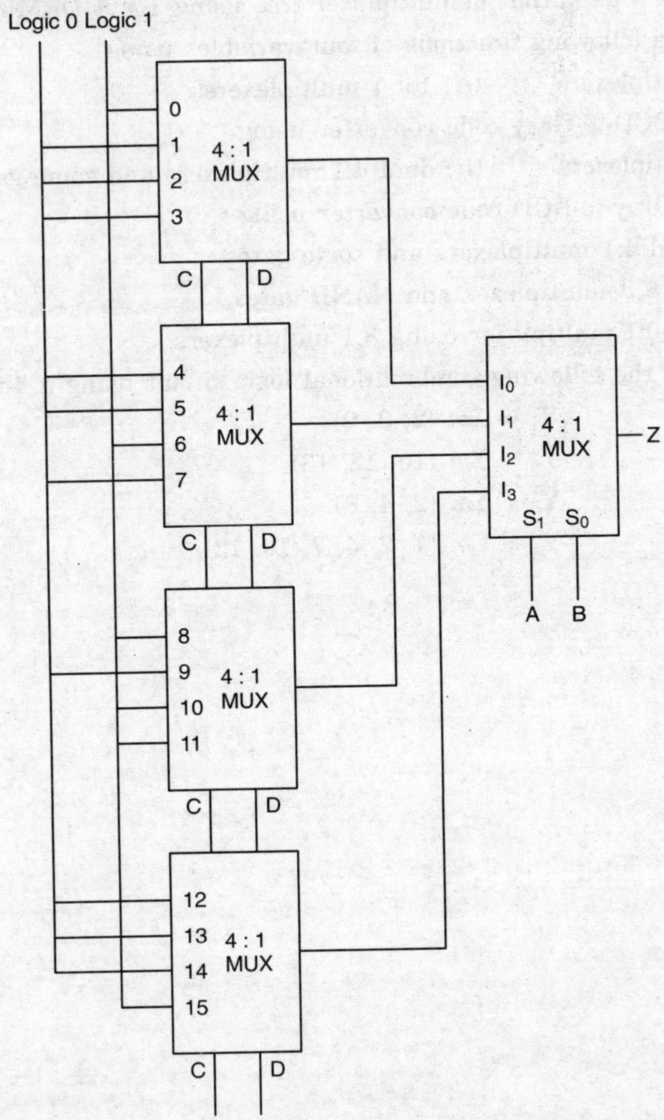


**Fig. 3.16** A 4-line to 1-line MUX implementation of a function of 4 variable

## 3.4 EXERCISE

1. Use a 8-input multiplexer to generate the function

$$Y = \overline{A}B + A\overline{D} + C\overline{D} + \overline{B}\,\overline{C}$$

2. Implement the following function with an multiplexer.

$$Y = \Sigma m\ (0, 1, 5, 7, 10, 14, 15)$$

3. Given $\quad Y = \Sigma m\ (1, 3, 5, 6)$

   Implement using a multiplexer and write expression for output.

4. Design a 32:1 multiplexer using two 16:1 multiplexers.
5. Implement a 64 output demultiplexer tree using 1 × 4 DEMUX.
6. Realize the following functions of four variables using

   (*i*) 8:1 multiplexers (*ii*) 16: 1 multiplexers.

7. Design a BCD-to-Gray code converter using

   (*i*) 8:1 multiplexers (*ii*) dual 4:1 multiplexers and some gates.

8. Design a Gray-to-BCD code converter using

   (*i*) two dual 4:1 multiplexers and some gates.

   (*ii*) one 1:16 demultiplexer and NAND gates.

9. Design a 40:1 multiplexer using 8:1 multiplexers.
10. Implement the following combinational logic circuit using a 4-to-16-line decoder.

$$Y_1 = \Sigma m\ (2, 3, 9)$$
$$Y_2 = \Sigma m\ (10, 12, 13)$$
$$Y_3 = \Sigma m\ (2, 4, 8)$$
$$Y_4 = \Sigma m\ (1, 2, 4, 7, 10, 12)$$

4
CHAPTER

# SEQUENTIAL LOGIC

## 4.1 INTRODUCTION

Sequential logic differs from combinational logic in that the output of the logic device is dependent not only on the present inputs to the device, but also on past inputs; *i.e.,* the output of a sequential logic device depends on its present internal state and the present inputs. This implies that a sequential logic device has some kind of memory of at least part of its "history" (*i.e.,* its previous inputs).

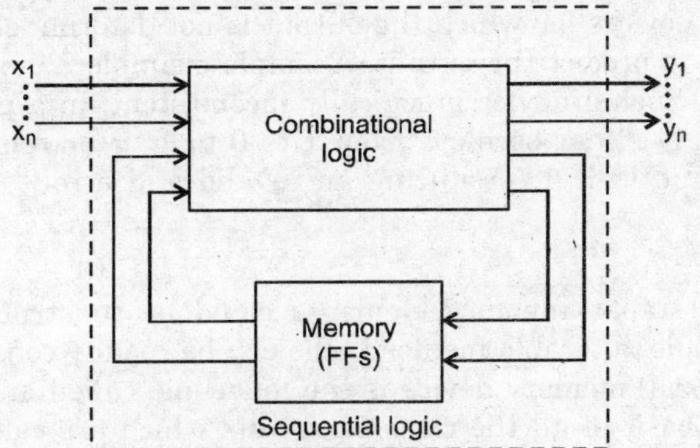


**Fig. 4.0** Sequential logic

A simple memory device can be constructed from combinational devices with which we are already familiar. By a memory device, we mean a device which can remember if a signal of logic level 0 or 1 has been connected to one of its inputs, and can make this fact available at an output. A very simple, but still useful, memory device can be constructed from a simple OR gate, as shown in Figure 4.1.

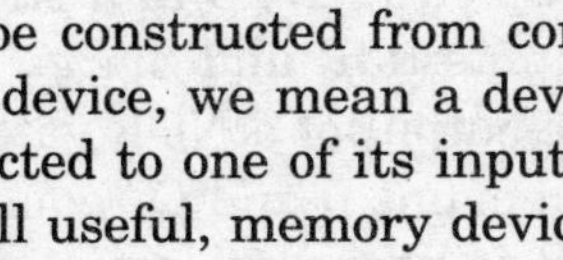


**Fig. 4.1**

In this memory device, if A and Q are initially at logic 0, then Q remains at logic 0. However, if the single input A ever becomes a logic 1, then the output Q will be logic 1 ever after, regardless of any further changes in the input at A. In this simple memory, the output is a function of the state of the memory element only; after the memory is "written" then it cannot be changed back. However, it can be "read." Such a device could be used as a simple read only memory, which could be "programmed" only once. Often a state table or timing diagram is used to describe the behaviour of a sequential device. Figure 4.2 shows both a state table and a timing diagram for this simple memory. The state table shows the state which the device enters after an input (the "next state"), for all possible states and inputs. For this device, the output is the value stored in the memory.

| *State Table* | | | |
|---|---|---|---|
| *Present State* $Q_n$ | *Input* | *Next State* $Q_{m+1}$ | *Output* |
| 0 | 0 | 0 | 0 |
| 0 | 1 | 1 | 1 |
| 1 | 0 | 1 | 1 |
| 1 | 1 | 1 | 1 |

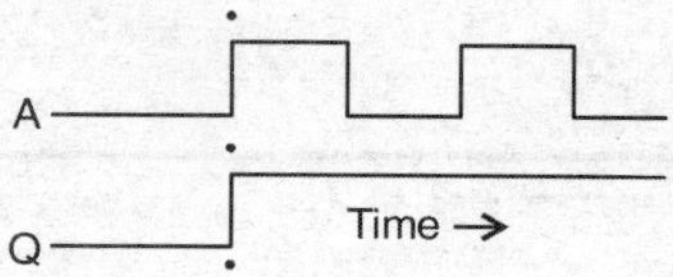


**Fig. 4.2**

Note that the output of the memory is used as one of the inputs; this is called feedback and is characteristic of programmable memory devices (Without feedback, a "permanent" electronic memory device would not be possible). The use of feedback in a device can introduce problems which are not found in strictly combinational circuits. In particular, it is possible to inadvertently construct devices for which the output is not determined by the inputs, and for which it is not possible to predict the output. A simple example is an inverter with its input connected to its output. Such a device is logically inconsistent; in a physical implementation the device would probably either oscillate from 1 to 0 to 1 . . . or remain at an intermediate value between logic 0 and logic 1, producing an invalid and erroneous output.

## 4.2 RS FLIP-FLOP

More complicated, stable, memory elements could be constructed using simple logic gates. In particular, simple, alterable memory cells can be readily constructed. One basic (but not often used in this form) memory device is the following, called an RS (reset-set) latch, or flip flop. It is the most basic of all the class of circuits which are called latches or flip-flops. A logic diagram for this device is shown in Fig. 4.3, together with its circuit symbol.

We can analyze the circuit shown in Fig. 4.3 in a straightforward manner, to determine the outputs $\overline{Q}$ and Q for various inputs to R and S; *e.g.*, suppose we raise S to logic 1, with Q at logic 0. Then $\overline{Q}$ must be 0, (the output of a NOR gate is 0 if any input is 1), and Q must be 1. If S is returned to 0, then $\overline{Q}$ remains 0 and Q remains 1; *i.e.*, the RS latch "remember" if S was set to 1, while R is 0. If R is raised to logic 1 while S is at logic 0, then Q is set to logic 0, and $\overline{Q}$ is set to logic 1; *i.e.*, the latch is reset. If both R and S are raised to logic 1, then both Q and $\overline{Q}$ will be at logic 0. This output is inconsistent with the identification of Q and $\overline{Q}$ as the two outputs, and therefore, this combination of inputs for R and S should be avoided.

A more serious problem occurs if R and S change from logic 1 to logic 0 simultaneously. This situation is called a race condition. If both R and S are at logic 1, then Q and $\overline{Q}$ are at logic 0. When R and S are both set to 0, then both Q and $\overline{Q}$ should switch to logic 1. However, when they switch to logic 1, they should cause a switch back to logic 0 again, because of the logic 1 input to each NOR gate. If both NOR gates were identical, this would occur over and over again, indefinitely—an oscillation of the outputs Q and $\overline{Q}$ from state 0 to 1 and back, with a period depending on the time delay for the NOR gate. In practice, one gate is a little faster than the other, and the final outcome depends on the relative speeds of the two gates other. However, the final outcome cannot be predicted.

A state table for the RS flip-flop is shown in Fig. 4.3, together with its a logic diagram and its circuit symbol. (The circuit symbol for a flip-flop or latch is a rectangular block, with the inputs on the left and outputs on the right. Special inputs may be on the top and bottom.)

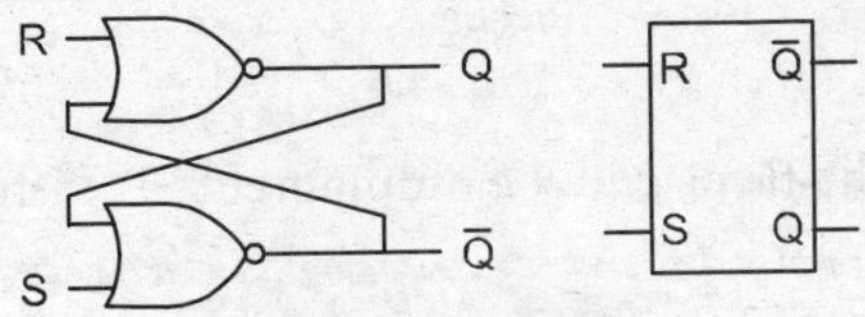


| S | R | $Q_{n+1}$ | $\overline{Q_{n+1}}$ |
|---|---|---|---|
| 0 | 0 | $Q_n$ | $\overline{Q}_n$ |
| 0 | 1 | 0 | 1 |
| 1 | 0 | 1 | 0 |
| 1 | 1 | 0 | 0 |

**Fig. 4.3**

There are three control signals often associated with flip-flops; they are the clock or enable signal; the preset, and the clear signal. The clock signal is ANDed with the inputs R and S, so that these signals can reach the flip-flop only when the clock pulse is 1; all other times the inputs to the inputs to the flip-flop are 0, and it retains its previous value.

The clock input is used for several purposes; it is used to "capture" data which is available for only a short time; and it is used to synchronize several flip-flops so they can all operate simultaneously, or synchronously. Figure 4.4 (a) shows a circuit diagram for a clocked RS flip-flop, together with its circuit symbol in Fig. 4.4 (b). Note the special symbol, similar to an arrowhead, which denotes the clock input.

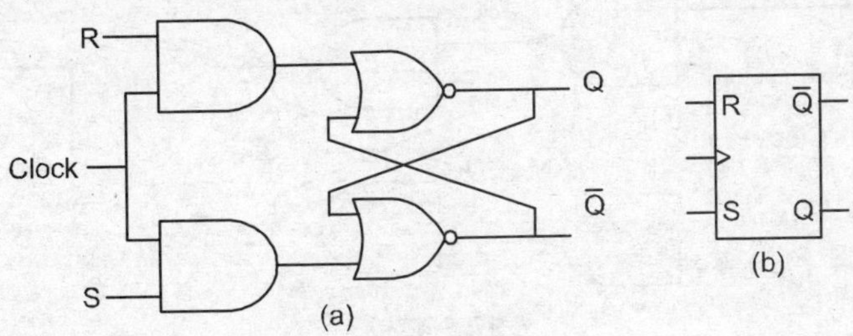


**Fig. 4.4**

The preset and clear signals are used to set the state of the flip-flop regardless of the state of the clock input. Because they are not synchronized by the clock pulse, they are said to be asynchronous. Figure 4.5 shows circuit symbol as a simple clocked RS flip-flop with preset and clear inputs.

The preset and clear act as an unclocked RS flip-flop, and consequently a logic 1 should not be applied to both at the same time.

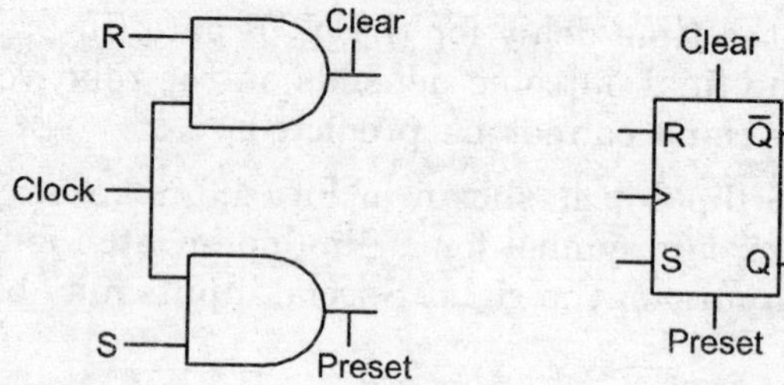


**Fig. 4.5**

A dual form of the RS flip-flop, can be implemented with NAND gates, as shown in Fig. 4.6.

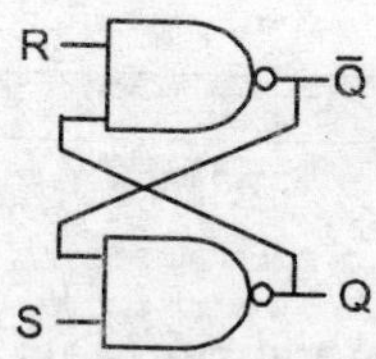


**Fig. 4.6**

Clock inputs, together with preset and clear inputs could similarly be provided for this device. Since, the inputs to this device are inverted, the preset and clear inputs would also be inverted.

## 4.3 D LATCH AND THE D FLIP-FLOP

It is possible to create a latch which has no race condition, simply by providing only one input to a RS latch, and generating an inverted signal to present to the other terminal of the latch. In this case, the S and R inputs are always inverted with respect to each other, and no race condition can occur. The circuit for a D latch is shown in Fig. 4.7.

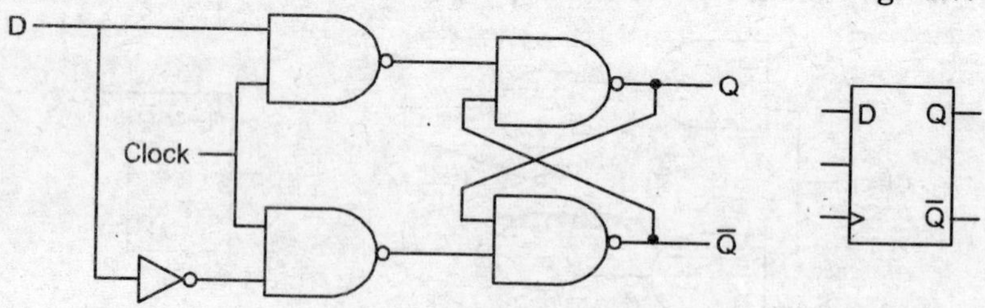


**Fig. 4.7**

The D latch is used to capture, or "latch" the logic level which is present on the Data line when the clock input is high. If the data on the D line changes state while the clock pulse is high, then the output, Q, follows the input, D. This effect can be seen in the timing diagram, Fig. 4.8 (a).

The D flip-flop, while a slightly more complicated circuit, performs a function very similar to the D latch. In the case of the D flip-flop, however, the rising edge of the clock pulse is used to "capture" the input to the flip-flop. This device is very useful when it is necessary to "capture" a logic level on a line which is very rapidly varying. Figure 4.8 (b) shows a timing diagram for a D-type flip-flop. This type of device is said to be "edge triggered"—either rising edge triggered (*i.e.*, a 0-1 transition) or falling edge triggered (*i.e.*, a 1-0 transition) devices are available.

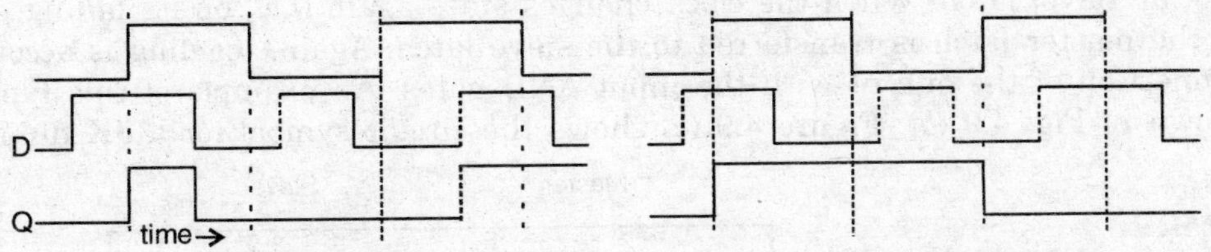


(*a*) The D latch (*b*) The D flip-flop

**Fig. 4.8**

Both the D latch and D flip-flop have the following truth table:

| $\overline{Preset}$ | $\overline{Clear}$ | *Clock* | *D* | *Q* | $\overline{Q}$ |
|---|---|---|---|---|---|
| 0 | 1 | x | x | 1 | 0 |
| 1 | 0 | x | x | 0 | 1 |
| 0 | 0 | x | x | 1 | 1 |
| 1 | 1 | ↑ or 1 | 0 | 0 | 1 |
| 1 | 1 | ↑ or 1 | 1 | 1 | 0 |
| 1 | 1 | 0 | X | $Q_a$ | $\overline{Q_a}$ |

The symbol ↑ means a leading edge, or 0–1 transition as the clock input to the flip-flop. For a D latch, it would be the level 1.

## 4.4 JK FLIP-FLOP

The JK flip-flop is the most versatile flip-flop, and the most commonly used flip-flop when discrete devices are used to implement arbitrary state machines. Like the RS flip-flop, it has two data inputs, J and K, and a clock input. It has no undefined states or race condition, however. It is always edge triggered; normally on the falling edge. (some JK flip-flops; *e.g.*, 74109, trigger on the positive edge.)

The JK flip-flop has the following characteristics:

1. If one input (J or K) is at logic 0, and the other is at logic 1, then the output is set or reset (by J and K respectively), just like the RS flip-flop, but on the (falling) clock edge.
2. If both inputs are 0, then it remains in the same state as it was before the clock pulse occurred; again like the RS flip-flop.
3. If both inputs are high, however, the flip-flop changes state whenever the (falling) edge of a clock pulse occurs; *i.e.*, the clock pulse toggles the flip-flop.

There are two basic types of JK flip-flops. The first type is basically an RS flip-flop with its outputs $\overline{Q}$ and Q ANDed together with J and K respectively. This type of JK flip-flop has no special name. Note that the connection between the outputs and the inputs to the AND gates determine the input conditions to R and S when J = K = 1. This connection is what causes the toggling, and eliminates the invalid condition which occurs in the RS flip-flop. A simplified form of this flip-flop is shown in Fig. 4.9 (*a*).

The second type of JK flip-flop is called a master-slave flip-flop. This consists of two RS flip-flops arranged so that when the clock pulse enables the first, or master, latch, it disables the second, or slave, latch. When the clock changes state again (*i.e.*, on its falling edge) the output of the master latch is transferred to the slave latch. Again, toggling is accomplished by the connection of the output with the input AND gates. An example of this type of flip-flop is shown in Fig. 4.9 (*b*). Figure 4.9 (*c*) shows the circuit symbol for a JK flip-flop.

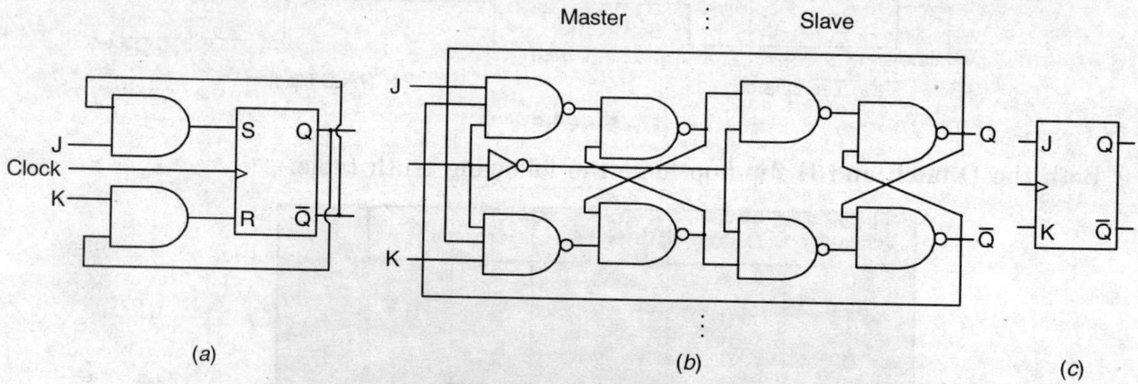


**Fig. 4.9** JK flip-flop

The JK flip-flop is a very versatile device, and is probably the most commonly used form of flip-flop in digital electronic and control circuits. The fact that it has two inputs often means that it is simpler to design the control logic required to ensure that it changes state properly in a circuit.

## 4.5 T FLIP-FLOP

This type of flip-flop is a simplified version of the JK flip-flop. It is not usually found as an IC chip by itself, but is used in many kinds of circuits, especially counter and dividers. Its only function is that it toggles itself with every clock pulse (on either the leading edge, on the trailing edge) it can be constructed from the RS flip-flop as shown in Fig. 4.10 (*a*).

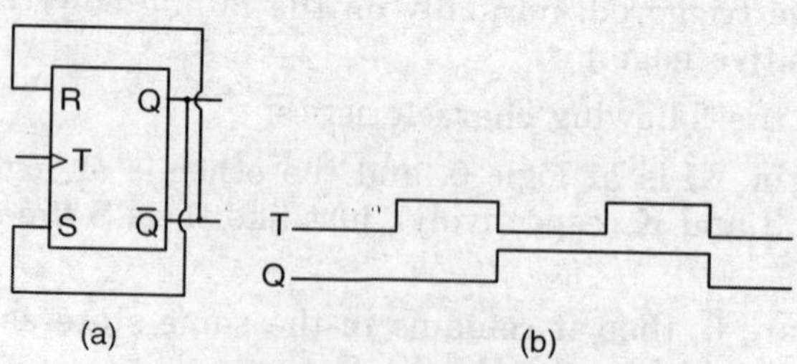


**Fig. 4.10** The T flip-flop

This flip-flop is normally set, or "loaded" with the preset and clear inputs. It can be used to obtain an output pulse train with a frequency of half that of the clock pulse train, as seen from the timing diagram, Fig. 4.10 (*b*). In this example, the T flip-flop is triggered on the falling edge of the clock pulse.

Several T flip-flops are often connected together in a simple IC to form a "divide by N" counter, where N is usually 5, 10, 12 or a power of 4.

## 4.6 FLIP-FLOP CONVERSIONS

This section shows how to convert a given type A FF to a desired type B FF using some conversion logic.

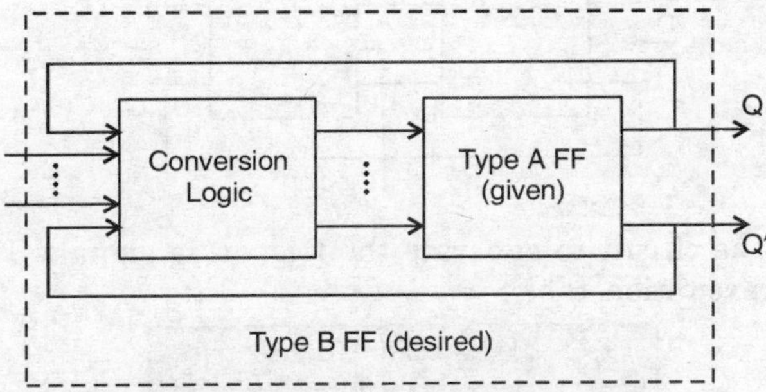


The key here is to use the excitation table, which shows the necessary triggering signal (S, R, J, K, D and T) for a desired flip-flop state transition $Q_t \rightarrow Q_{t+1}$:

| $Q_t$ | $Q_{t+1}$ | $S$ | $R$ | $J$ | $K$ | $D$ | $T$ |
|---|---|---|---|---|---|---|---|
| 0 | 0 | 0 | x | 0 | x | 0 | 0 |
| 0 | 1 | 1 | 0 | 1 | x | 1 | 1 |
| 1 | 0 | 0 | 1 | x | 1 | 0 | 1 |
| 1 | 1 | x | 0 | x | 0 | 1 | 0 |

**Example 1.** *Convert a D-FF to a T-FF:*

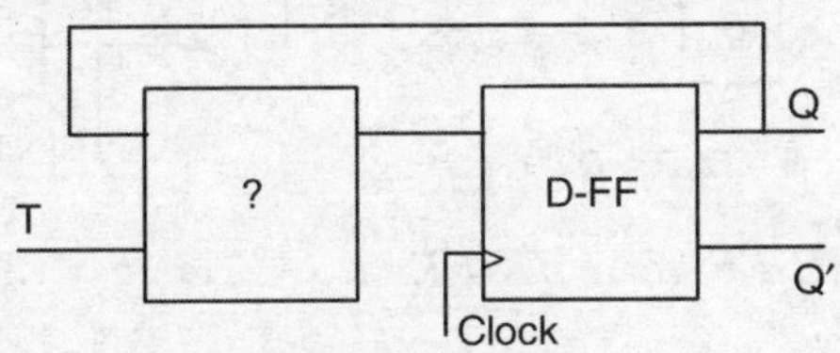


We need to design the circuit to generate the triggering signal D as a function of T and Q; D = *f* (T, Q). Consider the excitation table:

| $Q_t$ | $Q_{t+1}$ | $T$ | $D$ |
|---|---|---|---|
| 0 | 0 | 0 | 0 |
| 0 | 1 | 1 | 1 |
| 1 | 0 | 1 | 0 |
| 1 | 1 | 0 | 1 |

Treating D as a function of T and current FF state Q/($Q_t$), we have

$$D = T'Q + TQ' = T \oplus Q$$

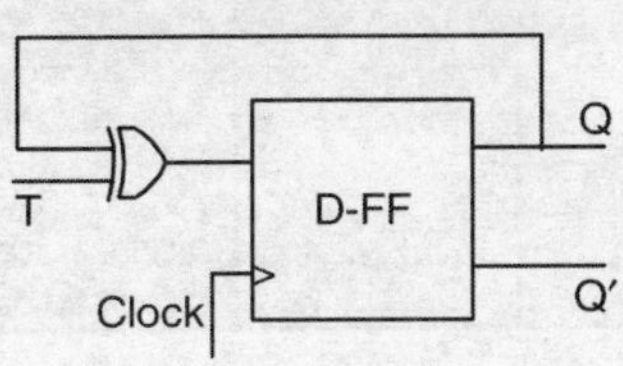

**Example 2.** *Convert a RS-FF to a D-FF:*

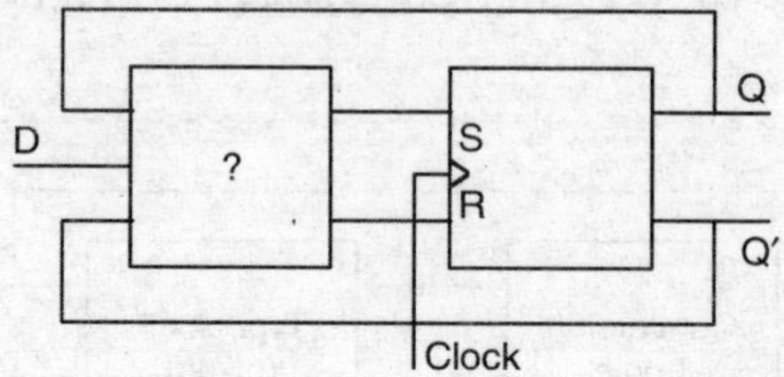


We need to design the circuit to generate the triggering signals S and R as functions of D and Q. Consider the excitation table:

| $Q_t$ | $Q_{t+1}$ | $D$ | $S$ | $R$ |
|---|---|---|---|---|
| 0 | 0 | 0 | 0 | x |
| 0 | 1 | 1 | 1 | 0 |
| 1 | 0 | 0 | 0 | 1 |
| 1 | 1 | 1 | x | 0 |

The desired signal S and R can be obtained as functions of T and current FF state Q from the Karnaugh maps:

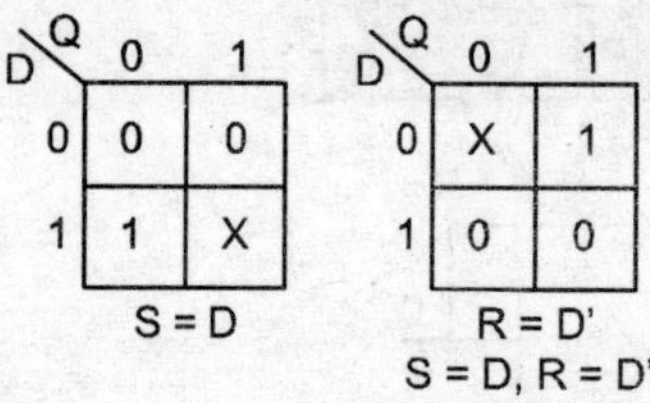


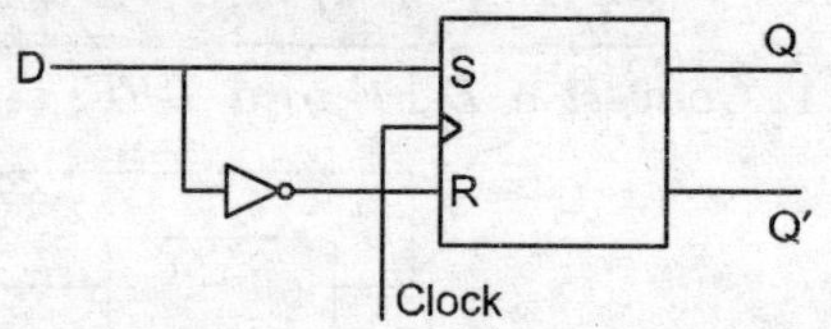


**Example 3.** *Convert a RS-FF to a JK-FF:*

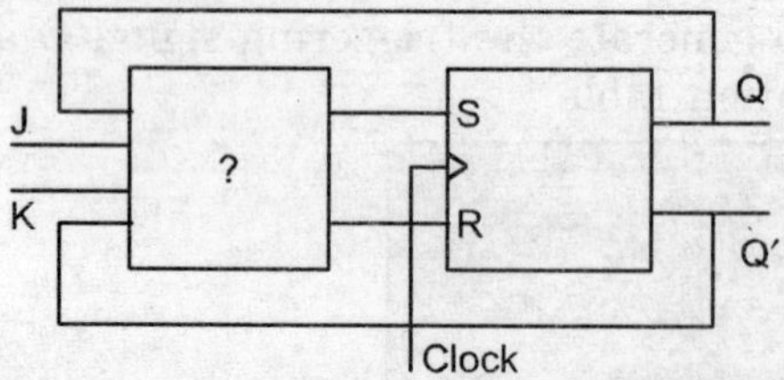


We need to design the circuit to generate the triggering signals S and R as functions of J, K and Q. Consider the excitation table:

| $Q_t$ | $Q_{t+1}$ | $J$ | $K$ | $S$ | $R$ |
|---|---|---|---|---|---|
| 0 | 0 | 0 | x | 0 | x |
| 0 | 1 | 1 | x | 1 | 0 |
| 1 | 0 | x | 1 | 0 | 1 |
| 1 | 1 | x | 0 | x | 0 |

The desired signal S and R as functions of J, K and current FF state Q can be obtained from the Karnaugh maps:

| D \ QJ | 00 | 01 | 11 | 10 |
|---|---|---|---|---|
| 0 | 0 | 1 | X | X |
| 1 | 0 | 1 | 0 | 0 |

S = Q'J

| K \ QJ | 00 | 01 | 11 | 10 |
|---|---|---|---|---|
| 0 | X | 0 | 0 | 0 |
| 1 | X | 0 | 1 | 1 |

S = QK

$$S = Q/J, \qquad R = QK$$

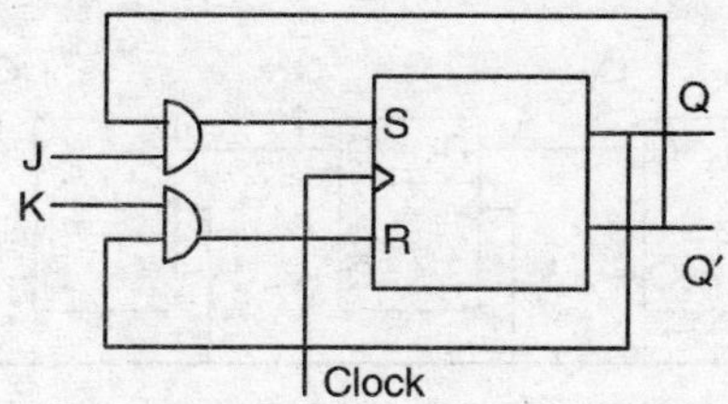


## 4.7 SHIFT REGISTERS

Registers are the group of flip-flops (single bit storage element). The simplest type of register is a data register, which is used for the temporary storage of data. In its simplest form, it consists of a set of N D flip-flops, all sharing a common clock. All of the digits in the N bit data word are connected to the data register by an N line "data bus". Figure 4.11 shows a four bit data register, implemented with four D flip-flops.

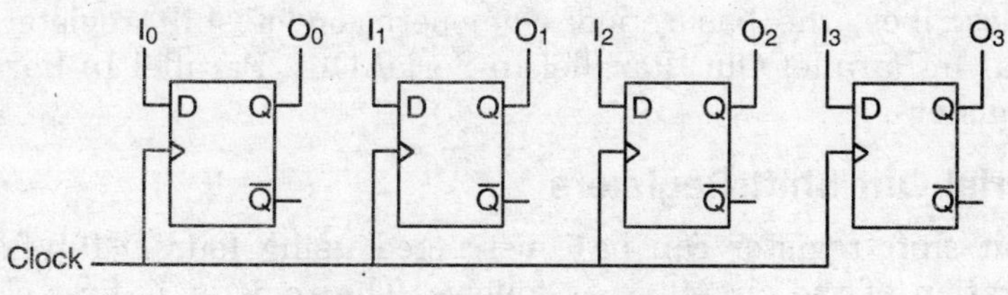


**Fig. 4.11** 4-bit D register

The data register is said to be a synchronous device, because all the flip-flops change state at the same time.

Another common form of register used in many types of logic circuits is a shift register. It is simply a set of flip-flops (usually D latches or RS flip-flops) connected together so that the output of one becomes the input of the next, and so on in series. It is called a shift register because the data is shifted through the register by one bit position on each clock pulse. Figure 4.12 shows a four bit shift register, implemented with D flip-flops.

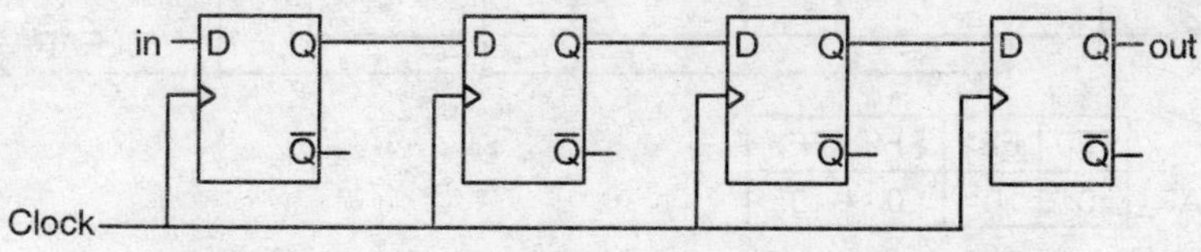


**Fig. 4.12** 4-bit serial-in serial-out shift register

On the leading edge of the first clock pulse, the signal on the DATA input is latched in the first flip-flop. On the leading edge of the next clock pulse, the contents of the first flip-flop is stored in the second flip-flop, and the signal which is present at the DATA input is stored in the first flip-flop, etc. Because, the data is entered one bit at a time, this called a serial-in shift register. Since, there is only one output, and data leaves the shift register one bit at a time, then it is also a serial out shift register. (Shift registers are named by their method of input and output; either serial or parallel.) Parallel input can be provided through the use of the preset and clear inputs to the flip-flop. The parallel loading of the flip-flop can be synchronous (*i.e.*, occurs with the clock pulse) or asynchronous (independent of the clock pulse) depending on the design of the shift register. Parallel output can be obtained from the outputs of each flip-flop as shown in Fig. 4.13.

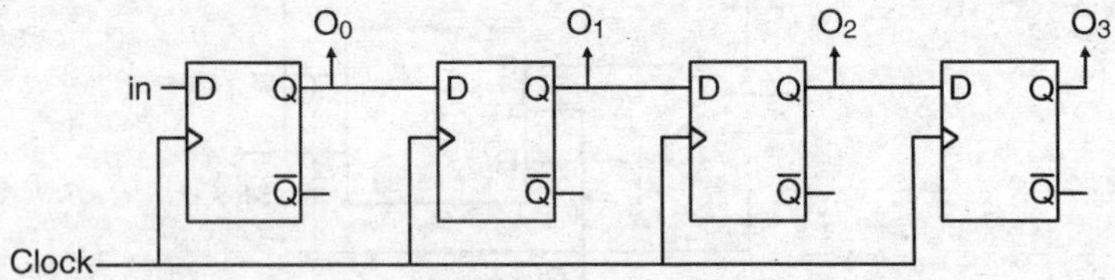


**Fig. 4.13** 4-bit serial-in parallel-out shift register

Communication between a computer and a peripheral device is usually done serially, while computation in the computer itself is usually performed with parallel logic circuitry. A shift register can be used to convert information from serial form to parallel form, and vice versa. Many different kinds of shift registers are available, depending upon the degree of sophistication required.

## 4.7.1 Modes of Operation

This section describes, the basic modes of operation of shift registers such as Serial In-Serial Out, Serial In-Parallel Out, Parallel In-Serial Out, Parallel In-Parallel Out, and bi-directional shift registers.

## 4.7.2 Serial In-Serial Out Shift Registers

A basic four-bit shift register can be constructed using four D flip-flops, as shown in Fig. 4.14. The operation of the circuit is as follows. The register is first cleared, forcing all four outputs to zero. The input data is then applied sequentially to the D input of the first flip-flop on the left (FF0). During each clock pulse, one bit is transmitted from left to right. Assume a data word to be 1001. The least significant bit of the data has to be shifted through the register from FF0 to FF3.

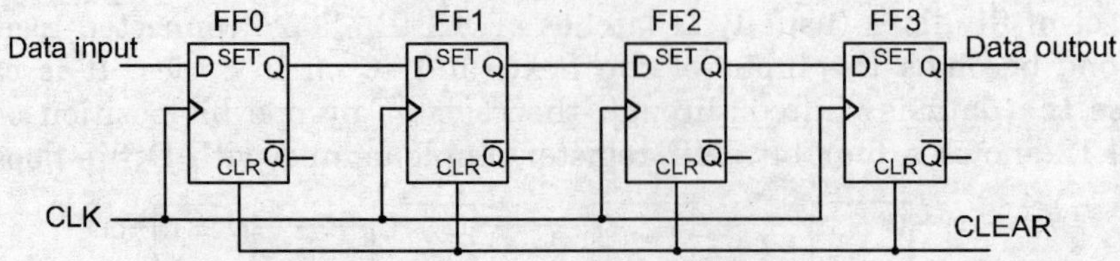


| | FF0 | FF1 | FF2 | FF3 |
|---|---|---|---|---|
| CLEAR | 0 | 0 | 0 | 0 |

**Fig. 4.14**

In order to get the data out of the register, they must be shifted out serially. This can be done destructively or non-destructively. For destructive readout, the original data is lost and at the end of the read cycle, all flip-flops are reset to zero.

| | FF0 | FF1 | FF2 | FF3 | |
|---|---|---|---|---|---|
| 0000 | 1 | 0 | 0 | 1 | 0000 |

To avoid the loss of data, an arrangement for a non-destructive reading can be done by adding two AND gates, an OR gate and an inverter to the system. The construction of this circuit is shown in Fig. 4.15.

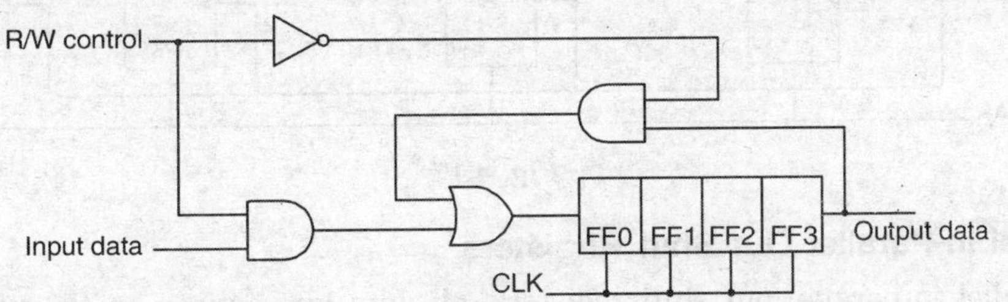


**Fig. 4.15**

The data is loaded to the register when the control line is HIGH (*i.e.,* WRITE). The data can be shifted out of the register when the control line is LOW (*i.e.,* READ).

### 4.7.3 Serial In-Parallel Out Shift Registers

For this kind of register, data bits are entered serially in the same manner as discussed in the last section. The difference is the way in which the data bits are taken out of the register. Once the data are stored, each bit appears on its respective output line, and all bits are available simultaneously. A construction of a four-bit serial in-parallel out register is shown in Fig. 4.16.

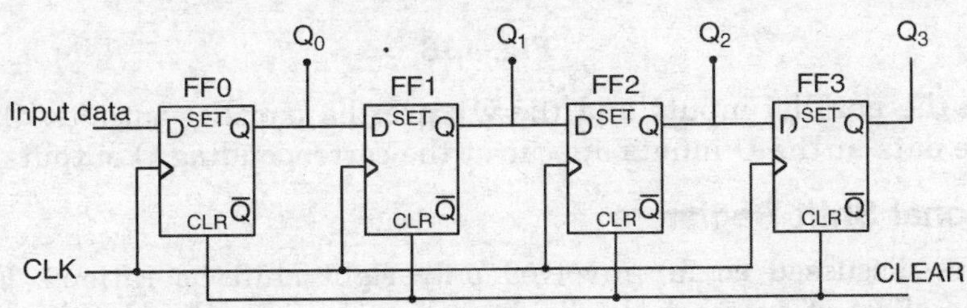


**Fig. 4.16**

### 4.7.4 Parallel In-Serial Out Shift Registers

A four-bit parallel in-serial out shift register is shown in Fig. 4.17. The circuit uses D flip-flops and NAND gates for entering data (*i.e.,* writing) to the register.

$D_0$, $D_1$, $D_2$ and $D_3$ are the parallel inputs, where $D_0$ is the most significant bit and $D_3$ is the least significant bit. To write data in, the mode control line is taken to LOW and the data is clocked in. The data can be shifted when the mode control line is HIGH as SHIFT is active high. The register performs right shift operation on the application of a clock pulse.

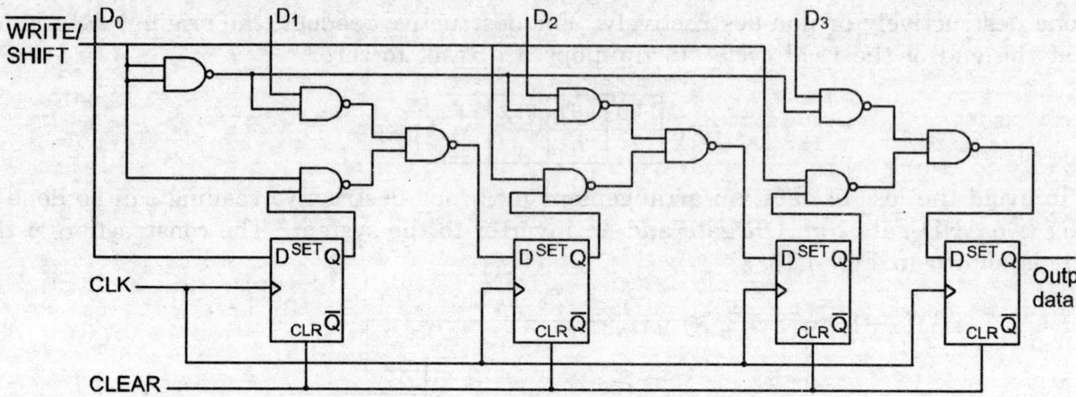


**Fig. 4.17**

### 4.7.5 Parallel In-Parallel Out Shift Registers

For parallel in-parallel out shift registers, all data bits appear on the parallel outputs immediately following the simultaneous entry of the data bits. The following circuit is a four-bit parallel in-parallel out shift register constructed by D flip-flops.

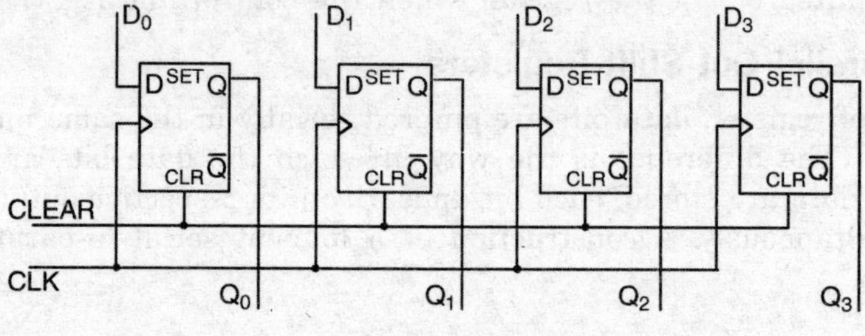


**Fig. 4.18**

The D's are the parallel inputs and the Q's are the parallel outputs. Once the register is clocked, all the data at the D inputs appear at the corresponding Q outputs simultaneously.

### 4.7.6 Bi-directional Shift Registers

The registers discussed so far involved only right shift operations. Each right shift operation has the effect of successively dividing the binary number by two. If the operation is reversed (left shift), this has the effect of multiplying the number by two. With suitable gating arrangement a serial shift register can perform both operations.

A bi-directional, or reversible, shift register is one in which the data can be shift either left or right. A four-bit bi-directional shift register using D flip-flops is shown in Fig. 4.19.

Here a set of NAND gates is configured as OR gates to select data inputs from the right or left adjacent bistables, as selected by the LEFT/RIGHT control line.

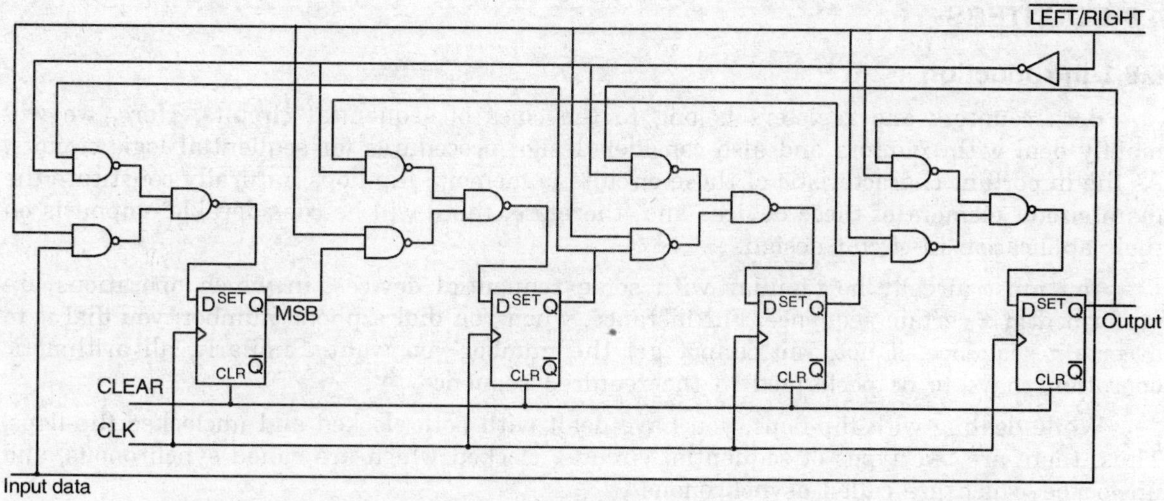


**Fig. 4.19**

### 4.7.7 Applications of Shift Registers

Shift registers can be found in many applications. Here is a list of a few.

### 4.7.8 To Produce Time Delay

The serial in-serial out shift register can be used as a time delay device. The amount of delay can be controlled by:

- the number of stages in the register (N)
- the clock frequency (f)

The time delay ΔT is given by

$$\Delta T = N \times f$$

### 4.7.9 To Simplify Combinational Logic

The ring counter technique can be effectively utilized to implement synchronous sequential circuits. A major problem in the realization of sequential circuits is the assignment of binary codes to the internal states of the circuit in order to reduce the complexity of circuits required. By assigning one flip-flop to one internal state, it is possible to simplify the combinational logic required to realize the complete sequential circuit. When the circuit is in a particular state, the flip-flop corresponding to that state is set to HIGH and all other flip-flops remain LOW.

### 4.7.10 To Convert Serial Data to Parallel Data

A computer or microprocessor-based system commonly requires incoming data to be in parallel format. But frequently, these systems must communicate with external devices that send or receive serial data. So, serial-to-parallel conversion is required. As shown in the previous sections, a serial in-parallel out register can achieve this.

## 4.8 COUNTERS

### 4.8.1 Introduction

Both counters and registers belong to the class of sequential circuits. Here, we will mainly deal with counters and also consider design procedures for sequential logic circuits. As the important characteristic of these circuits is memory, flip-flops naturally constitute the main circuit element of these devices and, therefore, there will be considerable emphasis on their application in circuit design.

You must already be familiar with some sequential devices, in which operations are performed in a certain sequence. For instance, when you dial a phone number, you dial it in a certain sequence, if not, you cannot get the number you want. Similarly, all arithmetic operations have to be performed in the required sequence.

While dealing with flip-flops, you have dealt with both clocked and unclocked flip-flops. Thus, there are two types of sequential circuits, clocked which are called synchronous, and unclocked which are called asynchronous.

In asynchronous devices, a change occurs only after the completion of the previous event. A digital telephone is an example of an asynchronous device.

If you are dialing a number, say 6354, you will first punch 6 followed by 3, 5 and 4. The important point to note is that, each successive event occurs after the previous event has been completed.

Sequential logic circuits find application in a variety of binary counters and storage devices and they are made up of flip-flops. A binary counter can count the number of pulses applied at its input. On the application of clock pulses, the flip-flops incorporated in the counter undergo a change of state in such a manner that the binary number stored in the flip-flops of the counter represents the number of clock pulses applied at the input. By looking at the counter output, you can determine the number of clock pulses applied at the counter input.

Digital circuits use several types of counters which can count in the pure binary form and in the standard BCD code as well as in some special codes. Counters can count up as well as count down. In this section, we will be looking at some of the counters in common use in digital devices.

Another area of concern to us will be the design of sequential circuits. We will be considering both synchronous and asynchronous sequential circuits.

### 4.8.2 Binary Ripple Up-Counter

We will now consider a 3-bit binary up-counter, which belongs to the class asynchronous counter circuits and is commonly known as a ripple counter. Figure 4.20 shows a 3-bit counter, which has been implemented with three T-type (toggle) flip-flops. The number of states of which this counter is capable is $2^3$ or 8. This counter is also referred to as a modulo 8 (or divide by 8) counter. Since, a flip-flop has two states, a counter having $n$ flip-flops will have $2^n$ states.

When clock pulses are applied to a ripple counter, the counter progresses from state to state and the final output of the flip-flop in the counter indicates the pulse count. The circuit recycles back to the starting state and starts counting all over again.

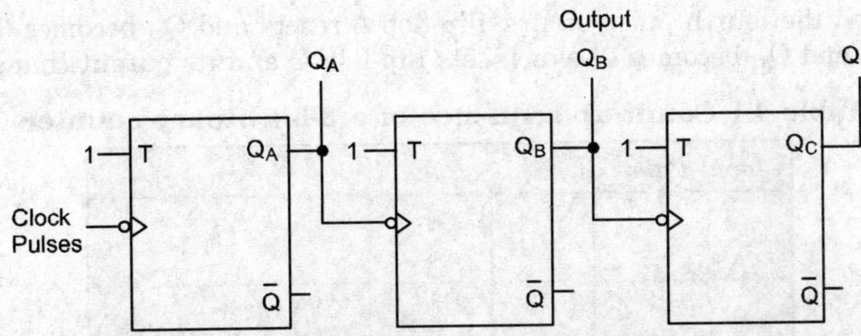


**Fig. 4.20** 3-Bit binary up-counter

There are two types of ripple counters: (*a*) asynchronous counters and (*b*) synchronous counters. In asynchronous counters all flip-flops are not clocked at the same time, while in synchronous counters all flip-flops are clocked simultaneously.

You will notice from the diagram that the normal output, Q, of each flip-flop is connected to the clock input of the next flip-flop. The T inputs of all the flip-flops, which are T-type, are held high to enable the flip-flops to toggle (change their logic state) at every transition of the input pulse from 1 to 0. The circuit is so arranged that flip-flop B receives its clock pulse from the $Q_A$ output of flip-flop A and, as a consequence, the output of flip-flop B will change its logic state when output $Q_A$ of flip-flop A changes from binary 1 to 0. This applies to all the other flip-flops in the circuit. It is thus an asynchronous counter; as all the flip-flops do not change their logic state at the same time.

Let us assume that all the flip-flops have been reset, so that the output of the counter at the start of the count is 0 0 0 as shown in the first row of Table 4.1. Also refer to Fig. 4.21 which shows the output changes for all the flip-flops at every transition of the input pulse from 1 $\rightarrow$ 0.

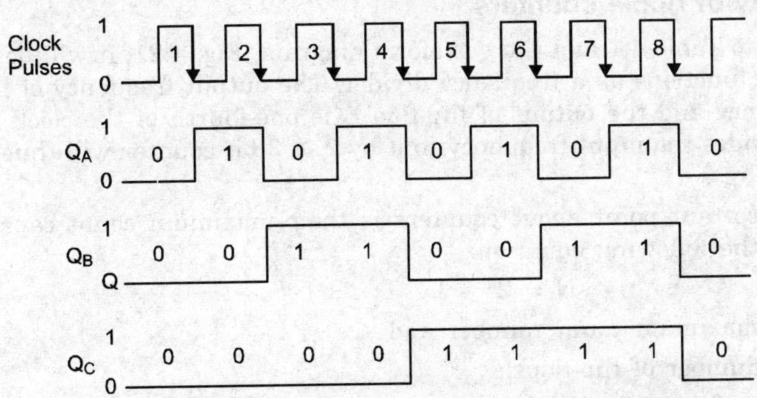


**Fig. 4.21** Waveform for 3-bit binary ripple up-counter

When the trailing edge of the first pulse arrives, flip-flop A sets and $Q_A$ becomes 1, which does not affect the output of flip-flop B. The counter output now is as shown in row 2 of the table. As a result of the second clock pulse, flip-flop A resets and its output $Q_A$ changes from 1 to 0, which sets flip-flop B and the counter output now is as shown in row 3 of the table.

When the third clock pulse arrives, flip-flop A sets and its output $Q_A$ becomes 1, which does not change the state of the B or the C flip-flop. The counter output is now as shown in row 3 of the table. When the fourth pulse occurs, flip-flop A resets and $Q_B$ becomes 0 which in turn resets flip-flop B and $Q_B$ becomes 0, which sets flip-flop C and its output changes to 1.

**Table 4.1 Count-up sequence of a 3-bit binary counter**

| *Input Pulse* | *Count* | | |
|---|---|---|---|
| | $2^2$ $Q_c$ | $2^1$ $Q_B$ | $2^0$ $Q_A$ |
| 0 | 0 | 0 | 0 |
| 1 | 0 | 0 | 1 |
| 2 | 0 | 1 | 0 |
| 3 | 0 | 1 | 1 |
| 4 | 1 | 0 | 0 |
| 5 | 1 | 0 | 1 |
| 6 | 1 | 1 | 0 |
| 7 | 1 | 1 | 1 |

Recycle

When the 5th clock pulse arrives, flip-flop A sets and $Q_A$ becomes 1; but the other flip-flops remain unchanged. The number stored in the counter is shown in the 6th row of the table. The 6th pulse resets flip-flop A and at the same time flip-flop B and C are set. The 7th pulse sets all the flip-flops and the counter output is now shown in the last row of the table.

The next clock pulse will reset all the flip-flops, as the counter has reached its maximum count capability. The counter has in all 8 states. In other words, it registers a count of 1 for every 8 clock input pulses. It means that it divides the number of input pulses by 8. It is thus a divide by 8 counter.

## Count capability of ripple counters

If you refer to Table 4.1 and the waveform diagram, Fig. 4.21, it will be apparent to you that the counter functions as a frequency divider. The output frequency of flip-flop A is half the input frequency and the output of flip-flop B is one-fourth of the clock input frequency. Each flip-flop divides the input frequency to it by 2. A 3-bit counter will thus divide the clock input frequency by 8.

Another important point about counters is their maximum count capability. It can be calculated from the following equation:

$$N = 2^n - 1$$

where N is the maximum count number and

$n$ is the number of flip-flops.

For example, if $n = 12$, the maximum count capability is

$$N = 2^{12} - 1 = 4095$$

If you have to calculate the number of flip-flops required to have a certain count capability, use the following equation:

$$n = 3.32 \log_{10} N$$

For example, if the required count capability is 5000

$$n = 3.32 \log_{10} 5000 = 12.28$$

which means that 13 flip-flops will be required.

### Counting speed of ripple counters

The primary limitation of ripple counters is their speed. This is due to the fact that each successive flip-flop is driven by the output of the previous flip-flop. Therefore, each flip-flop in the counter contributes to the total propagation delay. Hence, it takes an appreciable time for an impulse to ripple through all the flip-flops and change the state of the last flip-flop in the chain. This delay may cause malfunction, if all the flip-flops change state at the same time. In the counter we have just considered, this happens when the state changes from 011 to 100 and from 111 to 000. If each flip-flop in the counter changes state during the course of a counting operation, and if each flip-flop has a propagation delay of 30 nanoseconds, a counter having three flip-flops will cause a delay of 90 ns. The maximum counting speed for such a flip-flop will be less than

$$\frac{1}{90} \times 10^9 \text{ or } 11.11 \text{ MHz}$$

If the input pulses occur at a rate faster than 90 ns, the counter output will not be a true representation of the number of input pulses at the counter. For reliable operation of the counter, the upper limit of the clock pulses of the counter can be calculated from

$$f = \frac{1}{nt} \times 10^9$$

where $n$ is the number of flip-flops and

$t$ is the propagation delay of each flip-flop.

### 4.8.3 4-Bit Binary Ripple Up-Counter

A 4-bit binary ripple up-counter can be built with four T-type flip-flops. The diagram will follow the same pattern as for a 3-bit up-counter. The count-up sequence for this counter is given in Table 4.2 and a waveform diagram is given in Fig. 4.22. After the counter has counted up to

**Table 4.2 Count-up sequence of a 4-bit binary up-counter**

| *Input Pulse* | *Count* | | | |
|---|---|---|---|---|
| | $2^3$ $Q_D$ | $2^2$ $Q_C$ | $2^1$ $Q_B$ | $2^0$ $Q_A$ |
| 0 | 0 | 0 | 0 | 0 |
| 1 | 0 | 0 | 0 | 1 |
| 2 | 0 | 0 | 1 | 0 |
| 3 | 0 | 0 | 1 | 1 |
| 4 | 0 | 1 | 0 | 0 |
| 5 | 0 | 1 | 0 | 1 |
| 6 | 0 | 1 | 1 | 0 |
| 7 | 0 | 1 | 1 | 1 |
| 8 | 1 | 0 | 0 | 0 |
| 9 | 1 | 0 | 0 | 1 |
| 10 | 1 | 0 | 1 | 0 |
| 11 | 1 | 0 | 1 | 1 |
| 12 | 1 | 1 | 0 | 0 |
| 13 | 1 | 1 | 0 | 1 |
| 14 | 1 | 1 | 1 | 0 |
| 15 | 1 | 1 | 1 | 1 |
| 16 or 0 | 0 | 0 | 0 | 0 |

Recycle

1111, it recycles to 0000 like the 3-bit counter. You must have observed that each flip-flop divides the input frequency by, 2 and the counter divides the frequency of the clock input pulses by 16.

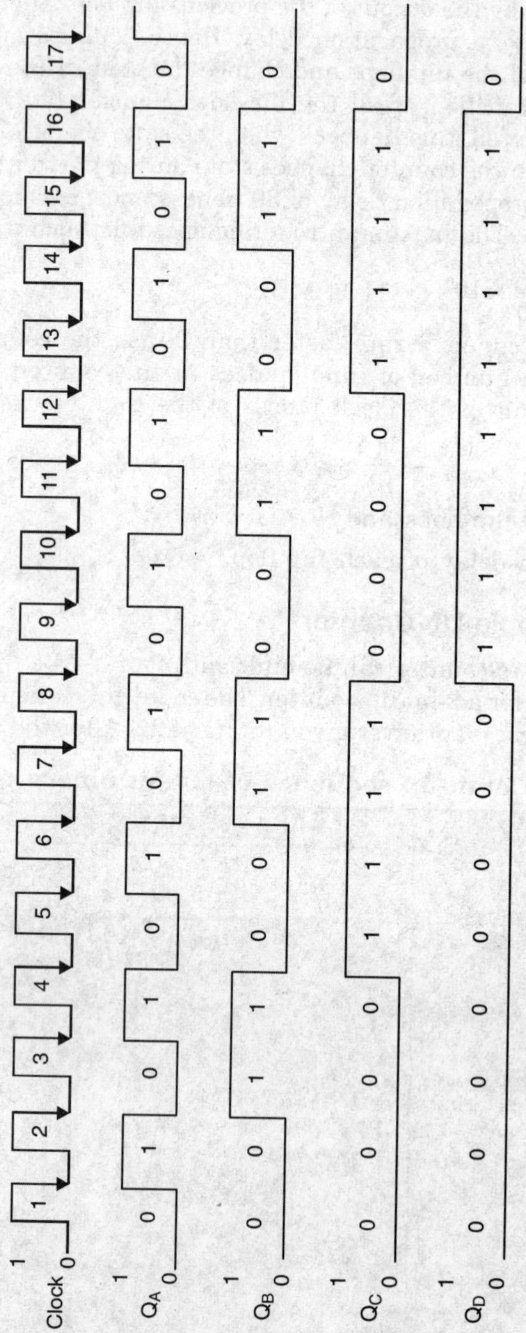


**Fig. 4.22** Waveform for 4-bit binary up-counter

### 4.8.4 3-Bit Binary Ripple Down Counter

The binary ripple up-counter we have just considered increases the count by one, each time a pulse occurs at its input. The binary ripple down counter which we are going to consider in this section decreases the count by one, each time a pulse occurs at the input. A circuit for a 3-bit down counter is given in Fig. 4.23. If you compare this counter with the up-counter in Fig. 4.20 the only difference you will notice is that, in the down counter in Fig. 4.23 the complement output $\overline{Q}$, instead of the normal output, is connected to the clock input of the next flip-flop. The counter output which is relevant even in the down counter is the normal output, Q, of the flip-flops.

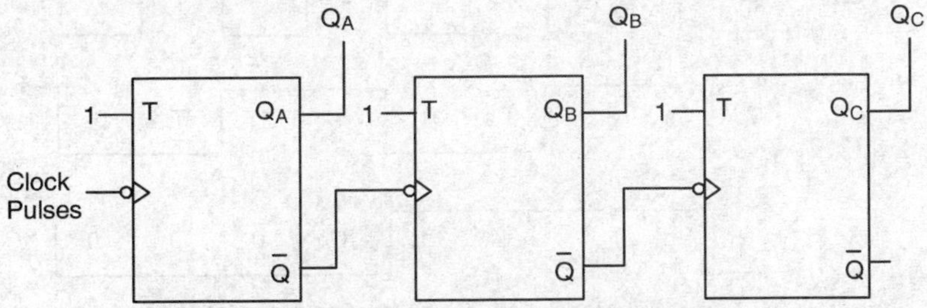


**Fig. 4.23** 3-bit binary ripple down counter

We can now analyze the circuit and examine its operation. It will help you to follow the operation of the counter, if you refer to Table 4.3 and waveform of the counter given in Fig. 4.24 for each input pulse count. Let us assume that the counter is initially reset, so that the counter output is 0 0 0. When the first input pulse is applied, flip-flop A will set, and its complement output will be 0. This will set flip-flop B, as there will be a 1 → 0 transition at the clock input. The counter output will now be 1 1 1.

**Table 4.3 Count-down sequence of a 3-bit binary counter**

| *Clock Pulse* | *Count* | | |
|---|---|---|---|
| | $2^2$ $Q_C$ | $2^1$ $Q_B$ | $2^0$ $Q_A$ |
| 0 | 0 | 0 | 0 |
| 1 | 1 | 1 | 1 |
| 2 | 1 | 1 | 0 |
| 3 | 1 | 0 | 1 |
| 4 | 1 | 0 | 0 |
| 5 | 0 | 1 | 1 |
| 6 | 0 | 1 | 0 |
| 7 | 0 | 0 | 1 |
| 8 | 0 | 0 | 0 |

Recycle

When the second clock pulse is applied, flip-flop A will reset and its complement output will become 1, which will not affect the other flip-flops. The counter output will now be 1 1 0 as shown in row 3 of the Table 4.3.

When the third clock pulse occurs, flip-flop A will set and its complement output will become 0, which will reset flip-flop B, its output becomes 0, and the complement output will be 1, which will not affect the other flip-flops. The counter will now show an output of 1 0 1, as in the fourth row of the table.

You will notice that every clock pulse decrements the counter by 1. After the eighth clock pulse, the counter output will be 0 0 0 and the counter will recycle thereafter.

The waveform for this 3-bit down counter is given in Fig. 4.24.

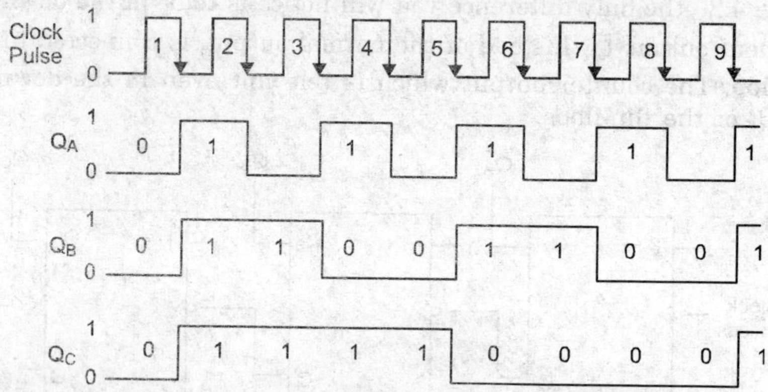


**Fig. 4.24** Waveform for 3-bit binary down-counter

### 4.8.5 Up-Down Counters

The counters which we have considered so far can only count up or down; but they cannot be programmed to count up or down. However, this facility can be easily incorporated by some modification in the circuitry. You might recall that in an up-counter the normal output of a flip-flop is connected to the clock input of the following flip-flop, and in a down counter it is the complement output which is connected to the clock input of the following flip-flop. The change from normal to complement connection to the clock input of the following flip-flop can be easily managed. A circuit for this purpose is shown in Fig. 4.25.

The normal and complement outputs of flip-flops are connected to AND gates D and E and the output of the AND gates goes to the clock input of the next flip-flop via OR gates F. When the up-down control is binary 1, gates D and F are enabled and the normal output of each flip-flop is coupled via OR gates F to the clock input of the next flip-flop. Gates E are inhibited, as one input of all these gates goes low because of the inverter. The counter, therefore, counts up.

When the up-down control is binary 0, gates D are inhibited and gated E are enabled. As a consequence the complement output of each flip-flop is coupled via OR gates F to the clock input of the next flip-flop. The counter, therefore, counts down.

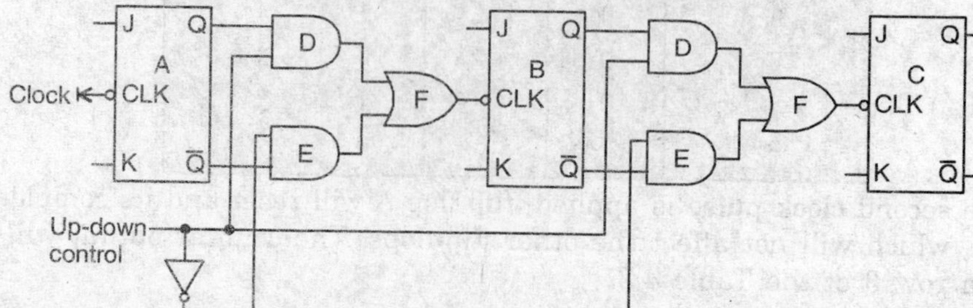


**Fig. 4.25** Up-down counter

### 4.8.6 Reset and Preset Functions

Reset and preset functions are usually necessary in most counter applications. When using a counter you would, in most cases, like the counter to begin counting with no prior counts stored in the counter. Resetting is a process by which all flip-flops in a counter are cleared and they are thus in a binary O state. JK flip-flops have a CLEAR or RESET input and you can activate them to reset flip-flops. If there are more than one flip-flop, the reset inputs of all flip-flops are connected to a common input line as shown in Fig. 4.26.

You will notice that the reset inputs of all the flip-flops in the counter are active low, and therefore, to reset the counter you take the reset input line low and then high. The output of the counter will then be 0 0 0 0.

At times you may want the counter to start the count from a predetermined point. If you load the required number into the counter, it can start counting from that point. This can be easily accomplished by using the arrangement shown in diagram. The preset inputs of all the flip-flops are connected to NAND gate outputs. One input of each NAND gate is connected to a common PRESET line and the desired number is fed into the other inputs of the NAND gates. To load a number into the counter, first clear the counter and then feed the required number into the NAND gates as indicated in the diagram. When you take the PRESET line high momentarily, the output of NAND gates 1 and 4 will be 1, so, flip-flops A and D will remain reset. The output of gates 2 and 3 will be 0 and so, flip-flops B and C will be set. The number stored in the counter will now be 0 1 1 0, which is the number required to be loaded in the counter.

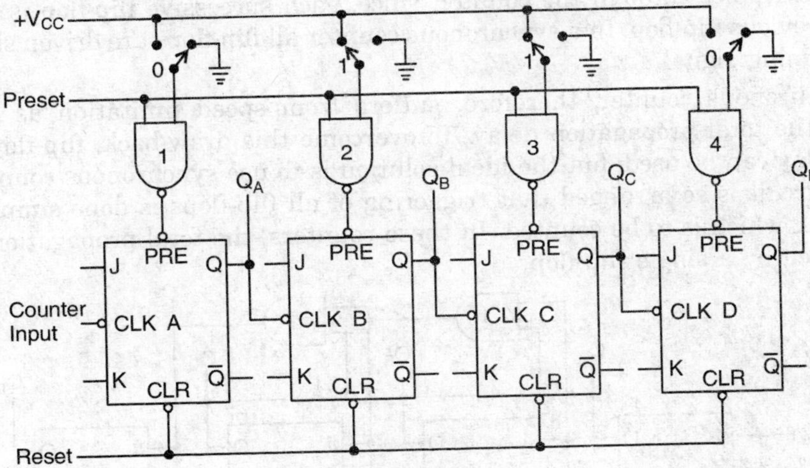


**Fig. 4.26**

It is also possible to load a number in a counter in a single operation, by using the arrangement shown in Fig. 4.27.

The arrangement for data transfer, which is a single pulse operation makes use of the Preset and Clear inputs of the flip-flops. When the clock pulse is low, the output of both NAND gates 1 and 2 is high, which has no effect on the Preset and Clear inputs of the flip-flop and there is no change in its output. If the $D_0$ input is high, the output of NAND gate 1 will go low when the clock pulse goes high. This will result in output $Q_A$ going high at the same time. Since, one input of NAND gate 2 will be low at this time, the clear input to the flip-flop remains high.

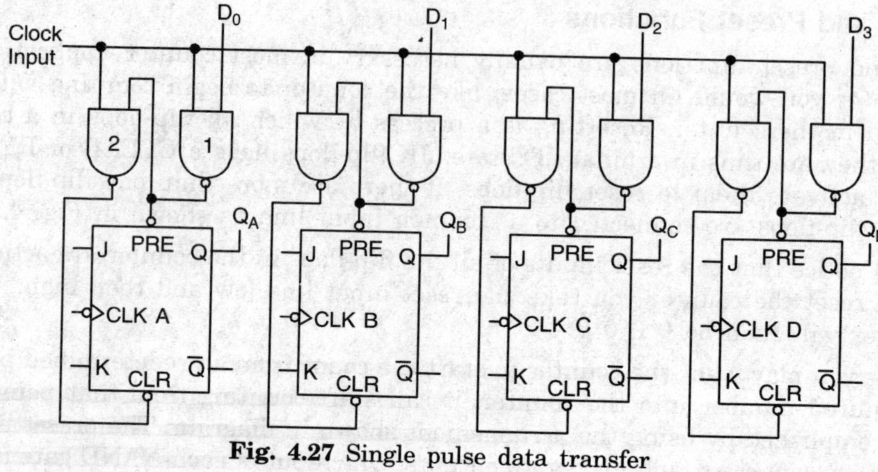


**Fig. 4.27** Single pulse data transfer

If the $D_0$ input is low and the clock pulse goes high, the output of NAND gate 1 will remain high, which will have no effect on the Preset input. The output of NAND gate 2 will go low, which will clear the flip-flop and $Q_A$ will go low.

### 4.8.7 Universal Synchronous Counter Stage

The up and down counters which we have considered so far are asynchronous counters, also known as ripple counters, for the simple reason that, following the application of a clock pulse, the count ripples through the counter, since, each successive flip-flop is driven by the output of the previous flip-flop. In a synchronous counter all flip-flops are driven simultaneously by the same timing signal.

The asynchronous counter, therefore, suffers from speed limitation as each flip-flop contributes to the total propagation delay. To overcome this draw-back, flip-flops with lower propagation delay can be used; but the ideal solution is to use synchronous counters. In these counters, the circuit is so arranged that triggering of all flip-flops is done simultaneously by the input signal, which is to be counted. In these counters, the total propagation delay is the delay contributed by a single flip-flop.

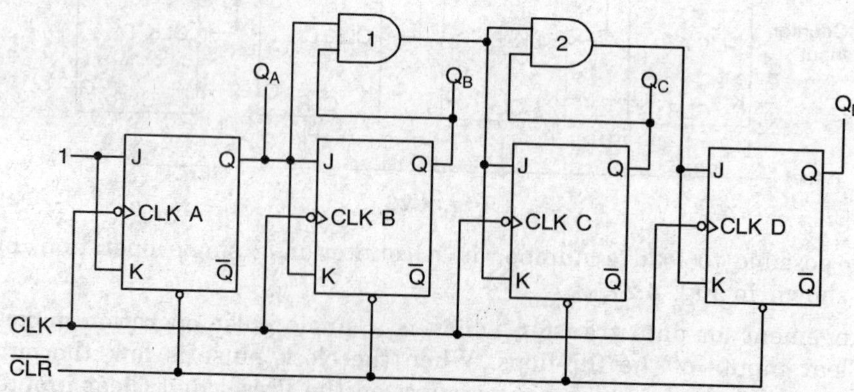


**Fig. 4.28 (*a*)** Synchronous counter

The design concept used in the synchronous counter shown in Fig. 4.28(a) uses counter stage blocks and this design concept lends itself to building large synchronous counters. Counter modules of the type used in this circuit and also shown separately in Fig. 4.28 (*b*) can be interconnected to build counters of any length.

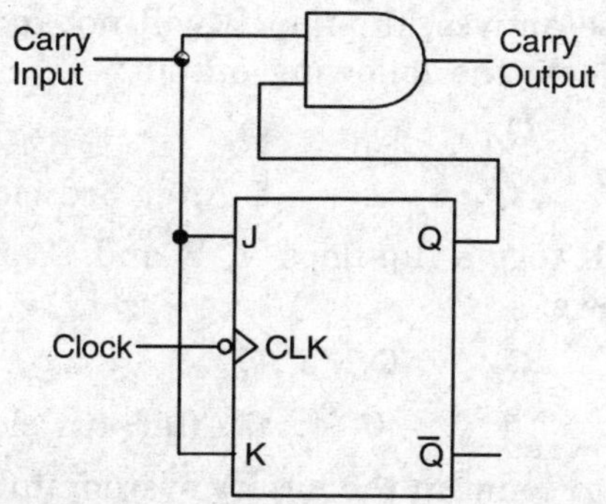


**Fig. 4.28 (b)** Universal counter stage block

Let us consider the synchronous counting circuit shown in Fig. 4.28(*a*). It is a 4-bit counter and the clock inputs of all the flip-flops are connected to a common clock signal, which enables all flip-flops to be triggered simultaneously. The Clear inputs are also connected to a common Clear input line. The J and K inputs of each flip-flop are connected together, so that they can toggle when the JK input is high. The JK input of flip-flop A is held high. Also notice the two AND gates 1 and 2, and the way they are connected. Gate 1 ensures that the JK input to flip-flop C will be binary 1 when both inputs $Q_A$ and $Q_B$ are binary 1. AND gate 2 ensures that the JK input to flip-flop D will be binary 1 only when outputs $Q_A$, $Q_B$ and $Q_C$ are binary 1.

We can now look into the output states required for the flip-flops to toggle. This has been summarized below:

1. Flip-flop A toggles on negative clock edge.
2. Flip-flop B toggles when $Q_A$ is 1
3. Flip-flop C toggles when $Q_A$ and $Q_B$ are 1
4. Flip-flop D toggles when $Q_A$, $Q_B$ and $Q_C$ are 1

This means that a flip-flop will toggle only if all flip-flops preceding it are at binary 1 level.

We can now look into the counting process of this counter. We begin by resetting the counter, which is done by taking CLR temporarily low.

| MSB | | | LSB |
|---|---|---|---|
| $Q_D$ | $Q_C$ | $Q_B$ | $Q_A$ |
| 0 | 0 | 0 | 0 |

Since, $Q_A$ is low and J and K are high, the first negative clock edge will set flip-flop A. The counter output will now be as follows:

| $Q_D$ | $Q_C$ | $Q_B$ | $Q_A$ |
|---|---|---|---|
| 0 | 0 | 0 | 1 After 1st clock pulse. |

When the second negative clock edge occurs, both A and B flip-flops will toggle and the counter output will change to the following:

| $Q_D$ | $Q_C$ | $Q_B$ | $Q_A$ |
|---|---|---|---|
| 0 | 0 | 1 | 0 After 2nd clock pulse. |

When the third clock pulse arrives, flip-flop B will not toggle as $Q_A$ is 0 but flip-flop A will toggle. The counter will show the following output:

| $Q_D$ | $Q_C$ | $Q_B$ | $Q_A$ |
|---|---|---|---|
| 0 | 0 | 1 | 1 After 3rd clock pulse. |

The fourth clock pulse will toggle flip-flops A, B and C, as both $Q_A$ and $Q_B$ are 1. The counter output is now as follows:

| $Q_D$ | $Q_C$ | $Q_B$ | $Q_A$ |
|---|---|---|---|
| 0 | 1 | 0 | 0 After 4th clock pulse. |

The counter will continue to count in the binary system until the counter output registers 1 1 1 1, when it will be reset by the next clock pulse and the counting cycle will be repeated.

### 4.8.8 Synchronous Counter ICs

Many types of counter ICs are available and it is very likely that one of these will meet your design requirements. You may not, therefore, find it necessary to design your own counter. However, should that become necessary, a variety of JK flip-flops are available, with which you can design one to meet your specific needs.

Some of the counter ICs available are listed below:

| Counter type | Parallel load | IC No. |
|---|---|---|
| 1 Decade Up | Synchronous | 74160 |
| | Synchronous | 74162 |
| 2 Decade Up/Down | Synchronous | 74168 |
| | Synchronous | 74ALS568 |
| | Asynchronous | 74ALS190 |
| | Asynchronous | 74ALS192 |
| 3 4-bit binary Up counter | Synchronous | 74161 |
| | Synchronous | 74163 |
| 4 4-bit binary Up/Down counter | Synchronous | 74169 |
| | Asynchronous | 74191 |
| | Asynchronous | 74193 |
| | Asynchronous | 74ALS569 |

All the counters listed here have parallel load capability, which implies that a binary data input applied to the counter will be transferred to the output when the load input on the counter is asserted. The load operation may be synchronous or asynchronous. If it is asynchronous, the data applied will be transferred to the output as soon as the load input is asserted.

In case it is synchronous, the data will not be transferred to the output until the next clock pulse occurs. In either case the counters will begin to count from the loaded count when clock pulses are applied.

The decade up-counters count from 0000 to 1001. Decade up-and down-counters can be programmed to count from 0000 to 1001, or from 1001 to 0000. 4-Bit binary counters in the up-count mode count from 0000 and 1111 and in the down-count mode count from 1111 to 0000.

We will now discuss the facilities available in counter IC 74193 and its operating procedures. Pin connections for this IC are given in Fig. 4.29. Figure 4.30(*a*) gives its traditional symbol and Fig. 4.30 (b) gives the IEEE/IEC symbol.

#### *4.8.8.1 Counter Functions*

*Clear (Reset) Function*

As the Clear input is active high, it is normally held low. To clear the counter it is taken high momentarily.

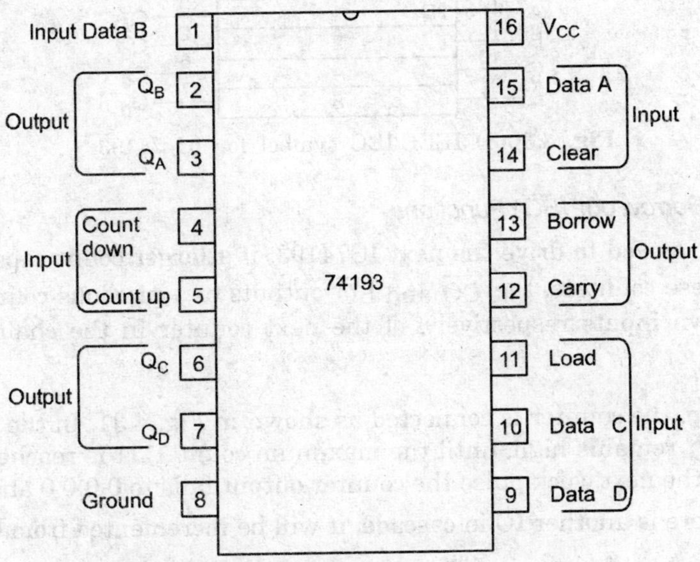


**Fig. 4.29** Pin connections for IC 74193

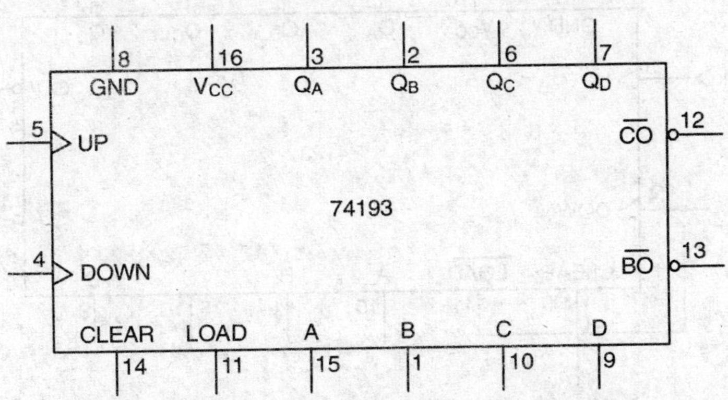


**Fig. 4.30(*a*)** Traditional symbol for IC 74193

*Load (Preset) Function*

To load the counter with a predetermined 4-bit binary number, it is fed into the parallel data inputs A, B, C and D. The number is shifted into the counter by taking the LOAD input momentarily low. Both Clear and LOAD inputs are asynchronous and will override all synchronous counting functions.

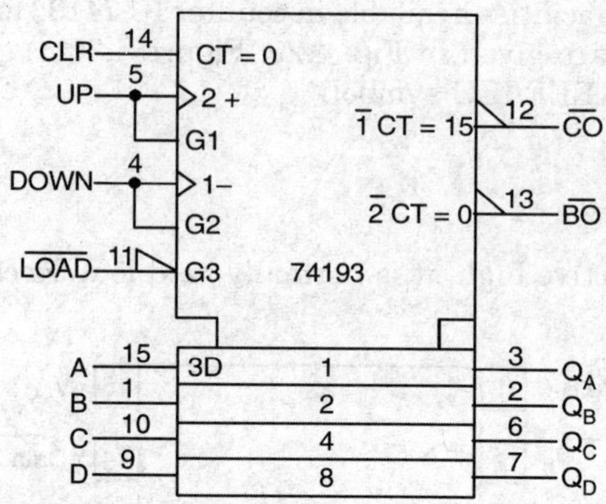


**Fig. 4.30(*b*)** IEEE/IEC symbol for IC 74193

*Carry out ($\overline{CO}$) and Borrow out ($\overline{BO}$) Functions*

These inputs are used to drive the next IC74193, if a larger count capability is required. While cascading these counters, the $\overline{CO}$ and $\overline{BO}$ outputs of a previous counter are connected to the UP and Down inputs respectively, of the next counter in the chain.

*Up-counting Function*

For counting up, the counter is connected as shown in Fig. 4.31. In the up-counting mode the carry output $\overline{CO}$ remains high, until the maximum count 1111 is reached, when the carry output goes low. At the next clock pulse the counter output falls to 0 0 0 0 and the carry output $\overline{CO}$ goes high. If there is another IC in cascade, it will be incremented from 0 0 0 0 to 0 0 0 1.

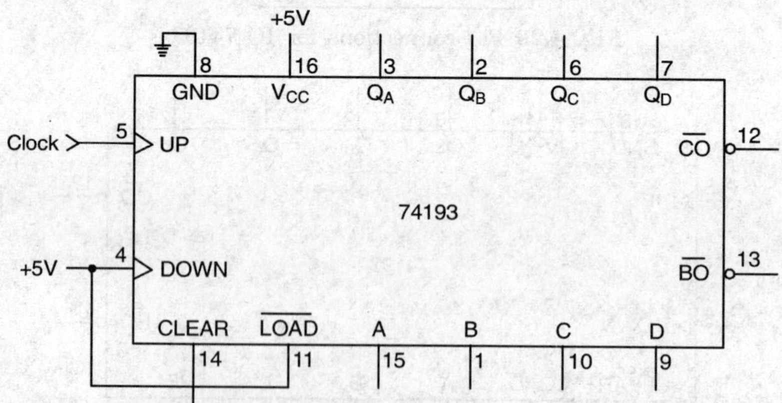


**Fig. 4.31** Counter connected to count up

*Down-counting Function*

For down-counting connection are made as shown in Fig. 4.32. In the down-counting operation the borrow output $\overline{BO}$ stays high until the minimum count 0 0 0 0 is reached, when the borrow output $\overline{BO}$ drops low. The borrow output detects the minimum counter value.

At the next input pulse the counter output rises to 1 1 1 1 and there is a 0 → 1 transition at the borrow output $\overline{BO}$. If another counter is connected in cascade it will be decremented.

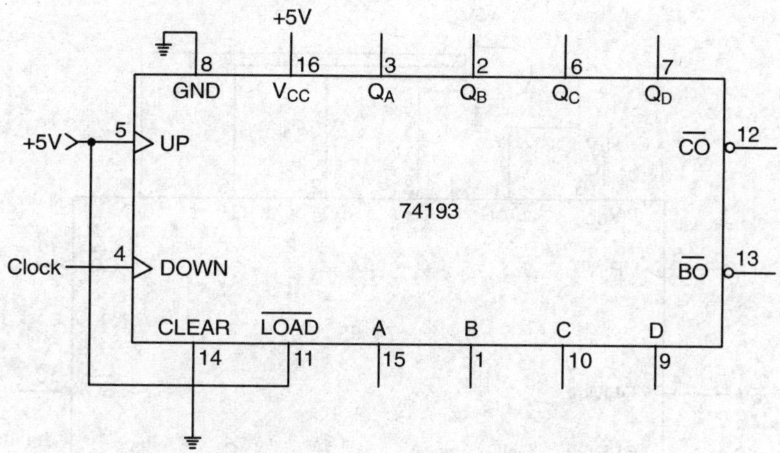


**Fig. 4.32** Counter connected to count down

*Presetting (Up-Counting Mode)*

The counter can be preset to any 4-bit binary number, which is first fed into the parallel inputs A, B, C and D, and the load input is held low momentarily, which shifts the number into the counter. It is not necessary to reset the counter before presetting it. Let us suppose that the number shifted into the counter 1 0 1 0 and the counter is made to count up. The counter output will be stepped up after each input pulse and after the 6th pulse the output will be 0 0 0 0. The counting up begins from the number preset in the counter and the 6th pulse resets the counter and then it starts counting up from this point.

*Presetting (Down-Counting Mode)*

The counter is set up in the down-counting mode and, as before, suppose the number fed into the counter is 1 0 1 0 and the counter is made to count down. The 10th, input pulse will reset the counter to 0 0 0 0 and the 11th, pulse will show a count of 1 1 1 1 and then it will begin to count down from this number.

*Presetting (Using Counter Output)*

The counter can also be preset by connecting it as shown in Fig. 4.33. The desired number, say 1 0 1 0 is fed into the A B C D inputs and the counter input is connected to a 1 Hz clock signal when the counter reaches the maximum, count, 1 1 1 1, the NAND gate output will go low and the binary number 1 0 1 0 will be shifted into the counter. The counter will now begin to count up from this preset number and when the count again reaches 1 1 1 1, the counter will return to the preset number 1 0 1 0 and will again begin to count up as before. You will notice that as soon as the counter reaches the maximum count 1 1 1 1 (or decimal 15), it is immediately preset to 1 0 1 0 (or decimal 10). Since, state 15 is being used to preset the counter, it is no longer a stable state. The stable states in this counting operation will be 10, 11, 12, 13 and 14, and the modulus (number of discrete states) of the counter will be 5.

The counter modulus in the up-counting mode for any preset number $n$ is given by

$$\text{Modulus} = 16 - n - 1$$

In this case $\quad \text{Modulus} = 16 - 10 - 1 = 5$

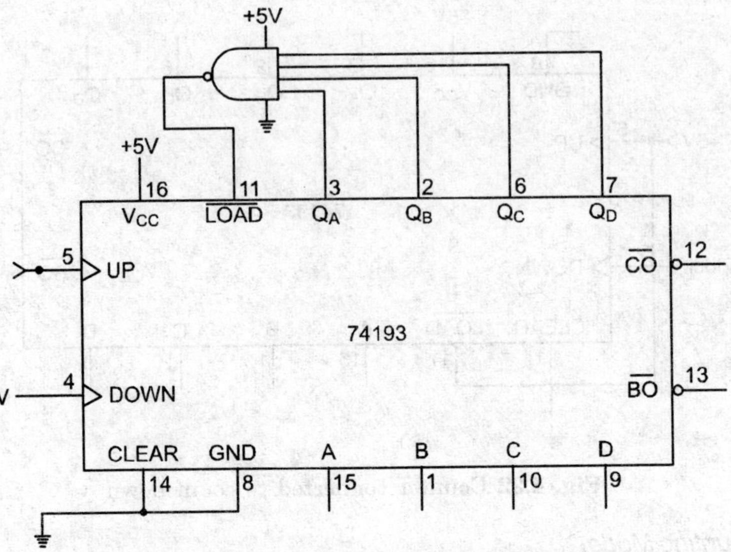


**Fig. 4.33** Presetting using counter output

In the down-counting mode, the counter will count down from the preset number, 1010 (or decimal 10). As before the counter will count down as follows; 9, 8, 7, 6, 5, 4, 3, 2, 1, 0. In this case, the counter modulus will be as follows:

$$\text{Modulus} = n + 1$$

In this case $$\text{Modulus} = 10 + 1 = 11$$

When the counter is preset in this manner, it should never be preset to number 15 as this is not a stable state, and it is likely to get latched up in this state.

*Modulo N Counter Using IC 74193*

In Sec. 4.8.8, you have seen how this IC can count up or down from a preset number. In fact it can function as a modulo counter by using a NAND gate to preset the counter to the desired number. There is a simpler way of implementing a modulo counter with this IC, but it has some drawbacks which we will discuss shortly. A circuit for a modulo counter using this IC in the down-counting mode is given in Fig. 4.34.

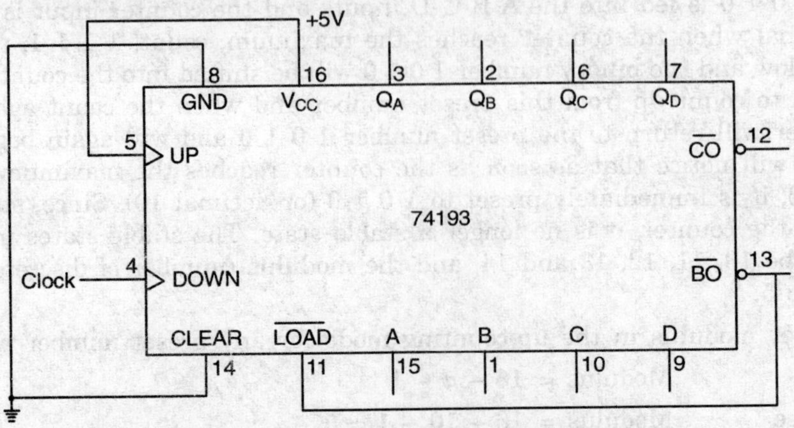


**Fig. 4.34** IC 74193 connected as a modulus counter

Clock pulses are applied at the down-count input and the up-count input is held high. Also observed that the borrow output $\overline{BO}$ is connected to the load input. The borrow output detects the state of the borrow output when the count reaches 0 0 0 0. Since, it is connected back to the load input, the binary number loaded into the A B C D inputs is shifted into the counter. The decimal number loaded into the counter represents its modulus.

To operate the counter load, the binary equivalent of the decimal number representing the required modulus into the ABCD inputs and apply clock pulses at the down-count input. If the binary number loaded into the counter is 1 0 0 0 (decimal 8) and the counter is decremented with clock pulses, the modulus number that is 1 0 0 0 will be loaded into the counter, as soon as the output reaches the state 0 0 0 0. It will again count down to 0 0 0 0 and will again be preset to 1 0 0 0.

You must have realized that as soon as the preset number is loaded into the counter, the borrow output, that is 0 0 0 0 will disappear. It is important, therefore, that the borrow output state, 0 0 0 0, must be of sufficient duration to enable the preset number to be shifted into the counter. This implies that the propagation delay of the gates responsible for presetting the counter to the number at the A B C D inputs must be of shorter duration than the duration of the clock pulse. To a certain extent this can be ensured by introducing some delay between the borrow output and the load input. This can be done by connecting an even number of inverters between the borrow output $\overline{BO}$ and the load input.

### 4.8.9 Modulus Counters

The modulus of a counter, as discussed before, is the number of discrete states a counter can take up. A single flip-flop can assume only two states 0 and 1, while a counter having two flip-flops can assume anyone of the four possible states. A counter with three flip-flops will have 8 states and so on. In short, the number of states is a multiple of 2. With $n$ flip-flops the number of possible states will be $2^n$. Thus, by building counters which count in the normal binary sequence, we can build counters with modulus of 2, 4, 8, 16 etc. In these counters, the count increases or decreases by 1 in pure binary sequence. The problem arises in building counters whose modulus is 3, 5, 7, 9 etc. For instance, if we need, a counter with a modulus of 3, we have to use a counter with a modulus of 4 and so arrange the circuit that it skips one of the states. Similarly, for a counter with a modulus of 5 we require $2^3$ or 8 states and arrange the circuit so that it skips 3 states to give us a modulus of $2^n - 3$ or 5 states. Thus, for a modulus N counter the number $n$ of flip-flops should be such that $n$ is the smallest number for which $2^n > N$. It, therefore, follows that for a decade (mod-10) counter the number of flip-flops should be 4. For this counter, we shall have to skip $2^4 - 10$ or 6 states. Which of these states are to be skipped is a matter of choice, which is largely governed by decisions which will make the circuit as simple as possible.

Many methods have been developed for designing such counters. We will consider the following:

***(1) Counter reset method***

In this method the counter is reset after the desired count has been reached and the count cycle starts all over again from the reset state.

***(2) Logic gating method***

This method provides the exact count sequence required without any need to reset the counter at some stage.

***(3) Counter coupling method***

This method is used to implement counters of the required modulus. For instance, we can interconnect mod-2 and mod-3 counters to implement a modulus 3 × 2 or mod-6 counter.

## 4.8.10 Counter Reset Method (Asynchronous Counters)

Let us first consider the typical case of a counter which has 3 states as shown in Fig. 4.35.

### *4.8.10.1 Mod-3 Counter*

It is obvious that a mod-3 counter will require two flip-flops which, when connected as a counter, will provide four states as shown in Table 4.4.

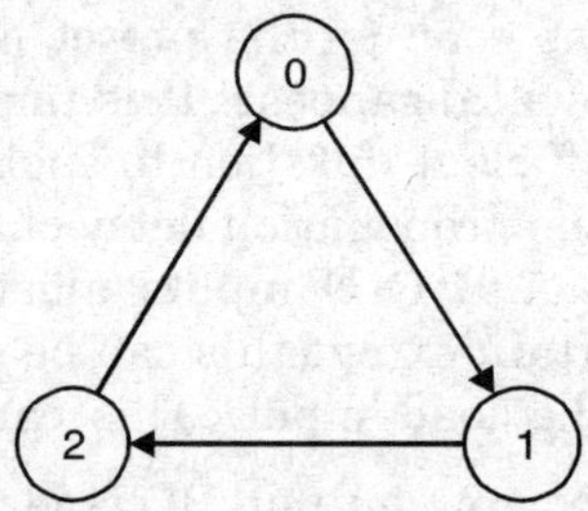


**Fig. 4.35** State diagram for a mod-3 counter

**Table 4.4 States for a two flip-flop counter**

| $Q_A$ *LSB* | $Q_B$ | *Count Value (Decimal)* |
|---|---|---|
| 0 | 0 | 0 |
| 1 | 0 | 1 |
| 0 | 1 | 2 |
| 1 | 1 | 3 |
| 0 | 0 | 0 |

This counter counts in the binary sequence 0, 1, 2, 3 and then it returns to 0, the starting point. Each count is referred to as a state. If we are building a mod-3 counter, the most convenient solution is to skip state 3 and then return to state 0 from state 2 and then again go through states 0, 1, 2 before returning to state 0. What we need is a combinational logic circuit, which will feed a reset pulse to the counter during state 3, and immediately after state 2, which is the last desired state. This reset pulse is applied to the CLR inputs which resets the counter to 0 after state 2.

A circuit diagram for a mod-3 counter together with the required combinational logic is given in Fig. 4.36.

When both outputs $Q_A$ and $Q_B$ are 1, the output of the NAND gate, which provides the reset pulse, goes low and both the flip-flops are reset. The counter returns to state 0 and it starts counting again in 0, 1, 2, 0 sequence. The waveforms for this counter are given in Fig. 4.37.

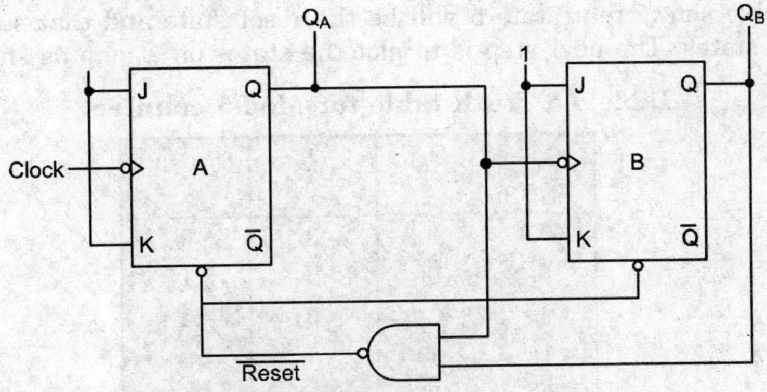


**Fig. 4.36** Modulo-3 counter

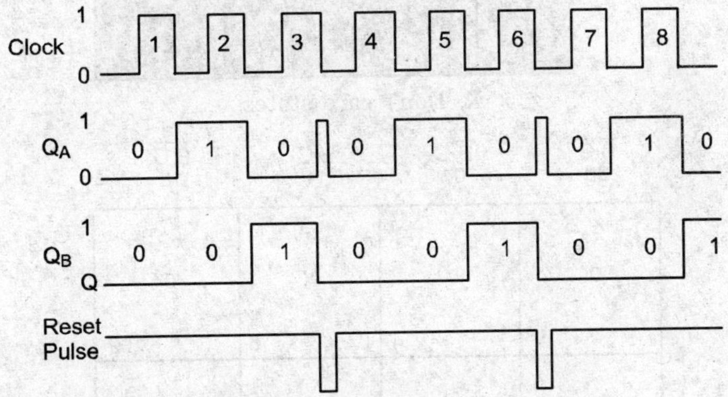


**Fig. 4.37** Waveform for Mod-3 counter

#### *4.8.10.2 Mod-5 Counter*

The minimum number of flip-flops required to implement this counter is three. With three flip-flops, the number of states will be 8. A modulo-5 counter will have only 5 states. A state diagram for this counter is given in Fig. 4.38. It will progress from state 000 through 100. The truth table for this counter, which will determine the stage at which the reset pulse should be applied, is given in Table 4.5.

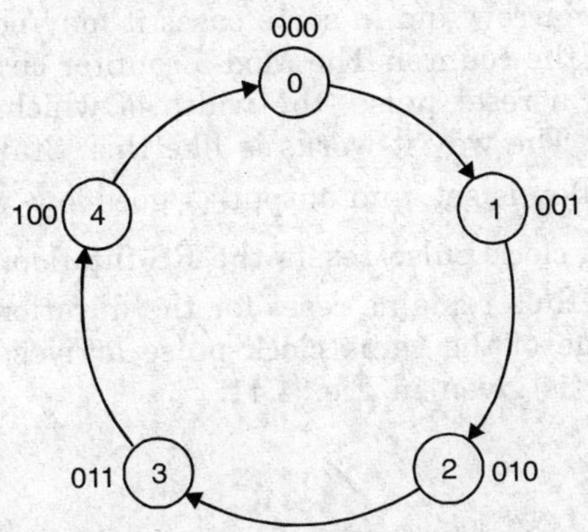


**Fig. 4.38** State diagram for Mod-5 counter

The truth table shows that state 5 will be the reset state and that states 6 and 7 will be the don't care states. The next step is to plot the states on a map as shown in Fig. 4.39.

**Table 4.5 Truth table for Mod-5 counter**

| $Q_A$ LSB | $Q_B$ | $Q_C$ | *State* |
|---|---|---|---|
| 0 | 0 | 0 | 0 |
| 1 | 0 | 0 | 1 |
| 0 | 1 | 0 | 2 |
| 1 | 1 | 0 | 3 |
| 0 | 0 | 1 | 4 |
| 1 | 0 | 1 | 5 |
| 0 | 1 | 1 | 6 X |
| 1 | 1 | 1 | 7 X |

X, Don't care states

| | $\overline{B}\,\overline{C}$ 00 | $\overline{B}$ C 01 | B C 11 | B $\overline{C}$ 10 |
|---|---|---|---|---|
| $\overline{A}$ 0 | 0 (cell 0) | 0 (cell 4) | X (cell 6) | 0 (cell 2) |
| A 1 | 0 (cell 1) | 1 (cell 5) | X (cell 7) | 0 (cell 3) |

**Fig. 4.39**

The map shows that the reset pulse is determined by $R = Q_A . \overline{Q_B} . Q_C$. The logic diagram for this counter is given in Fig. 4.40. The diagram shows that a reset pulse will be applied when both A and C are 1. You may have noticed that the reset pulse shown in Fig. 4.37 for the Mod-3 counter was very narrow and in some cases it may not be suitable to control other logic devices associated with the counter. The Mod-5 counter circuit Fig. 4.40 incorporates an RS flip-flop, which produces a reset pulse, the width of which is equal to the duration for which the clock pulse is low. The way it works is like this. State 5 is decoded by gate D, its output goes low, the RS flip-flop is set, and output $\overline{Q}$ goes low, which resets all the flip-flops. The leading edge of the next clock pulse resets the RS flip-flop, $\overline{Q}$ goes high which removes the reset pulse. The counter thus remains reset for the duration of the low time of the clock pulse. When the trailing edge of the same clock pulse arrives, a new cycle is started. The waveform for Mod-5 counter is given in Fig. 4.41.

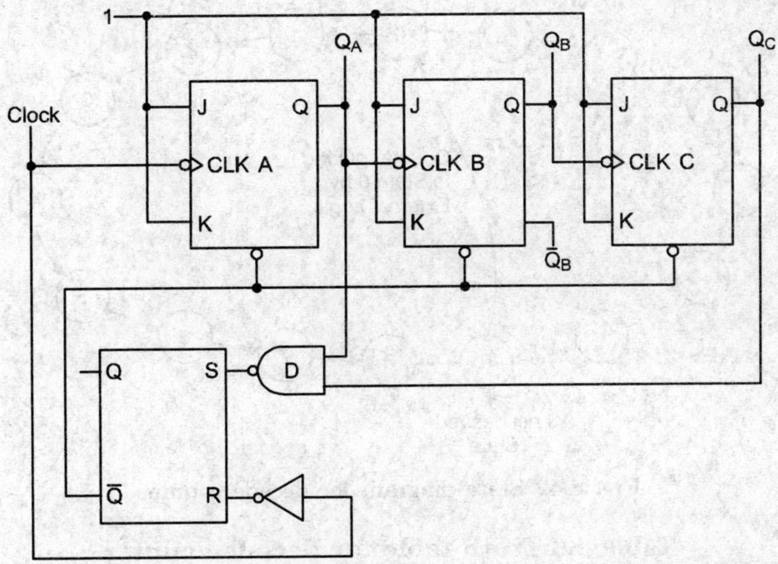


**Fig. 4.40** Modulus-5 counter

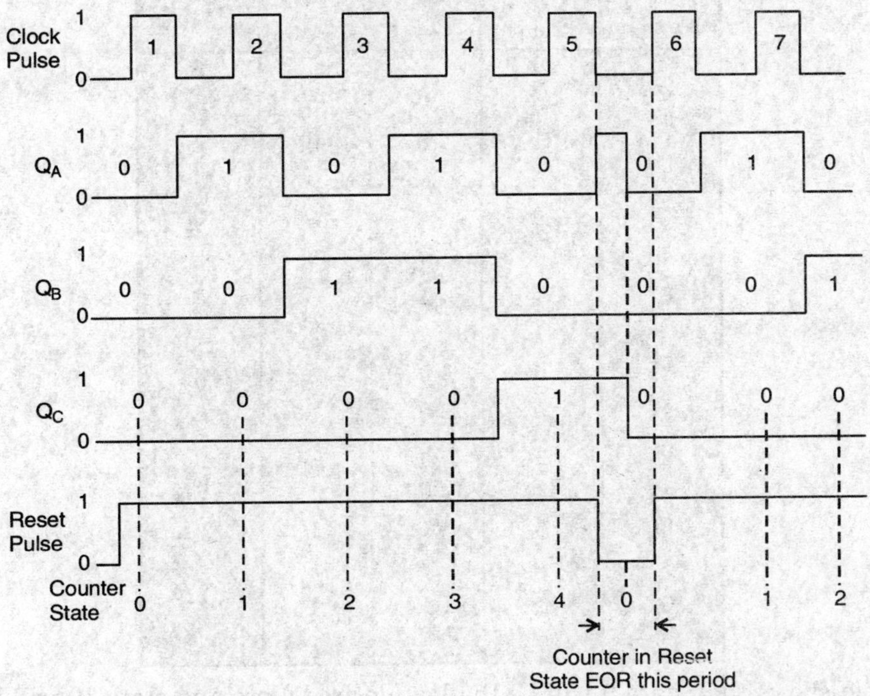


**Fig. 4.41** Waveform for Modulus-5 asynchronous counter

### *4.8.10.3 Mod-10 (Decade) Counter*

The decade counter discussed here is also an asynchronous counter and has been implemented using the counter reset method. As the decade counter has ten states, it will require four flip-flops to implement it. A state diagram for this counter is given in Fig. 4.42 and the truth table is given in Table 4.6.

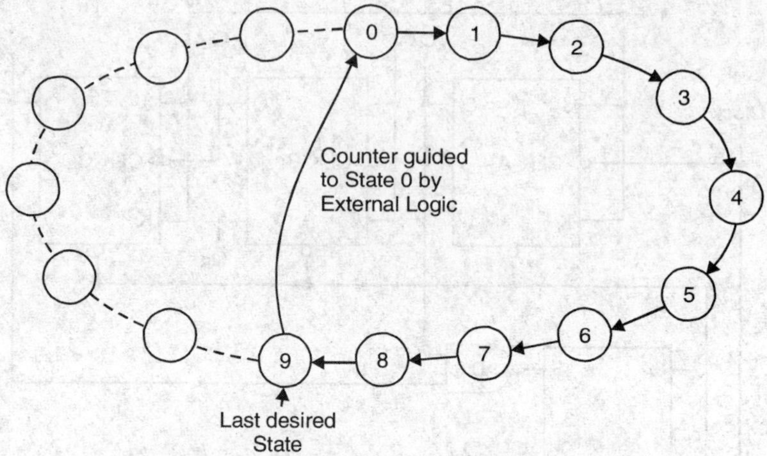


**Fig. 4.42** State diagram for decade counter

**Table 4.6 Truth table for decade counter**

| $Q_A$ LSB | $Q_B$ | $Q_C$ | $Q_D$ | *State* |
|---|---|---|---|---|
| 0 | 0 | 0 | 0 | 0 |
| 1 | 0 | 0 | 0 | 1 |
| 0 | 1 | 0 | 0 | 2 |
| 1 | 1 | 0 | 0 | 3 |
| 0 | 0 | 1 | 0 | 4 |
| 1 | 0 | 1 | 0 | 5 |
| 0 | 1 | 1 | 0 | 6 |
| 1 | 1 | 1 | 0 | 7 |
| 0 | 0 | 0 | 1 | 8 |
| 1 | 0 | 0 | 1 | 9 |
| 0 | 1 | 0 | 1 | 10 |
| 1 | 1 | 0 | 1 | 11 X |
| 0 | 0 | 1 | 1 | 12 X |
| 1 | 0 | 1 | 1 | 13 X |
| 0 | 1 | 1 | 1 | 14 X |
| 1 | 1 | 1 | 1 | 15 X |

The table shows that state 9 will be the last desired state and state 10 will be the reset state. State 11, 12, 13, 14 and 15 will be the don't care states. The next step is to plot the states on a map to determine the reset pulse. This has been done in Fig. 4.43.

The map shows that the reset pulse is determined by the following expression:

$$R = \overline{Q}_A . Q_B . \overline{Q}_C . Q_D$$

| | $B\bar{A}$ 00 | $\bar{B}A$ 01 | $BA$ 11 | $B\bar{A}$ 10 |
|---|---|---|---|---|
| $\bar{D}\bar{C}$ 00 | 0 (0) | 0 (1) | 0 (3) | 0 (2) |
| $\bar{D}C$ 01 | 0 (4) | 0 (5) | 0 (7) | 0 (6) |
| $DC$ 11 | 3 (12) | 3 (13) | X (15) | 3 (14) |
| $D\bar{C}$ 10 | 0 (8) | 0 (9) | X (11) | 1 (10) |

**Fig. 4.43**

The decade counter circuit Fig. 4.44 is essentially a binary ripple counter, which can count from 0000 to 1111; but since a decade counter is required to count only from 0000 to 1001, a reset pulse is applied at count 10 when the counter output is $\bar{Q}_A.Q_B.\bar{Q}_C.Q_D$. In order to have control over the reset pulse width, a 4-input NAND gate is used to decode state 10.

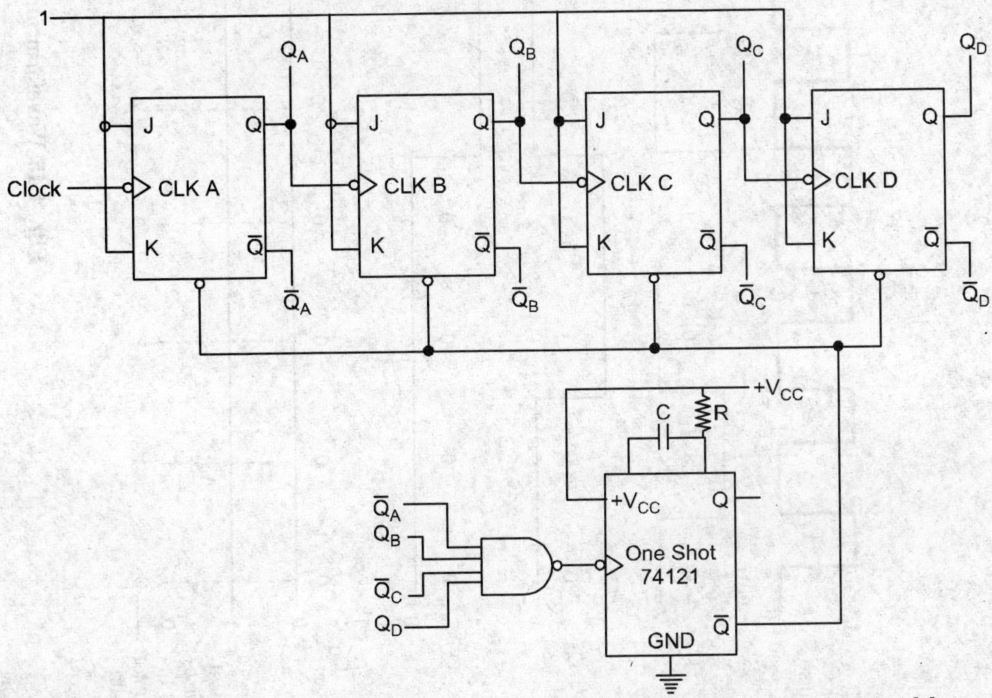


**Fig. 4.44** Decade (Mod-10) asynchronous counter using count reset and pulse width control

To decode count 10, logic inputs that are all one at the count of 10, are used to feed the NAND gate. At this count, the NAND gate output goes low providing a 1 → 0 change which triggers the one-shot unit. The $\overline{Q}$ output of the one shot unit is used, as it is normally high and it goes low during the one-shot timing period, which depends on the RC constants of the circuit. The timing period of the one-shot can be adjusted, so that the slowest counter state resets. Although only A and D flip-flops need to be reset, the reset pulse is applied to all the flip-flop to make doubly sure that all flip-flops are reset.

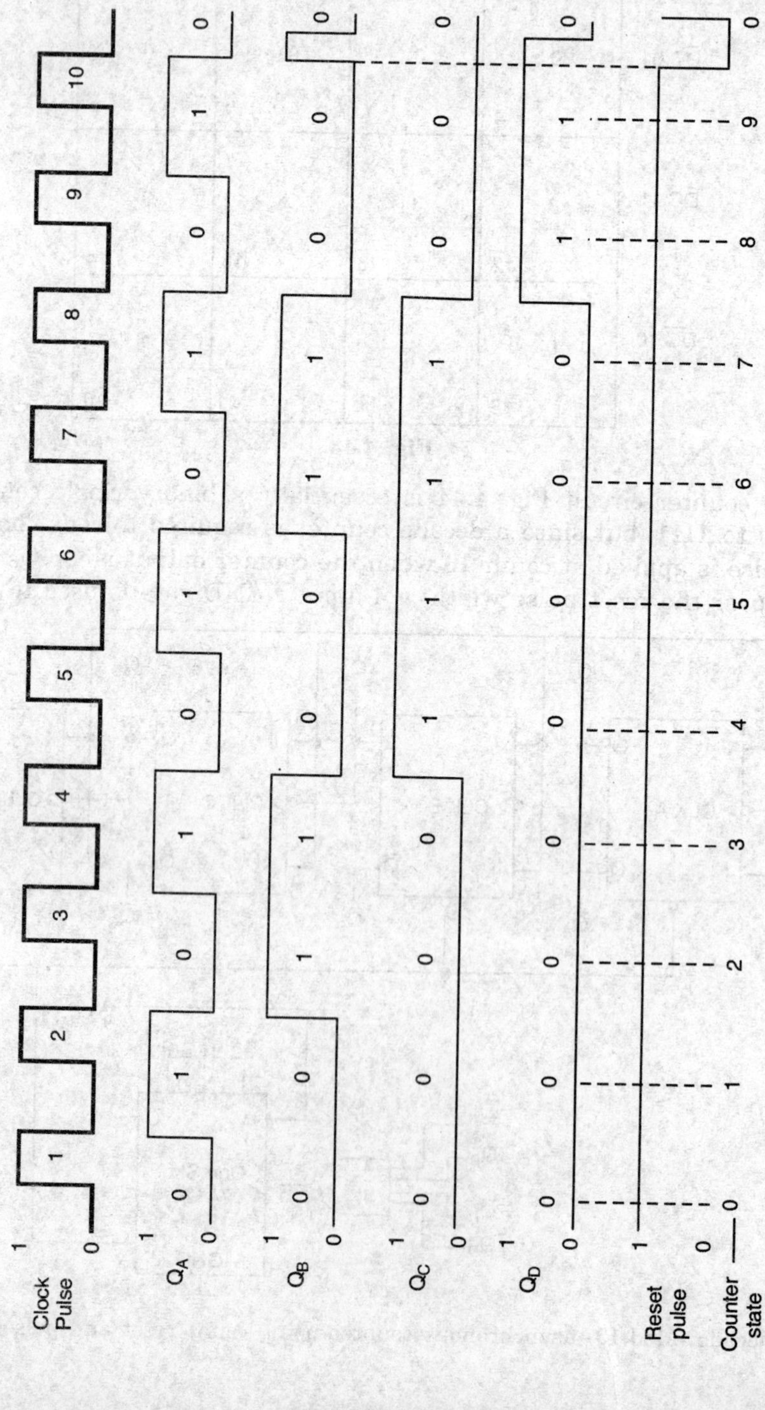


**Fig. 4.45** Waveform for decade counter

Since, decade (Modulus-10) counters have 10 discrete starts, they can be used to divide the input frequency by 10. You will notice that at the output of the D flip-flop, there is only one output pulse for every 10 input pulses. These counters can be cascaded to increase count capability.

The waveform for this counter is shown in Fig. 4.45.

## 4.8.11 Logic Gating Method

The counter reset method of implementing counters, which we have discussed in the previous section, has some inherent drawbacks. In the first place, the counter has to move up to a temporary state before going into the reset state. Secondly, pulse duration timing is an important consideration in such counters, for which purpose special circuits have to be incorporated in counter design.

We will now consider another approach to counter design, which provides for the exact count sequence. We will discuss the design of some modulus counters to illustrate the procedures.

### *4.8.11.1 Mod-3 Counter (Synchronous)*

Let us suppose that we are required to design a modulo-3 counter which conforms to the truth table given in Table 4.7.

**Table 4.7 Truth table for Mod-3 counter**

| *Input pulse count* | *Counter states* | |
|---|---|---|
| | *A* | *B* |
| 0 | 0 | 0 |
| 1 | 1 | 0 |
| 2 | 0 | 1 |
| 3 | 0 | 0 |

Based on this truth table, the output waveform for this Mod-3 counter should be as shown in Fig. 4.46.

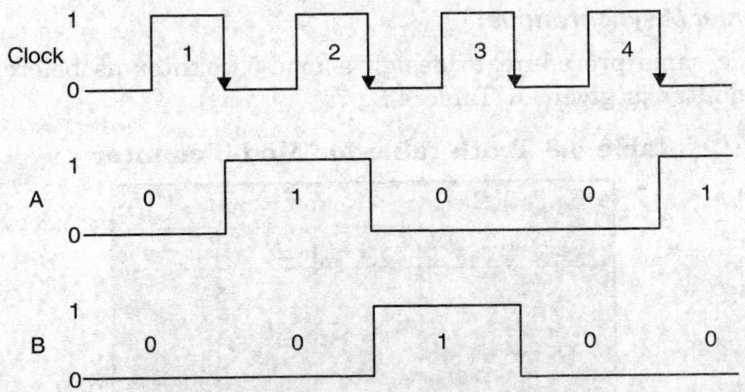


**Fig. 4.46** Waveform for Mod-3 counter

You will notice from the waveform of the counter, that flip-flop A toggles on the trailing edge of the first and second pulses. Also observe that flip-flop B toggles only on the second and third clock pulses. We have to bear this in mind, in figuring out logic levels for the J and K inputs of the flip-flops.

Suppose that initially both the flip-flops are reset. Since, flip-flop A has to toggle when the trailing edges of the first and the second clock pulses arrive, its J and K inputs should be at logic 1 level during this period. This is achieved by connecting the K input to logic 1 level and the J input to the complement output of flip-flop B, as during this period the $\overline{B}$ output of flip-flop B is at a high logic level. In this situation, the first clock pulse produces a logic 1 output and the second clock pulse produces a logic 0 output.

The J input of flip-flop B is connected to the normal output of flip-flop A. Therefore, when the first clock pulse arrives, the J input of flip-flop B is low. Its output will remain low as you will notice from the truth table and the waveform. The second pulse is required to toggle this flip-flop and its K input is, therefore held high. When the second clock pulse arrives, the flip-flop will toggle as both the J and K inputs are high. The output will go high. At the same time, its complement output will be low, which makes the J input of flip-flop A low.

When the third clock pulse arrives, the output of flip-flop A will go low. Since, after the second clock pulse the output of flip-flop A was already low, the third clock pulse produces a low output at flip-flop B. Both the A and B flip-flops are now reset and the cycle will be repeated.

A logic diagram for the Mod-3 counter is given in Fig. 4.47.

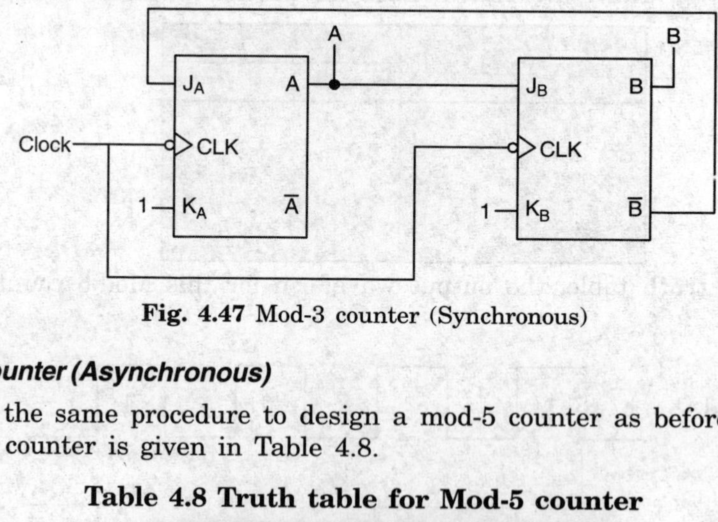


**Fig. 4.47** Mod-3 counter (Synchronous)

#### *4.8.11.2 Mod-5 Counter (Asynchronous)*

We will use the same procedure to design a mod-5 counter as before. The truth table required for this counter is given in Table 4.8.

**Table 4.8 Truth table for Mod-5 counter**

| Input Pulse Count | Counter States | | |
|---|---|---|---|
| | A | B | C |
| 0 | 0 | 0 | 0 |
| 1 | 1 | 0 | 0 |
| 2 | 0 | 1 | 0 |
| 3 | 1 | 1 | 0 |
| 4 | 0 | 0 | 1 |
| 5 | 0 | 0 | 0 |

The waveform for this counter based on this truth table is given in Fig. 4.48. You will notice from the truth table and the waveform that the A flip-flop complements each input pulse, except when the normal output of flip-flop C is logic 1, which is so after the trailing edge of the 4th, clock pulse. It, therefore, follows that the K input of flip-flop A should be a constant logic 1 and the J input should be connected to the complement output of flip-flop will be 0 when C is 1 so that the output of flip-flop A remains low after the trailing edge of the 5th clock pulse.

If you observe the changing pattern of the output of the B flip-flop, you will notice that it toggles at each transition of the A output from 1 → 0. It is, therefore, obvious that the A output should be connected to the clock input of the B flip-flop and the J and K inputs of this flip-flop should be at logic 1 level.

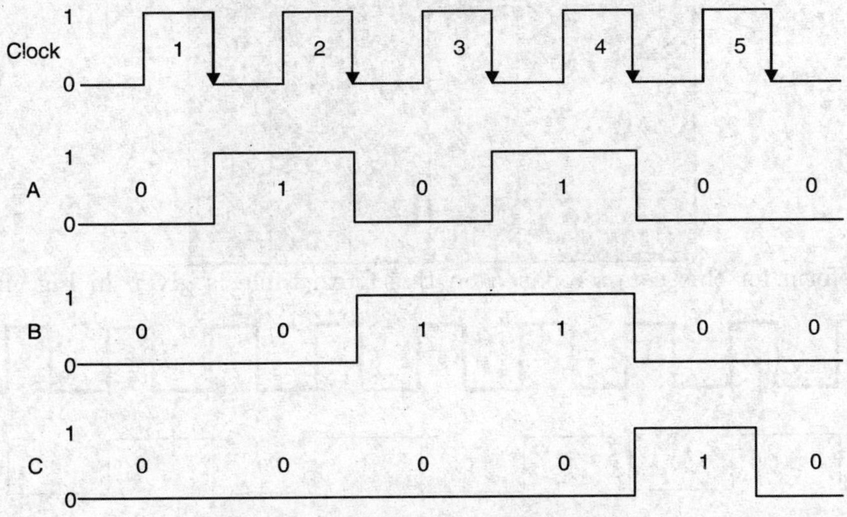


**Fig. 4.48** Waveform for Mod-5 counter

After the 3rd clock pulse, the outputs of A and B flip-flops are 1. An AND gate is used to make the J input to flip-flop C as 1 when both A and B are 1. The K input to flip-flop C is also held at logic 1 to enable it to toggle. The clock is also connected to the clock input to flip-flop C, which toggles it on the 4th, clock pulse and its output becomes 1. When the 5th, clock pulse arrives, the J input to flip-flop C is 0 and it resets on the trailing edge of this clock pulse. Thereafter the cycles are repeated. The logic diagram for the mod-5 counter is given in Fig. 4.49.

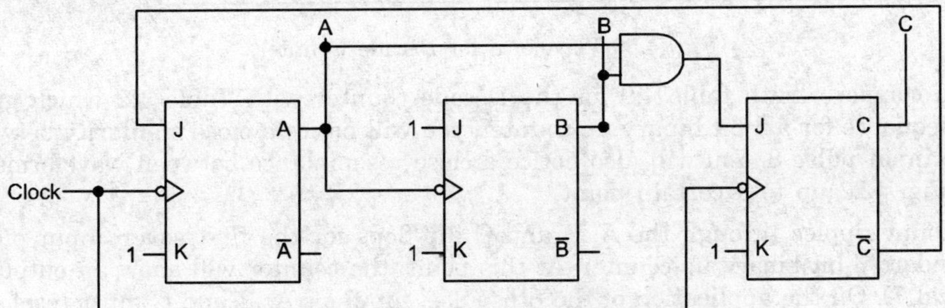


**Fig. 4.49** Logic diagram for Mod-5 counter

#### *4.8.11.3 Mod-10 (Decade) Counter (Asynchronous)*

The truth table for a Decade counter is given in Table 4.9.

**Table 4.9 Truth Table for Decade counter**

| Input pulse count | Counter States | | | |
|---|---|---|---|---|
| | A | B | C | D |
| 0 | 0 | 0 | 0 | 0 |
| 1 | 1 | 0 | 0 | 0 |
| 2 | 0 | 1 | 0 | 0 |
| 3 | 1 | 1 | 0 | 0 |
| 4 | 0 | 0 | 1 | 0 |
| 5 | 1 | 0 | 1 | 0 |
| 6 | 0 | 1 | 1 | 0 |
| 7 | 1 | 1 | 1 | 0 |
| 8 | 0 | 0 | 0 | 1 |
| 9 | 1 | 0 | 0 | 1 |
| 10 (0) | 0 | 0 | 0 | 0 |

The waveform for this counter based on this truth table is given in Fig. 4.50.

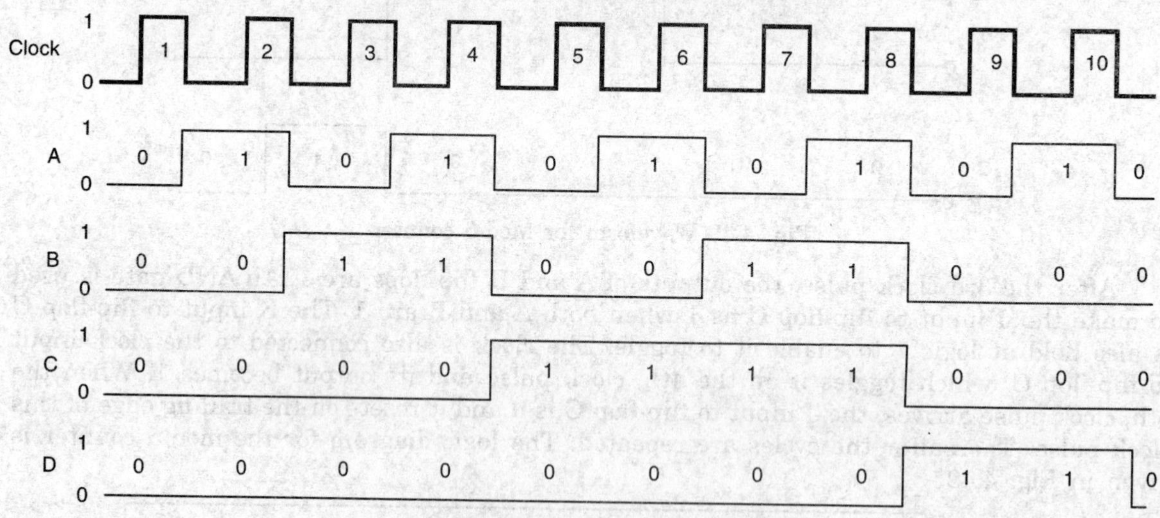


**Fig. 4.50** Waveform for Decade Counter

If you compare truth table 4.9 for the Decade counter with Table 4.2 which gives the count-up sequence for a 4-bit binary up-counter, you will notice a close similarity between the two, up to input pulse 8. You will also notice a close resemblance between waveforms of Fig. 4.50 and Fig. 4.22 up to a certain point.

The count ripples through the A, B and C flip-flops for the first seven input pulses, as in the standard 4-bit binary up-counter. At this point, the counter will show an output of 1 1 1 0 (decimal 7). On the application of the 8th pulse, flip-flops A, B and C must reset and the D output should be 1, that is the counter state should change from 1 1 1 0 to 0 0 0 1. In order that the J input to flip-flop D is 1, so that when K is 1 the D flip-flop output goes from 0 to

1; B and C outputs are applied to the input of an AND gate and its output goes to the J input. In order that the B and C outputs are 0, when D output is 1 for the 8th and the 9th count, the complement output of the D flip-flop which will be 0 when D is 1, is connected to the J input of the B flip-flop.

After the trailing edge of the 8th pulse D becomes 1 and A, B and C become 0, the 9th pulse is required to change the output from 0 0 0 1 to 1 0 0 1. Since, no change is required in the D output, the D flip-flop is triggered by the A output. When the 9th pulse arrives, the A output changes from 0 to 1, but this causes no change in the D output. When the 10th input pulse arrives, it changes the A output from 1 to 0, which changes the D output from 1 to 0. The counter output changes from 1 0 0 1 to 0 0 0 0. During the 9th and the 10th pulses, the B and C outputs will remain unchanged.

A logic diagram for the Decade counter is given in Fig. 4.51.

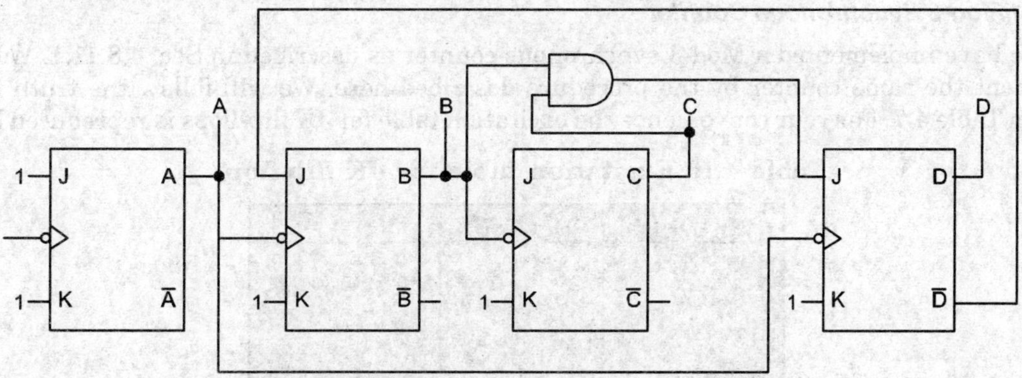


**Fig. 4.51** Logic diagram for Decade counter

## 4.8.12 Design of Synchronous Counters

In most of the counter designs, we have considered so far, the flip-flops are not triggered simultaneously. In synchronous counters all stages are triggered at the same time. The output of each stage depends on the gating inputs of the stage. If you refer to previous counter designs, you will observe that the gating inputs have been assigned values to give the desired outputs.

The basic framework of a synchronous counter would be somewhat like the partial logic diagram given in Fig. 4.52. You will notice that all the clock inputs are connected to a common line and the J and K inputs of the flip-flops have been left open. They are required to have the values necessary to give the required outputs after each input pulse. The J and K inputs of each flip-flop are therefore required to have the values which produce the desired counter states at each input pulse. The entire purpose of the exercise is to determine the input values for each stage. A typical design procedure can be summed up in the following steps:

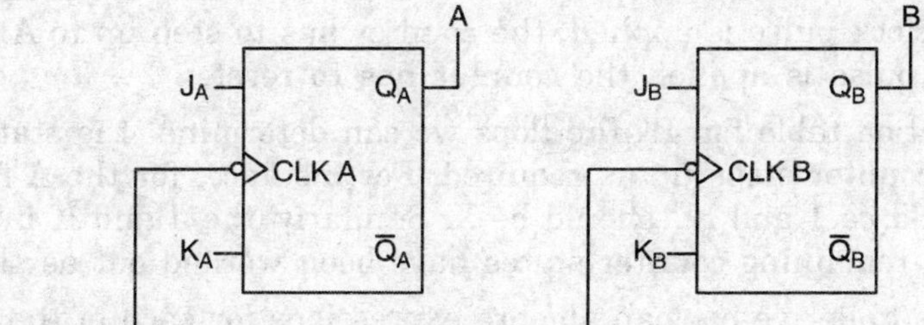


**Fig. 4.52**

(*a*) Write the desired truth table for the counter.

(*b*) Write the counter transition table which should list the starting state and the subsequent states the counter is required to take up.

(*c*) With the help of the excitation table and using the counter transition table, write down the input values for the J and K inputs to enable each flip-flop to attain the output state as required by the transition table.

(*d*) Prepare Karnaugh maps for the J and K inputs of each stage.

(*e*) Derive Boolean algebra expressions for each of the inputs to the flip-flops.

(*f*) Draw the synchronous counter circuit incorporating the J and K input values obtained from the above steps.

We will take up a specific case to illustrate the above procedure.

#### 4.8.12.1 Mod-3 Synchronous Counter

We have implemented a Mod-3 synchronous counter as described in Sec. 4.8.11.1. We will implement the same counter by the procedure described here. We will follow the truth table given in Table 4.7. For your convenience the excitation table for JK flip-flops is reproduced here.

**Table 4.10 Excitation table for JK flip-flop**

| *Present State* | *Next State* | *J* | *K* |
|---|---|---|---|
| 0 | 0 | 0 | X |
| 0 | 1 | 1 | X |
| 1 | 0 | X | 1 |
| 1 | 1 | X | 0 |

We now prepare a counter design table listing the two flip-flops and their states and also the four inputs to the two flip-flops as in table 4.11.

**Table 4.11 Counter design table**

| *Counter State* | | *Flip-flop Inputs* | | | |
|---|---|---|---|---|---|
| *A* | *B* | *A* | | *B* | |
| | | $J_A$ | $K_A$ | $J_B$ | $K_B$ |
| 0 | 0 | 1 | X | 0 | X |
| 1 | 0 | X | 1 | 1 | X |
| 0 | 1 | 0 | X | X | 1 |
| 0 | 0 | | | | |

The table shows that if the counter is in the state A = 0, B = 0 and a clock pulse is applied, the counter is required to step up to A = 1, B = 0. When the counter is in the state A = 1, B = 0 and a clock pulse is applied, the counter has to step up to A = 0, B = 1. Lastly when another clock pulse is applied the counter has to reset.

From the excitation table for JK flip-flops we can determine the states of the J and K inputs, so that the counter steps up as required. For instance, for the A flip-flop to step up from 0 to 1, $J_A$ should be 1 and $K_A$ should be X. Similarly, the J and K input values of both the flip-flops for the remaining counter states have been worked out as shown in the table.

The next step is to derive boolean algebra expressions for each of the inputs to the flip-flops. In the above exercise, our effort was to generate flip-flop inputs in a given row, so that when the counter is in the state in that row, the inputs will take on the listed values, so that the next clock pulse will cause the counter to step up to the counter state in the row below.

We now form boolean algebra expressions from this table for the $J_A$, $K_A$, $J_B$ and $K_B$ inputs to the flip-flops and simplify these expressions using Karnaugh maps. Expressions for these inputs have been entered in Karnaugh maps in Fig. 4.53 (*a*), (*b*), (*c*) and (*d*). The simplified expressions obtained for the inputs are also indicated under the maps.

The counter circuit when drawn up with the following resultant data will be the same as worked out before in Fig. 4.47.

$$J_A = \overline{B}$$
$$K_A = 1$$
$$J_B = A$$
$$K_B = 1$$

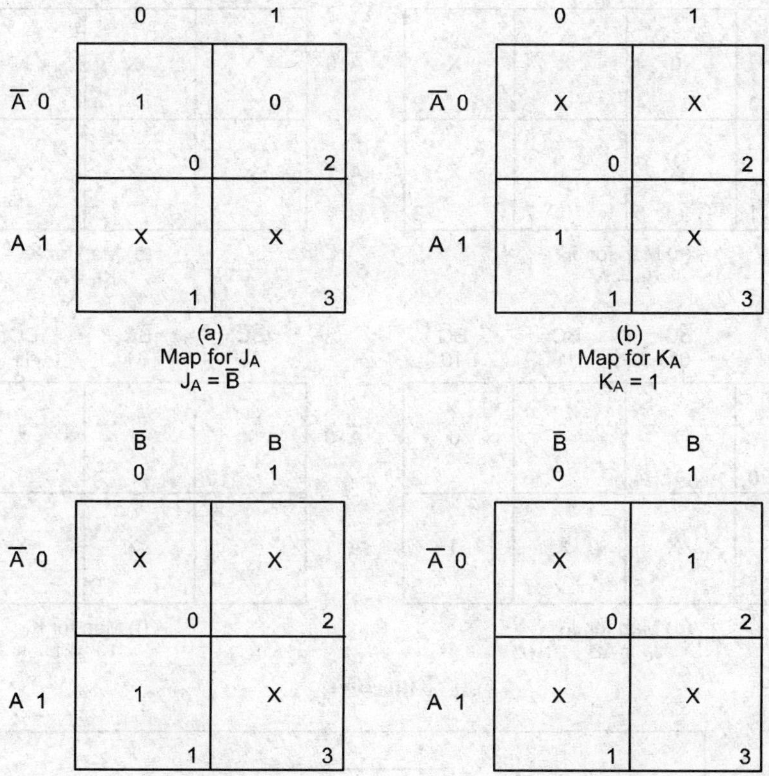


(a) Map for $J_A$ $J_A = \overline{B}$

(b) Map for $K_A$ $K_A = 1$

(c) Map for $J_B$ $J_B = A$

(d) Map for $K_B$ $K_B = 1$

**Fig. 4.53** (a), (b), (c) and (d)

### *4.8.12.2 Mod-5 Counter (Synchronous)*

The Mod-5 counter we are going to implement will be a synchronous counter, but it will have the same counter states as given earlier in Table 4.8. The counter design table for this counter lists the three flip-flops and their states as also the six inputs for the three flip-flops. The flip-flop inputs required to step up the counter from the present to the next state have been worked out with the help of the excitation table (Table 4.10). This listing has been shown in Table 4.12.

| | $\bar{B}\bar{C}$ 00 | $\bar{B}C$ 01 | $BC$ 11 | $B\bar{C}$ 10 |
|---|---|---|---|---|
| $\bar{A}$ 0 | 1 (0) | 0 (4) | X (6) | 1 (2) |
| A 1 | X (1) | X (5) | X (7) | X (3) |

(a) Map for $J_A$
$J_A = \bar{C}$

| | $\bar{B}\bar{C}$ 00 | $\bar{B}C$ 01 | $BC$ 11 | $B\bar{C}$ 10 |
|---|---|---|---|---|
| $\bar{A}$ 0 | X (0) | X (4) | X (6) | X (2) |
| A 1 | 1 (1) | X (5) | X (7) | 1 (3) |

(b) Map for $K_A$
$K_A = 1$

| | $\bar{B}\bar{C}$ 00 | $\bar{B}C$ 01 | $BC$ 11 | $B\bar{C}$ 10 |
|---|---|---|---|---|
| $\bar{A}$ 0 | 0 (0) | 0 (4) | X (6) | X (2) |
| A 1 | 1 (1) | X (5) | X (7) | X (3) |

(c) Map for $J_B$
$J_B = A$

| | $\bar{B}\bar{C}$ 00 | $\bar{B}C$ 01 | $BC$ 11 | $B\bar{C}$ 10 |
|---|---|---|---|---|
| $\bar{A}$ 0 | X (0) | X (4) | X (6) | 0 (2) |
| A 1 | X (1) | X (5) | X (7) | 1 (3) |

(d) Map for $K_B$
$K_B = A$

| | $\bar{B}\bar{C}$ 00 | $\bar{B}C$ 01 | $BC$ 11 | $B\bar{C}$ 10 |
|---|---|---|---|---|
| $\bar{A}$ 0 | 0 (0) | X (4) | X (6) | 0 (2) |
| A 1 | 0 (1) | X (5) | X (7) | 1 (3) |

(e) Map for $J_C$
$J_C = AB$

| | $\bar{B}\bar{C}$ 00 | $\bar{B}C$ 01 | $BC$ 11 | $B\bar{C}$ 10 |
|---|---|---|---|---|
| $\bar{A}$ 0 | X (0) | 1 (4) | X (6) | X (2) |
| A 1 | X (1) | X (5) | X (7) | X (3) |

(f) Map for $K_C$
$K_C = 1$

**Fig. 4.54**

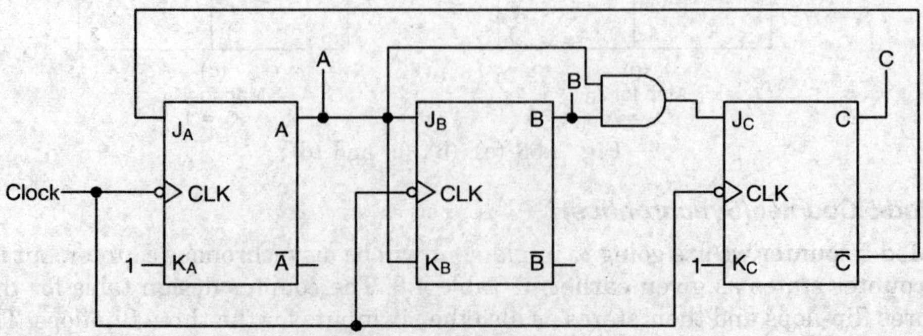


**Fig. 4.55** Synchronous Mod-5 counter

**Table 4.12 Counter design table for Mod-5 counter**

| *Input pulse count* | *Counter states* | | | *Flip-flop inputs* | | | | | |
|---|---|---|---|---|---|---|---|---|---|
| | *A* | *B* | *C* | $J_A$ | $K_A$ | $J_B$ | $K_B$ | $J_C$ | $K_C$ |
| 0 | 0 | 0 | 0 | 1 | X | 0 | X | 0 | X |
| 1 | 1 | 0 | 0 | X | 1 | 1 | X | 0 | X |
| 2 | 0 | 1 | 0 | 1 | X | X | 0 | 0 | X |
| 3 | 1 | 1 | 0 | X | 1 | X | 1 | 1 | X |
| 4 | 0 | 0 | 1 | 0 | X | 0 | X | X | 1 |
| 5 (0) | 0 | 0 | 0 | | | | | | |

The flip-flop inputs have been determined with the help of the excitation table. (Table 4.10). Some examples follow:

### *A flip-flop*

The initial state is 0. It changes to 1 after the clock pulse. Therefore, $J_A$ should be 1 and $K_A$ may be 0 or 1 (that is X).

### *B flip-flop*

The initial state is 0 and it remains unchanged after the clock pulse. Therefore, $J_B$ should be 0 and $K_B$ may be 0 or 1 (that is X).

### *C flip-flop*

The state remains unchanged. Therefore, $J_C$ should be 0 to $K_B$ should be X.

The flip-flop input values are entered in Karnaugh maps Fig. 4.54 [(*a*), (*b*), (*c*), (*d*), (*e*) and (*f*)] and a boolean expression is formed for the inputs to the three flip-flops and then each expression is simplified. As all the counter states have not been utilized, Xs (don't) are entered to denote un-utilized states. The simplified expressions for each input have been shown under each map. Finally, these minimal expressions for the flip-flop inputs are used to draw a logic diagram for the counter, which is given in Fig. 4.55.

### *4.8.12.3 Mod-6 Counter (Synchroncus)*

The desired counter states and the JK inputs required for counter flip-flops are given in the counter design table (Table 4.13).

**Table 4.13 Counter design table for Mod-6 counter**

| *Input Pulse Count* | *Counter States* | | | *Flip-flop Inputs* | | | | | |
|---|---|---|---|---|---|---|---|---|---|
| | *A* | *B* | *C* | $J_A$ | $K_A$ | $J_B$ | $K_B$ | $J_C$ | $K_C$ |
| 0 | 0 | 0 | 0 | 1 | X | 0 | X | 0 | X |
| 1 | 1 | 0 | 0 | X | 1 | 1 | X | 0 | X |
| 2 | 0 | 1 | 0 | 1 | X | X | 0 | 0 | X |
| 3 | 1 | 1 | 0 | X | 1 | X | 1 | 1 | X |
| 4 | 0 | 0 | 1 | 1 | X | 0 | X | X | 0 |
| 5 | 1 | 0 | 1 | X | 1 | 0 | X | X | 1 |
| 6 (0) | 0 | 0 | 0 | | | | | | |

As before, the JK inputs required for this have been determined with the help of the excitation table, (Table 4.10). These input values have been entered in Karnaugh maps Fig. 4.56 and a boolean expression is formed for the inputs to the three flip-flops and then each expression is simplified. Xs have been entered in those counter states which have not been utilized. The simplified expressions for each input have been shown under each map and finally a logic diagram based on these expressions has been drawn, as given in Fig. 4.57.

| | $\bar{B}\bar{C}$ 00 | $\bar{B}C$ 01 | $BC$ 11 | $B\bar{C}$ 10 |
|---|---|---|---|---|
| $\bar{A}$ 0 | 1 (0) | 1 (4) | X (6) | 1 (2) |
| A 1 | X (1) | X (5) | X (7) | X (3) |

(a) Map for $J_A$
$J_A = 1$

| | $\bar{B}\bar{C}$ 00 | $\bar{B}C$ 01 | $BC$ 11 | $B\bar{C}$ 10 |
|---|---|---|---|---|
| $\bar{A}$ 0 | X (0) | X (4) | X (6) | X (2) |
| A 1 | 1 (1) | 1 (5) | X (7) | 1 (3) |

(b) Map for $K_A$
$K_A = 1$

| | $\bar{B}\bar{C}$ 00 | $\bar{B}C$ 01 | $BC$ 11 | $B\bar{C}$ 10 |
|---|---|---|---|---|
| $\bar{A}$ 0 | 0 (0) | 0 (4) | X (6) | X (2) |
| A 1 | 1 (1) | 0 (5) | X (7) | X (3) |

(c) Map for $J_B$
$J_B = AC$

| | $\bar{B}\bar{C}$ 00 | $\bar{B}C$ 01 | $BC$ 11 | $B\bar{C}$ 10 |
|---|---|---|---|---|
| $\bar{A}$ 0 | X (0) | X (4) | X (6) | 0 (2) |
| A 1 | X (1) | X (5) | X (7) | 1 (3) |

(d) Map for $K_B$
$K_B = A$

| | $\bar{B}\bar{C}$ 00 | $\bar{B}C$ 01 | $BC$ 11 | $B\bar{C}$ 10 |
|---|---|---|---|---|
| $\bar{A}$ 0 | 0 (0) | X (4) | X (6) | 0 (2) |
| A 1 | 0 (1) | X (5) | X (7) | 1 (3) |

(e) Map for $J_C$
$J_C = AB$

| | $\bar{B}\bar{C}$ 00 | $\bar{B}C$ 01 | $BC$ 11 | $B\bar{C}$ 10 |
|---|---|---|---|---|
| $\bar{A}$ 0 | X (0) | 0 (4) | X (6) | X (2) |
| A 1 | X (1) | 1 (5) | X (7) | X (3) |

(f) Map for $K_C$
$K_C = A$

**Fig. 4.56**

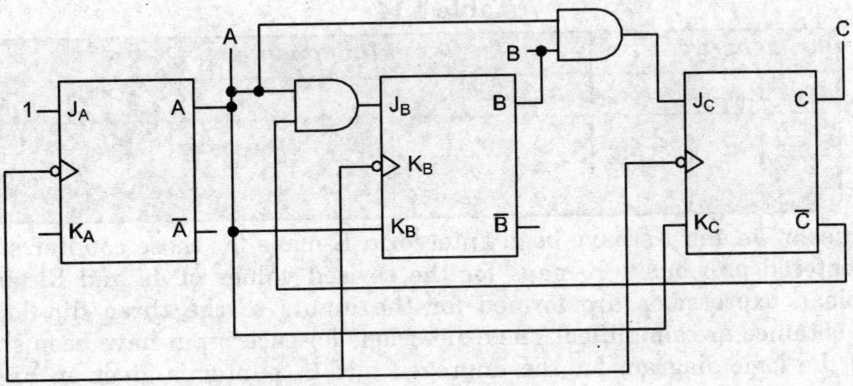


**Fig. 4.57** Synchronous Mod-6 counter.

### 4.8.13 Lockout

The mod-6 counter we have just discussed utilizes only six out the total number of eight states available in a counter having three flip-flops. The state diagram for the mod-6 counter given in Fig. 4.58, shows the states which have been utilized and also states 011 and 111 which have not been utilized. The counter may enter one of the unused states and may keep shuttling between the unused states and not come out of this situation. This condition may develop because of external noise, which may affect states of the flip-flops. If a counter has unused states with this characteristic, it is said to suffer from lockout.

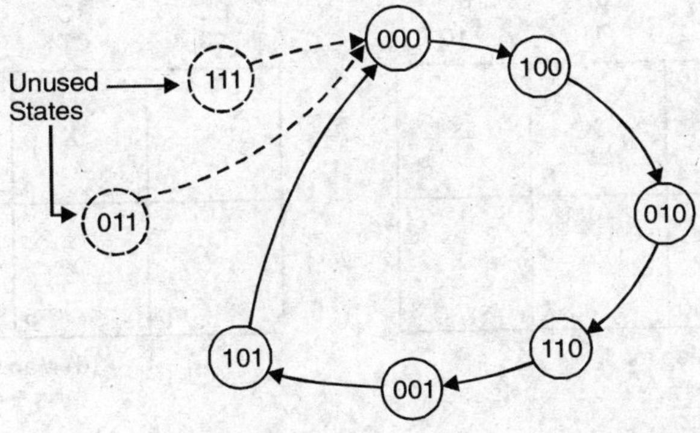


**Fig. 4.58** State diagram for Mod-6 counter.

The lockout situation can be avoided by so arranging the circuit that whenever the counter happens to be in an unused state, it reverts to one of the used states. We will redesign the mod-6 counter so that whenever it is in state 0 1 1 or 1 1 1, the counter swithces back to the starting point 0 0 0. You will notice from Fig. 4.56 that Js and Ks were marked X in squares corresponding to the unused states. We will now assign values for Js and Ks for the unused states, so that the counter reverts to state 0 0 0. This has been done in Table 4.14.

**Table 4.14**

| *Counter states* | | | *Flip-flop inputs* | | | | | |
|---|---|---|---|---|---|---|---|---|
| $A$ | $B$ | $C$ | $J_A$ | $K_A$ | $J_B$ | $K_B$ | $J_C$ | $K_C$ |
| 0 | 1 | 1 | 0 | X | X | 1 | X | 1 |
| 1 | 1 | 1 | X | 1 | X | 1 | X | 1 |
| 0 | 0 | 0 | | | | | | |

These values of Js and Ks have been entered in K-maps for those counter states where Xs had been entered previously. K-maps for the revised values of Js and Ks are given in Fig. 4.59. Boolean expressions are formed for the inputs to the three flip-flops and the expressions so obtained are simplified. The expressions for each input have been shown under each map and the logic diagram for the improved mod-6 counter is given in Fig. 4.60.

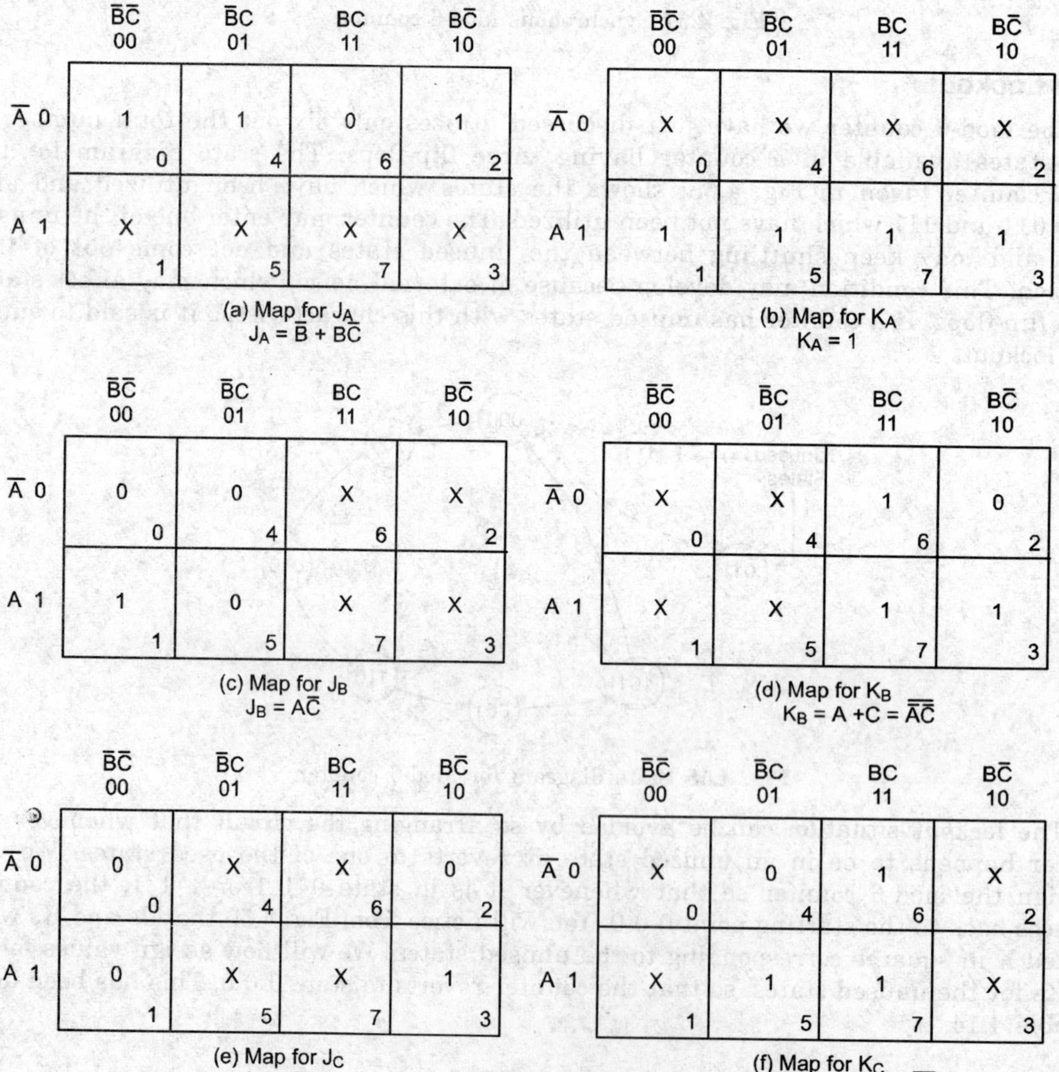


(a) Map for $J_A$
$J_A = \bar{B} + B\bar{C}$

(b) Map for $K_A$
$K_A = 1$

(c) Map for $J_B$
$J_B = A\bar{C}$

(d) Map for $K_B$
$K_B = A + C = \overline{\bar{A}\bar{C}}$

(e) Map for $J_C$
$J_C = AB$

(f) Map for $K_C$
$K_C = A + B = \overline{\bar{A}\bar{B}}$

**Fig. 4.59**

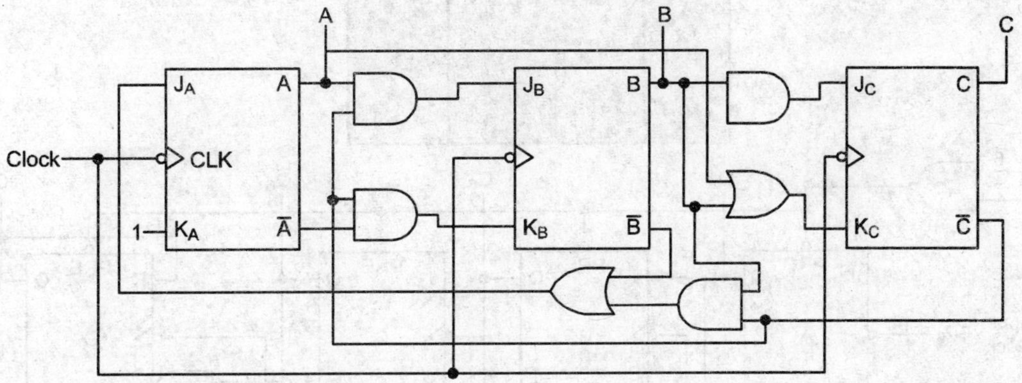


**Fig. 4.60** Mod-6 counter which will reset when it happens to reach an unutilized state

## 4.8.14 MSI Counter IC 7490 A

Of the many TTL MSI decade counters, IC 7490 A is most widely used for counting in the standard 8421 BCD code. The logic diagram for this counter is given in Fig. 4.61 and its pin connections and logic symbol are given in Figs. 4.62 and 4.63 respectively.

You will notice from Fig. 4.61 that it has three JK flip-flops A, B and C and, although the D flip-flop is an RS flip-flop, it functions like a JK flip-flop, since its normal output is connected to the R input. If you refer to Fig. 4.49, which shows a mod-5 counter, you will notice that the B, C and D flip-flops in IC 7490 A also form a similar mod-5 counter. Also notice that output $Q_A$ pin 12, of flip-flop A, which functions as a mod-2 counter, is not internally connected. It has to be externally connected to input B (pin 1) to enable it to function as a mod 2 × 5 or decade counter, when the input clock is applied at A (pin 14). It basically counts from binary 0000 to 1001 and back to 0000.

To reset the counter, gate 1 is provided with two inputs $MR_1$ and $MR_2$, any one of which will reset the counter with a high input. This makes it possible to reset the counter from any one of two sources. Normally both inputs are tied together. $MS_1$ and $MS_2$, inputs to gate 2 are used to preset the counter to binary 1001 (decimal 9) by taking any one or both inputs to gate 2 high. Normally both inputs are tied together. It is worth noting that, although this is an asynchronous counter, it has a count frequency of approximately 32 MHz, and therefore it finds wide application in frequency counters.

As you will see later, this counter also finds application as a modulo counter and it can be used to divide the input frequency by 5, 6, 7 etc.

**Table 4.15 Bi-quinary (5 × 2) sequence**

| *Output* | | | |
|---|---|---|---|
| $Q_A$ | $Q_D$ | $Q_C$ | $Q_B$ |
| 0 | 0 | 0 | 0 |
| 0 | 0 | 0 | 1 |
| 0 | 0 | 1 | 0 |
| 0 | 0 | 1 | 1 |
| 0 | 1 | 0 | 0 |
| 1 | 0 | 0 | 0 |

| | | | |
|---|---|---|---|
| 1 | 0 | 0 | 1 |
| 1 | 0 | 1 | 0 |
| 1 | 0 | 1 | 1 |
| 1 | 1 | 0 | 0 |

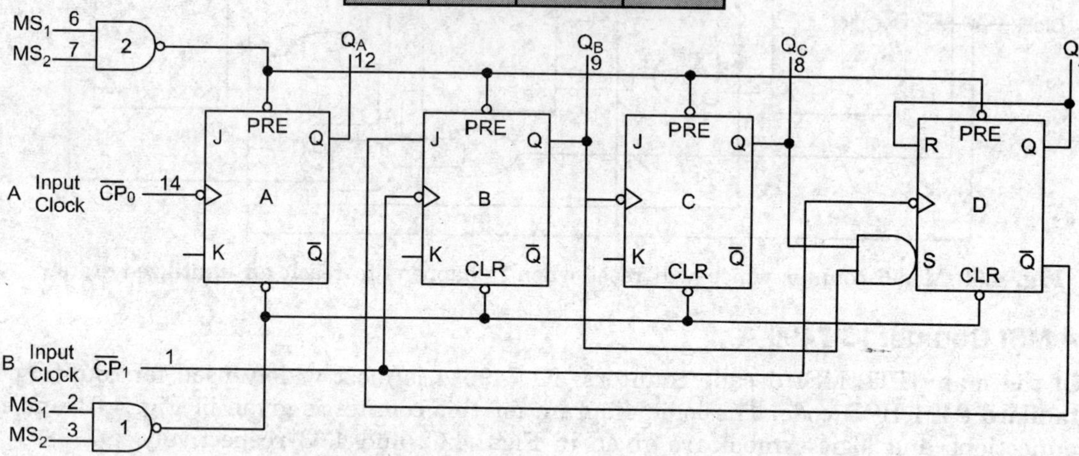


**Fig. 4.61** Logic diagram for counter IC 7490 A

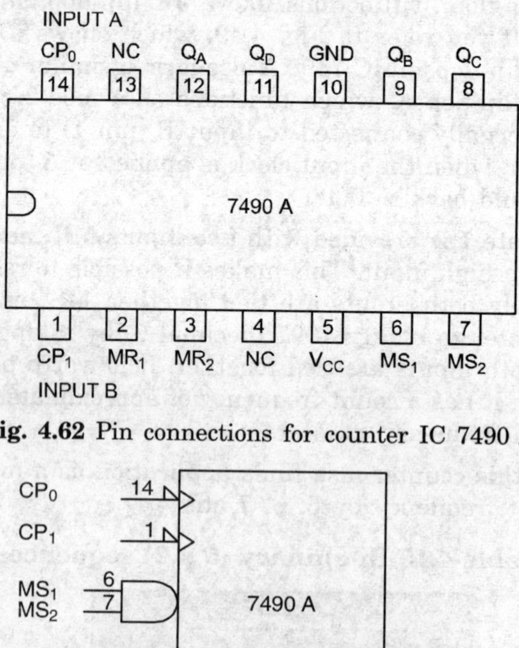


**Fig. 4.62** Pin connections for counter IC 7490 A

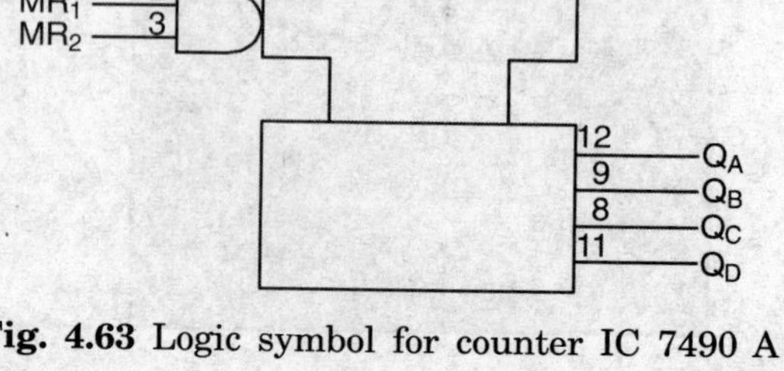


**Fig. 4.63** Logic symbol for counter IC 7490 A

When this counter is used as a decade counter in the 2 × 5 configuration, $Q_A$ (Pin 12) is connected to pin 1 as in Fig. 4.64 and clock pulse are applied at pin 14. The output at $Q_D$ (Pin 11) will be low from a count of 0000 to 1110. The output at pin 11 will be high at counts of 0001 and 1001 or decimal 9. At the next 1 to 0 transition of the clock pulse, the counter will be reset and at the same time, if there is another counter in cascade as shown in Fig. 4.65 its count will go up from 0000 to 1000 or decimal 1 on the 1 → 0 transition of the same clock pulse. In other words, when the first counter has reached its maximum count of 9, the next pulse will reset it to 0 and the second counter will be stepped up from 0000 to 1000 and the two put together will show a count of 10 and a maximum count of 99.

The waveform for this counter, connected in the 2 × 5 configuration, will be as shown in Fig. 4.50 and the counting sequence will be as shown in Table 4.9, which is in pure binary sequence. If you look at the D output in Fig. 4.50, you will observe that it is not symmetrical. If this counter is connected in the 5 × 2 mode, the output will have a symmetrical shape.

To operate this counter in the 5 × 2 mode, pin 14 is connected to $Q_D$ (pin 11) and the clock signal is applied at pin 1 as has been shown in Fig. 4.66. The output will now follow the bi-quinary (5 × 2) sequence as shown in Table 4.15, which is different from the pure binary sequence in Table 4.9. Bi-quinary (5 × 2) sequence waveforms are shown in Fig. 4.67. The counter will show a count of 0001 after the first clock pulse and the 10th pulse will reset the counter to 0000 on its trailing edge, which will also increment the next counter if another counter is connected in cascade. Two counters connected in cascade in the 5 × 2 configuration are shown in Fig. 4.68.

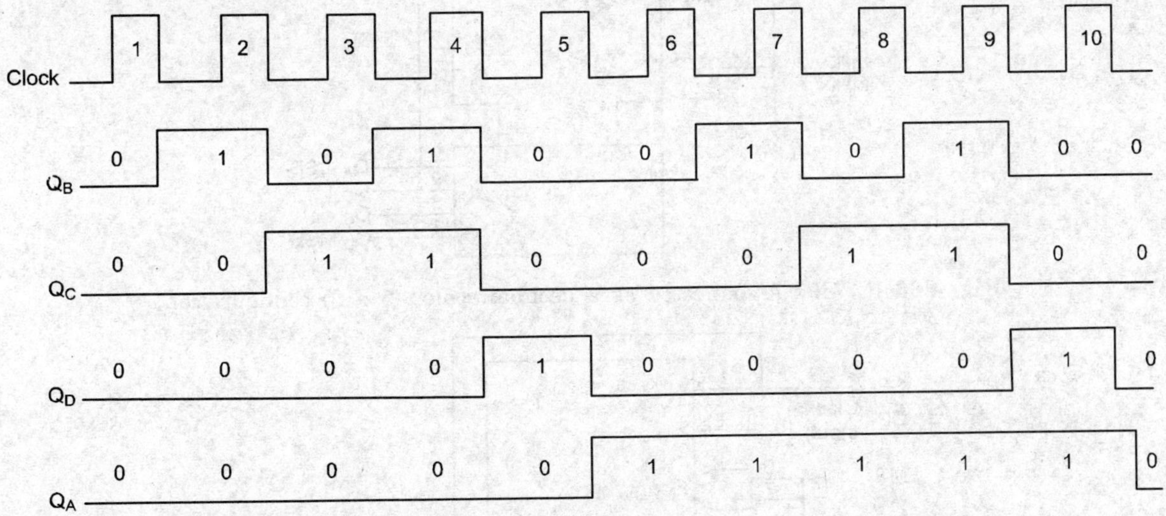


**Fig. 4.64** IC 7490 A connected as a decade counter (2 × 5) configuration

For two decade counters connected in cascade, there will be only one output pulse for every ten input clock pulses, which shows that the frequency of the train of input pulses is scaled down by a factor of 10. In other words, if the input frequency is $f$, the output frequency will be $f/10$.

In digital instruments, it is often necessary to divide a frequency by a given factor and for this function scalers are used. Scalers will accept input pulses and output a single pulse at the required interval. A single decade scaler will divide a train of pulses by 10 and four decade scalers will divide the input frequency by $10^4$.

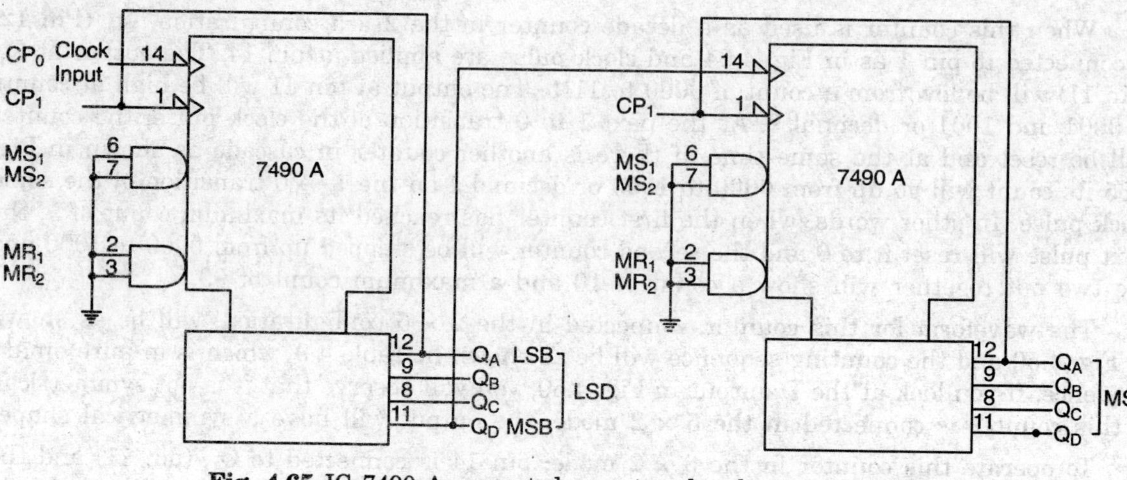


**Fig. 4.65** IC 7490 A connected as a two-decade counter (00-99)

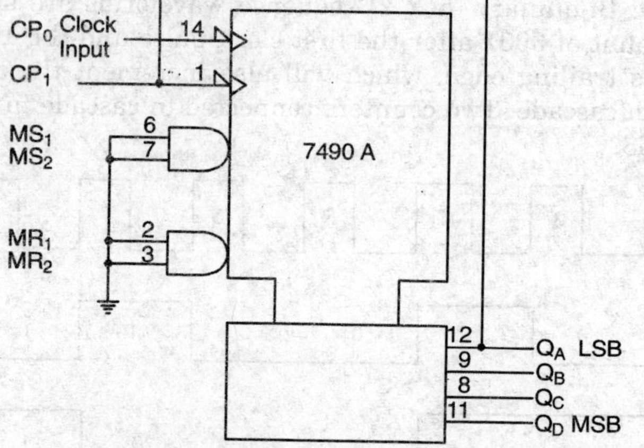


**Fig. 4.66** IC 7490 A connected as a decimal scaler (5 × 2) configuration

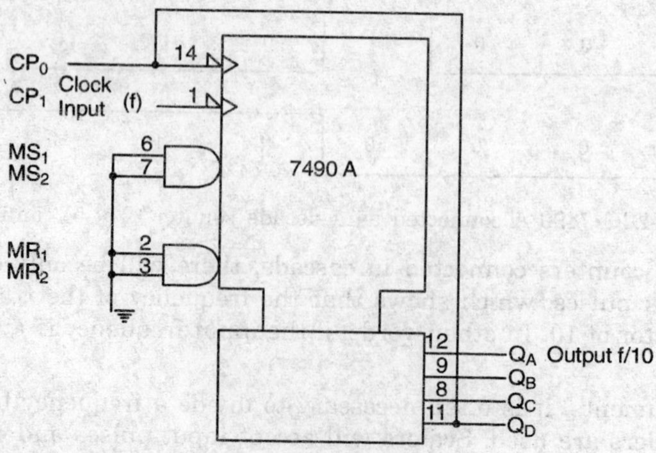


**Fig. 4.67** Waveforms in bi-quinary (5 × 2) sequence

### *4.8.14.1 Modulo-N counters based on IC 7490 A*

IC 7490 A has found several applications in circuits requiring frequency division. Some of the circuits in common use based on this IC have been discussed here.

#### *Modulo-5 Counter*

When used as a Mod-5 counter, connections are to be made as shown in Fig. 4.69. The count sequence for this counter is as given in Table 4.16.

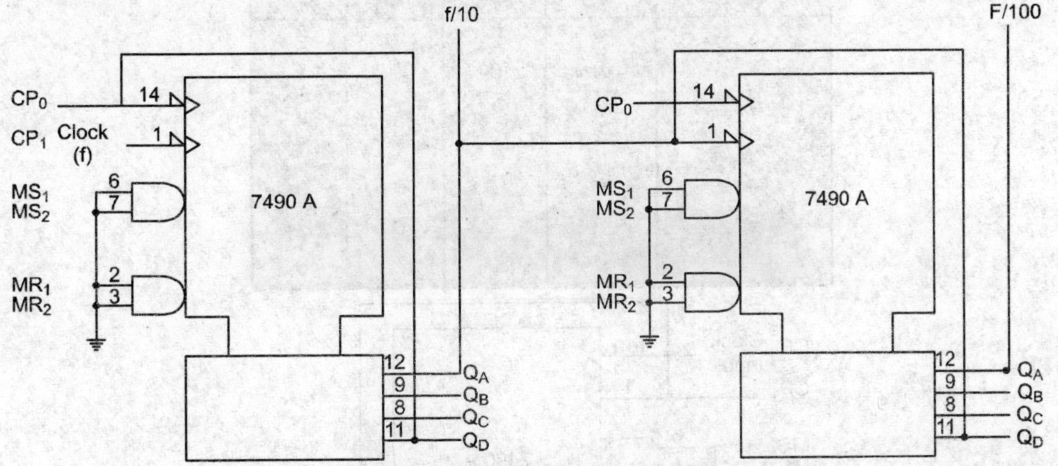


**Fig. 4.68** Divide by 100 scaler

**Table 4.16 Count sequence for Mod-5 counter**

| *Input pulse count* | *Counter output* | | |
|---|---|---|---|
| | $Q_D$ | $Q_C$ | $Q_B$ |
| 0 | 0 | 0 | 0 |
| 1 | 0 | 0 | 1 |
| 2 | 0 | 1 | 0 |
| 3 | 0 | 1 | 1 |
| 4 | 1 | 0 | 0 |
| 5 (0) | 0 | 0 | 0 |

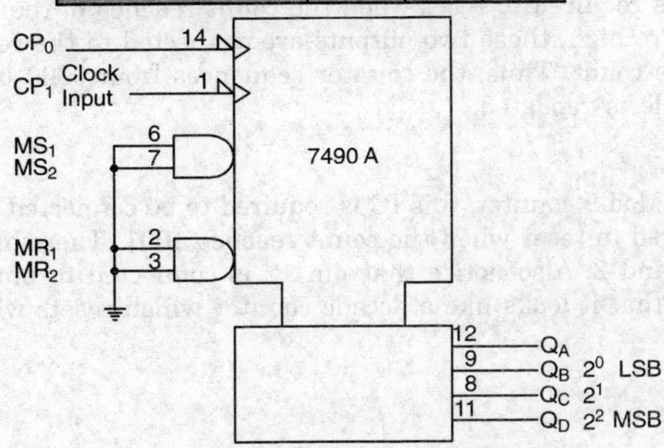


**Fig. 4.69** Mod-5 counter using IC 7490 A

### *Modulo-6 Counter*

IC 7490 A is to be connected as in Fig. 4.70 to obtain a Mod-6 counter. Its counter sequence is given in Table 4.17.

**Table 4.17 Count sequence for Mod-6 counter**

| *Input pulse count* | *Counter output* | | | |
|---|---|---|---|---|
| | $Q_D$ | $Q_C$ | $Q_B$ | $Q_A$ |
| 0 | 0 | 0 | 0 | 0 |
| 1 | 0 | 0 | 0 | 1 |
| 2 | 0 | 0 | 1 | 0 |
| 3 | 0 | 0 | 1 | 1 |
| 4 | 0 | 1 | 0 | 0 |
| 5 | 0 | 1 | 0 | 1 |
| 6 (0) | 0 | 1 | 1 | 0 |

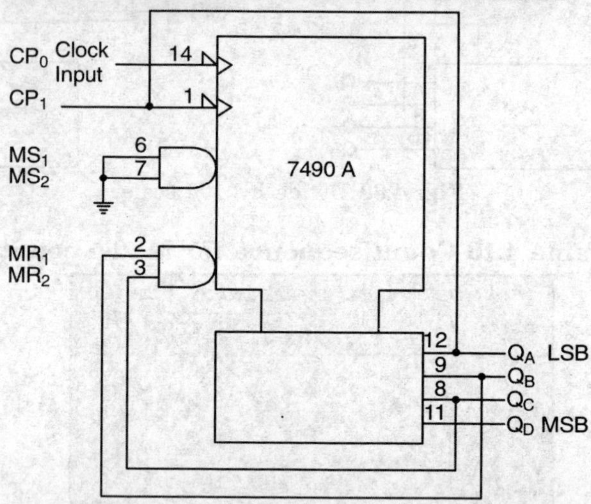


**Fig. 4.70** Mod-6 counter using IC 7490 A

As the counter is required to reset when the count reaches 6, that is 0 1 1 0 when both $Q_B$ and $Q_C$ outputs are high, these two outputs are connected to the reset inputs so that the counter resets at this count. Thus, the counter sequences from 0000 to 0101 and thereafter it resets and the cycle is repeated.

### *Modulo-9 Counter*

When used as a Mod-9 counter, this IC is required to be connected as shown in Fig. 4.71. The counter is required to reset when the count reaches 1001. Therefore, pins 11 and 12 are connected to pins 3 and 2. Also notice that pin 12 is connected to pin 1 and clock input is applied to pin 14, so that it looks like a decade counter which resets when the count reaches decimal 9.

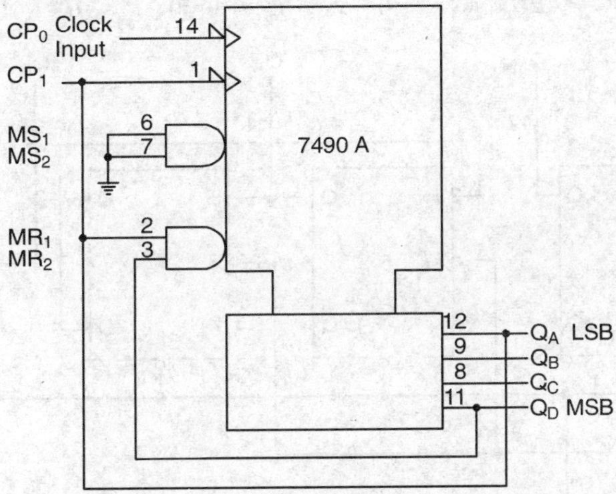


**Fig. 4.71** Mod-9 counter using IC 7490A

### 4.8.15 MSI Counter IC 7492A

Counter IC 7492 A, which is very similar to IC 7490 A, also finds considerable application in circuits requiring frequency division. A logic diagram of this IC is given in Fig. 4.72 and its pin connections and logic symbol are given in Figs. 4.73 and 4.74 respectively.

In this counter flip-flops B, C, and D are connected in the 3 × 2 configuration and, therefore, if input is applied at pin 1, and outputs are taken from $Q_B$, $Q_C$ and $Q_D$, this counter will function as mod-6 counter.

If output $Q_A$, pin 12, is connected to input pin 1, this IC functions as a 2 × 3 × 2 or mod-12 counter. Table 4.18 gives the truth table for this IC when $Q_A$, pin 12, is connected to input, pin 1. Some frequency division circuits based on this IC have been considered here.

**Table 4.18**

| *Input Pulse Count* | *Counter Output* | | | |
|---|---|---|---|---|
| | $Q_D$ | $Q_C$ | $Q_B$ | $Q_A$ |
| 0 | 0 | 0 | 0 | 0 |
| 1 | 0 | 0 | 0 | 1 |
| 2 | 0 | 0 | 1 | 0 |
| 3 | 0 | 0 | 1 | 1 |
| 4 | 0 | 1 | 0 | 0 |
| 5 | 0 | 1 | 0 | 1 |
| 6 | 1 | 0 | 0 | 0 |
| 7 | 1 | 0 | 0 | 1 |
| 8 | 1 | 0 | 1 | 0 |
| 9 | 1 | 0 | 1 | 1 |
| 10 | 1 | 1 | 0 | 0 |
| 11 | 1 | 1 | 0 | 1 |

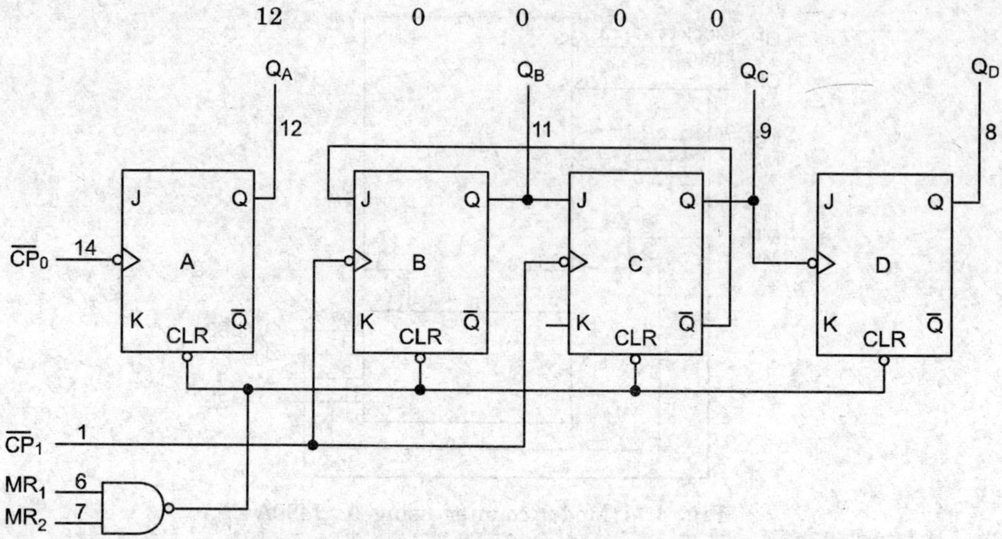


**Fig. 4.72** Logic diagram for IC 7492 A

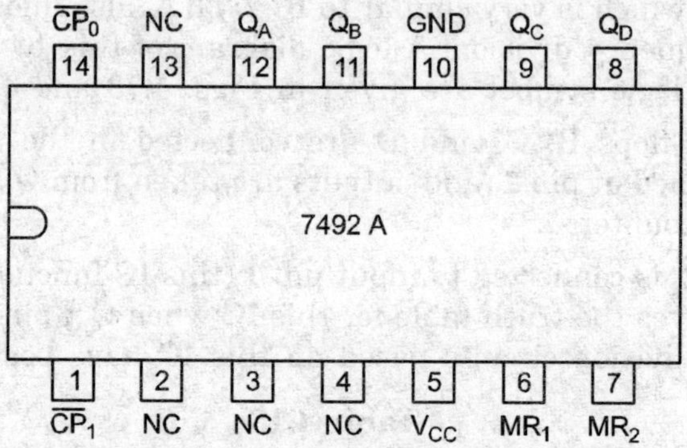


**Fig. 4.73** Pin connections for IC 7492 A

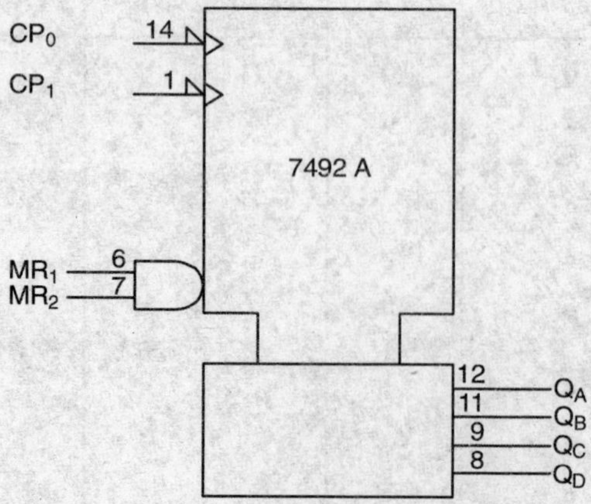


**Fig. 4.74** Logic symbol for IC 7492 A

#### 4.8.15.1 Divide-by-N circuits based on IC 7492 A

This IC like 7490 A is also a useful tool for circuits which require frequency division. Some circuits based on this IC have been considered here.

##### Divide-by-6-Circuit

As has been mentioned earlier, flip-flops B, C and D in this IC are connected in the 3 × 2 configuration. To operate as a divide-by-6, circuit input is applied at pin 1 and output is taken from $Q_D$, pin 8, as shown in Fig. 4.75.

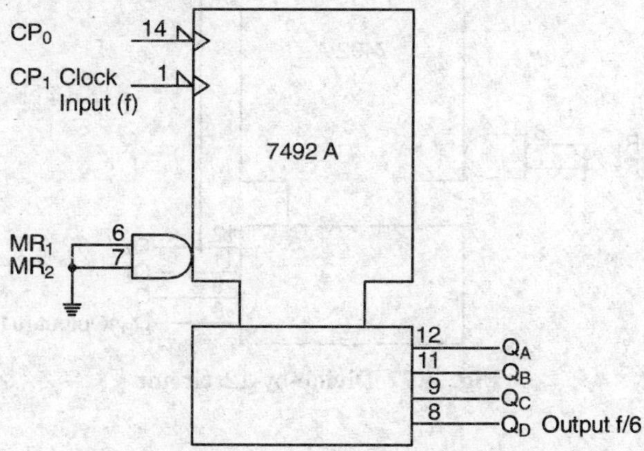


**Fig. 4.75** Divide-by-6 circuit

##### Divide-by-9 Circuit

Figure 4.75 gives the diagram for a circuit using IC 7492 A, which divides the input frequency by 9. Input is applied at pin 1 and, when the input pulse count reaches decimal 9, outputs $Q_D$ and $Q_A$ go high, and as they are connected to reset inputs, pins 7 and 6, the counter is reset. Output is taken from $Q_A$, pin 12.

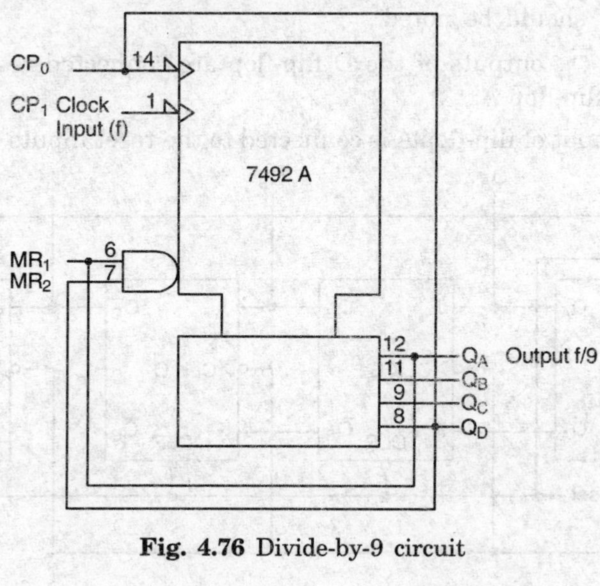


**Fig. 4.76** Divide-by-9 circuit

***Divide-by-12-Circuit***

A circuit based on IC 7492 A which will divide the input frequency by 12 is given in Fig. 4.77. Clock input is applied at pin 1 and the output is taken from $Q_D$, pin 12. When the circuit reaches pulse count 12, it is automatically reset and it repeats the cycle all over again.

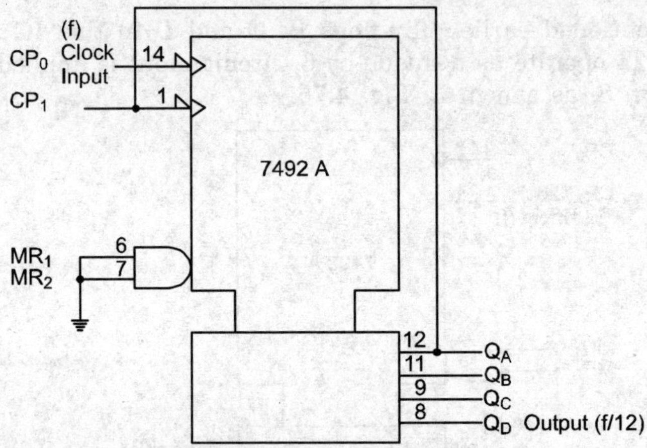


**Fig. 4.77** Divide-by-12 circuit

## 4.8.16 Ring Counter

Ring counters provide a sequence of equally spaced timing pulses and, therefore, find considerable application in logic circuits which require such pulses for setting in motion a series of operations in a predetermined sequence at precise time intervals. Ring counters are a variation of shift registers.

The ring counter is the simplest form of shift register counter. In such a counter, the flip-flops are coupled as in a shift register and the last flip-flop is coupled back to the first, which gives the array of flip-flops the shape of a ring as shown in Fig. 4.78. In particular, two features of this circuit should be noted.

(1) The $Q_D$ and $\overline{Q}_D$ outputs of the D flip-flop are connected respectively, to the J and K inputs of flip-flop A.

(2) The preset input of flip-flop A is connected to the reset inputs of flip-flops B, C and D.

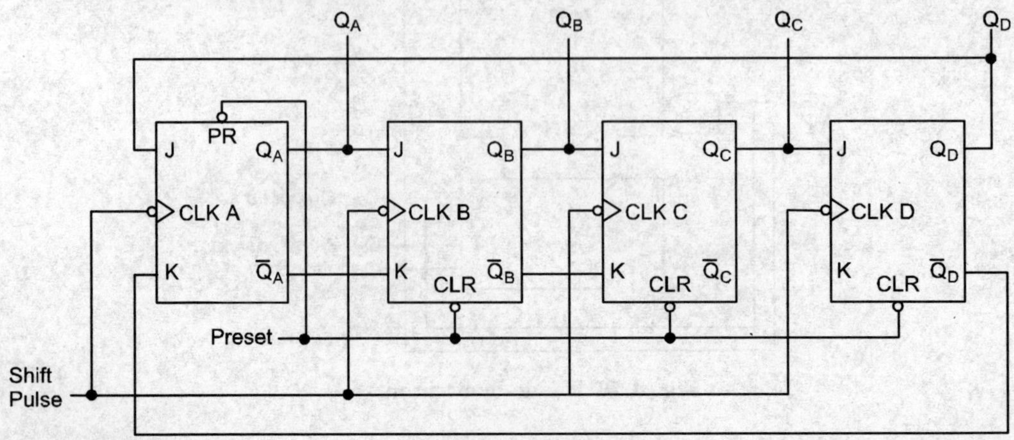


**Fig. 4.78** Ring counter

If we place only one of the flip-flops in the set state and the others in the reset state and then apply clock pulses, the logic 1 will advance by one flip-flop around the ring for each clock pulse and the logic 1 will return to the original flip-flop after exactly four clock pulses, as there are only four flip-flops in the ring. The ring counter does not require any decoder, as we can determine the pulse count by noting the position of the flip-flop, which is set. The total cycle length of the ring is equal to the number of flip-flop stages in the counter. The ring counter has the advantage that it is extremely fast and requires no gates for decoding the count. However, it is uneconomical in the number of flip-flops. Whereas a mod-8 counter will require four flip-flops, a mod-8 ring counter will require eight flip-flops.

The ring counter is ideally suited for applications where each count has to be recognized to perform some logical operation.

We can now consider how the modified shift register shown in Fig. 4.78 operates. When the preset is taken low momentarily, flip-flop A sets and all other flip-flops are reset. The counter output will now be as follows:

| $Q_A$ | $Q_B$ | $Q_C$ | $Q_D$ |
|---|---|---|---|
| 1 | 0 | 0 | 0 |

At the negative clock edge of the 1st pulse, flip-flop A resets $Q_A$ becomes 0, $Q_B$ becomes 1 and $Q_C$ and $Q_D$ remain 0. The counter output is now as follows:

| $Q_A$ | $Q_B$ | $Q_C$ | $Q_D$ |
|---|---|---|---|
| 1 | 0 | 0 | 0 |

After the 4th clock pulse, the counter output will be as follows:

| $Q_A$ | $Q_B$ | $Q_C$ | $Q_D$ |
|---|---|---|---|
| 1 | 0 | 0 | 0 |

You will notice that this was the position at the beginning of the operation, when the preset input was activated. A single logic 1 has travelled round the counter shifting one flip-flop position at a time and has returned to flip-flop A. The states of the flip-flops have been summarized in Table 4.19.

**Table 4.19 Ring counter states**

| *States* | *Counter output* | | | |
|---|---|---|---|---|
| | $Q_A$ | $Q_B$ | $Q_C$ | $Q_D$ |
| 1 | 1 | 0 | 0 | 0 |
| 2 | 0 | 1 | 0 | 0 |
| 3 | 0 | 0 | 1 | 0 |
| 4 | 0 | 0 | 0 | 1 |
| 5 | 1 | 0 | 0 | 0 |

The relevant waveforms are shown in Fig. 4.79.

If preset and clear inputs are not available, it is necessary to provide the required gating, so that the counter starts from the initial state. This can be simply arranged by using a NOR gate as shown in Fig. 4.80.

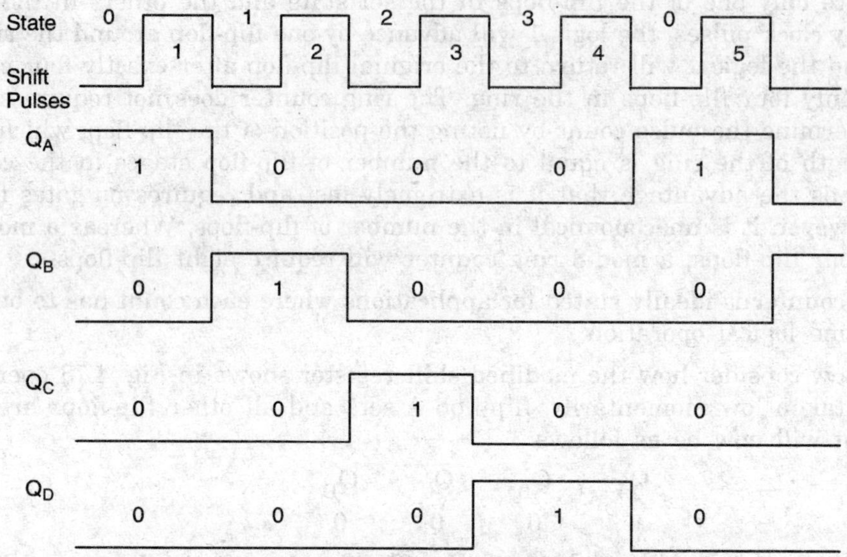


**Fig. 4.79**

The NOR gate ensures that the input to flip-flop A will be 0 if any of the outputs of A, B, C flip-flops is a logic 1. Now, on the application of clock pulses 0s will be moved right into the counter until all A, B and C flip-flops are reset. When this happens, a logic 1 will be shifted into the counter, and as this 1 is shifted right through the A, B and C flip-flops it will be preceded by three more 0s, which will again be followed by a logic 1 from the NOR gate when flip-flops, A, B and C are all reset.

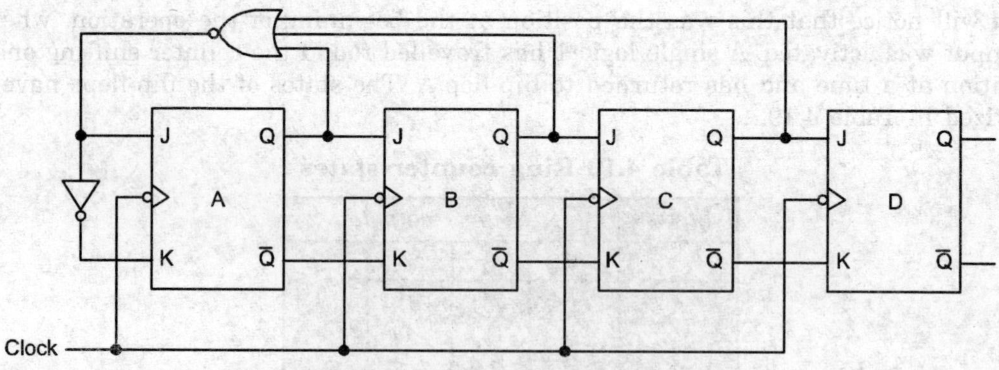


**Fig. 4.80** Ring counter with correcting circuit

### 4.8.17 Johnson Counter

The ring counter can be modified to effect an economy in the number of flip-flops used to implement a ring counter. In modified form, it is known as a switchtail ring counter or Johnson counter. The modified ring counter can be implemented with only half the number of flip-flops.

In the ring counter, circuit shown in Fig. 4.78, the $Q_D$ and $\overline{Q_D}$ outputs of the D flip-flop were connected respectively, to the J and K inputs of flip-flop A. In the Johnson counter, the outputs of the last flip-flop are crossed over and then connected to the J and K inputs of the first flip-flop. Figure 4.81 shows a Johnson counter using four JK flip-flops in the shift register configuration, shown $Q_D$ and $\overline{Q}_D$ outputs connected respectively, to the K and J inputs of flip-flop A. Because of this cross-connection, the Johnson counter is sometimes referred to as a twisted ring counter.

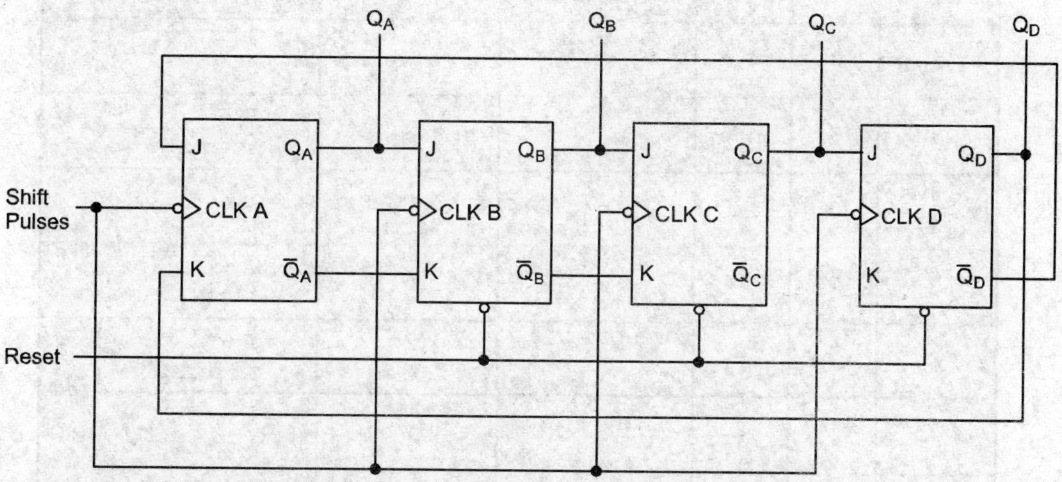


**Fig. 4.81** Four-stage Johnson counter

To enable the counter to function according to the desired sequence, it is necessary to reset all the flip-flops. Initially therefore, $Q_D$ is 0 and $\overline{Q}_A$ is 1, which makes the J input of flip-flop A logic 1. We will now study how shift pulses alter the counter output.

(1) Since, the J input of flip-flop A is 1, the 1st shift pulse sets the A flip-flop and the other flip-flops remain reset as the J inputs of these flip-flops are 0 and K inputs are 1.

(2) When the 2nd shift pulse is applied, since $\overline{Q}_D$ is still 1, flip-flop A remains set and flip-flop B is set, while flip-flop C and D remain reset.

(3) During the 3rd shift pulse, flip-flop C also sets, while flip-flops A and B are already set; but flip-flop D remains reset.

(4) During the 4th pulse, flip-flop D also sets while flip-flops A, B and C are already set.

(5) During the 5th pulse as $\overline{Q}_D$ is 0, flip-flop A resets, while flip-flops B, C and D remain set.

The entire sequence of states, which are 8 in all, is as shown in Table 4.20.

You will notice from Table 4.20 that Johnson counter with four flip-flops has eight valid states. Since, four flip-flops have been used, the total number of states is 16, out of which 8 are invalid, which have been listed in Table 4.21.

The valid states require decoding, which is different from normal decoding used for standard pure binary count sequence. You will notice that state 1 is uniquely defined, when the outputs of flip-flops A and D are low. Thus, a 2-input AND gate with inputs as shown in the table can decode state 1. State 2 is also fully defined by A high and B low. Similarly, the other outputs can be decoded by the gates with inputs as shown in Table 4.20.

**Table 4.20**

| *State* | $Q_D$ | $Q_C$ | $Q_B$ | $Q_A$ | *Binary Equivalent* | *Output Decoding* |
|---|---|---|---|---|---|---|
| 1 | 0 | 0 | 0 | 0 | 0 | $\bar{A}\bar{D}$ |
| 2 | 0 | 0 | 0 | 1 | 1 | $A\bar{B}$ |
| 3 | 0 | 0 | 1 | 1 | 3 | $B\bar{C}$ |
| 4 | 0 | 1 | 1 | 1 | 7 | $C\bar{D}$ |
| 5 | 1 | 1 | 1 | 1 | 15 | $AD$ |
| 6 | 1 | 1 | 1 | 0 | 14 | $\bar{A}B$ |
| 7 | 1 | 1 | 0 | 0 | 12 | $\bar{B}C$ |
| 8 | 1 | 0 | 0 | 0 | 8 | $\bar{C}D$ |

**Table 4.21 Invalid States**

| $Q_D$ | $Q_C$ | $Q_B$ | $Q_A$ | *Binary Equivalent* |
|---|---|---|---|---|
| 0 | 1 | 0 | 0 | 4 |
| 1 | 0 | 0 | 1 | 9 |
| 0 | 0 | 1 | 0 | 2 |
| 0 | 1 | 0 | 1 | 5 |
| 1 | 0 | 1 | 1 | 11 |
| 0 | 1 | 1 | 0 | 6 |
| 1 | 1 | 0 | 1 | 13 |
| 1 | 0 | 1 | 0 | 10 |

In order to ensure that the counter counts in the prescribed sequence given in Table 4.20, an initial reset pulse may be applied, which will reset all the flip-flops. If this is not done, there is no surety that the counter will revert to the valid counting sequence. If the counter should find itself in an unused state, it may continue to advance from one disallowed state to another. The solution to the problem lies in applying extra feedback, so that the counter reverts to the correct counting sequence. For this purpose, the self-correcting circuit given in Fig. 4.83 may be used. The input to the AND gate is $Q_A \overline{Q_B}\, \overline{Q_C}\, Q_D$ and thus it decodes the word 1 0 0 1, which overrides the input, which is 0 and the counter produces an output of 1 1 0 0, which is a part of the allowed counting sequence. From then onwards the counter functions in the desired sequence.

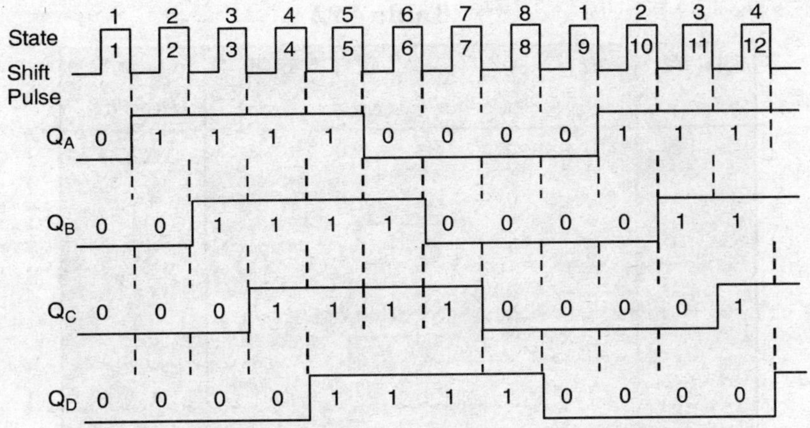


**Fig. 4.82** Waveforms for a 4-stage Johnson counter

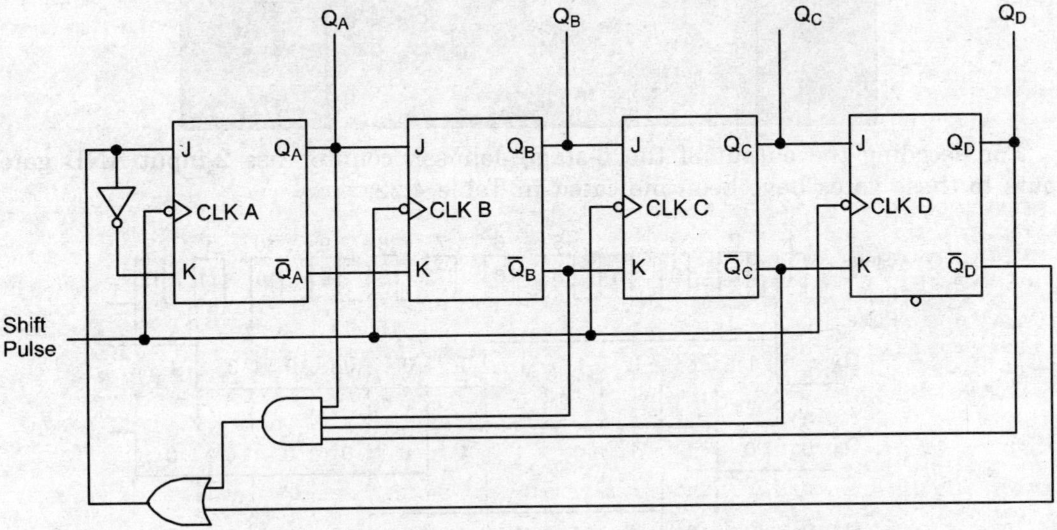


**Fig. 4.83** Self-starting and self-correcting Johnson counter

### 4.8.17.1 Five-stage Johnson Counter

While discussing the 4-stage Johnson counter, you must have observed that this counter divides the clock frequency by 8. Therefore, a Johnson counter with $n$ flip-flops will divide the clock frequency by $2n$ or, in other words, there will be $2n$ discrete states. If we have five flip-flops connected as a Johnson counter, we will have 10 discrete states. Consequently, we will have a decade counter. However, it should be noted that this counter will have in all 32 states, out of which the desired count sequence will utilize only 10 states and the remaining 22 will have to be disallowed. As in the case of a four flip-flop Johnson counter, some form of feedback will have to be incorporated, to disallow the illegal states. A self-correcting circuit like the one shown in Fig. 4.83 may be used with this counter Table 4.22 shows the sequence of the ten allowed states for this counter. The waveforms are shown in Fig. 4.84.

**Table 4.22**

| *State* | *E* | *D* | *C* | *B* | *A* | *Output Decoding* |
|---|---|---|---|---|---|---|
| 1 | 0 | 0 | 0 | 0 | 0 | $\bar{A}\bar{E}$ |
| 2 | 0 | 0 | 0 | 0 | 1 | $A\bar{B}$ |
| 3 | 0 | 0 | 0 | 1 | 1 | $B\bar{C}$ |
| 4 | 0 | 0 | 1 | 1 | 1 | $C\bar{D}$ |
| 5 | 0 | 1 | 1 | 1 | 1 | $D\bar{E}$ |
| 6 | 1 | 1 | 1 | 1 | 1 | $A\,E$ |
| 7 | 1 | 1 | 1 | 1 | 0 | $\bar{A}B$ |
| 8 | 1 | 1 | 1 | 0 | 0 | $\bar{B}C$ |
| 9 | 1 | 1 | 0 | 0 | 0 | $\bar{C}D$ |
| 10 | 1 | 0 | 0 | 0 | 0 | $\bar{D}E$ |

For decoding the output of the 5-stage Johnson counter use 2-input AND gates. The inputs to these gates have been indicated in Table 4.22.

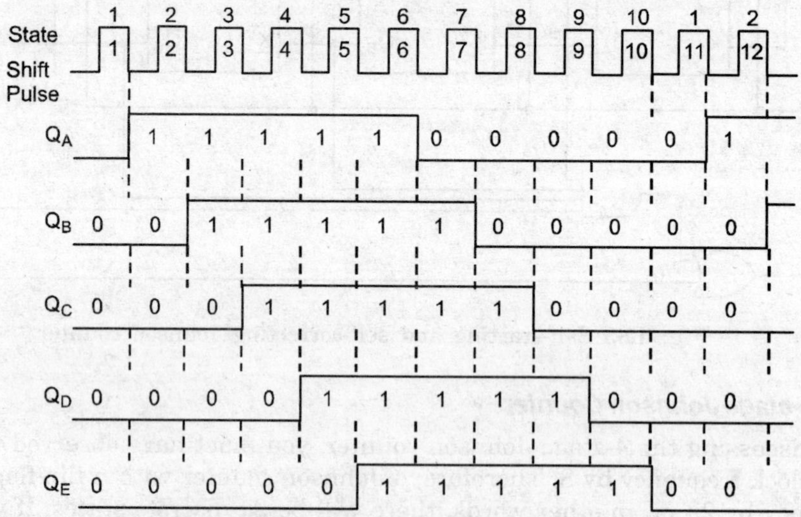


**Fig. 4.84** Waveform for a 5-stage Johnson counter

### 4.8.18 Ring Counter Applications

Ring counters find many applications as

(1) Frequency dividers
(2) Counters
(3) Code generators and
(4) Period and sequence generators

### *Frequency dividers*

If you look at the waveform Fig. 4.79 of the 4-stage ring counter shown in Fig. 4.78, you will notice that the B flip-flop produces one output pulse for two input pulses, that is it divides the frequency of the shift pulse by 2. Similarly, flip-flop C produces one output pulse for every three input pulses, that is it divides the input frequency by 3, and flip-flop D divides the input frequency by 4. If there are $n$ flip-flops they will divide the shift pulse by $n$. Thus, a shift register connected as a ring counter can be used as a frequency divider.

### *Counters*

A shift register, when connected as a ring counter, can also be used as a counter. For instance, the flip-flop outputs of the ring counter in Fig. 4.78 also give an indication of the number of pulses applied and, therefore counting requires no decoding.

### *Sequence generators*

Sequence generators are circuits which generate a prescribed sequence of bits in synchronism with a clock. By connecting the outputs of flip-flops in a ring counter to the logic circuits whose operations are to be controlled according to a certain sequence, a ring counter can perform a very useful function. Since, ring counters are activated by fixed frequency clocks, the timing intervals between the logic circuits to be controlled can be very precise.

This is of particular importance in computers where instructions have to be executed at the right time and in the correct sequence.

### *4.8.18.1 Feedback Counters*

The ring counters which we have considered so far have a cycle length which is the same as the number of flip-flops in the counter. For instance, the ring counter in Fig. 4.78 has a cycle length of 4. It is possible to design a ring counter which produces a longer cycle length of $2^n$–1, where $n$ is the number of flip-flops in the ring counter. The trick lies in decoding the outputs of the shift register and feeding the decoded output back to the input. This technique can be used to develop a wide variety of count sequences and output waveforms. To achieve a cycle length of $2^n - 1$, an exclusive-OR gate may be used as the feedback element, which provides a feedback term from an even number of stages to the first stage. Table 4.23 intended for counters up to 12 stages, shows the stages the outputs of which are to be fed back to the first flip-flop in the chain.

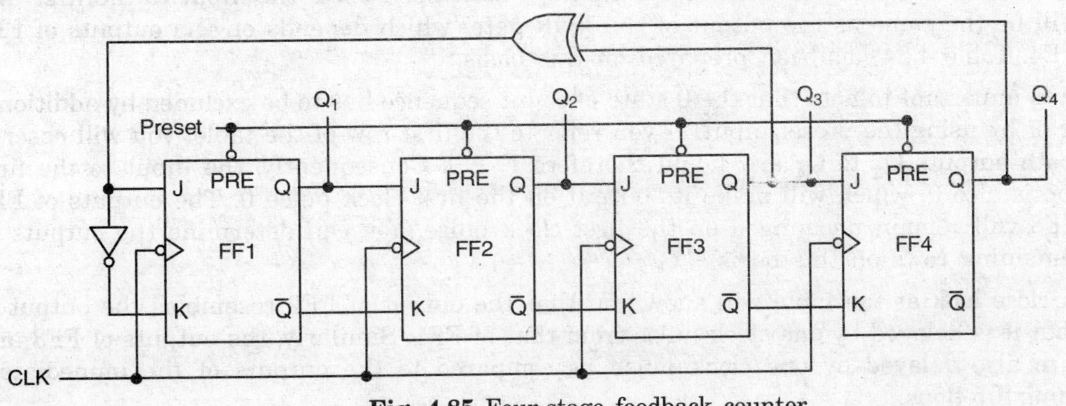


**Fig. 4.85** Four-stage feedback counter

This table can be used for designing counters of the type shown in Fig. 4.85, when the feedback element consists of a single XOR gate. The count sequence for this 4-stage counter is given in Table 4.24. When you refer to Table 4.23, you will notice that the feedback term for a 4-stage counter using an XOR gate as the feedback element is $F = (Q_3 \oplus Q_4)$. The truth table for an XOR gate reproduced below will enable you to determine the input to the first stage in the counter.

| *Input* | | *Output* |
|---|---|---|
| *A* | *B* | *F* |
| 0 | 0 | 0 |
| 0 | 1 | 1 |
| 1 | 0 | 1 |
| 1 | 1 | 0 |

**Table 4.23 Feedback terms for counter design**

| *No. of Stage* | *Feedback Stage* | | | |
|---|---|---|---|---|
| 2 | | $Q_1$ | $Q_2$ | |
| 3 | | $Q_2$ | $Q_3$ | |
| 4 | | $Q_3$ | $Q_4$ | |
| 5 | | $Q_3$ | $Q_5$ | |
| 6 | | $Q_5$ | $Q_6$ | |
| 7 | | $Q_6$ | $Q_7$ | |
| 8 | $Q_4$ | $Q_5$ | $Q_6$ | $Q_8$ |
| 9 | | $Q_5$ | $Q_9$ | |
| 10 | | $Q_7$ | $Q_{10}$ | |
| 11 | | $Q_9$ | $Q_{11}$ | |
| 12 | $Q_6$ | $Q_8$ | $Q_{11}$ | $Q_{12}$ |

In determining the counter states, all that is necessary is to determine the feedback input to the first flip-flop and, since JK flip-flops have been used, the input to the first flip-flop will be the same as the output of the XOR gate, which depends on the outputs of FF3 and FF4. Table 4.24 has been prepared on this basis.

It is important to note that the 0 state of count sequence has to be excluded by additional gating or by using the preset input. If you refer to the first row of the table, you will observe that both outputs $Q_3$ to $Q_4$ are 1 and therefore $F = 0$. Consequently, the input to the first flip-flop is also 0, which will make its output on the first clock pulse 0. The outputs of FF2 and FF3 will remain unchanged on the first clock pulse. You can determine the outputs in the remaining rows on this basis.

A close look at the table will show you that the output of FF2 resembles the output of FF1, but it is delayed by one clock pulse from that of FF1. Similarly, the outputs of FF3 and FF4 are also delayed by one clock pulse as compared to the outputs of the immediately preceding flip-flops.

**Table 4.24 Count sequence for 4-stage feedback counter**

| *Clock input* | *Output* | | | |
|---|---|---|---|---|
| | $Q_1$ | $Q_2$ | $Q_3$ | $Q_4$ |
| 0 | 1 | 1 | 1 | 1 |
| 1 | 0 | 1 | 1 | 1 |
| 2 | 0 | 0 | 1 | 1 |
| 3 | 0 | 0 | 0 | 1 |
| 4 | 1 | 0 | 0 | 0 |
| 5 | 0 | 1 | 0 | 0 |
| 6 | 0 | 0 | 1 | 0 |
| 7 | 1 | 0 | 0 | 1 |
| 8 | 1 | 1 | 0 | 0 |
| 9 | 0 | 1 | 1 | 0 |
| 10 | 1 | 0 | 1 | 1 |
| 11 | 0 | 1 | 0 | 1 |
| 12 | 1 | 0 | 1 | 0 |
| 13 | 1 | 1 | 0 | 1 |
| 14 | 1 | 1 | 1 | 0 |
| 15 | 1 | 1 | 1 | 1 |

This procedure can be used for designing counters which are required to cycle through a large number of states. For instance, a counter which uses 8 flip-flops will cycle through $2^8 - 1$ or 255 states. We have used only a single XOR gate as the feedback element, but the feedback logic can be designed differently to sequence through any desired sequence or waveform.

#### 4.8.18.2 Sequence generators

Here we are concerned with pseudo-random sequence generators. They will be random in the sense that the output generated will not cycle through the normal binary count. The sequence is termed pseudo, as it is not random in the real sense, because it will sequence through all the possible states once every $2^n - 1$ clock cycles. The random sequence generator given in Fig. 4.86 has $n$ stages and it will therefore sequence through $2^n - 1$ values before it repeats the same sequence of values.

Let us consider the sequence 100110011001. The bit sequence in this number has a length of 4 that is 1001, if you read it from the first bit on the left. You can also read the sequence from the 2nd and 3rd bits on the left, when the bit patterns will appear to be 0011 and 0110. No matter how you read it, the bit length does not change, nor does the sequence of bits change. You can describe the pattern of bits as 1001, 0011 or 0110.

We can now consider the structure of a sequence generator given in a simple form in Fig. 4.86 using D-type flip-flops connected as in a shift register. The output of the flip-flops are connected through a feedback decoder to the input of the first flip-flop. The output of the decoder is a function of the flip-flop outputs connected to it and the decoder circuitry. We can state this as follows:

$$F = f\,(Q_1, Q_2, Q_3, Q_n)$$

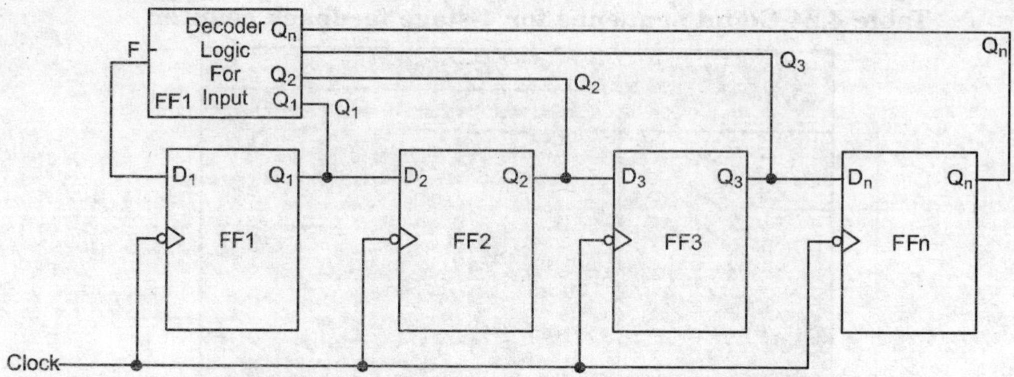


**Fig. 4.86** Basic structure of a sequence generator

The desired sequence of bits will appear at the output of each of the flip-flops, but the output of each of the successive flip-flops will show a delay in the appearance of the sequence by one clock interval over the one which precedes it.

The minimum number of flip-flops required to generate a sequence of length S is given by

$$S = 2^n - 1$$

Where $n$ is the number of flip-flops in the chain.

However, if the minimum number of flip-flops is used, it is not possible to say off hand, that it will be possible to generate a sequence of the required length; but for a given number of flip-flops there is invariably one sequence which has the maximum length.

It is important that in the generation of a sequence no state should be repeated, as that will put a limit on the number of states, because every state determines the development of the future sequence. Besides, the all 0 state has to be excluded, as in this case the input to the first flip-flop in the chain will be 0, which implies that the next state will also be 0, in which case the sequence generator would stop functioning.

We will now consider the steps in the generation of the sequence 1001001 of seven bits. The number of stages that will be required to generate this sequence can be determined as follows:

$$S = 2^n - 1$$

Since S = 7; $n$ should be 3, that is three flip-flops will be required.

However, there is no guarantee that a 7-bit sequence can be generated in 3 stages. If it is not possible, we can try to implement the sequence by using a 4-stage counter; but in this particular case, as you will see, it will be possible to generate this sequence with three stages. The basic arrangement for generating this sequence is shown in Fig. 4.87, which uses three JK flip-flops. The outputs of FF2 and FF3 constitute the inputs to the logic decoder, which in this case in an XOR gate. The output of the XOR gate, which constitutes the input F to FFI can be stated as follows:

$$F = (Q_2 \oplus Q_3)$$

You must have noticed that the outputs of FF2 to FF3 are one CLK pulse behind the outputs of flip-flops immediately preceding them. After the first sequence of 7 states has been completed, the sequence is repeated when the 8th (or 1st) CLK pulse arrives. Also observe that no output state has been repeated, which shows that it has been possible to implement the sequence with only 3 flip-flops.

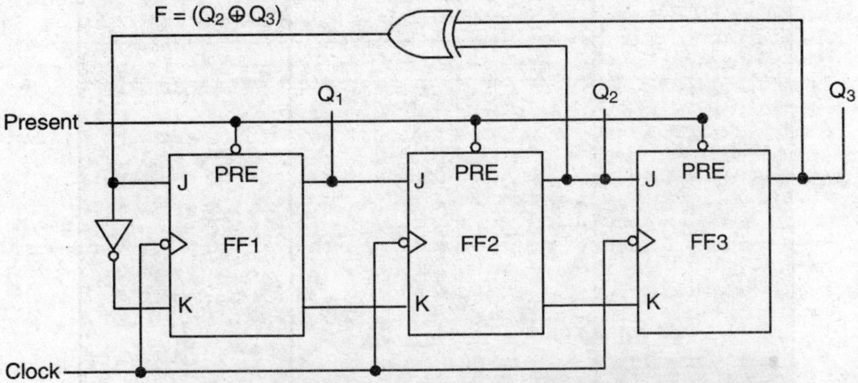


**Fig. 4.87** Three-stage sequence generator

When a larger or smaller number of flip-flops is used, the input to the first flip-flop can be worked out on the same basis; but the feedback logic will be different as shown in Table 4.25 for sequence generators using up to 8 stages. For instance, for a generator using four flip-flops, F will be as follows:

$$F = (Q_3 \oplus Q_4)$$

**Table 4.25 Logic design table for shift register sequences of maximum length (S = $2^n$ –1)**

| *Clock n* | *Feedback State* | | | |
|---|---|---|---|---|
| 2 | | $Q_1$ | $Q_2$ | |
| 3 | | $Q_2$ | $Q_3$ | |
| 4 | | $Q_3$ | $Q_4$ | |
| 5 | | $Q_3$ | $Q_5$ | |
| 6 | | $Q_5$ | $Q_6$ | |
| 7 | | $Q_6$ | $Q_7$ | |
| 8 | $Q_2$ | $Q_3$ | $Q_4$ | $Q_8$ |

The implementation of sequence 1001011 has been presented in Table 4.26.

The count sequence has been developed as follows: You will notice from the table that at the commencement of the operation, the counter is set as shown against CLK 1. Before CLK 2 is applied at FF1 input, the F input to it should be 0, so that its output changes from 1 to 0. Since, $Q_2$ and $Q_3$ are both 1, the F input to $FF_1$ will be 0. This condition is, therefore, satisfied. The second clock pulse, therefore, changes $Q_1$ from 1 to 0 and $Q_2$ and $Q_3$ remain on 1 as the inputs to these flip-flops are 1. Since, both $Q_2$ and $Q_3$ are again 1, the F input to $FF_1$, before the arrival of the 3rd clock pulse will again be 0. Therefore, on the arrival of CLK pulse 3, the output of $Q_1$ will remain 0, as the input to it is 0. On the same CLK pulse $Q_2$ will change from 1 to 0 as the input to it is 0 and $Q_3$ will remain on 1 as the input to $Q_3$ is still 1. Successive changes in the outputs have been worked out on this basis.

**Table 4.26**

| *Clock Interval* *CLK* | *Flip-flop Outputs* | | | *Input to FF1* $F = (Q_2 \oplus Q_3)$ |
|---|---|---|---|---|
| | $Q_1$ | $Q_2$ | $Q_3$ | |
| 1 | 1 | 1 | 1 | 0 |
| 2 | 0 | 1 | 1 | 0 |
| 3 | 0 | 0 | 1 | 1 |
| 4 | 1 | 0 | 0 | 0 |
| 5 | 0 | 1 | 0 | 1 |
| 6 | 1 | 0 | 1 | 1 |
| 7 | 1 | 1 | 0 | 1 |
| . | . | . | . | . |
| . | . | . | . | . |
| . | . | . | . | . |
| . | . | . | . | . |
| 1 | 1 | 1 | 1 | 1 |

## 4.9 EXERCISE

1. Can one store decimal number 12 in an 8-bit shift register.
2. The number stored in a 4-bit binary up-counter is 0101. What will be state of the counter after the following clock pulses?
   (*a*) 3rd clock pulse
   (*b*) 5th clock pulse
   (*c*) 8th clock pulse
   (*d*) 12th clock pulse
3. In a 4-bit ripple up-counter how many clock pulses will you apply, starting from state 0 0 0 0, so that the counter outputs are as follows?
   (*a*) 0 0 1 0
   (*b*) 0 1 1 1
   (*c*) 1 0 0 1
   (*d*) 1 1 1 0
4. Draw the logic diagram for a binary up-counter using four JK flip-flops and draw the truth table and the output waveforms.
5. Connect four edge-triggered D-type flip-flops to make an asynchronous up-counter.
6. How many JK flip-flops will you require to make the following modulo counters?
   (*a*) Mod-4 (*b*) Mod-6
   (*c*) Mod-9 (*d*) Mod-11
7. What will be maximum count capability of a counter having 12 JK flip-flops?

**8.** How many flip-flops will you require to attain a count capability of 8500?

**9.** An asynchronous counter has four flip-flops and the propagation delay of each flip-flop is 20 ns. Calculate the maximum counting speed of the counter.

**10.** A synchronous counter has four flip-flops and the propagation delay of each is 20 ns. What is its maximum counting speed?

**11.** By how much will a ripple down-counter having three flip-flops divide the input frequency?

**12.** Draw a logic diagram, truth table and output waveforms for a ripple down-counter with four flip-flops.

**13.** What will be the output states of a four flip-flop binary down-counter, after the following input clock pulses, if the initial state of the counter was 1111?

(*a*) 4 (*b*) 7 (*c*) 9 (*d*) 14

**14.** Draw the logic diagram of a presettable down counter with a maximum preset capability of 7.

**15.** What will be the modulus of IC 74193 in the up-counting mode, if the numbers preset in the counter are as follows?

(*a*) Decimal 5 (*b*) Decimal 7

(*c*) Decimal 9 (*d*) Decimal 12

**16.** What will be the modulus of IC 74193 in the down-counting mode, when the binary numbers preset in the counter are the same as in Problem 15?

**17.** A 74193 up-counter starts counting up from binary number 1 0 0 0. What will be the state of the counter after the 8th clock pulse?

**18.** Draw the logic diagram of a Mod-6 counter using the counter reset method. Write its truth table and draw the output waveforms.

**19.** Show how you will connect two ICs 74193 to build an 8-bit up-down counter.

**20.** What is the maximum counting capacity of a chain of five BCD counters?

**21.** A BCD counter is required to have the following states. After how many clock pulses will these states be reached, if the counter was initially reset?

(*a*) 0 0 1 0

(*b*) 0 1 0 0

(*c*) 0 1 1 0

(*d*) 1 0 0 1

**22.** Connect two ICs 74193 to make a moduluo-20 divider circuit.

**23.** Design a mod-10 (Decade) synchronous counter using JK flip-flops.

**24.** Draw decoding gates for the decade counter in Fig. 4.51.

**25.** Draw decoding gates for the counter of Fig. 4.49.

**26.** Redesign the synchronous mod-5 counter circuit discussed in Sec 4.8.12.2 so that whenever the counter reaches the unutilized state 1 0 1, 0 1 1 and 1 1 1 the counter is reset.

**27.** Design a Mod-7 counter using IC 7490 A.

28. Design a divide-by 120 counter using ICs 7490 A and 7492 A.
29. Design a correcting circuit for a 4-stage ring counter using a NAND gate instead of a NOR gate as used in Fig. 4.80.
30. Determine the maximal length sequence, which can be generated using four JK flip-flops and draw the sequence generated by the first flip-flop in the chain.
31. Draw waveforms to illustrate how a serial binary number 1011 is loaded into a shift register.
32. A binary number is to be divided by 64. By how many positions will you shift the number and in what direction?
33. Describe the working of shift register with PISO/SIPO operation.
34. Design a mod-5 synchronous counter having the states 011, 100, 101, 110, 111 respectively. Obtain a minimal cost design with J-K F/F.
35. Design a shift register counter to generate a sequence length of 8 having self-start feature.

# PART B

# MEMORIES

5

CHAPTER

# PROGRAMMABLE LOGIC DEVICES

## 5.0 INTRODUCTION

Digital circuit construction with small-scale integrated (SSI) and medium-scale integrated (MSI) logic has long been a basis of introductory digital logic design (refer Chap. 3). In recent times, designs using complex programmable logic such as programmable array logic (PLA) chips and field programmable gate arrays (FPGAs) have begun replacing these digital circuits.

This chapter deals with devices that can be programmed to realize specified logical functions. Since, evolution of programmable logic devices (PLDs) started with programmable ROM, it introduces ROMs and show how they can be used as a universal logic device and how simple programmable logic devices can be derived from ROMs. It also gives an overview of Complex Programmable Logic Devices (CPLDs) and Field Programmable Gate Arrays (FPGAs).

## 5.1 READ ONLY MEMORY (ROM)

A Read Only Memory (ROM) as shown in Fig. 5.1 is a matrix of data that is accessed one row at a time. It consists of k input lines and n output lines. Each bit combination of output lines is called a word while each bit combination of input variables is called an address. The number of bits per word is equal to the number of output lines n. A ROM is describe by the number of words $2^k$, the number of bits per word n.

The A inputs are address lines used to select one row (called a word) of the matrix for access. If A = $i$, then row $i$ is selected and its data appears on the output terminals D. In this case, we say that the contents of row $i$ are read from the memory.

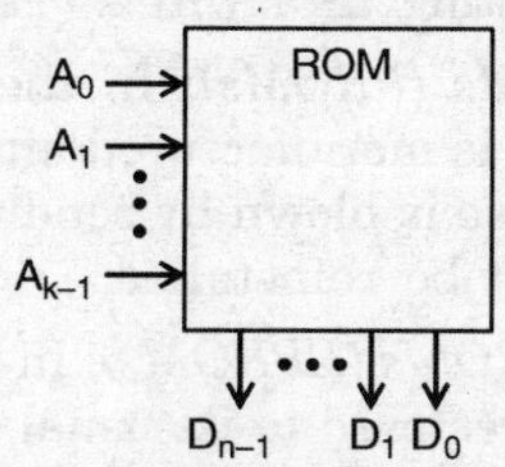


**Fig. 5.1**

If there are k address lines, then there are $2^k$ words in the ROM .The number of bits per word is called the word size. The data values of the words are called the contents of the memory and are said to be stored in the memory. The term read only refers to the property that once data is stored in a ROM, either it cannot be changed, or it is not changed very often.

ROM can be viewed as a combinational circuit with AND gates connected as a decoder and number of OR gates equal to the number of outputs. Internally a ROM contains a decoder and a storage array as shown in the Fig. 5.2.

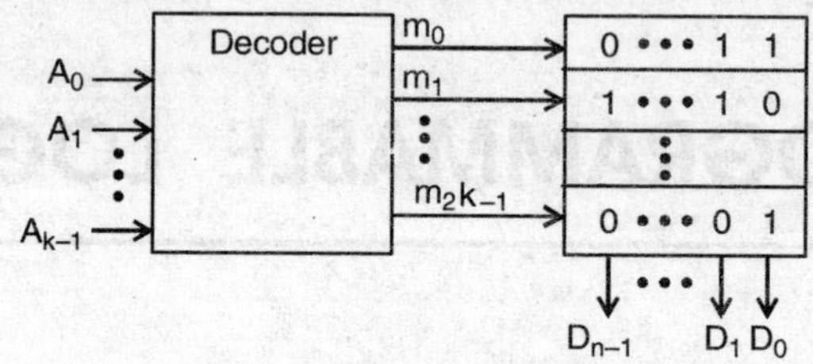


**Fig. 5.2**

When the address is *i*, the *i*th output of the decoder $m_i$ is activated selecting row *i* of the data array. Functionally the data array can be viewed as a programmable OR array. Each column acts as a stack of OR gates as shown in the Fig. 5.3.

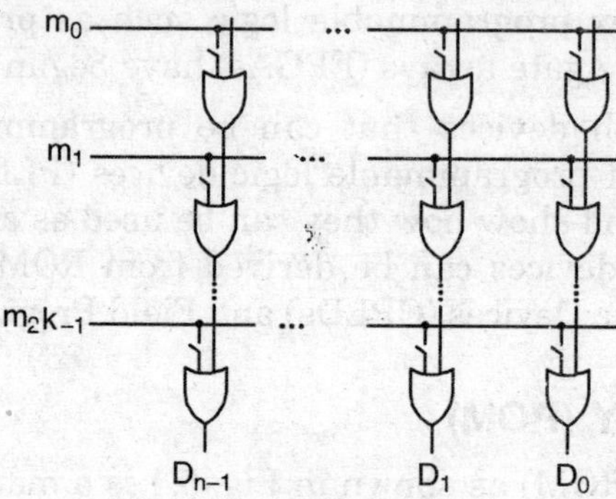


**Fig. 5.3**

Depending on the stored value (0/1) switch is open or closed. If a 0 is stored in a row, the switch is open and if a 1 is stored, the switch is closed. The type of ROM is determined by the way the switches are set or reset (*i.e.*, programmed).

(I) *Mask programmed ROMs:* In the mask programmed ROMs, switch is realized at the time the ROM is manufactured. Either a connection is made by putting in a wire, or the connection is left open by not putting in a wire.

(II) *Field programmable ROMs (PROMs):* In the field programmable ROMs, switch is realized by a fuse. When the ROM is manufactured all switches are closed, since, all the fuses are intact. To open a switch the fuse is blown by sending a larger than usual current through it. Once a fuse is blown, it cannot be reinstalled.

(III) *Erasable programmable ROMs (EPROMs):* In the erasable ROMs switch is realized by a special kind of fuse that can be restored to its usual closed state, usually by the insertion of extra energy (*e.g.*, shining ultraviolet light on the fuse). All fuses are reset when this is done.

(IV) *Electrically programmable ROMs (EPROMs):* In the electrically programmable ROMs fuses are reset by the application of larger than usual currents. Sometimes subsections of the ROM can be reset without resetting all fuses.

Consider a 32 × 8 ROM as shown in Fig. 5.4. The ROM consists of 32 words of bit size 8. That is, there are 32 distinct words stored which may be available through eight output lines. The five inputs are decoded into 32 lines and each output of the decoder represents one of the minterms of a function of five variables. Each one of the 32 addresses selects only one output from the decoder. The 32 outputs of the decoder are connected through links to each OR gate.

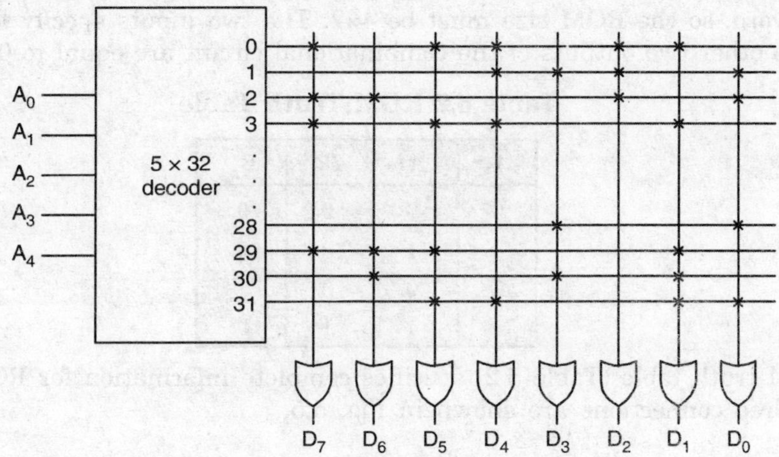


**Fig. 5.4**

### 5.1.1 Realizing Logical Functions with ROM

The ROM is a two-level implementation in sum of minterms form. ROMs with k address lines and n data terminals can be used to realize any n logical functions of *k* variables. For this one have to simply store the truth table for each function in a column of the ROM data array. The advantage of implementing logical functions by means of some form of programmable ROM, we have the possibility of reconfigurable logic. That is, the same hardware being reprogrammed to realize different logic at different times. But the disadvantage of using large ROMs to realize logical functions is that, the ROMs are much slower than gate realizations of the functions. The following example explains the procedure for realizing logical functions.

**Example 5.1.** Design a combinational circuit using a ROM that accepts a 2-bit number and generates an output binary number equal to the square of the input number.

**Solution. Step 1.** Derive the truth table for the combinational circuit. For the given example the truth table is

**Table 5.1**

| *Inputs* | | *Outputs* | | | | *Equivalent Decimal* |
|---|---|---|---|---|---|---|
| $A_1$ | $A_0$ | $B_3$ | $B_2$ | $B_1$ | $B_0$ | |
| 0 | 0 | 0 | 0 | 0 | 0 | 0 |
| 0 | 1 | 0 | 0 | 0 | 1 | 1 |
| 1 | 0 | 0 | 1 | 0 | 0 | 4 |
| 1 | 1 | 1 | 0 | 0 | 1 | 9 |

**Step 2.** If possible, reduce the truth table for the ROM by using certain properties in the truth table of the combinational circuit. For the given example, two inputs and four outputs are needed to accommodate all possible numbers.

Since, output $B_0$ is always equal to input $A_0$, therefore there is no need to generate $B_0$ with a ROM. Also $B_1$ is known as it is always 0. Therefore, we need to generate only two outputs with the ROM; the other two are easily obtained.

**Step 3.** Find the minimum size of ROM from step 2

The minimum size ROM needed must have two inputs and two outputs. Two inputs specify four word, so the ROM size must be 4×2. The two inputs specify four words of two bits each. The other two outputs of the combinational circuit are equal to 0 ($B_1$) and A0($B_0$).

**Table 5.2 ROM Truth Table**

| $A_1$ | $A_0$ | $B_3$ | $B_2$ |
|---|---|---|---|
| 0 | 0 | 0 | 0 |
| 0 | 1 | 0 | 0 |
| 1 | 0 | 0 | 1 |
| 1 | 1 | 1 | 0 |

The ROM truth table (Table 5.2) specifies complete information for ROM programming and the required connections are shown in Fig. 5.5.

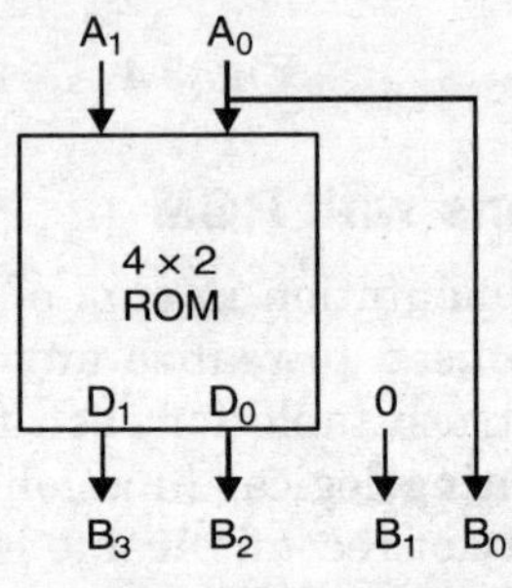


**Fig. 5.5** Block diagram

**Example 5.2.** Show that a 16 × 6 ROM can be used to implement a circuit that generates the binary square of an input 4-bit number with $B_0 = A_0$ and $B_1 = 0$ as shown in figure 5.6(*a*). Draw the block diagram of the circuit and specify the first four and last four entries of the ROM truth table.

**Solution. Step 1.** Draw the truth table for the combinational circuit. For the given example the truth table is

**Table 5.3**

| *Inputs* | | | | *Outputs* | | | | | | | | *Equivalent Decimal* |
|---|---|---|---|---|---|---|---|---|---|---|---|---|
| $A_3$ | $A_2$ | $A_1$ | $A_0$ | $B_7$ | $B_6$ | $B_5$ | $B_4$ | $B_3$ | $B_2$ | $B_1$ | $B_0$ | |
| 0 | 0 | 0 | 0 | 0 | 0 | 0 | 0 | 0 | 0 | 0 | 0 | 0 |
| 0 | 0 | 0 | 1 | 0 | 0 | 0 | 0 | 0 | 0 | 0 | 1 | 1 |
| 0 | 0 | 1 | 0 | 0 | 0 | 0 | 0 | 0 | 1 | 0 | 0 | 4 |
| 0 | 0 | 1 | 1 | 0 | 0 | 0 | 0 | 1 | 0 | 0 | 1 | 9 |
| 0 | 1 | 0 | 0 | 0 | 0 | 0 | 1 | 0 | 0 | 0 | 0 | 16 |

*Contd...*

| | | | | | | | | | | | | |
|---|---|---|---|---|---|---|---|---|---|---|---|---|
| 0 | 1 | 0 | 1 | 0 | 0 | 0 | 1 | 1 | 0 | 0 | 1 | 25 |
| 0 | 1 | 1 | 0 | 0 | 0 | 1 | 0 | 0 | 1 | 0 | 0 | 36 |
| 0 | 1 | 1 | 1 | 0 | 0 | 1 | 1 | 0 | 0 | 0 | 1 | 49 |
| 1 | 0 | 0 | 0 | 0 | 1 | 0 | 0 | 0 | 0 | 0 | 0 | 64 |
| 1 | 0 | 0 | 1 | 0 | 1 | 0 | 1 | 0 | 0 | 0 | 1 | 81 |
| 1 | 0 | 1 | 0 | 0 | 1 | 1 | 0 | 0 | 1 | 0 | 0 | 100 |
| 1 | 0 | 1 | 1 | 0 | 1 | 1 | 1 | 1 | 0 | 0 | 1 | 121 |
| 1 | 1 | 0 | 0 | 1 | 0 | 0 | 1 | 0 | 0 | 0 | 0 | 144 |
| 1 | 1 | 0 | 1 | 1 | 0 | 1 | 0 | 1 | 0 | 0 | 1 | 169 |
| 1 | 1 | 1 | 0 | 1 | 1 | 0 | 0 | 0 | 1 | 0 | 0 | 196 |
| 1 | 1 | 1 | 1 | 1 | 1 | 1 | 0 | 0 | 0 | 0 | 1 | 225 |

**Step 2.** If possible, reduce the truth table for the ROM by using certain properties in the truth table of the combinational circuit. For the given example, four inputs and eight outputs are needed to accommodate all possible numbers.

Since, $B_0 = A_0$ and $B_1 = 0$ as shown from truth table in step 1. We need only six outputs to generate with the ROM; the other two are easily obtained.

**Step 3.** Find the minimum size of ROM from step 2. The minimum size of ROM needed must have four inputs and six outputs. Four inputs specify sixteen word so the ROM size must be 16 × 6. The block diagram of the circuit and first four and last four entries of the ROM truth table is shown in Fig. 5.6.

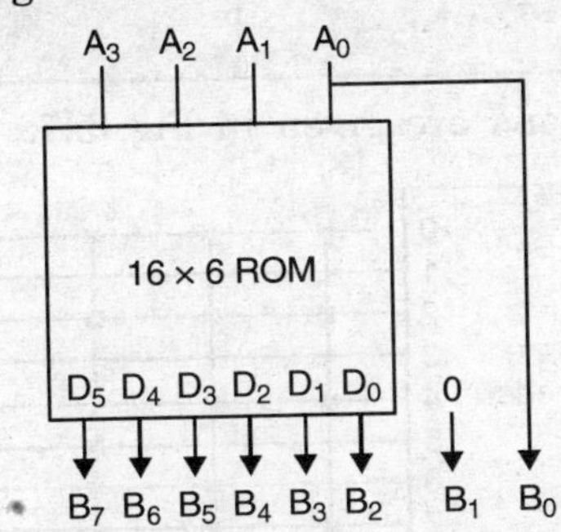


**Fig. 5.6** (*a*) Block diagram

ROM truth table

| | $A_3$ | $A_2$ | $A_1$ | $A_0$ | $D_5$ | $D_4$ | $D_3$ | $D_2$ | $D_1$ | $D_0$ |
|---|---|---|---|---|---|---|---|---|---|---|
| 0 | 0 | 0 | 0 | 0 | 0 | 0 | 0 | 0 | 0 | 0 |
| 1 | 0 | 0 | 0 | 1 | 0 | 0 | 0 | 0 | 0 | 0 |
| 2 | 0 | 0 | 1 | 0 | 0 | 0 | 0 | 0 | 0 | 1 |
| 3 | 0 | 0 | 1 | 1 | 0 | 0 | 0 | 0 | 1 | 0 |
| | ⋮ | | | | | | | ⋮ | | |
| 12 | 1 | 1 | 0 | 0 | 1 | 0 | 0 | 1 | 0 | 0 |
| 13 | 1 | 1 | 0 | 1 | 1 | 0 | 1 | 0 | 1 | 0 |
| 14 | 1 | 1 | 1 | 0 | 1 | 1 | 0 | 0 | 0 | 1 |
| 15 | 1 | 1 | 1 | 1 | 1 | 1 | 1 | 0 | 0 | 0 |

**Fig. 5.6** (*b*) ROM truth table

**Example 5.3.** For the function

$$F_1 = \Sigma(0, 2, 5, 6)$$
$$F_2 = \Sigma(0, 2, 4, 6, 7)$$
$$F_3 = \Sigma(0, 2, 4, 7)$$
$$F_0 = \Sigma(1, 2, 3, 5, 7)$$

Design a three bit addressable ROM.

**Solution.** From truth table, the minimum size of ROM needed having three inputs and four outputs. Three inputs specify $2^3 = 8$ word so the ROM size must be 8 × 4.

**Table 5.4**

| *Minterms* | *Inputs* | | | *Outputs* | | | |
|---|---|---|---|---|---|---|---|
| | $A_2$ | $A_1$ | $A_0$ | $F_3$ | $F_2$ | $F_1$ | $F_0$ |
| 0 | 0 | 0 | 0 | 1 | 1 | 1 | 0 |
| 1 | 0 | 0 | 1 | 0 | 0 | 0 | 1 |
| 2 | 0 | 1 | 0 | 1 | 1 | 1 | 1 |
| 3 | 0 | 1 | 1 | 0 | 0 | 0 | 1 |
| 4 | 1 | 0 | 0 | 1 | 1 | 0 | 0 |
| 5 | 1 | 0 | 1 | 0 | 0 | 1 | 1 |
| 6 | 1 | 1 | 0 | 0 | 1 | 1 | 0 |
| 7 | 1 | 1 | 1 | 1 | 1 | 0 | 1 |

The implementations of functions are given in Fig. 5.7.

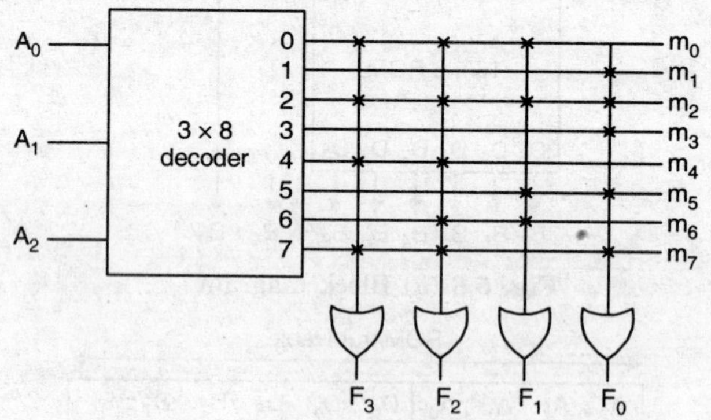


**Fig. 5.7**

**Example 5.4.** A ROM is to be used to implement the Boolean functions given below:

$$F_1\ (A, B, C, D) = ABCD + \overline{A}\,\overline{B}\,\overline{C}\,\overline{D}$$

$$F_2\ (A, B, C, D) = (A + B)\ (\overline{A} + \overline{B} + C)$$

$$F_3\ (A, B, C, D) = \Sigma 13, 15 + \Sigma 3, 5$$

(*a*) What is the minimum size of the ROM required?

(*b*) Determine the data in each location of the ROM.

**Solution.** (*a*) $F_1$ (A, B, C, D) $= ABCD + \bar{A}\,\bar{B}\,\bar{C}\,\bar{D}$

$F_2$ (A, B, C, D) $= (A + B)\,(\bar{A} + \bar{B} + \bar{C})$

$= A\bar{A} + A\bar{B} + AC + \bar{A}B + B\bar{B} + BC$

$= \bar{A}B + A\bar{B} + AC + BC$

$F_3$ (A, B, C, D) $= \Sigma(13, 15) + \Sigma(3, 5)$

To simplify $F_3$ (using K-Map).

| AB \ CD | $\bar{C}\bar{D}$ | $\bar{C}D$ | $CD$ | $C\bar{D}$ |
|---|---|---|---|---|
| $\bar{A}\bar{B}$ | 0 | 1 | × 3 | 2 |
| $\bar{A}B$ | 4 | × 5 | 7 | 6 |
| $AB$ | 12 | 1 13 | 1 15 | 14 |
| $A\bar{B}$ | 8 | 9 | 11 | 10 |

$F_3$ (A, B, C, D) $= ABD$

**Table 5.5 Truth table of ROM**

| *Inputs* | | | | *Outputs* | | |
|---|---|---|---|---|---|---|
| *A* | *B* | *C* | *D* | $F_3$ | $F_2$ | $F_1$ |
| 0 | 0 | 0 | 0 | | | 1 |
| 0 | 0 | 0 | 1 | | | - |
| 0 | 0 | 1 | 0 | | | - |
| 0 | 0 | 1 | 1 | | | - |
| 0 | 1 | 0 | 0 | | 1 | - |
| 0 | 1 | 0 | 1 | | 1 | - |
| 0 | 1 | 1 | 0 | | 1 | - |
| 0 | 1 | 1 | 1 | | 1 | - |
| 1 | 0 | 0 | 0 | | 1 | - |
| 1 | 0 | 0 | 1 | | 1 | - |
| 1 | 0 | 1 | 0 | | 1 | - |
| 1 | 0 | 1 | 1 | | 1 | - |
| 1 | 1 | 0 | 0 | | | - |
| 1 | 1 | 0 | 1 | 1 | | - |
| 1 | 1 | 1 | 0 | | 1 | - |
| 1 | 1 | 1 | 1 | 1 | 1 | 1 |

The size of the ROM required is 4 inputs and 3 outputs. So, the ROM size is $2^4 = 16 \times 3$. The four inputs specify 16 words of 3-bit each.

(*b*) The data in each location of the ROM is given by $F_1$, $F_2$, $F_3$ as in truth table.

## 5.2 PROGRAMMABLE LOGIC ARRAYS (PLAs)

The first type of user-programmable chip that could implement logic circuits was the Programmable Read-Only Memory (PROM), in which address lines can be used as logic circuit inputs and data lines as outputs. Figure 5.8 shows the basic configuration of PROM.

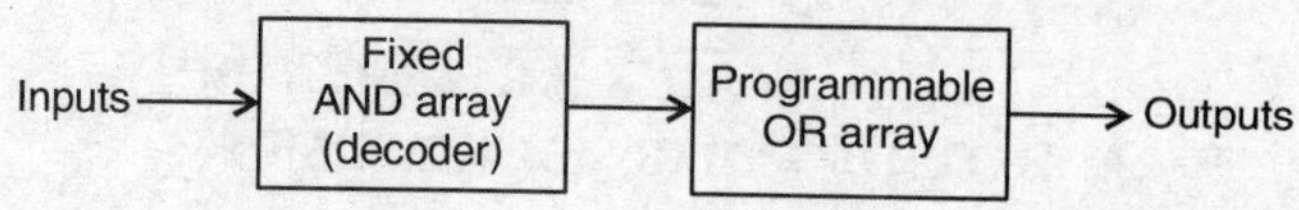


**Fig. 5.8** Basic configuration of programmable read-only memory (PROM)

Logic functions, however, rarely require more than a few product terms, and a PROM contains a full decoder for its address inputs. PROMs are thus an inefficient architecture for realizing logic circuits, and so are rarely used in practice for that purpose. The first device developed later specifically for implementing logic circuits was the Field-Programmable Logic Array (FPLA), or simply PLA for short. A PLA consists of two levels of logic gates: a programmable "wired" AND-plane followed by a programmable "wired" OR-plane.

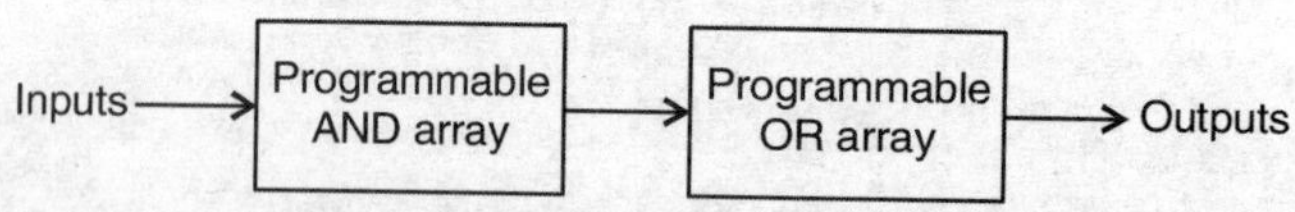


**Fig. 5.9** Basic configuration of programmable logic array (PLA)

A PLA is structured so that any of its inputs (or their complements) can be AND'ed together in the AND-plane; each AND-plane output can thus correspond to any product term of the inputs. Similarly, each OR plane output can be configured to produce the logical sum of any of the AND-plane outputs. With this structure, PLAs are well-suited for implementing logic functions in sum-of-products form. They are also quite versatile, since both the AND terms and OR terms can have many inputs (this feature is often referred to as *wide* AND and OR gates).

Programmable Logic Arrays (PLAs) have the same programmable OR array as a ROM, but also have a programmable AND array instead of the decoder as shown in Fig. 5.10. The programmable AND array can be used to produce arbitrary product terms, not just minterms. While the decoder produces all minterms of $k$ variables.

Since, the number of possible product terms m in PLA is much less than the number of possible minterms $2^k$, so some functions may not be realizable in PLA.

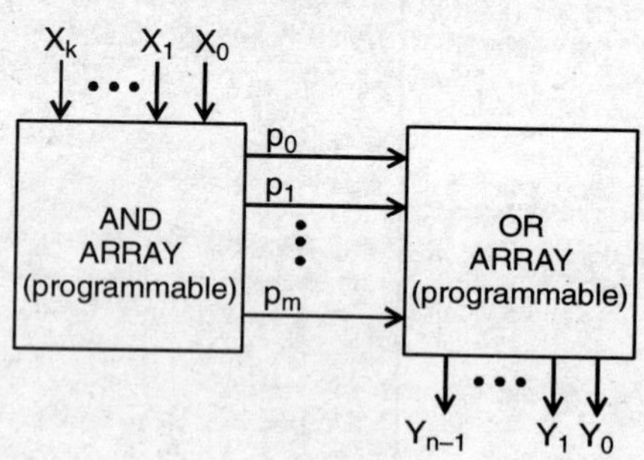


**Fig. 5.10**

The structure of a row of the programmable AND array is shown in Fig. 5.11 (*a*),

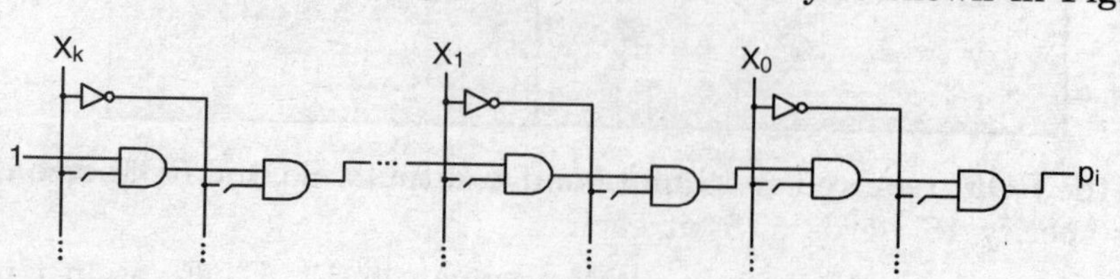


**Fig. 5.11** (*a*)

and of a column of the programmable OR array is shown in Fig. 5.11 (*b*).

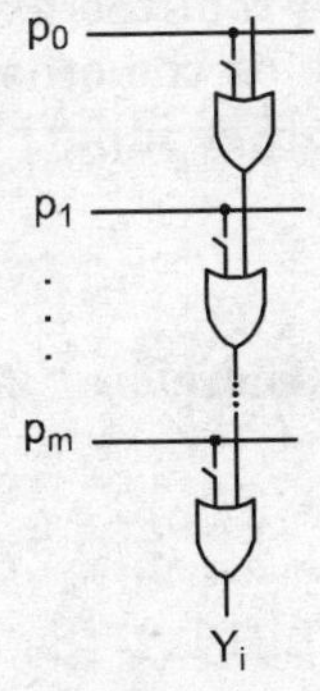


**Fig. 5.11** (*b*)

While the notation of a PLA is shown in Fig. 5.12.

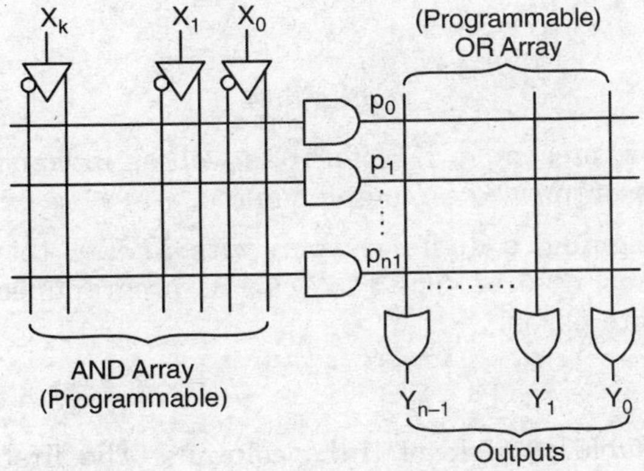


**Fig. 5.12**

## 5.2.1 Realizing Logical Functions with PLAs

During implementation (or programming) a dot (or cross) is placed at an intersection if the variable is to be included in the product term or to sum term. For example, a PLA with 3 inputs, 4 product terms and 2 outputs is shown in Fig. 5.13.

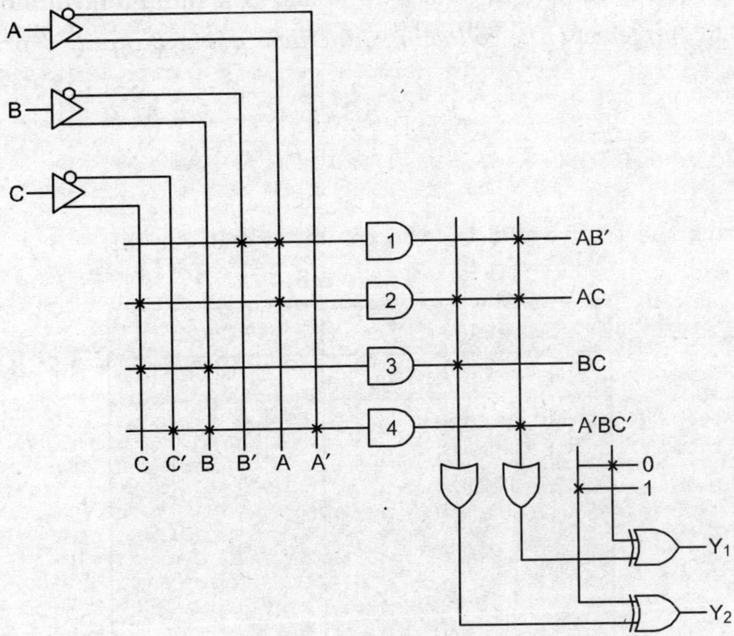


**Fig. 5.13**

From the exclusive OR operation, we know when one of the input is low the output is same as the other input and when one of the input is high the output is the complement of the other input. (Fig. 5.14).

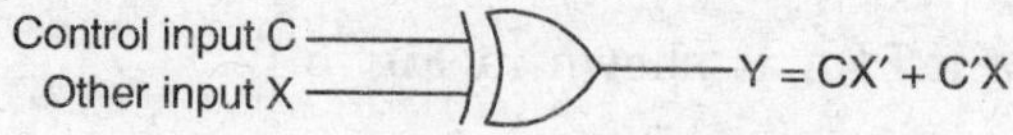


Therefore, if $C = 0, \quad Y = X$

$C = 1, \quad Y = X'$

**Fig. 5.14**

In PLA, the output is present in true form as well as in complement form. In Fig. 5.13, $Y_1$ is in true form while output $Y_2$ is complemented.

When realizing (designing) a digital system with a PLA, there is no need to show the internal connections as in Fig. 5.13. The PLA can be programmed with PLA program table which provides appropriate paths.

### *PLA Program Table*

A typical program table consists of three columns. The first column lists the product terms numerically. The second column specifies the required paths between inputs and AND gates. The third column specifies the paths between the AND gates and the OR gates. Under each output variable we write a T (for true) if the output is in true form and C (for complement) if the output is to be complement. For each product term, the inputs are marked as 1, 0 or – (dash). A variable in product term is marked as 1 if it appears in normal form, 0 if it is in complemented form and '–' shows that a variable is not present.

In PLA implementation of combinational circuits the total number of distinct product terms must be reduce by simplifying each function to a minimum number of terms.

**Example 5.5.** *Implement the following functions using 3-input, 3 product terms and 2 output PLA.*

$$F_1 = AB' + AC = \Sigma(4, 5. 7)$$

$$F_2 = AC + BC = \Sigma(3, 5, 7)$$

**Solution.**

**Step 1.** Derive the truth table for the combinational circuit.

**Table 5.6**

| *Inputs* | | | *Outputs* | |
|---|---|---|---|---|
| *A* | *B* | *C* | $F_2$ | $F_1$ |
| 0 | 0 | 0 | 0 | 0 |
| 0 | 0 | 1 | 0 | 0 |
| 0 | 1 | 0 | 0 | 0 |
| 0 | 1 | 1 | 1 | 0 |
| 1 | 0 | 0 | 0 | 1 |
| 1 | 0 | 1 | 1 | 1 |
| 1 | 1 | 0 | 0 | 0 |
| 1 | 1 | 1 | 1 | 1 |

**Step 2.** Simplify functions using K-map.

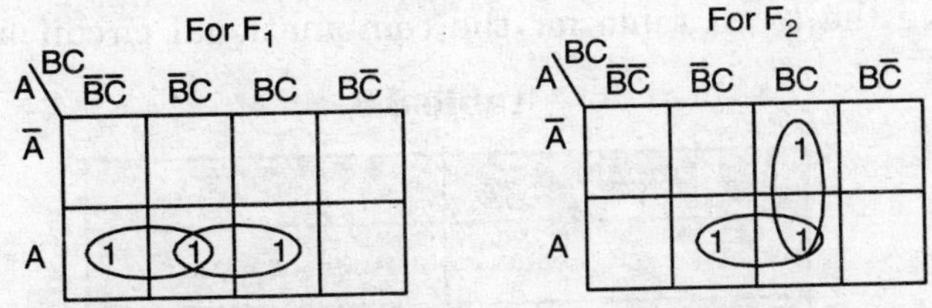


$F_1 = AB' + AC$ $\qquad$ $F_2 = AC + BC$

**Step 3.** Draw the PLA program table.

**Table 5.7**

| | *Product term* | *Inputs* | | | *Outputs* | | |
|---|---|---|---|---|---|---|---|
| | | *A* | *B* | *C* | $F_2$ | $F_1$ | |
| AB′ | 1 | 1 | 0 | - | - | 1 | |
| AC | 2 | 1 | - | 1 | 1 | 1 | |
| BC | 3 | - | 1 | 1 | 1 | - | |
| | | | | | T | T | T/C |

**Step 4.** Draw the logic diagram (Fig. 5.15)

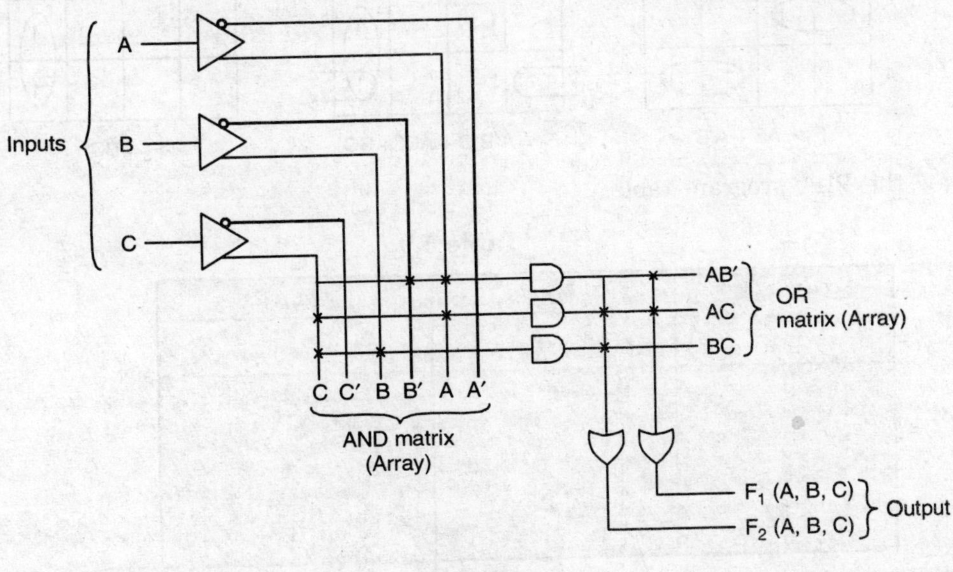


**Fig. 5.15**

For the implementation with PLA, the PLA program table is necessary and sufficient. Step 4 shows the logic diagram is only to show how PLA is implemented using AND array and OR array. Step 4 is optional.

**Example 5.6.** Implement the following function using PLA.

$$F_1(A, B, C) = \Sigma(0, 1, 6, 7)$$
$$F_2(A, B, C) = \Sigma(1, 2, 4, 6)$$

$$F_3(A, B, C) = \Sigma(2, 6)$$

**Solution.** Derive the truth table for the combinational circuit as shown in table 5.8.

**Table 5.8**

| *Inputs* | | | *Outputs* | | |
|---|---|---|---|---|---|
| *A* | *B* | *C* | $F_3$ | $F_2$ | $F_1$ |
| 0 | 0 | 0 | 0 | 0 | 1 |
| 0 | 0 | 1 | 0 | 1 | 1 |
| 0 | 1 | 0 | 1 | 1 | 0 |
| 0 | 1 | 1 | 0 | 0 | 0 |
| 1 | 0 | 0 | 0 | 1 | 0 |
| 1 | 0 | 1 | 0 | 0 | 0 |
| 1 | 1 | 0 | 1 | 1 | 1 |
| 1 | 1 | 1 | 0 | 0 | 1 |

Simplify functions using K-map

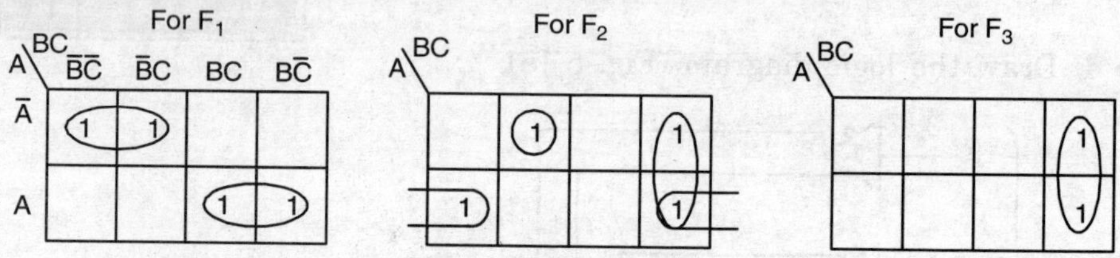


$F_1 = AB + A'B'$ $F_2 = A'B'C + AC' + BC'$ $F_3 = BC'$

Draw the PLA program table.

**Table 5.9**

| *Product term* | *Inputs* | | | *Outputs* | | | |
|---|---|---|---|---|---|---|---|
| | *A* | *B* | *C* | $F_3$ | $F_2$ | $F_1$ | |
| 1 | 0 | 0 | 1 | - | 1 | - | |
| 2 | 1 | - | 0 | - | 1 | - | |
| 3 | - | 1 | 0 | 1 | 1 | - | |
| 4 | 0 | 0 | - | - | - | 1 | |
| 5 | 1 | 1 | - | - | - | 1 | |
| | | | | T | T | T | T/C |

**Example 5.7.** Implement the following with PLA.

$$P1 = A' \bullet C'$$
$$P2 = A' \bullet C$$
$$P3 = A \bullet B'$$
$$P4 = A \bullet B \bullet C$$
$$X = P3 = A \bullet B'$$

$$Y = P2 + P4 = A' \bullet C + A \bullet B \bullet C$$

$$Z = P1 + P3 = A' \bullet C' + A \bullet B'$$

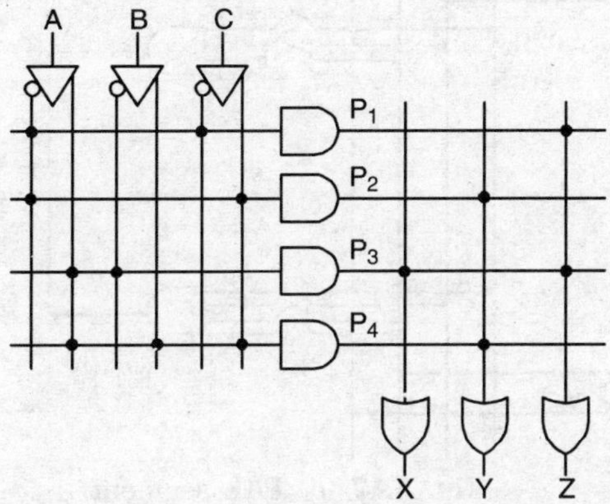


**Fig. 5.16**

**Note:** In this implementation, dot is placed at intersection but cross can be used for the same.

## 5.3 PROGRAMMABLE ARRAY LOGIC (PAL)

When PLAs were introduced in the early 1970s, by Phillips, their main drawbacks are that they are expensive to manufacture and offered poor speed-performance. Both disadvantages are due to the two levels of configurable logic, because programmable logic planes were difficult to manufacture and introduced significant propagation delays. To overcome these weaknesses, Programmable Array Logic (PAL) devices are developed. As Fig. 5.17 (*a*) illustrates, PALs feature only a single level of programmability, consisting of a programmable "wired" AND plane that feeds fixed OR-gates.

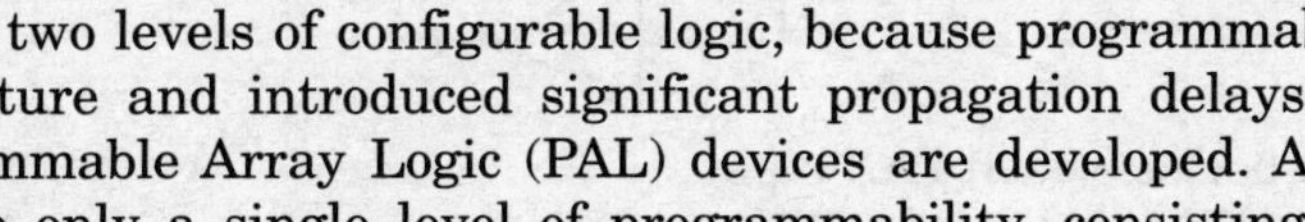


**Fig. 5.17** (*a*) Basic configuration of programmable array logic (PAL)

To compensate for lack of generality incurred because the OR Outputs plane is fixed, several variants of PALs are produced, with different numbers of inputs and outputs, and various sizes of OR-gates. PALs usually contain flip-flops connected to the OR-gate outputs so that sequential circuits can be realized. PAL devices are important, because when introduced they had a profound effect on digital hardware design, and also they are the basis for more sophisticated architectures. Variants of the basic PAL architecture are featured in several other products known by different acronyms. All small PLDs, including PLAs, PALs, and PAL-like devices are grouped into a single category called Simple PLDs (SPLDs), whose most important characteristics are low cost and very high pin-to-pin speed-performance.

While the ROM has a fixed AND array and a programmable OR array, the PAL has a programmable AND array and a fixed OR array. The main advantage of the PAL over the PLA and the ROM is that it is faster and easier to fabricate.

Figure 5.17 (*b*) represents a segment of an unprogrammed PAL.

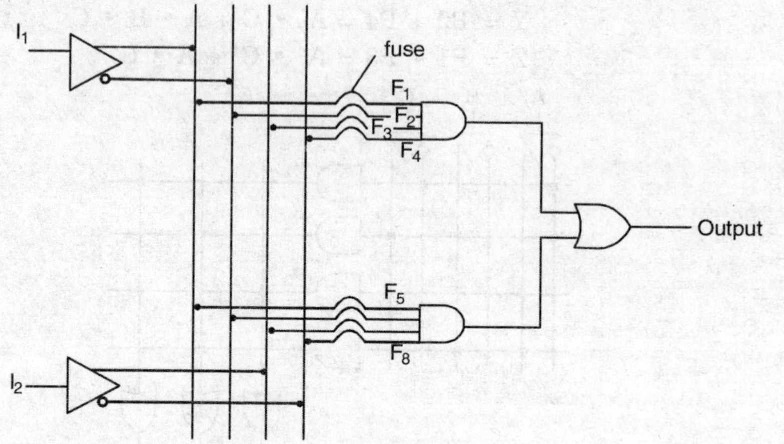


**Fig. 5.17** (*b*) PAL segment

The symbol

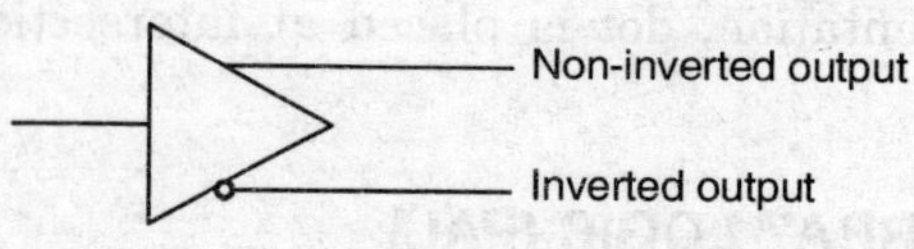


Represents an input buffer which is logically equivalent to

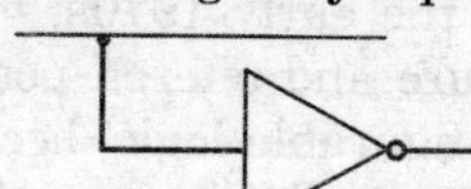

A buffer is used because each PAL input have to drive many AND gate inputs. When the PAL is programmed, the fusible links ($F_1$, $F_2$, ....., $F_8$) are selectively blown to leave the desired connection to the AND gate inputs. Connections to the AND gate inputs in a PAL are represented by X's as shown

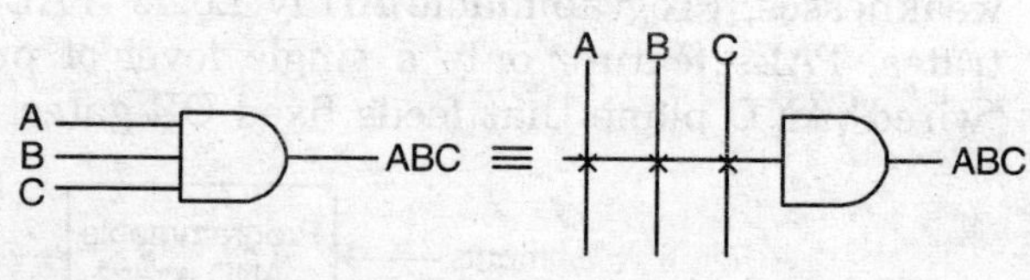


Figure 5.17 (*c*) shows the use of PAL segment of Fig. 5.17 (*b*) to realize the function $I_1I_2' + I_1'I_2$. The X's indicate that the $I_1$ and $I_2'$ lines are connected to the first AND gate, and the $I_1'$, and $I_2$ lines are connected to the other gate

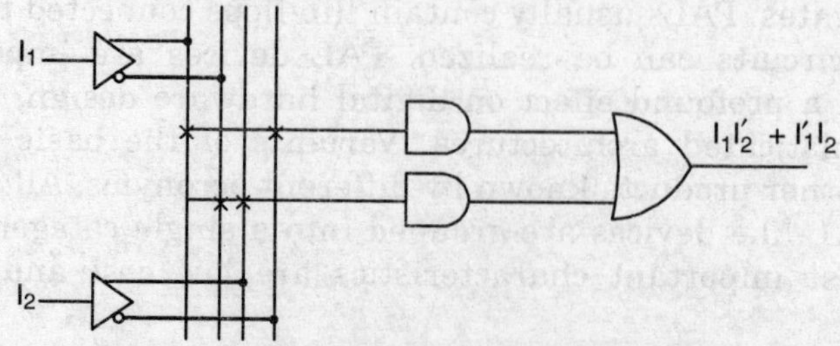


**Fig. 5.17** (*c*) Programmed PAL example

In early PALs, only seven product terms could be summed into an OR gate. Therefore, not all functions could be realized with these PALs. Also, the output was inverted in these early PALs so that what was really realized is

$(P1 + P2 + \ldots + P7)' = P1' \bullet P2' \bullet \ldots \bullet P7'$

Example of first-generation PAL is PAL 16L8 having following features.

- 10 input, 2 complemented outputs, 6 I/O pins
- Programmable (one AND term) 3-state outputs
- Seven product terms per output
- 20 pin chip
- 10 input (14 for 20V8)

A sum of products function with a small number of product terms may require a large number product terms when realized with a PAL.

For example: To implement the function $Z = A \bullet B \bullet C + D \bullet E \bullet F$

The inverted output of the function Z′ is given as

$$\begin{aligned} Z' &= (A \bullet B \bullet C)' \bullet (D \bullet E \bullet F)' = (A' + B' + C') \bullet (D' + E' + F') \\ &= A' \bullet D' + A' \bullet E' + A' \bullet F' + B' \bullet D' + B' \bullet E' + B' \bullet F' \\ &\quad + C' \bullet D' + C' \bullet E' + C' \bullet F' \\ &= p1 + p2 + p3 + p4 + p5 + p6 + p7 + p8 + p9 \end{aligned}$$

This has nine product terms and could not be realized in one pass with the early PALs.

The only way to realize this function in a PAL is to use two passes as shown in Fig. 5.18.

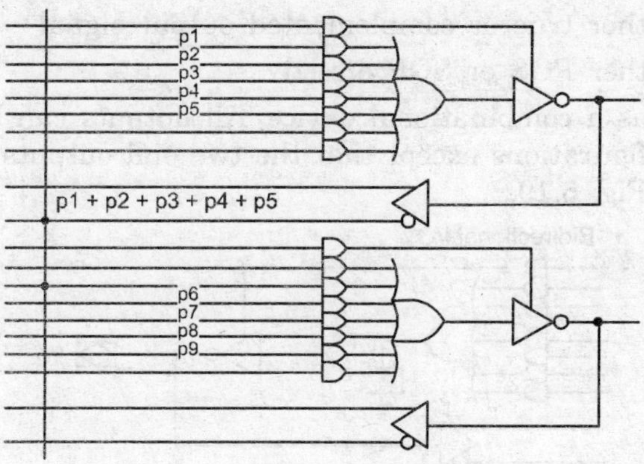


**Fig. 5.18**

### 5.3.1 Commercially Available SPLDs

For digital hardware designers for the past two decades, SPLDs are very important devices. SPLDs represent the highest speed-performance FPDs available, and are inexpensive. They are also straightforward and well understood.

Two of the most popular SPLDs are the PALs produced by Advanced Micro Devices (AMD) known as the 16R8 and 22V10. Both of these devices are industry standards and are widely second-sourced by various companies. The name "16R8" means that the PAL has a maximum of 16 inputs (there are 8 dedicated inputs and 8 input/outputs), and a maximum of 8 outputs. The "R" refers to the type of outputs provided by the PAL and means that each output is "registered" by a D flip-flop. Similarly, the "22V10" has a maximum of 22 inputs and 10 outputs. Here, the "V" means each output is "versatile" and can be configured in various ways, some configurations registered and some not.

Another widely used and second sourced SPLD is the Altera Classic EP610. This device is similar in complexity to PALs, but it offers more flexibility in the way that outputs are produced and has larger AND- and OR-planes. In the EP610, outputs can be registered and the flip-flops are configurable as any of D, T, JK, or SR.

In addition to the SPLDs mentioned above many other products are commercial available. All SPLDs share common characteristics, like some sort of logic planes (AND, OR, NOR, or NAND), but each specific product offers unique features that may be particularly suitable for some applications.

### 5.3.2 Generic Array Logic (GAL)

Generic Array Logic (GAL) is a programmable logic device that can be configured to emulate many earlier PLDs including those with internal flip-flops. GAL 16V8C and 20V8C are examples of Generic Array Logic. The only difference between the two is that the 16V8 is a 20-pin chip and the 20V8 is a 24-pin chip, which uses the extra pins for inputs. The characteristics of these devices are:

- 10 input (14 for 20V8)
- Programmable (one AND term) 3-state outputs
- Seven or eight product terms per output
- Programmable output polarity
  - Realize either true or complemented output signal
  - Realize either POS or SOP directly

When using GAL as a combinational device, All outputs can be programmed to one of the following three configurations except that the two end outputs have some minor limitations as illustrated by Fig. 5.19.

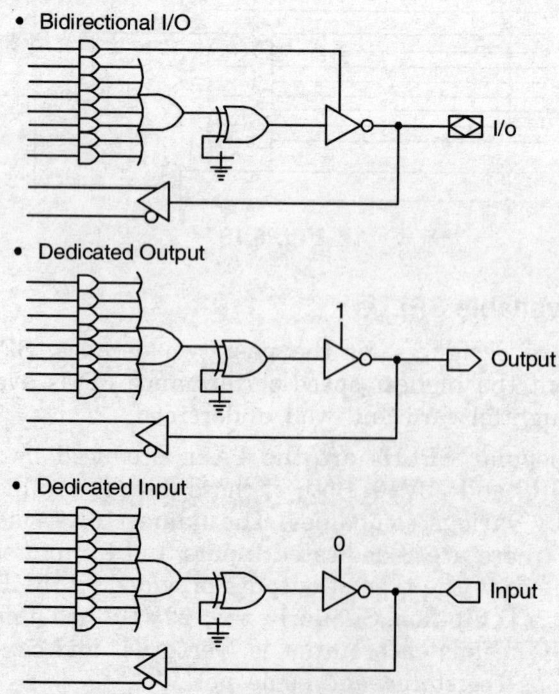


**Fig. 5.19**

For example, GAL 22V10C is a 24-pin chip having 12 input terminals and 10 input/output terminals. Among outputs, two of the outputs can have up to 8 product terms, two have 10, two have 12, two have 14 and two have 16, except the output buffer control.

The Combinational Configurations for GAL 22V10C is

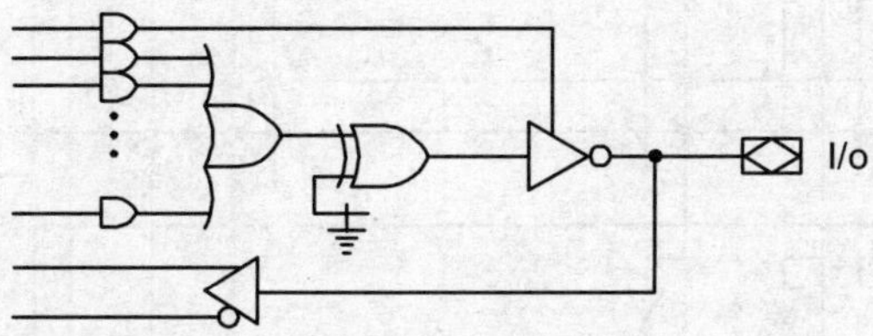


### 5.3.3 Applications of PLDs

PLDs are often used for address decoding, where they have several clear advantages over the 7400-series TTL parts that they replaced. First, of course, is that one chip requires less board area, power, and wiring than several do. Another advantage is that the design inside the chip is flexible, so a change in the logic doesn't require any rewiring of the board. Rather, the decoding logic can be altered by simply replacing that one PLD with another part that has been programmed with the new design.

## 5.4 COMPLEX PROGRAMMABLE LOGIC DEVICES (CPLDs)

As technology has advanced, it has become possible to produce devices with higher capacity than SPLDs (PALs). The difficulty with increasing capacity of a strict SPLD architecture is that the structure of the programmable logic-planes grows too quickly in size as the number of inputs is increased. It also significantly slows the chip down due to long rows of AND gates. The only feasible way to provide large capacity devices based on SPLD architectures is then to integrate multiple SPLDs onto a single chip, and are referred to as Complex PLDs (CPLDs) as shown in Fig. 5.20.

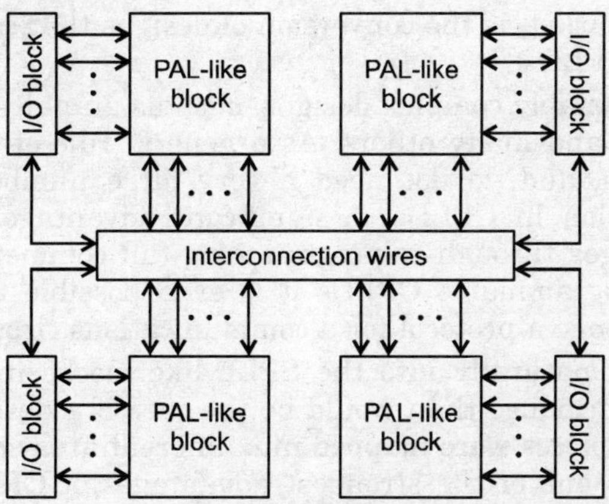


**Fig. 5.20** (*a*)

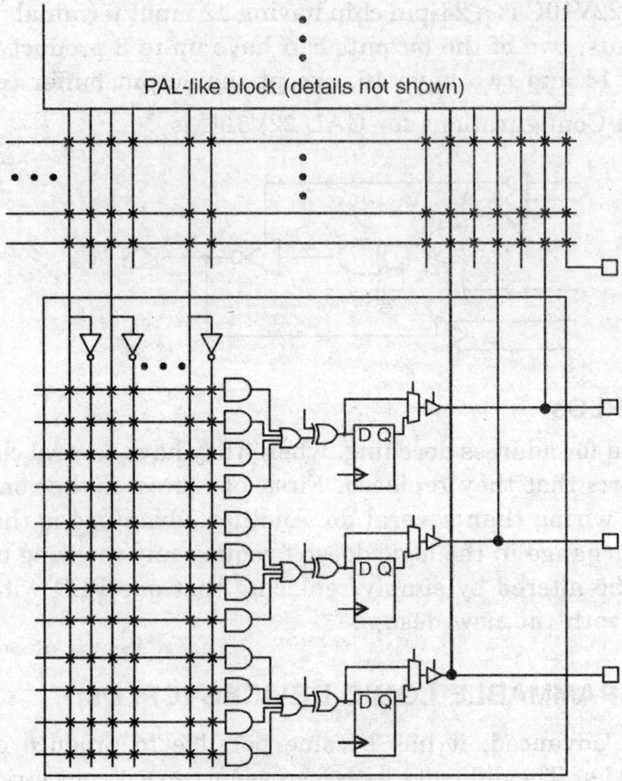


**Fig. 5.20** (*b*)

### 5.4.1 Applications of CPLDs

Because CPLDs offer high speeds and a range of capacities, they are useful for a very wide range of applications, from implementing random glue logic to prototyping small gate arrays. One of the most common uses in industry at this time, and a strong reason for the large growth of the CPLD market, is the conversion of designs that consist of multiple SPLDs into a smaller number of CPLDs.

CPLDs can realize reasonably complex designs, such as graphics controller, LAN controllers, UARTs, cache control, and many others. As a general rule-of-thumb, circuits that can exploit wide AND/OR gates, and do not need a very large number of flip-flops are good candidates for implementation in CPLDs. A significant advantage of CPLDs is that they provide simple design changes through re-programming (all commercial CPLD products are re-programmable). With programmable CPLDs it is even possible to re-configure hardware (an example might be to change a protocol for a communications circuit) without power-down.

Designs often partition naturally into the SPLD-like blocks in a CPLD. The result is more predictable speed-performance than would be the case if a design were split into many small pieces and then those pieces were mapped into different areas of the chip. Predictability of circuit implementation is one of the strongest advantages of CPLD architectures.

## 5.5 FIELD-PROGRAMMABLE GATE ARRAYS (FPGAs)

Field-Programmable Gate Arrays (FPGAs) are flexible, programmable devices with a broad range of capabilities. Their basic structure consists of an array of universal, programmable logic cells embedded in a configurable connection matrix. There are three key parts of FPGA structure: logic blocks, interconnect, and I/O blocks. The I/O blocks form a ring around the outer edge of the part. Each of these provides individually selectable input, output, or bi-directional access to one of the general-purpose I/O pins on the exterior of the FPGA package. Inside the ring of I/O blocks lies a rectangular array of logic blocks. And connecting logic blocks to logic blocks and I/O blocks to logic blocks is the programmable interconnect wiring.

In FPGAs, CPLD's PLDs are replaced with a much smaller *logic block*. The logic blocks in an FPGA are generally nothing more than a couple of logic gates or a look-up table and a flip-flop. The FPGAs use a more flexible and faster interconnection structure than the CPLDs. In the FPGAs, the logic blocks are embedded in a mesh or wires that have programmable interconnect points that can be used to connect two wires together or a wire to a logic block as shown in Fig. 5.21.

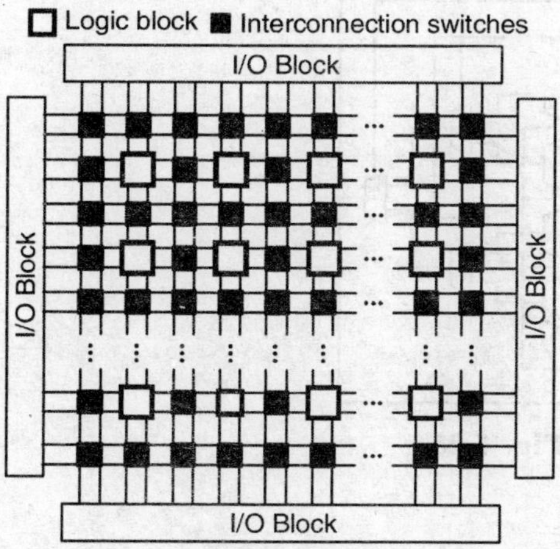


**Fig. 5.21**

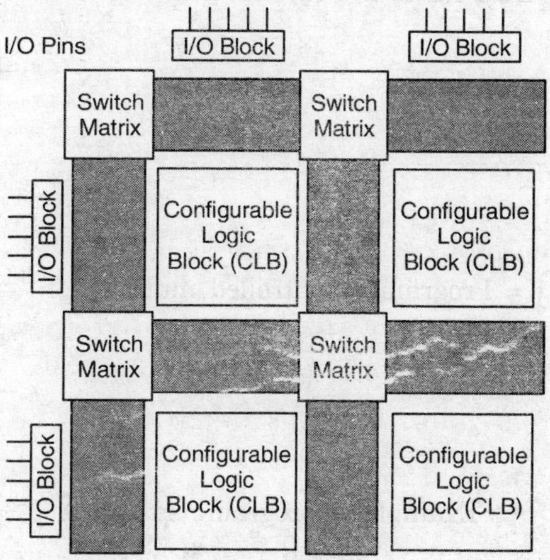


**Fig. 5.22**

There are several architectures for FPGAs available but the two popular architectures are that, used by Xilinx and Altera. The Xilinx chips utilize an "island-type" architecture, where logic functions are broken up into small islands of 4–6 term arbitrary functions, and connections between these islands are computed. Fig. 5.22 illustrates the basic structure of the Xilinx FPGA. Altera's architecture ties the chip inputs and outputs more closely to the logic blocks, as shown in Fig. 5.23. This architecture places the logic blocks around one central, highly connected routing array.

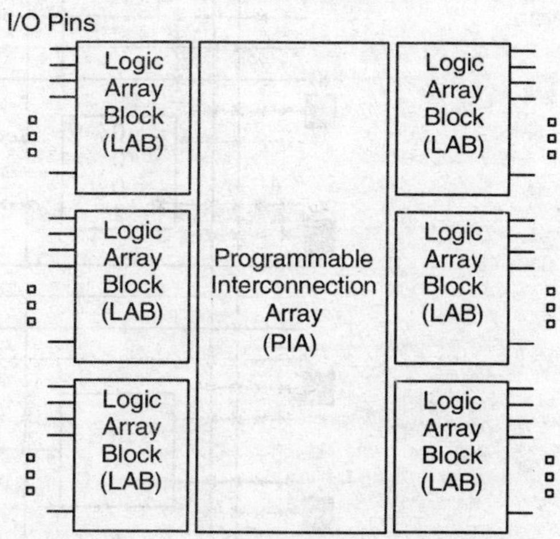


**Fig. 5.23**

The circuits used to implement combinational logic in logic blocks are called lookup tables (LUT). For example, the LUT in the Xilinx XC4000 uses three ROMs to realize the LUTs and generate the following classes of logical functions:

- Any two different functions of 4 variables each plus any other function of 3 variables.
- Any function of 5 variables. How?
- Any function of 4 variables, plus some (but not all) functions of 6 variables.
- Some (but not all) functions of up to 9 variables.

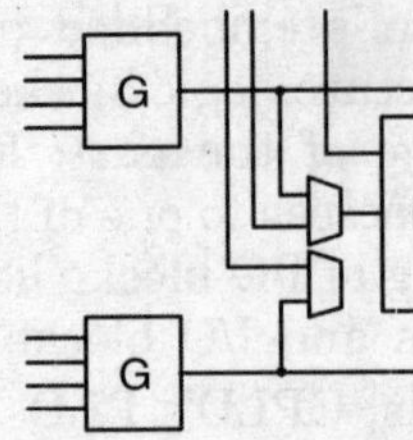


**Fig. 5.24**

The Fig. 5.24 shows the LUT's structure in Xilinx XC4000. The boxes G and H are ROMs with 16 1-bit words and H is a ROM with 8 1-bit words. While the structure of LUT's in Altera FPGAs are as shown in Fig. 5.25.

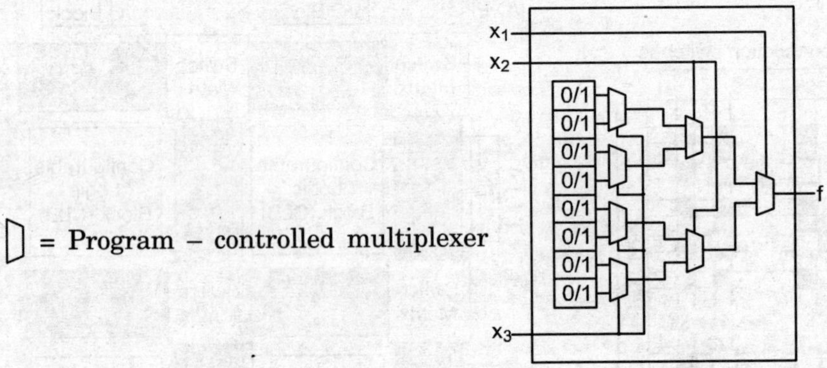


**Fig. 5.25**

- Example of programmed FPGA

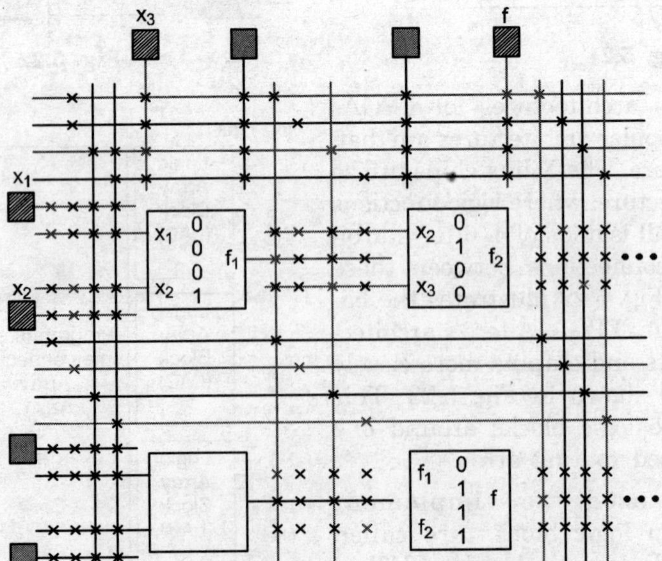

### 5.5.1 Applications of FPGAs

FPGAs have gained rapid acceptance and growth over the past decade because they can be applied to a very wide range of applications. A list of typical applications includes: random logic, integrating multiple SPLDs, device controllers, communication encoding and filtering, small to medium sized systems with SRAM blocks, and many more.

Other interesting applications of FPGAs are prototyping of designs later to be implemented in gate arrays, and also emulation of entire large hardware systems. The former of these applications might be possible using only a single large FPGA (which corresponds to a small Gate Array in terms of capacity), and the latter would involve many FPGAs connected by some sort of interconnect.

Another promising area for FPGA application, which is only beginning to be developed, is the usage of FPGAs as custom computing machines. This involves using the programmable parts to "execute" software, rather than compiling the software for execution on a regular CPU.

## 5.6 USER-PROGRAMMABLE SWITCH TECHNOLOGIES

The first type of user-programmable switch developed was the *fuse* used in PLAs. Although fuses are still used in some smaller devices, but for higher density devices, where CMOS dominates the IC industry, different approaches to implementing programmable switches have been developed. For CPLDs the main switch technologies (in commercial products) are floating gate transistors like those used in EPROM and EEPROM, and for FPGAs they are SRAM and antifuse. Each of these are briefly discussed below.

An EEPROM or EPROM transistor is used as a programmable switch for CPLDs (and also for many SPLDs) by placing the transistor between two wires in a way that facilitates implementation of wired-AND functions. This is illustrated in Fig. 5.18, which shows EPROM transistors as they might be connected in an AND-plane of a CPLD. An input to the AND-plane can drive a product wire to logic level '0' through an EPROM transistor, if that input is part of the corresponding product term. For inputs that are not involved for a product term, the appropriate EPROM transistors are programmed to be permanently turned off. A diagram for an EEPROM based device would look similar.

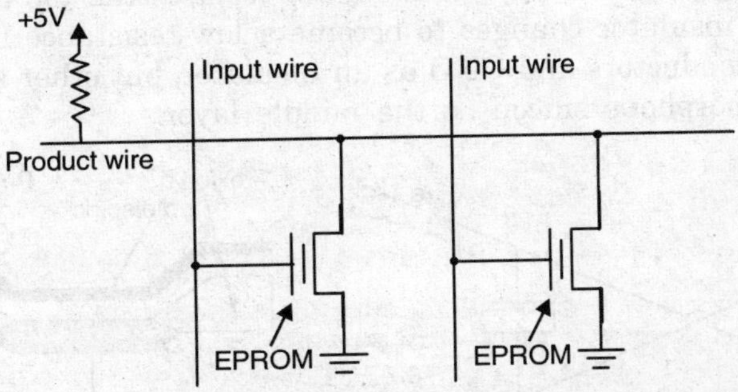


**Fig. 5.26** EPROM programmable switches

Although there is no technical reason why EPROM or EEPROM could not be applied to FPGAs, current commercial FPGA products are based either on SRAM or antifuse technologies, as discussed below.

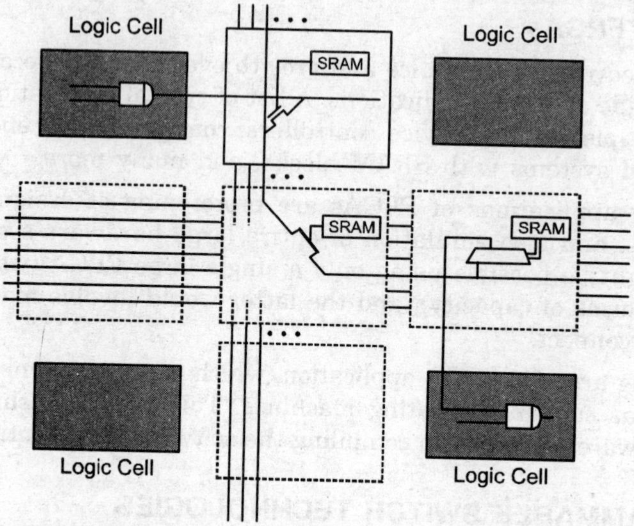


**Fig. 5.27** SRAM-controlled programmable switches

An example of usage of SRAM-controlled switches is illustrated in Fig. 5.27, showing two applications of SRAM cells: for controlling the gate nodes of pass-transistor switches and to control the select lines of multiplexers that drive logic block inputs.

The figures gives an example of the connection of one logic block (represented by the AND-gate in the upper left corner) to another through two pass-transistor switches, and then a multiplexer, all controlled by SRAM cells. Whether an FPGA uses pass-transistors or multiplexers or both depends on the particular product.

The other type of programmable switch used in FPGAs is the antifuse. Antifuses are originally open-circuits and take on low resistance only when programmed. Antifuses are suitable for FPGAs, because, they can be built using modified CMOS technology. As an example, Actel's antifuse structure, known as PLICE, is depicted in Fig. 5.28. The Fig. 5.28 shows that an antifuse is positioned between two interconnect wires and physically consists of three sandwiched layers: the top and bottom layers are conductors, and the middle layer is an insulator. When unprogrammed, the insulator isolates the top and bottom layers, but when programmed the insulator changes to become a low-resistance link. PLICE uses Poly-Si and n+ diffusion as conductors and ONO as an insulator, but other antifuses rely on metal for conductors, with amorphous silicon as the middle layer.

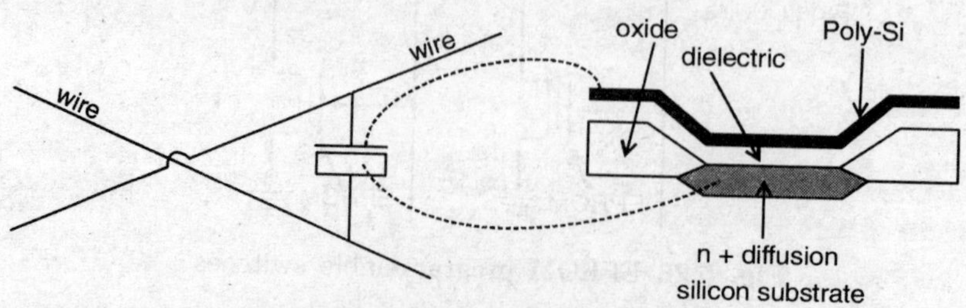


**Fig. 5.28** Actel antifuse structure

Table lists the most important characteristics of the programming technologies discussed in this section. The left-most column of the table indicates whether the programmable switches are one-time programmable (OTP), or can be re-programmed (RP). The next column lists whether the switches are volatile, and the last column names the underlying transistor technology.

**Table 5.10 Summary of Programming Technologies**

| *Name* | *Re-programmable* | *Volatile* | *Technology* |
|---|---|---|---|
| Fuse | no | no | Bipolar |
| EPROM | Yes (out of circuit) | no | UVCMOS |
| EEPROM | Yes (in circuit) | no | EECMOS |
| SRAM | Yes (in circuit) | yes | CMOS |
| Antifuse | no | no | CMOS+ |

## 5.7 EXERCISE

**1.** Realize the following functions using PLA

$$f_1\,(A, B, C) = \Sigma\,(0, 2, 4, 5)$$
$$f_2\,(A, B, C) = \Sigma\,(1, 5, 6, 7)$$

**2.** Realize the following functions using PLA

$$f_1 = \Sigma\,(1, 2, 3, 5)$$
$$f_2 = \Sigma\,(2, 5, 6, 7)$$
$$f_3 = \Sigma\,(0, 4, 6)$$

**3.** What is a PLA? Describe its uses.

**4.** What is ROM? Describe using block diagram. What size ROM would it take to implement a binary multiplier that multiplies two 4 bit-numbers?

**5.** Implement the combinational circuit specified by the truth table given

| *Inputs* | | *Outputs* | |
|---|---|---|---|
| $A_1$ | $A_0$ | $F_1$ | $F_2$ |
| 0 | 0 | 0 | 1 |
| 0 | 1 | 1 | 0 |
| 1 | 0 | 1 | 1 |
| 1 | 1 | 1 | 0 |

**6.** Derive the PLA program table for a combinational circuit that squares a 3-bit number. Minimize the number of product terms.

**7.** Implement the problem 6 with the ROM.

**8.** List the PLA program table for the BCD-to-excess-3 code converter.

**9.** Write short notes on user programmable switch technologies.

**10.** Write short notes on following:

(*i*) ROM (*ii*) PLA
(*iii*) PAL (*iv*) GAL
(*v*) CPLD (*vi*) FPGA

6

CHAPTER

# MEMORY

## 6.0 INTRODUCTION

Memories are most essential part of computer and microprocessor systems. They are used to store data and programs for the computer systems. In many general-purpose applications, they are also used to store the needed control information for the applications. There are various types of memory devices to accommodate various needs of data storage.

To be used with computer systems mainly we have two types of memories, semiconductor and magnetic memory. The semiconductor devices are fast storage devices and are connected directly to the CPU. For this reason, they are many a times called *main memory* or *primary memory*. Since, their storage capacity is relatively small they are generally used for temporary storage. Some of them are also used for permanent storage, as we will see later. The magnetic memories are used for very large data storage for long time, and are called *mass storage devices*. Since, they are not connected directly to the CPU they are generally called *secondary memory*.

In the computer systems very first memory elements were magnetic and were referred as core memory. These were very bulky and needed large PCBs. In contrast semiconductor memory is compact and fast. With the latest advances in VLSI the high-density reliable semiconductor memory devices are available at cheaper costs. Such devices internally use BJTs and MOS devices. Both read/write and read only memories are available with semiconductor technology and influenced the computational world greatly.

The advent of programmable read only memories (PROMs) made programmable logic devices (PLDs) to appear. A read only memory (ROM) consist of an array of AND and OR gates which are fixed. A PROM is one in which these arrays can be programmed but only once. The re-programmable PROMs are also available which greatly enhanced the utilization of these memory devices. The flexibility of programming the AND-OR array provided many complex systems to appear programmable logic array (PLA) and complex PLDs (CPLDs) are among them. Consequently, this made possible the appearance of field programmable graphic array (FPGA) and application specific integrated circuits (ASICs).

PLDs, CPLDs, PROMs, FPGAs etc., have been presented earlier. In this chapter, we will study the semiconductor memory devices extensively.

## 6.1 MEMORY BASICS

The ability to remember is the most important characteristics of digital circuits. The circuits or systems designed to facilitate storage of digital information are called *memory*.

In its simplest form a F/F is a basic memory device that can be used to store 1-bit of information. Any type of memory can be supposed to be composed of a no. of F/F. The general information that is stored in the memory is called as *Data*. The F/F or circuit arrangement that holds a 1-bit information is conveniently called a *storage cell* or simply memory cell. The total number of bits (or storage cells) that a memory device can store is referred to as its *storage capacity*. *e.g.*, a device that can store 1024 bits is said to have a storage capacity of 1024 bits. In memory data is always stored as a group of bits. In fact a single memory cell is rarely accessed, instead they are accessed in a group of fixed size. The number of bits in a group (of data) is called as the *Word Length* and each group is called as *Word*. *e.g.*, in a memory if there are 10 datas each of which are a group of 4-bits, then memory is said to have ability to store 10 words of word length 4-bits. What about storage capacity of this memory device? It is simply 10 words × 4-bits (word length) = 40-bits. So,

$$\text{Storage Capacity (in bits)} = \text{No. of Words} \times \text{Word Length} \quad ...(1)$$

The eqn. 1 is the basic relation to determine storage capacity of a memory device. Although word length can be any no. of bits (even 1-bit), nowadays all have settled down to the basic memory word length as byte.

In a memory device, there are several storage cells collected together to form a memory of larger capacity. In order to access them unambiguously each of the storage cell (or group of cell) is associated with a unique name, called *address* of the cell. So each cell may be called an address location or *memory location*, a place where data resides. In an analogy, let us consider a residential colony where each house is a memory cell, people living in it are data stored, and house numbers are address of memory cells.

Any memory device may permit two types of operations to be performed on it, the read and the write. A *Read operation*, also called *sensing*, means detecting the status (*i.e.*, information) of memory cell (whether it is 1 or 0) and the *write operation* means setting the status of memory cell either to 0 or to 1 according to the given data.

## 6.2 MEMORY CHARACTERISTICS

All kind of memory devices (*i.e.*, semiconductor, magnetic, and optical memory), used to build the memory system have some functional characteristics in common. One or more of these characteristics may be used to describe the performance of the memory devices. Following are the important functional characteristics that must be considered for any description of memory:

- ***Storage Capacity***: It is defined as the total number of bits (or words) that a memory device can store. In general storage capacity is specified in Kilobytes (KB), Megabytes (MB), or Gigabytes (GB). Kilobit is represented as Kb. In binary the kilo means 1024 (not $10^3$) and Mega means 1024 K (not $10^6$). If storage capacity of device is 1KB it means it has 1024 storage locations and at each location a word of length 1 byte (*i.e.*, 8-bits) can be stored. So the total capacity in bits would be 1024×8=8192 bits or 8 Kb.
- ***Cost***: The cost of the memory can be defined as the cost per bit. It is expected that the cost/bit should be as low as possible. If S is the storage capacity, C is the total cost of memory then the cost per bit Cp/b can be defined as

  Cp/b = [total cost (C)/Storage capacity (S)]

- ***Memory Access Time*:** The performance of a memory device is primarily determined by the rate at which the information can be read or write into the memory.

  The average time required to read a fixed amount of information from the selected memory location is termed as *Read Access Time* or *Access Time* and is denoted as '$t_A$'. In precise words, it is average time delay after memory address is issued till the data appears at output. The access time should be kept as low as possible. Similarly, the average time required to store a fixed amount of information at the selected memory location is termed as *Write Access Time*.

  *Read Access Time > Write Access Time*

  The average rate at which memory can be accessed is defined as the *Access Rate* '$b_A$' of a memory and is measured in words/sec.

  Access Rate ($b_A$) = $1/\ t_A$

- ***Memory Accessing Modes*:** It is defined as the way or sequence in which the information is accessed in the memory. The two types of access modes are

  - Random Access Mode
  - Serial Access Mode

  If the memory cells can be accessed in any order, then the access time is independent of the position of cell. This type of access mode is referred as random access mode, and the memories having such access mode are called *Random Access Memory*. In such memories any storage cell (or location) can be reached in a fixed amount of time and each storage cell can be accessed independently of the positions of other cells. Obviously this type of memories are faster. Semiconductor memories are of this type.

  If the memory cells can be accessed one after another or only in certain predetermined sequences, the access time is dependent of position of cell. Thus, the access time will be different for different cell locations. This is called serial access mode and the memories having such access mode are called *Serial Access Memory*. Magnetic memories are of this type.

- ***Memory Cycle Time & Bandwidth*:** The minimum time that must elapse between the initiation of two consecutive memory accesses is defined as the *Memory Cycle Time* $t_C$. The cycle time $t_C$ can be greater than the access time $t_A$. This is because after completion of one memory access some memory devices need a small amount of time, $t_{DELAY}$ to make them ready for next access. In general

  $t_C = t_A + t_{DELAY}$ ($t_{DELAY}$ is Additional delay due to the physical characteristics of memory)

  Note that $t_{DELAY}$ may not be resent in all type of memories.

  Maximum amount of information that can be transferred to or from memory every second is referred to as the maximum *Data Transfer Rate* in words/sec or the *Bandwidth* '$b_C$', defined as

  Bandwidth ($b_C$) = $1/t_C$

- ***Non Destructive Read Out (NDRO)*:** It is required that the read process should create a copy (*i.e.*, sense) of the data stored and must not disturb the data. Such a reading is called *Non Destructive Read Out* (NDRO) and is expected from all kind of memory.

In some memories, the reading may destroy the data stored at a location. Such a reading is called *Destructive Read Out* (DRO). In such cases, the read operation must be followed by a write operation to restore the original state of memory. Obviously such memories would be slower ones.

- ***Permanence of Storage***: It is concerned with how long a stored information can be retained when
  - (*a*) *Power is Switched off*: If the stored information does not vanish with power off, the memory is referred as *NON VOLATILE* memory. But if the stored information vanishes completely at power off the memory is called as *VOLATILE* memory.
  - (*b*) *Power is NOT Switched off*: If the data can be retained indefinitely the memory is called as *STATIC* memory. If it can be retained for some definite small amount of time, the memory is called as *DYNAMIC* memory. In the later case, the data must be rewritten periodically, this is called refreshing.
- ***Alterability***: Alterability is concerned to the capability of memory devices with which the stored data can be changed or updated when they are in use (*i.e.*, online). Memories, which can be altered online, are referred as *Read-Write Memories*. Memories, which can not be altered online (if at all they can be altered off line) are called erasable read only memory devices. However, some memory devices cannot be altered even when they are off line and are called nonerasable read only memory devices.

## 6.3 MASS STORAGE DEVICES

The devices used to store high volumes of data are referred as mass storage devices. The magnetic memories and optical memories (CD-ROMs) are such memory devices. The magnetic memories are used for very large data storage for long time, but due to their lower speed they are not connected directly to the CPU. Due to this they are generally called *secondary memory* or *backup storage device*. Optical memories (CD-ROMs) are another type of mass storage device. The optical disks are popular due to large storage capacity, transportability and reliability.

### 6.3.1 Magnetic Memory

In magnetic memory devices some sort of magnetic coating (usually ferric oxide) runs throughout the base. On this coating direction of magnetic flux or direction of magnetization can be used to store 1 or 0. These devices are called *Serial Access Memory* (SAM) devices, because, we cannot reach the data directly and to reach a data stored we must go one after another. For example, consider an audio tape and if you want to reach song number 3 you must traverse through song numbers 01 and 2.

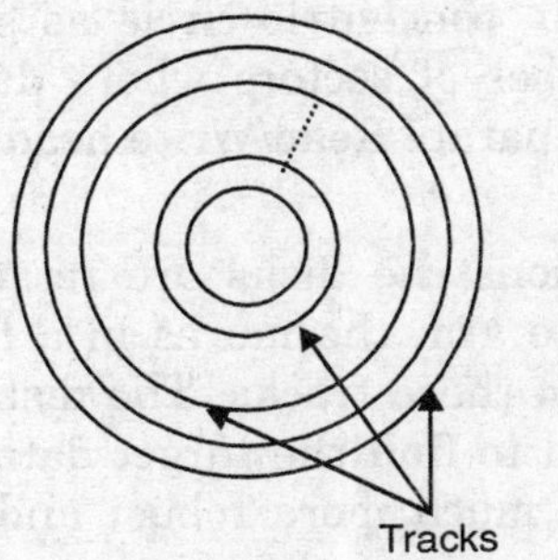


**Fig. 6.1** Organization of tracks

Hard disk and floppy disk are common type of magnetic memories used in computers. The storage media of magnetic disks are made up of aluminum or plastic base with a thin coating magnetic on its surface where the datas are actually stored.

In a ***Floppy Disk***, as shown in Fig. 6.1, the whole media is divided into a number of concentric circles, called track. Each track is further divided into a number of sectors. In these sectors bytes of data block are stored. To reach to a stored data first a particularly track is selected, and then particular sector is reached on this track, of course starting from the very first sector on this track. To reach to required sector an external rotating mechanism is employed, thus time delay to reach particular sector is called *rotational delay* or *latency time*. The time delay to select a particular track is called *seek time*. Nowadays the 3.5-inch floppy disk of storage capacity 1.44-MB is popular. It contains a total of 40 tracks where innermost track is numbered as Track '0' and outermost track is numbered Track '39'. For each of the data access search starts from 1st sector of Track '0'. The main advantage of using floppy disk is portability, but its use is restricted by its small storage capacity.

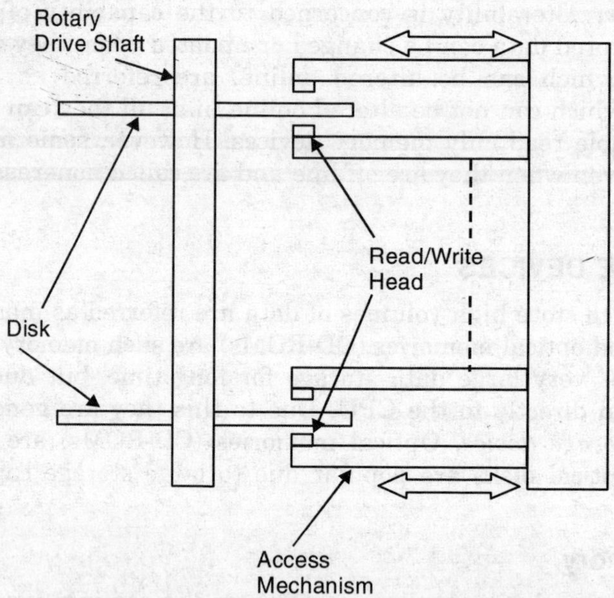


**Fig. 6.2** Structure of HARD DISKS

A ***Hard Disk*** can be supposed to have collection of such circular disk surfaces kept in a cylinder on a common shaft, called spindle for rotation. A simple organization of hard disk storage unit is shown in Fig. 6.2. The spindle rotates the disk surfaces at higher speeds, making data access faster than the floppy disks. On each disk surface, there are several hundreds of tracks arranged in concentric circle as shown in Fig. 6.1. Each of the tracks is further divided into a number of sectors where data actually resides. Each of the disk surfaces is provided with the separate Read/Write head that may be connected to form a Read/write arm.

During the access operations the disks are rotated continuously by the spindle, at a constant speed. The Read/Write arm the moves in a fixed linear path to select a particular set of tracks and the sectors on these tracks. The disk monitoring system determines which disk surface has to be accessed to find the target data. In comparison with floppy disks the construction of hard disks are much more robust and reliable but they are not portable.

In both the magnetic disks, the digital information can be *stored* on disk surface by applying a current pulse to magnetization coil present in Read/Write head. This causes a change in magnetization in the area under the read/write head. The direction of magnetization will be parallel to the direction of applied field. To *read* the magnetically stored information on the disk the Read/Write head has to sense the state of magnetization resulting from the area under the head. Movement of magnetic disk causes change in magnetic field, which induces a voltage in the coil of head. The polarity of induced voltage is monitored to obtain the magnetization state, which in turns gives the stored binary bit.

The principal disadvantage of magnetic disk memory is relatively slower slow speed that is attributed to slow rotational mechanism, seek and latency time and the fact that data transfer through such devices are serial. Also presence of mechanically moving parts makes magnetic memory unreliable.

But their advantage lies in two great facts that it offers very large-scale data storage for long time at very low cost per bit. There are other kind of magnetic memory devices also, namely ferrite core memory, magnetic tape memory, magnetic bubble memories etc.

### 6.3.2 Optical Memory

Optical memory usually takes the form of optical disks which resembles magnetic disks in that they store binary information in concentric tracks on a mechanically rotated disks. The read and write operations are done with the help of Lasers, capable of producing a light spot of the order of 1 micron.

Optical discs are available in many formats: CD-ROM (compact disk-read only memory), CD-R (compact disk-recordable), and CD-RW (compact disk-rewritable). Newer high capacity version of optical disks is DVDs, the Digital Versatile Disk. Similar to the CDs, the DVDs also have different formats as DVD-ROM, DVD-R, and DVD-RW. Most of the CDs can store upto 650 MB whereas the simple single layered DVD can store 4.7 GB of data.

The CD-ROM is manufactured using carefully prepared glass master. The master is pressed into injection molded polycarbonate plastic forming the CD-ROM. The resulting CD-ROM contains several small pits and lands (no pits) on the various tracks that can be processed optically. When a computer system want to read the disk, a Laser beam is aimed on the disk from the bottom and the reflection from the pits and lands are interpreted by the photo detector as logic 0s and 1s.

For the purpose of permanent storage (archival storage) the CD-Rs are very popular, and many a times known as WORM (*write once read many*) storage devices. The information can be recorded on CD-R (commonly known as CD burning) by using CD-writers. During the burning process, a laser heats gold reflective layer, and a dye layer in the CD-R causing it to have a dull appearance. When read by the CD-R drive the dark burnt areas (like pits) reflect less light. The CD-R reader interprets the shiny areas (lands) and the dull areas (burned) as logic 0s and 1s.

The CD-ROM and DVD-ROM both are manufactured by using the same technology and read data from a spiral track of pits and lands. However, the DVD-ROM has a greater storage capacity. It is because the pits and lands on the DVD-ROM are much smaller and more closely packed, thus allowing more information per track. The tracks also are closely spaced allowing more tracks per disk. The DVD-ROMs can store 4.7 GB (single sided layer), 9.4 GB (double sided layer), or 17 GB (double sided double layered), whereas the CD-ROMs can store only upto 650 MB.

The CDs are associated with all kind archival storage and have no special standards dictated for the storage of specific type of data on the media. However, the DVDs are most commonly associated with the video productions. DVD-video standards are used when disk holds only audio/video (such as movies). The DVD-ROM standards are used when the DVDs are used for data storage as with a computer system.

The *data transfer rate* of a CD-ROM drive is indicated as 1x, 2x, 4x, 16x, 32x etc. A CD-ROM drive with a designation of 1x would have a max data transfer rate of 150 Kbytes/sec. Therefore a 4x drive would have a data transfer speed of 150 Kbytes/sec × 4 = 600 Kbytes/sec. These data transfer rates are theoretical and the actual data transfer rates are usually lesser. The DVD-ROMs can provide data transfer rates of 1.38 Mbytes/sec, which is approximately same as the speed of 9x CD-ROM.

The advantages of optical disks are huge amount of data storage, low cost, easily transferable, a few mechanical parts results in reliability, and high speed. The main disadvantage could be the complexity of Read/Write head.

Although lot more pages can be shed to explain the architecture and characteristics of magnetic and optical memories, but a detailed discussion is beyond the scope of this text. However, interested readers can refer to *"Hayes, J.P.: Computer Architecture"*. A glance over magnetic and optical memory was presented to maintain the completeness of the topic. The semiconductor memory is the main consideration of this text so until and unless specified memory must be read as semiconductor memory throughout this text.

## 6.4 SEMICONDUCTOR MEMORY

Numerous developments in semiconductor technology has emerged into large numbers of LSI and MSI memory devices, called memory *chips*. Besides being faster and compatible with CPU they are economical also. A semiconductor memory is organized as a rectangular array (preferably square array) of storage cells that are integrated on a silicon wafer and are available in DIP packages. Due to this organization any memory cell can be accessed randomly, thus all the semiconductor memories are called *Random Access Memory* (RAM). The basic memory cell may be a flip-flop, or a charge storing element like capacitor that is said to hold logic 1 when charged and logic 0 when discharged. The type of transistors *e.g.*, bipolar, or MOS, or CMOS, used to form a memory cell dictates the storage capacity and speed of a memory chip.

### 6.4.1 Basic Memory Unit

A simple block diagram of a memory unit can be drawn as shown in Fig. 6.3. It contains data bus, address bus and control signals. A *bus* is a group of parallel conductors whose job is to carry binary information. Each of the conductors carries 1-bit information. The number of bits that a memory data bus carries simultaneously is called *memory bus width*. Usually, but not necessarily, the memory word length and memory bus widths are same.

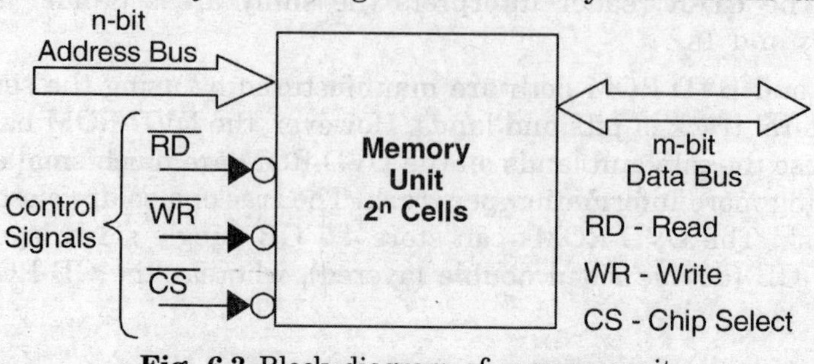


**Fig. 6.3** Block diagram of memory unit

The m-bit data bus is used to transfer data to and from the memory. The n-bit address bus carries the address of memory locations. An n-bit address bus can access upto $2^n$ storage cells *i.e.*, storage capacity is $2^n$ bits as each cell can store 1-bit. The Read (RD) and Write (WR) signals specify the operation to be performed. As shown the two signals are active low *i.e.* they are activated when logic '0'. At any time either of the two signals can be activated. In some memory chips read and write controls are available at one signal line. Chip select signal (CS) (sometimes labeled as enable EN also) is used to enable/disable the chip in multiple memory system. It is also a logic low signal. There may be multiple enable signals in a single chip that must be activated simultaneously to enable the chip.

### 6.4.2 Basic Memory Organization

Basic organization of semiconductor memory is shown in Fig. 6.4(*a*). It consists of a storage cell array, Read/Write control circuit along with control signals, an address decoder feeded by a register called memory address register, and a buffer register through which data transfer is carried out. In a semiconductor memory storage cells are organized as a rectangular array. The address bus is connected to internal address decoder through the address register. The RD and WR control line specifies the type of access: If $\overline{RD} = 0$ and $\overline{WR} = 1$ then read operation.

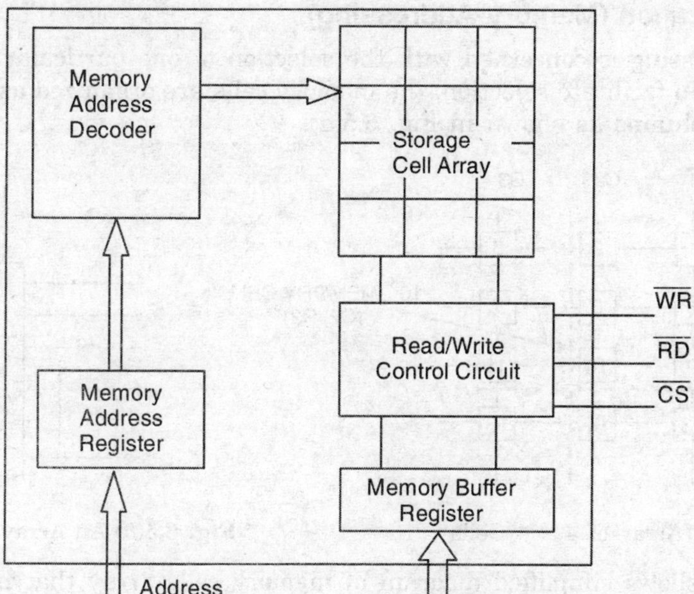


**Fig. 6.4**(*a*) Basic memory organization

If $\overline{RD} = 1$ and $\overline{WR} = 0$ then write operation. To access memory, address of the required cell is issued to the memory address register through the address bus. The address decoder selects the particular location in memory array. If read operation is requested then the content of selected location is copied to the memory buffer register which transfer it to the data bus. If write operation is requested then content of data bus is brought to buffer register and then transferred to the selected memory location. Memory buffer register contains bilateral three state buffers, one for each bit of data bus. By combining two three state buffers a

1-bit bi-directional input output line is formed. This is shown in Fig. 6.4(*b*). The enable or disable signals for the bilateral buffers can be generated through the realization shown in Fig. 6.4(c). These signals are given to all the bilateral buffers of buffer register. Note that if both RD and WR are activated, or CS inactivated, arrangement in Fig. 6.4(*c*) will generate disable signals for both the buffers *i.e.*, both TSL1 and TSL2 are disabled and data bus enters into high impedance state.

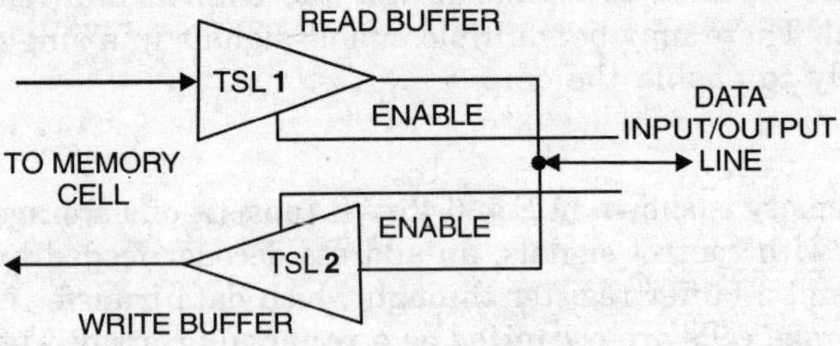


**Fig. 6.4**(*b*) Bilateral Memory Bus Buffer

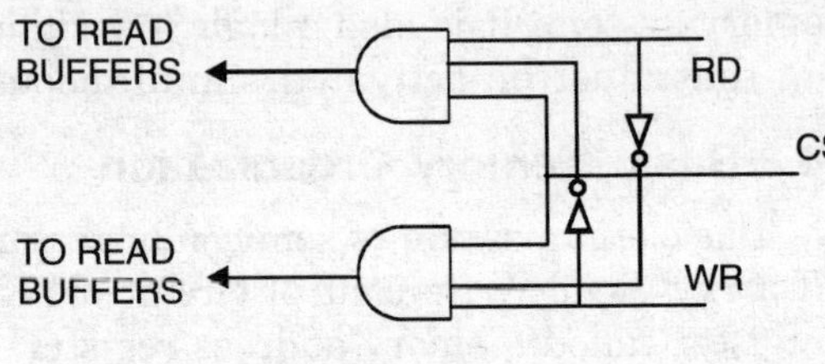


**Fig. 6.4(*c*)** Generation of Enable/Disable Signals for Buffers

### 6.4.3 Cell Organization (Memory Addressing)

Memory addressing is concerned with the selection of one particular memory cell from storage cell array. To facilitate selection, the memory cells are organized as rectangular array of m-rows and n-columns as shown in Fig. 6.5(*a*).

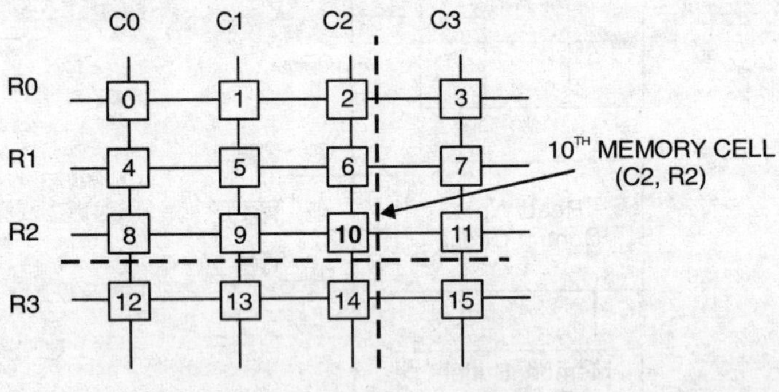


**Fig. 6.5**(*a*) An Array of 4 × 4 Cells

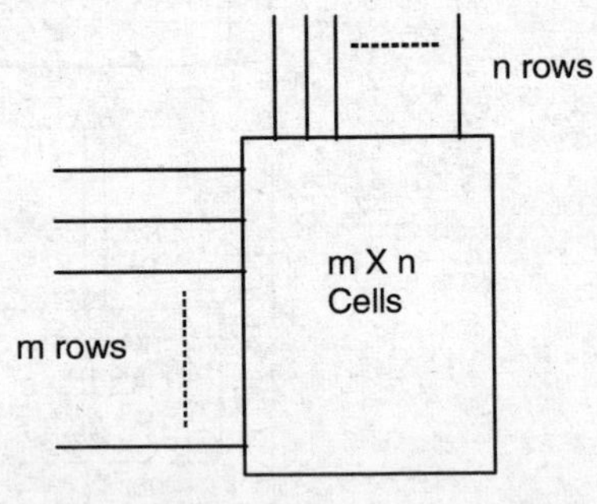


**Fig. 6.5**(*b*) An Array of m × n Cells

Figure 6.5(a) shows simplified diagram of memory cells array that have 4-rows and 4-columns, thus containing a total of 16 memory cells. The control circuitry associated with memory allows only one row and one column to be activated at a time. In order to select a particular cell we need to specify the appropriate row and column number. Let us consider the selection of 10th cell. It requires column C2 and row R2 to be activated and the cell, at the intersection of C2 and R2 is selected which is 10th cell. Dashed lines in Fig. 6.5(*a*) show this. So the 10th cell can be designated as the cell C2, R2 (or 2, 2 or 22). This designation is defined as the *address* of the 10th cell. Collectively the lines corresponding to rows and columns are called *address lines*. In a memory array, each cell will have a similar type of unique address. Hence, any cell can be accessed, just by specifying the row and column number (or address) associated with it. Since any cell can be accessed *randomly*, it is named *Random Access Memory*. Figure 6.5(*b*) shows a simple block representation of a rectangular array that we will use in following subsections to understand some important facts. If in Fig. 6.5 (*b*), m = 4, and n = 4 then it represents the array shown in Fig. 6.5 (*a*).

#### 6.4.3.1 Matrix Addressing

We know that to facilitate selection, the memory cells are organized as rectangular array of m-rows and n-columns. When rows and columns are made equal *i.e.*, m = n, then the array becomes a *Square Array* of capacity n × n = $n^2$. This type of arrangement is called *MATRIX Addressing*. This addressing have the advantage of requiring fewer number of address lines than the number of address lines required by any other rectangular arrangement. This fact is explained below by using an array of 16-cells (the one shown in Fig. 6.5 (a)). Observe carefully the different array arrangements shown in Fig. 6.6.

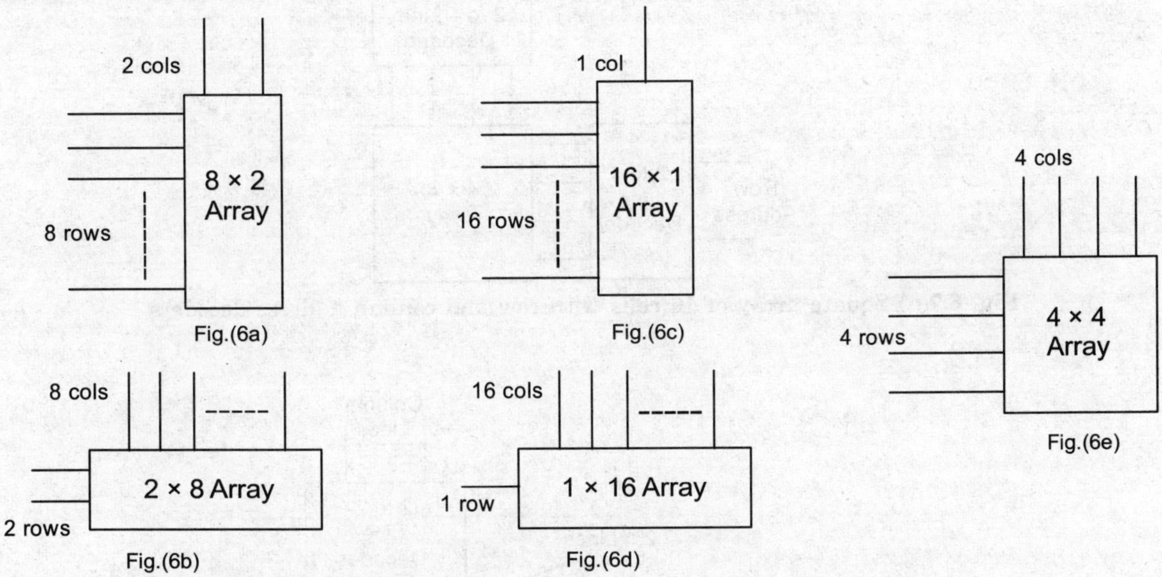


**Figure 6.6** Different Array Arrangements for 16 Memory cells

Figure 6.6 (*a*) and 6.6 (*b*) are equivalent array arrangement as one refers to 8-rows and 2-columns and other refers to 2-rows and 8-columns. Both require 10 address lines (8-rows+2-columns) to select any of the memory cells. Similarly, Fig. 6.6 (*c*) and 6.6 (*d*) are equivalent array arrangement and require 17 address lines. In fact 16 lines will suffice, as there is only one column/row. Figure 6.6 (*e*) is square array arrangement with equal number of rows and columns and require 8 address lines. So in order to reduce the number of address lines square array arrangement is best.

The arrangement in Fig. 6.6 (*e*) is referred as *Matrix addressing* as defined earlier. In contrast the 16 × 1 array arrangement as in Fig. 6.6 (*c*) is called *Linear Addressing*. It is because there is only one column and to select any of the cells, one needs to specify the row only.

#### 6.4.3.2 The Address Decoding

The address decoding is concerned with the activation of particular row and column to select a memory cell. Here our concern is to see this process exclusively for matrix addressing. Let us reconsider the Fig. 6.6 (*e*) that requires 4-rows and 4-columns. If we use two 2 to 4 line decoders then the address line requirements will be reduced further, as shown in

Fig. 6.7 (*a*). The decoders will activate only one of the row and column lines out of 4 lines. As evident from figure now the total number of required address lines are 4 only. The activation of a particular row and column line depends upon the row address and column address. Any column from C0 to C3 can be activated by specifying it as a 2-bit binary number (00 to 11) at column address lines. Similarly, specifying a 2-bit binary number at row address lines can activate any of the four rows. Thus, a total of 4-bit address can access any memory cell unambiguously. Since 4-bit address representation allows $2^4 = 16$ unique addresses, we can say that an n-bit address can be used to define a square array of $2^n$ memory cells.

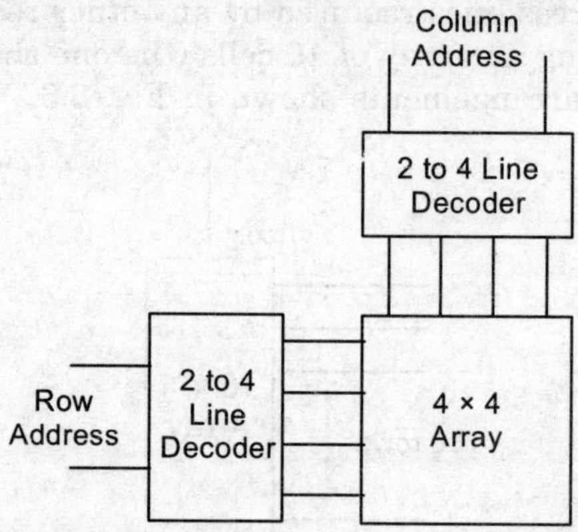


**Fig. 6.7**(*a*) Square array of 16 cells with row and column address decoders

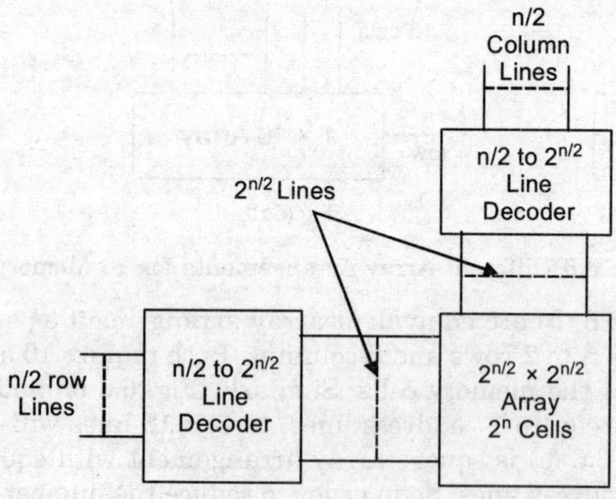


**Fig. 6.7**(*b*) Square array of $2^n$ cells with row and column address decoders

Figure 6.7 (*b*) shows a generalized arrangement of square array with address decoders. The array is organized as n/2 column address lines and n/2 row address lines thus making a total of n-bit address lines. It should be noticed that in such arrangements the value of n should an even integer (2, 4, 6, 8 ...). Since, at the output of each of the decoder we have $2^{n/2}$ lines, the number of cells (or capacity) in this array would be $2^{n/2} \times 2^{n/2} = 2^n$. This is exactly the reason why commercially available memories have capacity equal to some integer power of 2 *i.e.*, $2^{10} = 1024$, $2^{12} = 4096$ etc. The above discussion concludes that if n is the number of address lines then

$$\text{Number of storage cells} = 2^n$$

In general

$2^n \geq$ Number of storage locations

Or ...(2)

$2^n \geq$ Number of words

Where n = Number of address lines (An Integer)

**Example. 1.** *In the Fig. 6.8(a) explain how memory cell C2, R2 can be accessed. Given that the row and column numbers are in true order and activated output line have st... high*

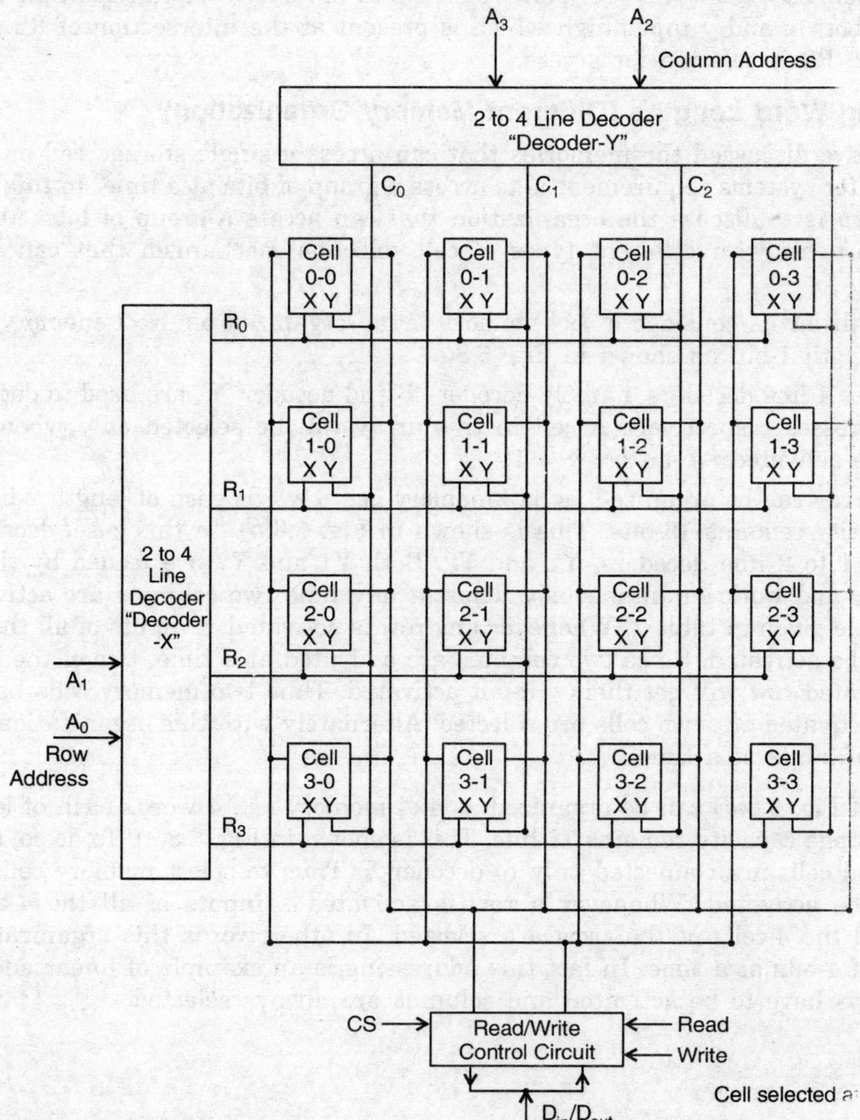


**Fig. 6.8**(*a*) 4 × 4 Array Organized as 16 × 1 Memory

**Solution.** Figure shows an array of 4 × 4 having storage capacity of 16-bits. Issuing its address can access the required cell. Since, row and column numbers are in true order, the binary equivalent of these numbers will give required memory address.

Memory cell to be accessed C2, R2

Column C2 specified in binary = 10 = $A_3$ $A_2$

Row R2 specified in binary = 10 = $A_1$ $A_0$

So the complete address $A_3$ $A_2$ $A_1$ $A_0$ = 1010

Upon receiving the address, the address decoders 'X' and 'Y' will activate row R2 and column C2, respectively. All other rows and columns will be deactivated at this time *i.e.*, R3 = R1 = R0 = 0 and C3 = C1 = C0 = 0. Now referring to fig. 6.8(*a*) we can see that only the cell 2-2 has got both x and y input high which is present at the intersection of R2 and C2. Thus the cell C2, R2 is selected for access.

### 6.4.4 Organizing Word Lengths (Different Memory Organization)

So far we have discussed the memories that can access a single storage cell or 1-bit at a time. In computer systems requirement is to access a group of bits at a time. In this section, our prime concern is to discuss the organization that can access a group of bits. Moreover, this section also deals with different types of cell selection mechanism that can be used conveniently.

To begin with let us consider a 4×4-memory array organized as 16×1 memory *i.e.*, 16 words each of length 1-bit, as shown in Fig. 6.8(*a*).

Here two 2 to 4 line decoders, namely decoder-'X' and decoder-'Y', are used to decode row and column addresses respectively. A cell in this array can be selected only when both x and y inputs are activated *i.e.* at x = y = 1.

The same array can be organized as 8×2 memory *i.e.*, 8 words each of length 2-bits. Still the storage capacity remains 16-bits. This is shown in Fig. 6.8(*b*). In this case, decoder-Y is replaced by two 1 to 2 line decoders, Y1 and Y2. Both Y1 and Y2 are feeded by the same address line (A2) and work simultaneously. Thus at any time two columns are activated as per the truth table given in table 1. Whenever any row is activated, x inputs of all the 4-cells in that row will be activated. Since two columns are activated at a time, two of the memory cells in the activated row will get their y input activated. Thus two memory cells have both x and y inputs activated *i.e.*, two cells are selected. Alternately with this organization we can access a group of 2-bits at a time.

The array of Fig. 6.8(*a*) can be organized as 4×4 memory *i.e.*, 4 words each of length 4-bits. Still the storage capacity remains 16-bits. This is shown in Fig. 6.8(*c*). To do so, decoder-Y is removed and cells are connected only to decoder-X. Thus to select memory cells only x inputs have to be activated. Whenever a row is activated x inputs of all the 4-cells are activated *i.e.*, all the 4-cells of that row are selected. In other words this organization can access a group of 4-bits at a time. In fact this addressing is an example of linear addressing because only rows have to be activated and columns are always selected.

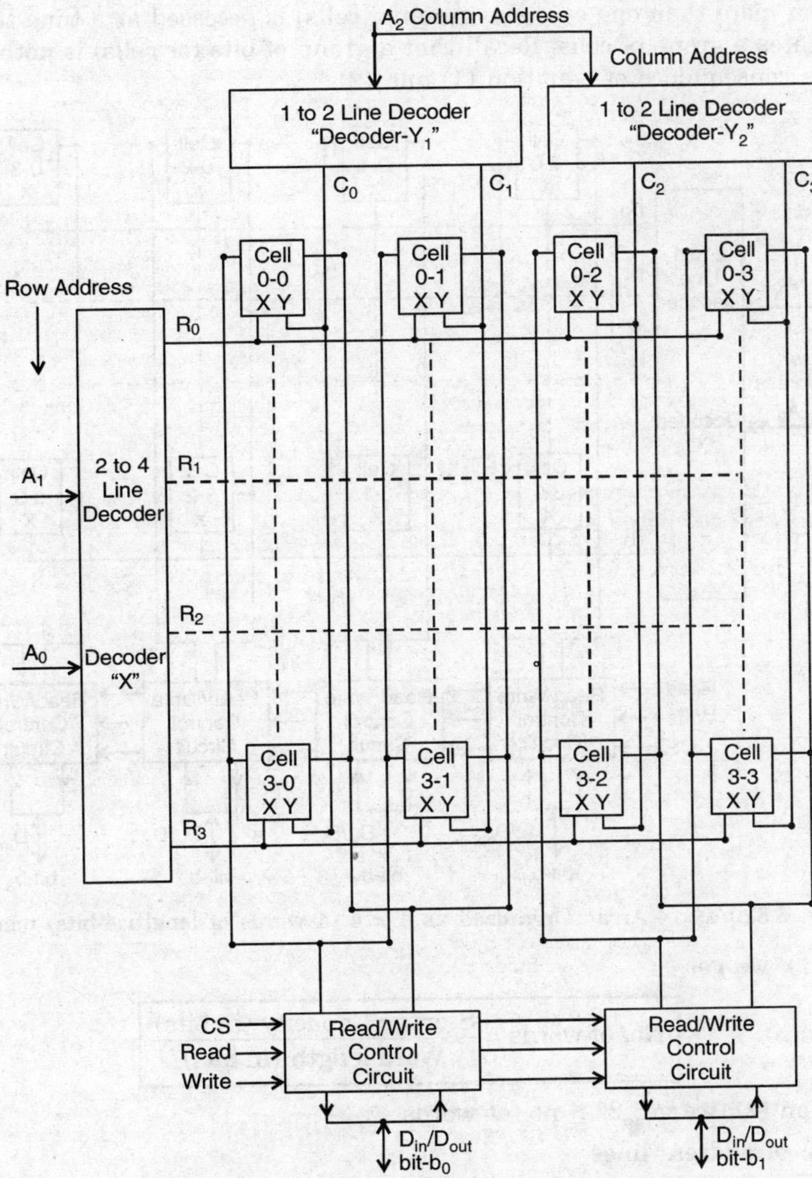


**Fig. 6.8**(*b*) 4 × 4 Array organized as 8 × 2 Memory

**Table 1. Truth Table for Fig. 6.8(b)**

| Column Address | Selected | |
|---|---|---|
| "$A_2$" | Columns | |
| 0 | $C_0$ | $C_2$ |
| 1 | $C_1$ | $C_3$ |

Notice the reduction in number of address lines in each case. In Fig. 6.8(*a*), 4-address lines were used whereas in Fig. 6.8(*b*), 3-address lines and in Fig. 6.8(*c*) only 2 address lines were used. It is because by increasing the word length the total numbers of words are reduced. When more than one cell (*i.e.*, group of cells) is accessed at a time than one storage location indicates a group of cells. Recall that a group of bits (or cells) is nothing but a word. It is a simple consequence of equation (1) and (2).

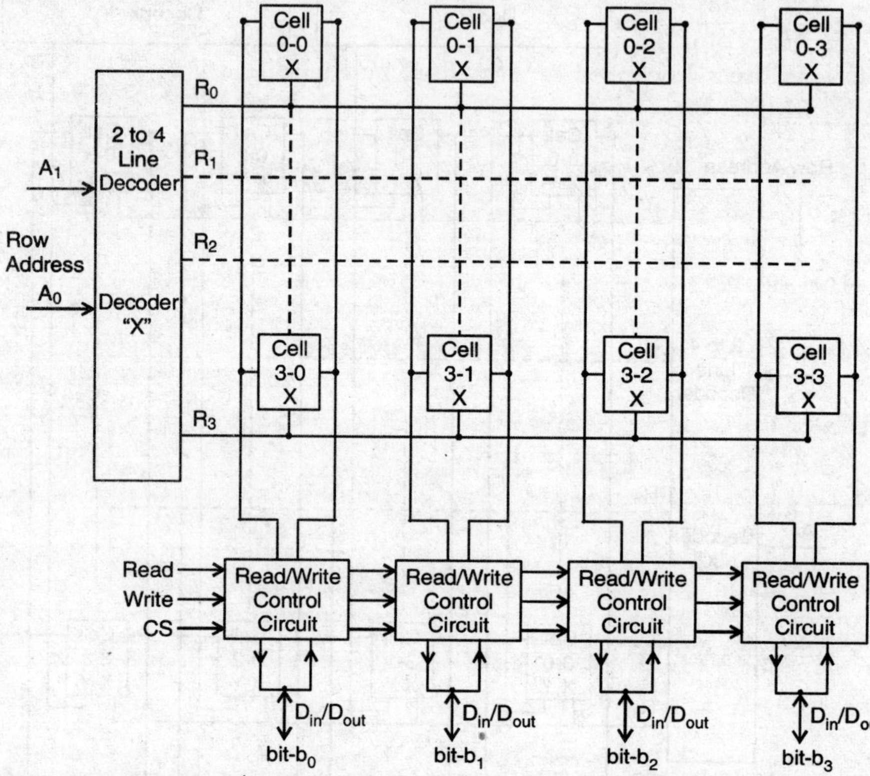


**Fig. 6.8**(*c*) 4 × 4 Array Organized as 4 × 4 (4 words of length 4-bits) memory

by equation (1), we get

$$\boxed{\text{No. of words} = \frac{\text{Storage Capacity (in bits)}}{\text{Word length (in bits)}}} \quad ...(3)$$

but by equation (2), we get $2^n \geq$ no. of words

where n = no. of address lines

Putting it into equation (3) results

$$\boxed{2^n \geq \frac{\text{Storage Capacity (in bits)}}{\text{Word length (in bits)}}} \quad ...(4)$$

The equation (4) clearly shows that number of address line 'n' is inversely proportional to word length. Thus, increasing word length will cause a reduction in no of address lines.

**Example 2.** *A memory has cell array of 32 × 32. What would be the required number of address lines if the word length is*

*(i) 1-bit* *(ii) 2-bits* *(iii) 4-bits* *(iv) 8-bits* *(v) 16-bits*

*Also find out the number of words in each case. What is the storage capacity of this memory in bits and in bytes?*

**Solution.** We know that since a **single** cell stores 1-bit, total number of cells constitutes the storage capacity of this memory.

Given array is 32 × 32 so,

$$\text{No. of storage cells} = 32 \times 32 = 1024$$

$$\text{Storage capacity} = 1024 \text{ bits or } 1 \text{ Kbits} = 128 \text{ bytes}$$

Number of address lines can be calculated by equation 4

when word length is 1-bit

$$2^n \geq 1024/1 \Rightarrow 2^n = 1024/1 \Rightarrow 2^n = 1024 \Rightarrow n = 10 \text{ lines}$$

when word length is 2-bits

$$2^n \geq 1024/2 \Rightarrow 2^n = 1024/2 \Rightarrow 2^n = 512 \Rightarrow n = 9 \text{ lines}$$

Similarly for other word lengths address lines required can be calculated.

The number of words can be calculated by equation 2 given as

$$2^n = \text{no. of words} \Rightarrow 2^n = \text{no. of words}$$

The value of $2^n$ for each case is calculated already. So 1024 words can be accessed when word length is 1-bit, 512 words can be accessed when word length is 2-bit, and so on.

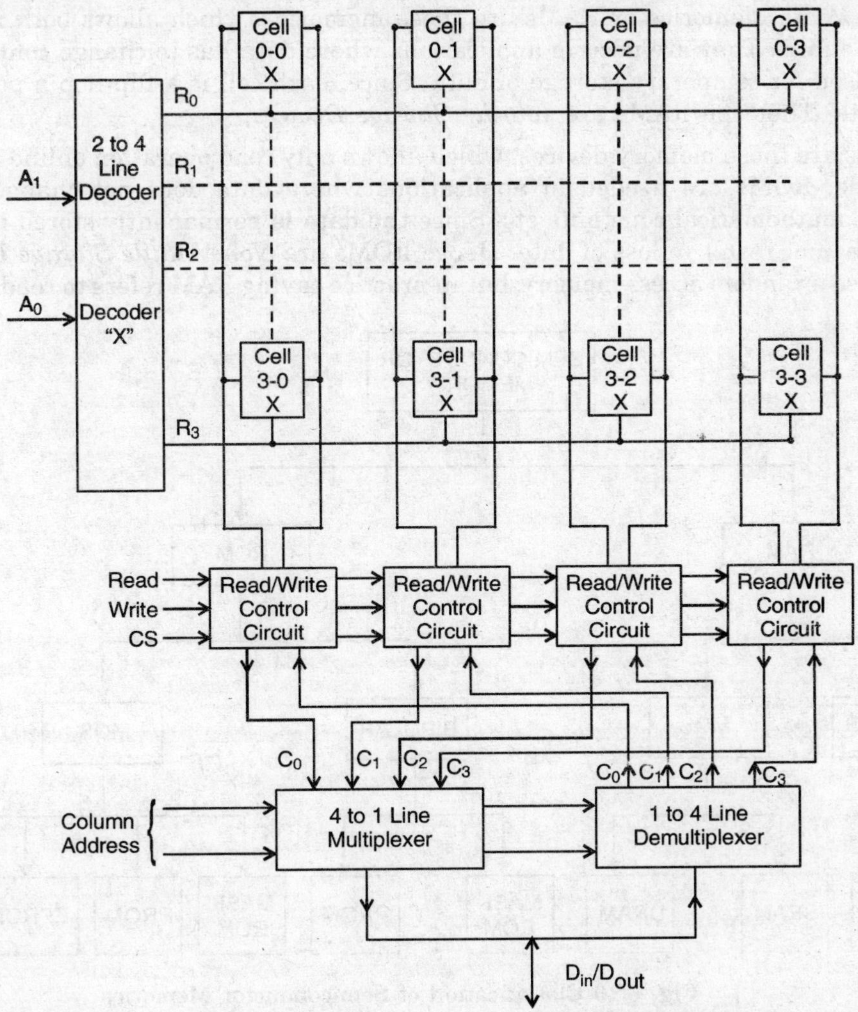


**Fig. 6.9** As 16 × 1 Memory Organization

A slightly different organization of 4 × 4 memory cells as 16 × 1 memory is shown in Fig. (6.9). Compare the Fig. (6.9) with Fig. 6.8(*a*). Here instead of using a column decoder, one 4 to 1 line MUX and a 1 to 4 line DeMUX is used. Whenever any row is activated all the 4-cells are selected. If read operation is requested, the multiplexer connects one of the selected cells to $D_{in}/D_{out}$ output line. If write operation is requested, then demultiplexer connects its input line (*i.e.*, $D_{in}/D_{out}$ line) to one of its output line which is connected to one of the cells which were selected by activating the row. The select input of both MUX and DeMUX are feeded with the column address lines.

### 6.4.5 Classification of Semiconductor Memory

The semiconductor memory devices can be categorized in several ways according to their functional and architectural characteristics. Figure 6.10 shows the most general classification. As shown they fall in two general categories.

- Read Write Memory or Random Access Memory (RAM)
- Read Only Memory (ROM)

Read Write Memories or RAMs are those memories, which allows both read and write operation online. They are used in applications where data has to change continuously. They are also used for temporary storage of data. Since, each cell is a flip-flop a power off means loss of data. Thus the RAMs are *Volatile Storage Devices*.

ROMs are those memory devices, which allows only read operation online and there is no write mode. ROMs are needed in applications where data does not change *e.g.*, monitor programs, mathematical constants etc. Since the data is permanently stored in ROM, power failure does not result in loss of data. Hence ROMs are *Non Volatile Storage Devices*. In fact ROM is also a random access memory, but in practice saying RAM refers to read write memory.

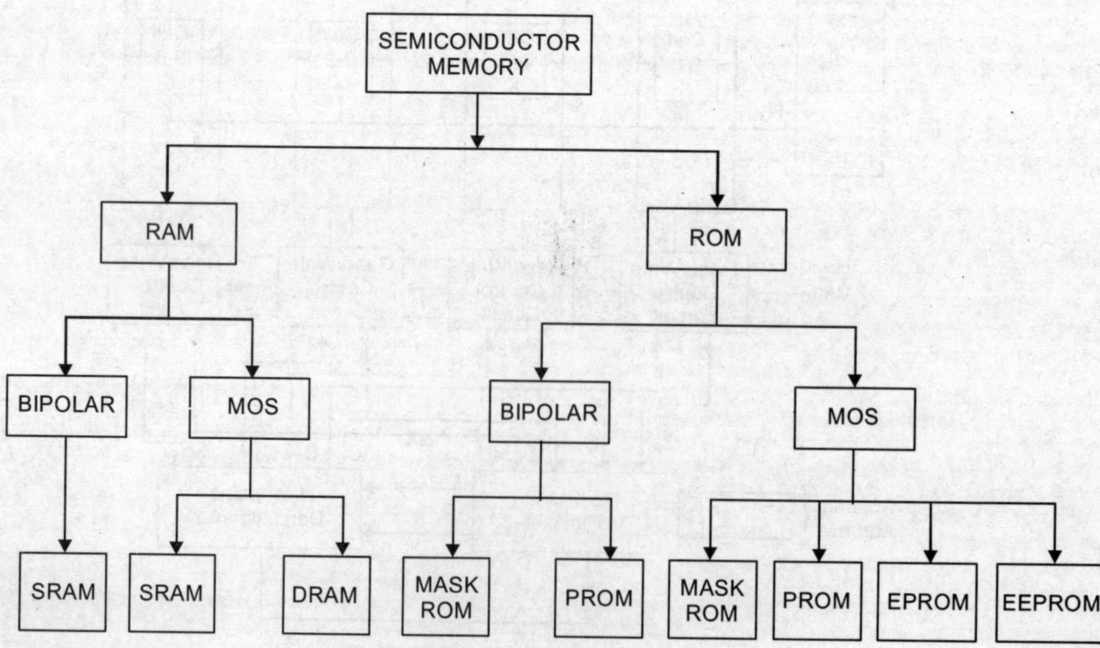


**Fig. 6.10** Classification of Semiconductor Memories

Both the RAM and ROM are further divided into other subcategories, as shown by figure. We will define each of them in this section whereas detailed discussions proceed in the subsequent sections.

Primarily both RAMs and ROMs are classified as *Bipolar* and *MOS* memory depending upon the type of transistors used to construct the individual cell. If the cells are formed by using bipolar (or MOS) transistors the chip is called *Bipolar (or MOS) memory chip*. High-speed operation is possible with Bipolar chips but their storage capacity is lesser. However economical MOS/CMOS chips have greater storage capacity, reduced size, and lesser power requirements.

*Static Ram* (SRAM) is a read write memory that uses two cross-coupled transistor (either bipolar or MOS) working as Flip-Flop to form the basic memory cell. SRAM holds the stored data indefinitely if power is on, hence the name static. SRAMs are very high speed but costly memories. A *Non Volatile RAM* (NVRAM) is formed by using battery backed up SRAM.

*Dynamic Ram* (DRAM) is a read write memory that uses a capacitor in conjunction with a MOS transistor to store 1-bit. Since the capacitors are leaky, they cannot hold the charges permanently. So, they must be recharged (refreshed) periodically to hold the stored data, hence the name dynamic. They are slower than SRAMs but their storage capacity is greater.

The ROMs are categorized according to the data storing process. The mechanism that stores the data into ROM is called as programming mechanism.

A simple ROM is programmed during the manufacturing process according to the data specified by the user. Such a ROM is referred as *Mask ROM* or *Mask Programmable ROM*.

A PROM (*Programmable ROM*) is a type of ROM that can be programmed by the users in the field. They are also referred as *Field Programmable ROM*. But once programmed they cannot be altered.

An EPROM (*Erasable Programmable ROM*) is another type of field programmable ROM that can be reprogrammed by the users after erasing the stored data. The erase operation is performed optically which erases all the data stored in EPROM. Selective erase *i.e.*, erasing just a segment of data is not possible with EPROMs.

An EEPROM (*Electrically Erasable Programmable ROM*) is another type of field programmable ROM that can be programmed by the users as often as required but after erasing the stored data. The erase operation is performed electrically which allows selective erase.

### 6.4.6 Semiconductor Memory Timing

In this section, we are concerned with timing sequences which must be considered for any type of memory operation. Although these timing requirements may not be precisely applicable to all types of memories, but it is useful to grasp the concept. The time duration and sequence in which various signals have to be activated is of great importance. Manufacturer's data sheets of the memory ICs specify these timing requirements. If any of these parameters are not followed then the manufacturer does not guarantee the intended operation. It is expected that design engineer will come out with the necessary access circuitry that meet these timing requirements for proper operation.

Based upon the discussions we had in earlier articles of this chapter we can list out some of the operational requirements.

- A valid memory address must be applied to the address input.

- Before initiating any operation the chip must be enabled through–$\overline{CS}$ signal line.
- The appropriate control signal then is applied for a certain time.

More or less all type of memory operations is followed in above-mentioned sequence. For the sake of easiness, we first consider the memory write operation and then read operation. The readers are advised to devote sometime to understand these waveforms.

#### 6.4.6.1 Memory Write Operation

*Memory Write operation* means setting the status of the selected memory cell either to 1 or to 0 according to the data supplied through the data bus. The timing waveforms for a typical memory write operation is shown in Figure 11-A. A close inspection reveals that to write a data to a memory location one must–

- Apply a valid address to the address bus to select a location.
- Initiate chip select signal by making $\overline{CS}$ = 0.
- Apply the write control signal by making $\overline{WR} = 0$ for a certain time.
- Apply the data to be written at the selected memory location to the data bus for a certain time.

In response the information present at data bus replaces the word at addressed memory location that might have been stored in it. The waveform also shows the different times that are typical and are explained as below:

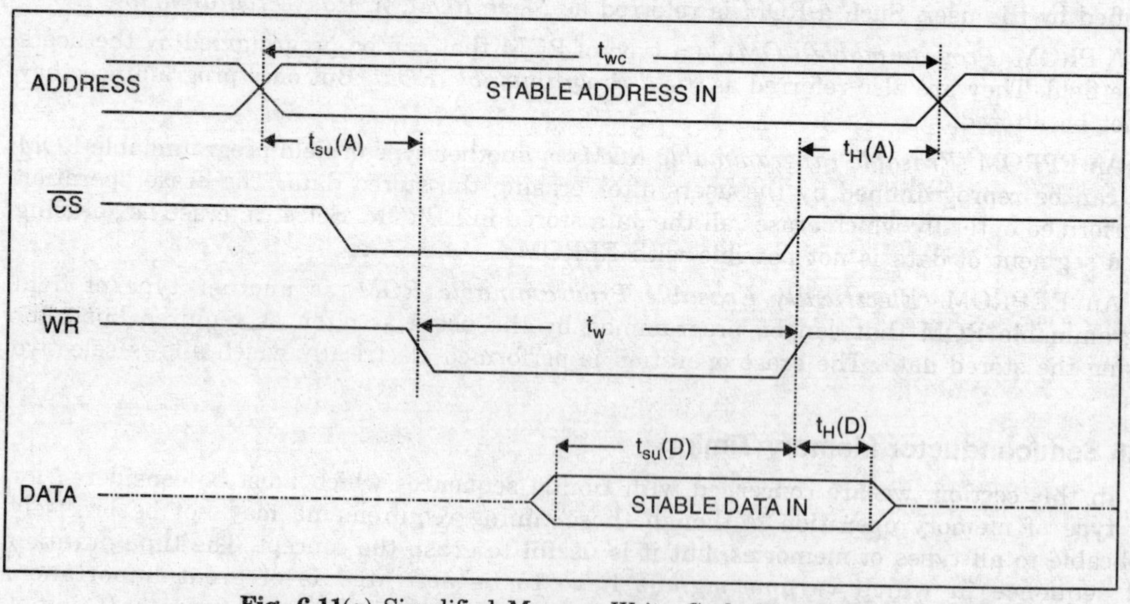


**Fig. 6.11**(*a*) Simplified Memory Write Cycle Waveforms

*Write Cycle Time* ($t_{WC}$): This is defined as the minimum amount of time for which a valid address must be present at the address bus for writing a memory word. As earlier defined this is the minimum time that must lapse between two successive write cycles.

*Address Set up Time* $t_{SU}$ *(A)*: It is defined as the minimum time for which the address must be stable at the address bus before $\overline{WR}$ goes low.

*Address Hold Time $t_H$ (A)*: This is defined as the minimum time for which the valid address must be stable at the address bus after $\overline{WR}$ rises.

*Write Pulse Width ($t_W$)*: This is defined as the minimum amount of time for which $\overline{WR}$ must be low in order to store the data in the memory. It must be noted that $t_W$ is measured from the later of write pulse or chip select going low to the write pulse going high. A write occurs during the overlap of low chip select and low write pulse *i.e.*, when both are low. Also the write pulse should be high during all address transitions.

*Data Setup Time $t_{SU}$ (D)*: This is defined as the minimum time for which the data to be written at addressed location must be held stable at the data bus before $\overline{WR}$ rises.

*Data Hold Time $t_H$ (D)*: This is defined as the minimum time for which the data to be written at addressed location must be held stable at the data bus after $\overline{WR}$ rises.

#### 6.4.6.2 Memory Read Operation

A *Read operation*, also called *sensing*, means detecting the status (*i.e.*, information) of selected memory cell that whether it is 1 or 0. The timing waveforms for a typical memory read operation is shown in Fig. 6.11(*b*). A close inspection reveals that to read a data from a memory location one must

- Apply a valid address to the address bus to select a memory location.
- Initiate chip select signal by making $\overline{CS} = 0$.
- Apply the read control signal by making $\overline{RD} = 0$ for a certain time.

In response the information from addressed memory location is transferred to the data bus. The waveform also shows the different times that are typical and are explained as below.

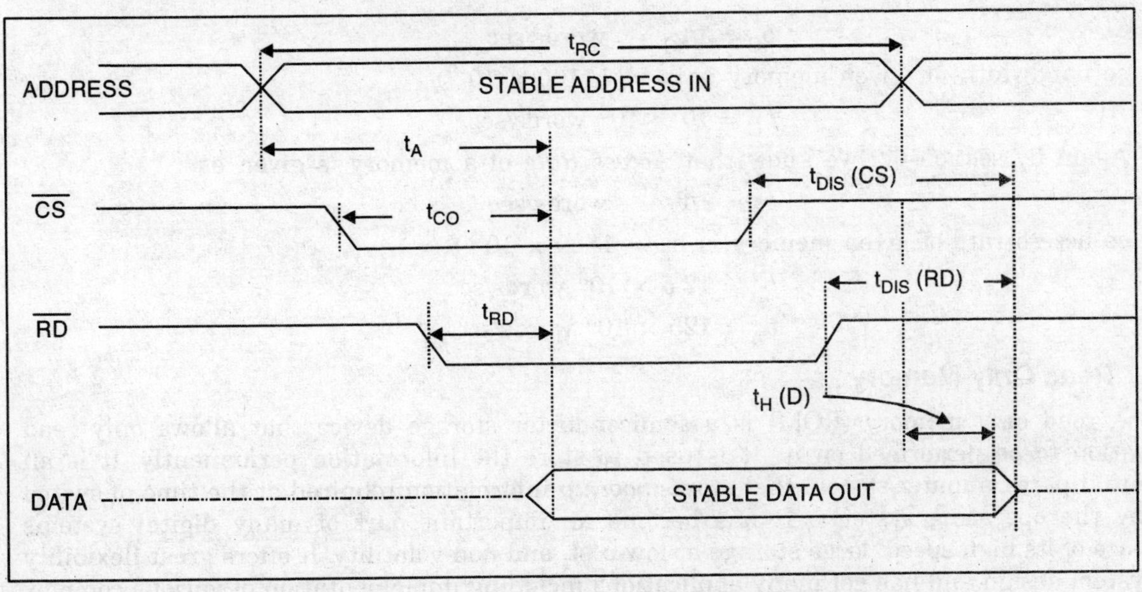


**Fig. 6.11**(*b*) Simplified Memory Read Cycle Waveforms

*Read Cycle Time* ($t_{RC}$): This is defined as the minimum amount of time for which a valid address must be present at the address bus for reading a memory word. As earlier defined this is the minimum time that must lapse between two successive read cycles.

*Read Access Time* ($t_A$): Read Access Time or *Access time* is defined as the maximum delay between the appearance of stable address and appearance of stable data. This definition is based upon the assumption that chip select goes low after the application of address. Access time is at the most equal to the read cycle time *i.e.*, $t_A \leq t_{RC}$.

*Chip Select to Output Valid Time* ($t_{CO}$): This is the maximum time delay between the beginning of chip select signal and appearance of stable data at the data bus. It is sometimes also defined as the access time from chip select $t_A$(CS).

*Read to Output Delay* ($t_{RD}$): This is the maximum time delay between the beginning of read signal and appearance of stable data at the data bus. It is sometimes also defined as the access time from read $t_A$(RD) or read to output valid time.

*Chip Select to Output Disable* $t_{DIS}$*(CS)*: This is the maximum time delay after the end of chip select signal for data bus to go to high impedance state *i.e.*, to get disabled. It is also defined as $t_{OTD}$, output 3-state from deselection.

*Read to Output Disable* $t_{DIS}$*(RD)*: This is the maximum time delay after the end of read signal for data bus to go to high impedance state *i.e.*, to get disabled.

$$\text{Generally } t_{DIS}(CS) = t_{DIS}(RD) = t_{OTD}$$

*Data Hold Time* $t_H$*(D)*: This is defined as the minimum time for which the stable data is available at the data bus after the end of the valid address. It is also defined as $t_V$(A), output data valid after change in address or output hold from change in address $t_{OHA}$.

**Example 3.** *For a memory the read and write cycle times are 100 nsec. Find out the bandwidth for this memory. What will be the access rate if access time is 80 nsec?*

**Solution.** By section 6.2 we know that *Data Transfer Rate* or *Bandwidth* of a memory is given as

$$b_C = 1/t_C \quad \text{words/sec}$$

so bandwidth for given memory is $b_C = 1/(100 \times 10^{-9})$

$$b_C = 10 \times 10^6 \text{ words/sec.}$$

Again by section 6.2 we know that *Access Rate* of a memory is given as

$$b_A = 1/t_A \quad \text{words/sec}$$

so access rate of given memory is $b_A = 1/(80 \times 10^{-9})$

$$b_A = 12.5 \times 10^6 \text{ words/sec.}$$

or

$$b_A = 125 \times 10^5 \text{ words/sec.}$$

### 6.4.7 Read Only Memory

A read only memory (ROM) is a semiconductor storage device that allows only read operation to be performed on it. It is used to store the information permanently. It is an essential part computer system that stores *boot up* information required at the time of switch on by the operating systems. It has become an important part of many digital systems because of its high speed, large storage at low cost, and non-volatility. It offers great flexibility in system design and has got many applications including implementation of various complex combinational logic, look up tables, character displays, embedded systems etc.

ROMs are mainly classified by the method that is used to store the information. The mechanism that stores the data into ROM is called as *programming mechanism*.

Basic organization of a ROM remains same as was discussed from 6.4.1 through 6.4.4 with the only difference that ROMs do not contain write signal. The actual consideration here would be the type of cells that a ROM device must use. Before going for discussion on the typical cells for different kind ROM cells we first consider some simpler ROM organization that can be worked out in labs to demonstrate the idea. The logic diagram of ROM unit is shown in Fig. 6.12.

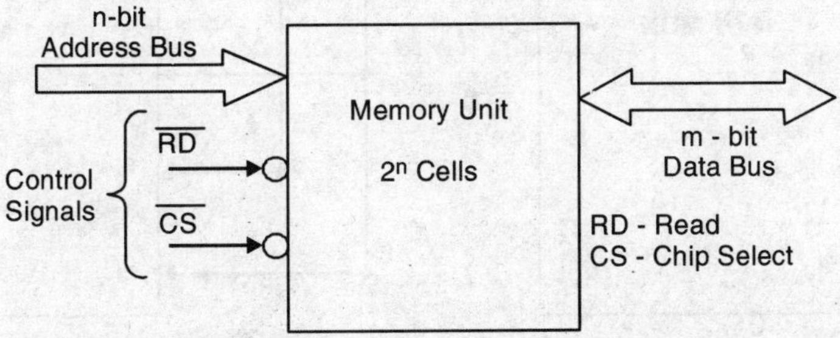


**Fig. 6.12** Logic Symbol of A ROM Memory Unit

### *6.4.7.1 Some Simple ROM Organizations*

**Diode Matrix ROM:** They are the simplest types of ROM. They were discussed previously in chapter 5.

**Multiplexer ROM:** It is yet another simple type of ROM. In this case, the multiplexer inputs are fixed to logic 1 or logic 0 as desired and the select inputs can be used as address lines to select the particular memory word. Figure 6.13 shows such a 4 × 1 ROM with the truth table of stored information.

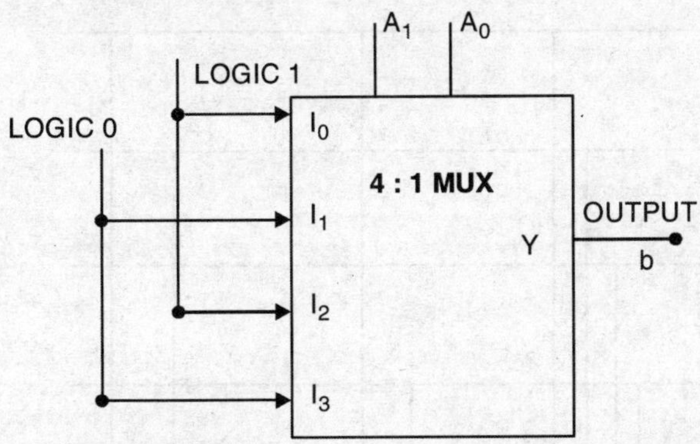


**Fig. 6.13**(*a*) 4 to 1 line multiplexer connected as 4 × 1 ROM

| MEMORY LOCATION or ADDRESS | | STORED WORD |
|---|---|---|
| $A_1$ | $A_0$ | b |
| 0 | 0 | 1 |
| 0 | 1 | 0 |
| 1 | 0 | 1 |
| 1 | 1 | 0 |

**Fig. 6.13**(*b*) Truth Table for ROM in Fig. 6.12(a)

It is interesting to note that forming a multiplexer tree with such fixed data connections can make a ROM of larger word length thus increasing the storage capacity. Such a ROM is shown in Fig. 6.14. The figure shows a 4 × 2 ROM with a storage capacity of 8-bits as opposite to the ROM of Fig. 6.13 which is a 4-bit ROM of word length of 1-bit. Note that the address lines are shorted together as usual to address the bits of same location from two MUX. Readers are encouraged to find out the words stored at different locations in this ROM.

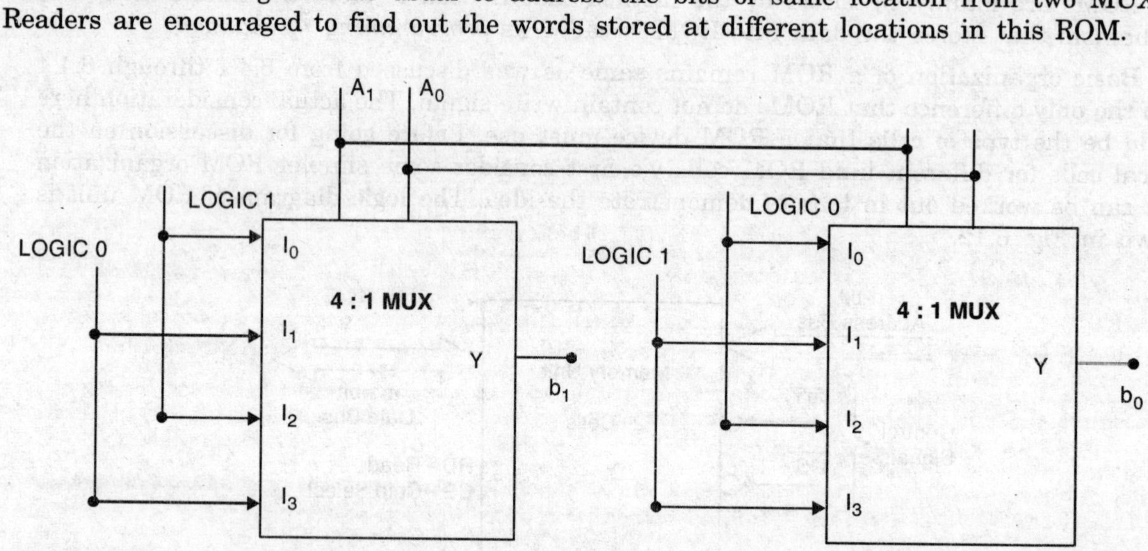


**Fig. 6.14** Two 4 to 1 line multiplexer connected as 4 × 2 ROM

**OR-Gate ROM:** It is yet another simpler ROM but more versatile than the multiplexer ROM. In this case, a decoder and n-input OR gates are used. The selection of decoder depends upon the number of words needed to store. The word length determines the number of OR-gates. The select inputs are used as address lines to select the particular memory word. Figure 6.15 shows such a 4 × 4 ROM.

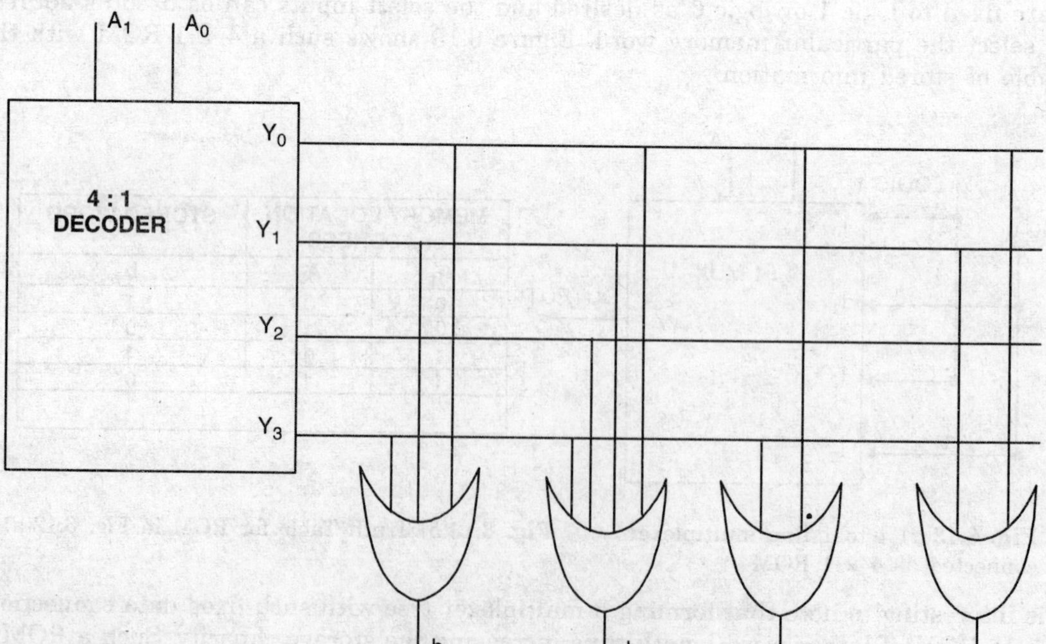


**Fig. 6.15** A 16-bit, 4 × 4 ROM using OR-Gates and 4 to 1 line decoder

Assuming that upon activation each of the decoder line becomes high we get that location 10 stores the word 0100. The readers are advised to find out the words stored at other locations.

An interesting fact can be noted from all the above organizations that each of them corresponds to AND-OR organization. Diode matrix is an AND-OR configuration and both multiplexers and decoders are internally AND-OR networks. This is nothing but *Sum of Product* (SOP) realization. This implies that the ROMs can also be used for SOP realization.

#### 6.4.7.2 Mask Programmed ROMs

In general the word ROM is used to refer to Mask Programmed ROMs. It is the type of memory, which is permanently programmed during the manufacturing process according to the information supplied by the users. Upon receiving the information to be stored into the ROM the manufacturer prepares a photographic template of the circuit, called *Photo Mask*. This photo mask is actually used for production of ROM ICs storing the needed information. Since, photo mask is used for programming such a ROM is called Mask Programmed ROM. Due to the various fabrication processes involved in such production like photomasking, etching, diffusion, Aluminium layering etc the overall cost is high. This makes them unsuitable when only a small number of ROMs are needed. For this reason, mask programmed ROMs are always used for high volume production.

Both the BJTs and MOS devices can be used as basic memory cell for this kind of ROM. Figure 6.16 shows the Bi-polar transistors connected to store logic 1 and logic 0. As shown the base connected transistor can be used to store logic 1. If row line is connected to the base of transistor then whenever ROW line goes high transistor turns ON and $+V_{CC}$ is connected to column line which is interpreted as Logic 1. But if base is unconnected the high on row line does not make it working and status of column line remains low which is interpreted as Logic 0.

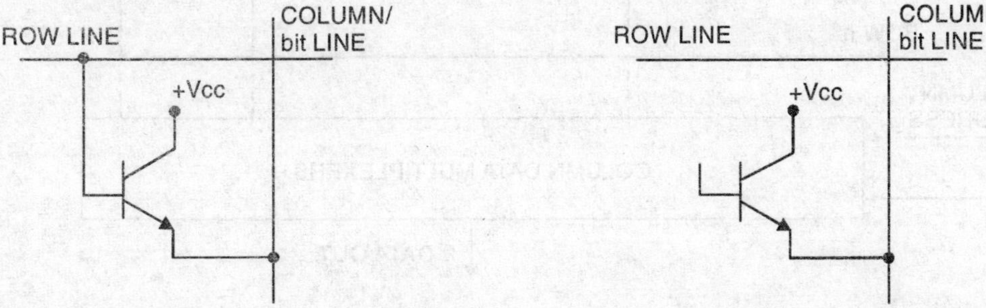


**Fig. 6.16**(*a*) A Bi-POLAR ROM Cell storing '1' **Fig. 6.16**(*b*) A Bi-POLAR ROM Cell storing '0'

In the similar way Gate connected MOS transistor can be used to store Logic 1 and floating Gate MOS transistor can be used to store Logic 0. This is shown in Fig. 6.17.

When organizing the ROM array the output data lines of individual cells in the same column are connected together as shown in Figure 6.18. This is done by assuming that such connections will form *Wired-OR*$_{ing}$ and such assumption is valid for most of the semiconductor technology.

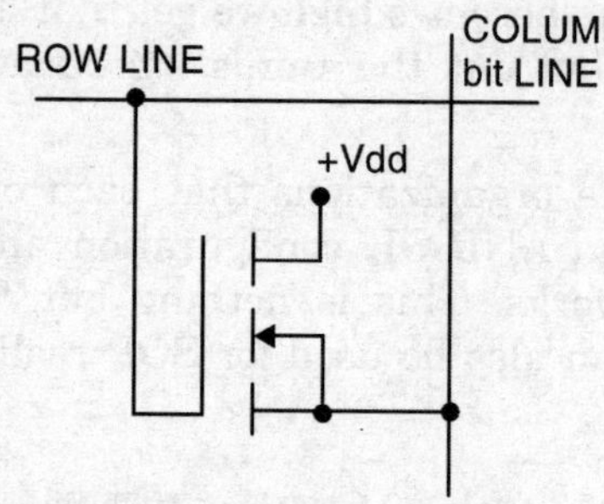


**Fig. 6.17**(*a*) A MOS ROM Cell storing '1'

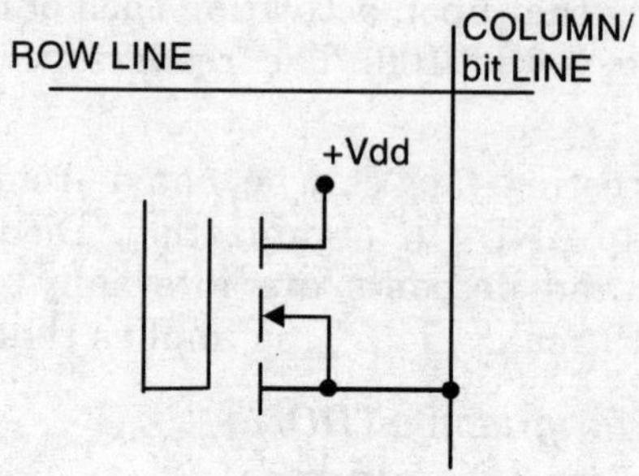


**Fig. 6.17**(*b*) A MOS ROM Cell storing '0'

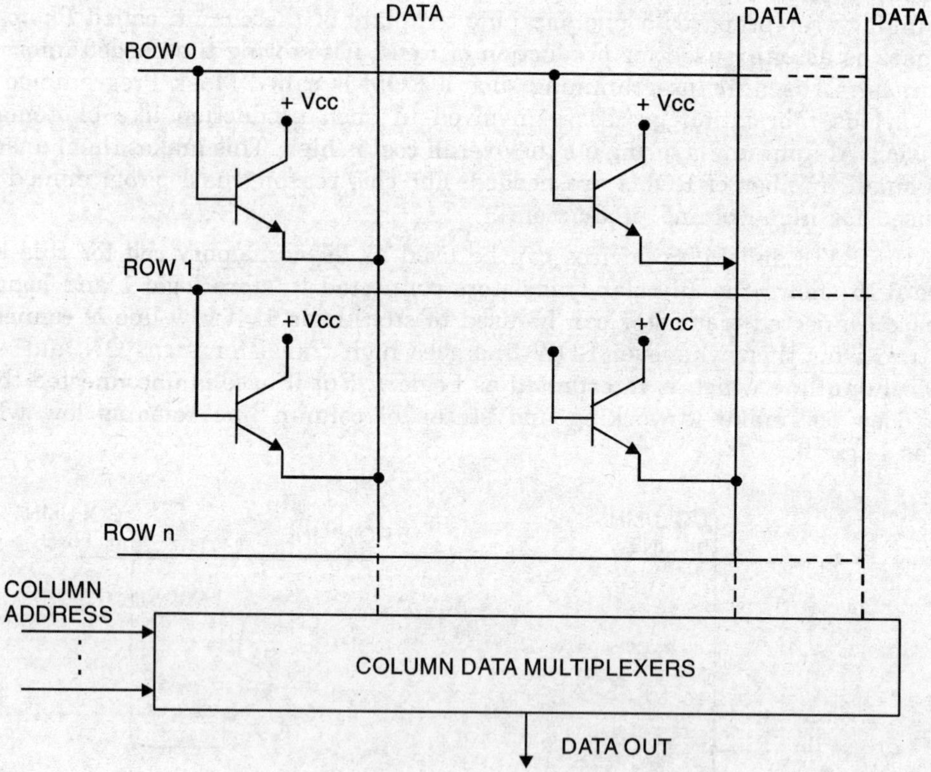


**Fig. 6.18** An Array of Bipolar ROM Cells

Finally column multiplexers may be used to select the data from a particular column only. This organization identical to the one, shown in Figure 6.9.

### 6.4.8 Programmable Read Only Memory (PROM)

The mask programmed ROMs have disadvantage that they are not flexible and with low volume production they become highly expensive. A Programmable ROM is a type of ROM which efforts to minimize these two disadvantages. These ROMs can be programmed by the users in the field, thus they are also called field programmable ROMs. These ROMs provide some flexibility to user but their disadvantage is that they can be programmed only once.

PROMs are available with both the Bipolar and MOS technology. Conceptually the programming technique in both technologies is same, but the real difference appears in the actual programming mechanism. In case of Bipolar technology, an instantaneous current pulse is used for programming whereas the current pulse is applied for certain period (typically for a few msecs) of time in case of MOS technology.

#### 6.4.8.1 Bipolar PROMs

Figure 6.19 shows a Bi-polar PROM cell that allows such kind of programming in PROMs. As shown the emitter is connected with a fusible link that can be blown off or burned by applying a high current to it. When the fuse remains intact it stores logic 1 and when it is burnt it stores logic 0. Initially all the cells have fuse intact i.e. they all stores logic 1 and at the time of programming users can selectively burn them out to store logic 0.

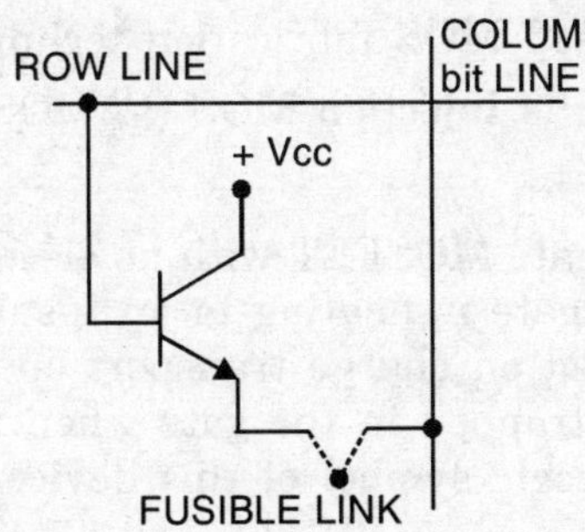


**Fig. 6.19** A Bipolar PROM cell with fusible link

This shows why these memories cannot be reprogrammed. Since, programming the PROM involves burning the fuse it is also referred as *burning*.

In Bipolar PROM cells, the fusible links are always placed between emitter of the transistor and the column/data line, as shown in Fig. 6.19. Such types of cells are called fuse cells. Basically there are types of fuse technology used in Bipolar PROMs as briefed below.

- *Metal Links* are formed by depositing a very thin layer of nichrome as material. This fuse can be burned during programming to store logic 0 by flowing large currents through them.
- *Silicon links* are formed by depositing a thick layer of polycrystalline silicon. This fuse can be burned to store logic 0 by flowing current pulse train of successive wider pulses. This programming process causes a temperature upto 1400°C at the fuse location, and oxidizing the silicon. This oxidization forms insulation around the opened link.
- *Avalanche Induced Migration (AIM) Process* this programming technique uses two PN junction diodes connected back to back as shown in Fig. 6.20. During the programming the diode $D_1$ is in reversed bias. There flows a large current in reverse direction due to avalanche of electrons. The heavy reverse current along with heat generated at the junction causes some aluminium ions to migrate. Due to this the base to emitter junction is shorted. Although this process requires higher currents and voltages than the earlier two, but this is faster.

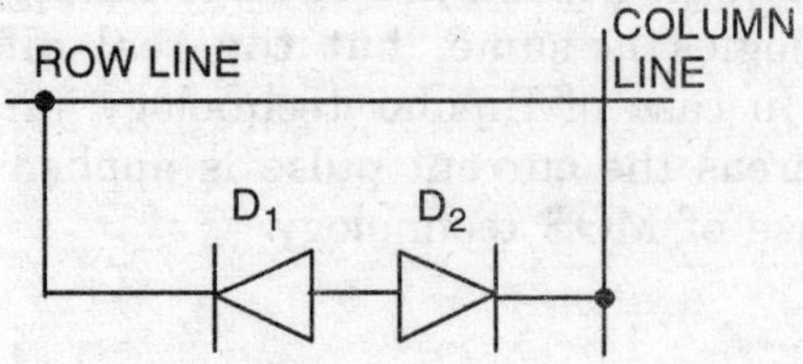


**Fig. 6.20** A Shorted Junction Cell

### 6.4.8.2 MOS PROMs

The fuse mechanism shown for Bipolar PROMs does not works for MOS technology where high current and resistance levels required for programming is incompatible with MOS impedance levels. Commonly used MOS fabrication techniques are

- Floating Gate Avalanche Injection MOS (FAMOS)
- MAOS

In FAMOS PROMs silicon gate MOSFET with no electrical connection to the gate is used as storage device. In this case, gate is floating in an insulating layer of silicon dioxide. The operation of such device is based on charge transport on application of high voltage to the floating gate. This charge gets trapped in the gate when voltage is removed, as there is no electrical connection for gate. Logic symbol of this device is shown in Fig. 6.21.

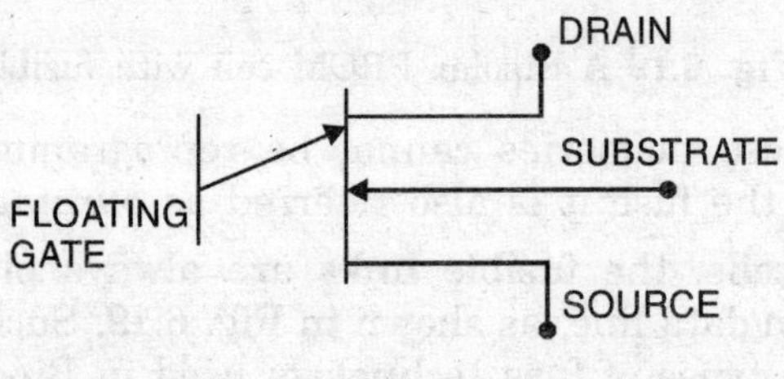


**Fig. 6.21** Logic Symbol of FAMOS Device

It is interesting to note that the charged trapped in floating gate of FAMOS device can be removed if the cell is exposed to high energy UV radiation for sometimes.

A MOS memory cell that uses *Alumina* ($Al_2O_3$) and silicon nitride as gate dielectric for charge storage is called MAOS memory element. Applying negative and positive polarity voltages can program the MAOS elements. The MAOS elements can be erased by applying opposite polarity voltage at gate and thus provides reprogramming.

Note that the MOS techniques provide reprogramming feature as opposite to Bipolar technology.

### 6.4.8.3 PROM Programming

As explained above the programming of PROM requires varying amount of currents to be supplied to store the information. This is done through a special device called PROM Programmer that mainly contains programmable pulse generator to meet requirements of different devices. A simplified programming set up is shown in Fig. 6.22.

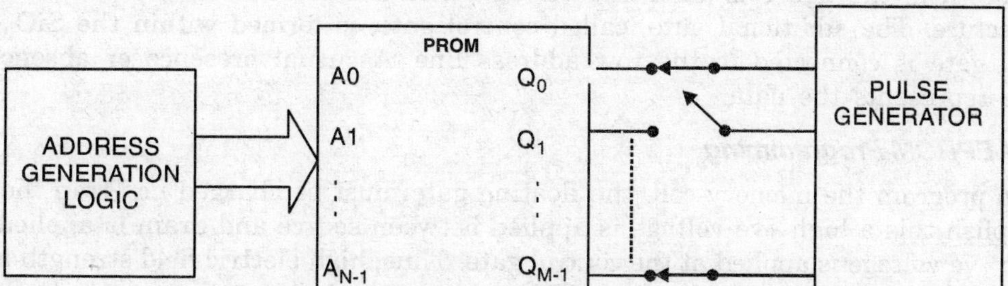


**Fig. 6.22** Simplified PROM Programming Set up

As earlier discussed initially PROMs will contain all 1's or all 0's. Let initially all 1's are stored then to store information first of all find out the bit positions where 0s have to be stored. Connect the corresponding output bit line *i.e.*, $Q_i$ to the pulse generator. The address generation unit selects the location of the word to be programmed. After the selection of word pulse generator supply the appropriate amplitude pulse to burn out the fuse, thus storing 0 at connected bit positions. The process is repeated for all memory words and the PROM can be programmed completely. Although not shown in figure all the power supply and other connections are assumed to be present for PROM before programming.

### 6.4.9 Erasable Programmable ROM (EPROM)

One disadvantage of PROM is that once programmed it cannot be reprogrammed. Any mistake during the programming cannot be corrected and the whole chip may become useless. An EPROM overcomes this problem by providing an erase operation. EPROM is a PROM device that can be reprogrammed as many times as needed.

Note that both ROMs and PROMs can be either Bipolar or MOS but EPROMs can only be MOS. An indication of this fact was given in previous section when discussing the FAMOS & MAOS devices. In its simplest form an EPROM can be viewed as a FAMOS PROM with an additional gate, called control gate. Figure 6.23 shows the basic structure of such a device and its logic symbol. The programming mechanism is same as previous and to erase UV radiation is used.

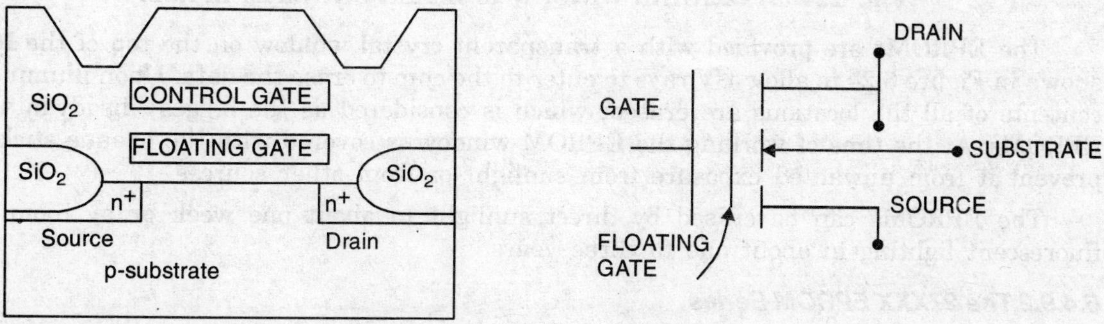


**Fig. 6.23** A Structure of EPROM Cell

Shown in the figure is an n-channel enhancement mode MOSFET with insulated gate architecture. The additional gate, called control gate, is formed within the $SiO_2$ layer. The control gate is connected to the row address line. As usual presence or absence of stored charge represents the data.

#### 6.4.9.1 EPROM Programming

To program the memory cell, the floating gate must be charged *i.e.*, trap the charge. To accomplish this a high +ve voltage is applied between source and drain is applied. A slightly higher +ve voltage is applied at the control gate. Thus, high electric field strength is developed which highly energizes the electrons. These energetic electrons thus reach to floating gate and charge is accumulated. As the more electrons (*i.e.*, negative charges) are accumulated the field strength reduces and further electron accumulation is inhibited. Since, an insulating layer ($SiO_2$) surrounds this gate, no discharge path is available for accumulated electrons. Thus charge carriers remain trapped at gate. Thus the programming requires charging the floating gates of individual memory cells. Programming of the EPROMs requires higher current levels for different times. For this purpose a special device, called EPROM Programmer, is used. All the EPROM chips must be physically removed from the memory boards and be connected to the EPROM programmer for reprogramming or programming. This is considered as the disadvantages of the EPROM.

To reprogram all cells of EPROMs must be erased. Illuminating EPROM to strong UV radiations carries out the erase operation. For this reason they are some times called as *UV erasable PROMs* or simply *UV EPROMs*. It typically requires a radiation of wavelength of about 254 nm to be present for about 20 minute. The photons of the incident radiation provide sufficient energy to the trapped electrons to escape to substrate through the $SiO_2$ layer.

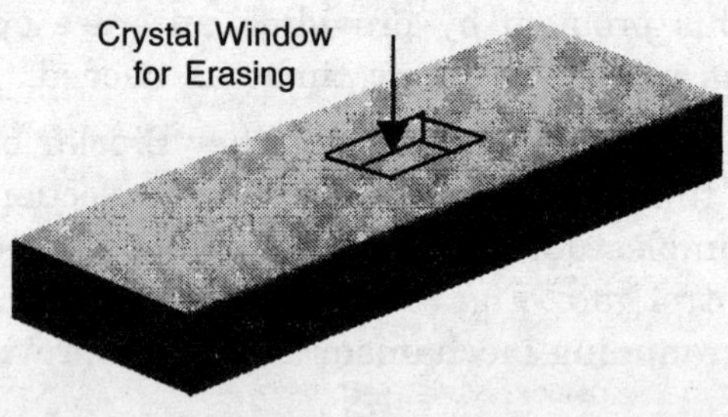


**Fig. 6.24** (*a*) CRYSTAL WINDOW to ERASE DATA from EPROM

The EPROMs are provided with a transparent crystal window on the top of the IC, as shown in Figure 6.24 to allow UV rays to enter to the chip to erase the data. Upon illumination contents of all the locations are erased, which is considered as the biggest disadvantage of EPROMs. At the time of working the EPROM window is covered with the opaque sticker to prevent it from unwanted exposure from sunlight or from other sources.

The EPROMs can be erased by direct sunlight in about one week or by room level fluorescent lighting in about one to three years.

#### 6.4.9.2 The 27XXX EPROM Series

A popular *EPROM family* is 27XXX series and commercially available from many manufacturers. In the IC number XXX represents the storage capacity in Kbits. For example, in IC 2732A XXX = 32 means it can stores a total of 32 Kbits. However, all ICs of this series are organized to have a word length of a byte *i.e.*, 8-bits. Hence 2732A is a XXX/8 = 32 Kbits/8 = 4Kbyte or 4KB memory device. Since length of each memory word is byte this IC contain 4 K (4 × 1024 = 4096) memory location. Thus by equation 4 get that IC 2732A must have 12 address lines (as $2^{12}$ = 4096) to select any of the 4096 words. In the similar way we can work out for all the members of this family to find out the storage capacity and the width of address bus. Data bus width will always be same as 8-bit. Pin diagram of IC 2732A is shown in Figure 6.24. The signal is $\overline{OE}/V_{PP}$ a dual purpose signal. Under the normal operation a logic 0 on this pin allows the data from selected location to appear at data output lines. The 2732A is in programming mode when it is connected to 21V. When 2732 is erased all the memory cells are returned to logic 1 status. The programming is done by applying the required input data on the $O_0 - O_7$ pins.

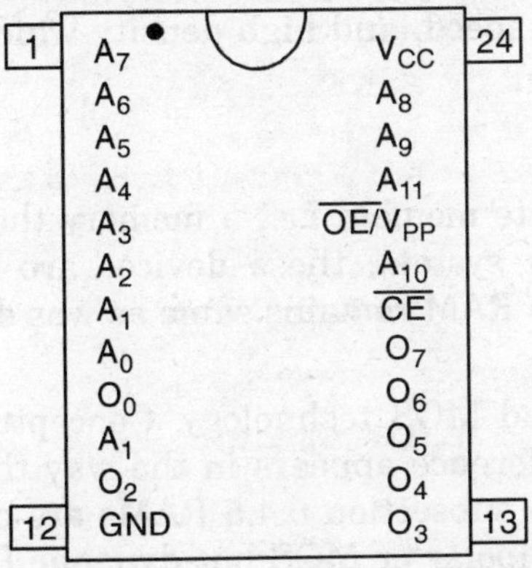


| | |
|---|---|
| $A_0$-$A_{11}$ | Address Lines |
| $\overline{CE}$ | Chip Enable |
| $\overline{OE}/V_{PP}$ | Out Enable/Programming |
| $O_0$-$O_7$ | Data Output Lines |

**Fig. 6.24** (*b*) INTEL 2732A EPROM IC, 4 K × 8 IC

Figure 6.25 list out a short summary of some models in 27XXX series. Also note that these chips are fully TTL compatible and has an access time less than 450 nsec that permits an access rate (most of the time Data Transfer Rate) of approximately 2 × $10^6$ memory words/sec or 16 × $10^6$ bits/sec.

| *EEPROM* | *MEMORY* | *STORAGE* | *CAPACITY* |
|---|---|---|---|
| *27XXX* | *ORGANIZATION* | *KBYTES* | *BITS* |
| 2708 | 1024 × 8 | 1 KB | 8192 |
| 2716 | 2048 × 8 | 2 KB | 16384 |
| 2732 | 4096 × 8 | 4 KB | 32768 |
| 2764 | 8192 × 8 | 8 KB | 65536 |
| 27128 | 16384 × 8 | 16 KB | 130172 |
| 272576 | 32768 × 8 | 32 KB | 262144 |
| 27512 | 65536 × 8 | 64 KB | 524288 |

**Fig. 6.25** 27XXX SERIES EPROMs

### 6.4.10 Electrically Erasable Programmable ROM (EEPROM)

One disadvantage of EPROM is that erase operation erase all the memory cells completely and reprogramming involves entering the complete data. There is no option of selective erase. Another disadvantage is that for reprogramming the chip must be removed physically from the main boards. An EEPROM, also called as $E^2PROM$, overcomes these problems which allows selective erase operation and there is no need to remove the chip as it requires different voltage levels which can be provided on board. In EEPROMs the erase operation is performed electrically as opposite to EPROMs. For this reason, they are also called as *Electrically Altered PROM i.e.*, the EAPROM. In these memories both the erase and programming can be done electrically by applying the controlled electrical pulses to the IC. Thus, changes can be made to selected memory locations only. The $E^2PROMs$ can be programmed one byte at a time.

Recently a newer $E^2PROM$ called *flash EEPROM* is introduced by Intel Corporation that has very simpler cells and thus have greater packing density. The *flash EEPROMs* devices can be programmed faster as compared to normal EEPROM and can be erased sector-by-sector. While the EEPROMs can be erased and programmed for parts of code, the entire *flash EEPROMs* memory must be erased and reprogrammed completely. The future seems to opt for *flash EEPROMs* because of their simpler cells, high speed, and high density which means lower cost per bit.

### 6.4.11 The Random Access Memory (RAM)

The Random Access Memory refers to the read write memory *i.e.*, a memory that allows both reading and writing data online. In a computer system, these devices are used for temporary or scratchpad storage. Basic organization of a RAM remains same as was discussed from 6.4.1 through 6.4.4 with no changes.

RAMs are also available with both the Bipolar and MOS technology. Conceptually the operation in both technologies is same, but the real difference appears in the way they store the binary information in the memory cell. As shown in subsection 6.4.5 RAMs are classified as *Static* and *Dynamic*. The static RAM can be either Bipolar or MOS but dynamic RAM can only be MOS. Both types of RAMs are discussed in subsequent subsections.

### 6.4.12 Static Random Access Memory (SRAM)

Random Access Memories that consist of circuits that can retain the information as long as power is applied are referred as *Static Random Access Memories*. Flip-flop forms the basic memory element in a SRAM device. A static RAM contains an array of flip-flops, one for each bit. Logic diagram a SRAM cell is shown in Fig. 6.26. The figure shows an S-R latch with required signals. As shown the cell can only be selected by placing logic 1 to both the ROW and COL lines. Data can be entered to this cell only when WR=1 and RD=0 when both row and col are activated. At the time of writing the data the cell output is disabled and is available only when RD=1 and WR=0.

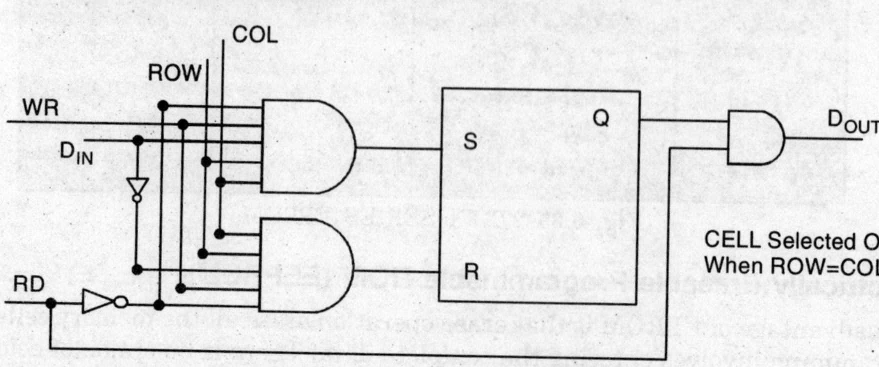


**Fig. 6.26** Logic Diagram of Basic SRAM Cell

Since, SRAM contains array of flip-flops, a large number of flip-flops are needed to provide higher capacity memory. For this reason simpler flip-flop circuits using BJTs and MOS transistors are used for SRAM. This helps to save chip area and provides memory IC at relatively reduced cost, increased speed and reduces the powers dissipation as well. The static RAMs have very small access times typically less than 10 nsec. SRAM with battery back up is commonly used provide non-volatile RAM (NVRAM).

#### *6.4.12.1 The Bipolar SRAM Cell*

For the reasons stated above we use simpler flip-flop circuits to implement flip-flops in memory. The circuit shown in Fig. 6.27(*a*) forms basic Bipolar latch that can be used to store 1-bit of binary information. Note that it contains two cross-connected collector coupled transistors $Q_1$ and $Q_2$. At any time one of the transistor remains on and other remains off *i.e.*, status of their collector are always complement to each other thus satisfying the basic definition of flip-flop. That's why the data lines are labeled as b and $\overline{\text{b}}$.

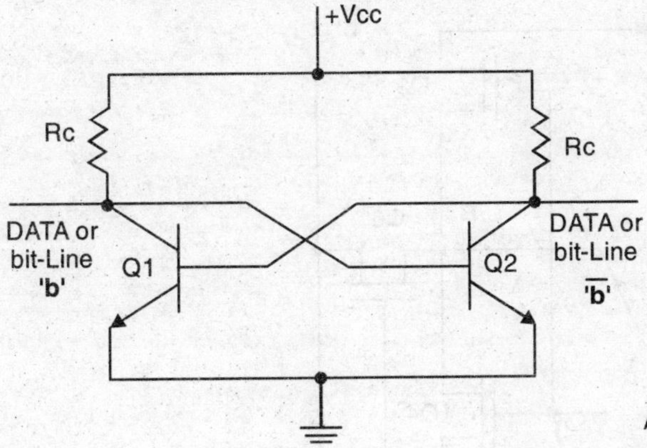


**Fig. 6.27** (*a*) Basic Bipolar Latch (or Storage Cell)

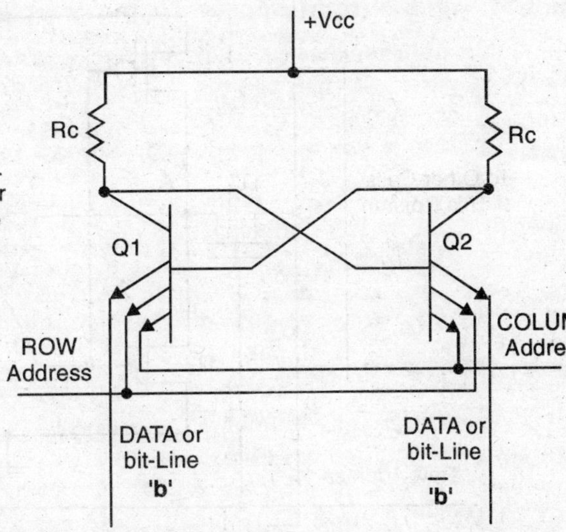


**Fig. 6.27** (*b*) Basic Bipolar SRAM Cell

Figure 6.27(*b*) shows the same latch but along with the necessary control and the data signals. Use of multi-emitter transistors accommodates the necessary signals of BJT SRAM cell. To read or write to this cell both the row and column lines must be high.

To ***write*** the two bit lines are placed with required status and row and column lines are placed high. This causes the two lower emitters of both the transistors to stop current conduction. If a logic 1 was to be store then bit line b placed as $b = 1$, this makes upper emitter of $Q_1$ to cease to conduct but the upper emitter of transistor $Q_2$ will remain conducting as its bit line is placed as $\overline{b} = 0$. This makes $Q_1$ to go to off state and $Q_2$ to go to on state, thus giving status of $Q_1$ as logic 1 and $Q_2$ as logic 0. The similar process can be used to store logic 0 to this cell. Every time the state of transistor $Q_1$ can be read to sense the status of this cell.

To ***read*** the data from this cell row and column lines are placed high and current flowing through the upper emitter can be sensed by read amplifier to declare it as 0 or 1.

### *6.4.12.2 The MOS SRAM Cell*

A CMOS realization of SRAM cell is shown in Fig. 6.28. The cell comprises two cross-connected inverters, $Q_1$ and $Q_2$ as inverter 1 and $Q_3$ and $Q_4$ as inverter 2, thus forming a latch capable of storing 1-bit of information. When the cell stores logic 1 the voltage at point A is maintained high and that at B is maintained low by having $Q_1$ and $Q_4$ ON and $Q_2$ and $Q_3$ OFF. Thus, if $Q_5$ and $Q_6$ are turned ON by activating the row address line, the bit lines will have their status respective to voltage at A and B. Finally upon activation of column address lines $Q_7$ and $Q_8$ turn ON and pass this information to read/sense amplifier. Note that the bit line is connected to all the cells of a column by forming wire-OR connection. The write operation for this cell is same as BJT cell in that bit lines are first fixed to required status and then the cell is forced to enter in that status.

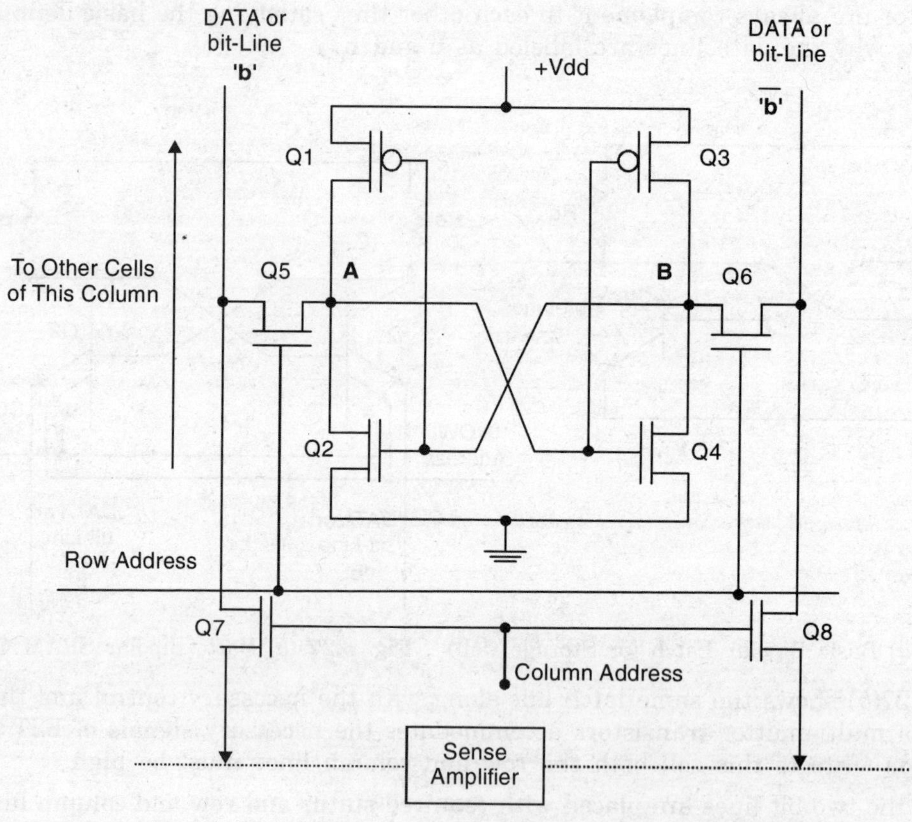


**Fig. 6.28** CMOS SRAM Storage Cell

The power supply $V_{dd}$ is 5 volts in standard CMOS SRAMs and 3.3 volts in low-voltage versions. The biggest advantage of using CMOS cell is very low power consumption because the current can flow in the cell only when they are accessed. Otherwise one of the transistor from each inverter remains OFF ensuring that there is no active path between the supply voltage $V_{dd}$ and ground. Although CMOS is slower than the BJT but latest advances have reduced the difference in the Access time of the two types of SRAM. Also since CMOS devices have very large packing density, almost all the SRAM devices with capacity more than 1024 bits are MOS devices.

#### *6.4.12.3 SRAM ICs*

- ***IC 7489- 64 bit TTL SRAM*** Fig. 6.29 shows the pin diagram and logic diagram along with truth table and signal description. This is a 64-bit SRAM organized as 16 × 4 memory. The data sheet for this memory device specify a maximum read data delay or access time of 50 nsec. Note that the device contains separate data busses for input and output. The output of this IC always the complement of bits stored in the memory. Moreover, this IC package provides open collector output thus it requires external pull up resistors to be used as shown in functional diagram. Note the third entry of the truth table with the mode of operation as inhibit storage. In this mode, the device simply works as inverter in that the data present at the input complemented and presented at the output. In this mode, neither the data can be stored nor the data read whether address is applied or not.

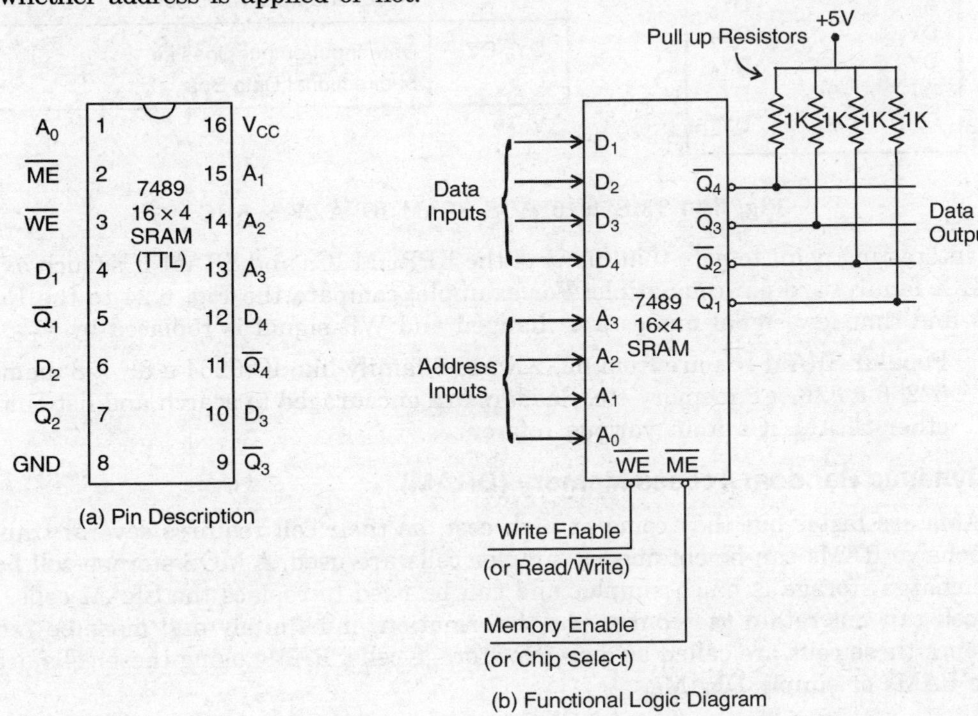


(a) Pin Description

(b) Functional Logic Diagram

| Signal | Description |
|---|---|
| $\overline{ME}$ | Selects or Enables the chip when ME = 0 |
| $\overline{WE}$ | Selects write operation when WE = 0<br>Selects read operation when $\overline{WE}$ = 1 |
| $A_0$ to $A_3$ | Address lines to select any of the 16-words |
| $D_1$ to $D_4$ | 4-bit Data Input Bus |
| $\overline{Q}_1$ to $\overline{Q}_4$ | 4-bit Data Output Bus-Data output is complement of bits stored. |

(c) Signal Description

| Operating Mode | Inputs $\overline{ME}$ | Inputs $\overline{WE}$ | Output Condition |
|---|---|---|---|
| Write | 0 | 0 | Complement of Data Inputs |
| Read | 0 | 1 | Complement of Selected word |
| Inhibit Storage | 1 | 0 | Complement of Data Input. No read or write is done |
| Do Nothing | 1 | 1 | All Outputs High |

(d) Truth Table

**Fig. 6.29** 64 bit (16 × 4) TTL SRAMIC

- **TMS 4016-2KB MOS SRAM** Fig. 6.30 shows the pin diagram of this MOS SRAM device. This device is representative of all other 2K × 8 SRAM MOS ICs such as Intel 2016, and most popular in this range the 6116 IC. The figure shows the signal description also, with the help of which truth table for this IC can be worked out.

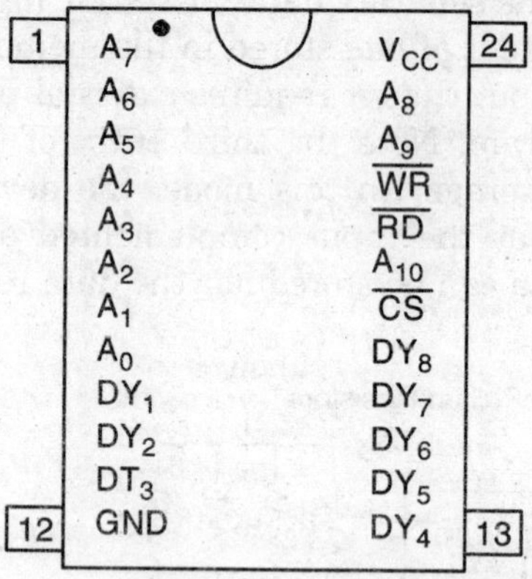


| $A_0$-$A_{11}$ | Address Lines |
|---|---|
| $\overline{CS}$ | Chip Select when set to 0 |
| $\overline{WR}$ | Writes the word when set to 0 |
| $\overline{RD}$ | Reads the word when set to 0 |
| $DY_0$-$DY_7$ | Data input/output Lines i.e. bi-directional Data Bus |

**Fig. 6.30** TMS 4016 MOS SRAM IC, A 2K × 8 IC

An interesting point to note that many of the EPROM ICs and SRAM ICs (such as 27XXX and 62XXX family) are pin compatible. For example, compare the Fig. 6.24 to the Fig. 6.30. One can find that few signal names are changed and WR signal is replaced by $V_{PP}$.

- Popular SRAM ICs are from 62XXX MOS family like IC-6264 a 8K × 8 memory, IC-62256 a 32K × 8 memory etc. Readers are encouraged to search and list out several other SRAM ICs from various references.

## 6.4.13 Dynamic Random Access Memory (DRAM)

SRAMs are faster but they come at high cost, as their cell requires several transistors. Less expensive RAMs can be obtained if simpler cells are used. A MOS storage cell based on dynamic charge storage is much simpler and can be used to replace the SRAM cells. Such a storage cell can not retain the charge (*i.e.*, information) indefinitely and must be recharged again, hence these cells are called as dynamic storage cells. RAMs using these cells are called Dynamic RAMs or simply DRAMs.

### *6.4.13.1 Basic DRAM Cell*

A basic DRAM cell is shown in Fig. 6.31, in which information is stored in the form of charge stored on a capacitor. The cell consists of a MOS transistor and a storage capacitor C. information can be stored as presence or absence of charge on capacitor C. but the charge stored on the capacitor tend to decay with time. It is because of two facts- first even though the transistor is OFF there flows a small leakage current, and secondly the capacitor itself has a leakage resistance. The result is charge (*i.e.*, information) can only be retained for a few milliseconds. Thus, to retain the information for a longer period of time the capacitor must be recharged periodically before charge goes below a threshold value. The process of restoring charge is called as refreshing. Even though DRAM requires additional circuitry to deal periodic refresh and destructive read the advantage of greater storage capacity on a single chip make it worth, as it still offers a low cost per bit solution.

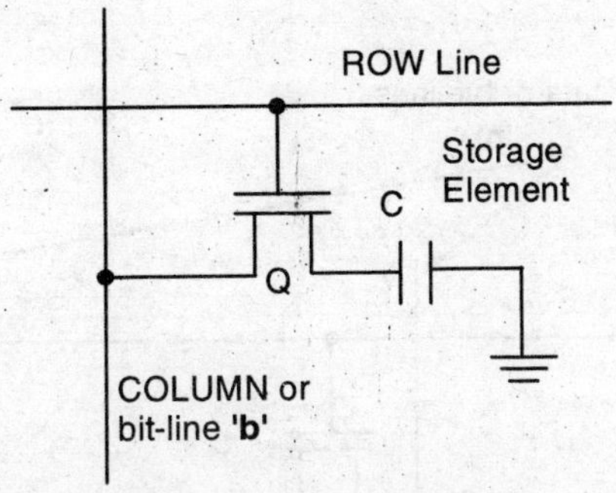


**Fig. 6.31** Basic DRAM Storage Cell

- ***Read and Write Operation*** to store the information into the cell the row address line is activated to turn ON the transistor, and a voltage (either high or low corresponding to 1 or 0) is placed on the bit line. This causes a known amount of charge transfer to the storage capacitor if status of bit line is 1 and no charge transfer if bit line is 0. During read, the transistor is turned ON and charge on the capacitor is transferred to the bit line. A sense amplifier connected to bit line detects whether the stored charge is below or above a threshold value or not and accordingly interpret it 1 or 0. Since, the read process discharges the capacitor, information is lost, it called as *Destructive Read Out (DRO)* process. For this reason, the information that was read out is amplified and written back to the storage cell. A DRAM cell therefore is refreshed every time it is read. Alternately, the activation of row line refreshes the cell every time. This forms the basis of periodic refreshing of DRAM, as we will see later, to keep it from loosing the information. Also note that transistor itself acts as transmission gate so no additional transistors are needed as was required in MOS SRAM cell, see Fig. 6.28.

### 6.4.13.2 One MOS Transistor DRAM Cell

The circuit used for DRAM MOS cells may use one or more transistors. The simplest is one transistor cell as shown in Fig. 6.32(*a*). It consists of an NMOS transistor and a MOS capacitor, $C_{MOS}$, fabricated on a chip. The equivalent circuit is shown in Fig. 6.32(*b*), in which $C_j$ represents the junction capacitance of transistor. If MOS capacitor plate lead and substrate leads are connected to ground, it then forms a parallel connection of $C_j$ and CMOS. The storage capacitor is $C = C_j + C_{MOS}$ which can be used to store charge in dynamic cells.

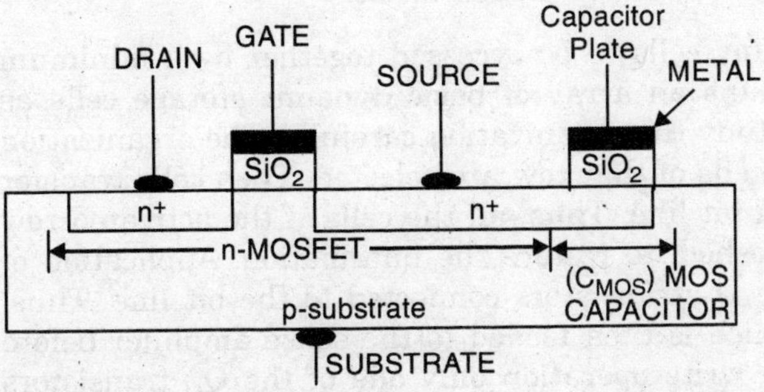


**Fig. 6.32**(*a*) Fabrication of One Transistor Dynamic Memory Cell

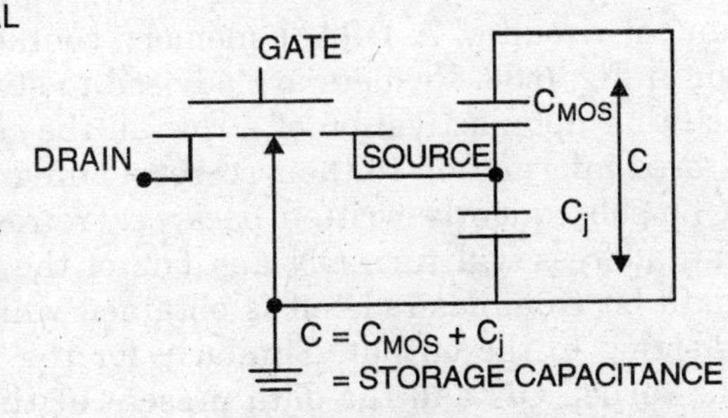


**Fig. 6.32**(*b*) Equivalent Circuit Diagram

### *6.4.13.3 DRAM Organization*

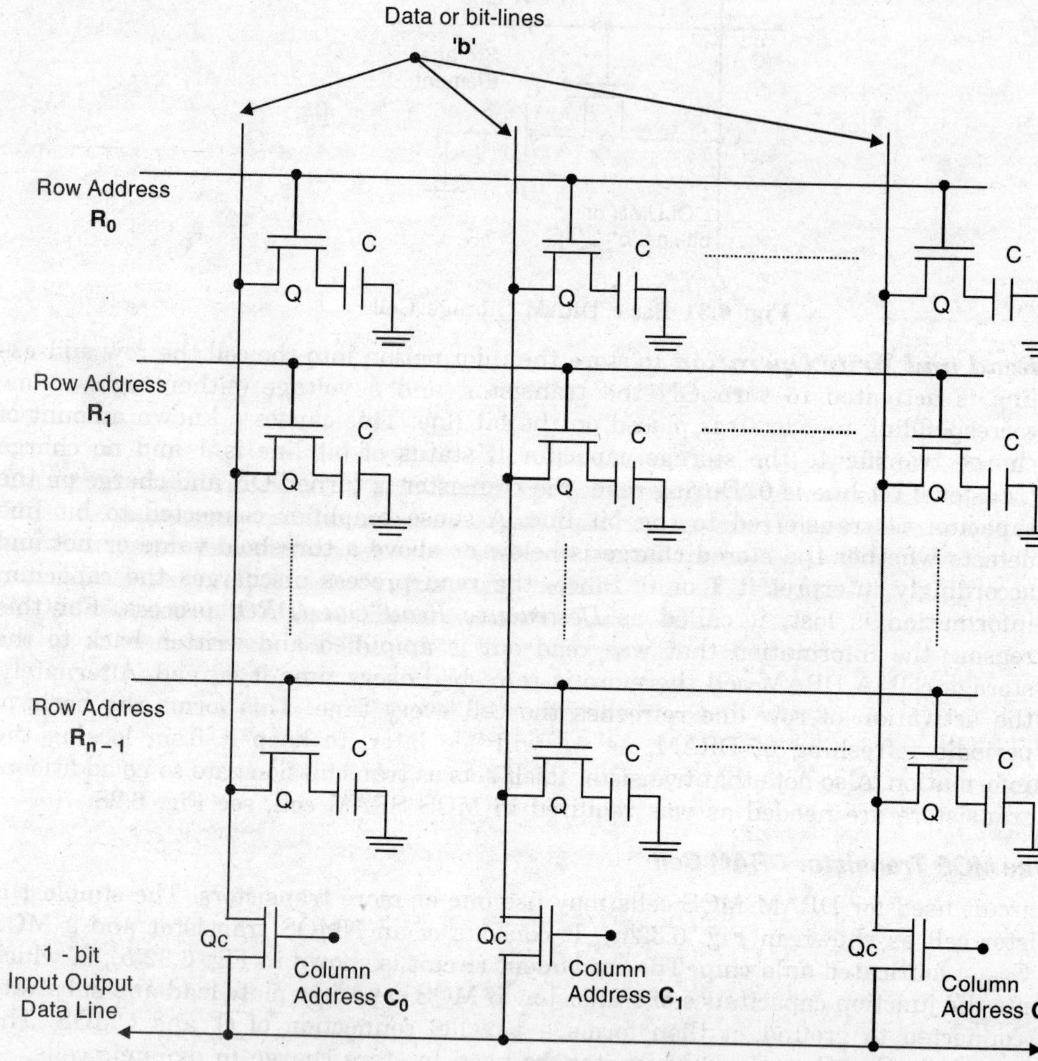


**Fig. 6.33** Organization of n × 1 MOS DRAM Memo

The organization of a DRAM allows many cells to be accessed together by a minimum amount of circuitry. A DRAM memory contains an array of basic dynamic storage cells as shown in Fig. 6.33. Readers are advised to study the organization carefully. The organization is such that upon activation of a row all the cells of that row are selected. Then cells transfer the stored information to their corresponding bit line. Thus, all the cells of the activated row must be subsequently written back *i.e.*, refreshed, to restore the information. Application of column address will turn ON any one of the $Q_C$ transistors connected to the bit line. Thus, the data bit from desired cell is obtained which is then feeded to the sense amplifier before transferring to the output. Similarly for the write operation only one of the $Q_C$ transistors will be turned ON and the data present at the input is transferred to the desired cell. From the above discussion it is clear that for any operation with the DRAM the row address must be applied first and then column address is applied. Moreover, due to the fact that charge stored in DRAM cell is very small the actual read and write processes are too intricate. Thus selecting more than one cell at a time to read and write may create their own unique problems. For this reason DRAMs are organized to have a word length of 1-bit. An external circuitry (device) called DRAM controller is used along with DRAMs to attain periodic refresh of DRAM. Since activation of a row refreshes all the cells in that row, the DRAM controller simply activates all the rows to refresh entire DRAM. The DRAM controller also takes cares about all the timing requirements of DRAM chip like after what time span the refresh operation must be initiated.

### *6.4.13.4 The DRAM Structure*

The generalized structure of DRAM memory is shown by Fig. 6.34. Let us first turn our attention to the generalized block diagram of a DRAM shown in Fig. 6.34(*a*). Since DRAMs have higher storage capacity the requirements of address lines are also large. That means too many pins have to be devoted to the address bus. To deal with, manufacturers have multiplexed the address bits in two groups; the row address and the column address. That's why the diagram shows n/2-bit address bus. The two signals $\overline{\text{RAS}}$ and $\overline{\text{CAS}}$ are used to tell when row address and when the column address respectively, is applied. RAS stands for *row address strobe* and CAS stands for *column address strobe*. A low on any of these two lines strobes the address present on address bus into an internal latch. The latch can be row address latch if RAS is activated or column address latch if CAS is activated, as shown in Fig. 6.34(*b*). Output of these two latches are used by the two decoders to address the required cell. Note that the $\overline{\text{CAS}}$ also performs the chip select function is most of the DRAMs. As previously stated for any operation the first the row address followed by $\overline{\text{RAS}}$ is applied. After that the column address of desired cell followed by $\overline{\text{CAS}}$ is applied. The DRAM controller handles this sequence for the users and fulfills the required timing between the signals. In fact DRAM controllers are invisible for users from operational point of view, even though they actually communicate with them only. It is DRAM controller that actually communicates with DRAM IC by means of various signals. A practically useful DRAM is IC-4116 whose pin

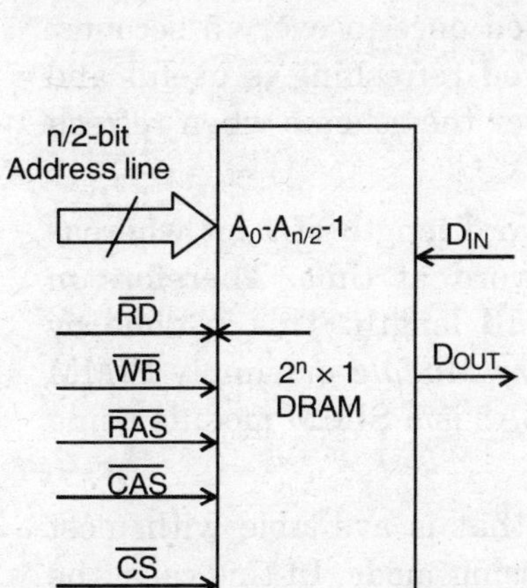


**Fig. 6.34**(*a*) General Block Diagram of a $2^n \times 1$ DRAM

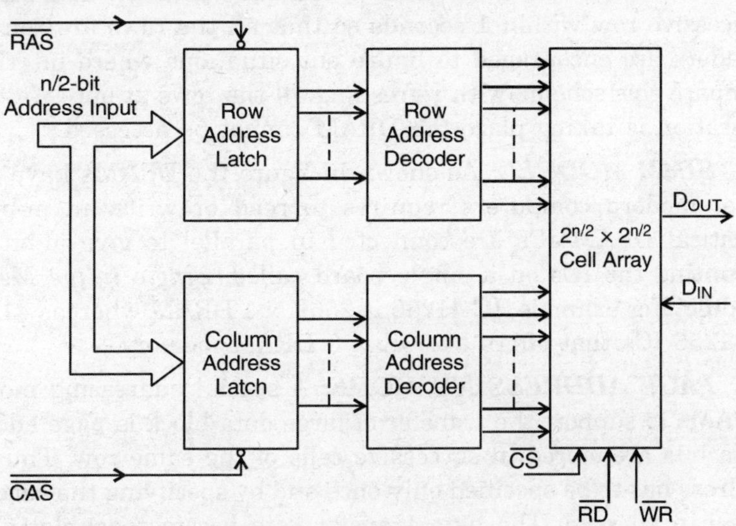


**Fig. 6.34**(*b*) General structure of A $2^n \times 1$ DRAM

diagram is shown in Fig. 6.35. This IC employs architecture identical to the one shown in Fig. 6.34(*b*) but utilizes a 128 × 128 cell array. Note that the IC does not have any chip select signal thus it is performed by the $\overline{\text{CAS}}$ signal.

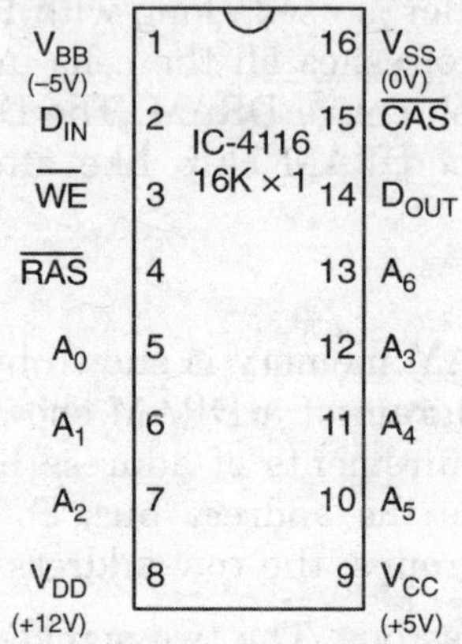


**Fig. 6.35** Pin Diagram of IC 4116 A 16K×1 DRAM

***REFRESHING DRAMs:*** To refresh, the DRAM controller utilizes the fact that activation of a row refreshes all the cells connected to that row. The DRAM controller simply outputs a row address and activates the $\overline{\text{RAS}}$ signal to refresh a row. Such a memory cycle is called as $\overline{\text{RAS}}$ cycle. The total number of such cycles needed to refresh all the rows constitute one refresh cycle that refreshes the entire DRAM. The DRAM controller initiates a refresh cycles after every predetermined time interval as specified by data sheet of DRAM. Yet another method is to interleave the refresh operation in which only one row is refreshed at a time and each successive row is refreshed after a fixed amount of time. Consider for example a DRAM having 5 rows and after 5 seconds datas are lost. Then it is require to refresh each successive row within 1 seconds so that all the rows are refreshed once in every 5 seconds. Readers are encouraged to figure out situations where interleaved refreshing is useful and compare this scheme with refreshing all the rows at once. In either the scheme when refresh operation is taking place the DRAM cannot be accessed.

***SIMM MODULE:*** As shown in figure the DRAMs have a word length of 1-bit whereas most modern computers requires to read or write an m-bit word at time. Therefore m identical DRAM ICs are connected in parallel to give m-bit word length. This is done by mounting the ICs on a single board called, *Single Inline Memory Module* or simply SIMM module. For example, IC 41256 is 256K × 1 DRAM whereas 41256A8 is a SIMM module using 8 41256 ICs that offers a 256K × 8 DRAM memory.

***PAGE ADDRESSING MODE:*** A special addressing mode that is available with most DRAMs to support the transfer of large data block is page addressing mode. In this case, the data bits are stored in successive cells of the same row. Thus for the data transfer the row address has to be specified only once and by specifying the successive column address the data bits can be read. The data transfer rate becomes double in this case as compared to the normal case in which each time a cell is accessed both the row and column address must be issued.

***PSEUDOSTATIC DRAMs:*** Newer DRAMs are available in which the refresh logic is incorporated in the memory chip itself. In this case the dynamic nature of these memories are almost invisible. Such a dynamic memory is referred as pseudostatic, or simply PDRAMs. Note that when internal refreshing is going on the device cannot be accessed.

### 6.4.14 SRAMs and DRAMs

Having been studied the SRAMs and DRAMs it is worth to devote sometime in comparative study of the two memories. Here are the few, which must be appreciated for the two types.

- The SRAMs cells can either be Bipolar or MOS but DRAM cells can only be MOS.
- The DRAM cells are much simpler than the SRAM cells.
- SRAMs can retain information as long as power is ON where as DRAMs loose the retained information after a small time and thus requires refreshing.
- Data storage in DRAMs involves charge storage where as in SRAMs it involves ON/OFF the transistors.
- DRAM cells can be constructed around a single transistor where SRAMs may require 6 transistors per cell. Thus DRAMs offer higher storage density. In fact the DRAMs are among the densest VLSI circuits in terms of transistor per chip. Due to this almost all the RAMs greater than 16KB are DRAMs.
- DRAMs are cost effective memory solution than the SRAMs.
- The actual read/write mechanism of DRAMs are much more tedious than that of SRAMs.
- DRAMs are always organized with the word length of 1-bit so that they are used with SIMM module where as SRAMs are organized for many different word lengths.
- DRAMs require many hardware pins so that address lines have be multiplexed where as it is seldom the case with SRAMs.
- Timing requirements of DRAMs are very complex as compared to the timing requirements of SRAMs.
- The DRAMs suffer from destructive read out so that each read must be followed by a write whereas there is no such problem with SRAMs.
- The DRAM requires extra hardware circuitry, called DRAM Controllers, for its proper operation where as SRAM does not need such supports.
- DRAMs are slower than the SRAMs due to destructive read out, address multiplexing and mainly due to refresh requirements.
- Future expansion of DRAM is easier as they are used with SIMM module in which case expansion involves replacement of board on the slot of main board. Needless to mention that using SIMM further increases the storage capacity than achieved by using a single DRAM chip.
- The DRAM cells offer lesser power consumption compared to either BJT or MOS SRAM cell.

At this point we strongly recommend the readers to find out similar comparison between other memory devices like BJT and MOS SRAMs, BJT and MOS ROMs and PROMs etc.

## 6.4.15 Memory System Design

An important aspect of study of memories to design a memory system that suits for a particular application. A design engineer is suppose to design a memory system that meets number of required storage words and the word length with the available resources. The memory system design main involves the two things

- The Address Space Allocation or Address decoding.
- Obtaining the required storage capacity with a given word length.

The first point requires the understanding of address range available with memory IC and that with the available with processing system. The second problem mainly requires different types of connection that can be made with the memory ICs to achieve the required capacity and word length. We access these steps one by one in following subsections to elaborate the idea. It has been our experience that students are often feared about how to determine number of address lines, how to find out address ranges and how it is written. Thus, we first address this issue in order to make the newcomers feel easy.

### *6.4.15.1 Determining Address Lines and Address Range*

To determine the number of address lines in a memory IC we first see its organization (*e.g.*, 1K × 8) to find out the number of storage locations or words in that memory. For example, in 1K × 8 memory 1K = 1024 storage locations or words are present. Now by using equation 2 we determine the number of address lines in a memory. We have equation 2 as

$$2^n \geq \textit{number of storage locations}$$

Where $n$ = number of address lines and is always integer.

| *Address bits* → | $A_9$ | $A_8$ | $A_7$ | $A_6$ | $A_5$ | $A_4$ | $A_3$ | $A_2$ | $A_1$ | $A_0$ | *Address In Hex* |
|---|---|---|---|---|---|---|---|---|---|---|---|
| Starting Address | 0 | 0 | 0 | 0 | 0 | 0 | 0 | 0 | 0 | 0 | $000_H$ |
| Ending Address | 1 | 1 | 1 | 1 | 1 | 1 | 1 | 1 | 1 | 1 | $3FF_H$ |

**Fig. 6.36** Address Bit Map or Address Range for 1K × 8 Memory

So for 1K × 8 memory $2^n \geq$ 1K = 1024 results in $n$ = 10. *i.e.*, it has 10 address lines. The address bits are written as $A_0$, $A_1$...$A_{n-1}$ *i.e.*, for $n$ = 10 they are labeled as $A_0$, $A_1$...$A_9$. To determine the address range we use the fact that addresses are specified as binary bit and each binary bit can have max change from 0 to 1. Thus to determine range we consider this max change for address bits at a time as shown in Fig. 6.36 for 1K × 8 memory. While writing the memory addresses the usual way is to write in hexadecimal instead of binary for the sake of easiness.

Thus, the address ranges from $000_H$ to $3FF_H$ for a 1K × 8 memory. The bitwise representation of memory address as shown in Fig. 6.36 is called as *Address Bit Map*. We will use such type of bit maps in designing problems. From the above *we can conclude that adding $3FF_H$ to the initial address will give the last address of 1K memory locations*. The same can be said alternately, that by changing the 10 address bits we traverse through any of the 1K address location.

#### 6.4.15.2 Parallel and Series Connections of Memory

In this subsection, we are concerned with how connect more than one memory ICs to get the desired word length and desired number of address location. In general we can connect the memory in three different configurations. They are

- Parallel Connection
- Series Connection
- Series-parallel Connection

The *parallel connection* of memory ICs are used when we need to increase the word length while keeping the address location same. In this case the address lines and control signals are tied together by forming wired-OR and data lines from all the ICs are taken at the output to provide desired word length. Let we have two ICs organized as 1K × 4 and we need a memory of 1K × 8. A Parallel connection shown in Fig. 6.37 can solve this issue.

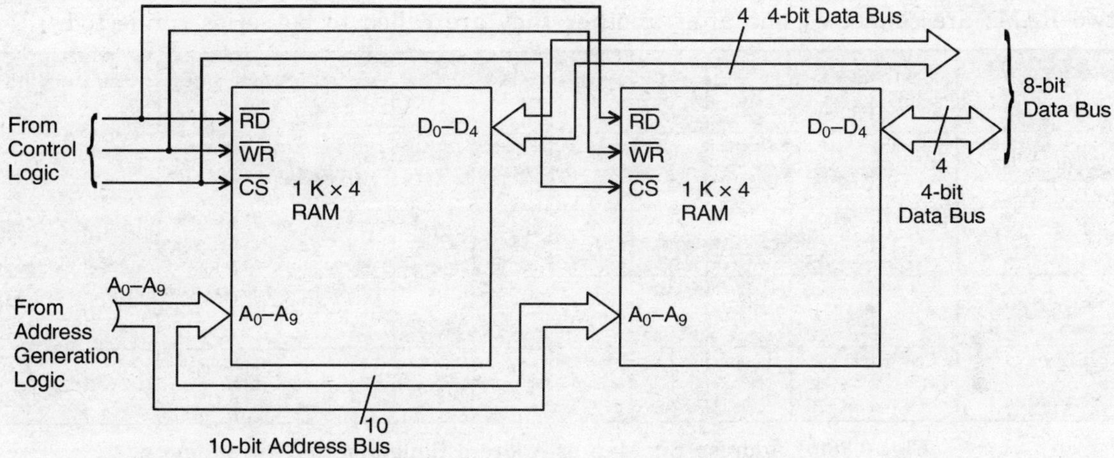


**Fig. 6.37** Parallel connection of 1024 × 4 RAMS to obtain 1024 × 8 RAM

Observe the figure carefully and notice that 4-bit data bus from two ICs are taken at the output in parallel giving a total of 8-bit data bus, that why it is called parallel connection. Any group of the four bits can be defined least significant or most significant.

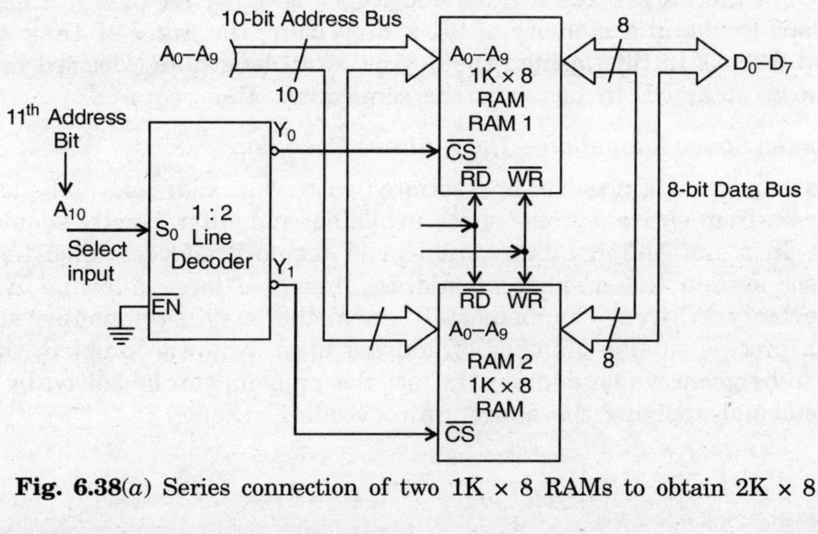


**Fig. 6.38**(*a*) Series connection of two 1K × 8 RAMs to obtain 2K × 8 RAM

The *series connection* of memory ICs are used when we need to increase the address location while keeping the word length same. In this case, the address lines, data lines and control signals are all tied together by forming wired-OR. A decoder can then be used to select one of the ICs. This provides the desired numbers of address locations. Let we have two ICs organized as 1K × 8 and we need a memory of 2K × 8. A series connection shown in Fig. 6.38(*a*) can solve this issue.

Since, there are two ICs of 1K locations each, when combined together they can give 2K locations. But having 2K locations requires 11-address bits. The select input of 2:1 line decoder provides this 11th address bit as labeled in Figure. When this bit 0 the upper RAM is selected and when 1 lower RAM is selected. Thus 2K locations can be accessed. The address bit map for this connection is shown in Fig. 6.38(*b*). Observe how the address is changing for the two values of $A_{10}$ which is connected to the select input of decoder. Thus we can say that we have address bank of 2K locations. As clearly seen by the bit map 1st 1K addresses of this bank are assigned to the upper RAM and 2nd 1K are assigned to the lower RAM. Since the two RAMs are connected one after another they are called to be series connected.

| *Address bits* → | $A_{10}$ | $A_9$ | $A_8$ | $A_7$ | $A_6$ | $A_5$ | $A_4$ | $A_3$ | $A_2$ | $A_1$ | $A_0$ | *Address In Hex* |
|---|---|---|---|---|---|---|---|---|---|---|---|---|
| Starting Address | 0 | 0 | 0 | 0 | 0 | 0 | 0 | 0 | 0 | 0 | 0 | $000_H$ |
| Ending Address | 0 | 1 | 1 | 1 | 1 | 1 | 1 | 1 | 1 | 1 | 1 | $3FF_H$ |
| Starting Address | 1 | 0 | 0 | 0 | 0 | 0 | 0 | 0 | 0 | 0 | 0 | $400_H$ |
| Ending Address | 1 | 1 | 1 | 1 | 1 | 1 | 1 | 1 | 1 | 1 | 1 | $7FF_H$ |

**Fig. 6.38**(*b*) Address Bit Map or Address Range for 1K × 8 Memory

The *series-parallel connection* of memory ICs are used when we need to increase both the word length and the number of address locations. This is the combination of first two connections. If readers are through with the first two configurations this can easily be understood. For this type of connection we can consider the connection shown in Fig. 6.38(*a*) in which each of the 1K × 8 ICs are derived from Fig. 6.37. Readers are instructed to draw the connections to obtain a memory of 2K × 8 by using the 4-ICs of 1K × 4 on the basis of Fig. 6.37 and 6.38(*a*). In this fashion the desired word length and desired number of storage locations can be obtained. In fact it is the connection often required.

### *6.4.15.3 Address Space Allocation—The Address Decoding*

The address-decoding problem is associated with what addresses to be assigned to which memory devices from entire address space available, and what exactly should be the scheme to assign it. In a nutshell it is the problem of memory address allocation. In a general microprocessor system the number of address lines are large allowing it to access large amount of memory. Whereas the memory ICs available may be of smaller storage capacities *i.e.*, they can process smaller number of address lines. Now the problem could be which of the ICs are to be given which address. In fact the problem can be solved by careful analysis of requirement and applying the appropriate decoding scheme.

There are two types of decoding schemes, *Exhaustive Decoding* and *Partial Decoding*. In the exhaustive or fully decoded system, all the address lines of processor must be decoded. In case of partial decoding scheme, all the address lines of processor are not decoded. But in this case the addresses may not be unique and more than one address can be assigned to same memory word.

To understand it let us consider a residential colony in which house numbers can be a 4-digit numbers and any of the house can be allotted a number between 0000 to 9999. Now suppose only the numbers from 1000 to 2000 are allotted to houses. In this case saying house numbers 500 or even 3500 or 4500 is same as 1500 as we know that only house numbers are one from 1000 to 2000. Saying just 500 as house number means *Partial Decoding* in case of memory address decoding. Whereas saying house number 1500 is *Exhaustive Decoding*. Now consider the case when allotted house numbers are 1000 to 3000 then saying just 500 to mention same house creates trouble that whether it refers to 1500 or 2500 as both are present. In memories it means two memory ICs are assigned same address. So both the ICs will start working at a time causing *BUS Contention* to occur. *BUS Contention* is a situation in which more than one device attempts to drive the system bus simultaneously in which case buses may be damaged. To avoid all such problems we must give complete house number *i.e.,* 1500 to refer to that house. Thus before saying 500 we must ensure that there is no other house number whose last 3 digits are 500. The same is ensured in memory systems too, to avoid bus contention. Thus irrespective of the decoding schemes the goal of design is to assign unambiguous (or unique) addresses to memory devices. The way two schemes are realized are explained in next subsection.

#### 6.4.15.4 Formation of Memory System

In this section we are concerned with how to deal with the requirements of different systems. Here we must analyze the different requirement given to us and check the resources available and then take the appropriate steps to solve the problem. In fact a design engineer is supposed to come with the appropriate access circuitry for the memory modules given to him/her in order to obtain the required system. It has our best observation and reading that it is far better if we consider the problems to illustrate the ideas to students. So we start with the example in this subsection to consider the different situation and its fulfillment. *Note that we illustrate many important facts and make the important conclusions through these examples only.* We first start with the assumption that processing system can be a microprocessor or any other system capable of providing the required number address bits and control signals required for memory. Our job is mainly to find out the decoding circuitry for the circuits.

**Example 1.** *It is required to obtain a memory system of 2K × 8 bits for a certain application. Given that memory ICs available are 1K × 8. Obtain the desired system.*

**Solution.** By reading the problem it is revealed that we have already solved this problem even before saying any thing!!!!. If surprised see Fig. 6.38(*a*), it is same as required by problem. Sit comfortably now because we are already through with it. For the reference we reproduce the Fig. 6.38(*a*) and 6.38(*b*) again.

It's now time to list out the different steps in order to solve these types of problems. Carefully read all steps we take to solve this problem again.

1. > *Determine the total number of address lines required for the memory system to be designed.*

Given total requirement is 2K × 8 means we need a *total of 11 address lines* because $2^{11}$ = 2048 = 2K.

**2.** > *Determine the number of address bits available with the given memory ICs.*

Given ICs are 1K × 8 means we have 10 address lines available with the individual ICs because $2^{10}$ = 1024 = 1K.

**3.** > *Determine the number of bits available for the chip decoder.*

Since total required address bits are 11 and individual memories can handle 10-bits of address, we are left with 1 address bit. This extra bit can be feeded to the decoder as shown in the Fig. 6.39(*a*).

**4.** > *Draw the Address Bit Map for Entire Memory Space and indicate change in bits for individual memory ICs.* This is needed to assign particular address to individual ICs. The same is shown in Fig. 6.39(*b*).

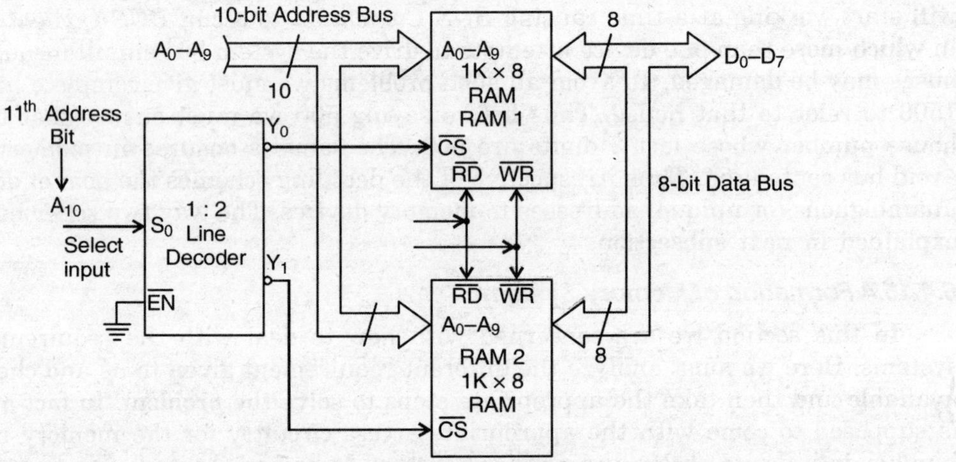


**Fig. 6.39**(*a*) Series connection of two 1K × 8 RAMs to obtain 2K × 8 RAM

Decoder bit ← Address bits handled by memory ICs →

| | $A_{10}$ | $A_9$ | $A_8$ | $A_7$ | $A_6$ | $A_5$ | $A_4$ | $A_3$ | $A_2$ | $A_1$ | $A_0$ | HEX Addr | IC |
|---|---|---|---|---|---|---|---|---|---|---|---|---|---|
| Start Addr | 0 | 0 | 0 | 0 | 0 | 0 | 0 | 0 | 0 | 0 | 0 | $000_H$ | RAM 1 |
| End Addr | 0 | 1 | 1 | 1 | 1 | 1 | 1 | 1 | 1 | 1 | 1 | $3FF_H$ | |
| Start Addr | 1 | 0 | 0 | 0 | 0 | 0 | 0 | 0 | 0 | 0 | 0 | $400_H$ | RAM 2 |
| End Addr | 1 | 1 | 1 | 1 | 1 | 1 | 1 | 1 | 1 | 1 | 1 | $7FF_H$ | |

**Fig. 6.39**(*b*) Address Bit Map for figure 6.39(a) of example 1

Observe that bit $A_{10}$ does not change anywhere within the address rage for RAM1 and remains 0 always. The same is true for and RAM2 where bit $A_{10}$ 1 always. This justifies the step 3 to take the left over bits for decoder. As one can *see* that *the decoder bit selects how much memory address (1K in this case) can be selected by each output of the decoder*. In fact this is the main purpose of drawing address bit maps.

5. **> *Draw the Connection diagram for the memory ICs as per Address Bit Map*.** This is the one we have done already in Fig. 6.39(*a*). But this done for this example only. We will draw the connection diagram in this step only for the other examples.

6. **> *Draw the Address Map*.** In step we diagrammatically represents the entire memory address space and show which address is assigned to which IC as shown in Fig. 6.39(*c*).

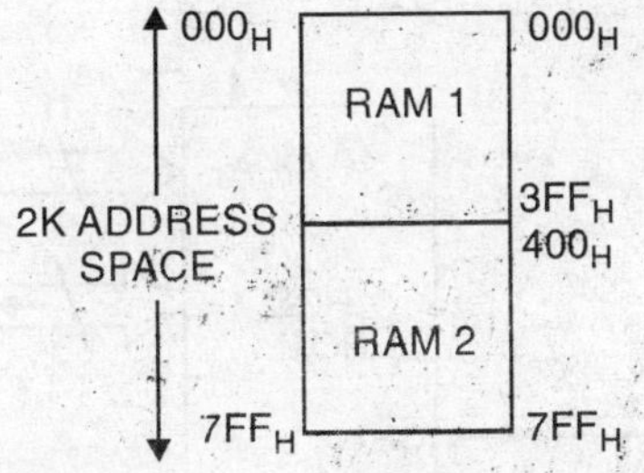


**Fig. 6.39**(*c*) Address Map for Fig. 6.39(*a*)

From this address map *we also conclude that adding $7FF_H$ to the initial address will give the last address of 2K memory locations.*

If you are waiting for step 7, we are sorry to say that problem is over and you have given the complete solution to the problem posed to you. We advise the readers to go to the beginning of this example and carefully read it again, as these are the findings we would be using in following examples.

**Example 2.** *Given two 2K × 8 ROM ICs and two 2K × 8 RAM ICs obtain a memory system of 8K × 8 bits.*

**Solution.** We start step by step as defined by the previous problem.

1. **>** Given total requirement is 8K × 8 means we need a *total of 13 address lines* because $2^{13}$ = 8192 = 8K.
2. **>** Given ICs are 2K × 8 means we have 11 address lines available with the individual ICs because $2^{11}$ = 2048 = 2K.
3. **>** Since total required address bits are 13 and individual memories can handle 11-bits of address, we are left with 2-address bit, which can be feeded to the decoder.
4. **> *Draw the Address Bit Map for Entire Memory Space and indicate change in bits for individual memory ICs*.** This is needed to assign particular address to individual ICs. The same is shown in Fig. 6.40(*a*).

| | Decoder bit | | ← Address bits handled by memory ICs → | | | | | | | | | | | | |
|---|---|---|---|---|---|---|---|---|---|---|---|---|---|---|---|
| | $A_{12}$ | $A_{11}$ | $A_{10}$ | $A_9$ | $A_8$ | $A_7$ | $A_6$ | $A_5$ | $A_4$ | $A_3$ | $A_2$ | $A_1$ | $A_0$ | HEX Addr | IC |
| Start Addr | 0 | 0 | 0 | 0 | 0 | 0 | 0 | 0 | 0 | 0 | 0 | 0 | 0 | $0000_H$ | ROM 1 |
| End Addr | 0 | 0 | 1 | 1 | 1 | 1 | 1 | 1 | 1 | 1 | 1 | 1 | 1 | $07FF_H$ | |
| Start Addr | 0 | 1 | 0 | 0 | 0 | 0 | 0 | 0 | 0 | 0 | 0 | 0 | 0 | $0800_H$ | ROM 2 |
| End Addr | 0 | 1 | 1 | 1 | 1 | 1 | 1 | 1 | 1 | 1 | 1 | 1 | 1 | $0FFF_H$ | |
| Start Addr | 1 | 0 | 0 | 0 | 0 | 0 | 0 | 0 | 0 | 0 | 0 | 0 | 0 | $1000_H$ | RAM 1 |
| End Addr | 1 | 0 | 1 | 1 | 1 | 1 | 1 | 1 | 1 | 1 | 1 | 1 | 1 | $17FF_H$ | |
| Start Addr | 1 | 1 | 0 | 0 | 0 | 0 | 0 | 0 | 0 | 0 | 0 | 0 | 0 | $1800_H$ | RAM 2 |
| End Addr | 1 | 1 | 1 | 1 | 1 | 1 | 1 | 1 | 1 | 1 | 1 | 1 | 1 | $1FFF_H$ | |

**Fig. 6.40**(*a*) Address Bit-Map for 8K × 8 Memory System of example 2

It is clear from the address bit map that each decoder output (selected by A12 and A11 bits) selects one 2K-memory address space.

**5.** > Connection diagram for the memory ICs is shown in Fig. 6.40(*b*).

**6.** > The Address Map is shown in Fig. 6.40(*c*).

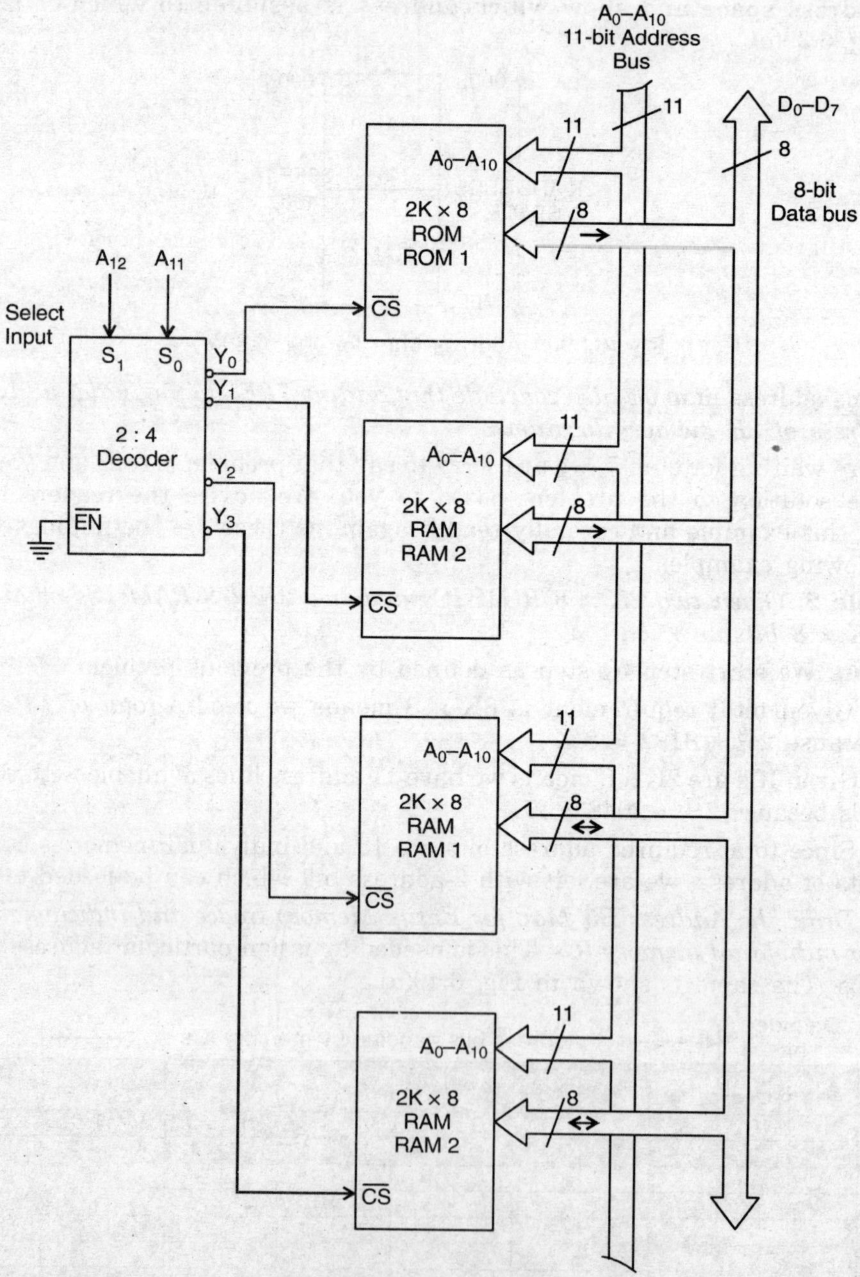


**Fig. 6.40**(*b*) Formation of 8KB memory system using RAMS and ROMS

From this address map *we also conclude that adding* $1FFF_H$ *to the initial address will give the last address of 8K memory locations.* Alternately we can say that we must change 13 address bits at a time to traverse through 8K memory locations.

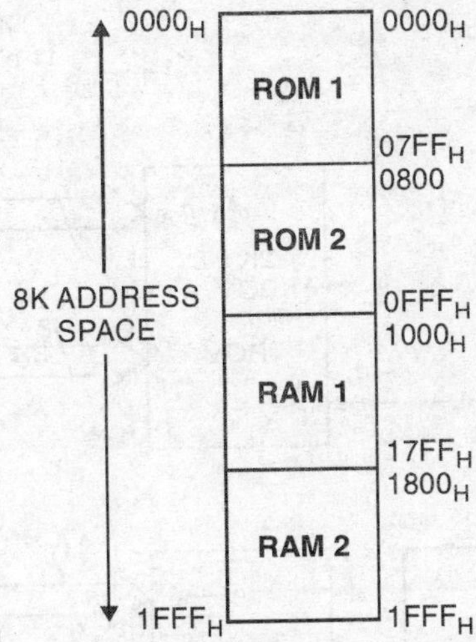


**Fig. 6.40**(*c*) Address Map for Fig. 6.40(*b*).

**Example 3.** *Given two 2K × 8 ROM ICs and two 2K × 8 RAM ICs obtain a memory system of 8K × 8 bits. It is required that 1st 2K address must be assigned to a ROM, 2nd 2K address to a RAM, 3rd 2K address to a ROM, and the 4th 2K address to a RAM.*

**Solution.** Read the statement once again it is essentially the same as previous problem, but the only difference is now it specifies the address where the particular memory devices are to be connected.

We know that for 8K address we need 13 address lines and with the arrangement shown in fig 40-B it reveals that we can access four 2K memory segments whose addresses can be obtained as shown in bit map of Fig. 6.40(*a*).

| | Decoder bit | | ← Address bits handled by memory ICs → | | | | | | | | | | | |
|---|---|---|---|---|---|---|---|---|---|---|---|---|---|---|
| | $A_{12}$ | $A_{11}$ | $A_{10}$ | $A_9$ | $A_8$ | $A_7$ | $A_6$ | $A_5$ | $A_4$ | $A_3$ | $A_2$ | $A_1$ | $A_0$ | HEX Addr | IC |
| Start Addr | 0 | 0 | 0 | 0 | 0 | 0 | 0 | 0 | 0 | 0 | 0 | 0 | 0 | $0000_H$ | ROM |
| End Addr | 0 | 0 | 1 | 1 | 1 | 1 | 1 | 1 | 1 | 1 | 1 | 1 | 1 | $07FF_H$ | 1 |
| Start Addr | 0 | 1 | 0 | 0 | 0 | 0 | 0 | 0 | 0 | 0 | 0 | 0 | 0 | $0800_H$ | RAM |
| End Addr | 0 | 1 | 1 | 1 | 1 | 1 | 1 | 1 | 1 | 1 | 1 | 1 | 1 | $0FFF_H$ | 1 |
| Start Addr | 1 | 0 | 0 | 0 | 0 | 0 | 0 | 0 | 0 | 0 | 0 | 0 | 0 | $1000_H$ | ROM |
| End Addr | 1 | 0 | 1 | 1 | 1 | 1 | 1 | 1 | 1 | 1 | 1 | 1 | 1 | $17FF_H$ | 2 |
| Start Addr | 1 | 1 | 0 | 0 | 0 | 0 | 0 | 0 | 0 | 0 | 0 | 0 | 0 | $1800_H$ | RAM |
| End Addr | 1 | 1 | 1 | 1 | 1 | 1 | 1 | 1 | 1 | 1 | 1 | 1 | 1 | $1FFF_H$ | 2 |

**Fig. 6.41**(*a*) Address Bit-Map for 8K × 8 Memory System of example 3

Now the only thing we need to do is to connect the device at correct outputs of the decoder, which can be obtained from bit map shown in Fig. 6.41(*a*). Go through the details of this map carefully.

The similar connection diagram and memory address map would also appear but with the ICs changed to positions required by problem. Fig. 6.41(*b*) and 6.41(*c*) show this.

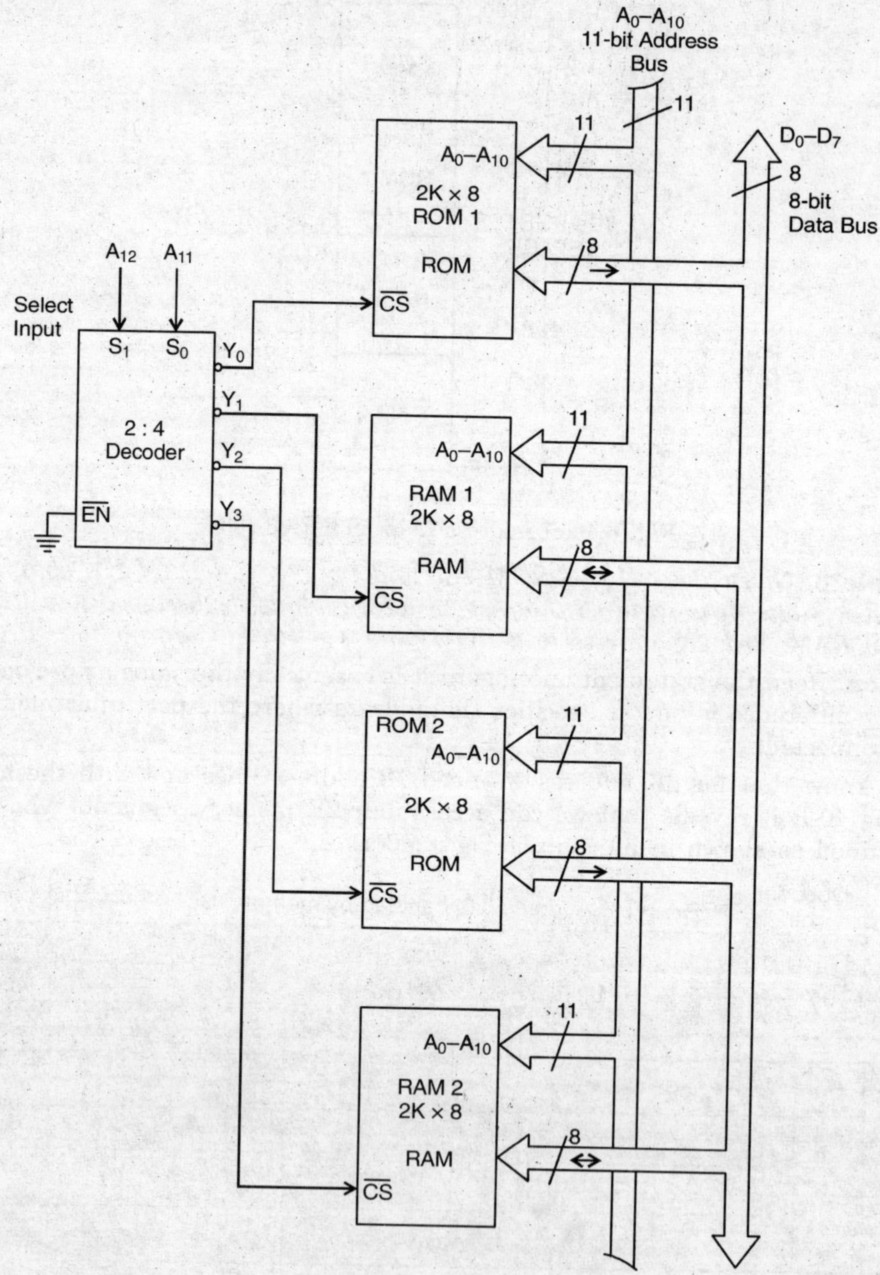


**Fig. 6.41**(*b*) Formation of 8KB memory system using RAMS and ROMS

**Example 4.** *Given two 2K × 8 ROM ICs and two 2K × 8 RAM ICs obtain a memory system of 8K × 8 bits. It is required that two ROMs must be connected to addresses beginning from 0000H and 1000H. Also the RAMs should be connected to begin from* $0800_H$ *and* $1800_H$.

**Solution.** Example 4 is just another way or giving statement for problem example 3. But we will consider it separately to understand that what should be the way to solve these types of issues.

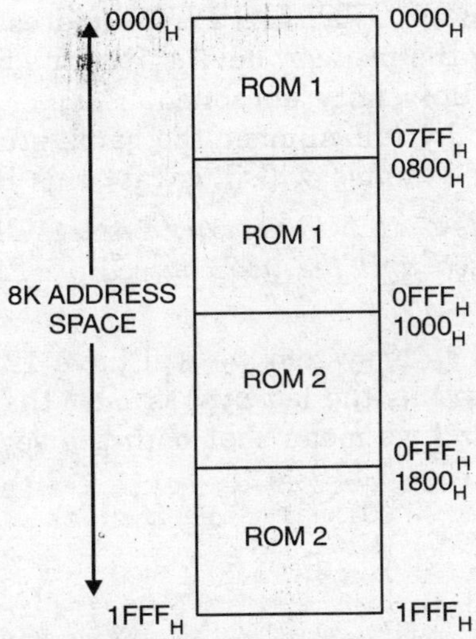


**Fig. 6.41**(*c*) Address Map for Fig. 6.41(*b*)

Except the step 4 *i.e.,* generating address bit map, all other steps are exactly same so that we consider only address bit map that too in much simplified way. Recall that in example 1 we concluded that adding $7FF_H$ to the initial address would give the last address of 2K memory locations. We use this to generate the bit map as given ICs are 2K × 8.

*For ROMs*: given that a ROM should start from $0000_H$ and $1000_H$

First when connected at $0000_H$:

$$\text{Last address} = 0000_H + 07FF_H = 07FF_H$$

So the address range is $0000_H$ to $07FF_H$

Second when connected at $1000_H$:

$$\text{Last address} = 1000_H + 07FF_H = 17FF_H$$

So the address range is $1000_H$ to $17FF_H$

*For RAMs*: in the similar way we get for RAMs

First when connected at $0800_H$:

Address range is $0800_H$ to $0FFF_H$

Second when connected at $1800_H$:

Address range is $1800_H$ to $1FFF_H$

Compare these addresses with those shown in the bit map of Fig. 6.41(*a*), you reached the same map. Thus, the entire Fig. 6.41 can redrawn for example 4.

It is interesting to see that instead of adding 07FF if we would have changed the least 11 significant address bits (as $2^{11}$ = 2K) of initial address to 1 even in that case also we could have reached the same point. Infact this is what we have done till example 3. Either the way we proceed it is same because we found the number 07FFH from the fact that the highest hexadecimal number that can be written by 11 address bits is 07FFH. Many a times you will find that adding a number to initial address is easier because it is less time consuming than case of drawing complete bit map. But this short hand is useful only when you are through with concept and saying a hexadecimal number displays its bit pattern in your mind.

***SHADOWING or ADDRESS OVERLAPPING*** address overlapping means assigning more than one address space to the memory device. It is the situation similar with a student who has his roll number and university enrolment number unique to him. So that when called by enrolment number or by roll number the same student will respond and none of the other students respond. An example will illustrate this best.

**Example 5.** *A system needs a 4K × 8 memory system. But the requirement is such that a single 2K × 8 RAM IC be used and the two consecutive 2K memory addresses should be overlapped to this device only.*

**Solution.** We know that for 4K system we will have 12 address lines. The 2K devices can process only 11 address bits thus the left over is 1-bit that can be used to access two 2K segments. By address overlapping we mean that both the segments would be referenced for same device. This is shown in Fig. 6.42.

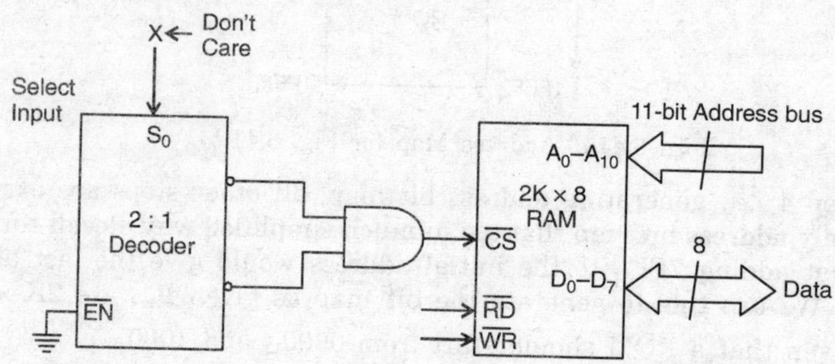


**Fig. 6.42** Illustration of Memory Address Overlapping with 2K × 8IC

Notice the use of AND gate used to generate chip select for memory device. As shown, upon activation decoder outputs goes low so whether activated output is $Y_0$ or $Y_1$ AND gate output is always low. This means memory is selected irrespective of the status of select input of decoder.

If we draw (readers are instructed to draw) the bit map for 4K as two 2K address block we see that first 2K block is 000 to $7FF_H$ and second 2K block is $800_H$ to $FFF_H$. With the configuration shown in figure 42 both the address blocks refers to the same IC thus address blocks are overlapped to each other and hence the name address overlapping. In the similar way, we can overlap any two equal sized address blocks present in entire address map (or space).

We now turn our attention to exhaustive and partially decoded memory system. For illustration purpose, we again consider the problem posed in example 2. Because write now we are very much through with it and once we understand the idea we can apply it to design. Read the problem statement carefully as it is going to create the difference.

**Example 6.** *It is required to obtain an 8K × 8 memory system for 8085 microprocessor system that has an addressing capability of 64K locations. Given memories are 2K × 8 ROM ICs and 2K × 8 RAM ICs. Obtain the exhaustive or fully decoded as well as partially decoded system.*

**Solution.** We first determine the number of address lines this processor has. 64K means $2^{16}$ *i.e.,* the processor has 16 address bits whereas the requirement for memory is just 13-bits, see step 1 in example 2. This means 3 address bits of processor will remain unused (or unchanged). This is shown by the address bit maps in Fig. 6.43, which now contains 16 bits instead of 13.

*For exhaustive decoding:* As stated for this scheme we must decode all the address bits of microprocessor. The address bit map for this scheme is shown in Fig. 6.43(*a*). It shows that bit $A_{13}$ to bit $A_{15}$ are unchanged for entire 8K-address space. Since, in this scheme we must decode all address bits, we can use these 3-bits to generate $\overline{EN}$ signal for Decoder which can also be used enable or disable the memory system by enabling/disabling decoder.

| | Unchanged bit | | | Decoder bit | | Address bits handled by memory ICs | | | | | | | | | | | | |
|---|---|---|---|---|---|---|---|---|---|---|---|---|---|---|---|---|---|---|
| | $A_{15}$ | $A_{14}$ | $A_{13}$ | $A_{12}$ | $A_{11}$ | $A_{10}$ | $A_9$ | $A_8$ | $A_7$ | $A_6$ | $A_5$ | $A_4$ | $A_3$ | $A_2$ | $A_1$ | $A_0$ | HEX Addr | IC |
| Start Addr | 0 | 0 | 0 | 0 | 0 | 0 | 0 | 0 | 0 | 0 | 0 | 0 | 0 | 0 | 0 | 0 | $0000_H$ | ROM |
| End Addr | 0 | 0 | 0 | 0 | 0 | 1 | 1 | 1 | 1 | 1 | 1 | 1 | 1 | 1 | 1 | 1 | $07FF_H$ | 1 |
| Start Addr | 0 | 0 | 0 | 0 | 1 | 0 | 0 | 0 | 0 | 0 | 0 | 0 | 0 | 0 | 0 | 0 | $0800_H$ | RAM |
| End Addr | 0 | 0 | 0 | 0 | 1 | 1 | 1 | 1 | 1 | 1 | 1 | 1 | 1 | 1 | 1 | 1 | $0FFF_H$ | 1 |
| Start Addr | 0 | 0 | 0 | 1 | 0 | 0 | 0 | 0 | 0 | 0 | 0 | 0 | 0 | 0 | 0 | 0 | $1000_H$ | ROM |
| End Addr | 0 | 0 | 0 | 1 | 0 | 1 | 1 | 1 | 1 | 1 | 1 | 1 | 1 | 1 | 1 | 1 | $17FF_H$ | 2 |
| Start Addr | 0 | 0 | 0 | 1 | 1 | 0 | 0 | 0 | 0 | 0 | 0 | 0 | 0 | 0 | 0 | 0 | $1800_H$ | RAM |
| End Addr | 0 | 0 | 0 | 1 | 1 | 1 | 1 | 1 | 1 | 1 | 1 | 1 | 1 | 1 | 1 | 1 | $1FFF_H$ | 2 |

**Fig. 6.43**(*a*) Address Bit-Map for exhaustive decoded 8K × 8 Memory System of example 6

The diagram for decoder along with enable generation is shown in Fig. 6.43(*b*). The figure indicates which decoder output to be connected to which IC. In fact connections will be same as Fig. 6.40(*b*) and the decoder of Fig. 6.43(*b*) will replace decoder of Fig. 6.40(*b*).

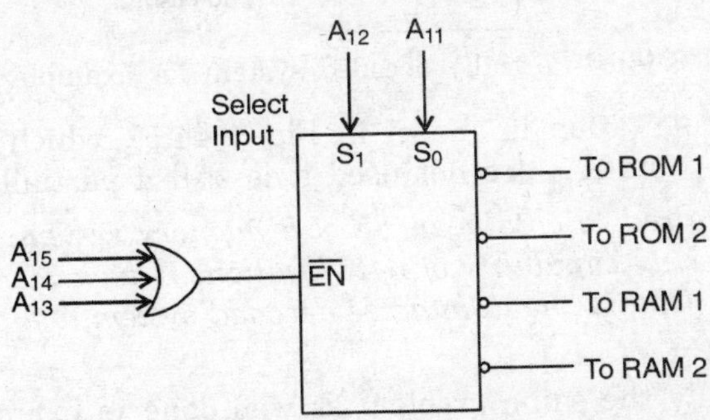


**Fig. 6.43**(*b*) Exhaustive Decoded System for example 6

Notice the use of OR gate. Output of OR gate is low only when all its inputs are low otherwise high. Thus saying an address higher than $1FFF_H$ will not be responded by this system. If we say 8000H it means bit $A_{15}$ goes high and output of OR gate goes high thus disabling the decoder and consequently the entire memory system.

*For partial decoding:* Here the idea is not to use all the address bits of processor for address decoding. As the 3 most significant address bits $A_{15}$, $A_{14}$, $A_{13}$ are unchanged we can say that they are not used *i.e.*, don't care. So it hardly matters if we use them for decoding or not. The address bit map shown in Fig. 6.44(*a*) show this.

| | Unchanged bit | | | Decoder bit | | Address bits handled by memory ICs | | | | | | | | | | | | |
|---|---|---|---|---|---|---|---|---|---|---|---|---|---|---|---|---|---|---|
| | $A_{15}$ | $A_{14}$ | $A_{13}$ | $A_{12}$ | $A_{11}$ | $A_{10}$ | $A_9$ | $A_8$ | $A_7$ | $A_6$ | $A_5$ | $A_4$ | $A_3$ | $A_2$ | $A_1$ | $A_0$ | HEX Addr | IC |
| Start Addr | X | X | X | 0 | 0 | 0 | 0 | 0 | 0 | 0 | 0 | 0 | 0 | 0 | 0 | 0 | $0000_H$ | ROM |
| End Addr | X | X | X | 0 | 0 | 1 | 1 | 1 | 1 | 1 | 1 | 1 | 1 | 1 | 1 | 1 | $07FF_H$ | 1 |
| Start Addr | X | X | X | 0 | 1 | 0 | 0 | 0 | 0 | 0 | 0 | 0 | 0 | 0 | 0 | 0 | $0800_H$ | RAM |
| End Addr | X | X | X | 0 | 1 | 1 | 1 | 1 | 1 | 1 | 1 | 1 | 1 | 1 | 1 | 1 | $0FFF_H$ | 1 |
| Start Addr | X | X | X | 1 | 0 | 0 | 0 | 0 | 0 | 0 | 0 | 0 | 0 | 0 | 0 | 0 | $1000_H$ | ROM |
| End Addr | X | X | X | 1 | 0 | 1 | 1 | 1 | 1 | 1 | 1 | 1 | 1 | 1 | 1 | 1 | $17FF_H$ | 2 |
| Start Addr | X | X | X | 1 | 1 | 0 | 0 | 0 | 0 | 0 | 0 | 0 | 0 | 0 | 0 | 0 | $1800_H$ | RAM |
| End Addr | X | X | X | 1 | 1 | 1 | 1 | 1 | 1 | 1 | 1 | 1 | 1 | 1 | 1 | 1 | $1FFF_H$ | 2 |

**Fig. 6.44**(*a*) Address Bit-Map for partially decoded 8K × 8 Memory System of example 6

This means irrespective of the status of $A_{15}$, $A_{14}$, and $A_{13}$ the memory system can be used. Thus, Fig. 6.40(*b*) is direct implementation of partially decoded system, as it does not include these bits.

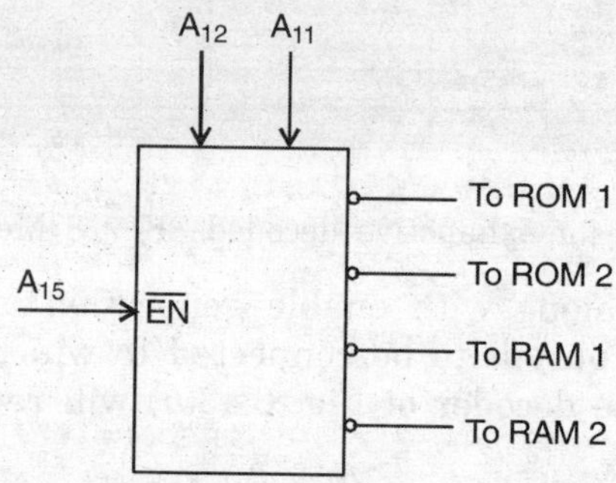


**Fig. 6.44**(*b*) Partially decoded system for example 6.

A variation of implementation is shown in Fig. 6.44(*b*), which uses $A_{15}$ to enable the address decoder. Since $A_{14}$ and $A_{13}$ are not used it is still a partially decoded system.

**Example 7.** *It is required to obtain an 8K × 8 memory system for 8085 microprocessor system that has an addressing capability of 64K locations. Given memories are 2K × 8 ROM ICs and 2K × 8 RAM ICs. Obtain the exhaustive decoded system, which maps the 8K-memory system to begin from $8000_H$.*

**Solution.** It essentially the same problem as was done in example 6. The change now is to assign the particular address. For this already we have seen example 4. So we do not go to complete design rather we just draw the bit-map and decoder circuit required by stating the net outcomes of detailed design.

The only change in bit map of Fig. 6.45(*a*) as compared to that of Fig. 6.43(*a*) is just the status of $A_{15}$, which is set to 1 now. It is because 8K system has to begin from $8000_H$. No other change can be observed in this bit map. So we connect $A_{15}$ through not gate to the input of OR gate to generate the enable signal for this address range. This is shown in Fig. 6.44(*b*).

The readers are directed draw an address map for this design as was drawn in Fig. 6.40(*c*) of example 2.

| | Unchanged bit | | | Decoder bit | | Address bits handled by memory ICs | | | | | | | | | | | | |
|---|---|---|---|---|---|---|---|---|---|---|---|---|---|---|---|---|---|---|
| | $A_{15}$ | $A_{14}$ | $A_{13}$ | $A_{12}$ | $A_{11}$ | $A_{10}$ | $A_9$ | $A_8$ | $A_7$ | $A_6$ | $A_5$ | $A_4$ | $A_3$ | $A_2$ | $A_1$ | $A_0$ | HEX Addr | IC |
| Start Addr | 1 | 0 | 0 | 0 | 0 | 0 | 0 | 0 | 0 | 0 | 0 | 0 | 0 | 0 | 0 | 0 | $0000_H$ | ROM |
| End Addr | 1 | 0 | 0 | 0 | 0 | 1 | 1 | 1 | 1 | 1 | 1 | 1 | 1 | 1 | 1 | 1 | $07FF_H$ | 1 |
| Start Addr | 1 | 0 | 0 | 0 | 1 | 0 | 0 | 0 | 0 | 0 | 0 | 0 | 0 | 0 | 0 | 0 | $0800_H$ | RAM |
| End Addr | 1 | 0 | 0 | 0 | 1 | 1 | 1 | 1 | 1 | 1 | 1 | 1 | 1 | 1 | 1 | 1 | $0FFF_H$ | 1 |
| Start Addr | 1 | 0 | 0 | 1 | 0 | 0 | 0 | 0 | 0 | 0 | 0 | 0 | 0 | 0 | 0 | 0 | $1000_H$ | ROM |
| End Addr | 1 | 0 | 0 | 1 | 0 | 1 | 1 | 1 | 1 | 1 | 1 | 1 | 1 | 1 | 1 | 1 | $17FF_H$ | 2 |
| Start Addr | 1 | 0 | 0 | 1 | 1 | 0 | 0 | 0 | 0 | 0 | 0 | 0 | 0 | 0 | 0 | 0 | $1800_H$ | RAM |
| End Addr | 1 | 0 | 0 | 1 | 1 | 1 | 1 | 1 | 1 | 1 | 1 | 1 | 1 | 1 | 1 | 1 | $1FFF_H$ | 2 |

**Fig. 6.45**(*a*) Address Bit-Map for exhaustibe decoded 8K × 8 Memory System of example 7

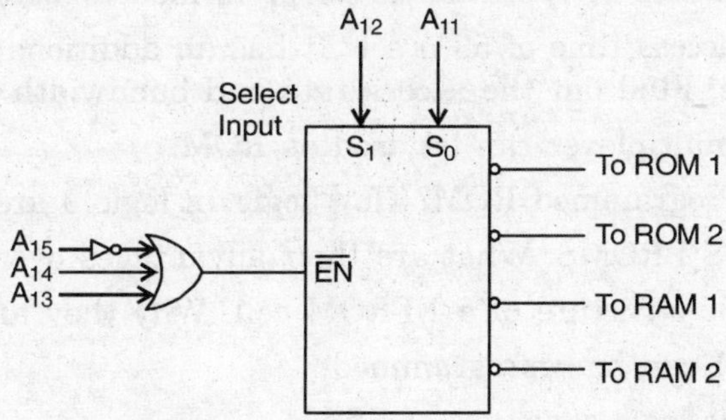


**Fig. 6.45**(*b*) Exhaustive Decoded system of Example 7

Although all the above examples do not contain all types design variation we hope that it will serve as the best building block to understand the problem memory bank formation. Notice that same system was taken to illustrate the different ideas because once we are familiar with a system then it is easy to view it in different situations. In general, the problems define IC numbers not the organization (*e.g.,* 2K × 8) of memories for which user must know the address bus width and data bus width. For this reason, readers are advised to prepare a list of ICs and memorize the bus width and control signals.

## 6.5 EXERCISE

1. What is meant by primary memory, secondary memory and mass storage devices?
2. Define the terms storage capacity, memory word, storage location and word length.
3. Determine the storage capacity of the memories shown in Fig. 6.46.

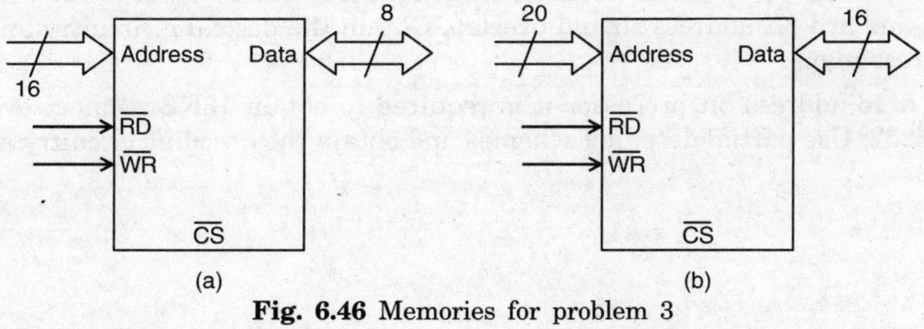


**Fig. 6.46** Memories for problem 3

4. Define the terms (*i*) Access Time (*ii*) Cycle time (*iii*) Bandwidth (*iv*) Volatile (*v*) Dynamic (*vi*) Static.
5. Explain organization of tracks in magnetic memories with the help of figure.
6. What are optical memories?
7. Explain basic semiconductor memory organization with the help of figure.
8. With the help of figure, explain the memory cell addressing.
9. In the Figure 6.8(b) how memory cell "Cell 3-2" is accessed?
10. Explain the memory cell organization shown in Figure 6.9. How a particular cell can be selected in this case?
11. A memory has cell array of 64 × 64, what will be the required number of lines of word length is (a) 2-bits (b) 4-bits (*c*) 8-bits.
12. Explain the sequence of operation to be performed to write a data into memory.
13. A memory has access time of 50 n sec. It has an additional delay called precharge time of 20 n sec. Find out the access rate and bandwidth of this unit.
14. Explain how a multiplexer can be used as ROM.
15. What is Mask Programmed ROM? How logic 1s logic 0 are stored in such ROMs?
16. Explain the MOS PROMS. What are their advantages over Bipolar PROMs?
17. Explain the basic structure of a EPROM cell. Why they are so popular?
18. How an EPROM can be reprogrammed?
19. Explain the basic logic structure of SRAM.
20. With the help of figure, explain the operation of a Bipolar SRAM cell and MOS SRAM cell.
21. What is Dynamic RAM? Why they are most widely used?
22. With the help of figure, explain the basic DRAM storage cell.
23. Draw the organization of a DRAM. How a particular cell can be read or write in this organization?
24. What are DRAM controllers? Why they are needed for operation of DRAM?
25. What are partial decoding and exhaustive decoding?
26. For a 16 Address-bit processor systems it is required to form 32 KB memory system using one 2764, Four 4016 and two 6264 memory ICs. Obtain the decoding circuitry and draw the address map. Use exhaustive decoding.
27. A system needs to create 16KB of memory using 6264 ICs. It is required that the 2nd and 3rd 8K address should overlap. Obtain the decoding circuitry and draw the address maps.
28. For a 16 address bit processor it is required to obtain 16KB memory system using IC 6232. Use partial decoding schemes and obtain the decoding circuitry and address maps.

PART C

# WAVE SHAPING CIRCUITS AND WAVEFORM GENERATORS

7

CHAPTER

# WAVE SHAPING CIRCUITS

## 7.0 INTRODUCTION

The process whereby the form of a signal is altered by transmission through a network is called "wave shaping".

There are different types of wave shaping circuits used in digital and analog circuits. These circuits are classified as follows:

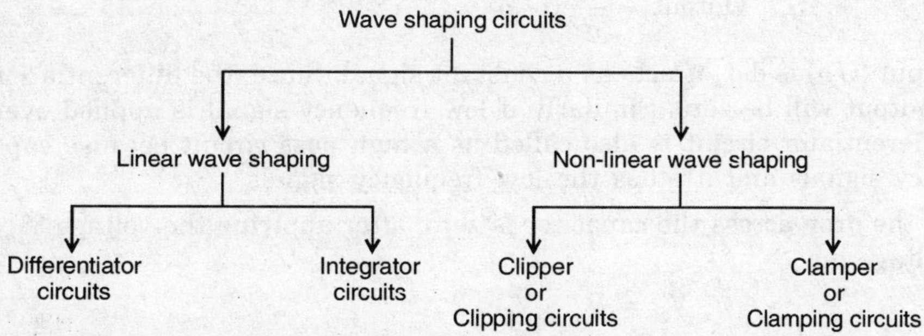


This chapter first goes through linear wave shaping (differentiator, integrator), followed by non-linear wave shaping (clipper, clamper).

## 7.1 DIFFERENTIATOR OR HIGH PASS CIRCUIT

The differentiator circuit also known as high pass circuit as shown in Fig. 7.1 is used for pulse shaping at number of places.

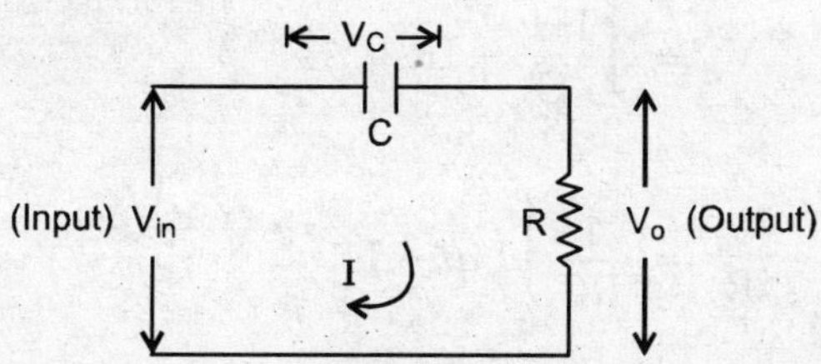


**Fig. 7.1**

In circuit component resistor (R), inductor (L), capacitor (C) mainly R and C are preferred. L is usually not used due to high cost.

For the given circuit

$$V_{in} = V_o + V_C$$

$$IZ = IR + IX_C$$

For D.C. signal, f is zero so

$$X_C = \frac{1}{2\pi fc} = \infty$$

For A.C. signal having low frequency

$$X_C = \frac{1}{2\pi fc} = \frac{1}{\text{low}} = \text{high}$$

For A.C. signal having high frequency

$$X_C = \frac{1}{2\pi fc} = \frac{1}{\text{high}} = \text{low}$$

Differentiating circuit provides the output which is proportional to differential of input $\left[\frac{d}{dt}(i/p)\right]$. *i.e.,*

$$\text{Output} \propto \frac{d}{dt}(i/p) \quad \text{...(7.1)}$$

If the input $(i/p)$ is d.c., it acts as a constant signal. Since, the differentiation of constant is zero, the output will be zero. Similarly if low frequency signal is applied even then o/p is zero. The differentiator circuit is also called as a high pass circuit because capacitor passes high frequency signals and it stops the low frequency signals.

Initially the drop across the capacitor is zero, after applying the voltage $V_{in}$ according to Kirchoff's voltage law

$$V_{in} = V_o + V_C$$

Since $$V_C = \frac{q}{C} = \frac{\int_o^t I\,dt}{C}$$

$$V_o = IR$$

Hence $$V_{in} = \int_o^t \frac{I\,dt}{C} + IR$$

$$\frac{V_{in}}{R} = \frac{1}{RC}\int_o^t I\,dt + I$$

Suppose if the time constant (RC) is small as compare to the time period of input $(i/p)$ signal. In such condition first term on RHS is very much larger than the IInd (second) term. So neglecting I

$$\frac{V_{in}}{R} = \frac{1}{RC}\int_o^t I\,dt$$

$$\text{RC V}_{\text{in}} = \text{R}\int_{o}^{t} \text{I}\, dt$$

Now differentiating the above equation with respect to $t$, we get

$$\text{RC}\frac{d}{dt}(\text{V}_{in}) = \text{RI}$$

$$\text{RC}\frac{d}{dt}(\text{V}_{in}) = \text{V}_o$$

Since RC is constant, therefore, by the law of proportionality

$$\text{V}_o \propto \frac{d}{dt}(\text{V}_{in}) \qquad \text{...(7.2)}$$

Hence the output voltage is proportional to differentiation of input voltage.

Therefore the circuit is a differentiator circuit.

## Time Constant

The time period after which the voltage across capacitor in R, C circuit becomes 63% of the initial applied voltage is called as time constant of RC circuit. Therefore

$$\text{Time constant} = \text{RC} = \tau \qquad \text{...(7.3)}$$

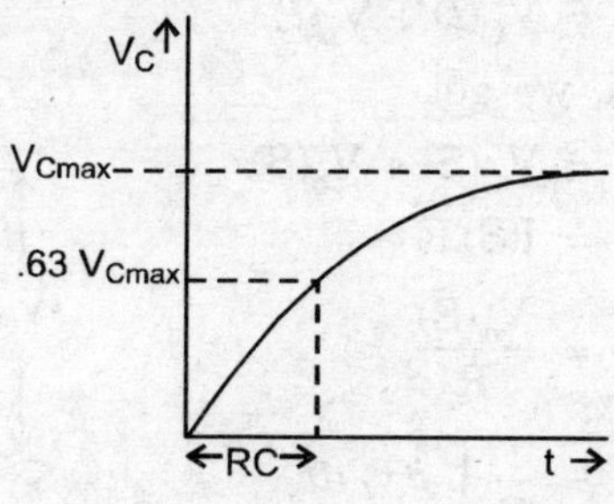


## Phasor Diagram

Whenever current I flows through the resistance R, there is zero phase shift between I and R. While if the same current I is flowing through the capacitor then $X_C$ lags the current. I by 90°. Therefore between I and Z phase shift θ exist, as shown in phasor diagram (Fig. 7.2(*a*)).

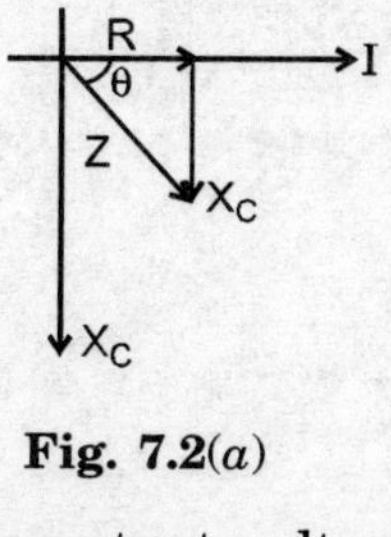


**Fig. 7.2**(*a*)

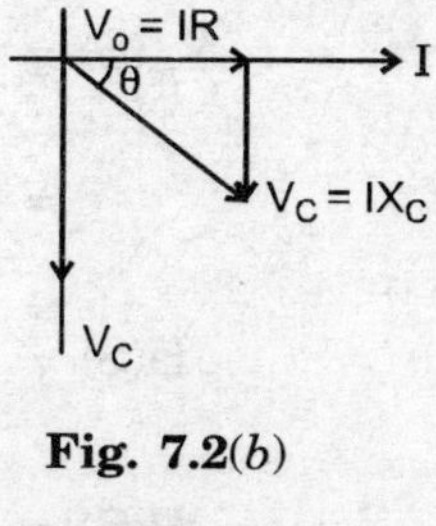


**Fig. 7.2**(*b*)

Similarly, between output voltage $V_o$ and input voltage $V_s$ there is a phase shift θ is existing, shown in Fig. 7.2(*b*).

$$\tan\theta = \frac{V_C}{V_o} = \frac{IX_C}{IR} = \frac{X_C}{R}$$

since
$$X_C = \frac{1}{2\pi fc}$$

$$\tan\theta = \frac{1}{2\pi fcR} \qquad \text{...(7.4)}$$

If the initial input signal is sinusoidal the output may be sinusoidal but with a phase shift θ for example.

where
$$\theta = \tan^{-1}\left(\frac{1}{2\pi fcR}\right)$$

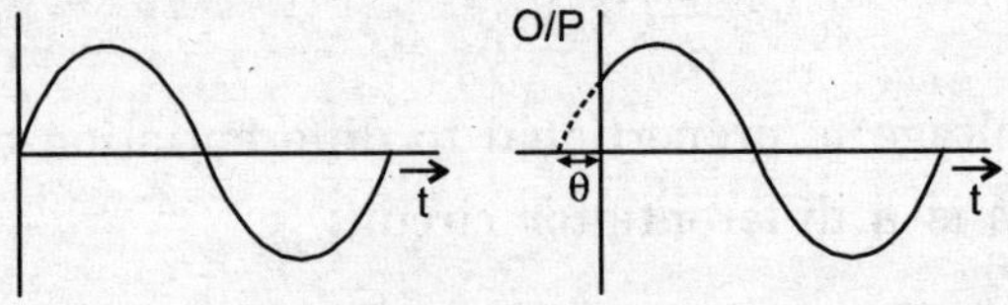


**Fig. 7.3**

## Transfer Function

By applying KVL in the circuit, we get

$$V_{in}(t) = V_C(t) + V_o(t)$$

Applying Laplace Transform, we get

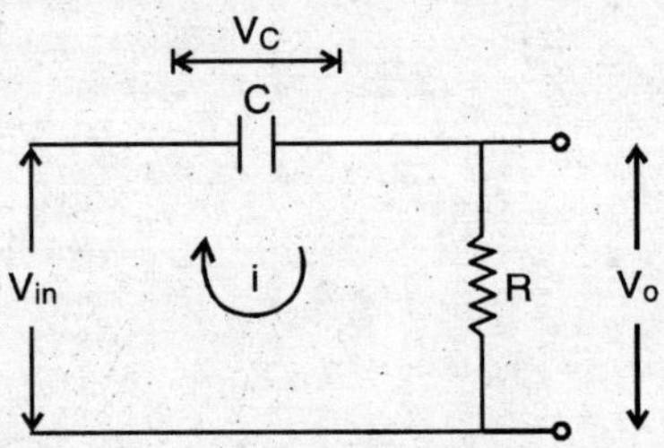


$$V_{in}(S) = V_C(S) + V_o(S)$$

we have
$$V_o(S) = I(S).R$$

so
$$I(S) = \frac{V_o(S)}{R}$$

Again,
$$V_C(t) = \frac{1}{C}\int_0^t i(t)\,dt$$

So,
$$V_C(S) = \frac{1}{CS} I(S)$$

$$V_C(S) = \frac{V_o(S)}{RCS} = \frac{V_o(S)}{\tau S} \quad \text{as } \tau = RC$$

So
$$V_{in}(S) = \frac{V_o(S)}{S\tau} + V_o(S)$$

$$= \frac{V_o(S) + S\tau\, V_o(S)}{S\tau}$$

thus
$$H(S) = \frac{V_o(S)}{V_{in}(S)} = \frac{S\tau}{1+S\tau}$$

or
$$H(S) = \frac{S}{S + 1/\tau} \qquad \text{...(7.5)}$$

Thus the TF for HIGH PASS circuit has a pole at $S = -\frac{1}{\tau}$.

## Response to Step Input

A step input is shown in Fig. 7.4 (*a*) and defined as

$$V_{in}(t) = V\,U(t) \quad t \geq 0$$
$$= 0 \quad t \leq 0$$

taking laplace of input, we get

$$V_{in}(S) = \frac{V}{S} \qquad \text{...(7.6)}$$

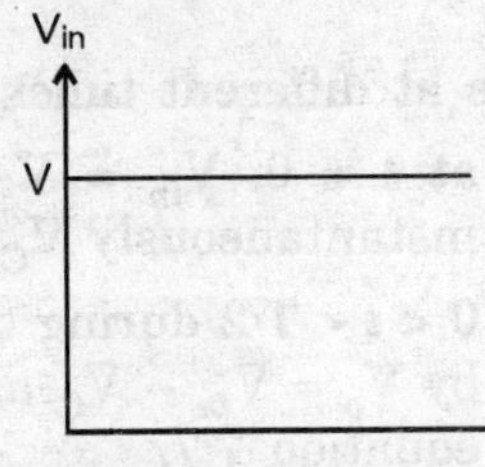


**Fig. 7.4**(*a*) Step input

we have

$$Y(S) = H(S).\frac{V}{S}$$

so by equations 7.5 and 7.6, we get

$$Y(S) = \frac{S}{S+1/\tau}.\frac{V}{S}$$

$$Y(S) = \frac{V}{S+1/\tau}$$

taking inverse laplace, we get

$$Y(t) = V.e^{-t/\tau}$$

or

$$V_o(t) = V_R = V.e^{-t/\tau} \qquad \text{...(7.7)}$$

So the response or HIGH PASS can be drawn in Fig. 7.4 (*b*).

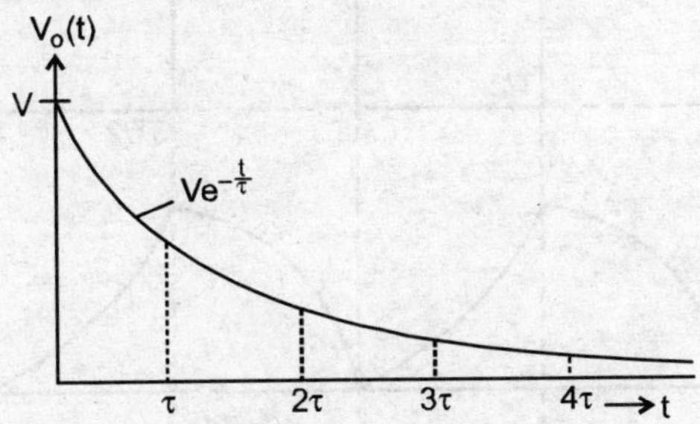


**Fig. 7.4**(*b*) Response of step input

Figure 7.4(*b*) shows clearly that in each τ interval the output decreases approximately by 50% and after 5τ time period the output falls to about 99% of initial applied value. Under steady state the output reaches 0 V as capacitor is full charged. Thus at steady state $V_C = V_{in}$ and $V_o = 0$ V.

## Response to Square Wave

To determine the response to a square wave we can use equation 7.7 because a square wave consist of a series of pulses and each pulse contains a finite duration step voltage. Thus, when a pulse is present it will affect the output of circuit according to equation 7.7.

Let us qualitatively see how the circuit responds to square wave input. Let the time constant τ < T/2 such that capacitor can charge fully in T/2 time and can discharge completely in T/2 time. The resulting waveforms are shown in Fig. 7.6.

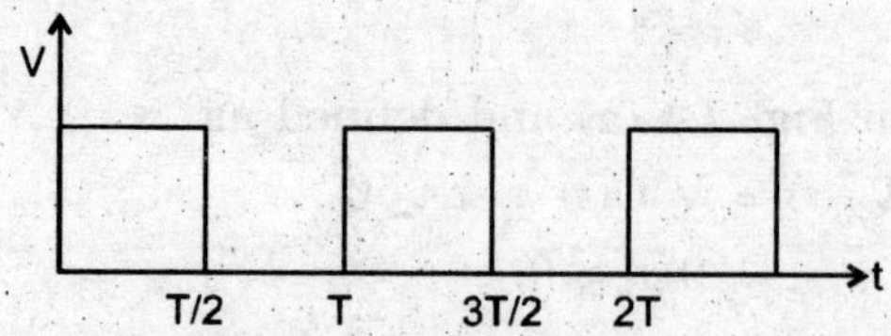


**Fig. 7.5** Square Wave

By KVL in high pass circuit, we get

$V_o = V_{in} - V_C$, we use this relation only to describe the waveforms at different times.

1. at $t = 0$, $V_{in} = V$ input suddenly rises to 0 V. Since capacitor change its state instantaneously $V_C = 0$ and by $V_0 = V_{in} - V_C$, we get $V_{in} = V$.
2. $0 < t < T/2$ during this time capacitor charges towards input, so $V_C$ increases. Then by $V_o = V_{in} - V_C$ as $V_C\uparrow \rightarrow V_o\downarrow$ as shown. The fall in output is same as given by equation 7.7.
3. at $t = T/2$ capacitor is charged fully so $V_C = V$, so by KVL $V_o = 0V$, as shown.

But at this time input goes zero suddenly. Since capacitor cannot change its state instantly so $V_C = V$ and thus by $V_o = V_{in} - V_C$, we get $V_o = -V$. Thus at $\tau = T/2$ $V_o = -V$.

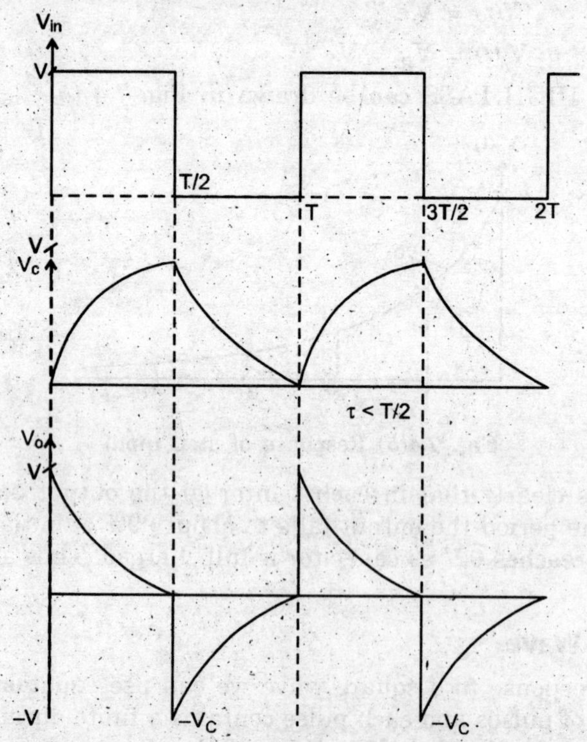


**Fig. 7.6** Response to square wave

4. $T/2 < t < T$ since $V_{in} = 0$ during this time capacitor gets path to discharge and hence $V_C$ decreases towards 0V and thus $V_o$ increases from –V towards 0V by $V_o = -Ve^{-t/\tau}$. H. Hence as $V_C\downarrow \rightarrow V_o\uparrow$.

5. at $t$ = T capacitor is completely discharged so $V_C$ = 0V and $V_o$ = 0V. But immediately at this time the $V_{in}$ rises to V and by $V_o = V_{in} - V_C = V - 0$, we get $V_o$ = V.

In the similar way cycle repeats for other times conclusion: from step 1 and step 5 we conclude that when $V_{in}$ rises from 0 to V output also rises by V. From step 3 we can conclude that when the input falls from V to 0 the output also falls by V volt. Hence the circuit is linear.

Here if we see the figure we find that output takes a form of spike. The spikes can be narrow if capacitor charges and discharges rapidly. This can be done if we make $\tau$<<T/2 so that capacitor charges and discharges fully in much smaller time than T/2. The relevant waveforms are shown in Fig. 7.7.

From figure we see that since $\tau$<<T/2, capacitor can charge and discharge quickly in a short time $\partial << T/2$. As the input goes to V the output is $V_o$ = V at $t$ = 0. At $t = \partial$ $V_C$ = V so $V_o = V_{in} - V_C = V - V$ *i.e.*, $V_o$ = 0V at $t = \partial$. Similarly at $t$ = T/2 input falls by V volt we get $V_o$ = –V. At $t = T/2 + \partial$ capacitor discharges completely so $V_C$ = 0. Since $V_{in}$ = 0 at this time $V_o$ = 0. Hence by using High pass circuit with $\tau$ << T/2 we generate narrow spikes which can be used to trigger the devices like flip-flops.

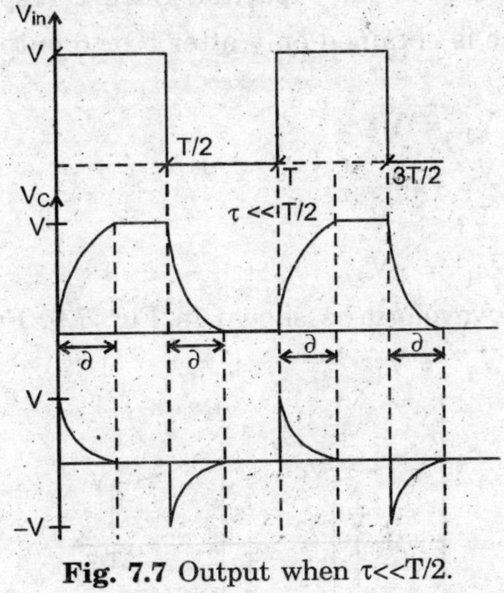


**Fig. 7.7** Output when $\tau$<<T/2.

## Response when $\tau$ = T/2

When time constant $\tau$ is exactly equal to the half time period it implies that capacitor can not charge and discharge completely and the output will be tilted replica of input as shown in fig. 7.8.

At $t$ = 0 $V_{in}$ rises to V suddenly so the output $V_0$ = V. During $t$ = 0 to $t$ = T/2 capacitor charges slowly toward $V_{in}$ so the output decreases accordingly. Thus at $t$ = T/2 $V_0 = V_1' = V_1 e^{-t/\tau} = V.e^{-t/\tau}$. At = T/2 it falls by amount V so the output also falls by an amount V. So we get $V_2 = V_1' - V$ or $V_1' - V_2 = V$. After this capacitor starts discharging and so the output starts rising from $V_2$ towards $V_2'$. Since capacitor can not dischargefully output does not rise to 0V.

Thus $V_2' = V_2\, e^{-t/\tau}$

At $t$ = T input rises by V volt so the output also rises by V volt hence at $t$ = T

$$V_0 = V_3 = V_2' + V \text{ or } V_3 - V_2' = V$$

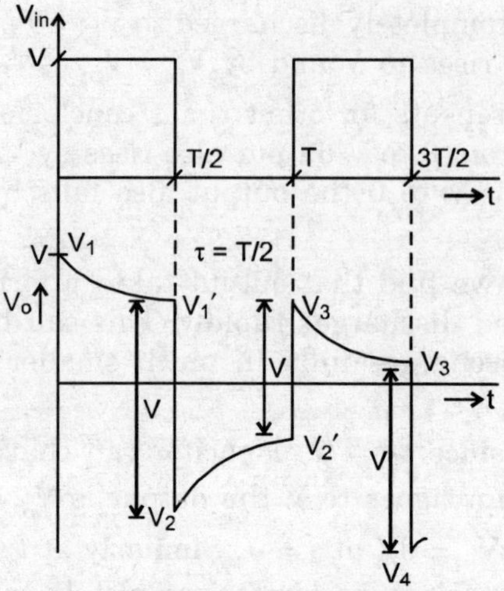


**Fig. 7.8** Output when τ = T/2

After that cycle repeats. A close inspection reveals that consecutive output cycles are shifting downwards, which is due to the capacitor. Such a response is transient response.

The steady state response is obtained only after 5 or 6 output cycles. When steady state output is obtained

$$V_1 + V_1' = V$$

$$V_2 + V_2' = V \qquad ...(7.8)$$

and

$$V_1 = -V_2$$

$$V_1' = -V_2' \qquad ...(7.9)$$

The steady state output waveform is shown in Fig. 7.9. From figure

$$V_1' = V_1 e^{-t/\tau}$$

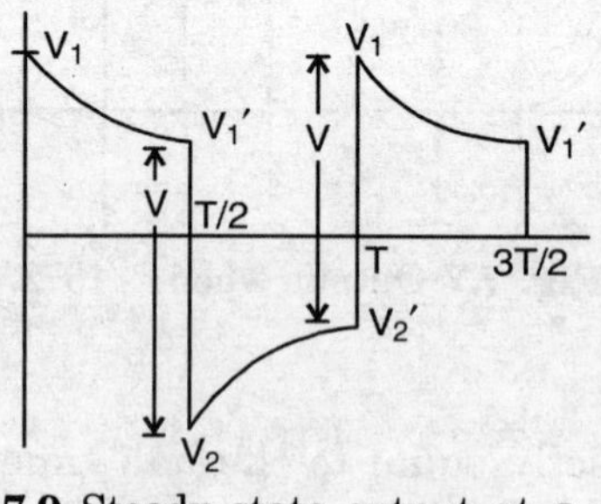


**Fig. 7.9** Steady state output at τ = T/2

by using equation 7.8, we get $V_1 + V_1' = V$

so

$$V_1 = \frac{V}{1+e^{-t/\tau}} \text{ under steady state} \qquad ...(7.10)$$

and

$$V_1' = \frac{V}{1+e^{t/\tau}} \text{ under steady state} \qquad ...(7.11)$$

## Percentage Tilt

Here we are interested in finding out the amount by which the voltage is changed with respect to initial value. For this purpose we consider Fig. 7.8

we have $$V_0 = Ve^{-t/\tau}$$

as shown in figure the capacitor charges for T/2 period and discharges for T/2 period.

So at $t$ = T/2 $$V_1' = V_1 e^{-T/2\tau} \quad \text{...(7.12a)}$$

now expanding equation 7.12.a

$$V_1' = V_1\left(1-\frac{T}{2\tau}+\frac{1}{2}.\left(\frac{T}{2\tau}\right)^2-\frac{1}{6}\left(\frac{T}{2\tau}\right)^3+....\right)$$

neglecting higher order term, we get

$$V_1' = V_1\left(1-\frac{T}{2\tau}\right)$$

Since output charges from $V_1$ to $V_1'$ so $\Delta V = V_1 - V_1'$

$$\Delta V = V_1 - V_1(1 - T/2\tau)$$

$$\Delta V = V_1\frac{T}{2\tau} \quad \text{...(7.12b)}$$

when voltage is $V_1$ net change = $\Delta V$

$$\text{so for 1V net change} = \frac{\Delta V}{V_1}$$

Thus $\frac{\Delta V}{V_1}$ represents change or tilt in output per volt

$$\frac{\Delta V}{V_1} = \frac{V_1\frac{T}{2\tau}}{V_1} = \frac{T}{2\tau}$$

but time const. $\tau$ = RC

so $$\frac{\Delta V}{V_1} = \frac{T}{2RC} = \text{tilt} \quad \text{...(7.13)}$$

hence percentage tilt is given as

$$\%\text{ tilt} = \frac{\Delta V}{V_1}\times 100 = \frac{T}{2RC}\times 100 \quad \text{...(7.14)}$$

If we draw the output $V_s$ frequency curve as shown in Fig. 7.10 we find that $f_1$ is the frequency at which output is at 70.7% (3*db* value) of its peak. Since, this occurs at lower part of curve it is called lower 3*db* frequency.

Therefore the $f_1$ is given as $f_1 = \frac{1}{2\pi RC}$

or $$RC = \frac{1}{2\pi f_1}$$

also $$T = 1/f$$

putting these in equation 7.14, we get

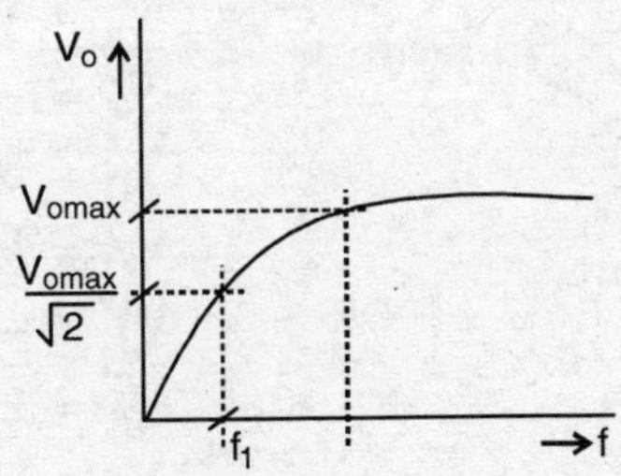

**Fig. 7.10** Frequency response

$$\%\text{ tilt} = \frac{\pi f_1}{f}\times 100 \quad \text{...(7.15)}$$

**Example 7.1.** *A square wave of time period one milisec and peak amplitude of 10V is applied to high pass circuit which have the time constant of 2 msec. Plot the first two output cycles and capacitor waveform. Also find out steady state waveform.*

**Solution.** Given $\tau = 2$ m sec

$T = 1$ m sec

So $e^{-T/2\tau} = e^{-1/4}$

so $e^{-T/2\tau} = 0.778$

at $t = 0$ capacitor is at 0V, $V_c = 0V$

so $V_1 = 10$ V

at $t = T/2$

$$V_1¢ = V_1.e^{-t/\tau} = V_1 e^{-T/2\tau}$$

$$= 10 \times 0.778$$

so $V_1' = 7.78$ V

and $V_2 = V_1' - V_{in} = 7.78 - 10$

so $V_2 = 2.22$ V

but $V_2 = -V_C$ at $t = T/2$

so $V_C = 2.22$ V at $t = T/2$

at $t = T$

$$V_2' = V_2 e^{-t/\tau} = V_2.e^{-T/2\tau}$$

$$= -2.22 \times 0.778$$

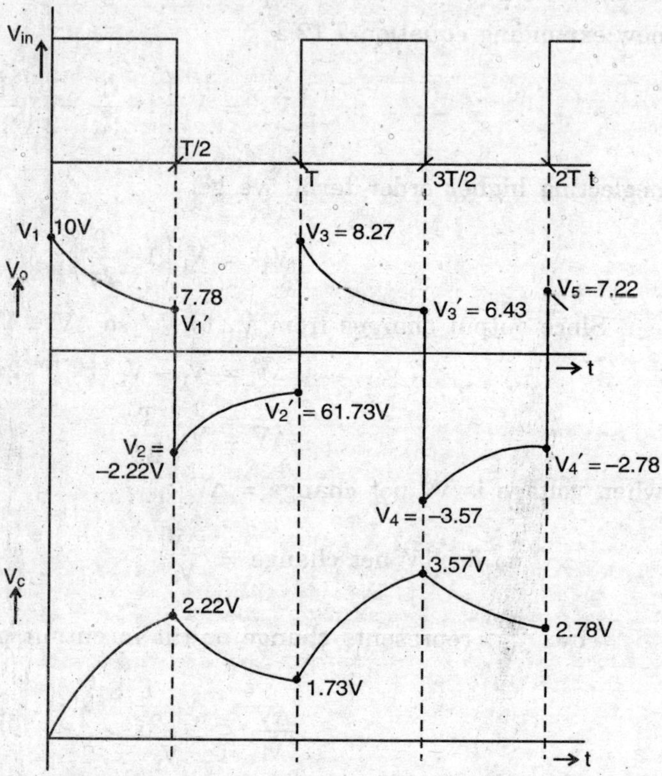


**Fig. 7.11** (*a*) First two cycle waveforms of example 7.1

so $V_2' = -1.73$ V

thus $V_C = 1.73$ V at this time

and $V_3 = V_2' + V_{in} = -1.73 + 10$

so $V_3 = 8.27$ V

at $t = 3T/2$ $V_3' = V_3' e^{-T/2\tau} = 8.27 \times 0.778$

so $V_3' = 6.43$ V

and $V_4 = V_3' - V_{in} = 6.43 - 10$

so $V_4 = -3.57$ V

thus $V_C = 3.57$ V at $t = 3T/2$

at $t = 2T$ $V_4' = V_4 e^{-t/T} = V_4 e^{-T/2T} = -3.57 \times 0.778$

so $V_4' = -2.78$ V

thus $V_C = 2.78$ V at $t = 2T$

and $V_5 = V_4' + V_{in} = -2.78 \text{ V} + 10$

so $V_5 = 7.22$ V

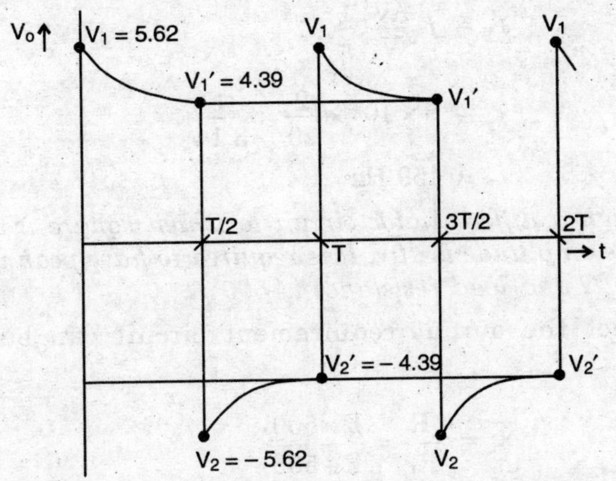


**Fig. 7.11** (*b*) Steady state output of example 7.1

The waveform using these values are shown in Fig. 7.11 to calculate steady value we can use equations 7.10 and 7.11.

$$V_1 = \frac{V}{1+e^{-t/\tau}} = \frac{V_{in}}{1+e^{-T/2\tau}} = \frac{10}{1+0.778}$$

so $$V_1 = 5.62 \text{ V}$$

$$V_1' = \frac{V_{in}}{1+e^{t/\tau}} = \frac{10}{1+1.128}$$

so $$V_1' = 4.39$$

by equation 7.9

$$V_2 = -V_1 = -5.62 \text{ V}$$

and $$V_2' = -V_1' = -4.39 \text{ V}$$

The steady state waveform using these values are drawn in Fig. 7.11.

**Example 7.2.** *A square wave of 5 KHz is applied to a differentiator circuit and resultant waveform measured. CRO was tilted from 20 V to 18 V. Find out lower 3db frequency of differentiator circuit.*

**Solution.** Given $f = 5 \text{ KHz}$

change in voltage $= 20 \text{ V} - 18 \text{ V}$

*i.e.,* $$\Delta V = 2 \text{ V}$$

so $$\text{tilt} = \frac{\Delta V}{V} = \frac{2}{20}$$

by equation 7.15 $$\text{tilt} = \frac{\pi f_1}{f}$$

so $$\frac{\pi f_1}{f} = \frac{\Delta V}{V}$$

or
$$f_1 = f.\frac{\Delta V}{V}.\frac{1}{\pi}$$

$$f_1 = 5 \times 10^3 \times \frac{2}{20} \times \frac{1}{3.14}$$

$$f_1 = 159 \text{ Hz}$$

**Example 7.3** *Design a differentiator circuit to which square wave of 1 msec repetition rate is feeded and whose amplitude is 10V. It is required to have peak value of output 8 V. The source impedance is 50 Ω and load resistance is 500 Ω.*

**Solution.** To meet the output requirement circuit can be drawn as shown in Fig. 7.12(*a*).

Thus
$$\text{Req} = \frac{R}{R_L} = \frac{R \times 500}{R + 500}$$

or
$$\text{Req} = \frac{500\ R}{R + 500}$$

At $t = 0$ capacitor C is initially not charged so it acts as short circuit as shown in Fig. 7.12(*b*).

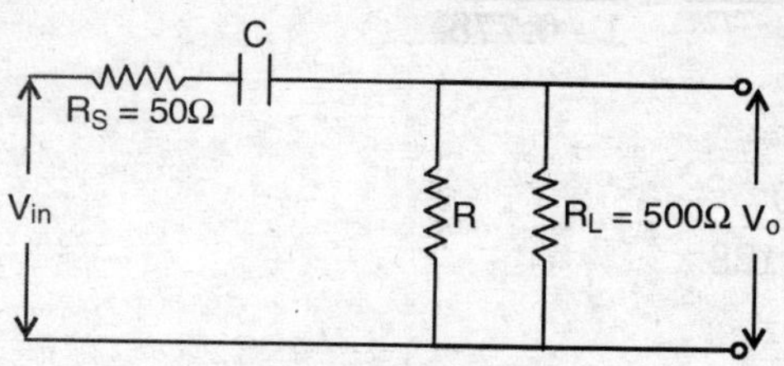


**Fig. 7.12**(*a*)

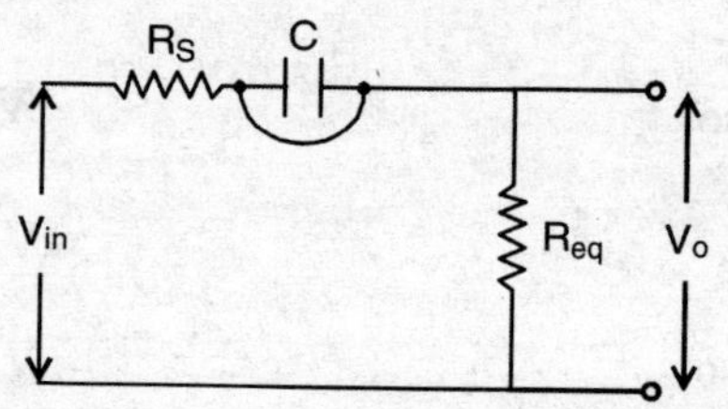


**Fig. 7.12**(*b*) Circuit Fig. 7.12(a) at $t = 0$

We need 8 V output so

$$V_o = \frac{R_{eq}}{R_{eq} + R_S}.V_{in}$$

or
$$8 = \frac{500R/500+R}{\frac{500\ R}{500+R}+50}.10$$

but solving we, get
$$R = 333.33\ \Omega$$

Capacitor value is determined by time constant τ. Since it is differentiator circuit $\tau << T/2$.

Let us select
$$\tau = \frac{T}{10}$$

so
$$\tau = 0.1 \text{ msec at } T = 1 \text{ msec.}$$

but
$$\tau = RC \text{ so } c = \tau/R$$

or
$$C = \frac{0.1 \times 10^{-3}}{333.33}$$

or
$$C \cong 0.3 \ \mu F$$

We have not considered $R_L$ and $R_S$ while calculating C because $R_L$ is part of load circuit, external to differentiator and $R_S$ is part of generator which is also external to differentiator circuit.

## 7.2 INTEGRATOR OR LOW PASS CIRCUIT

The integrating circuit contains the resistance R in series arm, capacitor C in shunt arm as shown in Fig. 7.13(*a*).

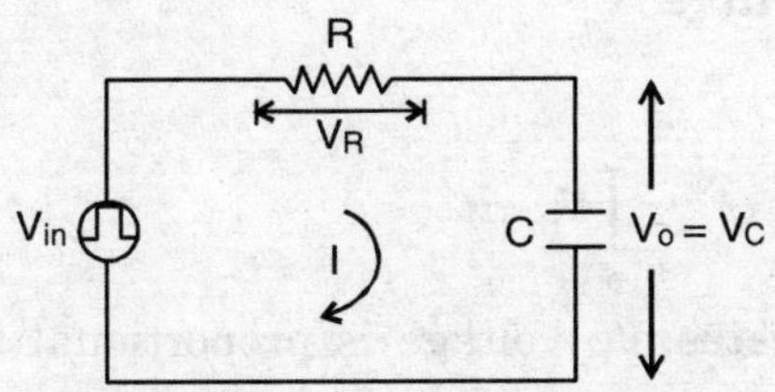


**Fig. 7.13** Low pass circuit.

At the time of the application of *i*/*p* signal $V_i$, current flows in the circuit. The resistor R cannot discriminate low and high frequency signals while the capacitor C offers the reactance.

$$X_c = \frac{1}{2\pi fc}$$

$$f = \text{low}; \qquad X_c = \text{high}$$

$$f = \text{high}; \qquad X_c = \text{low}$$

Since, in such conditions high frequency signals are bypassed *i.e.,* high frequency signals are eliminated hence the o/p is containing only low frequency signals; so it is called as low pass circuit or one can say that the o/p is obtained as integral of the i/p signal. Hence, it is called as integrator circuit.

By applying KVL, we get

$$V_{in} = V_R + V_o$$

$$= IR + \int_0^t \frac{I}{C} dt \qquad \text{...(I)}$$

On multiplying both sides by C

$$C.V_{in} = IRC + \int_0^t I dt \qquad \text{...(II)}$$

If time constant RC is very large w.r.t. applied signal time period, in such conditions

$$IRC >> \int_0^t I dt$$

so eqn. (II) becomes on neglecting smaller terms

$$C \cdot V_{in} = IRC \qquad ...(III)$$

Integrating both sides of eqn. (III) w.r.t. *t*, we get

$$\int_0^t C\, V_{in}\, dt = \int_0^t I\, RC\, dt$$

$$\int_c^t \frac{V_{in}\, dt}{RC} = \frac{1}{C}\int_0^t I\, dt$$

or $$\frac{1}{\tau}\int_0^t V_i\, dl = V_o \qquad ...(7.16)$$

$$V_o \propto \int_0^t V_{in}\, dt \qquad ...(7.17)$$

The above equation indicates o/p voltage is proportional to integration of i/p voltage.

When current I flows through resistor R there is no phase difference between voltage and current. But when this current flows through capacitor C, its reactance $X_C$ and hence voltage $V_C = I.X_C$ lags behind the current by 90° as shown in fig. 7.13 (*b*). Hence, there exist a phase difference θ between input and output.

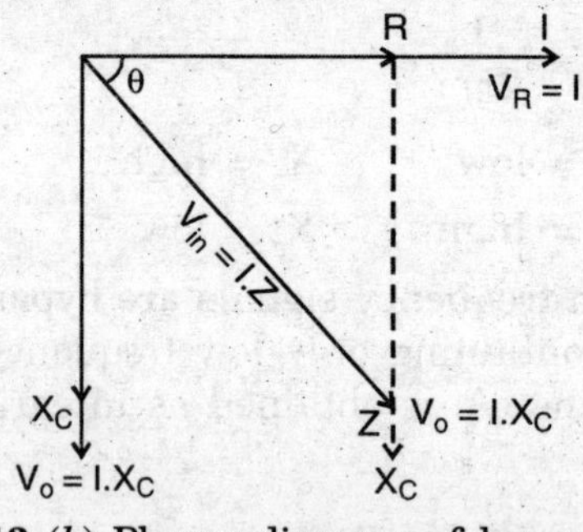


**Fig. 7.13** (*b*) Phasor diagram of low pass circuit

$$\tan\theta = \frac{V_o}{V_R} = \frac{I \cdot X_C}{I \cdot R}$$

but $$X_C = \frac{1}{2\pi fc}$$

so $$\tan\theta = \frac{1}{2\pi fc \cdot R} \qquad ...(7.18)$$

or $$f = \frac{\cot\theta}{2\pi RC}$$

but time constant $$\tau = RC$$

so $$f = \frac{\cot\theta}{2\pi\tau} \qquad ...(7.19)$$

When a sinusoid of frequency $f$ is applied at input of Low pass circuit there will be a phase shift θ given by equation 7.18. The equation also indicate that the amount of phase shift will increase with the frequency of input. Thus, whenever a sinusoid of frequency $f$ is applied at input of low pass then output will also be a sinusoid of same frequency $f$ but with a phase difference θ, of course amplitude will be changed as determined by transfer function of the circuit

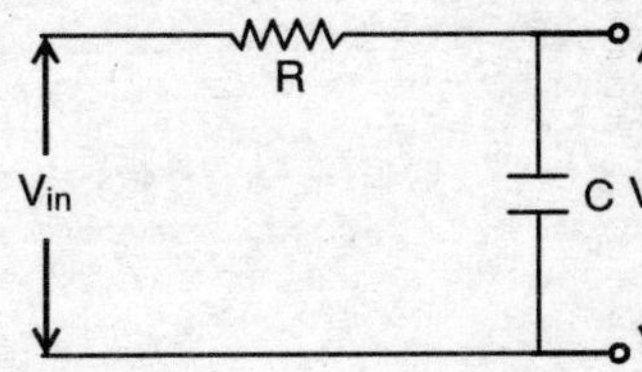


## Transfer Function

By KVL in circuit $V_{in}(t) = V_R + V_o(t)$

applying laplace transform

$$V_{in}(S) = V_R(S) + V_o(S)$$

we have $$V_R = I(S)\cdot R$$

and $$V_o(t) = V_C(t) = \frac{1}{C}\int_o^t (it)\cdot dt$$

so $$V_o(S) = \frac{I(S)}{C\cdot S}$$

or $$I(S) = V_o(S)\cdot CS$$

thus $$V_R = I(S)\cdot R = V_o(S)\cdot CS\cdot R$$

or $$V_R = S\cdot\tau\, V_o(S) \text{ as } \tau = RC$$

so $$V_{in}(S) = S\cdot\tau\, V_o(S) + V_o(S)$$

or $$\frac{V_o(S)}{V_{in}(S)} = H(S) = \frac{1}{1+S\tau}$$

or $$H(S) = \frac{1}{\tau}\cdot\frac{1}{(S+1/\tau)} \qquad ...(7.20)$$

## Response to step input

By inspecting the low pass and high pass circuit we find that both the circuits are same. The difference lies in the point of output. In high pass we measure output across resistor and in case of low pass we measure output across the capacitor. So in both the cases voltage across resistance is same, when input is step voltage and is given by equation 7.7 *i.e.*,

$$V_R = Ve^{-t/\tau}$$

where V is amplitude of step input thus by KVL in low pass circuit, we get

$$V_o = V_C = V - Ve^{-t/\tau} \qquad ...(7.20)$$

This is the relation we use to determine the response as plotted in fig. 7.14. Initially capacitor is at OV so at $t = 0$, we get output OV. As time goes on capacitor charges exponentially to peak value (V) of step input. Since for low pass we take t >> T, at $t = \infty$ output reaches maximum *i.e.*, to peak amplitude V. As indicated in figure the rise time of integrator circuit is defined as the time taken by the output waveform to reach to 90% of peak value from 10% of peak value. So

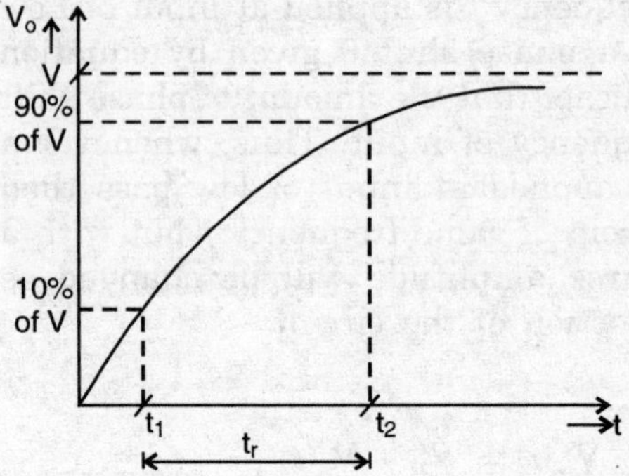


**Fig. 7.14** Response of low pass circuit to step input of V volt

$$\text{Rise time } t_r = t_2 - t_1$$

to develop relation for rise time we use equation 7.20 to find $t_1$ and $t_2$.

to determine $t_1$: at $t = t_1$ $\quad V_o = 10\% \, V_{in}$

$$= 0.1 \text{ V}$$

So by (7.20) $\quad 0.1 \text{ V} = \text{V} - \text{V}e^{-\frac{t_1}{\tau}}$

or $\quad e^{-t_1/\tau} = 0.9$

or $\quad e^{t_1/\tau} = 1.1$

taking natural log both sides, we get

$$t_1 \cong 0.1\tau \qquad \text{...(7.21.}a\text{)}$$

to determine $t_2$:

at $t = t_2$ $\quad V_o = 90\% \text{ of } V_{in} = 0.9 \text{ V}$

by (7.20) $\quad 0.9 \text{ V} = \text{V} - \text{V}e^{-\frac{t_2}{\tau}}$

$$e^{-t_2/\tau} = 0.1$$

or $\quad e^{t_2/\tau} = 10$

taking natural log both sides, we get

$$t_2 = 2.303 \; \tau \qquad \text{...(7.21.b)}$$

we've $\quad t_r = t_2 - t_1$

$$= 2.303 \; t - 0.1\tau$$

so $\quad t_r = 2.203\tau$

or $\quad t_r = 2.203 \text{ RC as } \tau = \text{RC} \qquad \text{...(7.22)}$

## RESPONSE TO SQUARE WAVE INPUT

As indicated earlier output of low pass circuit is nothing but the voltage measured across capacitor. Thus at once we can say that square wave response is already plotted in section 7.1. But there is something else also that we must consider in low pass or integrator circuit. The difference comes from the fact that for RC circuit to behave as perfect integrator $\tau >> T/2$.

Taking $\tau >> T/2$ is essential if we want voltage across the capacitor to vary in straight line fashion. If we do not impose this condition, the capacitor will charge and discharge exponentially. Also taking high value of $\tau$ permits us to use integrator as attenuator. It is because we have

$$1 + (S) = \frac{1}{\tau}\frac{1}{S+1/\tau}$$

Thus if $\tau$ is high $1/\tau$ is low, hence magnitude of H(S) will be of lower amplitude and hence the output is much lower than the input.

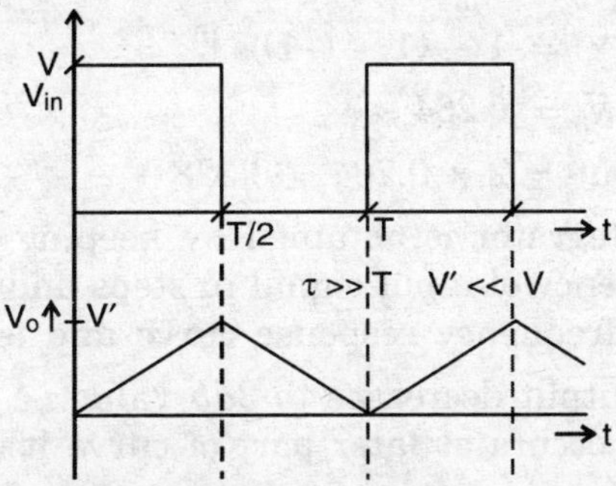


**Fig. 7.15** Square wave response of integrator.

The simplified response curve of an integrator is shown in Fig. 7.15. When pulse amplitude is V capacitor charges slowly due to high $\tau$ the charging is almost in straight line fashion. Also due to high $\tau$ capacitor can charge only some smaller magnitude V′ such that $V' << V$. It is also evident in example 7.4. During T/2 to T input is 0V so capacitor discharges in almost straight line fashion. Thus in response to square wave we get triangular wave at the output. This is obvious because if we simply integrate the square wave we get triangular wave. Readers are advised to show it mathematically. Several waveforms at the output of low pass circuit is drawn in Fig. 7.16 for different values of $\tau$. In the Fig. 7.16, output voltage makes swing between negative and positive values which is obvious because input also makes such swings as shown in figure.

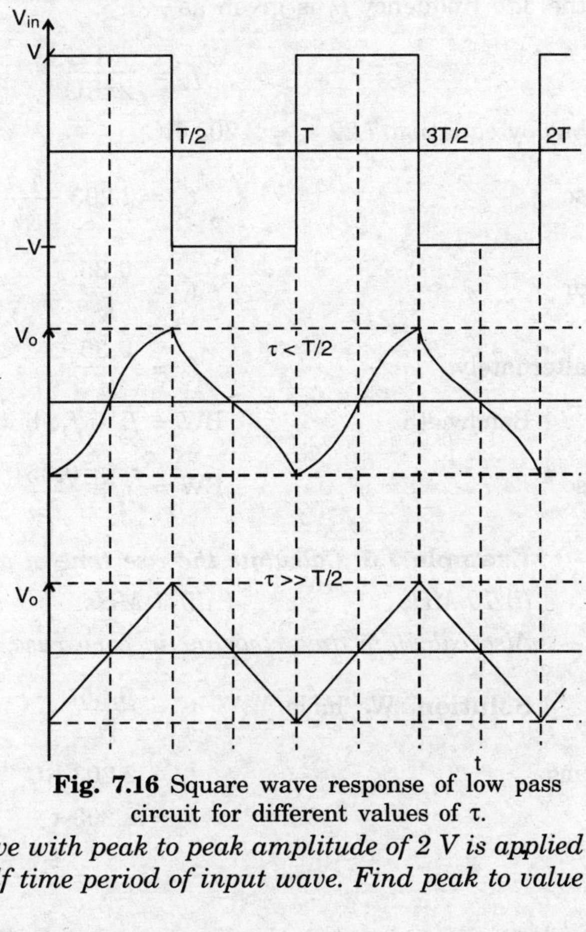


**Fig. 7.16** Square wave response of low pass circuit for different values of $\tau$.

**Example 7.4.** *A symmetrically square wave with peak to peak amplitude of 2 V is applied to integrator. The time constant is equal to half time period of input wave. Find peak to value of output waveform.*

**Solution.** Square wave with 2 V peak to peak is shown below. Note that net voltage change is applied to the capacitor and value attained by input at any time is applied to capacitor.

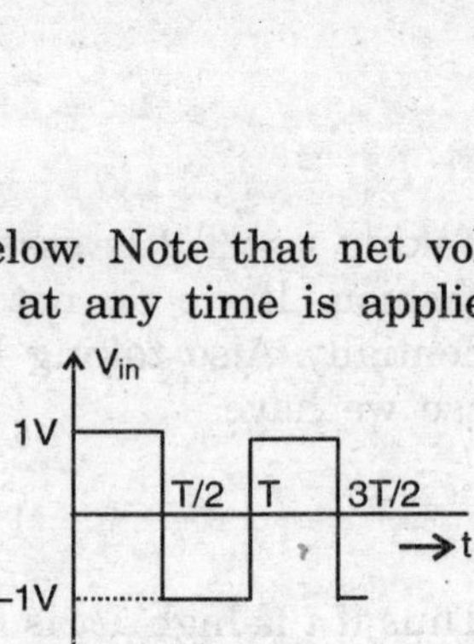


So $\tau = RC = \frac{T}{2}$ given

and $t = \frac{T}{2}$

So
$$V_o = V_{in} \text{ (final)} - (V_{in} \text{ (final)} - V_{in} \text{ (initial)}\, e^{-t/\tau}$$
$$= 1 - (1 - (-1))e^{-T/2/T/2}$$
$$V_o = 0.264$$
$$\text{peak to peak output} = 2 \times 0.264 = 0.528 \text{ V}$$

Frequency response of integrator is obtained by keeping the input voltage at constant amplitude. Now vary the frequency of input signal in steps and note down the value of output voltage. Such a plot is called frequency response curve and is shown in Fig. 7.17.

The frequency at which output decreases to 3*db* value *i.e.*, 70.7% of maximum value, is called 3*db* frequency. Since, it occurs at later part of curve it is called upper 3*d*B frequency $f_2$.

the 3*db* frequency $f_2$ is given as

$$f_2 = \frac{1}{2\pi RC}$$

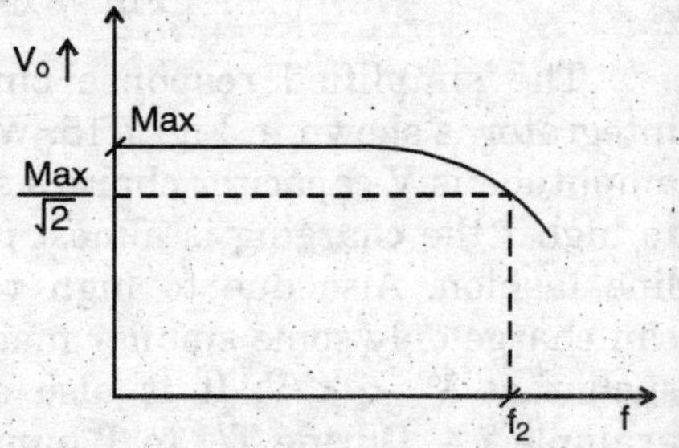


**Fig. 7.17** Frequency response curve of integrator

but by equation 7.22 $t_r = 2.203$ RC

so $$t_r = 2.203.\frac{1}{2\pi f_2}$$

or $$t_r = \frac{0.35}{f_2} \qquad ...(7.23)$$

alternately $$f_2 = \frac{0.35}{t_r}$$

Bandwidth $BW = f_2 - f_1$, but $f_1 = 0$ for low pass

so $$BW = f_2 = \frac{0.35}{t_r} \qquad ...(7.24)$$

**Example 7.5.** *Calculate the rise time of a low pass circuit if the 3 frequency is db*

*(i) 10 MHz* *(ii) 1 MHz* *(iii) 0.1 MHz.*

*Also calculate time constant in each case.*

**Solution.** We have $t_r = \frac{0.35}{f_2}$

and $t_r = 2.203$ RC

$t_r = 2.203\ \tau$

(*i*) $f_2$ = 10 MHz $\quad t_r = \dfrac{0.35}{10 \times 10^6}$

or $\quad t_r = 0.035\ \mu$ sec

$$\tau = \frac{t_r}{2.203}$$

or $\quad \tau \cong 15.89$ *n*sec

Similarly

(*ii*) $f_2$ = 1 MHz $\quad t_r = 0.35\ \mu$sec

and $\quad \tau \cong 158.9$ *n* sec

(*iii*) $f_2$ = 0.1 MHz $\quad t_r = 3.5\ \mu$ sec

and $\quad \tau \cong 1589$ *n*sec

## Integrator As Attenuator

In many application such as CRO probes, it is desired to scale down the magnitude of signal. An attenuator is such a device. It is desired that such scale down should occur without distortion. A simple attenuator using resistances is shown in Fig. 7.18.

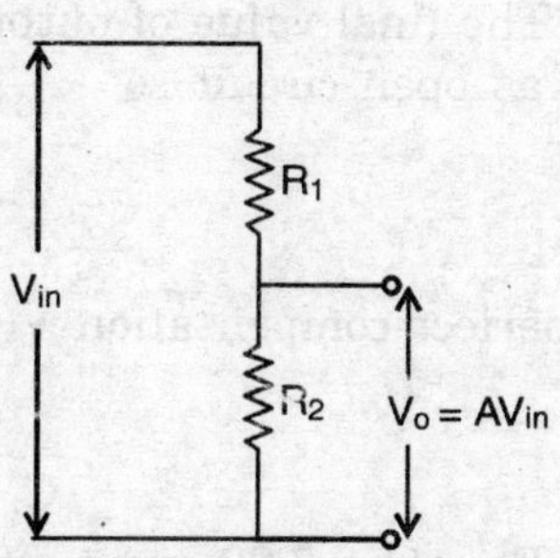


**Fig. 7.18** Simple attenuator

$$V_o = \frac{R_2}{R_1 + R_2} . V_{in}$$

or $\quad V_o = A.V_{in} \quad$ ...(7.25a)

where $\quad A = \dfrac{R_2}{R_1 + R_2}$

= Attenuation factor

When this attenuator is used in circuits say at the input of CRO, the input capacitance $C_i$ of CRO shunts the resistor $R_2$ as shown in Fig. 7.19(*a*). Presence of $C_i$ creates problem that it makes the output of attenuator dependent of frequency and thus the output given by equation 7.25 is distorted. If we shunt the resistor $R_1$ by a capacitor $C_1$ the output can be compensated. Such an attenuator is called **compensated attenuator,** and shown in Fig. 7.19 (*b*).

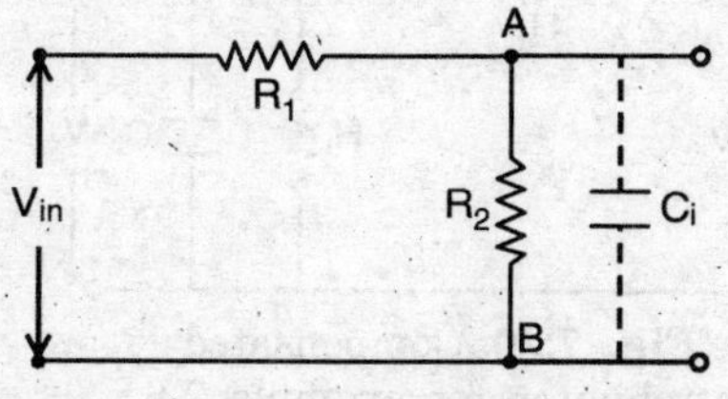


**Fig. 7.19**(*a*)

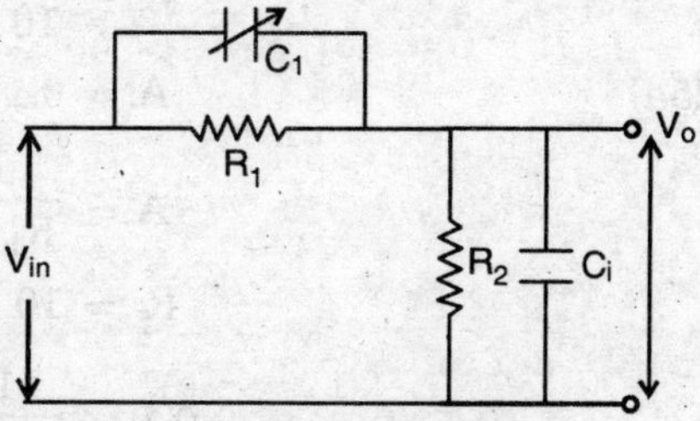


**Fig. 7.19**(*b*) Compensated attenuator

The resistors $R_1$ and $R_2$ and capacitors $C_1$ and $C_2$ forms four arm of a bridge. The bridge is balanced when

$$R_1C_1 = R_2C_i \qquad ...(7.26)$$

The equation 7.26 gives the condition for perfect compensation. Note that in Fig. 7.19(*a*) capacitor $C_1$ is made variable because practically we must satisfy the equation 7.26 by adjusting the value of $C_1$ as $C_i$ input capacitance of load stage which is fix. Thus for attenuator shown in Fig. 7.19(*b*), for perfect compensation by equation 7.29.

$$C_1 = \frac{R_2}{R_1}.C_i = C_C \qquad ...(7.27)$$

If $C_1 = C_C$ perfect compensation occurs. If $C_1 < C_C$ under-compensation and if $C_1 > C_C$ overcompensation occurs. The initial output voltage *i.e.*, at $t = 0^+$ is determined by capacitor, as they cannot change their state instantaneously, so

$$V(0^+) = \frac{C_1}{C_1 + C_i}.V_{in} \qquad ...(7.28a)$$

where $0^+$ is time immediately after $t = 0$ or immediately after switching.

The final value of output is determined by resistors as capacitors are fully charged and acts as open circuit so

$$V(\infty) = \frac{R_2}{R_1 + R_2}.V_{in} \qquad ...(7.28b)$$

for perfect compensation $V(0^+) = V(\infty)$

so
$$\frac{C_1}{C_1 + C_i} = \frac{R_2}{R_1 + R_2} = A \qquad ...(7.29)$$

Equation 7.29 gives attenuation factor for perfect compensation. The equation 7.29 also indicates that attenuation factor is now independent of frequency and thus the output also is independent upon frequency.

**Example 7.6.** *An oscilloscope has input impedance of 10 MΩ shunted by an input capacitance 20 pF. Design a 10 times voltage divider probe end. Also find out net capacitance and resistance offered by the circuit to CRO.*

**Solution.** As already indicated as compensated attenuator arrangement must be formed as shown below in Fig. 7.20.

We need 10 times voltage divider so

$$V_o = \frac{1}{10}V_{in}$$

by (7.25a) $\quad A = 0.1$

but
$$A = \frac{R_i}{R_1 + R_i} = 0.1$$

given $\quad R_i = 10\ \text{M}\Omega$, so

$$0.1 = \frac{10 \times 10^6}{R_1 + 10\times10^6}$$

or $\quad R_1 = 90\ \text{M}\Omega$

for perfect compensation $R_i.C_i = R_1C_1$

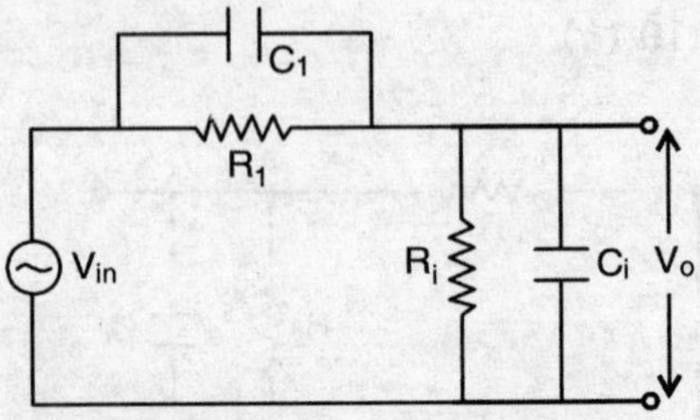

**Fig. 7.20** Compensated attenuator for example 7.6

or $$C_1 = \frac{R_i}{R_1}.C_i = \frac{10 \times 10^6 \times 20 \times 10^{-12}}{90 \times 10^6}$$

so $$C_1 = 2.22 \text{ pF.}$$

To find resistance and capacitance offered we look back from output terminal and apply a Thevenin's theorem, we get

$$R_{eq} = R_1 \| R_i \quad \text{and} \quad C_{eq} = C_1 \| C_i$$

so $$R_{eq} = \frac{R_1.R_i}{R_1 + R_2} = \frac{90 \times 10^6 \times 10 \times 10^6}{90 \times 10^6 + 10 \times 10^6}$$

so $$R_{eq} = 9\text{M}\Omega$$

$$C_{eq} = C_1 + C_i = 20\text{PF} + 2.22 \text{ pF}$$

so $$C_{eq} = 22.22 \text{ pF}$$

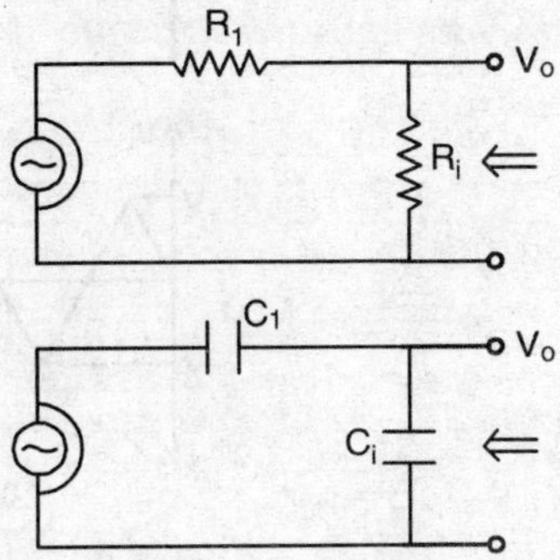


**Fig. 7.21** Equivalent Thevenin's circuits

## 7.3 CLIPPERS

There are varieties of non-linear (diode/transistor) networks clippers that have the ability to "clip" off a portion of the input signal without affecting the remaining portion of the applied signal. There are basically two types of clippers series and parallel.

### Series Clippers

The series clipper is one where the diode is in series with the load ($R_L$). Depending on the orientation of the diode, the positive or negative region of the input signal is "clipped" off. For the series configuration of Fig. 7.22.

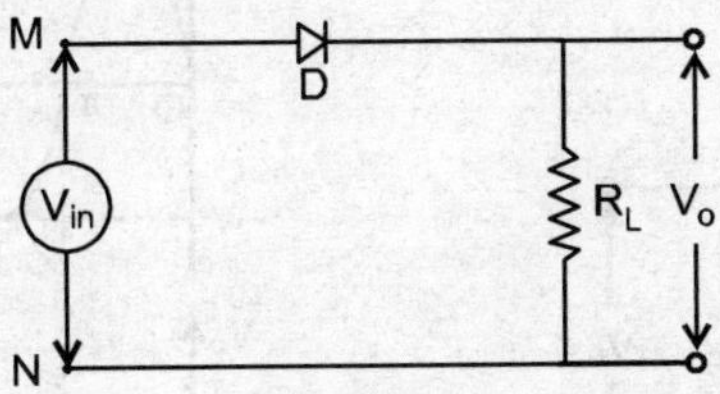


**Fig. 7.22**

When sinusoidal voltage is applied across the MN terminals between 0 to $\pi$, M terminal becomes positive with respect to N terminal. During 0 to $\pi$, diode becomes forward biased and current flows through the diode and load $R_L$. So output voltage $V_o$ is obtained across $R_L$. During $\pi$ to $2\pi$, M terminal becomes –ve w.r.t. N terminal and diode becomes reverse biased. Therefore, diode doesn't conduct in between $\pi$ to $2\pi$ and *o*/*p* becomes zero. The cycle repeats. The output is obtained only during +ve half cycle of the *i*/*p* signal so this circuit is referred as negative clipper. The output (response) of clipper circuit is shown in Fig. 7.23.

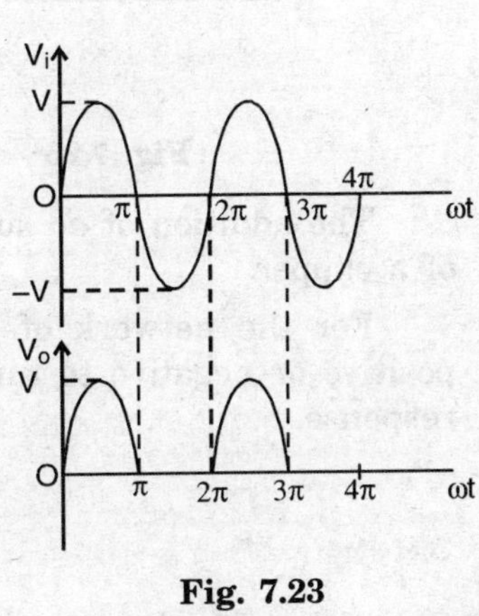


**Fig. 7.23**

One can applied any type of signal to a clipper and it is not limited to sinusoidal waveform only. When the given input signals Fig. 7.24(*a*) are applied to the same configuration of Fig. 7.22, the response will be as shown in Fig. 7.24(*b*).

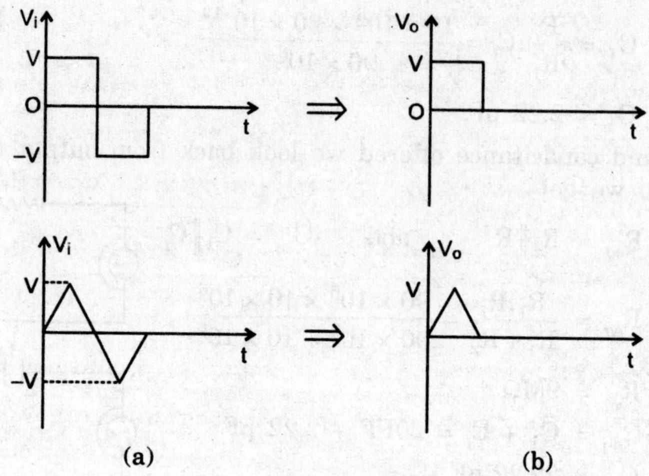


**Fig. 7.24**

For the series configuration of Fig. 7.25.

In this circuit positive alternatives are clipped between O to $\pi$ and $2\pi$ to $3\pi$ etc. duration. Because the diode is operated in reverse biased condition between $\pi$ to $2\pi$ and $3\pi$ to $4\pi$, the negative alternation is obtained as $o/p$ (positive alternation clipped). The output is obtained only during –ve half cycle of the $i/p$ signal so this circuit is referred as positive clipper. The $o/p$. The $o/p$ of clipper circuit is shown in Fig. 7.26.

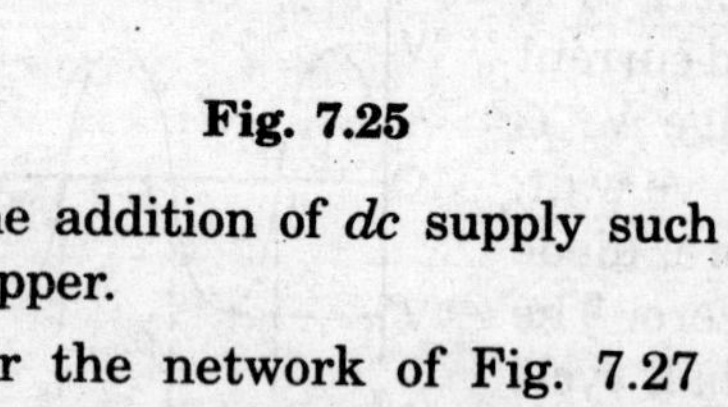


**Fig. 7.25**

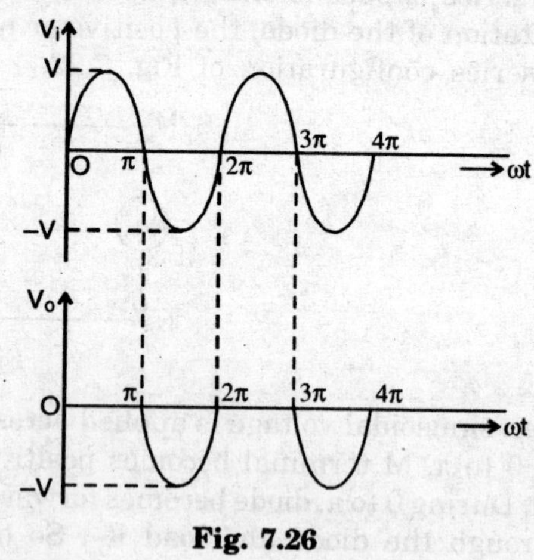


**Fig. 7.26**

The addition of *dc* supply such as shown in Figure 7.27 can have effect on the output of a clipper.

For the network of Fig. 7.27 on the direction of the diode, the signal $V_i$ must be positive or negative to turn it on. The following steps should be applied to reach the final response.

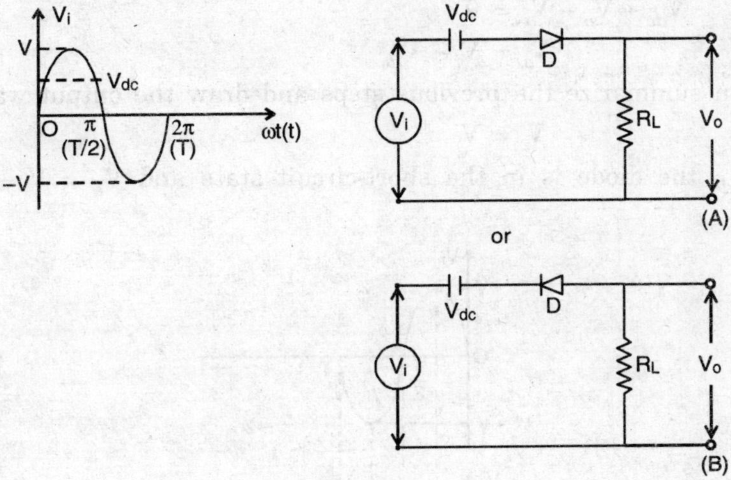


**Fig. 7.27**

**Step 1.** Determine the diode state (ON/OFF) based on the direction of the diode and the applied voltage levels. For the Fig. 7.27 A, the diode turn ON for the voltage $V_i$ greater than $V_d$.

**Step 2.** Determine the transition voltage (applied voltage) that will cause a charge in state for the diode. Since, for the ideal diode the transition of states occur at the point on the characteristics where $i_d$ = 0 A and $V_d$ = 0. For the Fig. 7.27(A), the level of $V_i$ that will cause a transition in state is determined by applying the condition is = 0 and $V_d$ = 0.

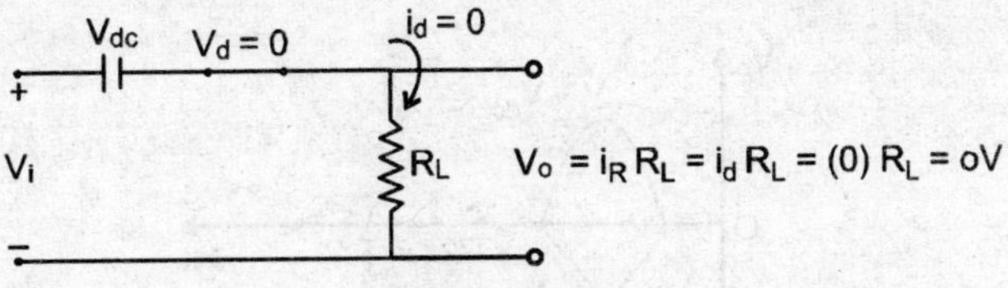


**Fig. 7.28**

From Fig. 7.28, $V_i = V_{dc}$

Therefore, for an input voltage greater than $V_{dc}$ the diode is in the short-circuit-(ON) state, while it is in the open-circuit (OFF) state for input voltages less than $V_{dc}$.

**Step 3.** Determine the output at instantaneous values of the input by sketching the input signal above the output and continually aware of polarity of $V_o$.

For the ON state of diode (short-circuit), the output voltage $V_o$ can be determined by applying KVL, as shown in Figure 7.29.

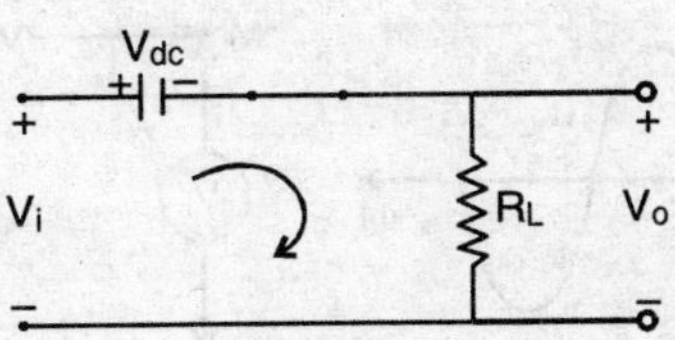


**Fig. 7.29**

$$V_{dc} + V_o - V_i = 0$$
$$V_o = V_i - V_{dc}$$

Now, we can summarize the previous steps and draw the output waveform, *i.e.*,

At $\quad V_i = V$

For $V > V_{dc}$ the diode is in the short-circuit state and $V_o = V - V_{dc}$ as shown in Fig. 7.30.

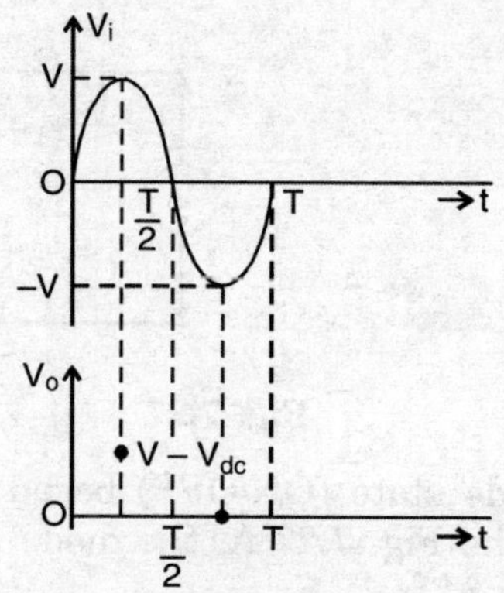


**Fig. 7.30**

At, $\quad V_i = V_{dc}$, the diode change state and

$V_i = -V, V_o = 0$

The final o/p will be as shown in Fig. 7.31.

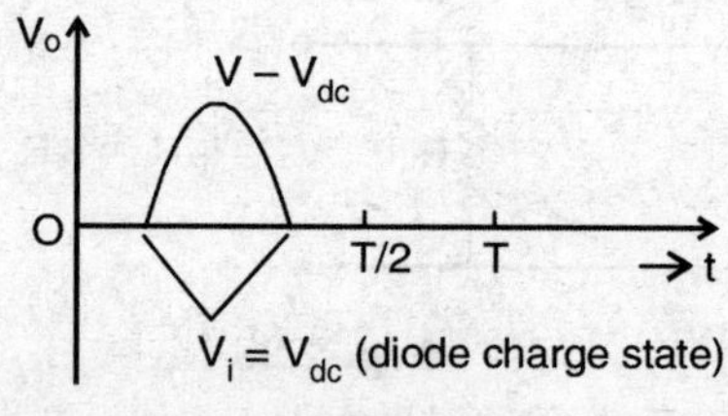


**Fig. 7.31**

***Parallel Clippers***

The parallel clipper is one where the diode is in branch parallel to the load. The analysis of parallel clipper is similar to that applied to series clipper. For the parallel configuration of Fig. 7.32.

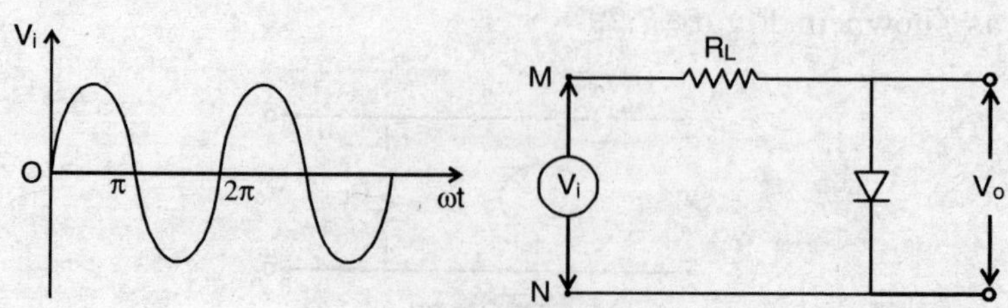


**Fig. 7.32**

During the +ve half cycle the diode acts in the forward biased (short-circuit), so the o/p voltage $V_o = 0$.

During the –ve half cycle the diode acts in the reversed biased (open-circuit), so the o/p follows the input voltage $V_i$. Since the diode is connected across o/p terminals this circuit is called shunt positive clipper (clipped +ve alternation of input $V_i$) as shown in Fig. 7.33.

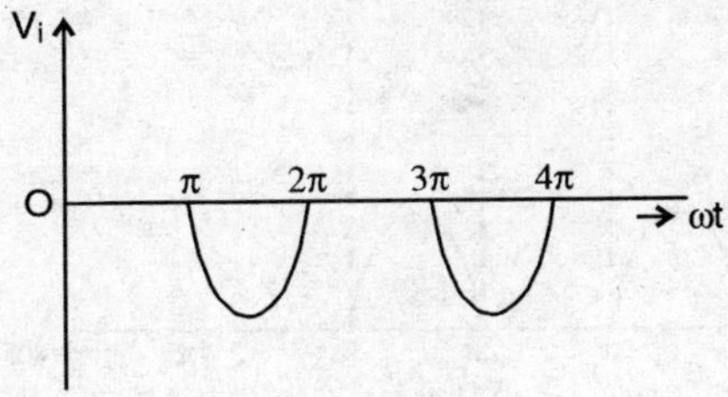


**Fig. 7.33**

One can apply any type of signal to a clipper and it is not limited to the sinusoidal waveform only. When the given input signals Fig. 7.34(*a*) are applied to the same configuration of Fig. 7.32. The response will be as shown in Fig. 7.34(*b*).

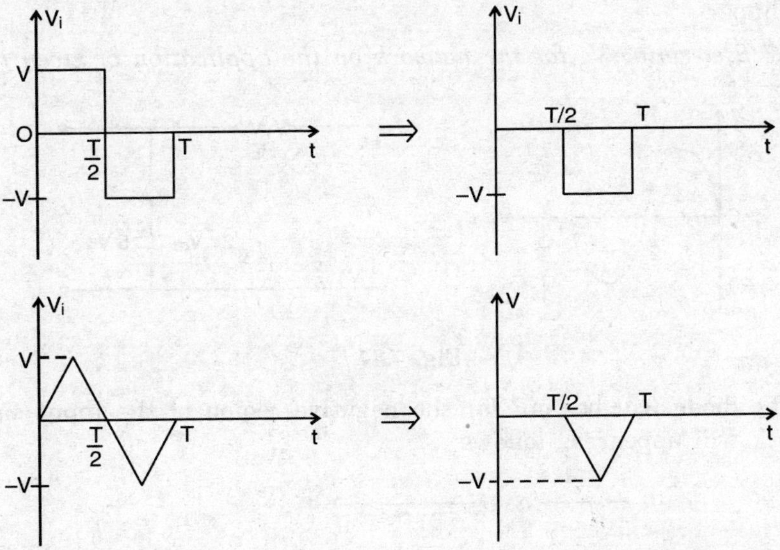


(*a*) (*b*)

**Fig. 7.34**

For the parallel configuration of 7.35.

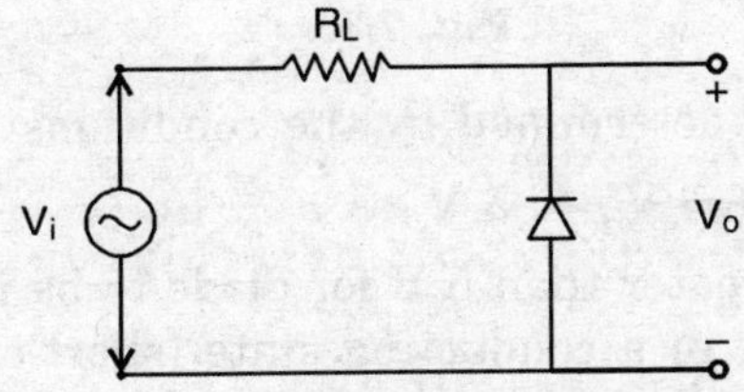


**Fig. 7.35**

**The o/p of the clipper circuit is shown in Fig. 7.36.**

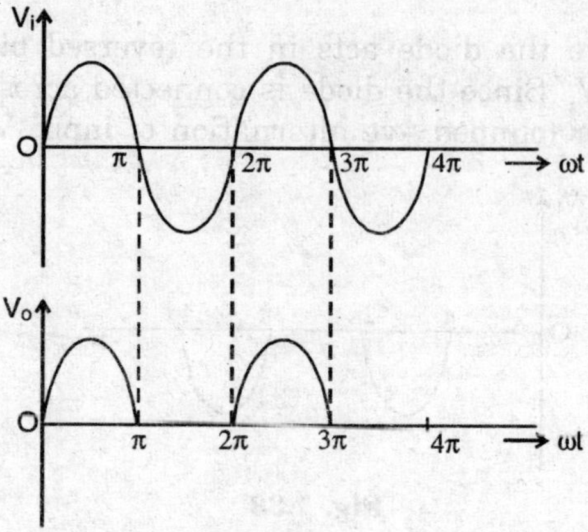


**Fig. 7.36**

**Since, the output is obtained only during the half cycle of the i/p signal (clipped –ve alternation of input $V_i$) and the diode is connected across o/p terminals this circuit is called shunt negative clipper.**

**Example 7.7.** ***Determine $V_o$ for the network on the application of given input.***

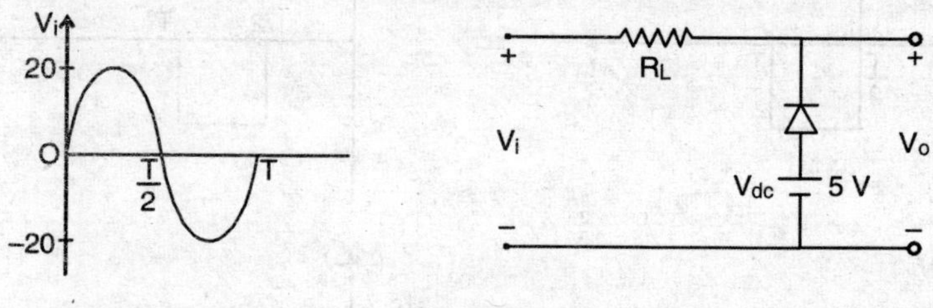


**Fig. 7.37**

**Solution.** **The diode will be "on" for the negative region of the input signal. For this region the network will appear as follows:**

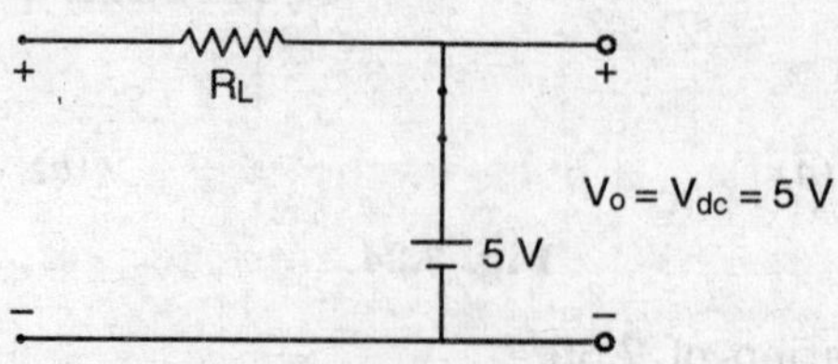


**Fig. 7.38**

**The transition state can be determined by the conditions $i_d = 0$, $V_d = 0$**

$$V_i(\text{transition}) = V_{dc} = 5\text{ V}$$

***i.e.,*** **the input voltage must be greater than 5 V for diode to be in the "OFF" state. Any input voltage less than 5 V will result in a conducting state (short-circuited diode).**

For the open-circuit state the network will appear as follows:

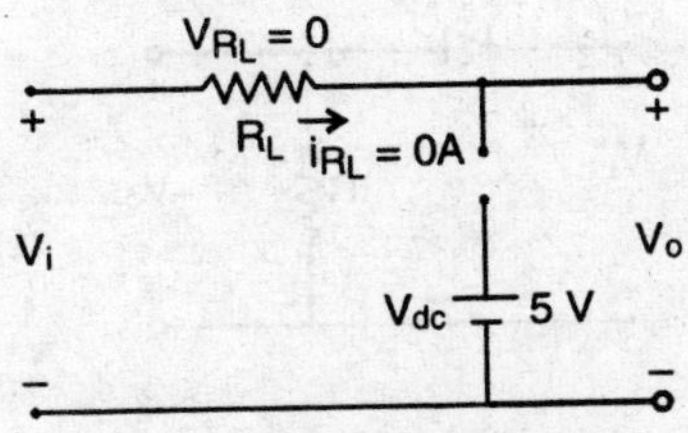


**Fig. 7.39**

The o/p waveform of the network will be as follows:

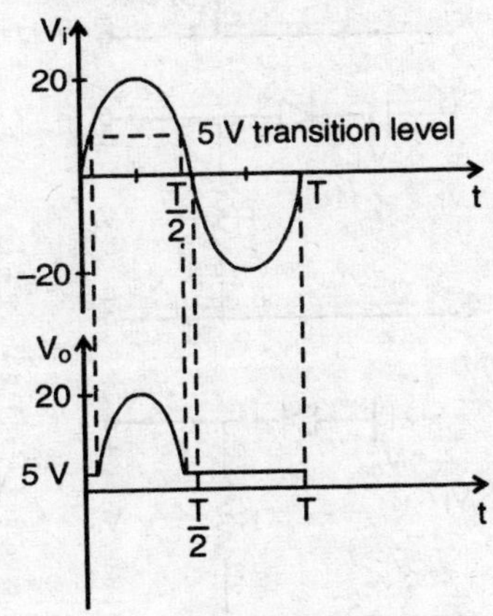


**Fig. 7.40**

So far the ideal diode circuitry are considered (that is the turn on voltage is taken as 0). In particle silicon diode, this turn on voltage ($V_{ON}$) is 0.7V. For the above example, if we consider the effect of this turn on voltage the o/p $V_o$ will be as follows:

In this case, transition voltage will be

$$V_i + V_{ON} - V_{dc} = 0$$

$$V_i \text{ (transition)} = V_{dc} - V_{ON} = 5 - 0.7 = 4.3 \text{ V}$$

For input voltages greater than 4.3 V, the diode will be open circuit and $V_o = V_i$. For input voltages of less than 4.3 V, the diode will be in the "ON" state and $V_o$ = 5 V – 0.7 V = 4.3 V.

The o/p waveform of the network is shown in Fig. 7.41.

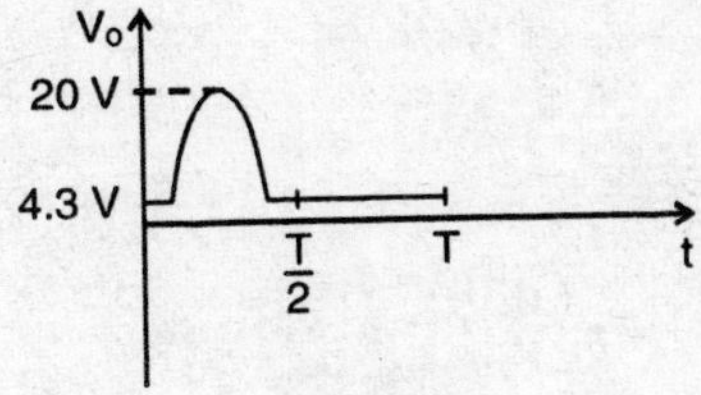


**Fig. 7.41**

## Summary of Different Clipping circuits (for Ideal diodes)

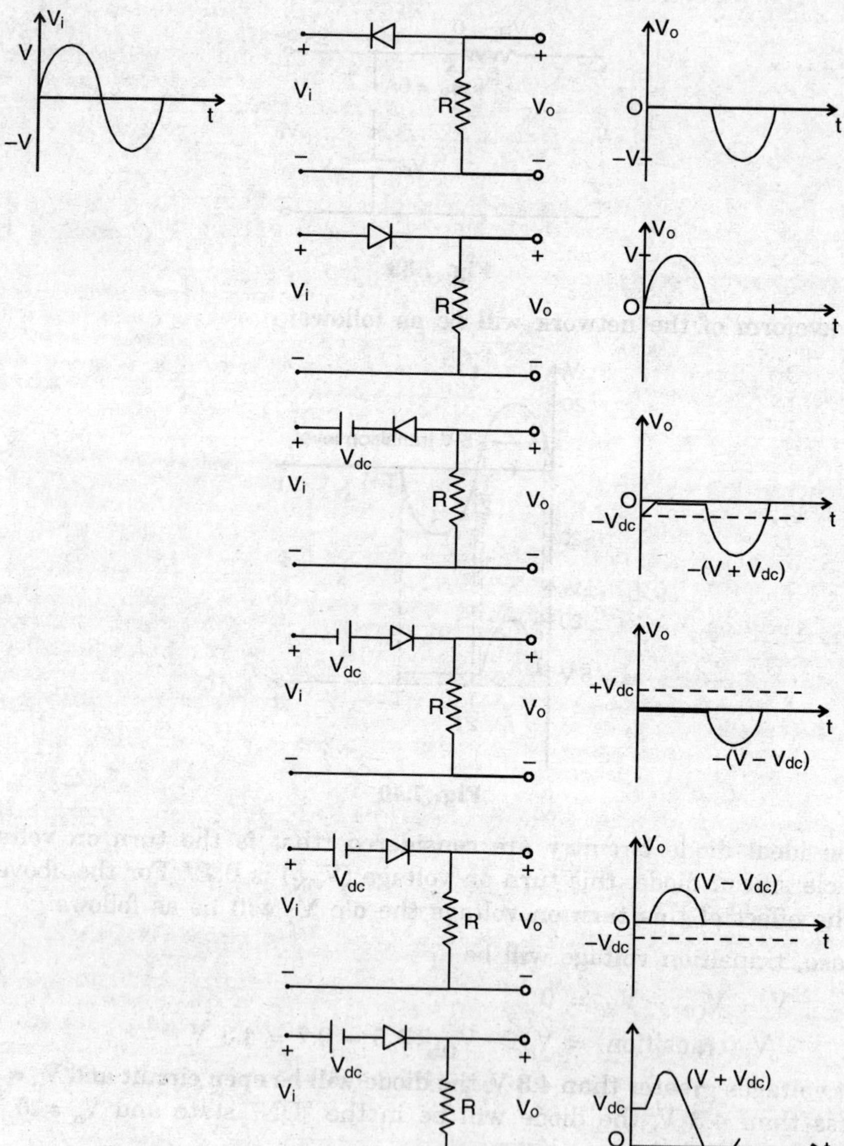

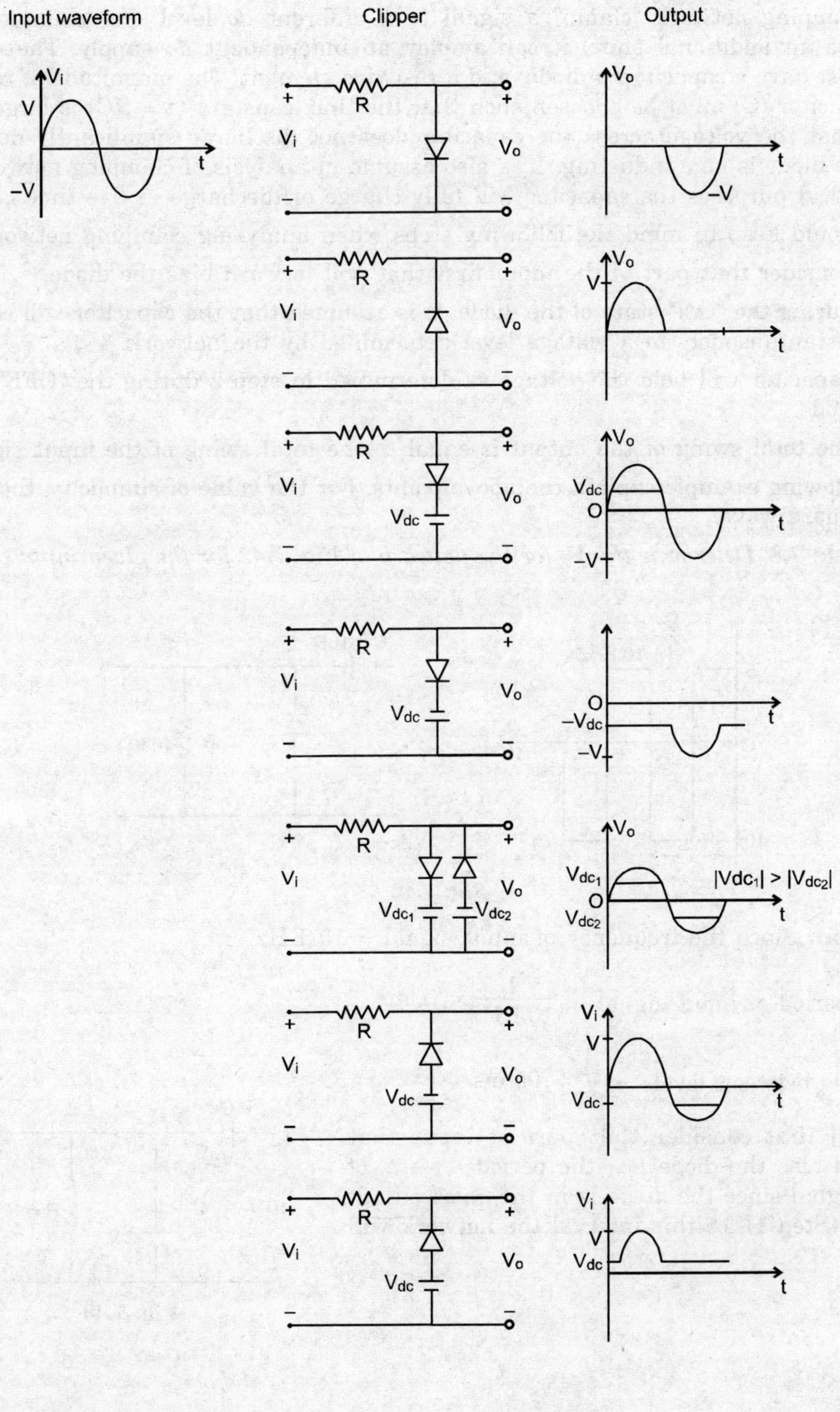
Input waveform
Clipper
Output
Vi
V
–V
t
R
Vo
Vdc
O
–Vdc
Vdc1
Vdc2
|Vdc1| > |Vdc2|

## 7.4 CLAMPERS

The clamping network "clamp" a signal to a different *dc* level. For clamping signal (to introduce an additional shift) it can employ an independent *dc* supply. The clamping network must have a capacitor, a diode, and a resistive element. The magnitude of resistance (R) and capacitor (C) must be choosen such that the time constant ($\tau$ = RC) is large enough to ensure that the voltage across the capacitor does not discharge significantly during the interval, the diode is nonconducting. It is also assume in analysis of clamping networks that for all practical purposes the capacitor will fully charge or discharge in five time constants.

One should keep in mind the following steps when analyzing clamping networks:

1. Consider that part of the input first that will forward bias the diode.
2. During the "ON" state of the diode, it is assumed that the capacitor will charge up instantaneously to a voltage level determined by the network.
3. Capacitor will hold the voltage as determined in step 2 during the "OFF" state of diode.
4. The total swing of the output is equal to the total swing of the input signal.

The following example explain the above points. For the value of simplicity, the input is taken as square wave.

**Example 7.8.** *Determine the* $V_o$ *for the network of Fig. 7.42 for the given input assuming ideal diode.*

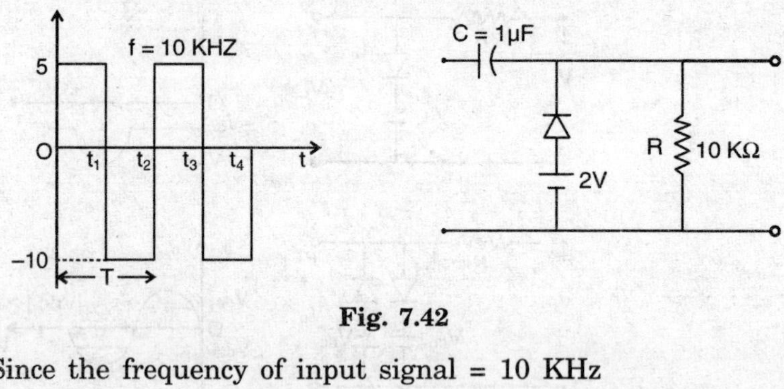


**Fig. 7.42**

**Solution.** Since the frequency of input signal = 10 KHz

$$\text{The period of input signal} = \frac{1}{10\text{ KHz}} = .1\text{ ms}$$

$$\text{and intervals between levels} = \frac{.1}{2} = .05\text{ ms}$$

We will first consider that part of input that will forward bias the diode *i.e.*, the period $t_1 \to t_2$ of the input signal since the diode is in the short circuit state (ON). (Step 1) for this interval the network will appear as

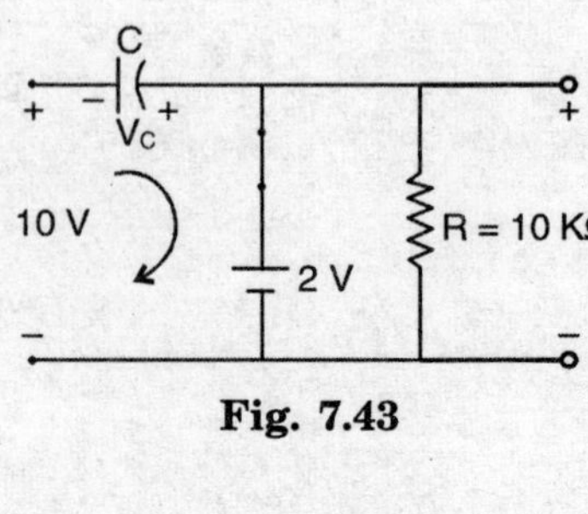


**Fig. 7.43**

The output is across R, but it is also in parallel to 2 V dc supply. Therefore

$$V_o = 2\text{V for interval } t_1 \rightarrow t_2$$

On applying KVL in input loop, we get

$$-V_C + 10 + 2 = 0$$

$$V_C = 12 \text{ V}$$

Therefore the capacitor will charge upto 12 V. (Step 2) For the period $t_2 \rightarrow t_3$ the network will appear as

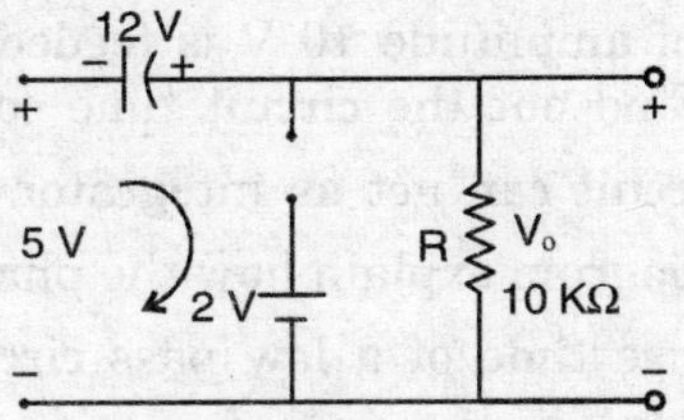


**Fig. 7.44**

On applying KVL for outside loop, we get

$$-5 - 12 + V_o = 0$$

$$V_o = 17 \text{ V (When diode is in "OFF" state)}$$

The time constant of the discharging network of Fig. 7.44 is given by

$$\tau = RC = (10 \text{ KW}) (.1 \text{ μF}) = 10^4 \times 10^{-7} = 10^{-3} \text{ sec} = 1 \text{ ms}$$

The total discharge time = 5τ = 5 × 1 = 5 ms.

Since the interval $t_2 \rightarrow t_3$ will only last for .05 ms, the assumption of step 3 that the capacitor will hold its voltage during the discharge period between pulses of the input signal.

The resulting output will be as shown in Fig. 7.45.

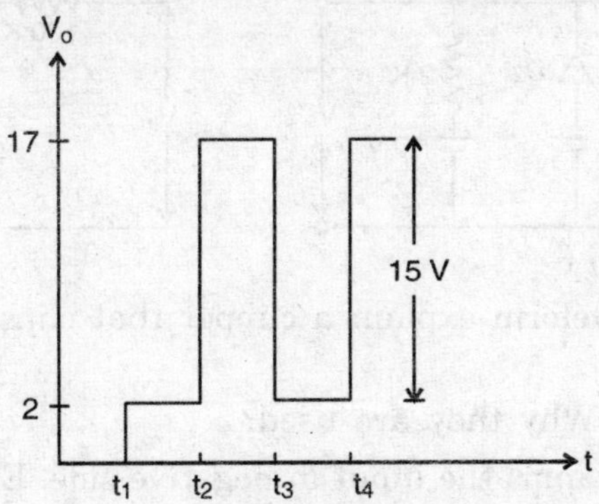


**Fig. 7.45**

The output swing of 15 V matches the input swing (step 4).

## 7.5 EXERCISE

1. Draw the circuit diagram of a high pass circuit and explain why it is called high pass.

2. Derive the transfer function of high pass circuit and calculate the response to sinewave.
3. Explain with the help of waveforms how a high pass circuits can be used to trigger Flip-Flops.
4. Derive the relation for percentage tilt of high pass output.
5. A 10 Hz symmetrical square wave whose peak amplitude is 2 V, is impressed upon a high pass circuit. If the circuit has lower 3 db frequency of 5 Hz, calculate and draw the steady state output waveform.
6. A 10 KHz square wave of amplitude 10 V is feeded to a differentiator circuit. The output is tilted to 7 V. Find out the circuit time constant and 3 db frequency.
7. Show that a low pass circuit can act as integrator.
8. With the help of phasor diagram explain how the phase shift θ varies with frequency.
9. Derive the relation for rise time of a low pass circuit.
10. A symmetrical square wave of repetetion period 2 μsec with 20 $V_{pp}$ is applied to a low pass circuit whose 3db frequency is $\frac{1}{2\pi}$ MHz. Calculate and sketch the output.
11. Design an oscillator probe having attenuation factor of 25% at the probe end. The CRO has an input resistance of 10 MΩ and shunt capacitance of 100 PF.
12. What will be the bandwidth of a low pass circuit if it has a time constant 100 μ sec?
13. What are clippers and how they are different from rectifiers?
14. With the help of waveforms explain the operation of biased clippers.
15. Plot the transfer characteristics of clipper circuits shown below. Assume diodes are ideal.

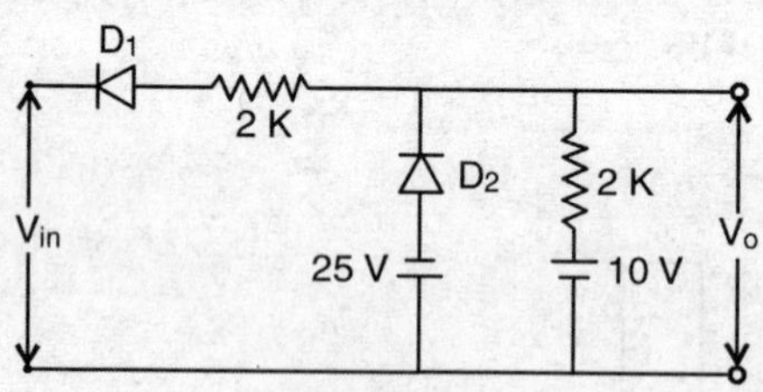


(*a*)

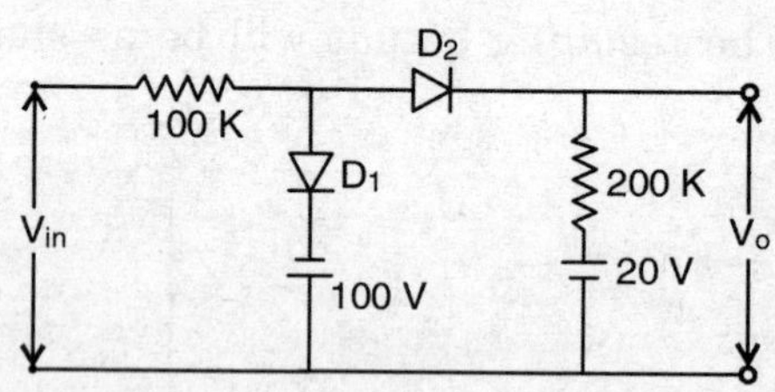


(*b*)

16. With the help of waveform explain a clipper that clips both positive and negative side of the input.
17. What are clampers? Why they are used?
18. Draw a circuit that clamps the input in negative side. Explain its operation through waveforms.
19. Identify the circuit shown below and explain its operation.

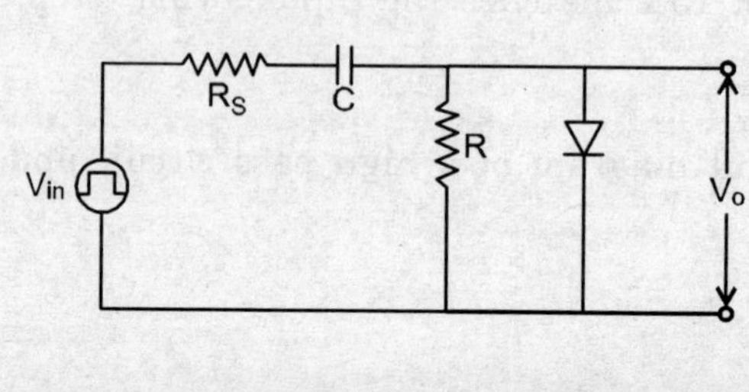

8

CHAPTER

# MULTIVIBRATORS

## 8.0 INTRODUCTION

Almost all digital systems require some kind of a timing waveform. The regenerative circuits intended especially for timing applications are referred to as multivibrators. Multivibrators are classified as astable, bistable and monostable.

An astable multivibrator toggles between one state and the other, without any external commands. It has two quasi-stable states and does not requires any triggering. Also known as a free-running multivibrator, its timing is set by a suitable network, usually comprising a capacitor or quartz crystal. This is used as a source of clock pulses in sequential circuits.

In a bistable multivibrator both states are stable, so external commands (triggering) are required to force the circuit to a given state. This is the flip-flop, which in turn takes on different names, depending on the way in which the external commands are effected. These are often used as memory elements in digital systems.

A monostable multivibrator, also called a one-shot, is stable only in one of its two states. Under steady-state condition its output is fixed, it is in either the LOW or the HIGH state. If forced into the other state via an external command called a trigger, it returns to its stable state spontaneously, after a delay set by a suitable timing network. This state of the circuit is referred to as quasi-stable state, since it recovers back to the stable state without any external triggering pulse. This circuit is very useful because it can generate a relatively long pulse from a narrow pulse, therefore, it is also known as pulse stretcher.

## 8.1 ASTABLE MULTIVIBRATORS (PULSE GENERATORS)

A circuit diagram for a pulse generator using discrete components is given in Figure 8.1.

In order to our analysis, we will assume that $R_{C_1} = R_{C_2}$; $R_{B_1} = R_{B_2}$; $C_1 = C_2$ and $Q_1$ is similar to $Q_2$. On power on current flows from collector to emitter in both transistors. However, inspite of the symmetry we have assumed, one transistor will draw more current than the other. Let us suppose that $Q_2$ draws more current than $Q_1$. As more and more current flows through $R_{C_2}$, the collector of $Q_2$ will gradually become more and more negative than the collector of $Q_1$. This build up of negative voltage at the collector of $Q_2$ is coupled to the base of $Q_1$ via $C_1$, thus making the base of $Q_1$ more and more negative, which causes a reduction in the forward bias of $Q_1$. This has two consequences.

It reduces the collector current of $Q_1$ and makes the collector of $Q_1$ even more positive. The build-up of positive voltage at the collector of $Q_1$ is passed on to the base of $Q_2$ via $C_2$, which has the effect of increasing the forward bias of $Q_2$ and consequently its collector current increases further. In a short time this regenerative feedback causes $Q_2$ to saturate while $Q_1$ is cut-off.

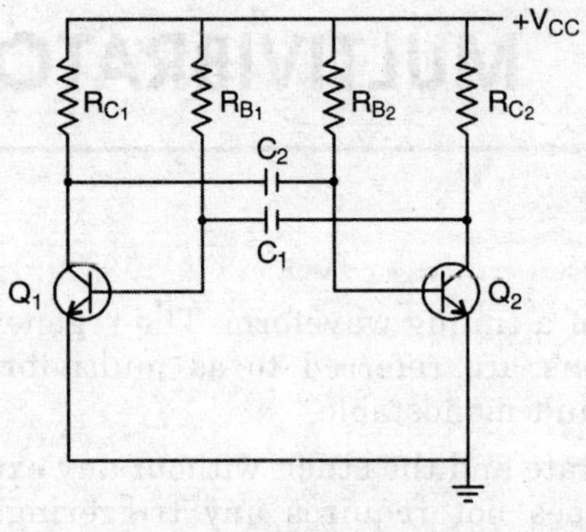


**Fig. 8.1** Pulse generator

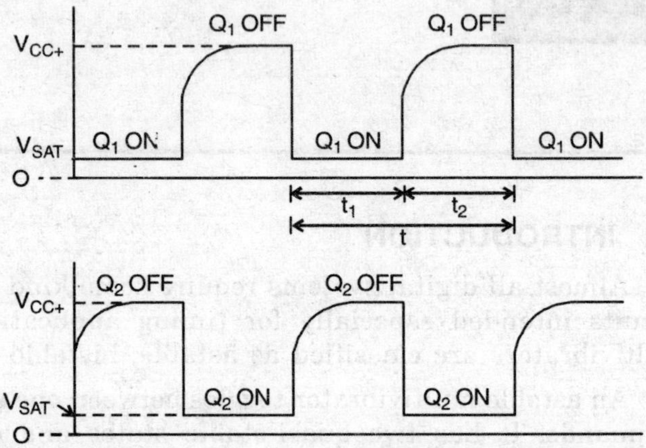


**Fig. 8.2** Clock pulses at the collectors of $Q_1$ and $Q_2$

After $Q_2$ has reached saturation, the resistance between the collector and emitter of $Q_2$ approaches zero. Therefore $C_1$ starts discharging through $Q_2$ and $R_2$. As $C_1$ discharges towards the positive supply line, the voltage at the base of $Q_1$ begins to rise to a more positive value, which brings it out of cut off and into conduction. Collector current now starts to flow in $Q_1$ and as a result, the collector voltage of $Q_1$ drops and this charge is coupled via $C_2$ to the base of $Q_2$, which reduces its collector current. The voltage at the collector of $Q_2$ rises and this positive voltage charge is coupled via $C_1$ to the base of $Q_1$. The same sequence of events, as described earlier, follows and $Q_1$ reaches saturation and $Q_2$ is cut off. This process goes on indefinitely as long as power is supplied to the circuit. The waveforms at the collectors of $Q_1$ and $Q_2$ will be as shown in Figure 8.2.

At a time only one of the two transistor is on and 'on time' and 'off time' of $Q_1$ and $Q_2$ are the same. The expressions for the "off times" of $Q_1$ and $Q_2$ are as follows:

$$\text{For } Q_1, \text{ off time} = t_2 = .694\ C_1\ R_{B_1}$$

$$\text{For } Q, \text{ off time} = t_1 = .694\ C_2\ R_{B_2}$$

The expression for the total, period of a clock cycle is

$$t = t_1 + t_2 = .694\ (C_1R_{B_1} + C_2R_{B_2})$$

On assumption $R_{B_1} = R_{B_2} = R$

$$C_1 = C_2$$

we have $t = 1.4\ RC$

and the clock frequency $f = \dfrac{1}{t} = \dfrac{0.7}{RC}$

where $f$ is in Hz.

R is in Megaohms and

C is in Microfarads.

## 8.2 MONOSTABLE MULTIVIBRATOR

A circuit diagram for a monostable multivibrator using discrete components is given in Fig. 8.3. It has its stable state when $Q_1$ is cut off and $Q_2$ is conducting. It can be triggered into the unstable state for a duration when $Q_1$ will be conducting and $Q_2$ will be cut off.

When power is switched on, the circuit will remain in the stable state until a trigger pulse is applied. When the circuit goes into the unstable state, duration of which depends on the values of $C_2$ and $R_3$. At the end of this duration the circuit reverts to the stable state. Thus, the monostable will generate rectangular ouptut pulses of specified duration, each time a trigger is applied.

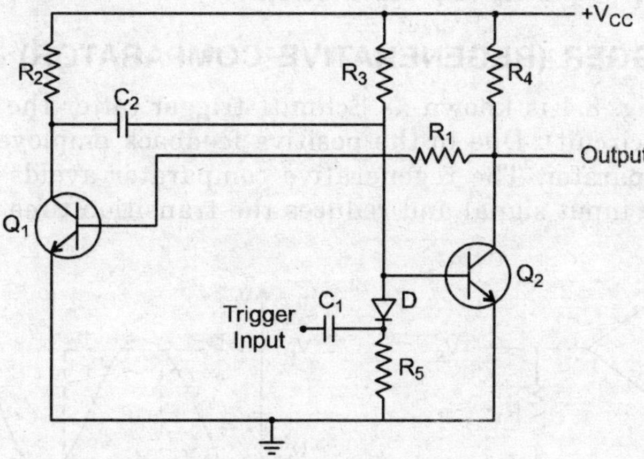


**Fig. 8.3** Monostable Multivibrator

When power is applied $Q_2$ is forward-biased by resistor $R_3$, and $Q_2$ soon saturates, which brings down the voltage at its collector to nearly zero volt. This cuts off transistor $Q_1$ as the base-emitter voltage is not enough to allow it to conduct. The voltage at the collector of $Q_1$ is now almost equal to $V_{CC}$. This charges capacitor $C_2$ through $R_2$ and the base-emitter junction of $Q_2$. It acquires the polarity indicated in the diagram. When a trigger pulse is applied, the positive-going edge of the pulse is blocked by the diode, but the trailing edge or negative-going edge passes through the diode, which reverse-biases the emitter-base junction of $Q_2$. This switches off $Q_2$ and the voltage at its collector rises, which forward-biases $Q_1$ by the current flowing through $R_4$ and $R_1$. This saturates $Q_1$ and the voltage at its collector drops nearly to zero volt. Capacitor $C_2$ now begins to discharge through $R_3$ and $Q_1$. Because one end of capacitor $C_2$ was at a negative potential at the common current of the operation, $Q_2$ will remain cut off until $C_2$ is completely discharged. After sometime $C_2$ will be discharged and then charged in the opposite direction. When the voltage across $C_2$ is enough, it will forward-bias $Q_2$, which will now conduct and $Q_1$ will be cut off. As soon as $Q_2$ begins to conduct, the output pulse is terminated.

The duration of the output-pulse will depend on the value of $C_2$ and $R_3$ and is given by the expression

$$t_1 = .694\ C_2R_3$$

The value of $R_3$ should be low enough to ensure that transistor $Q_2$ saturates during operation. However, the values of $R_2$ and $C_2$ should be such as would allow $C_2$ to recharge through $R_2$ and the base-emitter junction of $Q_2$ between trigger pulses. This places a limit on the duty cycle, which should not exceed 90%. Since the value of $R_2$ cannot be made very small because of the circuit requirements, this places a limit on the maximum value of $C_2$.

## 8.3 BISTABLE MULTIVIBRATORS (BASIC ELECTRONIC LATCH)

In its simplest form, a bistable multivibrator is called a bistable latch or simply latch. It is because when a particular state is set at the output of a bistable multivibrator then state is hold until the input is applied to change its state. It is said that the input is latched by the circuit through its output state.

For the detail on latch/flip-flop refer Chapter 4.

## 8.4 SCHMITT TRIGGER (REGENERATIVE COMPARATOR)

The circuit of Fig. 8.4 is known as Schmitt trigger (after the inventor of a vacuum-tube version of this circuit). Due to the positive feedback employed it is also referred to as regenerative comparator. The regenerative comparator avoids problems due to noise superimposed on the input signal and reduces the transition time that causes the output to change faster.

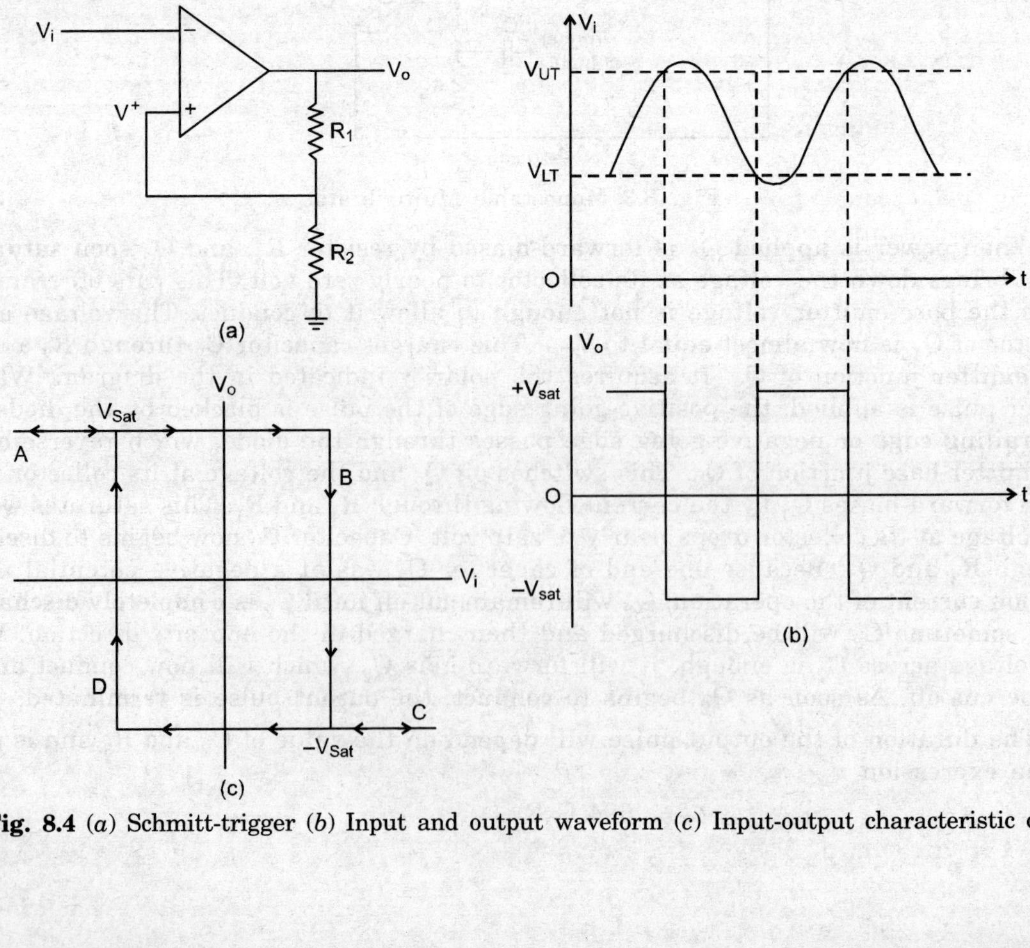


**Fig. 8.4** (*a*) Schmitt-trigger (*b*) Input and output waveform (*c*) Input-output characteristic curve

A resistive voltage divider provides a positive feedback path from the junction of $R_1$ and $R_2$ to the operational amplifier's non-inverting input. The voltage at the non-inverting input determines the positive going level at which $V_i$ will cause the comparator's output to switch to approximately $-V_{sat}$. This positive going level is called the upper threshold voltage ($V_{UT}$) and it is given as

$$V_{UT} = \frac{R_2}{R_1 + R_2} . V_{sat}$$

When $V_i < V_{UT}$, the voltage on the non-inverting input is more positive than $V_i$ and the output equals $+V_{sat}$. When $V_i > V_{UT}$, the output switches to $-V_{sat}$.

When the output voltage equals $-V_{sat}$ the voltage across $R_2$ is called lower threshold voltage $V_{LT}$. The input voltage then drops below $V_{LT}$ before the output will switch to $V_{sat}$. Then $V_{LT}$ is equal to

$$V_{LT} = \frac{R_2\,(-V_{sat})}{R_1 + R_2}$$

The amount of dead zone or hysteresis ($V_H$) is the difference between the two threshold levels

$$V_H = V_{UT} - V_{LT}$$

The input-output characteristics curve for Schmitt trigger is shown in figure 8.4(c). For illustration assume initially the circuit is in a state corresponding to the left hand portion of line A. Then $V_o = V_{sat}$, $V^+ = V_{UT}$ and $V_i$ is negative. Since $V^+ = V_{UT}$, the input voltage $V_i$ must slightly exceed $V_{UT}$ to force the differential input voltage to charge signs. This is indicated by the direction of arrows to the right on line A. When $V_i$ reaches $V_{UT}$ the OP AMP output quickly charges $+V_{sat}$ to $-V_{sat}$ along line B. Any further increase in $V_i$ causes the input to charge along line C, but the output remains in negative saturation. In this state $V_o = -V_{sat}$, hence $V^+ = -V_{sat}$.

To return to line A *i.e.*, previous state, $V_i$ must assume a slightly more positive value than $-V_{LT}$. Thus $V_i$ must move along line C to the left to a value $V_{LT}$. At this point the output returns to positive saturation along line D. Further increase in $V_i$ result in the movement to the left along line A. This is the region in which the operation was initially assumed. The effect of noise is minimised by choosing a sufficiently large value of threshold voltages. The rectangle on the input-output characteristic curve is called a hysteresis loop.

**Example 1.** *For the circuit of Figure 8 (a), if* $\pm V_{sat}$ *= 14V. Find* $V_{UT}$ *and* $V_{LT}$ *if* $R_1$ *=* $100\ K\Omega$*,* $R_2 = 100\ \Omega$*.*

**Solution.** The upper threshold voltage

$$V_{UT} = \frac{R_2}{R_1 + R_2} . V_{sat}$$

$$V_{UT} = \frac{100\ \Omega}{100K + 100}(14\ V)$$

$$V_{UT} = 14\ mV$$

and the lower threshold voltage

$$V_{LT} = \frac{R_2 - (-V_{sat})}{R_1 + R_2}$$

$$V_{LT} = \frac{100\,(-14)}{100 \times 1000 + 100}$$

$$V_{LT} = -14 \text{ mV}.$$

## 8.5 FUNCTION GENERATOR

The function generator, basically, comprises a triangular waveform generator whose frequency can be controlled smoothly as well as in steps. The function generator can produce a square wave train at the same frequency as the triangular wave train. One can also obtain sine waveform from the triangular waveform by using suitable sine-wave synthesis circuit along with this generator. The circuit of a function generator is shown in Fig. 8.5. In the block schematic of function generator, a FF source (a bistable multivibrator) that is capable of producing equal positive and negative potentials relative to a reference potential feeds its output to an adjustable potentiometer. Depending on the setting of this potentiometer, a fraction $E_i$ of the FF output voltage is applied to the linear integrator which use an OP AMP.

As shown in Fig. 8.5, the integrator comprises R and C in association with a high-gain, phase-inverting OP AMP. When the gain of the OP AMP is high, the potential variation at its input terminal is very small compared to $E_i$. For this case, the input current $I_t$ is given by

$$I_t = \frac{E_i}{R}$$

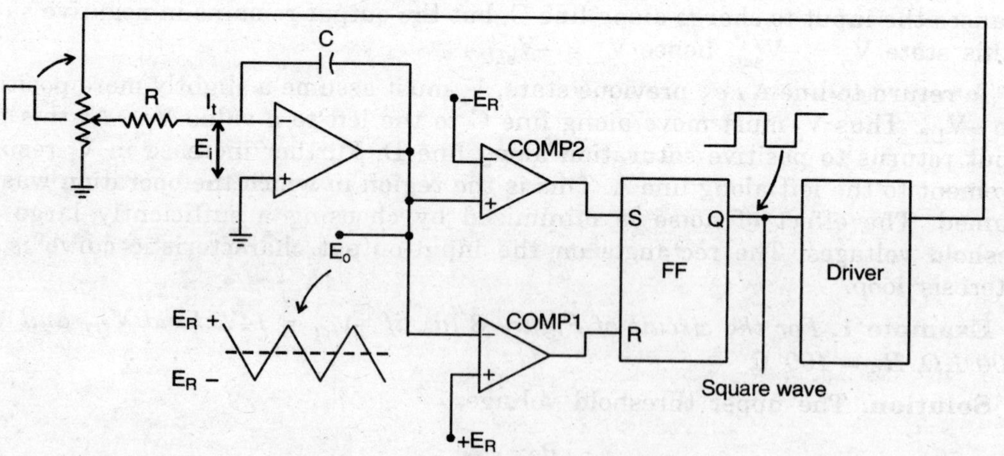


**Fig. 8.5** Function generator circuit

As the input bias current of the OP AMP is negligible, most of this current flows through C. Therefore, the output voltage of the OP AMP changes linearly with time at a fixed slope given by

$$\frac{dE_0}{dt} \; \frac{I_t}{C}$$

Two voltage comparators COMP1 and COMP2 is fed by a uniformly changing voltage $E_o$. The comparators serve to trigger the FF (bistable multivibrator) to an opposite state and to reverse $E_i$ when the magnitude of $E_o$ reaches any of the reference voltages $\pm E_R$ is produced at the OPAMP output terminals. Since, the slope of the triangular wave form is directly proportional to $I_t$ the repetition rate of the waveform is proportional to $E_t$, which permits the potentiometer to serve as a frequency control for the generator. By switching in integrating capacitors of different values at C, several tuning ranges can be obtained. This circuit offers method of waveform generation over a wide frequency range, as a wide range of capacitors can be used. The lowest frequency of operation of the circuit is limits due to leakage resistance associated with capacitor C and high frequency limit is due to slew rate of the OP AMP.

The output of the FF will be a square wave train switching between $\pm E_R$. An interface circuit is used between the FF and the potentiometer. The synthesis of a sine-wave from the triangular waveform is usually carried out by employing a voltage dependent attenuator circuit. A biased diode-resistor network or FET circuitry can be used for this purpose.

## 8.6 TIMER IC-555

This timer is useful in timing applications. It can function as an astable, monostable and bistable multivibrator. The timer consists of two comparators that drive the SET(S) and RESET(R) terminals of a flip-flop. The transition of flip-flop controls the "ON" and "OFF" cycles of the discharge transistor $Q_o$. The voltage divider made up of three series resistor (R) is used to fix the comparator reference voltage as $\frac{2}{3}V_{CC}$ ($V_{TH}$) for comparator COMP1 and $\frac{V_{CC}}{3}$ ($V_{TL}$) for comparator COMP2.

These reference voltages are used to control the timing. The positive terminal of the *dc* power supply is connected to pin 8 ($+V_{CC}$) and the negative terminal to the ground (pin 1). The output (pin 3) of the 555 timer can assume one of the two possible levels. ('HIGH' level/'LOW' level).

The upper threshold node is externally accessible via pin 5 so that the user can modulate the value of $V_{TH}$. Regardless of the value of $V_{TH}$, we always have $V_{TL} = V_{TH}/2$. Assuming that pin 5 is not connected externally to a *dc* circuit, the non inverting input of the COMP1 (threshold comparator) is called the threshold terminal. Similarly the non inverting terminal of the lower comparator COMP2 (trigger comparator) is called trigger terminal.

When an external input *dc* circuit is connected to the control terminal (pin 5), the transition levels will be modified. The condition of the discharge terminal (pin 7) is a function of output state. When the output is high the discharge transistor is reverse biased. In this case, the discharge terminal appears essentially as an open circuit. When the ouptut is low the terminal then appears as a short to ground.

The reset terminal (pin 4) allows the 555 timer to be disabled. If this terminal is grounded or the potential is reduced below 0.4 V, the output assumes the low state irrespective of the operation. If it is not necessary the reset terminal is connected to $V_{CC}$.

An external voltage applied to pin 5 (control voltage) changes the threshold as well as the trigger voltage. When not used, the control pin should be bypassed to ground with a μ*f* capacitor.

The basic principle of operation of this timer is on a negative transition of pulse applied at the trigger terminal and when the voltage at the trigger terminal passes through $\frac{V_{CC}}{3}$. The output of a comparator COMP2 changes state because its positive input terminal is fixed at $\frac{V_{CC}}{3}$ $(V_{TL})$. This change of state sets the flip-flop, so that the output of flip-flop, $\overline{Q}$ goes to low level.

On the other hand, when the voltage applied at the threshold terminal of COMP1 goes positive and passes through the reference level $\frac{2\,V_{CC}}{3}(V_{TH})$ the output of the comparator changes its state. This change of state resets the flip-flop so that $\overline{Q}$ is latch into high level. The functional block diagram of 555 is shown in Fig. 8.6.

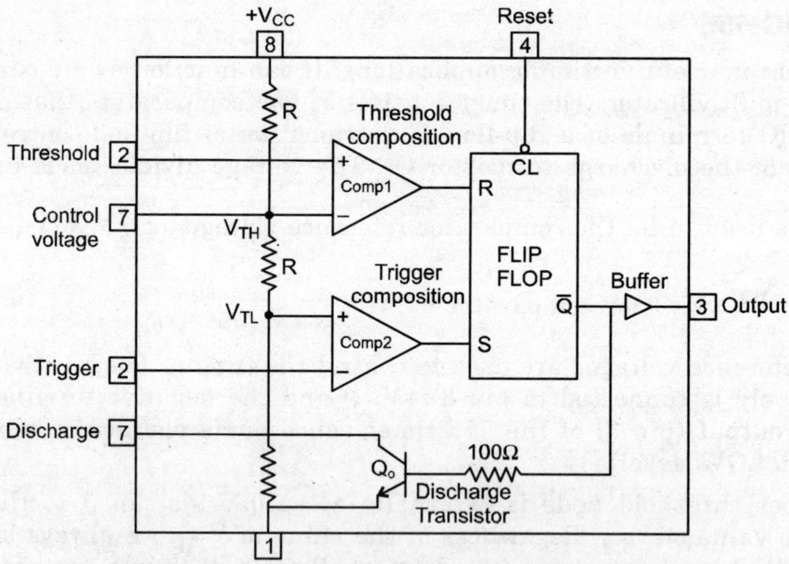


**Fig. 8.6** Functional block diagram of 555 timer

## 8.7 MULTIVIBRATORS USING IC-555

### 8.7.1 Timer 555 as Astable Multivibrator

Figure 8.7(a) shows how the 555 is configured for astable operation using only three external components. The discharge transistor (pin7) of the timer is connected to the junction of two resistors $R_A$ and $R_B$. A timing capacitor C, connected as shown in Fig. 8.7(*a*).

When power is switch on, the timing capacitor begins to charge towards $\frac{2\,V_{CC}}{3}(V_{TH})$ through resistors $R_A$ and $R_B$. When, the capacitor voltage has reached this value, the upper comparator of the timer triggers the flip-flop and the capacitor begins to discharge to ground through resistor $R_B$. When the capacitor voltage reaches $\frac{1}{3}V_{CC}$, the lower comparator is triggered and another charge cycle begins.

The waveforms generated by this astable multivibrator are shown in Fig. 8.7 (*b*).

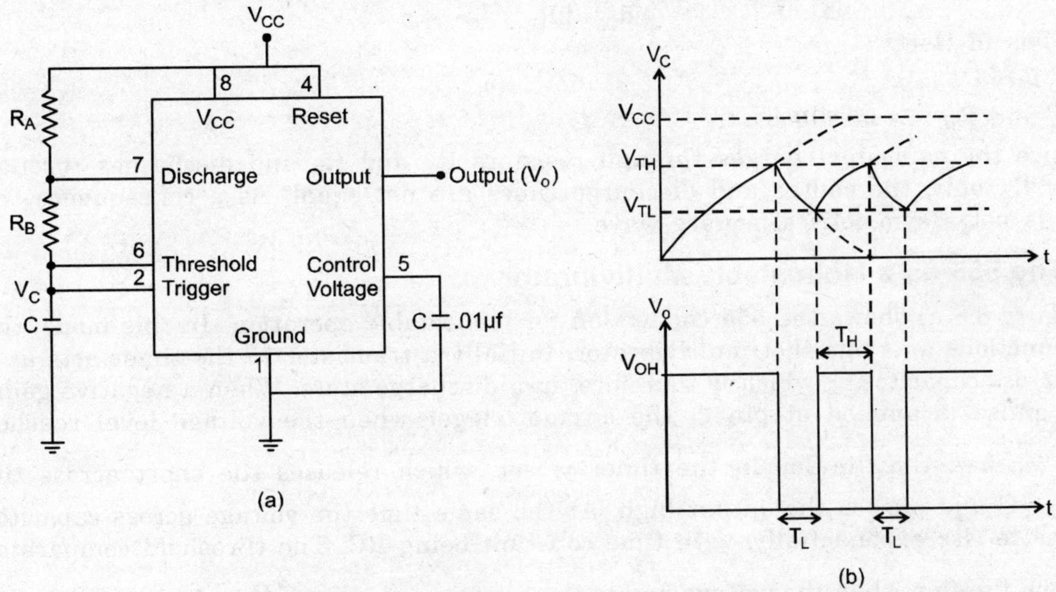


**Fig. 8.7** The 555 timer as an astable multivibrator

To prevent power-supply noise from causing false triggering when $V_C$ approaches either thresholds, a 0.01 µF by pass capacitor is used between pin 5 and ground.

The waveforms show that the charge and discharge cycles are repeated between $V_{TH}\left(\frac{2V_{CC}}{3}\right)$ and $V_{TL}\left(\frac{V_{CC}}{3}\right)$. During charge cycle $T_H$ the time constant is $(R_A + R_B)\,C$ and output stays high and during discharge cycle $T_L$ the time constant is $R_BC$. The formulae applicable for charge and discharge periods are as follows:

$$\text{Charge time } T_H = (R_A + R_B)\,C \ln\left[(V_{CC} - V_{TL})/(V_{CC} - V_{TH})\right] = (R_A + R_B)\,C \ln 2$$

$$\text{discharge time } T_L = R_BC \ln\left(\frac{V_{TH}}{V_{TL}}\right) = R_BC \ln 2$$

$$\text{Total period } T = T_L + T_H$$

$$T = R_BC \ln 2 + (R_A + R_B)\,C \ \ln \frac{V_{CC} - V_{TH}/2}{V_{CC} - V_{TH}}$$

$$\text{substituting } V_{TH} = \frac{2\,V_{CC}}{3}$$

$$T = (R_A + 2R_B)\,C \ln 2$$

Solving for output frequency, $f_0 = \frac{1}{T}$ and duty cycle, $D(\%) = 100\frac{T_H}{T_L + T_H}$, we get

$$f_0 = \frac{1.44}{(R_A + 2R_B)\,C}$$

$$D(\%) = 100\,\frac{R_A + R_B}{R_A + 2R_B}$$

where $f$ is in Hertz
C is in farad
and $R_A$ and $R_B$ are in ohms.

Since the capacitor charges through resistors $R_A$ and $R_B$ and discharges through resistor $R_B$ only, the charge and discharge times are not equal. As a consequence the output is not a symmetrical square wave.

### 8.7.2 The 555 as a Monostable Multivibrator

Figure 8.8(a) shows the 555 connection for monostable operation. In this mode, the timer functions as a one-shot multivibrator. Initially a transistor in the timer acts as a short across capacitor C, which is therefore, in a discharge state. When a negative going trigger pulse is applied at pin 2, the circuit trigger when the voltage level reaches $(V_{TL})\frac{1}{3}V_{CC}$ and the flip-flop in the timer is set, which releases the short across the capacitor C and pushes the output high. At the same time the voltage across capacitor C begins to rise exponentially, with time constant being RC. The threshold comparator resets the flip-flop when the voltage across the capacitor reaches $\frac{2}{3}V_{CC}$. As a consequence the capacitor is discharged and the output is driven low. The circuit will remain in this state until the application of the next negative going pulse at pin 2.

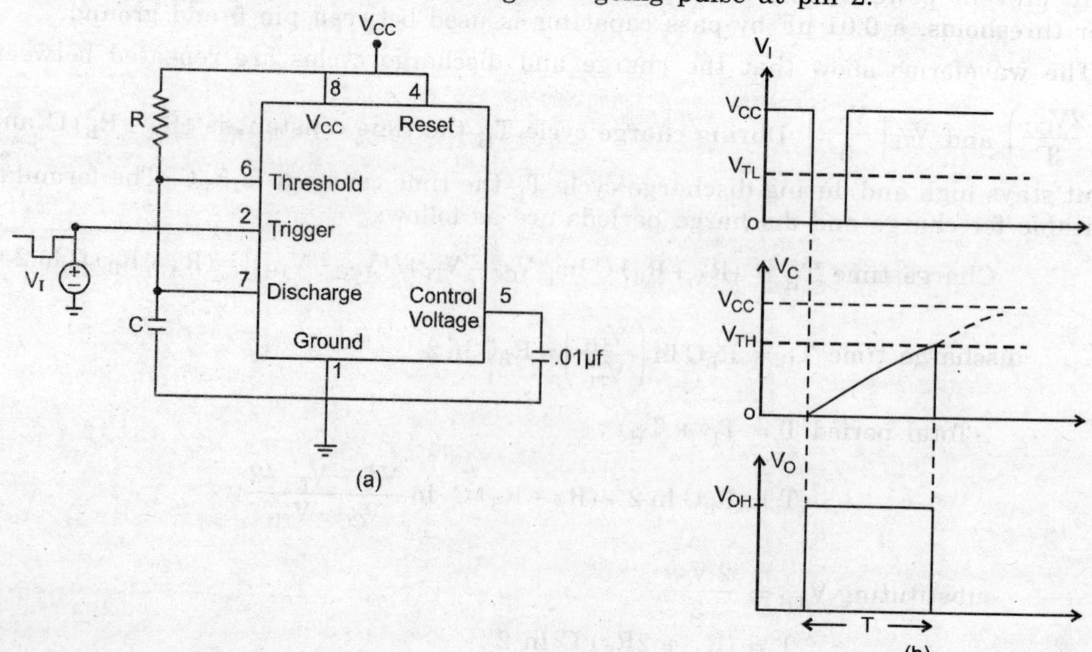


**Fig. 8.8** The 555 timer as a monostable multivibrator

After the circuit has been triggered, it will continue in this state for a period dependent on the values of R and C, even if it is triggered again during this interval of time.

The pulse width T is given as

$$T = RC \ln \frac{V_{CC}}{V_{CC} - V_{TH}}$$

Putting $V_{TH} = \frac{2}{3} V_{CC}$, gives

$$T = RC \ln 3$$

$$T = 1.10\ RC$$

### 8.7.3 555 as a Bistable Multivibrator

Timer 555, functioning as a bistable miltivibrator finds application as a compatible driver in TLL circuits. Its output is adequate to drive relays directly from its output pin. A circuit for this purpose is shown in Fig. 8.9. When a negative going pulse is applied at its trigger input, pin 2, the flip-flop in the timer is set and its output goes high. When a positive going pulse is applied at the thresholds input, pin 6, the flip-flop in the timer is reset and drives the output-low.

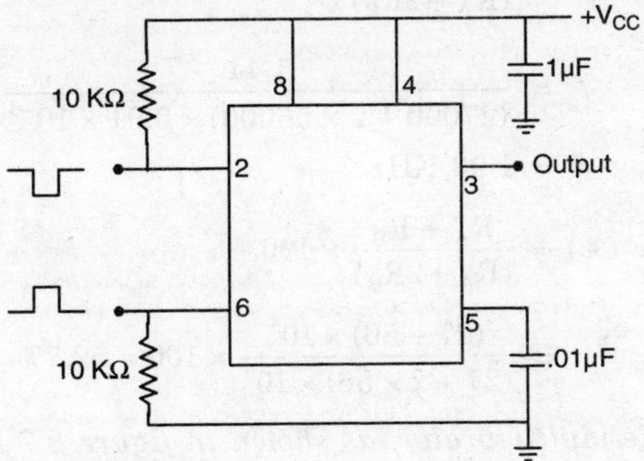


**Fig. 8.9** 555 as a bistable multivibrator

### 8.7.4 Voltage Control

If desired, the timing characteristics of 555 can be modulated via the control input. Changing $V_{TH}$ from its nominal value of $\left(\frac{2}{3}\right) V_{CC}$ will result in longer or shorter capacitance charging times, depending on whether $V_{TH}$ is increased or decreased.

When the timer is configured for astable operation, modulating $V_{TH}$ varies $T_H$ while leaving $T_L$ unchanged. Consequently, the output is a train of constant-width pulses with a variable repetition rate. This is referred to as pulse-position modulation (PPM).

When the timer is configured for monostable operation, modulating $V_{TH}$ varies T. If the monostable is triggered by a continuous pulse train, the output will be a pulse train with the same frequency as the input but with the pulse width modulated by $V_{TH}$. This is referred to as pulse-width modulation (PWM).

It must be remember that once $V_{TH}$ is overridden externally, $V_{TH}$ and $V_{CC}$ are no longer related; hence the timing characteristics are no longer independent of $V_{CC}$.

***Monostable Multivibrators ICs***

| *IC No.* | *Description* |
|---|---|
| 74121 | Monostable multivibrator (one-shot) |
| 74122 | Retriggerable multivibrator with clear |
| 74123 | Dual retriggerable multivibrator with clear |
| 74221 | Dual monostable multivibrator with clear |

## 8.8 SOLVED EXAMPLES

**Example 1.** *Calculate the frequency and the duty cycle of the output of an astable multivibrator using Timer 555. The relevant data is as follows:*

$$R_A = 27\ K\Omega$$
$$R_B = 56\ K\Omega$$
$$C = 0.01\ \mu F$$

**Solution.**

$$f_o = \frac{1.44}{(R_A + 2R_B)\,C}$$

$$f_o = \frac{1.44}{(27000 + 2 \times 56000) \times 0.01 \times 10^{-6}}$$

$$f_o = 1.03 \text{ KHz}$$

$$\text{Duty cycle (\%)} = \frac{R_A + R_B}{(R_A + 2R_B)} \times 100$$

$$= \frac{(27 + 56) \times 10^3}{(27 + 2 \times 56) \times 10^3} \times 100 = 59.7\%$$

**Example 2.** *An astable multivibrator, as shown in figure 8.7 is used to provide a 2 MHz clock frequency at 60% duty cycle. Calculate the values of $R_B$ and C if $R_A$ = 3000 ohms.*

**Solution.**

$$T = \frac{1}{f} = \frac{1}{2 \times 10^6} = 0.5\ \mu s$$

$$D(\%) = \frac{R_A + R_B}{R_A + 2R_B} \times 100 = 60 = \frac{T_H}{T}$$

$$R_A + R_B = 0.6\ R_A + 1.2\ R_B$$
$$0.4R_A = 0.2\ R_B$$
$$R_B = 2R_A$$
$$R_B = 2 \times 30000 \text{ ohm}$$
$$R_B = 60000 \text{ ohm}$$

$$\frac{T_H}{T} = D = 0.6$$

$$T_H = 0.6 \times T = 0.6 \times 0.5 = 0.30 \ \mu s$$

$$\text{Charging time } T_H = .693\,(R_A + R_B)\,C$$

$$C = \frac{T_H}{0.693\,(R_A + R_B)} = \frac{0.3 \times 10^{-6}}{0.693 \times 9000} \text{ Farad}$$

$$C = 48.10 \text{ PF.}$$

**Example 3.** *Determine the value of the timing capacitor required for an astable multivibrator as shown in figure 8.7; so that it delivers a clock frequency of 50 KHz when $R_A$ = 2 KΩ and $R_B$ = 2.5 KΩ.*

**Solution.** The frequency of oscillation is given by

$$f_o = \frac{1.44}{(R_A + 2R_B)\,C}$$

Therefore the value of timing capacitor will be

$$C = \frac{1.44}{(R_A + 2R_B) f_o}$$

$$C = \frac{1.44}{50 \times 10^3\,(2 \times 10^3 + 2 \times 2.5 \times 10^3)}$$

$$C = 4122 \text{ PF}$$

**Example 4.** *For a 555 monostable multivibrator, calculate the width of the output pulse when R = 10 KΩ and C = 0.05 μF.*

**Solution.** Pulse width $t = 1.1$ RC

where R is in ohms

C is in Farads

and t is in seconds.

$$t = 1.1 \times 10 \times 10^3 \times 0.05 \times 10^{-6}$$

$$t = 0.55 \text{ ms}$$

## 8.9 EXERCISE

1. Calculate the operating frequency and duty cycle for 555 timer in the astable mode, when $R_A$ = 10 KΩ, $R_B$ = 47 KΩ and C = 0.01 μF (Refer to Fig. 8.7).
2. Design an astable oscillator using 555 timer to oscillate at a frequency of 1 KHz with a duty cycle as close to 50% as possible.
3. Draw a circuit diagram for a delayed pulse generator to produce three delayed pulses. Also sketch the output waveforms.
4. Draw a neat diagram of a Schmitt trigger. Describe the operation for the same and explain what hysteresis is.
5. Draw the functional blood diagram of 555 timer and explain its operation.
6. In the Schmitt Trigger circuit of Figure 8.4.

   (*i*) if $V_{sat}$ = 13 V, find the upper triggering voltage ($V_{UT}$) and lower triggering voltage ($V_{LT}$).

(*ii*) if $V_i$ = 5 sin *wt*, find the waveform of the output voltage.

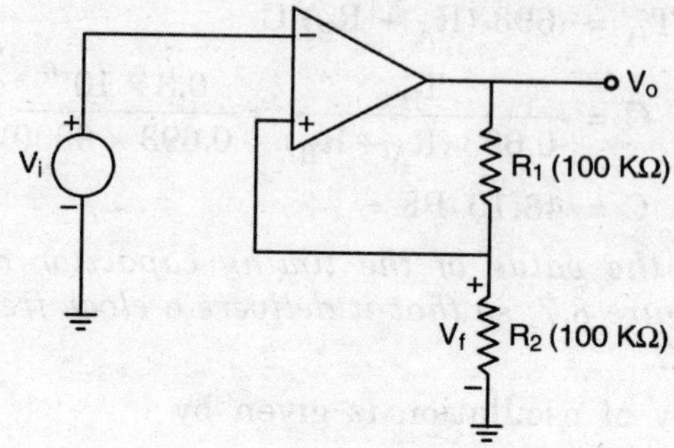


**Fig. 8.10**

**7.** Explain operation of function generator.

**8.** Write short notes on

(*i*) Monostable multivibrator

(*ii*) Astable multivibrator

(*iii*) Bistable multivibrator

**9.** Design a 100 KHz, 55% duty cycle square-wave generator using 555.

**10.** Verify that the circuit of Figure 8.11 acts as an astable multivibrator.

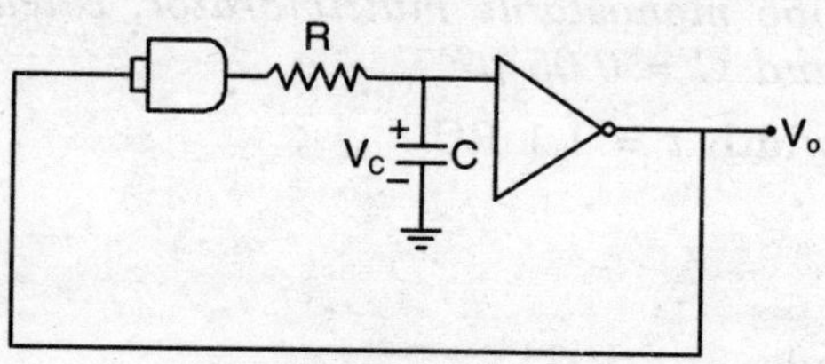


**Fig. 8.11**

9

CHAPTER

# A/D AND D/A CONVERTERS

## 9.0 INTRODUCTION

An ADC is used to convert analog electrical signal (quantity) such as voltage or current into digital quantity (binary number). It is essentially a hardware encoder. The conversion process is the process of dividing (or mapping) the analog i/p into a set of discrete o/p levels. It accepts analog i/p with a reference voltage $V_R$ and provides a digital output (Fig. 9.1).

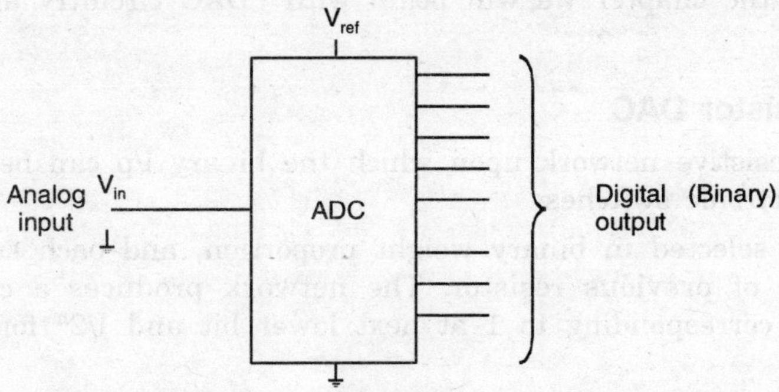


**Fig. 9.1**

A DAC, on the other hand, inputs a binary number and outputs an analog voltage or current signal. (Fig. 9.2)

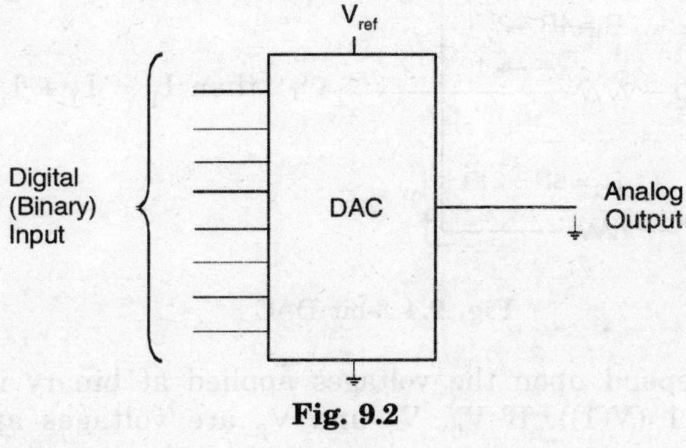


**Fig. 9.2**

Together, they are often used in digital systems to provide complete interface with analog sensors and output devices for control systems. Figure 9.3 shows a digital control system with analog input/output.

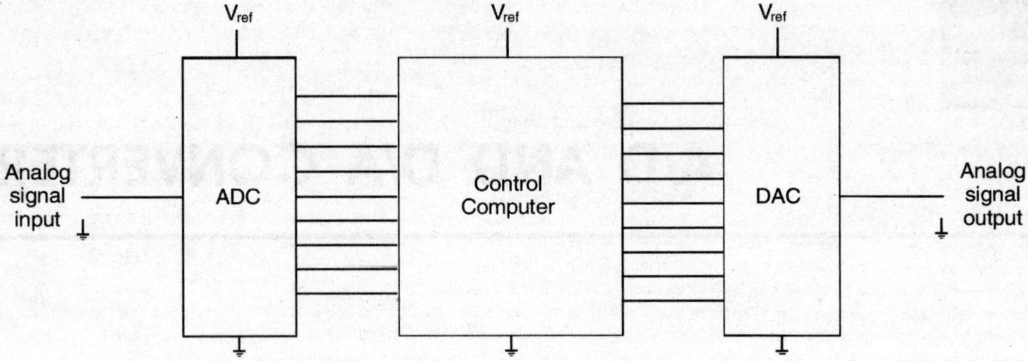


**Fig. 9.3** Digital control system with analog I/O

## 9.1 DIGITAL-TO-ANALOG CONVERTERS

It is much easier to convert a digital signal into an analog signal than it is to do the reverse. Therefore, in the chapter we will begin with DAC circuitry and then move to ADC circuitry.

### 9.1.1 Weighted Resistor DAC

It consists of a resistive network upon which the binary i/p can be applied through digitally controlled electronic switches.

The resistors are selected in binary weight proportion, and each successive resistor has double the value of previous resistor. The network produces a current I/2 when MSB = 1, I/4 or $I/2^2$ corresponding to 1 at next lower bit and $I/2^n$ for logic 1 at least significant bit.

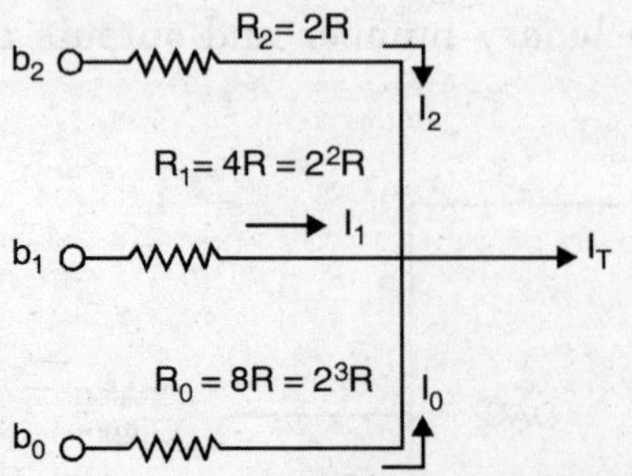


then $I_T = I_0 + I_1 + I_2$ ...(1)

Let R = 1K

**Fig. 9.4** 3-bit DAC

Currents $I_1$, $I_2$, $I_0$ depend upon the voltages applied at binary $i/p_s$ corresponding to logic 0 (V(0)) and logic 1 (V(1)). If $V_0$, $V_1$ and $V_2$ are voltages applied at $b_0$, $b_1$, $b_2$ respectively, then

$$I_0 = \frac{V_0}{R_0} = \frac{V_0}{2^3R}, \qquad I_1 = \frac{V_1}{2^2R}, \qquad I_2 = \frac{V_2}{2R}$$

so $$I_T = \frac{V_0}{2^3R} + \frac{V_1}{2^2R} + \frac{V_2}{2R} \qquad ...(2)$$

let $$V(1) = V_R \text{ and } V(0) = 0V$$

then $$\boxed{V_i = b_i V_R} \qquad ...(3)$$

so when $$b_i = 0, V_i = 0 = V(0) = \text{Logic } 0$$

$$b_i = 1, V_i = V_R = V(1) = \text{Logic } 1$$

with the help of equation (3), equation (2) can be modified

$$I_T = \frac{b_0 V_R}{2^3R} + \frac{b_1 V_R}{2^2R} + \frac{b_2 V_R}{2R}$$

or $$\boxed{I_T = V_R \left[\frac{b_0}{2^3R} + \frac{b_1}{2^2R} + \frac{b_2}{2R}\right]} \qquad ...(4)$$

or $$\boxed{I_T = \frac{V_R}{R}\left(\frac{b_2}{2} + \frac{b_1}{2^2} + \frac{b_0}{2^3}\right)} \qquad ...(5)$$

$$= \frac{1}{R}\left[\frac{V_R}{2} b_2 + \frac{V_R}{4} b_1 + \frac{V_R}{8} b_0\right]$$

Equations (4) and (5) can be generalized for an $n$-bit DAC shown below in Fig. 9.5

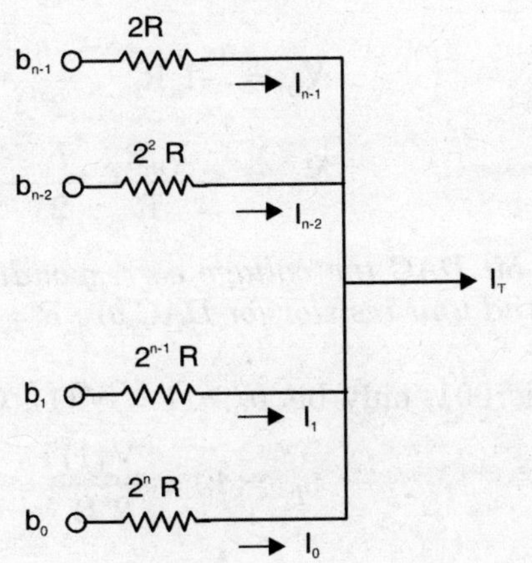


**Fig. 9.5** $n$-bit DAC

so $$I_T = I_0 + I_1 + \ldots + I_{n-1}$$

or $$I_T = V_R\left[\frac{b_0}{2^n R} + \frac{b_1}{2^{n-1}R} + \ldots + \frac{b_{n-1}}{2R}\right] \qquad \ldots(6)$$

or $$I_T = \frac{V_R}{R}\left[\frac{b_0}{2^n} + \frac{b_1}{2^{n-1}} + \ldots + \frac{b_{n-1}}{2}\right] \qquad \ldots(7)$$

let $$I_R = \frac{V_R}{R}, \text{ then}$$

$$I_T = I_R\left[\frac{b_0}{2^n} + \frac{b_1}{2^{n-1}} + \ldots + \frac{b_{n-1}}{2}\right]$$

$$I_T = I_R \sum_{i=0}^{n-1} \frac{b_i}{2^{n-i}} \qquad \ldots(8)$$

where $b_0$ is ISB and $b_{n-1}$ is MSB and $n$ = no. of bits at the i/p of DAC. Equation (8) gives the basic relation for a current type $n$-bit DAC.

In order to produce a voltage at the o/p the an OP AMP as current to voltage converter can be connected at the o/p of DAC as shown below in Figure 9.6.

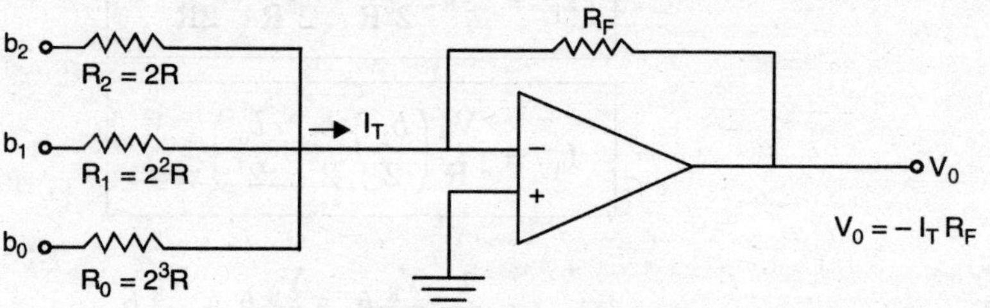


**Fig. 9.6** 3-bit voltage o/p DAC

Here $$V_0 = -I_T R_F$$

by eqns. (7) and (8)

$$V_0 = -I_R R_F \sum_{i=0}^{n-1} \frac{b_i}{2^{n-i}}$$

or $$V_0 = -\frac{V_R R_F}{R}\left[\frac{b_0}{2^n} + \frac{b_1}{2^{n-1}} + \ldots + \frac{b_{n-1}}{2}\right]$$

**Example 1.** *For a 3-bit DAC the voltage corresponding to logic 1 is 1V and for logic 0 is 0V. If feedback resistor and unit resistor for DAC are R = 1KΩ, then calculate the o/p voltage when i/p is 001, 111.*

**Solution:** When i/p is 001, only bit $b_0$ = 1 = V(1). Other bits are 00.

So $$I_T = I_0 = \frac{V(1)}{2^3 R} = \frac{1}{8 \times 10^3} = 0.125\ mA$$

$$= 125\ \mu A$$

$$\text{o/p } V_0 = 0.125 \times 10^{-3} \times 1 \times 10^3$$

or $$V_0 = 0.125\ V$$

Similarly, for i/p 111 all the bits have logic 1

*i.e.,* $b_0 = b_1 = b_2 = 1 = V(1)$

so $I_T = I_0 + I_1 + I_2 = \frac{1}{2^3R} + \frac{1}{2^2R} + \frac{1}{2R} = 0.875\ mA$

and o/p $V_0 = 0.875 \times 10^{-3} \times 1 \times 10^3$

$= 0.875$ V

### 9.1.2 R-2R Ladder DAC

In binary weighted resistor DAC wide range of resistors are required. An alternative to the binary-weighted resistor DAC is the R/2R DAC where only two values of resistors are required. It is well suited for integrated circuit realization.

For simplicity, consider a 3-bit DAC as shown in Fig. 9.7. It has 3-electronic switches $d_0$, $d_1$, $d_2$ controlled by binary input word. These switches are single pole double throw (SPDT) type. If the binary input to a particular switch is 1, it connects the resistance to the reference voltage ($-V_R$). And if the input bit is 0, the switch connects the resistor to the ground. In Figure 9.7, the switch position $d_0$, $d_1$, $d_2$ corresponds to the binary word 100. The circuit can be simplified to the equivalent form of Fig. 9.8 and finally to Fig. 9.9.

Then voltage at node *c* can be easily calculated by the set procedure of network analysis as

$$\frac{-V_R\left(\frac{2}{3}R\right)}{2R+\frac{2}{3}R} = -\frac{V_R}{4}$$

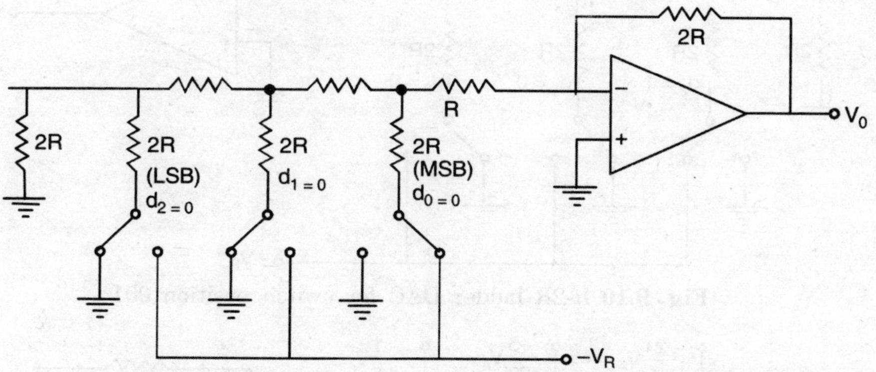


**Fig. 9.7** R-2R ladder DAC for switch position 100

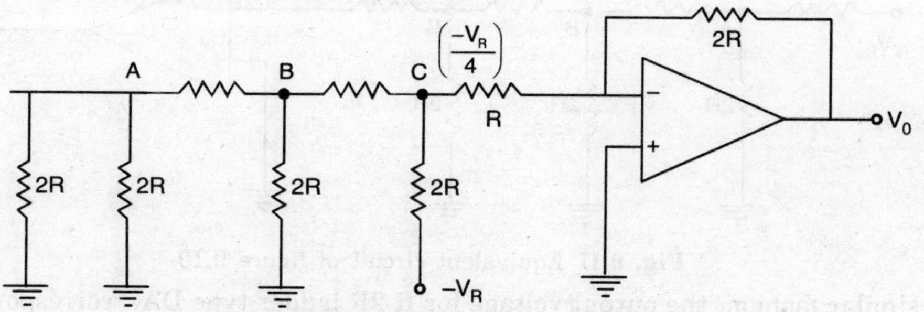


**Fig. 9.8** Equivalent circuit of figure 9.7

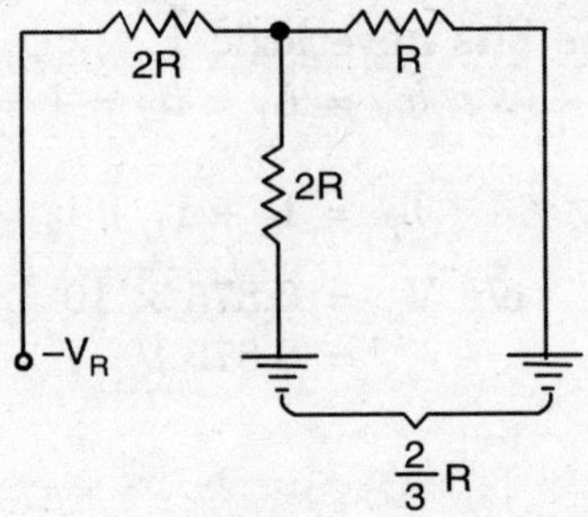


**Fig. 9.9** Equivalent circuit of figure 9.8

## The output voltage

$$V_0 = \frac{2R}{R} \cdot \frac{V_R}{4} = \frac{V_R}{2} = \frac{V_{FS}}{2}$$

The switch position corresponding to the binary word 001 in 3 bit DAC is shown in Figure 9.10. The circuit can be simplified to the equivalent form of Fig. 9.11. The voltages at the nodes (A, B, C) formed by resistor branches are easily calculated in a similar fashion and the output voltage becomes

$$V_0 = \left(\frac{-2R}{R}\right)\left(\frac{-V_R}{16}\right) = \frac{V_R}{8} = \frac{V_{FS}}{8}$$

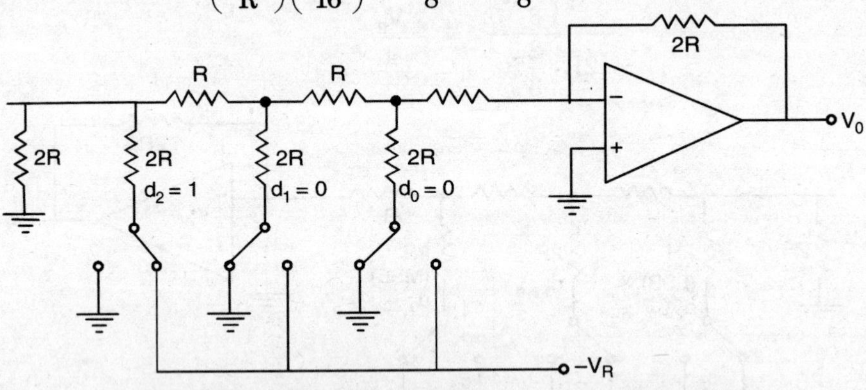


**Fig. 9.10** R-2R ladder DAC for switch position 001

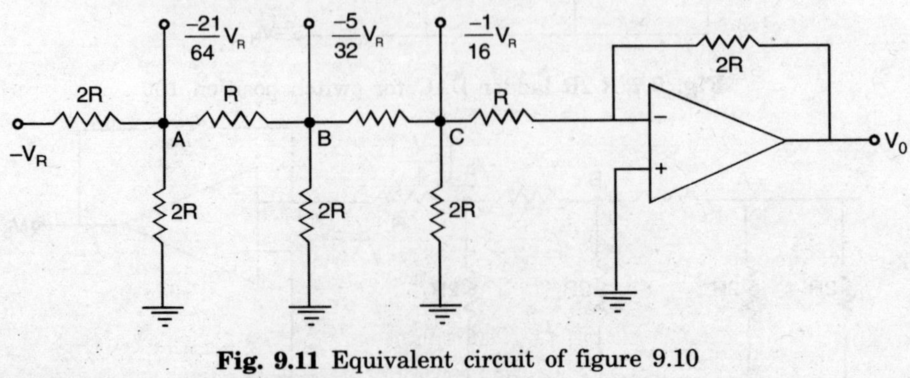


**Fig. 9.11** Equivalent circuit of figure 9.10

In a similar fashion, the output voltage for R-2R ladder type DAC corresponding to other 3-bit binary words can be calculated.

**Transfer Characteristic of 3-bit DAC**

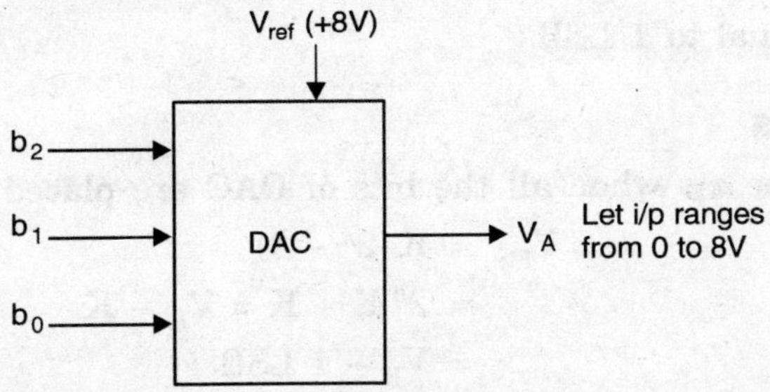


It has $2^n = 2^3 = 8$ levels

and $2^n - 1 = 2^3 - 1 = 7$ steps

since $n = 3$ the $V_{ref}$ can be divided into 8 equal parts.

So $w$ 1 at LSB should produce $\frac{1}{8}V_R$. So resistive network should be such that the resistance in bit $b_0$ (or $2^0$) position can cause $\frac{1}{8} \times 8 = 1V$.

Similarly 1 at $b_1$ should cause $2 \times \frac{1}{8}V_R$

1 at $b_2$ should cause $2 \times \left(2 \times \left(\frac{1}{8}V_R\right)\right)$

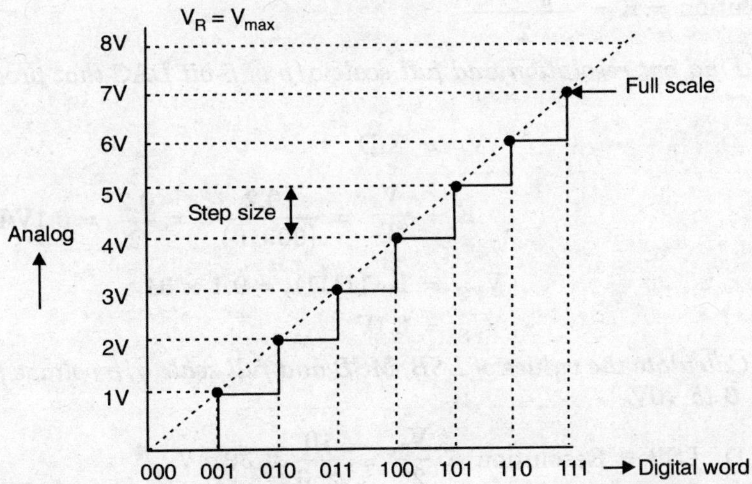


**Fig. 9.12** Transfer characteristic of 3-bit DAC

From curve note that

(1) A 1 at MSB produces half of max i/p voltage *i.e.*, half of $V_R = \frac{1}{2}8 = 4V$.

(2) Full Scale o/p is, 1 LSB less than $V_R$ *i.e.*, $V_{FS} = V_R - 1\text{ LSB} = 8 - 1 = 7V$.

(3) $V_0 \propto V_{iu}$ *i.e.*, $\Rightarrow V_0 = K{\cdot}V_{iu} = K{\cdot}D$ where K = 1LSB or resolution.

(4) Each successive o/p is $\frac{1}{8}V_R$ higher than the previous.

(5) Step size is equal to 1 LSB.

### 9.1.3 DAC Parameters

**Full scale o/p** is the o/p when all the bits of DAC are placed at logic 1.

$$V_{FS} = K\cdot(2^n - 1)$$
$$= 2^n\cdot K - K = V_R - K$$
$$= V_R - 1\text{ LSB}$$

**Resolution** is smallest incremental change in o/p voltage as a fraction of the full scale o/p range against the smallest change in i/p.

$$\text{Resolution} = K = \frac{V_{FS}}{2^n - 1}$$

For $n = 8$, $2^n - 1 = 255$ so $K = \frac{V_{FS}}{255}$

It means smallest change in o/p would be $\frac{1}{255}$th of the full scale o/p. Hence resolution is 1 part in 255 or 0.4%.

Alternatively no. of bits itself can be defined as resolution. For example, an *n*-bit DAC has an *n*-bit resolution.

$$\text{Also Resolution} = K = \frac{V_R\,(V_{max})}{2^n}$$

**Example 2.** *Find out resolution and full scale o/p of 5-bit DAC that produces 0.2V when i/p is 0010.*

**Solution:**

$$V_0 = K\cdot D$$
$$K = \frac{V_0}{D} = \frac{0.2}{(00010)_2} = \frac{0.2}{2} = 0.1\text{V/LSB}$$
$$V_{FS} = K\cdot(11111)_2 = 0.1 \times 31$$

or
$$V_{FS} = 3.1\text{V}$$

**Example 3.** *Calculate the values of LSB, MSB and full scale o/p voltage for an 8-bit DAC having the range 0 to 10V.*

**Solution:** (1) $\text{LSB} = \text{Resolution} = \frac{V_R}{2^n} = \frac{10}{256} \cong 39\,m\text{V}$

(2) $\text{MSB} = \frac{1}{2}V_{max} = \frac{1}{2}V_R = \frac{1}{2} \times 10 = 5\text{V}.$

(3) $V_{FS} = V_R - 1\text{ LSB} = 10 - 39 \times 10^{-3} = 9.961\text{V}$

**Linearity:** The linearity of DAC is a measure precision with which the linear input-output relationship is satisfied.

In a DAC equal increment in numerical value of i/p should result in equal increments in analog o/p.

The linearity error is the difference between the actual value and expected value and is generally maintained less than $\frac{1}{2}$ LSB.

**Accuracy:** It is measure of difference between the actual and expected o/p. It is defined as the %age of full scale or max o/p voltage. If a DAC have 10V max. o/p voltage and an accuracy of 0.2% then max error = 0.002 × 10 = 20 mV for any o/p voltage.

**Settling time** is the time taken by DAC to settle to desired accuracy. The time taken for analog o/p to settle to within $\pm\frac{1}{2}$LSB of the final value after a change in digital i/p is usually defined settling time.

## 9.2 ANALOG-TO-DIGITAL CONVERTER

An ADC is required to perform three basic functions:

1. Sampling
2. Quantization
3. Encoding in digital format

In many popular ADC ICs sample and hold circuits are not provided, so the last two functions are performed by ADCs and an external sampling circuit is to be provided to measure AC or ever varying quantities. Before discussing different ADCs the basic functions of ADC are discussed here.

### Conversion Process

The conversion process is same as weighing anything with a balance scale. Let $W_X$ = 3.25 kg is to be weighed with reference $W_R$ = 1 kg. Then no. of reference weights has to be added (one at a time) until $3 < W_R < 4$. But there will be an error due to unavailability of smaller reference weights. This is called quantization error in an ADC. If smaller values of reference weights are used more accurate measurements can be achieved.

TF of an ideal ADC is shown in Figure 9.13. It has an staircase waveform. The size of step in TF is called Quantum size "Q" or step size Q. For an *n*-bit converter

$$Q = \frac{V_{FS}}{2^n - 1} \cong \frac{V_{FS}}{2^n}, \text{ where } V_{FS} = \text{full scale voltage}$$

One step in ADC TF is equivalent to one unit of reference weight $W_R$. $V_{FS}$ is maximum weight that can be measured.

In the waveform in Figure 9.13, 3-bit ADC is considered. On vertical axis 8 discrete o/p levels are defined and represented by set of 3-bit binary number (000 to 111). The analog signal is represented at horizontal axis. The analog voltage is divided into quanta (*i.e.*, quantized) at decision levels 0.5V, 1.5V, 2.5V etc., at horizontal axis. The decision levels are located at Q/2, 3Q/2, 5Q/2 etc. For example, for $V_{FS}$ = 8V, Q = 1

$$\text{So 1st decision level} = \frac{Q}{2} = 0.5\text{V}$$

$$\text{2nd decision level} = \frac{3Q}{2} = 1.5\text{V and so on.}$$

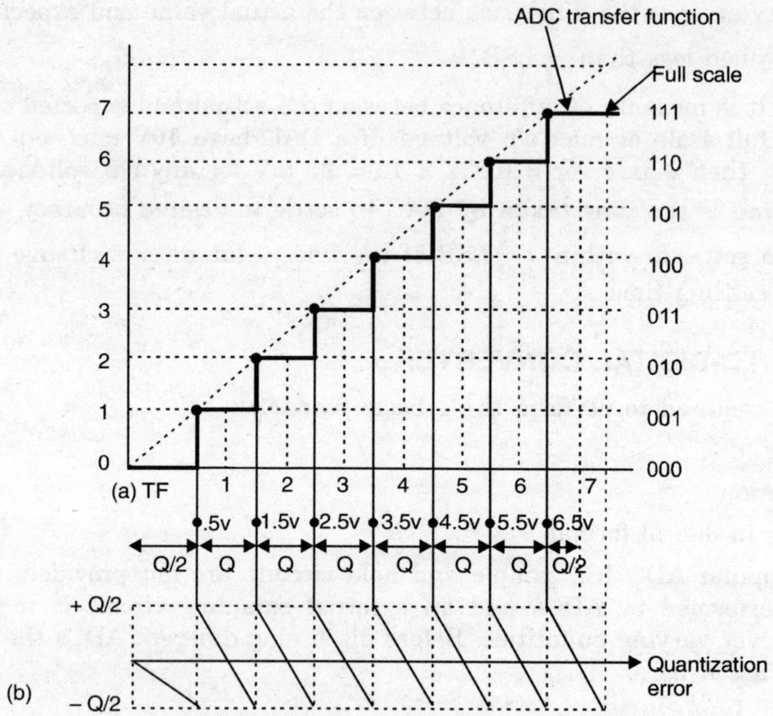


**Fig. 9.13** Transfer Function of an Ideal ADC

Thus any voltage ranging between 0 to $\frac{Q}{2}$V (0 to .5V) will have code 000. Any voltage ranging between $\frac{Q}{2}$ to $\frac{3Q}{2}$ *i.e.,* $\left(\frac{V_{FS}}{2^3}\right)\Big/2$ to $\left(\frac{3V_{FS}}{2^3}\right)\Big/2$ (0.5 to 1.5V) will have code 001 and so on.

If the signal value changes and enters into another step then a new code is generated for the signal. For example, if signal value is 0.4V then code is 000 and if it changes to 1.2V then it enters into next step and code will be 001. Hence

1 step size = width of 1 bit = 1 LSB = Q

Since moving from one step to immediate next step gives next code in series, it is equivalent to add 1-bit to LSB to get new code.

On either side of center of quantization interval, maximum error $\in_{max}$ is $\frac{1}{2}$ of the interval so

$$\in_{max} = \pm\left(\frac{V_{FS}}{2^n}\right)\cdot\frac{1}{2} = \pm\ \frac{Q}{2} = \pm\ \frac{1}{2}\ \text{LSB}$$

In order to reduce the quantization error higher bit converter is used.

### Sample and Hold

The analog i/p can be time independent (DC) or can be time dependent (AC). To provide steady state values to ADC Sample and Hold circuits are used. In its simplest form it is an electronic switch with a capacitor, as shown in Fig. 9.14.

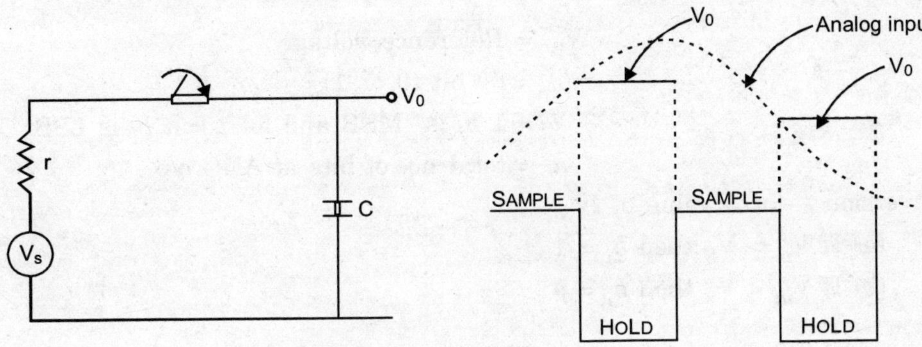


**Fig. 9.14** Sample and Hold Circuit

In sampling mode switch is closed and capacitor charges to applied input. In the hold mode capacitor retains its charge and thus represent the signal value, when it was sampled. The S/H circuit must have a very low drop rate. The drop rate is the rate at which *o/p* of S/H circuit decreases.

## Acquisition Time

It is the time taken by S/H circuit for the capacitor to change from the level of holding voltage to new value of *i/p* voltage, after the input is applied to hold capacitor.

## Aperture Time

It is delay between the hold command and the moment at which the i/p is applied to hold capacitor. It is usually very small and accounts to few nano seconds. It means after how much time i/p is actually applied on capacitor.

## Binary Coding

The method of assigning a binary number to *i/p* voltage is referred to as binary coding. This process is shown in Fig. 9.13 of ADC TF.

In analog to digital conversion the analog *i/p* is compared with a series of fractions of reference voltages which is decreasing in factors of $\frac{1}{2}$. Thus the conversion is a division process *i.e.*, dividing the *i/p* by a series of reference weights. The fraction to be compared can be expressed as

$$\text{Fraction} = V_F = \left(\frac{1}{2^1} + \frac{1}{2^2} + \dots + \frac{1}{2^{n-1}} + \frac{1}{2^n}\right) = \sum_{i=1}^{n} \frac{1}{2^i} = \sum_{i=1}^{n} 2^{-i}$$

The fraction $V_F$ is selected according to the previous decisions and reference voltage. So $V_F$ can be expressed in more general form

$$V_F = \left(\frac{1}{2^1} b_1 + \frac{1}{2^2} b_2 + \dots + \frac{1}{2^n} b_n\right) . V_R = \sum_{i=1}^{n} \frac{b_i}{2^i} V_R$$

or $V_F = \left[ \sum_{i=1}^{n} b_i \, 2^{-i} \right] \cdot V_R$

where $V_R$ = Reference voltage

$b_i$ = $i^{th}$ bit (0 or 1)

for $i = 1$ $b_i$ is MSB and for $i = n$ $b_i$ is LSB.

$n$ = total no. of bits at ADC o/p

for conversion – for a value of $i$

(a) If $V_{in} > V_F$ then $b_i = 1$

(b) If $V_{in} < V_F$ then $b_i = 0$

For an $n$-bit ADC smallest fraction of binary weight is given as $\frac{1}{2^n}$.

For example, if $n = 8$ $\frac{1}{2^8} = 0.00390625$

$\cong 0.004$

So 1 LSB = $\frac{1}{2^8} \cdot V_R = 0.004 \times 5 = 0.02V$ if $V_R = +5V$

$\cong 20mV$

**Example 4.** *Find out the binary value given by an 8-bit ADC if reference voltage is 5V and analog i/p is 3.41.*

**Solution:** Given $n = 8$, $V_R = 5V$, $V_{in} = 3.41$

For $i = 1$ $V_F = \frac{V_R}{2} = 2.5V$

since $V_{in}$ (3.41) > 2.5V so $b_1 = 1$ (MSB)

$i = 2$ $V_F = b_1 \frac{V_R}{2} + \frac{V_R}{4} = 3.75$

since $V_{in}$ (3.41) < 3.75 so $b_2 = 0$

$i = 3$ $V_F = b_1 \frac{V_R}{2} + b_2 \frac{V_R}{4} + \frac{V_R}{8} = 1 \times \frac{5}{2} + 0 \times \frac{5}{4} + \frac{5}{8}$

$= 3.125$

since $V_{in}$ (3.41) > 3.125 so $b_3 = 1$

Similarly, we get $b_4 = 0$, $b_5 = 1$, $b_6 = 1$ and $b_7 = 1$

for $i = 8$ $V_F = 3.41796875$ since $V_{in} < V_F$ so $b_8 = 0$ (LSB)

Therefore digital word is 1010 1110.

### 9.2.1 Parallel-comparator ADC

Parallel-comparator ADC circuit is the simplest and also called as Flash ADC. It is formed of a series of comparators, each one comparing the input signal to a unique reference voltage. The comparator outputs connect to the inputs of a priority encoder circuit, which then produces a binary output. The Figure 9.15 shows a 3-bit flash ADC circuit.

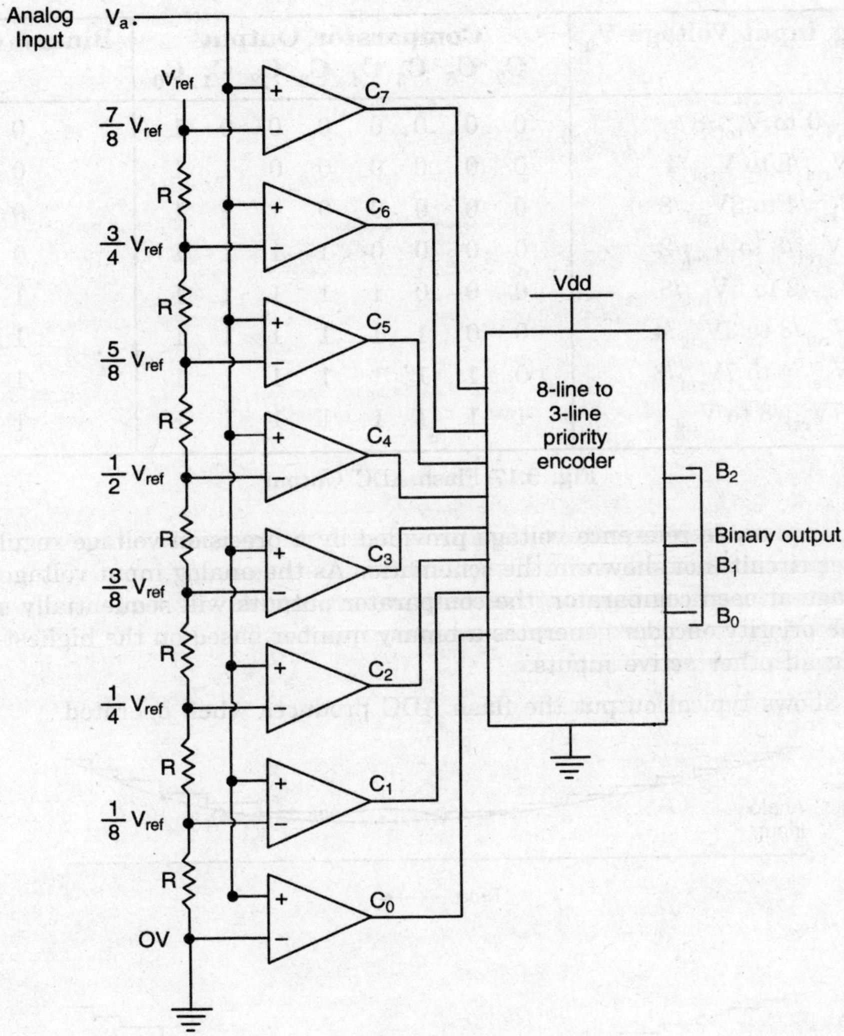


**Fig. 9.15**

**The circuit consists of a resistive divider network, 8 comparator and a 8-line to 3-line encoder (3-bit priority encoder). For *n*-bit converter no. of comparators required $2^n - 1$. The comparator and its truth table is shown in figure 9.16**

| **Voltage input** | **Logic output** |
|---|---|
| $V_a > V_d$ | C = 1 |
| $V_a < V_d$ | C = 0 |
| $V_a = V_d$ | Previous value |

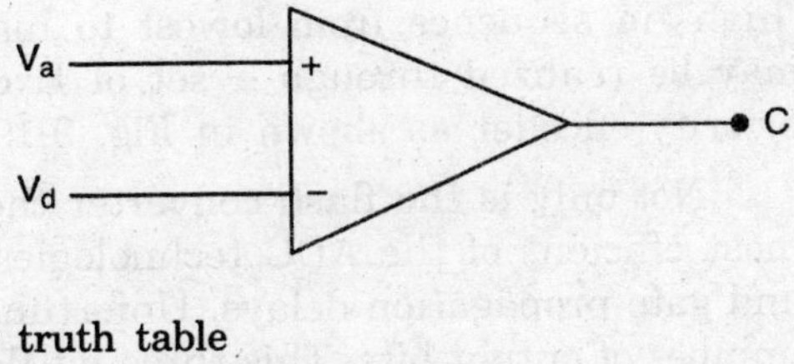


**Fig. 9.16** Comparator and its truth table

**The resistive network provides the fraction of reference voltage required for comparison or provides the decision level.**

The truth table for the flash type ADC is shown in Figure 9.17

| Analog Input Voltage $V_a$ | Comparator Output $C_7$ $C_6$ $C_5$ $C_4$ $C_3$ $C_2$ $C_1$ $C_0$ | Binary Output |
|---|---|---|
| 0 to $V_{ref}/8$ | 0 0 0 0 0 0 0 1 | 0 0 0 |
| $V_{ref}/8$ to $V_{ref}/4$ | 0 0 0 0 0 0 1 1 | 0 0 1 |
| $V_{ref}/4$ to $3V_{ref}/8$ | 0 0 0 0 0 1 1 1 | 0 1 0 |
| $3V_{ref}/8$ to $V_{ref}/2$ | 0 0 0 0 1 1 1 1 | 0 1 1 |
| $V_{ref}/2$ to $5V_{ref}/8$ | 0 0 0 1 1 1 1 1 | 1 0 0 |
| $5V_{ref}/8$ to $3V_{ref}/4$ | 0 0 1 1 1 1 1 1 | 1 0 1 |
| $3V_{ref}/4$ to $7V_{ref}/8$ | 0 1 1 1 1 1 1 1 | 1 1 0 |
| $7V_{ref}/8$ to $V_{ref}$ | 1 1 1 1 1 1 1 1 | 1 1 1 |

**Fig. 9.17** Flash ADC Output

Here $V_{ref}$ is a stable reference voltage provided by a precision voltage regulator as part of the converter circuit (not shown in the schematic). As the analog input voltage exceeds the reference voltage at each comparator, the comparator outputs will sequentially saturate to a high state. The priority encoder generates a binary number based on the highest-order active input, ignoring all other active inputs.

Fig. 9.18 shows typical output the flash ADC produces when operated.

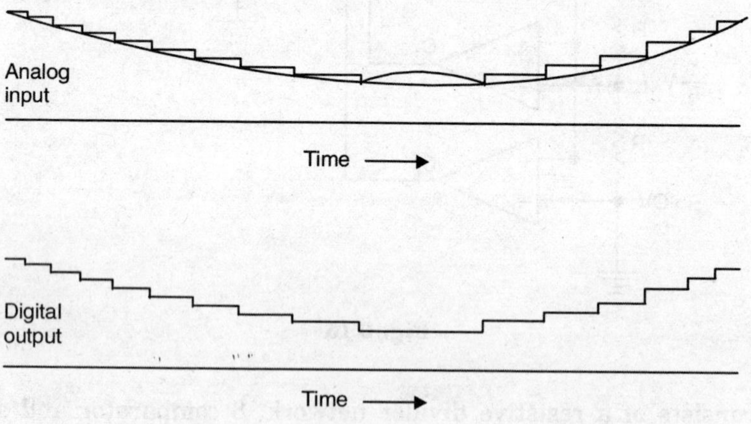


**Fig. 9.18**

Due to the nature of the sequential comparator output states (each comparator saturating "high" in sequence from lowest to highest), the same "highest-order-input selection" effect may be realized through a set of Exclusive-OR gates, allowing the use of a simpler, non-priority encoder as shown in Fig. 9.19.

Not only is the flash converter the simplest in terms of operational theory, but it is the most efficient of the ADC technologies in terms of speed, being limited only in comparator and gate propagation delays. Unfortunately, it is the most component-intensive for any given number of output bits. This three-bit flash ADC requires eight comparators. A four-bit version would require 16 comparators. With each additional output bit, the number of required comparators doubles. Considering that eight bits is generally considered the minimum necessary for any practical ADC (256 comparators needed!).

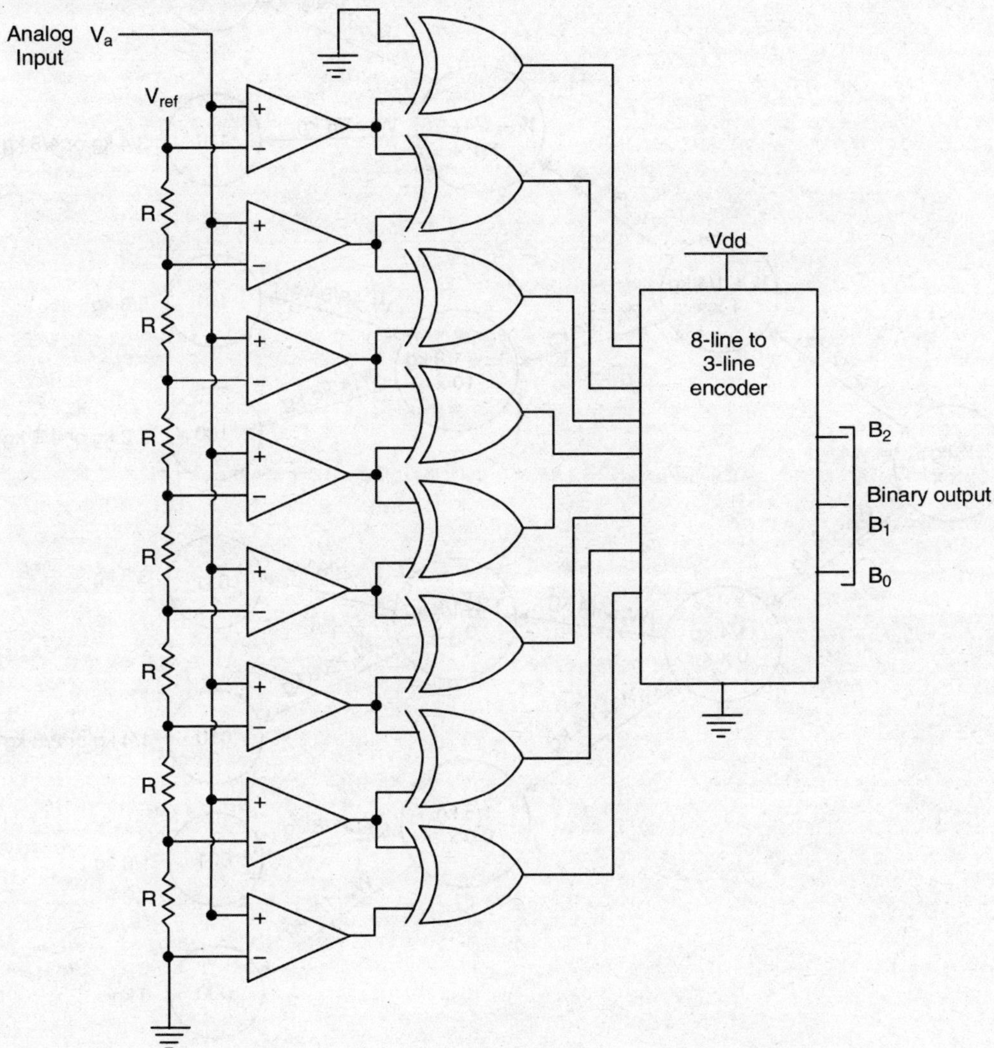


**Fig. 9.19**

### 9.2.2 Successive Approximation ADC

In this type of ADC a given weight is successively compared by fraction of weights which are divided successively by 2. The process is shown below in Fig. 9.20.

Let us assume an unknown object having weight 0 to 1 kg.

We start the process first by comparing with weight $\frac{1}{2}$ kg. If $W_a \geq \frac{1}{2}$ kg, MSB = 1 and add the $\frac{1}{4}$ kg for next comparison. If $W_a < \frac{1}{2}$ kg, MSB = 0 and remove $\frac{1}{2}$ kg and add $\frac{1}{4}$ kg for next comparison. This process is continued. Note that in both the above cases weight $\frac{1}{4}$ kg is to be added to scale. To illustrate we begin with unknown bits XXX.

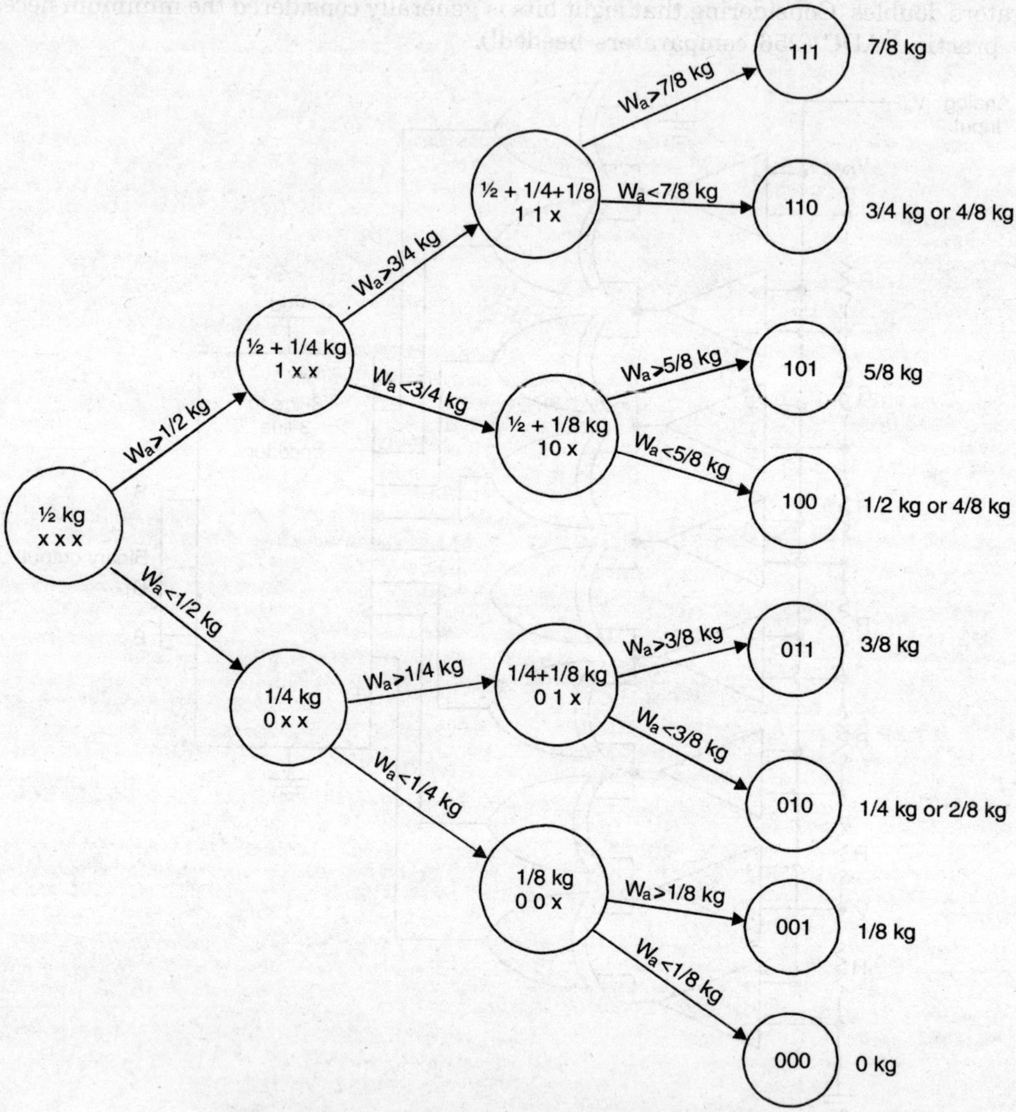


**Fig. 9.20** 3-bit Successive Approximation ADC

For implementation purpose, the approximation process can be modified. When $\frac{1}{2}$ kg weight is added on scale, then put 1 on MSB. If comparison $W_a \geq \frac{1}{2}$ kg then retain this 1 on MSB else put 0 on MSB. Similarly when weight $\frac{1}{4}$ is added put 1 on corresponding bit and if comparison is true, then retain the 1 else put 0. (See Fig. 9.21)

Both Figs. 9.20 and 9.21 are identical with a small change that in Fig. 9.21 whenever a weight is added a 1 is placed on the corresponding bit. If after comparison the weight is removed this 1 is replaced by 0.

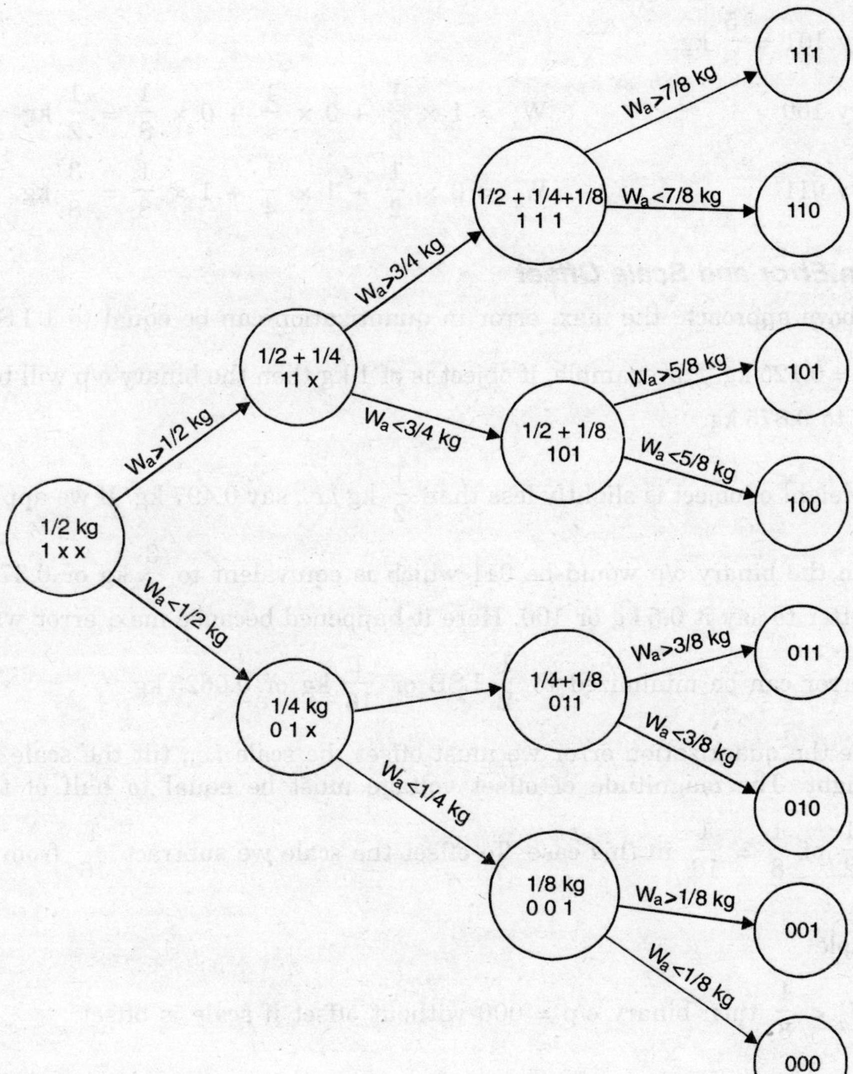


**Fig. 9.21** 3-bit Successive Approximation ADC

### *Calculation of o/p*

In this ADC the width of LSB will be $\frac{1}{2^3}$ *i.e.*, LSB = $\frac{1}{8}$ kg

It means adding $\frac{1}{8}$ kg scale is equivalent to put 1 at LSB. Similarly adding $\frac{1}{2}$ kg to scale is equivalent to put 1 at MSB.

If binary o/p is 101 then measured weight

$$W_a = 1 \times \frac{1}{2} + 0 \times \frac{1}{4} + 1 \times \frac{1}{8} = \frac{5}{8} \text{ kg.}$$

So binary 101 = $\frac{5}{8}$ kg.

for binary 100 $\quad W_a = 1 \times \frac{1}{2} + 0 \times \frac{1}{4} + 0 \times \frac{1}{8} = \frac{1}{2}$ kg

for binary 011 $\quad W_a = 0 \times \frac{1}{2} + 1 \times \frac{1}{4} + 1 \times \frac{1}{8} = \frac{3}{8}$ kg.

### *Quantization Error and Scale Offset*

In the above approach, the max. error in quantization can be equal to 1 LSB *i.e.*, max. error = $\frac{1}{8}$ kg = 0.125 kg. For example, if object is of 1 kg then the binary o/p will be 111 which is equivalent to 0.875 kg.

Let the weight of object is slightly less than $\frac{1}{2}$ kg *i.e.*, say 0.497 kg. If we apply the above approach then the binary o/p would be 011 which is equivalent to $\frac{3}{8}$ kg or 0.375 kg. But it will be far better to say it 0.5 kg or 100. Here it happened because max. error was 1 LSB or $\frac{1}{8}$ kg. This error can be minimized to $\frac{1}{2}$ LSB or $\frac{1}{16}$ kg or 0.0625 kg.

To reduce the quantization error we must offset the scale *i.e.*, tilt the scale in favour of unknown weight. The magnitude of offset voltage must be equal to half of the smallest voltage i.e., $\frac{1}{2}$ of $\frac{1}{8} = \frac{1}{16}$ in this case. To offset the scale we subtract $\frac{1}{16}$ from each of the weight.

As example

If $0 < W_a < \frac{1}{8}$ then binary o/p = 000 without offset if scale is offset.

$0 < W_a < \frac{1}{16}$ and binary o/p = 000

Similarly if $\frac{1}{8}$ kg $< W_a < \frac{1}{4}$ kg o/p = 001 without offset if scale is offset then

$\frac{1}{16} < W_a < \frac{3}{16}$ and binary o/p = 001.

The same is summarised in table of figure 9.22.

| Range of Unknown Weight | Binary o/p |
|---|---|
| 0 to $\frac{1}{16}$ kg | 000 |
| $\frac{1}{16}$ kg to $\frac{3}{16}$ kg | 001 |

*Contd...*

| | |
|---|---|
| $\frac{3}{16}$ kg to $\frac{5}{16}$ kg | 010 |
| $\frac{5}{16}$ kg to $\frac{7}{16}$ kg | 011 |
| $\frac{7}{16}$ kg to $\frac{9}{16}$ kg | 100 |
| $\frac{9}{16}$ kg to $\frac{11}{16}$ kg | 101 |
| $\frac{11}{16}$ kg to $\frac{13}{16}$ kg | 110 |
| $\frac{13}{16}$ kg to $\frac{15}{16}$ kg | 111 |

**Fig. 9.22** 3-bit ADC o/p for unknown weights after scale offset.

For comparison the same table is drawn without scale offset in Fig. 9.23.

| Range of Unknown Weight | ADC o/p |
|---|---|
| 0 to $\frac{1}{8}$kg $\left(0 < W_a < \frac{1}{8}\right)$ | 000 |
| $\frac{1}{8}$ kg to $\frac{2}{8}$ kg $\left(\frac{1}{8} < W_a \frac{2}{8}\right)$ | 001 |
| $\frac{2}{8}$ kg $\leq W_a < \frac{3}{8}$ kg | 010 |
| $\frac{3}{8}$ kg $\leq W_a < \frac{4}{8}$ kg | 011 |
| $\frac{4}{8}$ kg $\leq W_a < \frac{5}{8}$ kg | 100 |
| $\frac{5}{8}$ kg $\leq W_a < \frac{6}{8}$ kg | 101 |
| $\frac{6}{8}$ kg $\leq W_a < \frac{7}{8}$ kg | 110 |
| $\frac{7}{8}$ kg $\leq W_a < 1$ kg | 111 |

**Fig. 9.23**

Block diagram of a successive approximation ADC is shown in Fig. 9.24.

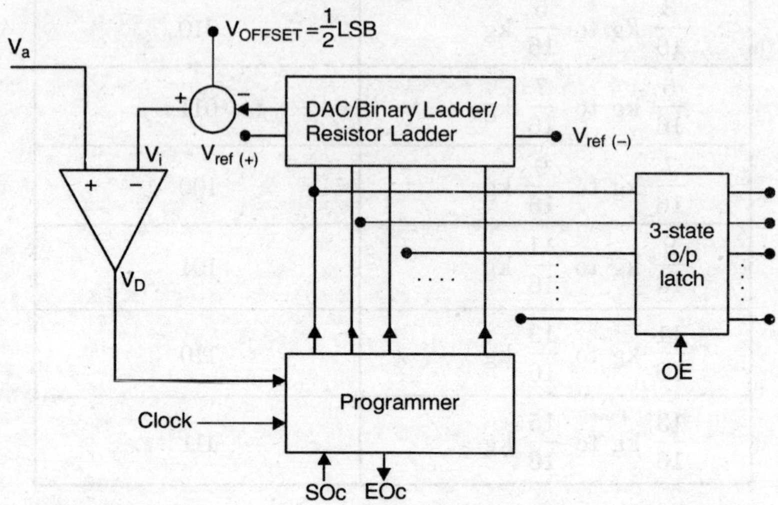


**Fig. 9.24** Block Diagram of Successive Approximation ADC

The comparator serves the function of scale and its o/p is fed to programmer to set or reset the bits at the o/p of programmer. The o/p programmer will change only at arrial of clock pulse. The DAC accepts the digital o/p of programmer and converts it into the quivalent voltage.

The offset voltage is subtracted from the o/p of DAC and the resultant is applied to inverting input of op amp. The unknown voltage is applied at non inverting i/p of op amp.

Here the op amp is used as comparator, which compares voltage present at its input terminals. If the voltage at non-inverting i/p is higher than the voltage at inverting i/p then o/p of comparator is high otherwise it goes low."

"As earlier indicated offset adjustment is to tilt the scale towards unknown voltage. To do this we must add the offset voltage to unknown voltage. Instead we have subtracted the offset from the o/p of DAC (*i.e.*, subtracted from known weight side) to get the equivalent effect."

As soon as SOC is applied the programmer is reset *i.e.*, all the bits of programmer are set to 0. On the arrival of 1st clock pulse MSB of programmer is set to 1, and the data is applied to DAC. DAC provides equivalent analog voltage which compared to unknown i/p after offset is subtracted from DAC o/p. If $V_a > V_i$, comparator voltage $V_0$ goes high and sets the next bit of programmer to 1. If $V_a < V_i$ the o/p of comparator goes low which sets the MSB of programmer to 0 and sets the next bit to 1 for next successive approximation. Thus a 1 is tried at each bit of DAC until the binary equivalent of analog voltage is obtained. For an N-bit converter, N clock pulses are required and hence it is slower than flash ADCs.

As soon as conversion is completed EOC signal goes high. To read the data 3-state o/p latches must be enabled by providing a high on OE signal.

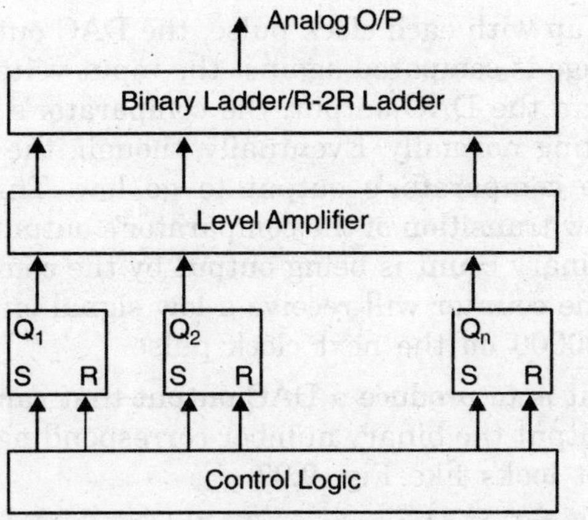


**Fig. 9.25** Detailed Block Diagram of Successive Approximation ADC

### 9.2.3 Counting ADC

Counting ADC also known as the Stairstep-ramp, or Digital ramp ADC. This type of ADC is also easy to understand but unfortunately suffers from several limitations.

The basic idea is to connect the output of a free-running binary counter to the input of a DAC, then compare the analog output of the DAC with the analog input signal to be digitized and use the comparator's output to tell the counter when to stop counting and reset. The following schematic in figure 9.26 shows the basic idea:

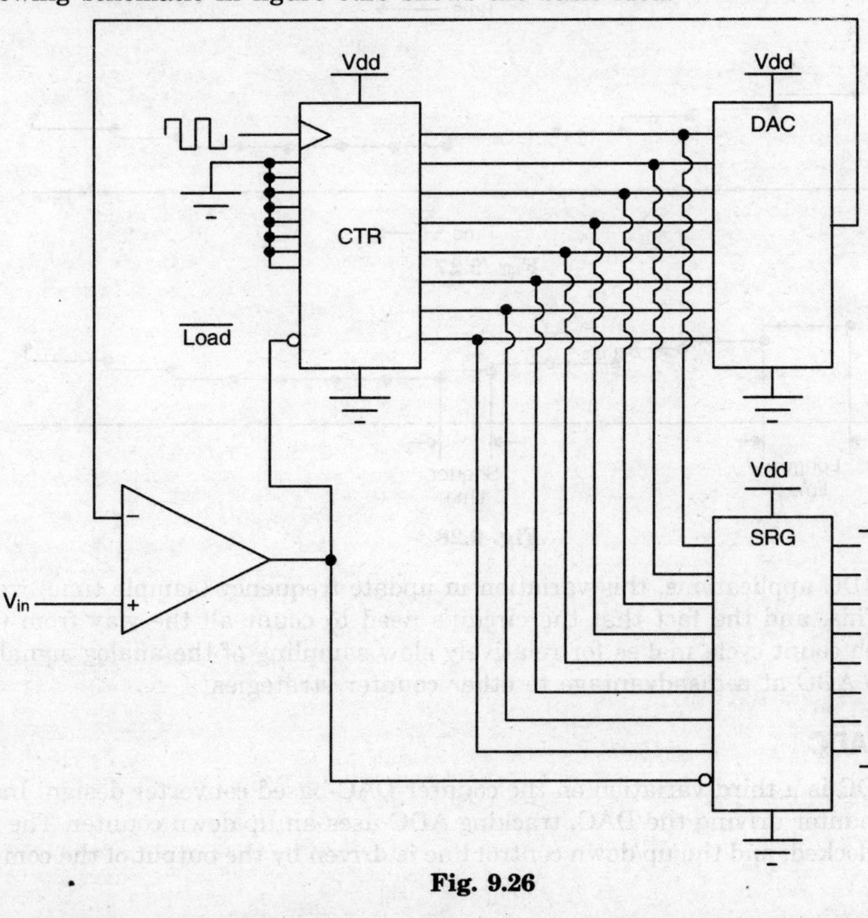


**Fig. 9.26**

As the counter counts up with each clock pulse, the DAC outputs a slightly higher (more positive) voltage. This voltage is compared against the input voltage by the comparator. If the input voltage is greater than the DAC output, the comparator's output will be high and the counter will continue counting normally. Eventually, though, the DAC output will exceed the input voltage, causing the comparator's output to go low. This will cause two things to happen: first, the high-to-low transition of the comparator's output will cause the shift register (SRG) to "load" whatever binary count is being output by the counter, thus updating the ADC circuit's output; secondly, the counter will receive a low signal on the active-low LOAD input, causing it to reset to 00000000 on the next clock pulse.

The effect of this circuit is to produce a DAC output that ramps up to whatever level the analog input signal is at, output the binary number corresponding to that level, and start over again. Plotted over time, it looks like Fig. 9.27.

Note how the time between updates (new digital output values) changes depending on how high the input voltage is. For low signal levels, the updates are rather close-spaced. For higher signal levels, they are spaced further apart in time as shown in Fig. 9.28.

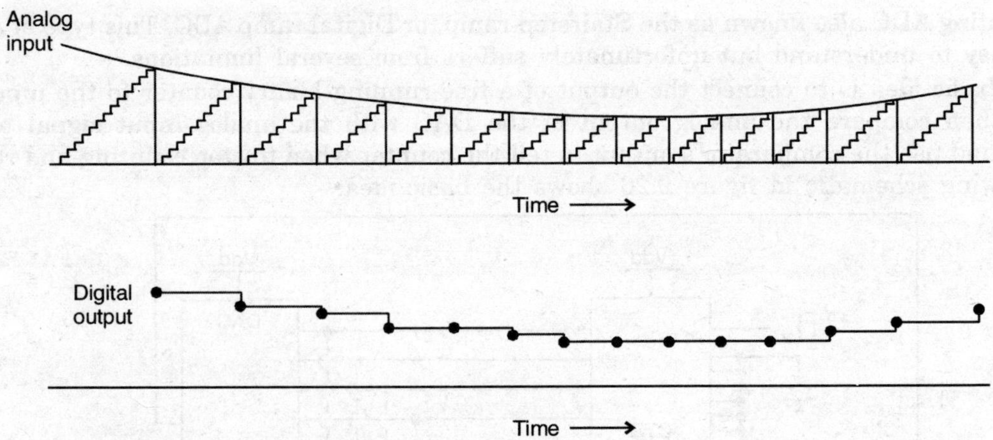


**Fig. 9.27**

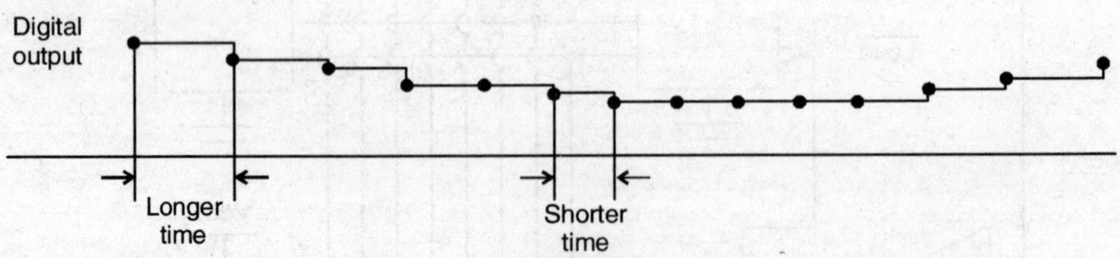


**Fig. 9.28**

For many ADC applications, this variation in update frequency (sample time) would not be acceptable. This, and the fact that the circuit's need to count all the way from 0 at the beginning of each count cycle makes for relatively slow sampling of the analog signal, places the digital-ramp ADC at a disadvantage to other counter strategies.

### 9.2.4 Tracking ADC

Tracking ADC is a third variation on the counter-DAC-based converter design. Instead of a regular "up" counter driving the DAC, tracking ADC uses an up/down counter. The counter is continuously clocked, and the up/down control line is driven by the output of the comparator.

So, when the analog input signal exceeds the DAC output, the counter goes into the "count up" mode. When the DAC output exceeds the analog input, the counter switches into the "count down" mode. Either way, the DAC output always counts in the proper direction to track the input signal. The tracking ADC is shown in Figure 9.29.

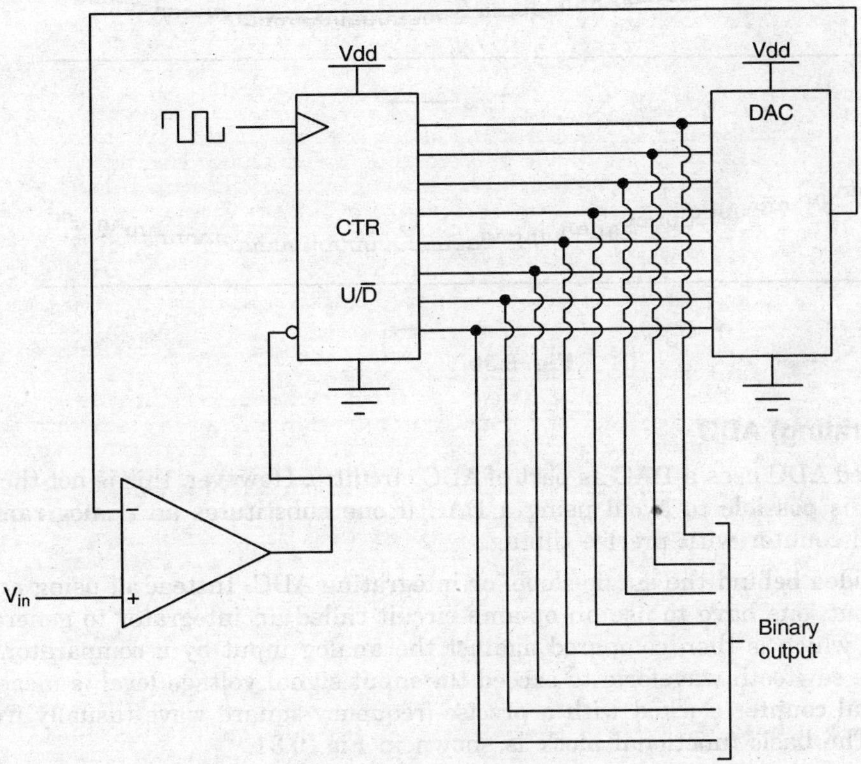


**Fig. 9.29**

In Tracking ADC how no shift register is needed to buffer the binary count at the end of a cycle. Since, the counter's output continuously tracks the input (rather than counting to meet the input and then resetting back to zero), the binary output is reasonably updated with every clock pulse.

An advantage of this converter circuit is speed, since the counter never has to reset. Tracking ADC having much faster update time than any of the other "counting" ADC circuits. Also, with no shift register in this circuit, the binary output would actually ramp up rather than jump from zero to an accurate count as it did with the counter and successive approximation ADC circuits. Also note how at the very beginning of the plot (Figure 9.30) where the counter had to "catch up" with the analog signal, the rate of change for the output was identical to that of the first counting ADC.

The main drawback to this ADC design is the fact that the binary output is never stable: it always switches between counts with every clock pulse, even with a perfectly stable analog input signal. This phenomenon is informally known as bit bobble.

**Note:** Bit bobble can be overcome, through the creative use of a shift register. For example, the counter's output may be latched through a parallel-in/parallel-out shift register only when the output changes by two or more steps. Building a circuit to detect two or more successive counts in the same direction takes a little ingenuity, but is worth the effort.

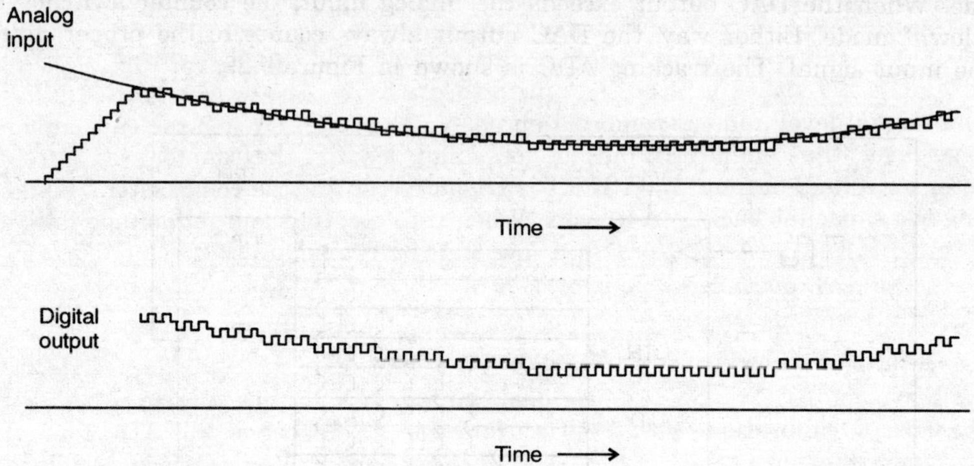


**Fig. 9.30**

### 9.2.5 Slope (integrating) ADC

Earlier discussed ADC uses a DAC as part of ADC circuitry. However, this is not the only option one have. It is possible to avoid using a DAC if one substitutes an analog ramping circuit and a digital counter with precise timing.

This the basic idea behind the single-slope, or integrating ADC. Instead of using a DAC with a ramped output, one have to use an op-amp circuit called an integrator to generate a sawtooth waveform which is then compared against the analog input by a comparator. The time it takes for the sawtooth waveform to exceed the input signal voltage level is measured by means of a digital counter clocked with a precise-frequency square wave (usually from a crystal oscillator). The basic functional block is shown in Fig. 9.31.

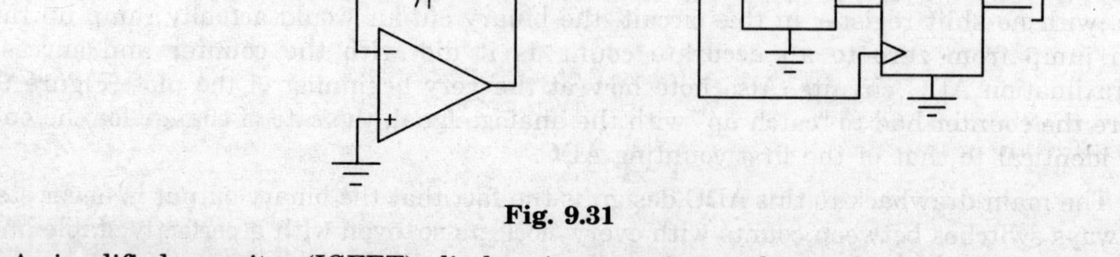


**Fig. 9.31**

A simplified capacitor (IGFET) -discharging transistor scheme shown here is. In reality, a latching circuit timed with the clock signal have to be connected to the IGFET gate to ensure full discharge of the capacitor when the comparator's output goes high. The basic idea, however, is clear from Fig. 9.31. When the comparator output is low (input voltage greater than integrator output), the integrator is allowed to charge the capacitor in a linear fashion. Meanwhile, the counter is counting up at a rate fixed by the precision clock frequency. The time it takes for the capacitor to charge up to the same voltage level as the input depends on the input signal level and the combination of $-V_{ref}$, R, and C. When the capacitor reaches that voltage level, the comparator output goes high, loading the counter's output into the shift register for a final output. The IGFET is triggered "on" by the comparator's high output, discharging the capacitor back to zero volts. When the integrator output voltage falls to zero, the comparator output switches back to a low state, clearing the counter and enabling the integrator to ramp up voltage again.

This ADC circuit behaves very much like the digital ramp ADC, except that the comparator reference voltage is a smooth sawtooth waveform rather than a "stairstep" (Figure 9.32).

The single-slope ADC suffers all the disadvantages of the digital ramp ADC, with the added drawback of calibration drift. The accurate correspondence of this ADC's output with its input is dependent on the voltage slope of the integrator being matched to the counting rate of the counter (the clock frequency). With the digital ramp ADC, the clock frequency had no effect on conversion accuracy, only on update time. The only advantage of this circuit is that it avoids the use of a DAC, which reduces circuit complexity.

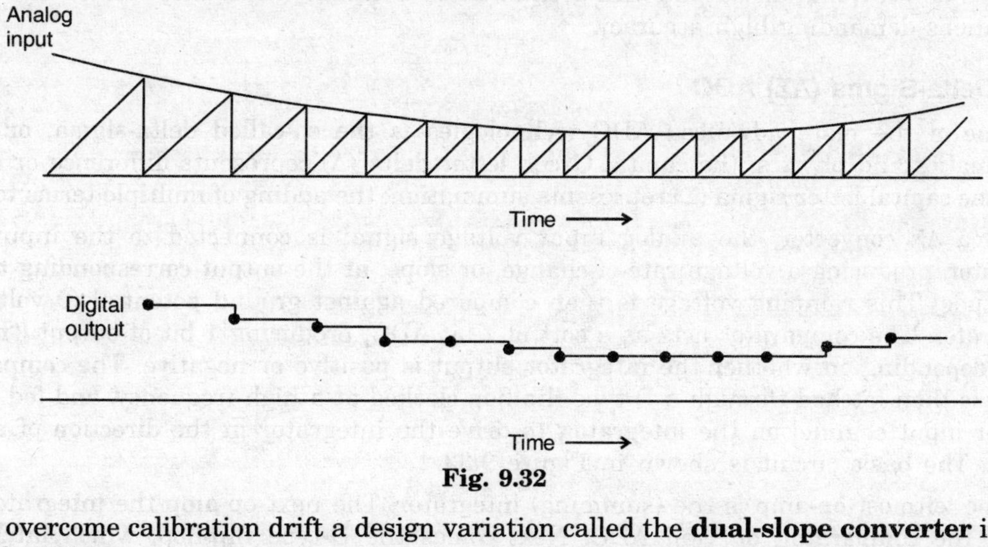


**Fig. 9.32**

To overcome calibration drift a design variation called the **dual-slope converter** is used. In the dual-slope converter, an integrator circuit is driven positive and negative in alternating cycles to ramp down and then up, rather than being reset to 0 volts at the end of every cycle. In one direction of ramping, the integrator is driven by the positive analog input signal (producing a negative, variable rate of output voltage change, or output slope) for a fixed amount of time, as measured by a counter with a precision frequency clock. Then, in the other direction, with a fixed reference voltage (producing a fixed rate of output voltage change) with time measured by the same counter. The counter stops counting when the integrator's output reaches the same voltage as it was when it started the fixed-time portion of the cycle. The amount of time it takes for the integrator's capacitor to discharge back to its original output voltage, as measured by the magnitude accrued by the counter, becomes the digital output of the ADC circuit.

This technique of analog-to-digital conversion escapes the calibration drift problem of the single-slope ADC because both the integrator's integration coefficient (or "gain") and the counter's rate of speed are in effect during the entire "winding" and "unwinding" cycle portions. If the counter's clock speed were to suddenly increase, this would shorten the fixed time period where the integrator "winds up" (resulting in a lesser voltage accumulated by the integrator), but it would also mean that it would count faster during the period of time when the integrator was allowed to "unwind" at a fixed rate. The proportion that the counter is counting faster will be the same proportion as the integrator's accumulated voltage is diminished from before the clock speed change. Thus, the clock speed error would cancel itself out and the digital output would be exactly what it should be.

Another important advantage of this method is that the input signal becomes averaged as it drives the integrator during the fixed-time portion of the cycle. Any changes in the analog signal during that period of time have a cumulative effect on the digital output at the end of that cycle. Other ADC strategies merely "capture" the analog signal level at a single point in time every cycle. If the analog signal is "noisy" (contains significant levels of spurious voltage spikes/dips), one of the other ADC converter technologies may occasionally convert a spike or dip because it captures the signal repeatedly at a single point in time. A dual-slope ADC, on the other hand, averages together all the spikes and dips within the integration period, thus providing an output with greater noise immunity. Dual-slope ADCs are used in applications demanding high accuracy.

### 9.2.6 Delta-Sigma (ΔΣ) ADC

One of the more advanced ADC technologies is the so-called delta-sigma, or ΔΣ. In mathematics and physics, the capital Greek letter delta (Δ) represents difference or change, while the capital letter sigma (Σ) represents summation: the adding of multiple terms together.

In a ΔΣ converter, the analog input voltage signal is connected to the input of an integrator, producing a voltage rate-of-change, or slope, at the output corresponding to input magnitude. This ramping voltage is then compared against ground potential (0 volts) by a comparator. The comparator acts as a sort of 1-bit ADC, producing 1 bit of output ("high" or "low") depending on whether the integrator output is positive or negative. The comparator's output is then latched through a D-type flip-flop clocked at a high frequency, and fed back to another input channel on the integrator, to drive the integrator in the direction of a 0 volt output. The basic circuit is shown in Figure 9.33.

The leftmost op-amp is the (summing) integrator. The next op-amp the integrator feeds into is the comparator, or 1-bit ADC. Next comes the D-type flip-flop, which latches the comparator's output at every clock pulse, sending either a "high" or "low" signal to the next comparator at the top of the circuit. This final comparator is necessary to convert the single-polarity 0 V/5 V logic level output voltage of the flip-flop into a +V/–V voltage signal to be fed back to the integrator.

If the integrator output is positive, the first comparator will output a "high" signal to the D input of the flip-flop. At the next clock pulse, this "high" signal will be output from the Q line into the noninverting input of the last comparator. This last comparator, seeing an input voltage greater than the threshold voltage of 1/2 +V, saturates in a positive direction, sending a full +V signal to the other input of the integrator. This +V feedback signal tends to drive the integrator output in a negative direction. If that output voltage ever becomes negative, the feedback loop will send a corrective signal (–V) back around to the top input of the integrator to drive it in a positive direction. This is the delta-sigma concept in action: the first comparator senses a difference (Δ) between the integrator output and zero volts. The integrator sums (Σ) the comparator's output with the analog input signal.

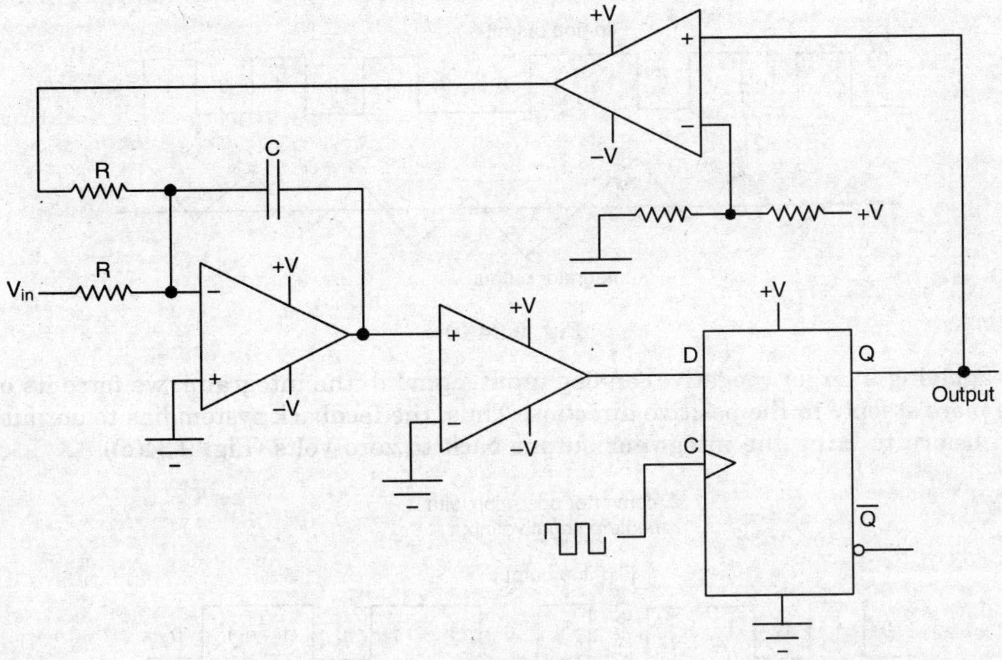


**Fig. 9.33**

Functionally, this results in a serial stream of bits output by the flip-flop. If the analog input is zero volts, the integrator will have no tendency to ramp either positive or negative, except in response to the feedback voltage. In this scenario, the flip-flop output will continually oscillate between "high" and "low," as the feedback system "hunts" back and forth, trying to maintain the integrator output at zero volts as shown in Fig. 9.34(*a*):

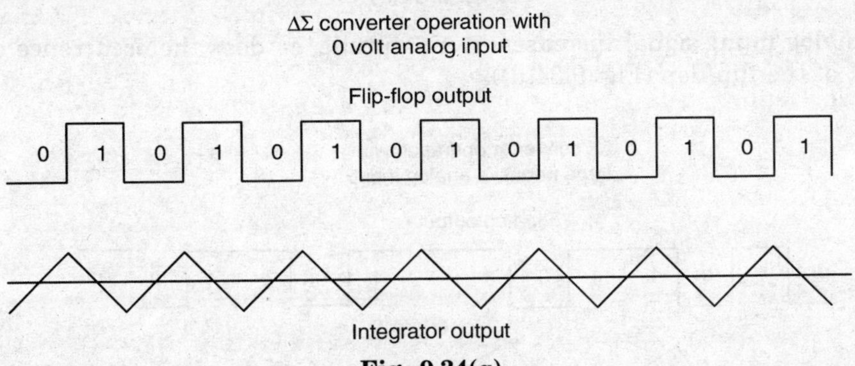


**Fig. 9.34(*a*)**

If, however, we apply a negative analog input voltage, the integrator will have a tendency to ramp its output in a positive direction. Feedback can only add to the integrator's ramping by a fixed voltage over a fixed time, and so the bit stream output by the flip-flop will not be quite the same Fig. 9.34(*b*).

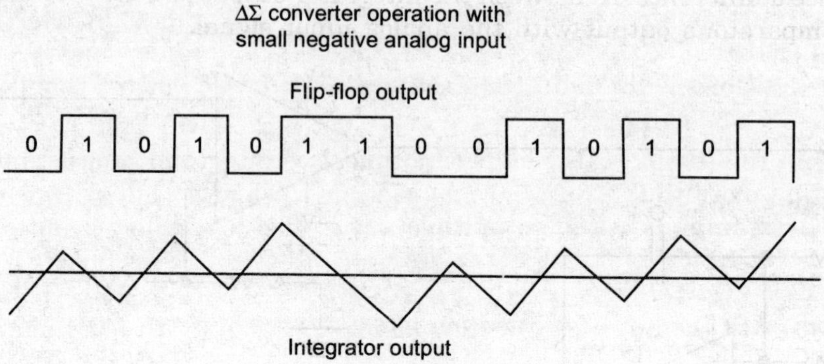


**Fig. 9.34(*b*)**

By applying a larger (negative) analog input signal to the integrator, we force its output to ramp more steeply in the positive direction. Thus, the feedback system has to output more 1's than before to bring the integrator output back to zero volts (Fig. 9.34(c)).

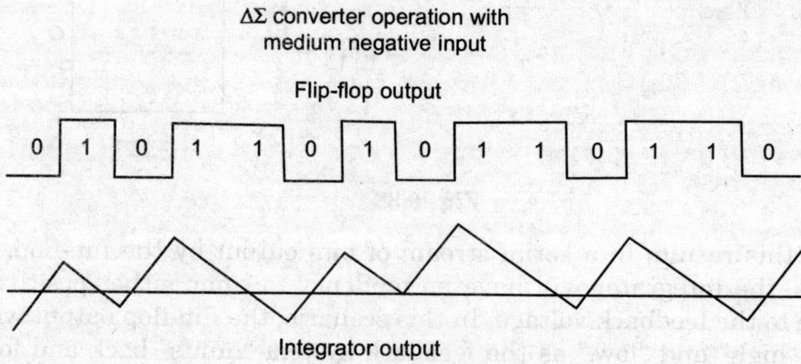


**Fig. 9.34(*c*)**

As the analog input signal increases in magnitude, so does the occurrence of 1's in the digital output of the flip-flop (Fig. 9.34(d)).

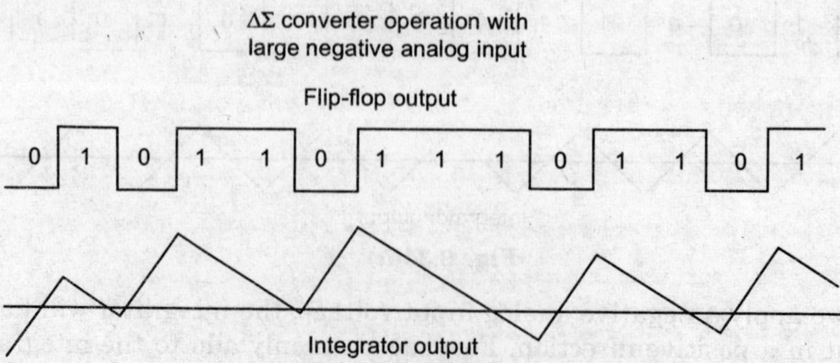


**Fig. 9.34(*d*)**

A parallel binary number output is obtained from this circuit by averaging the serial stream of bits together. For example, a counter circuit could be designed to collect the total number of 1's output by the flip-flop in a given number of clock pulses. This count would then be indicative of the analog input voltage.

Variations on this theme exist, employing multiple integrator stages and/or comparator circuits outputting more than 1 bit, but one concept common to all ΔΣ converters is that of oversampling. Oversampling is when multiple samples of an analog signal are taken by an ADC (in this case, a 1-bit ADC), and those digitized samples are averaged. The end result is an effective increase in the number of bits resolved from the signal. In other words, an oversampled 1-bit ADC can do the same job as an 8-bit ADC with one-time sampling.

## 9.3 PRACTICAL CONSIDERATIONS OF ADC CIRCUITS

### 9.3.1 Resolution

The most important consideration of an ADC is its resolution. Resolution is the number of binary bits output by the converter. The resolution of an A/D conversion is defined as the smallest voltage difference that can be detected. The resolution is also referred to as the magnitude of the least significant bit (LSB) in the conversion. The fact that an A/D conversion has a finite (non-zero) resolution results in what is called quantization error. Quantization error results because a continuously varying analog signal is represented digitally as a series of discrete steps differing by the resolution of the conversion process. The resolution depends on two other quantities:

***(i) Number of digital bits in the conversion***

This is the length of the digital word that the A/D conversion produces as its output. Typical values for this are 8, 12 and 16 bits. The higher the number of bits the longer the conversion takes and the more accurate it is. This number is fixed for a given converter. The number of discrete values that can represented (quantized) by a given length digital word is equal to 2 raised to the number of bits. For example, if the converter is a 12 bit system then $2^{12}$ = 4096 values can be represented.

***(ii) Input voltage range***

This is the total range in volts of the A/D converter and depends on the amount of gain that the converter has. Typically the amount of gain is adjustable.

The resolution in volts is defined as:

***Resolution = (Input Voltage Range) / (2 $^{\text{Number of bits}}$ –1)***

For example,

$$\text{Input voltage range} = \pm 10 \text{ V} = 20 \text{ V}$$

$$\text{Number of bits} = 12$$

$$\text{Resolution} = 20 \text{ V} / (2^{12} - 1) = 0.0049 \text{ Volts}$$

Note that if the input voltage range is decreased to 0.050 (50 millivolts) the resolution = 0.10 / 4095 = 0.0000244 volts or 2.e-5 volts.

The choice of the input range value is critical in ensuring that we obtain enough resolution to accurately measure the input signal.

In both cases above, the resolution expressed as a percentage of the input voltage range is the same.

Resolution / Input voltage range * 100 0.0049 / 20 * 100 = 0.0245 % 2.e-5 / 0.10 * 100 = 0.02 %

This is certainly low enough for almost any application.

However, unless our signals use the input voltage range we do not obtain this per cent resolution. Consider the case of measuring a signal of 0.1 volts using a input voltage range of 10 volts. The per cent error in our measurement of this signal using a 12 bit A/D is:

$$0.0049 / 0.1 * 100 = 4.9 \%$$

which is probably not acceptable. In this case an input range of 1.0 or 0.1 volts should be used, giving either 0.49 or 0.049 per cent resolution.

An alternative to adjusting the gain of the A/D is to provide the A/D with signals that use the entire ±10 volt range. This is generally preferable due to signal noise. Each amplification stage introduces noise into the signal and each succeeding amplification amplifies the noise from the previous stage. Thus it is generally preferable to have the first stage provide as much gain as possible. And the A/D, which is the last analog stage, should have the least amount of gain necessary to resolve the signals. That is, the best procedure is to choose the gain range on the load cells, etc., so that a ±10 volt range on the A/D results in acceptable resolution of the signals.

Because ADC circuits take an analog signal, which is continuously variable, and resolve it into one of many discrete steps, it is important to know how many of these steps there are in total.

For example, an ADC with a 10-bit output can represent up to 1024 ($2^{10}$) unique conditions of signal measurement. Over the range of measurement from 0% to 100%, there will be exactly 1024 unique binary numbers output by the converter (from 0000000000 to 1111111111, inclusive). An 11-bit ADC will have twice as many states to its output (2048, or $2^{11}$), representing twice as many unique conditions of signal measurement between 0% and 100%.

Resolution is very important in data acquisition systems (circuits designed to interpret and record physical measurements in electronic form). Suppose we were measuring the height of water in a 40-foot tall storage tank using an instrument with a 10-bit ADC as shown in figure 9.35. 0 feet of water in the tank corresponds to 0% of measurement, while 40 feet of water in the tank corresponds to 100% of measurement. Because the ADC is fixed at 10 bits of binary data output, it will interpret any given tank level as one out of 1024 possible states. To determine how much physical water level will be represented in each step of the ADC, we need to divide the 40 feet of measurement span by the number of steps in the 0-to-1024 range of possibilities, which is 1023 (one less than 1024). Doing this, we obtain a figure of 0.039101 feet per step. This equates to 0.46921 inches per step, a little less than half an inch of water level represented for every binary count of the ADC.

This step value of 0.039101 feet (0.46921 inches) represents the smallest amount of tank level change detectable by the instrument. Admittedly, this is a small amount, less than 0.1% of the overall measurement span of 40 feet. However, for some applications it may not be fine enough. Suppose we needed this instrument to be able to indicate tank level changes down to one-tenth of an inch. In order to achieve this degree of resolution and still maintain a measurement span of 40 feet, we would need an instrument with more than ten ADC bits.

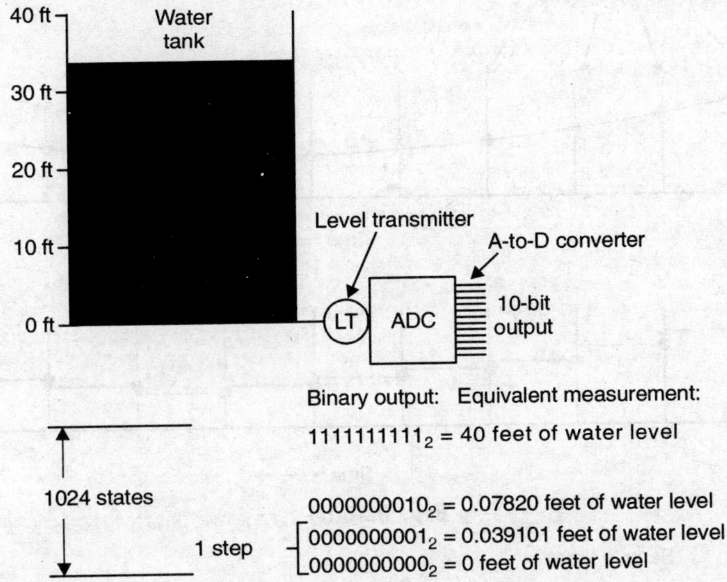


**Fig. 9.35**

To determine how many ADC bits are necessary, we need to first determine how many 1/10 inch steps there are in 40 feet. The answer to this is 40/(0.1/12), or 4800 1/10 inch steps in 40 feet. Thus, we need enough bits to provide at least 4800 discrete steps in a binary counting sequence. 10 bits gave us 1023 steps, and we knew this by calculating 2 to the power of 10 ($2^{10}$ = 1024) and then subtracting one. Following the same mathematical procedure, $2^{11} - 1 = 2047$, $2^{12} - 1 = 4095$, and $2^{13} - 1 = 8191$. 12 bits falls shy of the amount needed for 4800 steps, while 13 bits is more than enough. Therefore, we need an instrument with at least 13 bits of resolution.

## 9.3.2 Sample Frequency

Another important consideration of ADC circuitry is its sample frequency, or conversion rate. This is simply the speed at which the converter outputs a new binary number. Like resolution, this consideration is linked to the specific application of the ADC. If the converter is being used to measure slow-changing signals such as level in a water storage tank, it could probably have a very slow sample frequency and still perform adequately. Conversely, if it is being used to digitize an audio frequency signal cycling at several thousand times per second, the converter needs to be considerably faster.

Consider the Fig. 9.36(*a*) for ADC conversion rate versus signal type, typical of a successive-approximation ADC with regular sample intervals:

Here, for this slow-changing signal, the sample rate is more than adequate to capture its general trend. But consider this example, Figure 9.36(b) with the same sample time:

When the sample period is too long (too slow), substantial details of the analog signal will be missed. Notice how, especially in the latter portions of the analog signal, the digital output utterly fails to reproduce the true shape. Even in the first section of the analog waveform, the digital reproduction deviates substantially from the true shape of the wave.

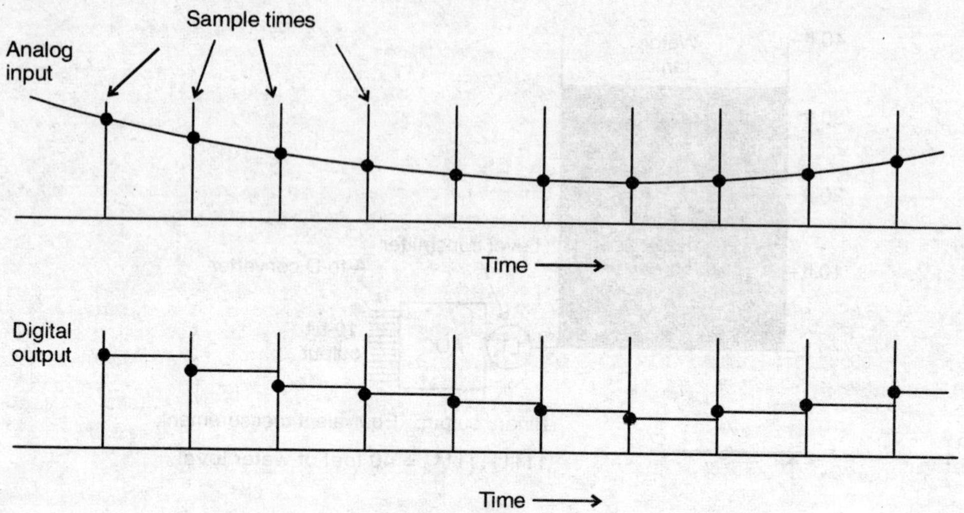


**Fig. 9.36(*a*)**

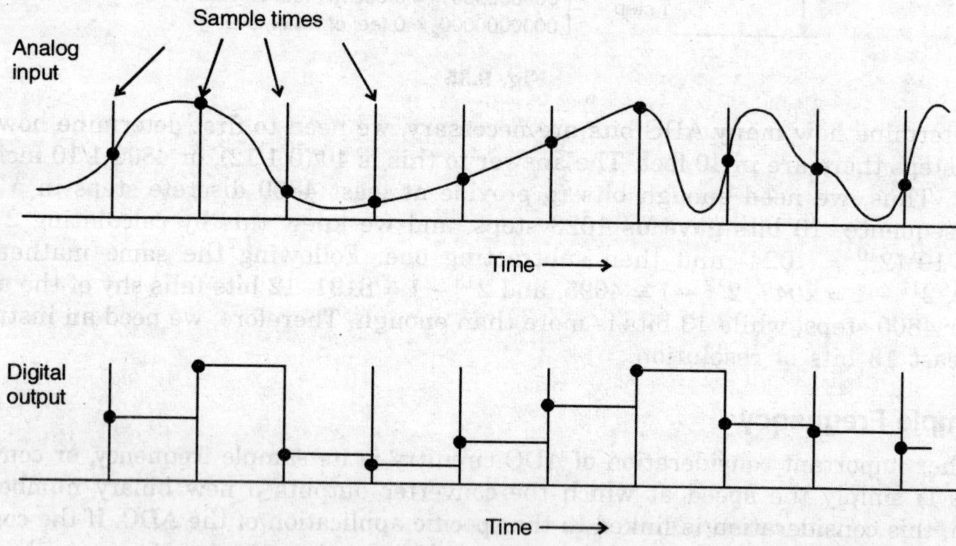


**Fig. 9.36(*b*)**

It is imperative that an ADC's sample time is fast enough to capture essential changes in the analog waveform. In data acquisition terminology, the highest-frequency waveform that an ADC can theoretically capture is the so-called Nyquist frequency, equal to one-half of the ADC's sample frequency. Therefore, if an ADC circuit has a sample frequency of 5000 Hz, the highest-frequency waveform it can successfully resolve will be the Nyquist frequency of 2500 Hz.

If an ADC is subjected to an analog input signal whose frequency exceeds the Nyquist frequency for that ADC, the converter will output a digitized signal of falsely low frequency. This phenomenon is known as aliasing.

It should be understood that the Nyquist frequency is an absolute maximum frequency limit for an ADC, and does not represent the highest practical frequency measurable. To be safe, one shouldn't expect an ADC to successfully resolve any frequency greater than one-fifths to one-tenth of its sample frequency.

A practical means of preventing aliasing is to place a low-pass filter before the input of the ADC, to block any signal frequencies greater than the practical limit. This way, the ADC circuitry will be prevented from seeing any excessive frequencies and thus will not try to digitize them. It is generally considered better that such frequencies go unconverted than to have them be "aliased" and appear in the output as false signals.

### 9.3.3 Step Recovery

Another measure of ADC performance is step recovery. This is a measure of how quickly an ADC changes its output to match a large, sudden change in the analog input. In some converter technologies especially, step recovery is a serious limitation. One example is the tracking converter, which has a typically fast update period but a disproportionately slow step recovery.

An ideal ADC has a great many bits for very fine resolution, samples at lightning-fast speeds, and recovers from steps instantly. It also, unfortunately, doesn't exist in the real world. Of course, any of these traits may be improved through additional circuit complexity, either in terms of increased component count and/or special circuit designs made to run at higher clock speeds. Different ADC technologies, though, have different strengths. Here is a summary of them ranked from best to worst:

#### *Resolution/complexity ratio*

Single-slope integrating, dual-slope integrating, counter, tracking, successive approximation, flash.

#### *Speed*

Flash, tracking, successive approximation, single-slope integrating and counter, dual-slope integrating.

#### *Step recovery*

Flash, successive approximation, single-slope integrating and counter, dual-slope integrating, tracking.

## 9.4 SOLVED EXAMPLES

**Example 1.** *Determine the output voltage for the circuit of Fig. 9.37.*

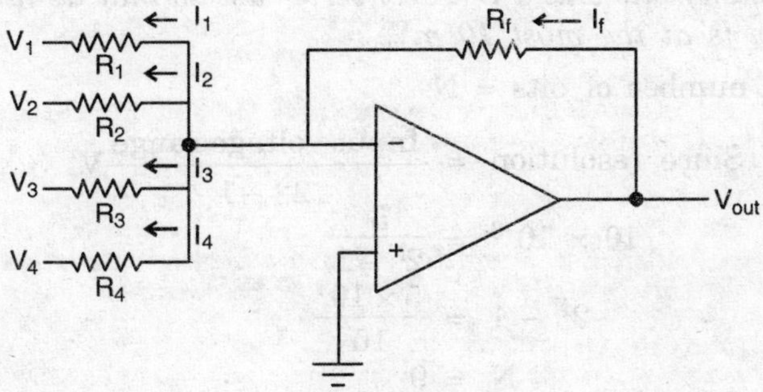


**Fig. 9.37**

*The values of the voltages and resistors are as follows:*

$$V_1 = -2V \quad R_1 = 2\ K\Omega$$
$$V_2 = +6V \quad R_2 = 2\ K\Omega$$
$$V_3 = -4V \quad R_3 = 2\ K\Omega$$
$$V_4 = -3V \quad R_4 = 10\ K\Omega$$
$$R_f = 15\ K\Omega$$

**Solution.**

$$I_1 = \frac{-2}{2 \times 10^3} = -1\ mA = -10^{-3}\ A$$

$$I_2 = \frac{6}{2 \times 10^3} = 3\ mA$$

$$I_3 = \frac{-4}{2 \times 10^{-3}} = -2\ mA$$

$$I_4 = \frac{-3}{10 \times 10^{-3}} = -0.3\ mA$$

$$V_{out} = ?$$

Since

$$I_f = I_1 + I_2 + I_3 + I_4$$
$$I_f = (-1 + 3 - 2 - 0.3)$$
$$I_f = -0.30\ mA = -\ 0.30 \times 10^{-3}\ A$$
$$V_{out} = -I_f \times R_f$$
$$V_{out} = -\ (-0.30 \times 10^{-3}) \times 15 \times 10^3$$
$$V_{out} = 4.5\ V$$

Therefore the output voltage for the circuit will be 4.5 V.

**Example 2.** *Find the resolution of an 8-bit DAC provides an analog output which has a maximum value of 10 V.*

**Solution.** The resolution is defined as

$$\text{Resolution} = \frac{\text{Input voltage range}}{2^{\text{Number of bits}} - 1}\ \text{Volt}$$

$$= \frac{10}{2^8 - 1} = \frac{10}{255}\ V$$

$$\text{Resolution} = 0.035\ V$$

**Example 3.** *How many bits will a D/A converter use so that its full-scale output voltage is 5V and its resolution is at the most 10 mV.*

**Solution.** Let the number of bits = N

$$\text{Since resolution} = \frac{\text{Input voltage range}}{2^N - 1}\ V$$

$$10 \times 10^{-3} = \frac{5}{2^N - 1}$$

$$2^N - 1 = \frac{5 \times 10^3}{10}$$

$$\Rightarrow \quad N = 9$$

Therefore DAC will use 9 bits.

**Example 4.** *For the 8-bit weighted-resistor DAC shown in Fig. 9.38, find r.*

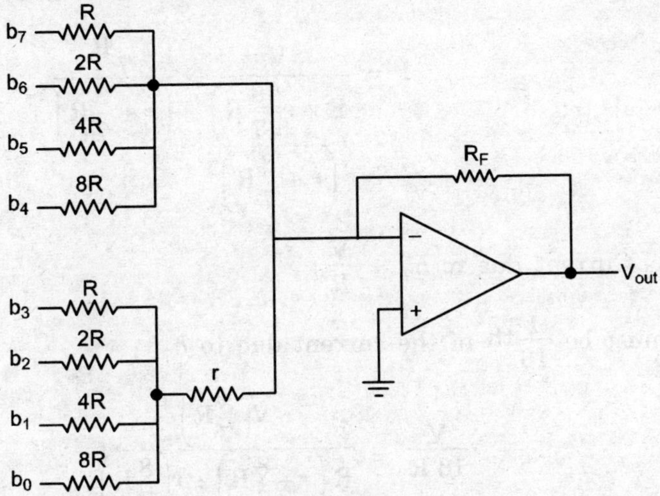


**Fig. 9.38**

**Solution.** Let assume that bits $b_0 = b_1 = b_2 = 0$ and $b_3 = 1$. The equivalent circuit corresponding to the lower order four bits is shown in Figure 9.39.

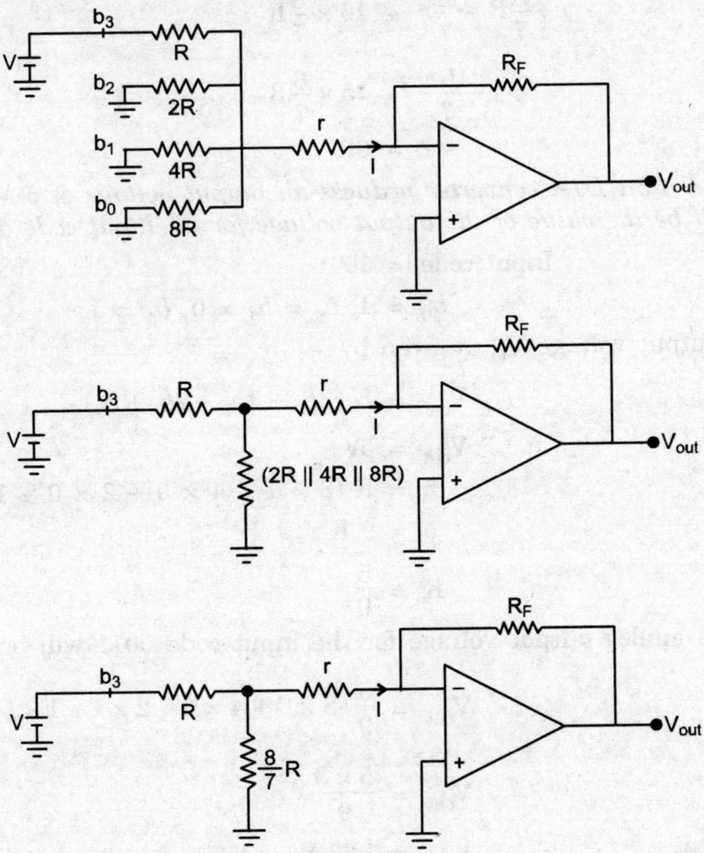


**Fig. 9.39**

The current I will be given by

$$I = \frac{V}{R + \dfrac{r\left(\frac{8}{7}R\right)}{\left(r + \frac{8}{7}R\right)}} \times \frac{\frac{8}{7}R}{\left(r + \frac{8}{7}R\right)}$$

$$\text{Current due to } b_7 = \frac{V}{R}$$

The current I must be $\frac{1}{16}$th of the current due to $b_7$.

*i.e.,*

$$\frac{V}{16\,R} = \frac{V\left(\frac{8}{7}R\right)}{R\left(r + \frac{8}{7}R\right) + r\left(\frac{8}{7}R\right)}$$

$$R\left(r + \frac{8}{7}R\right) + r\left(\frac{8}{7}R\right) = 16\,R\left(\frac{8}{7}R\right)$$

$$r + \frac{8}{7}R + \frac{8}{7}r = 16 \times \frac{8}{7}R$$

$$\frac{15r}{7} = 15 \times \frac{8}{7}R$$

$$\Rightarrow \qquad r = 8R.$$

**Example 5.** *A 4-bit D/A converter prduces an output voltage of 5 V for an input code of 1001. What will be the value of the output voltage for an input code of 0011?*

**Solution.** Input code = 1001

*i.e.,* $b_0 = 1,\ b_2 = b_1 = 0,\ b_3 = 1$

The analog output voltage $V_O$ is given by

$$V_{out} = K\,(8b_3 + 4b_2 + 2b_1 + b_0)$$

$$V_{out} = 5V$$

$$5 = K\,(8 \times 1 + 4 \times 0 + 2 \times 0 + 1)$$

$$5 = 9\,K$$

Therefore $$K = \frac{5}{9}$$

Therefore, the analog output voltage for the input code 0011 will be

$$V_{out} = \frac{5}{9}(8 \times 0 + 4 \times 0 + 2 \times 1 + 1 \times 1)$$

$$V_{out} = \frac{5 \times 3}{9}V$$

$$V_{out} = 1.67\ V$$

## 9.5 EXERCISE

**1.** What will be the binary equivalent weight of each bit in the following cases?

(*a*) 3-bit resistive divider

(*b*) 4-bit resistive divider

(*c*) 5-bit resistive divider

(*d*) 6-bit resistive divider

**2.** Draw a R-2R ladder network for 6 bits.

**3.** Calculate the per cent resolution of a 7-bit D/A converter.

**4.** Calculate the resolution and per cent resolution of an 8-bit D/A converter, the output of which varies between +10 and –10V.

**5.** The LSB of a 6-bit D/A converter represents 0.1 V. What voltage value will be represented by the following binary words?

(*a*) 101010

(*b*) 110101

(*c*) 011010

(*d*) 110110

**6.** Design a 3-bit parallel-comparator A/D converter for 2's complement format.

**7.** A D/A converter has a full scale analog output of 10V and accepts 6 binary bits as inputs. Find the voltage corresponding to each analog step.

**8.** Explain the practical considerations of ADC circuits.

**9.** Write short notes on

(*a*) Binary-weighted resistor DAC

(*b*) R/2R ladder DAC

**10.** Write short notes on

(*a*) Parallel-comparator ADC

(*b*) Counting ADC

(*c*) Tracking ADC

(*d*) SLOPE ADC

(*e*) DELTA-SIGMA ADC

# PART D

# LOGIC FAMILIES

10

CHAPTER

# FUNDAMENTALS OF SWITCHING ELEMENTS AND LOGIC FAMILIES

## 10.0 INTRODUCTION

In earlier chapters, we have studied the basic logic gates and seen how they can be realized using switches in ON/OFF fashion (or TRUE/FALSE). The semiconductor devices can be used to replace these switches and can realize these logic functions. A circuit employing semiconductor devices to realized logic functions is called as **digital circuit.** Since semiconductor devices are used to replace the switch, these devices and their switching characteristics are discussed first in this chapter. In fact using semiconductor devices offers several advantages, that will be apparent throughout this chapter.

Advent of semiconductor IC technology in late 1950's and early 1960's made it possible to fabriate large number of circuit components on a small piece of semiconductor, whose area is few $mm^2$. Thus a large number of circuits could be integrated on small piece of semiconductor. This small piece of semiconductor is called as CHIP and a chip with circuits fabricated on it is chritened as **Integrated Circuit or IC** in short. Various types of digital circuits are available in form of ICs. In particular, advent of MOS technology made more number of components and logic circuits on one IC. Thus giving rise to very large scale integration which resulted in high capacity memory devices, microprocessor and many other complex circuits available on a small chip.

## 10.1 FUNDAMENTALS OF SEMICONDUCTORS AND SEMICONDUCTOR SWITCHING DEVICES

### 10.1.1 Semiconductors

By the idea of electrical properties of solids, we know that materials are broadly categorized as conductor, semiconductor, and insulator, on the basis of their conductivity. Semiconductors are those which have electrical conductivity intermediate to that of an conductor and insulator. In fact in a semiconductor the filled energy band, called valance band and the unfilled energy band, called conduction band are separated by a small energy gap, called band gap energy $E_G$.

By providing energy from an external source, the charge carriers at filled band can be raised to conduction band. Thus the materials can start conduction.

There are numerous elemental and compound semiconductors are available out of which Silicon and Germanium are two common elemental semiconductors. The silicon is used mostly because energy gap of silicon is a bit larger than the germanium thus providing a good operational mechanism, as we will see later.

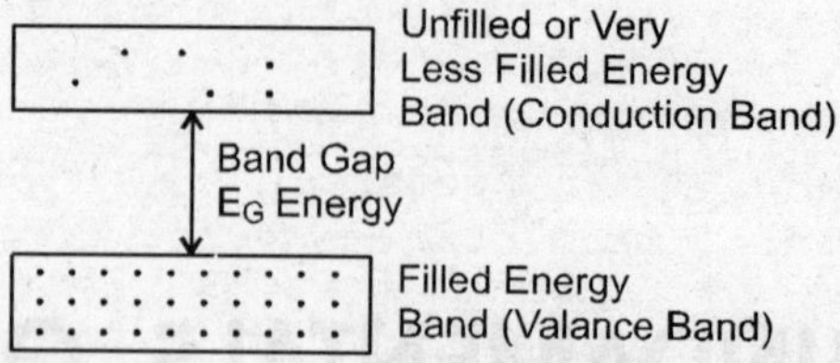


**Fig. 10.1** Energy band diagram for semiconductors

Both the silicon and germanium atoms have 4 electrons in their outer shell, which forms covalent bands with neighbouring atoms in a semiconductor material. This is shown in Figure 10.2. By providing energy from an electrical source these covalent bands can be broken and free charge carriers are available for conduction. Many of these covalents bonds are broken even at room temperature so at room temperature semiconductors (shorthand SCs) can behave some what like conductors. A semiconductor in its extreme pure form is called as **intrinsic semiconductor.** At room temperature conductivity of intrinsic semiconductors are poor. Thus to increase the no. of free charge carriers (or conductivity) it usual to add some impurity to intrinsic semiconductors. This dramatically increases the conductivity of semiconductors, and make it suitable for various applications. A semiconductor with impurity added to it is called as **extrinsic semiconductor.** The process of adding impurities to semiconductors is called **doping.** These extrinsic semiconductors are also called as **doped semiconductors.**

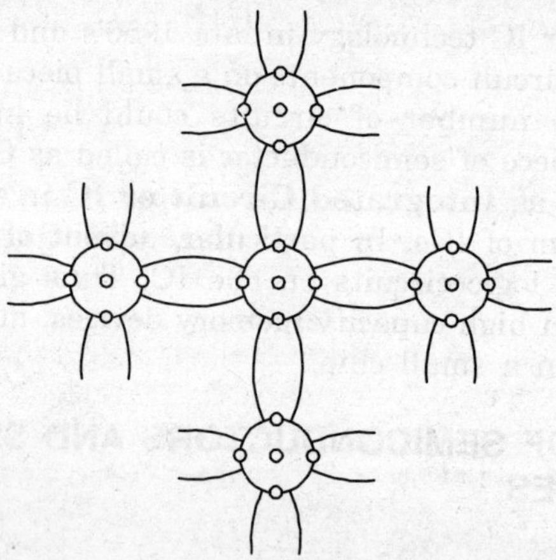

**Fig. 10.2** Formation of covalent bonds in semiconductor.

In a semiconductor, whenever a covalent bond is broken the electron gets free from its parent atom and leaves a vacancy, thus a +ve charge equal to the magnitude of electron charge is left with the parent atom. Thus the atom is ionized. An electron from neighbouring atom can fill this vacancy, but creates a vacancy there, if this process repeats this vacancy can be moved from one place to another and thus giving a mechanism of conduction. This vacancy is called **hole** which has an equal but opposite charge to that of an electron. In a semiconductor, both holes and electrons provide the conduction mechanism. In fact free electrons travels in conduction band where hole movement is due to the movement of electrons in valence band. Both the charge carriers travel in a direction opposite to each other but constitute current in same direction.

In a semiconductor, both electrons and holes move randomly through the semiconductor crystal during which an electron can fill a hole causing free electrons and holes to disappear.

This process is called **Recombination.** In a semiconductor the rate of charge carrier generation (generation of both electrons and holes) is equal to the rate of recombination and remains constant in time.

In an intrinsic semiconductor the number of free electron ($n$) and free holes ($p$) is same *i.e.,*

$$n = p = n_i \qquad ...(10.1)$$

where $n_i$ is intrinsic concentration of holes or electrons in intrinsic semiconductor. The $n_i$ can be approximated as

$$n_i^2 = BT^3 e^{-E_G/K_B.T} \text{ per cm}^3 \qquad ...(10.2)$$

where B = material constant = $5.4 \times 10^{31}$ for silicon

T = Temperature in Kelvin

$E_G$ = Band gap energy of SC = 1.12 eV for silicon

$K_B$ = Boltzmann constant = $1.38 \times 10^{-23}$ joules/kelvin

= $8.62 \times 10^{-5}$ eV/K

By using eqn. (10.2) for silicon we get that at room temperature *i.e.,* at 27°C we get approximately $1.51 \times 10^{10}$ free carrier/cm$^3$. A silicon crystal has $5 \times 10^{23}$ atoms/cm$^3$. So $n_i = 1.51 \times 10^{10}$ shows that at room temperature only one of every billion atom is ionized.

In a semiconductor recombination causes a pair of free charge carriers, called electron hole pair (EHP) to disappear and breaking of a covalent gives an EHP. Also breaking of a covalent bond ionizes an atom by freeing an electron, for this reason generation of free charge carriers is called **ionization process.**

In a semiconductor movement of charge carrier can be obtained by two mechanism **diffusion** and **drift.** If there is uniform concentration of charge carriers throughout the crystal of a semiconductor there is not net flow of charges *i.e.,* no current. If in one portion concentration is high and in another portion concentration is low then the charge carriers will diffuse to low concentration region and thus constituting **diffusion current $I_D$.** If an electric field is applied to semiconductors free electrons and holes are accelerated and acquires a velocity called **drift velocity** and is given as

$$V_{drift} = \mu E \qquad ...(10.3)$$

where μ = mobility of charge carriers in cm$^2$/V.sec

E = applied electric field in V/Cm

$V_{drift}$ = drift velocity in cm/sec

Note that mobility of a hole is lower than that of an electron.

The electric current caused by drift velocity is called as **drift current.**

As earlier stated, to increase the conductivity of a semiconductor doping is done. There are two types of doping: used to increase free charge carriers; depending upon whether we want to increase no. of holes or no. of electrons. In a doped semiconductor if impurity increases no. of free-electrons it is called **n-type** semiconductor in which case electrons becomes majority carrier and holes become minority carrier. If impurity increases no. of free holes it is called **p-type** semiconductor. To obtain n-type semiconductor a pentavalent impurity (*e.g.,* antimony or phosphorous with 5 electrons in outer orbits) is introduced. Out of 5 valence electrons of impurity atoms four electrons forms covalent bonds with surrounding semiconductor atoms and one electron remains-free. Thus, the free electron can be donated for current conduction. For this reason such impurity atoms are called **donor atoms.** Similarly introducing a trivalent impurity (*e.g.*, boron or medium) gives a p-type semiconductor in which holes are majority carriers. In this case only three electron exists in outer orbits which form covalent bonds with three neighbouring atoms. But this impurity is having a vacant position *i.e.*, hole which is free and cannot be used to form fourth covalent bond in lattice structure. Thus a free hole is created. But this impurity can accept an electron to form fourth covalent bond causing hole movement. For this reason trivalent impurities are also called **acceptor impurities.**

*"It should be noted that p-type or n-type semiconductors are electrically natural. The majority carriers in each type are neutralized by* ***bound charges*** *associated with the impurity atoms,* ***see Fig. 10.3.***

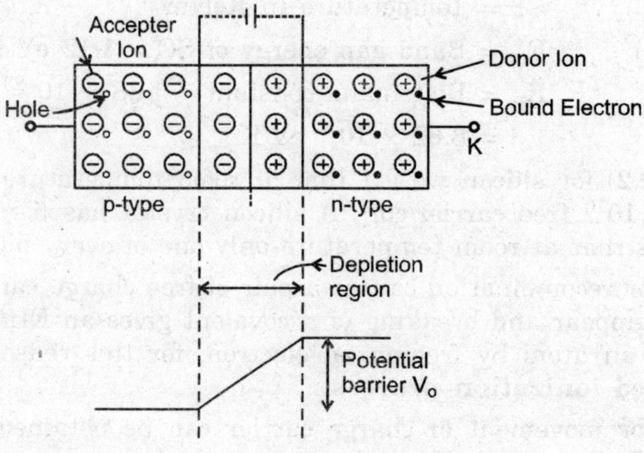


**Fig. 10.3** A PN Junction diode under open-circuit terminals

## 10.1.2 Semiconductor Diode or PN Junction

When a PN-junction is formed then due to concentration gradient, the charge carriers diffuses on either side of the junction. But soon after crossing the junction the free charge carrier disappear by re-combination. This leaves the ion without neutralizing carrier. The process of diffusion continue until a potential barrier against the flow of charge carrier is formed. This is shown in Fig. 10.3. The PN junction in open circuit is sold to be in equilibrium. Since the recombination occurs immediately after the junction, this region is out of or depleted of free charge carrier and thus it is called **depletion region.** It is in this region the potential barrier is built up and the charge carrier must overcome this barrier to cross the junction. Symbol of PN junction diode is shown in Fig. 10.4.

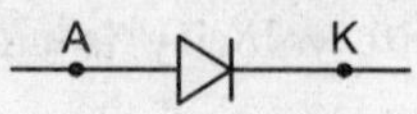


**Fig. 10.4** Symbol of PN junction diode.

When no external voltage applied the inbuilt junction voltage $V_O$, shown in **Fig. 10.3** is given as

$$\therefore \quad V_O = V_T \log_e \left( \frac{N_A . N_D}{n_i^2} \right) \qquad ...(10.4(a))$$

where

$$V_T = \frac{K_B . T}{q} = \text{Thermal voltage} \qquad ...(10.4(b))$$

$q$ = electronic charge

$N_A$, $N_D$ = Doping concentration on *p*-side and *n*-side respectively.

For silicon the junction inbuilt voltage $V_O$ typically varies between 0.6 to 0.8 V.

Let us connect a dc supply $V_F$ to the diode such that positive terminal of supply is connected to *p*-type and negative is connected to *n*-type as shown in Fig. 10.5. This configuration of the diode is **forward biasing.**

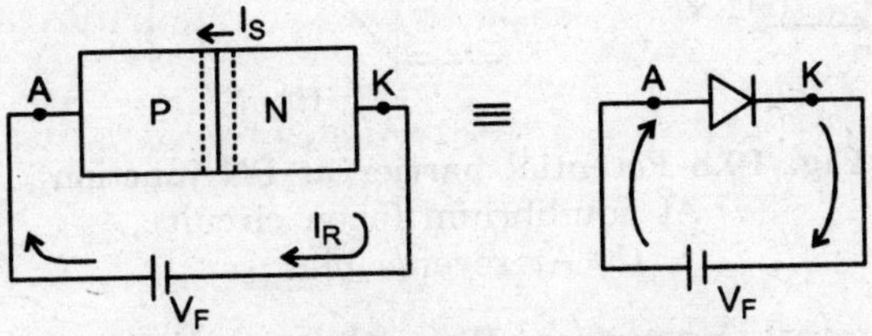


**Fig. 10.5** Diode in forward bias

The voltage $V_F$ is thus called as the forward voltage. As we increase the $V_F$ the width of the depletion start reducing. Alternately, the potential barrier $V_O$ reduces as shown in Figure 10.6(*b*).

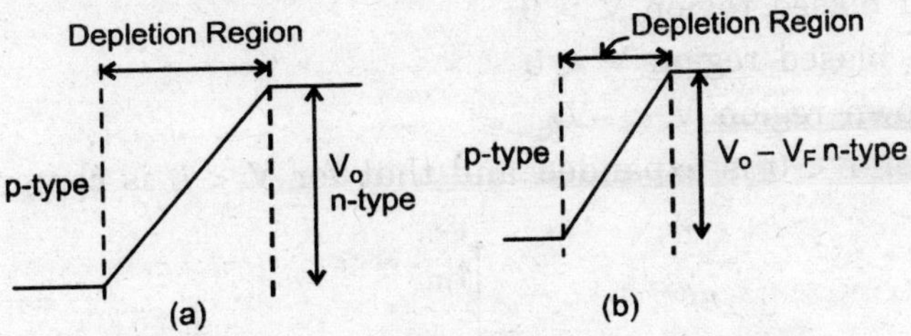


**Fig. 10.6** Potential barrier at PN junction
(*a*) At equilibrium (open circuit) (*b*) At forward bias

If we increase $V_F$ further, situation can soon be reached at which depletion region width is zero. And the moment $V_F > V_O$, the charge carriers are swept across the junction under the influence of electric field. Thus current flows through the device in a direction shown in Fig. 10.5. The current flowing through the device in this case is called as forward current.

If the batter polarities are reversed *i.e.,* positive terminal is connected to *n*-type and negative terminal is connected the p-type, then we get what called **reverse biasing.** This is shown in Fig. 10.7. Note that battery is now-labelled $V_R$ (reverse voltage), in order to distinguish it from forward voltage $V_F$.

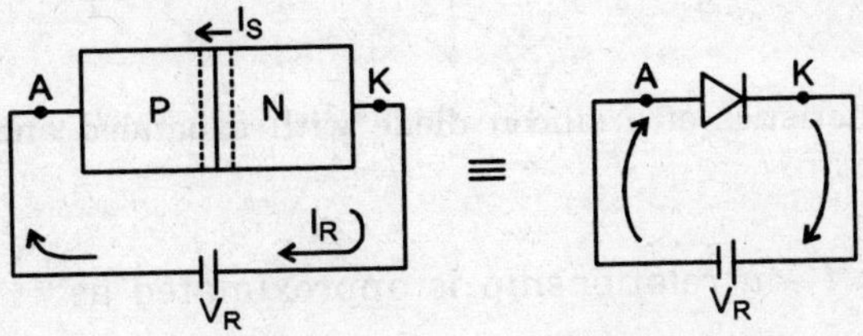


**Fig. 10.7** Diode in reverse bias

In this case the electrons of the n-type are attracted towards the positive plate of battery and holes are attracted towards the negative plate. Consequently the width of depletion region increases. And increase, in depletion region increases the potential barrier across the junction as shown in Figure 10.8(*b*).

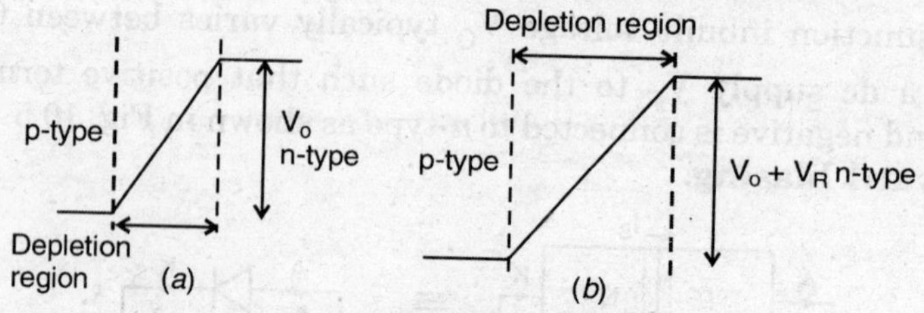


**Fig. 10.8** Potential barrier at PN junction
(*a*) At equilibrium (open circuit)
(*b*) At reverse bias

In this situation, apparently no current flows through the junction. But in reality due to the flow of minority carriers there exist a small reverse current called as **leakage current.**

### *10.1.2.1 I–V Characteristics of Diodes*

As shown in figure the characteristics is divided into three parts.

1. The forward biased region $V > 0$
2. The reverse biased region $V < 0$
3. The breakdown region $V < -V_K$

Note that scale for $I < 0$ is expanded and that for $V < 0$ is compressed.

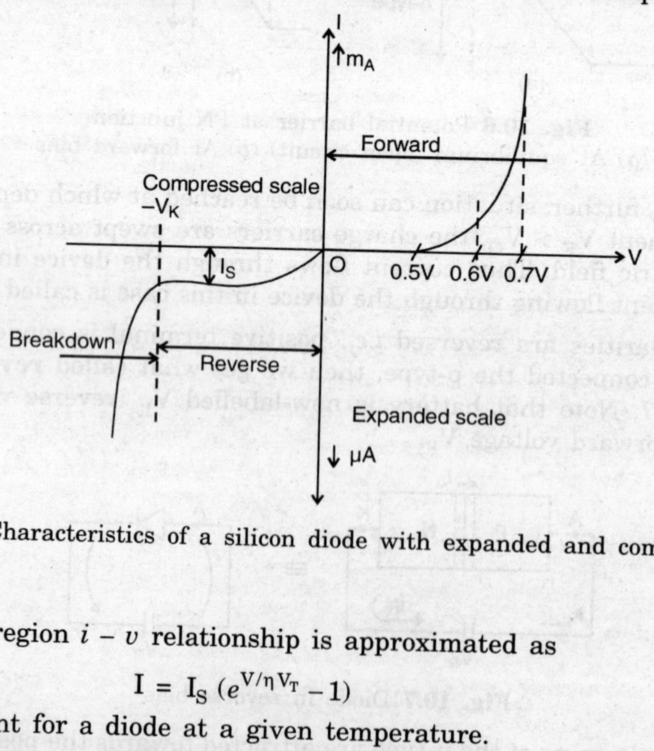


**Fig 10.9** I-V Characteristics of a silicon diode with expanded and compressed scale

### *Forward Region*

In the forward region *i* – *v* relationship is approximated as

$$I = I_S\,(e^{V/\eta V_T} - 1) \qquad \text{...(10.5)}$$

where $I_S$ is a constant for a diode at a given temperature.

$V_T$ is thermal voltage defined by equation 10.4(b).

at $t = 27°C$ or $T = 300°K$ the thermal voltage

$$V_T \cong 26 \text{ mV} \qquad ...(10.6(a))$$

η is a parameter and η = 1 for germanium and η = 2 for silicon.

The current $I_S$ in eqn. 10.5 is called as SCALE CURRENT. The name is given because $I_S$ is directly proportional to the cross-sectional area of junction. This means doubling the junction area will double the $I_S$ which consequently doubles the diode current I as shown by equation 10.5, for a given forward voltage V.

An inspection of *i – v* characteristics reveals that almost no current flows (*i.e.*, less than 1% or so) for voltages V < 0.6 V. For voltages varying between 0.6 V to 0.8V there flows an appreciable amount of current. Thus we say that 0.6 V is a threshold value of voltage that must be applied for conduction. This is called as **cut-in voltage** ($V_\gamma$). Thus for silicon diode cut in voltage is

$$V_\gamma = 0.6 \text{ V} \qquad ...(10.6(b))$$

Since for a fully conducting diode voltage drop lies in a narrow range of 0.6 to 0.8V we can approximate that for silicon diodes

$$V_D = 0.7 \text{ V} \qquad ...(10.6(c)$$

where $V_D$ = Drop across conducting diode.

In forward region we get appreciable amount of current such that I >> $I_S$ so we can approximate equation 10.5 for forward biased region as

$$I = I_S e^{eV/\eta V_T} \qquad ...(10.7(a))$$

alternately $$V = \eta V_T \log_e \frac{I}{I_S} \qquad ...(10.7(b)$$

**Example 10.1.** *Calculate the scale current at room temperature for a 2 mA silicon diode in forward biased mode.*

**Solution.** By equation 10.6(c) we have drop across conducting diode

$$V_D = 0.7 \text{ V}$$

and at room temperature $V_T$ = 26 mV by equation 10.6(a)
by equation 10.7(a)

$$I_S = I.e^{-V/\eta V_T}$$

for silicon η = 2, given I = 2 mA

so $$I_S = 2 \times 10^{-3} \; e^{-(07/2 \times 2 \times 26 \times 10^{-3})}$$

or $$I_S \cong 2.85 \times 10^{-9} \text{ A } i.e., \; 1_S 2.Q5 \; mA \text{ at } t = 27°C$$ for this diode.

It is worth noting that since both $I_S$ and $V_T$ are function of temperature the V–I characteristics varies with temperature. At a given constant current the drop across diode decreases approximately by 2.5 mV by every 1°C rise in temperature *i.e.*,

$$\frac{dV}{dT} = -2.5 \text{ mV/°C}$$

### *The Reverse Region*

When the applied voltage is reversed and diode voltage V is made negative we get the reverse bias operation of diode. If V is negative and is few times larger than $V_T$ in magnitude we approximate equation 10.5 as

$$I = -I_S \qquad ...(10.8)$$

This means that current in reverse direction is constant in the junction and is equal to $I_S$, see Fig. 10.7. Since $I_S$ is constant it is also called **saturation current.** Practically diodes have quite small reverse current but much larger than $I_S$ *e.g.*, for $I_S = 10^{-15}$A, reverse current $I_R \cong 10^{-9}$ A. The reverse current also increases with increase of reverse voltage. Major contribution to the reverse current is due to leakage effect. The leakage current is also proportional to the junction area. In general reverse current doubles for every 10°C rise in temperature.

### Breakdown Region

The breakdown region is reached when reverse voltagc exceeds a certain threshold value for a diode, called **breakdown voltage.** This is indicated by the knee of V-I characteristics and thats why it is also called **knee voltage** and is represented by $V_K$ in Fig. 10.9. In the breakdown region a small increase in reverse voltage results large increase in reverse current. If the dissipated power is limited, the diode breakdown is non-destructive.

Also the fact that V–I characteristics in breakdown region is almost a vertical line, enables one to use this region for voltage regulation.

### 10.1.2.2 Diode as a Switch

The P-N junction diode can be operated as a switch in electronics circuits by operating it into forward biased region and reverse biased region.

When the diode is operated in forward bias at that time the drop across diode is negligibly small and is almost constant. If the forward current $I_F$ is limited by a series O resistor R, then the forward biased diode can be used as switch in ON condition. This is shown in Fig. 10.10 (*a*). If the diode is reversed biased then a small current flows through the diode, which is almost constant. This can be used to represent a switch in OFF position.

Now let us apply a voltage $V_{in}$ as shown in Fig. 10.10(*b*) and see how the diode circuit shown in Fig. 10.10(*a*) respond to it.

At $t = 0$ $V_{in} = V_1$ and diodes is in forward biased and the drop across conducting diode is small. This is shown by $V_D$ in Fig. 10.11(*d*). The current $I_F$ flowing in the circuit is approximated as

$$I_F \cong \frac{V_1}{R}$$

This is shown in Fig. 10.11(*c*).

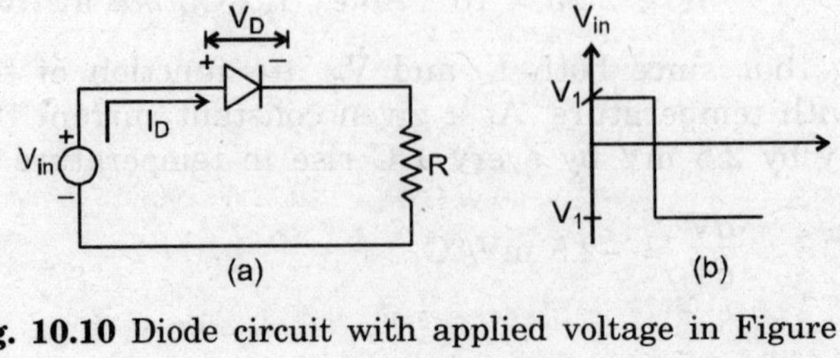


**Fig. 10.10** Diode circuit with applied voltage in Figure (*b*).

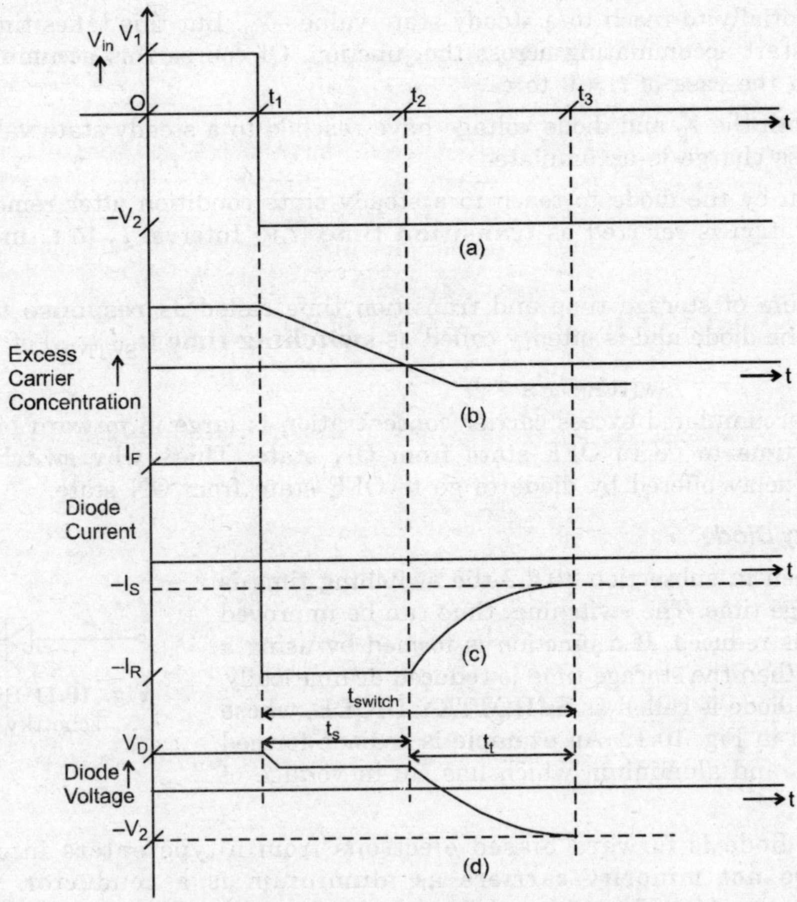


**Fig. 10.11** Switching waveforms for Fig. 10.10

Also shown by Fig. 10.11(*b*) is, when diode is conducting minority charge carriers will accumulated across the junction. This excess concentration will be quite large if diode stays ON for long.

*at* $t = t_1$ $V_{in}$ switches to $-V_2$ but the diode voltage does not changes immediately as shown in Fig. 10.11. This is because during $t = 0$ to $t_1$ minority charge carriers were accumulated across the junction. This must be removed to change the state of diode. This takes sometime to be done.

"The time required for the removal of excess charge carrier from junction is referred as **storage time (ts)**". In Fig. 10.11 interval $t_1$ to $t_2$ is storage time.

In fact to remove excess charge carriers a large reverse current flows till all the excess charges are removed. This is shown in Fig. 10.11(*c*) in interval $t_1$ to $t_2$ where it remains constant and can be approximated as

$$I_R \cong \frac{-V_2}{R}$$

At $t = t_2$ excess carriers are removed the current $I_R$ changes exponentially and goes towards a steady state value of $-I_S$. As shown in Figs. 10.11(*c*) and (*d*), the diode voltage also changes exponentially to reach to a steady state value $-V_2$. But this takes time and excess charge carrier start accumulating across the junction. Of course this accumulation is very small as was in the case of $t = 0$ to $t_1$.

At $t = t_3$ Both the $I_R$ and diode voltage have reached to a steady state value and small amount of excess charge is accumulated.

"Time taken by the diode to reach to a steady state condition after removal of excess carrier concentration is referred as **transition time** ($t_t$)". Interval $t_2$ to $t_3$ in Fig. 10.11 is transition time.

And "the sum of storage time and transition time called as **response time** or **total time delay** of the diode and is oftenty called as **switching time** ($t_{SWITCH}$) of the diode *i.e.,*

$$t_{SWITCH} = t_S + t_t \qquad \text{...(10.9)}$$

Since, the accumulated excess carrier concentration is large in forward biased it takes a quite longer time to go to OFF state from ON state. Thats why switching speed is measured from delay offered by diode to go to OFF state from ON state.

#### 10.1.2.3 Schottky Diode

We have seen in subsection 10.2.2 the switching time is limited by storage time. The switching, time can be improved if storage time is reduced. If a junction is formed by using a SC and a metal then the storage time is reduced dramatically. Such a junction diode is called as SCHOTTKY DIODE, whose symbol is shown in Fig. 10.12. An example is a diode formed using n-type SC and aluminium which has cut-in voltage of 0.35 V.

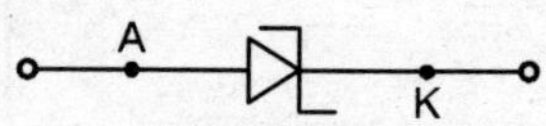


**Fig. 10.11** Symbol of a schottky diode

When the diode is forward biased electrons from n-type enters into aluminium where they are not minority carriers as aluminium is a conductor. Thus, when junction is reverse biased problem of removing excess minority carriers does not exist. So the SCHOTTKY diodes have negligible storage time and have very high switching speed.

### 10.1.3 Bipolar Junction Transistor (BJT)

Yet another non linear semiconductor device is a 3-terminal bipolar junction transistor. The basic principal is to apply a voltage between two terminals to control the current flowing into the third terminal.

A transistor is formed by sandwitching a p-type semiconductor between two *n*-type semiconductors or by sandwitching an *n*-type semiconductor between two *p*-type semiconductors. The former is called *npn* transistor and later is called a *pnp* transistor. A simplified structure with their symbols along with conventional current direction is shown in Fig. 10.12.

An observation of above figure reveals that a transistor is nothing but two PN junction diodes connected back to back. The three regions are named emitter, base and collector which forms two junction the emitter to base junction (EBJ) and collector to base junction (CBJ). To be useful practically emitter is heavily doped, base is lightly doped and width of base is made small *i.e.,* thin base, and collector is made thick offering high resistance.

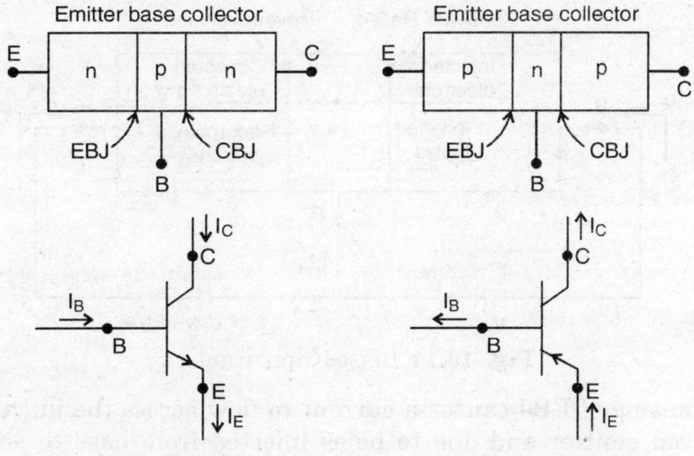


(a) npn transistor (b) pnp transistor

**Fig. 10.12** The bipolar junction transistor

#### *10.1.3.1 Configuration and Operation of BJTs*

Depending upon the biasing of emitter to base junction (EBJ) and collector to base junction (CBJ) the transistor can be operated in different modes. This is sumarised in Table 10.1.

**Table 10.1 Modes of operation of BJT**

| *EBJ Biasing* | *CBJ Biasing* | *Mode* |
|---|---|---|
| REVERSE | REVERSE | CUTOFF |
| FORWARD | REVERSE | ACTIVE |
| FORWARD | FORWARD | SATURATION |
| REVERSE | FORWARD | INVERSE ACTIVE |

The Active mode is used for amplification whereas CUTOFF and SATURATION is used for switching application.

In order to configure the device as two port network one of the three terminals of the device is made common to both the input acid output. Thus three different configuration are possibles as shown in Fig. 10.13. Out of these three configurations the common emitter (CE) configuration is the most used configuration. Note that all the transition in Fig. 10.13 are *n-p-n* transistor.

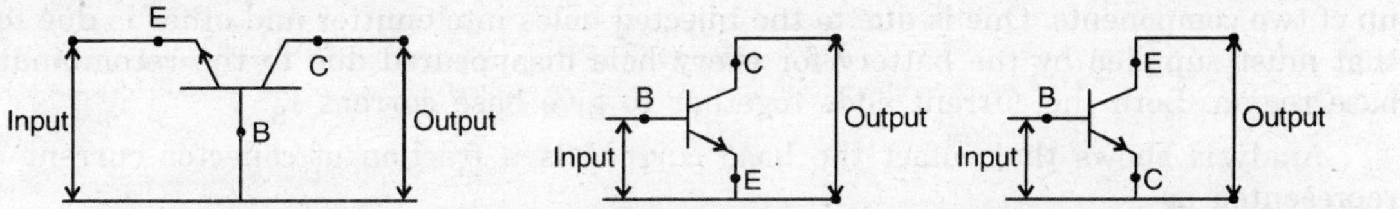


(*a*) Common Base (CB) (*b*) Common Emitter (CE) (*c*) Common Collector (CC)

**Fig. 10.13** Different configuration of transistors

## Operation

To understand the operation consider the biasing of *npn* transistor, shown in Fig. 10.14. The diagram shows simplified carrier movement due to diffusion only. The EБJ is forward biased by dc supply $V_{BE}$ and $C_{BJ}$ is reverse biased by supply $V_{CB}$.

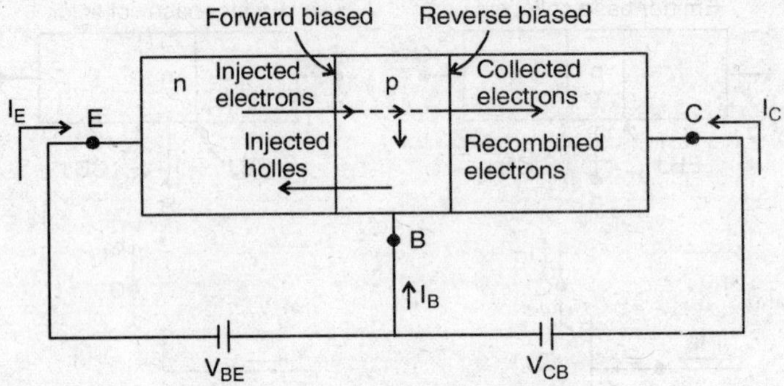


**Fig. 10.14** Biased npn transistor

The forward biasing of EBJ causes a current to flow across the junction due to electrons injected to base from emitter and due to holes injected from base to emitter. Flow of both the carriers constitute the current in same direction. Moreover since emitter is much heavily doped and base is lightly doped the emitter current is entirely due to the electrons. Upon entering into the base the electrons injected becomes minority carrier. Some of these electrons will recombine with holes in base and rest can reach to CBJ. The positive collector voltage $V_{CB}$ causes these electrons to be swept across the CBJ depletion region in to the collector. Thus they get collected to constitute collector current $I_C$. Since width of the base region is very thin, recombination in base region is very small. Thus almost all the injected electrons can be collected into collector region. The collector current $I_C$ is given as

$$I_C = I_S\, e^{V_{BE}/V_T} \qquad ...(10.9(a))$$

where $I_S$ = saturation current or current scale factor

and $I_S \alpha$ junction area EBJ (or device size)

$$V_{BE} = V_B - V_E = \text{Base to emitter voltage}$$

$$VT = \frac{K_B.T}{q} = \text{Thermal voltage} = 26 \text{ mV at room temperature.}$$

Note that $I_C$ is independent of base to collector voltage $V_{CB}$. This means as long as collector is positive with respect to base (*i.e.*, $V_{CB} = V_C - V_B > 0$) electrons injected from emitter will be swept into collector to make collector current. This is a very important observation because it also *implies that if, "VCB < 0 i.e., CBJ is forward biased then injected electrons may not be swept across the junction and collector current remains unaffected".* This fact can be utilized for switching. As evident from the figure the base current is made up of two components. One is due to the injected holes into emitter and other is due to holes that must supplied by the battery for every hole disappeared due to the recombination in base region. Both the current adds together to give base current $I_B$.

Analysis shows that infact the base current is a fraction of collector current and is represented as

$$I_B = \frac{I_C}{\beta} \qquad ...(10.10)$$

where β is a constant for particular transistor and is called common emitter current gain. The β depends upon width of Base and relative dopings of base and emitter region. To achieve high β (which is usually the case) base should be very thin and emitter must be heavily doped with lightly doped base.

The emitter current is sum of base current and collector current as shown in Fig. 10.14. Thus

$$I_E = I_B + I_C \qquad ...(10.11(a))$$

by equation (10.10), we get

$$I_E = \frac{I_C}{p} + I_C$$

or
$$I_E = \frac{\beta + 1}{\beta} I_C \qquad ...(10.11(b))$$

if we define
$$\alpha = \frac{\beta}{\beta + 1} \qquad ...(10.11(c))$$

then we get
$$I_C = \alpha I_E \qquad ...(10.11(d))$$

where $\alpha$ = common base current gain alternatively for $\beta$

$$\beta = \frac{\alpha}{1 - \alpha} \qquad ...(10.11(e))$$

Since $\alpha$ is constant and is less than but closer to unity it is a consequence of equation 10.11(e) that a small change in $\alpha$ will result in large change in $\beta$.

Although we have presented the working with a *n-p-n* transistor, the same is applicable for *p-n-p* transistor but with all current directions and voltage polarities reversed as in *p-n-p* transistors majority carriers are holes.

**Example 10.2.** *Design the circuit given in 10.15 to have a collector current of 1 mA with collector voltage of 5V. Given that transistor has $\beta$ = 50 and base to emitter drop $V_{BE}$ = 0.7 V.*

**Solution.** Given $\beta = 50$, $I_C = 1$ mA, $V_C = 5$V and $V_{BE} = 0.7$ V

The current $I_C$ is flowing through the resistor $R_C$ and is given as

$$I_C = \frac{15 - 5}{R_C}$$

or
$$R_C = \frac{10}{I_C}$$

at
$$I_C = 1 \text{ wA}$$

we get
$$R_C = 10 \text{ K}\Omega$$

we have
$$I_B = \frac{I_C}{\beta}$$

so at $I_C$ = 1 mA
$$I_B = \frac{1 \times 10^{-3}}{50}$$

or
$$I_B = 20 \ \mu\text{A}$$

again we have
$$V_{BE} = V_B - V_E$$

so
$$V_E = V_B - V_{BE} = 0 - 0.7 = -0.7 \text{ V}$$

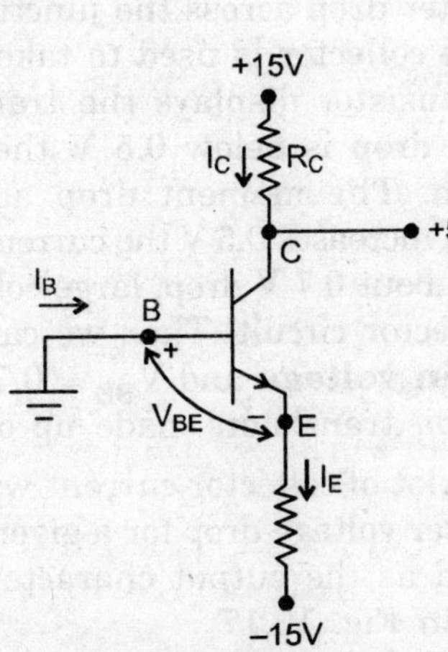


**Fig. 10.15** Circuit for example 10.2

*i.e.,* $V_E = -0.7$ V

we have $$\alpha = \frac{\beta}{\beta+1}$$

so at $\beta = 50,\ \alpha \cong 0.98$

we have $I_C = \alpha I_E$

or $$I_E = \frac{1\times10^{-3}}{0.98}$$

*i.e.,* $I_E \cong 1.02$ mA

The same value can also be calculated by

$$I_E = I_C + I_B$$
$$= 1 \text{ mA} + 20\ \mu\text{A}$$
$$= 1.02 \text{ mA}$$

emitter current $I_E$ can be given as

$$I_E = \frac{V_E - (-15)}{R_E}$$

or $$R_E = \frac{V_E + 15}{I_E}$$

$$= \frac{-0.7+15}{1.02\times10^{-3}}$$

finally $R_E \cong 14$ KΩ

#### 10.1.3.2 BJT Characteristic

The first characteristic we consider is the plot of collector current with respect to base to emitter drop across the junction. In CE configuration the base is used to supply the input and the collector is used to take the output. Thus the plot shown in Fig. 10.16 for a silicon npn transistor displays the transfer characteristics. As shown in figure when the base to emitter drop is below 0.5 V then there flow a small amount of current in the collector junction. The moment drop across base to emitter junction increases 0.5 V the current increases appreciably and at about 0.7 V drop, large collector current flows in the collector circuit. Thus we can regard $V_{BE}$ = 0.5 V as **cut-in voltage** and $V_{BE}$ = 0.7 V as **active voltage** for a *npn* transistors made up of silicon.

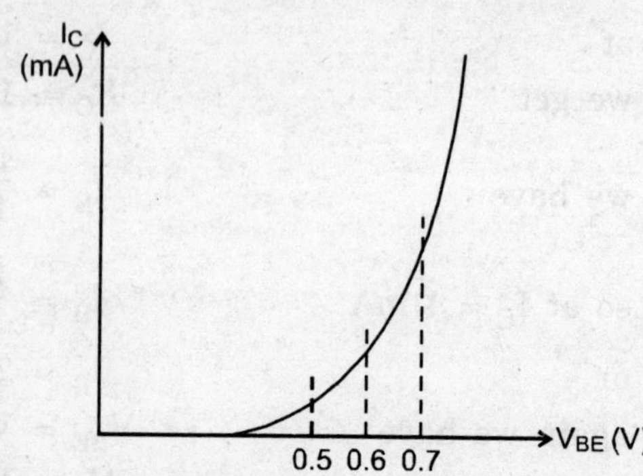


**Fig. 10.16** Transfer characteristics of CE configuration

A plot of collector current with respect to collector to emitter voltage drop for a given value of base current is called as the output characteristic of transistor, as shown in Fig. 10.17

The output characteristics can be divided into three regions. The active region, cut off region, and saturation region. The active region operation is what we discussed earlier to describe the operation. This region is used for amplification in which small change in base current results in larger current.

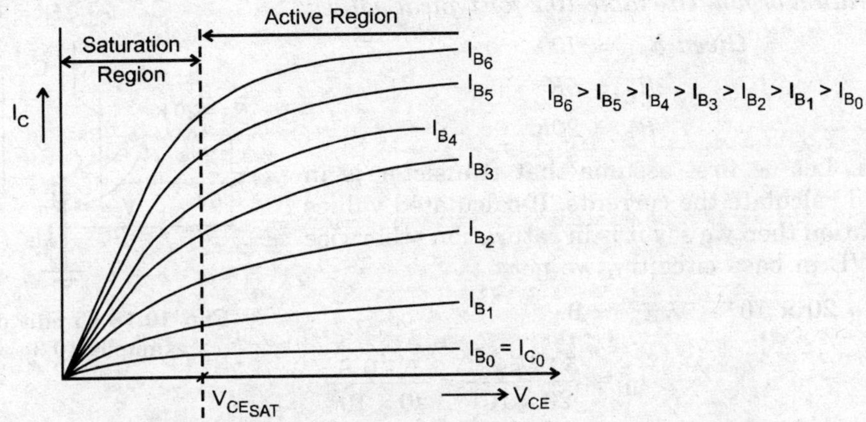


**Fig. 10.17** Output characteristics of CE configuration

In the saturation region both CBJ and EBJ are forward biased. Since the voltage across EBJ and CBJ are very small under forward biased, the collector to emitter voltage also is very small as

$$V_{CE} = V_{BE} - V_{BC} \quad ...(10.12)$$

In the saturation region the collector current does not change appreciably and can be considered that collector current is approximately independent of base current. In saturation region the collector current may be given as

$$I_{C_{sat}} = \frac{V_{CC} - V_{CEsat}}{R_C} \cong \frac{V_{CC}}{R_C} \quad ...(10.13(a))$$

because $V_{C_{sat}}$ is very small and is approximately 0.2 V for silicon *npn* transistor operating well into saturation. A good check of saturation operation is

$$\beta_{min}\ I_B \geq I_{C_{sat}}$$

alternately

$$h_{FEmin}\ I_B \geq I_{C_{sat}} \quad ...(10.13(b))$$

where $h_{FE}$ is just an alternate representation for current gain β.

The cut off region approached when both the CBJ and EBJ are reverse biased and no emitter current flows. Even though both the junctions are reverse biased there flows a small amount of current at CBJ called reverse saturation current $I_{CO}$. Thus to make $I_E$ = 0 $I_B = -I_{CO}$ as $I_C = I_{CO}$ at this time. Thus we can say that cut off is reached when $I_C = I_{CO}$, $I_B = -I_{CO}$, thus making $I_E = 0$ and $V_{BE}$ = OV for Si and $V_{BE} \cong -0.1$ V for Ge.

Table 10.2 may serve as reference to choose typical values for different mode of operation.

**Table 10.2 Typical npn transistor junction voltages at 25°C**

| *Semiconductor* | $V_{BE_{cut\ in}}$ $(V_\gamma)$ | $V_{BE_{ACTIVE}}$ | $V_{CE_{SAT}}$ | $V_{BE_{SAT}}$ | $V_{BE_{CUTOFF}}$ |
|---|---|---|---|---|---|
| Si | .5V | 0.7 | 0.2 | 0.8 | 0.0 |
| Ge | 0.1 | 0.2 | 0.1 | 0.3 | –0.1 |

**Example 10.3.** *For the circuit shown in figure 10.18 determine whether the silicon npn transistor with $h_{FE}$ = 100 is in saturation or not. Use table 10.2 for typical values.*

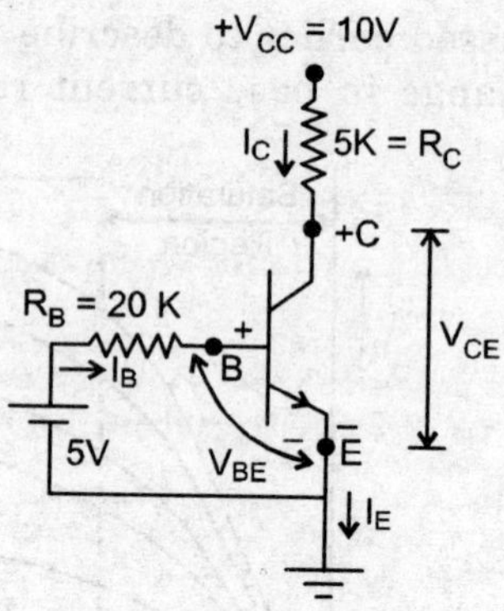


**Fig. 10.18** Circuit of example 10.3

$$\text{Given } h_{FE} = 100$$
$$R_C = 5K$$
$$R_B = 20K$$

**Solution.** Let us first assume that transistor is in saturation and calculate the currents. If calculated values confirm saturation then we say it is in saturation otherwise not. Apply KVL in base circuitry, we get

$$5 - I_B\, 20 \times 10^3 - V_{BEsat} = 0$$

so
$$I_B = \frac{5 - V_{BESAT}}{20 \times 10^3} = \frac{5 - 0.8}{20 \times 10^3}$$

or
$$I_{Bsat} = 0.21 \text{ mA} \qquad ...(1)$$

Applying KVL to output side, we get

$$V_{CC} - I_{Csat}R_C - V_{CEsat} = 0$$

or
$$I_{Csat} = \frac{V_{CC} - V_{CEsat}}{R_C} = \frac{10 - 0.2}{5 \times 10^3}$$

or
$$I_{Csat} = 1.96 \text{ mA} \qquad ...(2)$$

by equation 10.13(b) $h_{FE}I_B \geq I_C$ in saturation.

$$h_{FE}I_B = 100 \times 0.21 \times 10^{-31} = 21 \times 10^{-3}$$

Since $h_{FE}I_B$ ($21 \times 10^{-3}$) is greater than $I_{Csat}$, the transistor is in saturation region.

### *10.1.3.3 Transistor as a Switch*

To understand the switching characteristics let us consider the transistor as inverter as shown in Fig. 10.19, along with input voltage.

Consider the input for time $t < t_1$. Waveform shows that both EBJ and CBJ are reverse biased as $V_{in} = -V_2$.

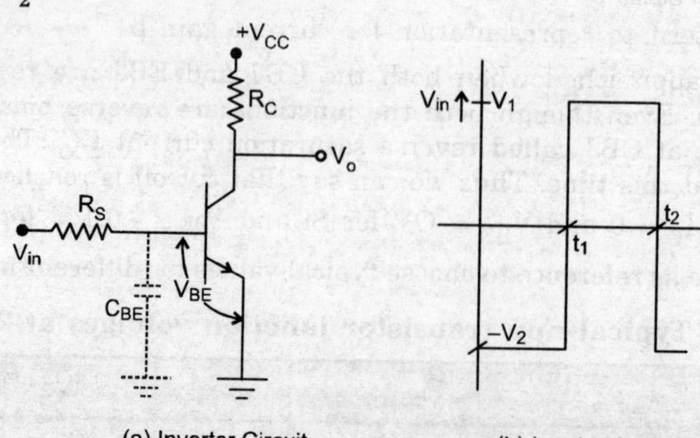


**Fig. 10.19** *npn* transistor as inverter

At this moment almost all the supply voltage $+V_{CC}$ appear at output and no collector current flows in circuit. This is shown in Fig. 10.20 for $t < t_1$. This represents the transistor in OFF state. Note that at this moment transition capacitance $C_{BE}$ is charged to $-V_2$. The moment input changes instantaneously to $V_1$ the transistor cannot change its state instantaneously. The capacitance $C_{BE}$ starts charging towards $V_1$ (from $-V_2$). The moment $V_{BE} > V_\gamma$ transistor starts conducting after sometimes it enters into saturation. This is shown in figure 10.20 for $t > t_1$. Here the **delay time** ($t_d$) is the time taken by collector current to rise to 10% of $I_{C_{sat}}$ from O. Also shown is **rise time** ($t_r$) is time taken by collector current to reach to 90% $I_{C_{sat}}$ from 10% of $I_{C_{sat}}$. Sum of delay time and rise time is referred as **ON time** ($t_{ON}$) of the transistor. *i.e.*,

$$t_{ON} = t_d + t_r$$

Note that during this time the collector voltage will be reduced to $V_{CEsat}$ from $V_{CC}$, as shown in figure.

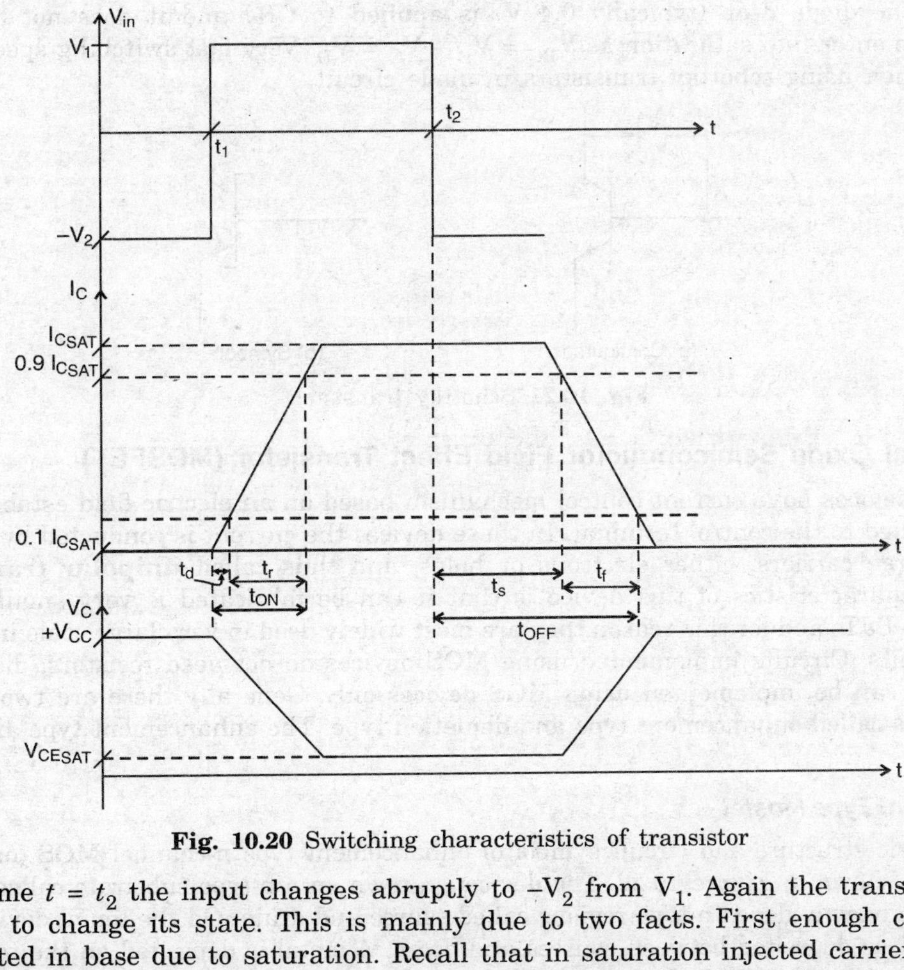


**Fig. 10.20** Switching characteristics of transistor

At time $t = t_2$ the input changes abruptly to $-V_2$ from $V_1$. Again the transistor takes sometime to change its state. This is mainly due to two facts. First enough charges are accumulated in base due to saturation. Recall that in saturation injected carriers may not all be swept across CBJ. It takes sometime to remove these carriers. Second, even before the input goes below cut off many charge carriers are already injected. These two facts give rise to delay to switching effect. Thus, after certain time transistor becomes OFF and collector voltage rises to $+V_{CC}$. As shown in figure 10.20 **storage time ($t_s$)** is the time taken by collector current to reduce to 90% of $I_{C_{sat}}$ after the input has change its state from positive to negative value. **Fall time ($t_f$)** is the time taken by collector to reduce to 10% of $I_{C_{sat}}$ from 90% of $I_{C_{sat}}$. Sum of storage time and fall time is defined as **OFF time ($t_{OFF}$)** of the transistor *i.e.*,

$$t_{OFF} = t_S + t_f$$

From the figure, it is clear that OFF time is larger than the ON time. This is mainly due to the storage time, which is significant due to the saturation region, operation.

#### *10.1.3.4 Schottky Transistor*

In previous subsection, we pointed out that main victim of switching delay of a transistor. If we connect a schottky diode between base and collector as shown in Figure 10.21(a), then transistor can be prevented to enter into saturation region. When the transistor is in active region the diode is in reverse bias. When the transistor goes to saturation, the diode conducts. The diode drop (typically 0.4 V) is applied to CBJ and it does not allow the transistor to enter into saturation as $V_{BC} = V_B - V_C = V_D$. Very fast switching speed can be obtained when using schottky transistors in diode circuit.

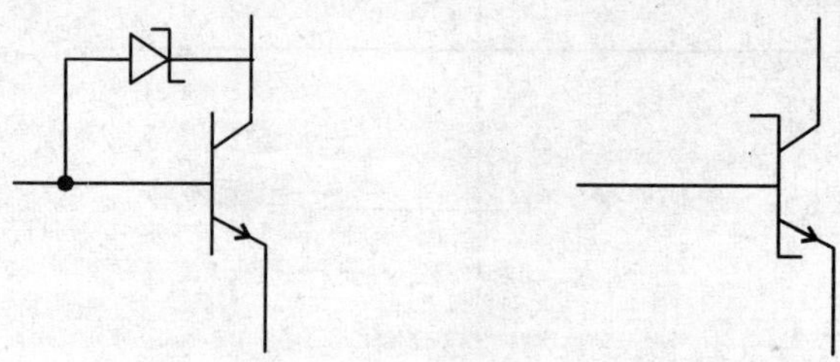

(a) Configuration (b) Symbol

**Fig. 10.21** Schottky transistor

### 10.1.4 Metal Oxide Semiconductor Field Effect Transistor (MOSFET)

These devices have current control mechanism based on an electric field established by voltage applied to the control terminal. In these devices the current is conducted by only one type of charge carriers, either electrons or holes, and thus called **unipolar transistors.** Important characteristics of this device is that it can be fabricated is very small area as compared to BJTs and for this reason they are most widely used in very large scale integrated (VLSI) circuits. Circuits implemented using MOS devices do not need resistors, diodes, etc. rather they can be implemented using MOS devices only. Generally there are two types of MOS devices called enhancement type and depletion type. The enhancement type are widely used.

#### *Enhancement Type Mosfet*

The basic structure and circuit symbol of enhancement type n-channel MOS (or NMOS) transistor is shown in Figure 10.22. The device is grown on a p-type substrate called body. It contains two heavily doped n-type regions called source and drain. On the top of device a thin layer of $SiO_2$ is deposited between sources and drain. A metal is deposited on the top of this layer and the terminal taken from it is called gate. Due to the thin layer of $SiO_2$ there exist a small current in gate terminal. It is evident from figure substrate forms two PN junctions with source and drain. In normal operation they are kept reverse biased by connecting the body and source terminal to the ground. Thus, the substrate have no effect on operation as it is always shorted with source and device becomes three terminal device. When proper voltages are applied the current flows between source and drain through the region labelled channel which is of length L. When no voltage applied no current flow through channel.

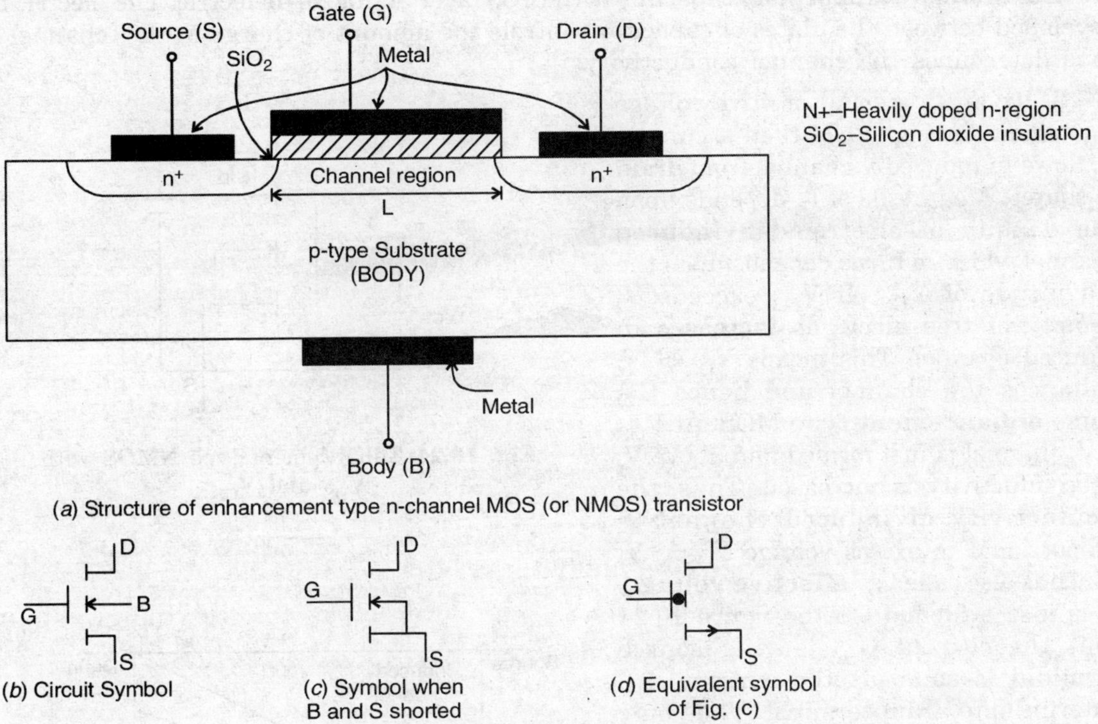


**Fig. 10.22** Enhancement type NMOS

Let the gate is connected to positive voltage as shown in Fig. 10.23, with source and drain grounded. The positive voltage at gate causes the free holes to be repelled from the

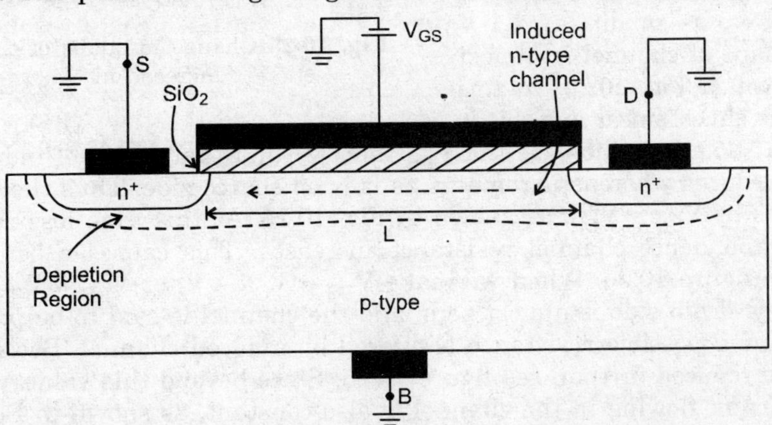


**Fig. 10.23** Enhancement type NMOS with positive voltage at gate

channel region and thus leaving behind a carrier depletion region, as shown in Fig. 10.23. At the same time positive gate voltage attracts electrons from $n^+$ regions into channel region. When sufficient number of electrons is accumulated in the channel region, it creates an *n*-region connecting drain and source. This is called induced *n*-type channel. When a voltage is applied at drain the current can flow through this region. The value of $V_{GS}$ at which the *n*-channel is induced is called as **threshold voltage ($V_t$).** The gate and body of MOSFET form a parallel plate capacitor with $SiO_2$ layer acting as dielectric. The electric field developed between the plates of capacitor controls the amount of charge in the channel and thus determines the channel conductivity.

If we apply a small positive voltage $V_{DS}$ shown in Fig. 10.24 then a current $I_D$ flows in induced *n*-channel from drain to source. Magnitude of $I_D$ depends upon the density of electrons in induced channel which in turns depends upon the magnitude of $V_{GS}$. If $V_{GS}$ exceeds $V_t$ density of free electrons increases in induced channel. This means $V_{GS} > V_t$ enhances the channel and hence the name **enhancement type** MOS. At $V_{GS} = V_t$ channel is just formed and above $V_t$ its conductivity is increased. Thus, the conductivity of induced channel is proportional to excess voltage $V_{GS} - V_t$ which is also called as **effective voltage.** It is also evident from the figure 10.24 that the current ($I_S$) leaving source terminal is same as the current ($I_D$) entering into drain terminal. Thus only electrons contribute the current in the channel and the device is called **unipolar.** In essence, the voltage $V_{DS}$ appears as drop across the length of channel. When $V_{DS}$ is small, say 0.1 V or 0.2V then shape of channel is almost uniform as shown in Fig. 10.25. In this case $I_D$ Vs $V_{DS}$ is almost linear and this is shown in Fig. 10.26. If we increase the $V_{DS}$ then we find that width of induced channel on the drain side reduces whereas it remains as it is on source side. Thus the voltage at drain end also reduces by $V_{GS} - V_{DS}$, as shown in Fig. 10.25. At this time less room is available for conduction and hence channel resistance increases. This causes a bend in $I_D$ Vs $V_{DS}$ curve, shown in figure 10.26. When we make $V_{DS} = V_{GS} - V_t$ or $V_{DS} - V_{GS} = V_t$ the width of channel on the drain side is almost zero, and the channel is said to be **pinched OFF.** At this time maximum possible resistance is offered by induced channel. Because the channel width cannot be reduced further, see figure 10.25. Since beyond this value $V_{DS}$ resistance is constant the current flowing in the channel is also constant, as shown in Figure 10.26. The value of $V_{DS}$ beyond which constant current flows into the channel is referred $V_{DS_{SAT}}$. The drain to source voltage at which the pinch off occurs when $V_{GS} = 0$, is called as **pinch off voltage ($V_{PO}$).**

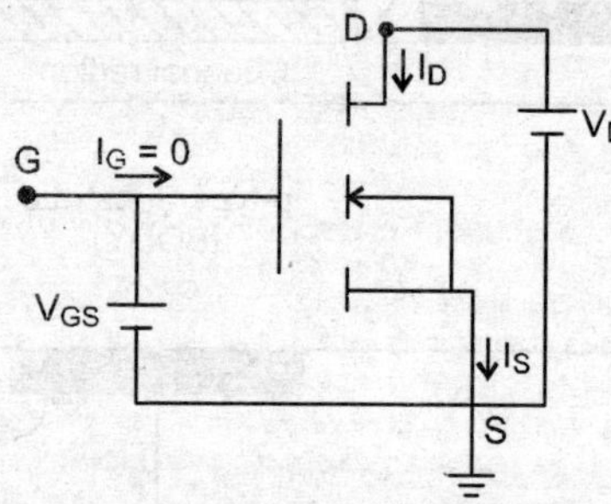


**Fig. 10.24** Enhancement type NMOS with $V_{DS}$ and $V_{GS}$

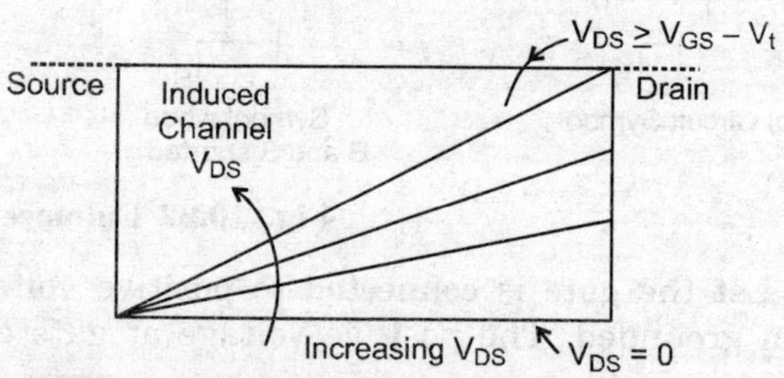


**Fig. 10.25** Change in shape of channel with increase in $V_{DS}$

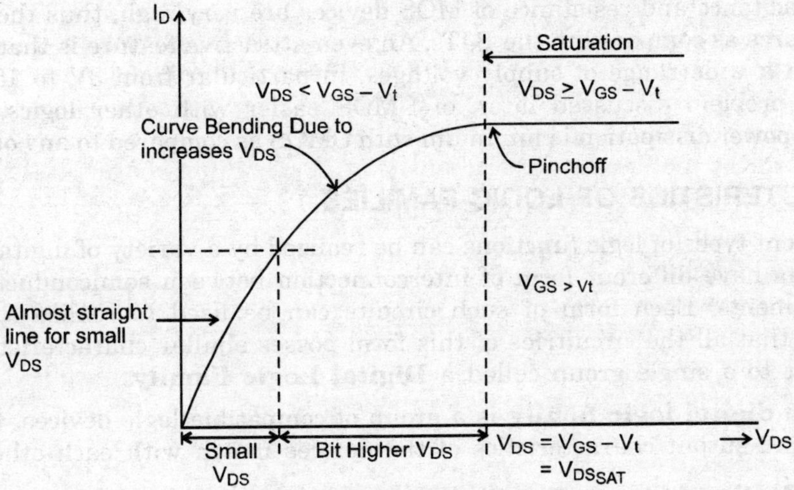


**Fig. 10.26** $I_P$ $V_S$ $V_{DS}$

The **P-channel enhancement type MOSFET** is formed by using *n*-type substrate and $p^+$ type source and drain. In case of PMOS the induced channel is *p*-type region. The circuit symbols of PMOS are shown below.

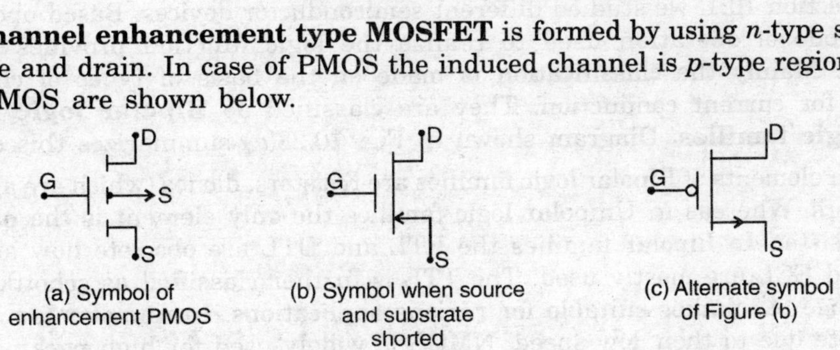


**Fig. 10.27** Circuit symbols of enhancement PMOS

Note that in NMOS current flows due to electrons and in PMOS due to holes. Since mobility of electrons is higher than holes, thus NMOS is faster than PMOS. Since mobility of electrons is 3 time greater than holes PMOS devices needs 3 times large area to generate the same amount of current that of NMOS. Thus packing density of NMOS is greater than that of PMOS.

### 10.1.5 The Complementary MOS (CMOS)

The most widely appreciated MOS technology is COMPLEMENTARY MOS or CMOS technology. As the name implies the CMOS technology uses both PMOS and NMOS transistors. At present time the CMOS has replaced almost all the NMOs circuit designs. For the fabrication the two transistors are grown on same p-type substrate and their drain are separated by deposition $SiO_2$. An *n*-type well is created in the *p*-type substrate to facilitate PMOS its packing density is bit lower than NMOS. But in terms of power dissipation the CMOS performance is dramatically improved. This gives enough motivation for CMOS to be used as powerful circuit designing tool.

Before we end the discussions an MOS devices we state few more properties for which they superceeds the BJT. For the fabrication point of view, the chip area required by a MOS transistor is just about 5% of that required by BJTs, making high packing density of MOS.

The input capacitance and resistance of MOS devices are very high, thus they can be easily driven by a source as compared to the BJTs. An even attractive feature is that CMOS devices can operate on a wide range of supply voltages, in particular from 3V to 15V. This makes interfacing, a problem discussed later, of CMOS easier with other logics. An as earlier mentioned the power dissipation is minimum with CMOS as compared to any other technology.

## 10.2 CHARACTERISTICS OF LOGIC FAMILIES

The different types of logic functions can be realized by a variety of digital circuits. Each of these circuits have different form of interconnection between semiconductor devices and the circuit elements. Each form of such circuits can be used to realise a different logic function, such that all the circuitries of this form posses similar characteristics. Thus, they can be brought to a single group called a **Digital Logic Family.**

In short, a **digital logic family** is a group of compatible logic devices. **Compatibility** means input and output characteristics of the devices match with each other.

### 10.2.1 Classification of Logic Families

In the Section 10.1, we studied different semiconductor devices. Based upon the devices and their mode of operation used to realize the logic function provides the basis for classification. Mainly the classification is made on the basis of types of charge carriers contributing for current conduction. They are classified as **Bipolar logic families** and **Unipolar logic families.** Diagram shown in Fig. 10.28(*a*) summarizes this classification.

The main elements of Bipolar logic families are resistors, diodes (which are also capacitors) and transistors. Whereas in Unipolar logic families the only element is the particular type of MOS transistor. In Bipolar families the RTL and DTL are obselete now and in present time TTL and ECL are mostly used. The TTL is further classified as schottky TTL giving attractive range of families suitable for various applications. In unipolar families PMOS is totally obselete due to their low speed. NMOS is widely used for high packing density and complicated logic devices, like memories and microprocessors. CMOS is an attractive choice for the fabrication of low power consumption devices like calculators but they have a bit slower speed.

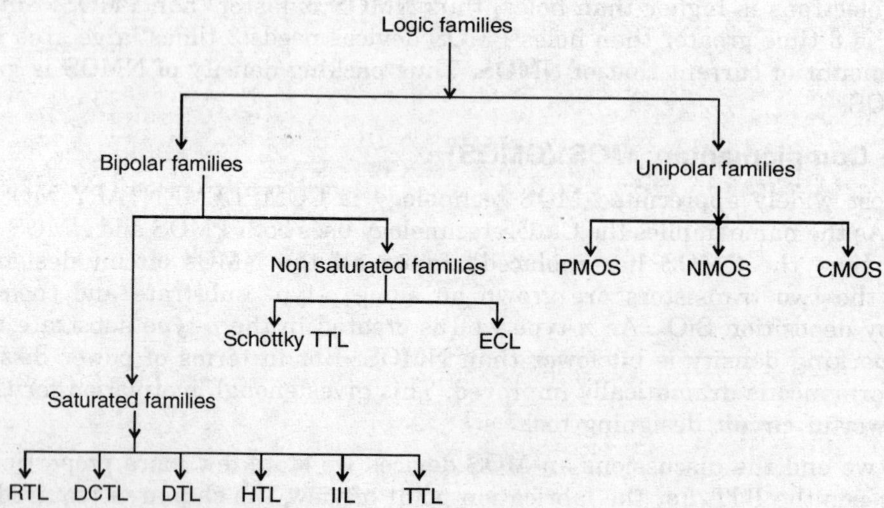


**Fig. 10.28** (*a*) Classification of logic families

Yet another classification of digital ICs can be made on the basis of level of integration of logic gates in a single IC. This is shown in table 10.3.

**Table 10.3 Classification of digital ICs based on level of integration**

| *Integration Scale* | *Number of Gates Fabricated* |
|---|---|
| SSI – Small Scale Integration | Less than 12 gates |
| MSI – Medium Scale Integration | 12 < Gates ≤ 100 |
| LSI – Large Scale Integration | 100 < Gates ≤ 1000 |
| VLSI – Very Large Scale Integration | 1000 < Gates ≤ 10,000 |
| ULSI – Ultra Large Scale Integration | Gates > 10,000 |

## 10.2.2 Characteristics of Digital ICs and Families

Emergence of various logic families and integration techniques have resulted in widespread use of digital ICs. It is thus necessary to study different performance parameters and characteristics of logic families. They adequately reflects their relative advantages and disadvantages and may serve as a basis to choose a particular family for the application. In fact our study and analysis of different families will be around these parameters only.

- **Propagation Delay** is the maximum time taken by output to change its state in response to input. The propagation delay determines the speed of operation of a gate. In general switching speed is measured when 50% duty cycle time square wave is applied at a input and a square wave is generated at output, as shown in Fig. 10.28. The times are measured from 50% of voltage levels. The time $t_{PHL}$ is delay when output goes LOW from HIGH and $t_{PLH}$ is the time delay taken by output to go HIGH from LOW state. The propagation delay $t_p$ is average of the two times and measured in *n* sec.

$$t_p = \frac{t_{PHL} + t_{PLH}}{2} = \text{Propagation Delay } (n \text{ sec})$$

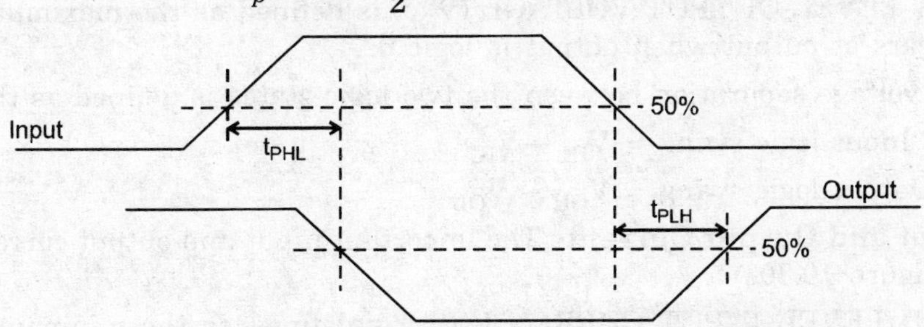


**Fig. 10.28** (*b*) Input-output waveforms for propagation delay

- **Power Dissipation ($P_D$)** is defined as the power dissipated in an IC and measured in mW. It is desired to have low power dissipation to reduce cooling, but it may increase the propagation delays.
- **Speed Power Product** is defined as the product of propagation delay (in nano seconds) and power dissipation (in mW) and is measured in pico joules. It is also referred as the figure of merit of a digital IC.

$$\text{figure of merit} = \text{Propagation delay} \times \text{Power dissipation}$$
$$= t_p \times P_D = n \text{ sec} \times \text{mW}$$
$$= p\text{J}$$

- **Fan In** is defined as the number inputs that a logic gate can have
- **Fan Out** is defined as number of similar gates that a logic gate can drive. High fan out is desirable.
- **Input and Output Voltages** various input and output voltage levels are shown in figure 10.29.

  HIGH LEVEL INPUT VOLTAGE ($V_{IH}$) is defined as the minimum input voltage recognized as logic 1.

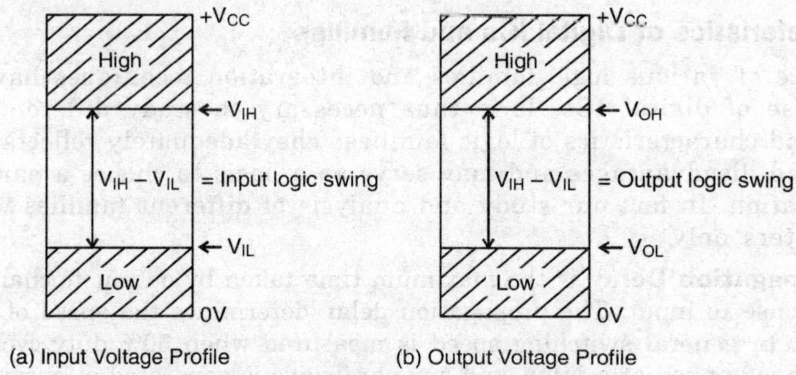


**Fig. 10.29** Illustration of voltage profiles

LOW LEVEL INPUT VOLTAGE ($V_{IL}$) is defined as maximum value of input voltage recognized as logic 0.

HIGH LEVEL OUTPUT VOLTAGE ($V_{OH}$) is defined as the minimum value of output voltage when output is logic 1.

LOW LEVEL OUTPUT VOLTAGE ($V_{OL}$) is defined as the maximum voltage that appears at output when output is logic 0.

The voltage separation between the two logic states is defined as the *logic swing.*

$$\text{Input logic swing} = V_{IH} - V_{IL}$$
$$\text{Output logic swing} = V_{OH} - V_{OL}$$

- **Input and Output Currents** The important input and output currents are shown in Figure 10.30.

  HIGH LEVEL INPUT CURRENT ($I_{IH}$) is defined as the minimum current that must be supplied to a gate corresponding to logic 1 input.

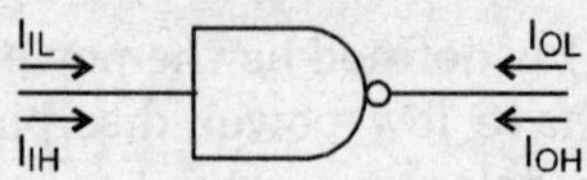


**Fig. 10.30** Illustration of currents in a gate

LOW LEVEL INPUT CURRENT ($I_{IL}$) is defined as the minimum current that must be supplied to the gate corresponding to logic 0 input.

HIGH LEVEL OUTPUT CURRENT ($I_{OH}$) is defined as the maximum amount of current that a gate can sink when output is logic 1.

LOW LEVEL OUTPUT CURRENT ($I_{OL}$) is defined as the maximum amount of current that a gate can sink when output is logic 0.

Why we have shown the output currents as sink current will be clear when discussing the circuits of various families.

- **Supply Currents** it is important to consider the current drawn in LOW and HIGH state.

  HIGH STATE SUPPLY CURRENT ($I_{CC}(1)$) is the current drawn from supply when output of gate is logic 1.

  LOW STATE SUPPLY CURRENT ($I_{CC}(O)$) is the current drawn from supply when output of gate is logic O.

  We can calculate average power dissipation by calculating the dissipation in two states.

  The low state power dissipation $P(O) = V_{CC}.I_{CC}(0)$

  The high state power dissipation $P(1) = V_{CC}.\ I_{CC}(1)$

  The average power dissipation $P_{avg} = \dfrac{P(1) + P(0)}{2}$

  This is how we will calculate the power dissipation of various families in next sections.

- **Noise Margin** Unwanted electric signals, called noise, can appear when connecting the logic devices. These noise signals can cause the voltage levels to rise or reduce from intended value. This may cause circuit malfunction. For example, if noise causes an input voltage to reduce below the $V_{1H}$, then input is not recognized as logic 1 and thus the circuit malfunctions. The ability of a circuit to tolerate the effect of noise is called as **noise immunity.** The amount by which a circuit can tolerate the effect of noise is called **noise margin.** The noise margins are illustrated in Fig. 10.31. Margins shown in the figure are called **dc noise margin,** they are

$$\Delta 1 = V_{OH} - V_{1H} = \text{High state noise margin}$$

$$\Delta O = V_{IL} - V_{OL} = \text{Low state noise margin}$$

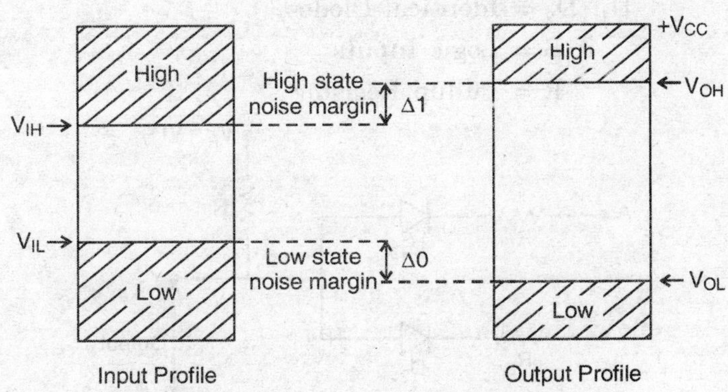


**Fig. 10.31** Illustration of noise margins

In fact noise is a random signal, considered as ac signal with some amplitude and pulse width. If the pulse width is large compared to propagation delay they can be treated as dc. If the pulse width is less than propagation delay, then pulse width is not enough to change the state of circuit. In this situation, the noise pulse amplitude must be large enough to change the state of circuit. Thus, the logic circuits have high **ac noise margins.** It is specified in data sheet in form of a curve of noise margin vs noise pulse width.

- **Operating Temperature** is the range of temperature in which the digital IC can function properly. In general 0 to +70°C is the range for consumers and industrial applications. A range of –55°C to 125°C is accepted for military applications.

## 10.3 IMPLEMENTATION OF LOGIC FAMILIES

So far we have studied the switching characteristics of semiconductor switching devices and logic families. We now turn our attention to the implementation of gates of different families. Here we start with the basic diode logic then move to various families of BJTs and then to MOS family which are most important for fabrication of ICs.

### 10.3.1 Basic Diode Logic

To start with diode logic let us first define the two voltage levels corresponding to two logic levels.

Let $V(1)$ = Voltage corresponding to logic 1 = $+V_{CC}$

$V(0)$ = Voltage corresponding to logic 0 = Gnd or OV

Let all the diodes are silicon diode and have the drop of 0.7 V when in conduction. In all the cases we measure the output voltage with respect to ground, assuming that forward resistance of diode ($R_f$) is very small.

#### *DIODE AND GATE*

A two terminal diode AND gate is shown in Fig. 10.32 and we assume that the resistance $R >> R_S$ so that drop across $R_S$ can be neglected in calculation.

$V_R$ = Reference Voltage

$R_S$ = Source Resistance

Y = Output of Gate

$D_1$, $D_2$ = Identical Diodes

$A_1B$ = Logic Inputs

R = Pullup Resistor

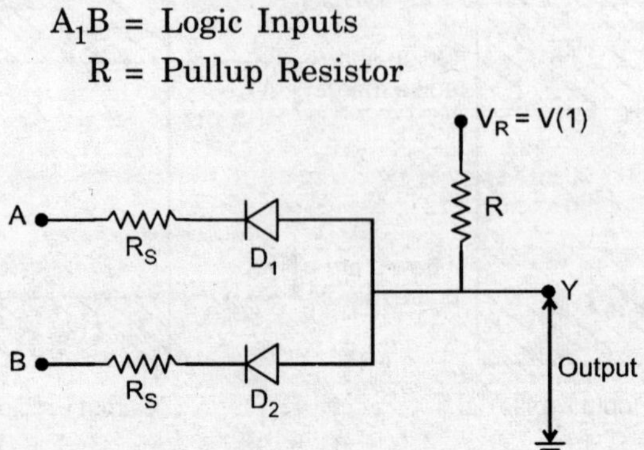


**Fig. 10.32** Diode and gate

Resistor R is called pull up resistor because in some sense it pulls the output from logic low to logic high.

As evident from the circuit, status of inputs A and B will make the diode conducting (ON) or non conducting (OFF). For simplicity let us first consider that–both the inputs are at logic 1 *i.e.*, **A = B = V(1).** We get Figure 10.32 reduced as in Fig. 10.33(*a*).

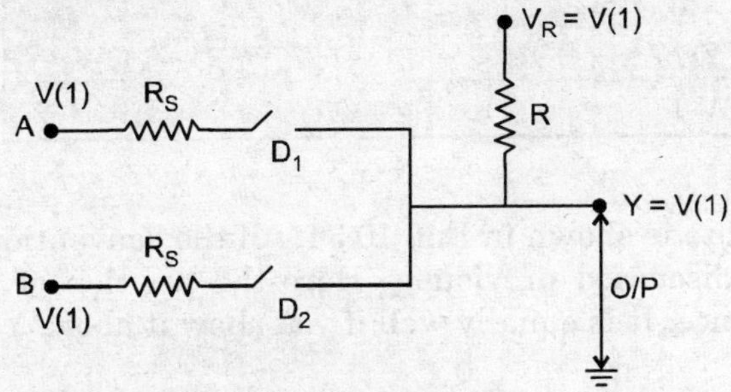


**Fig. 10.33** (*a*) And Gate of Fig. 10.32 at A = B = V(1)

Both the diodes are reverse biased and represents open circuit as shown. Since, there is no path for current flow through resistor it will not have any drop across it and $V_R$ = V(1) appears at output. This is obvious because when all inputs to the AND gate are high then output is high. Thus

when A = B = V(1) Y = V(1)

**when A = V(1) and B = V(0),** the diode $D_2$ conducts and $D_1$ remains in OFF condition. The equivalent circuit in this case is shown below in Fig. 10.33(*b*).

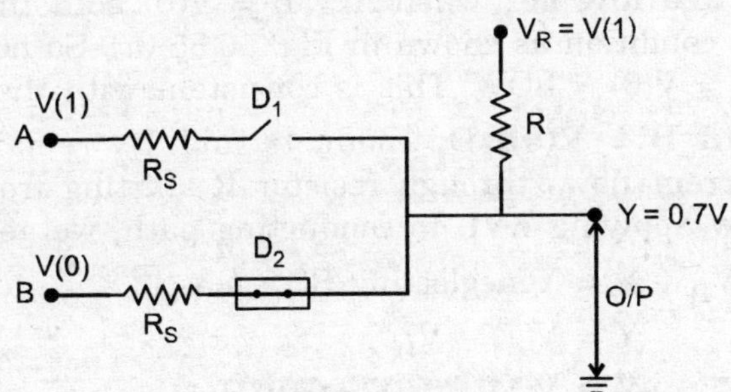


**Fig. 10.33** (*b*) And Gate of Fig. 10.32 at A = V(1) and B = V(0)

Since a current flows through R, through diode $D_2$ towards ground (V(0)), we get drop across diode $D_2$ at output so when A = V(1) and B = V(0) Y = $V_0$ = 0.7 V = LOW which confirms that if any of the input of AND gate goes low output goes low.

**When A = V(0) and B = V(1).** In this case $D_1$ conducts and $D_2$ goes OFF and output again becomes the drop across diode *i.e.*, Y = 0.7 V.

**When A = V(0) and B = V(0)** In this case both $D_1$ and $D_2$ conducts having a drop of 0.7 V. Again this drop appears at output. So the output Y = 0.7 V. All these value of outputs along with logic state is summarized in table 10.4 which confirms AND gate. Note that we define 0.7 V as logic low at the output whereas 0 V as logic low at the input. For logic 1 voltages at input output are same.

**Table 10.4 Input/output table of and gate of figure 10.32**

| *Inputs* | | *Output* | |
|---|---|---|---|
| *A* | *B* | *Y* | *Logic State* |
| V(0) | V(0) | 0.7 V | LOW |
| V(0) | V(1) | 0.7 V | LOW |
| V(1) | V(0) | 0.7 V | LOW |
| V(1) | V(1) | V(1) | HIGH |

## Diode OR Gate

A two terminal OR Gate is shown in Fig. 10.34. All the conventions and assumptions are same as Diode and gate discussed previously. Here the position of $V_R$ is shown below the output Y, just for convenience. It is equally well if you show it above Y with same connections.

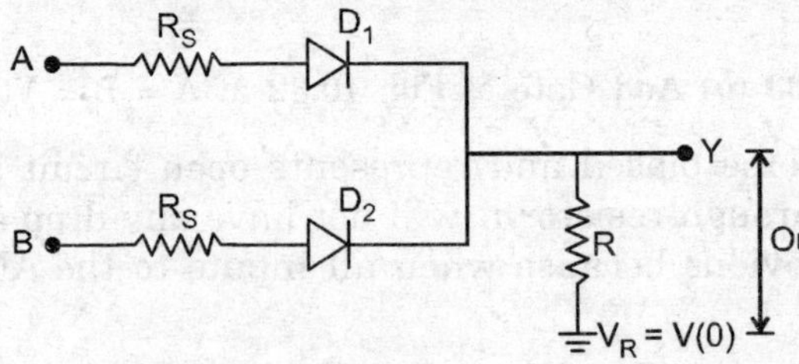


**Fig. 10.34** Two terminal diode or gate

As evident from figure the drop across resistor R will be the output voltage.

**When both inputs are low** *i.e.,* when A = B = V(0) both the diodes are OFF and represents switch in open condition as shown in Fig. 10.35 (*a*). So no current flows through R and the output Y = $V_R$ = V(0) = LOW. This is consistent with the definition of OR gate.

**When A = V(1) and B = V(0),** $D_1$ conducts and $D_2$ remains OFF as shown in Fig. 10.35(*b*). Thus, a current flows through resistor R starting from input A through $D_1$ through R to ground. Now applying KVL to conducting path, we get

$$V(1) - V_D - Y = Y \text{ neglecting RS}$$

So
$$Y = V(1) - V_D$$

or
$$Y = V(1) - 0.7V = \text{HIGH}$$

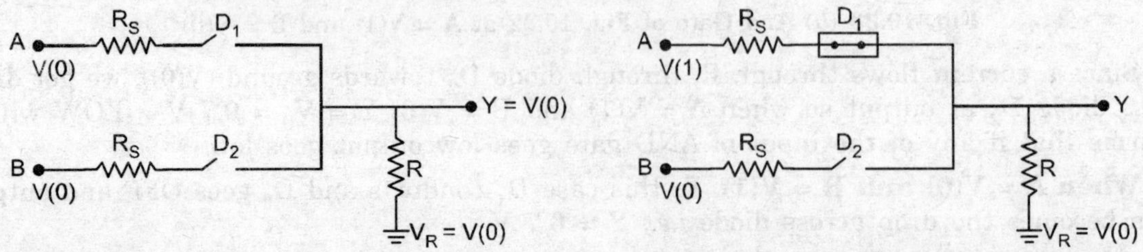


**Fig. 10.35** (*a*) Diode or Gate with A = B = V(0)

**Fig. 10.35** (*b*) Diode or Gate with A = V(1) and B = V(0)

In digital circuits we take V(1) = 5 V generally, so saying Y = V(1) – 0.7 V means Y = 4.3 V which is good enough to regard as HIGH output.

Similar situation occurs when A = V(0) and B = V(1) and when A = V(1) and B = V(1).

Thus, the gate shown in Fig. 10.34 behaves as OR gate. Readers are advised to find out the input/output table for this gate by taking V(1) = 5V.

### 10.3.2 Resistor Transistor Logic (RTL)

The RTL family is now-a-days historical but its study and analysis can give good understanding and enough motivation for the other logic families. The Basic RTL gate is a NOR gate as shown in Fig. 10.36. For the logic operation, we first assume that logic low input is sufficient to switch off the transistor and logic high is sufficient to switch ON the transistor.

**When both the inputs are high** *i.e.,* A = B = V(1), both $Q_1$ and $Q_2$ goes to ON state *i.e.,* both enters into saturation. Thus the voltage at collectors is nothing but $V_{CEsat}$. So output Y = $V_{CEsat}$. Hence, when

A = B = V(1) $\quad Y = V_{CEsat} = 0.2$ V

$\cong$ V(0) = LOW

**When both the inputs are low** *i.e.,* A = B = V(0), both $Q_1$ and $Q_2$ goes to OFF state. Thus no current flow through $R_C$ and drop across $R_C$ is zero. So whole $+V_{CC}$ will appear at output *i.e.,* Y = $+V_{CC}$ = 3.6 V = HIGH.

Thus when $\quad$ A = B = V(0) $\;$ Y = $+V_{CC}$ = HIGH

**When only one input goes high** *i.e.,* A = V (1) and B = V(0) or when A = V(0) and B = V(1), the transistor feeded with high input conducts causing a current to flow through ON transistor. Consequently the transistor enters into saturation. Thus the output voltage becomes $V_{CEsat}$. So,

when $\quad$ A = V(1) B = V(0) $\quad$ Y = $V_{CEsat}$ = LOW

A = V(0) B = V(1) $\quad$ Y = $V_{CEsat}$ = LOW

From the above discussion it is clear that output of circuit shown in Fig. 10.36 represents a NOR gate. It is because when all the inputs are low, only then output is high otherwise the output is low.

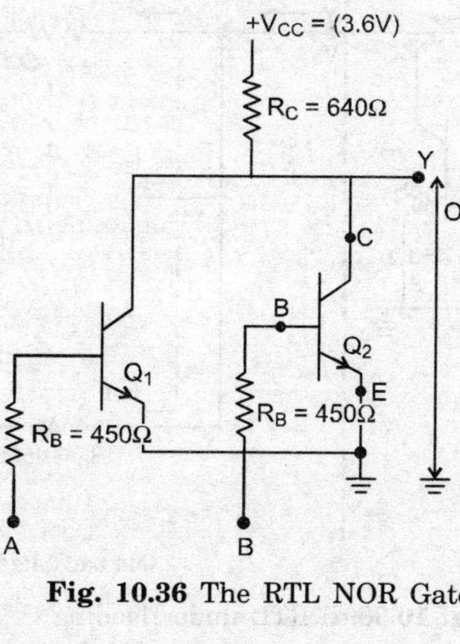


**Fig. 10.36** The RTL NOR Gate

To find out the FAN OUT, NOISE MARGINs etc. let us consider the loading of RTL gate as shown in Fig. 10.37. For the ease of analysis we connect the input B of all the load gates are connected to logic LOW and all the A inputs connected to the output of Driver gate.

Note that all the load gates and the driver gate are identical with all the parameter assumed same.

Since all the B inputs are low, transistor $Q_2$ (of Fig. 10.36) represents switch in open condition. So transistor $Q_2$ may not be drawn in this condition as shown in Fig. 10.38(*a*). To understand the idea let us consider an example.

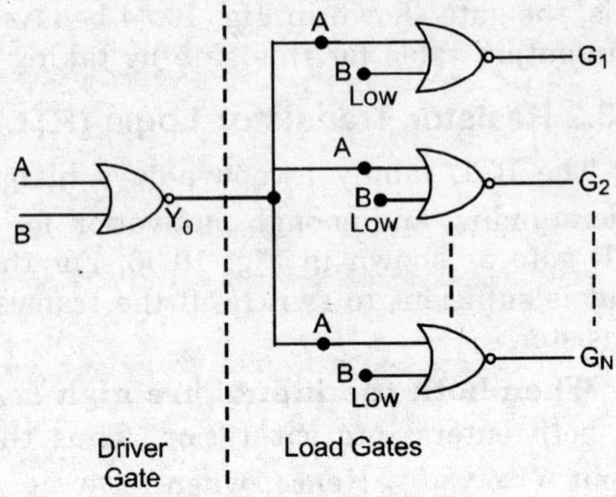


**Fig. 10.37** An RTL gate driving N-Load gates

**Example 10.4.** *Find out the Noise margin and Fan out of the RTL NOR gate shown in Figure 10.38(a). Given the transistors have* $h_{FE} = 7$.

**Solution.** To begin with we take the assumptions and connection explained for Figure 10.37.

To find out FAN OUT let both the inputs of Driver gate are low *i.e.,* A = B = V(0). Then both the $Q_1$ and $Q_2$ goes to cut off and output of driver goes HIGH. Thus all the load gates are driven by this HIGH output and consequently all the load transistors are driven into saturation. In this situation a current $I_{BT}$ will be drawn from the $+V_{CC}$ of driver side, as shown in Fig. 10.38(a). Since all load transistors are identical, they will draw equal amount of base current. Thus,

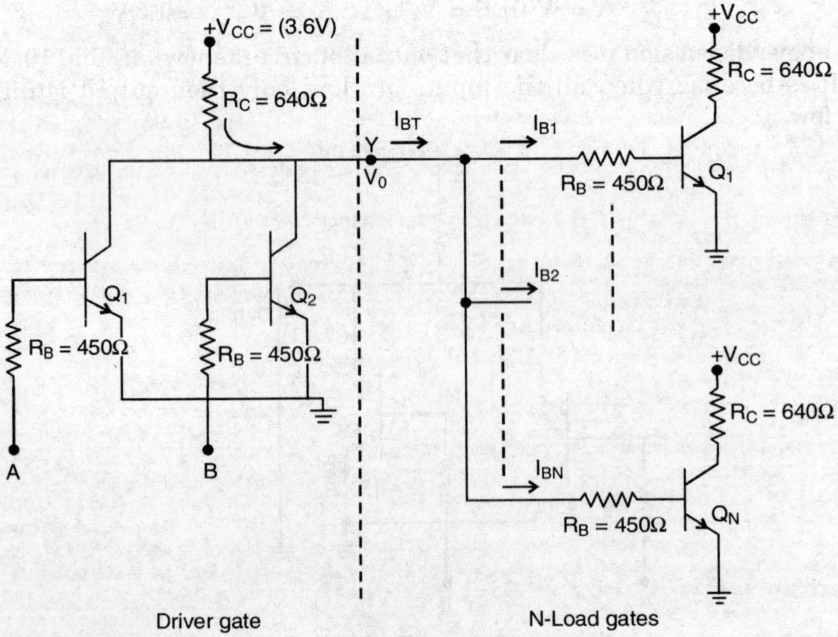


**Fig. 10.38**(*a*) RTL under loading

$$I_{BT} = I_{B1} + I_{B2} + \ldots\ldots + I_{BN}$$

and since $$I_{B1} = I_{B2} \ldots\ldots = I_{BN}$$

we get $$I_{BT} = N.I_{B1}$$

or $$I_{B1} = \frac{I_{BT}}{N} \qquad ...(10.14)$$

When a load transistor is driven into saturation it can be represented as shown in Fig. 10.38(*b*).

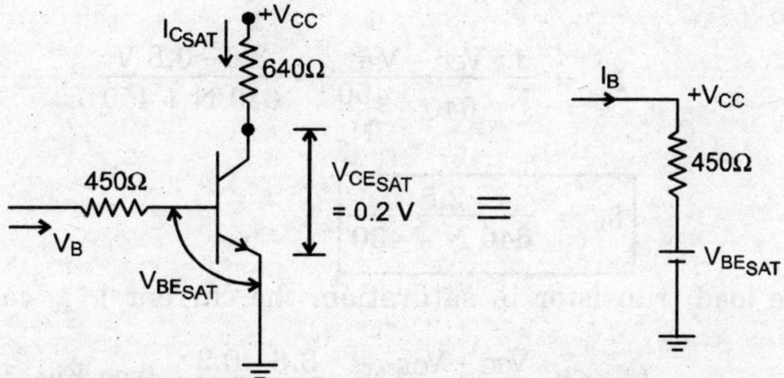


**Fig. 10.38**(*b*) Equivalent representation of transistor in saturation

Similarly if all the load transistors are in saturation we get equivalent figure as shown in Fig. 10.38(*c*).

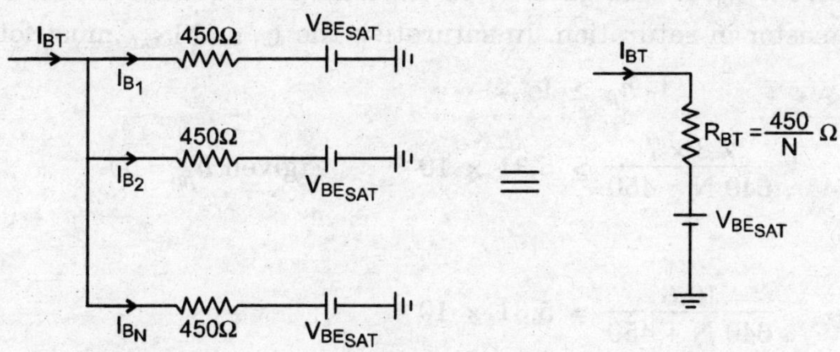


**Fig. 10.38**(*c*) Equivalent circuit for N-load gates in saturation.

Thus we can redraw the Fig. 10.38(*a*) when both A and B inputs of driver gates are low, as shown in Fig. 10.38(*d*).

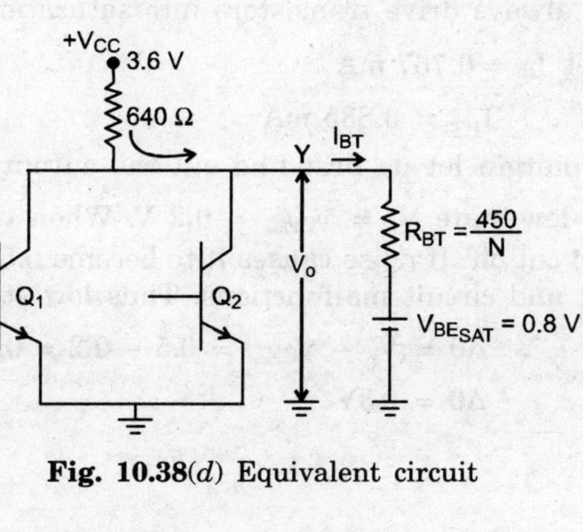


**Fig. 10.38**(*d*) Equivalent circuit

Thus the current $I_{BT}$ can be calculated as

$$I_{BT} = \frac{V_{CC} - V_{BE_{sat}}}{640 + \frac{450}{N}}$$

Now by using equation (10.14) base current to individual transistor can be given as

$$I_{B1} = \frac{I_{BT}}{N}$$

So $$I_{B_1} = \frac{1}{N} \cdot \frac{V_{CC} - V_{BE_{sat}}}{640 + \frac{450}{N}} = \frac{3.6 - 0.8\ V}{640\ N + 450}$$

or $$\boxed{I_{B_1} = \frac{2.8}{640\ N + 450}} \qquad \text{...(10.15)}$$

For each of the load transistor in saturation, the current $I_{CSAT}$ can be calculated as

$$I_{CSAT} = \frac{V_{CC} - V_{CESAT}}{R_C} = \frac{3.6 - 0.2}{640} \quad \text{(see Fig. 10.38(}b\text{))}$$

or $$I_{CSAT} = 5.31\ mA$$

Now the current $I_{B_1}$ of load gate $G_1$ as calculated in equation 10.15 must be sufficient to drive the transistor in saturation. In saturation the $I_{B_1}$ and $I_{CSAT}$ must follow the relation.

$$I_B . h_{fe} \geq I_{CSAT}$$

*i.e.,* $$\frac{2.8 \times 7}{640\ N + 450} \geq 5.31 \times 10^{-3} \qquad (\text{given } h_{fe} = 7)$$

for worst case

$$\frac{19.6}{640\ N + 450} = 5.31 \times 10^{-3}$$

or $$19.6 = 3.3984\ N + 2.3895$$

or $$N = 5.064$$

thus taking N = 5 will always drive transistors into saturation. So FAN OUT = 5.

With N = 5, we get $I_{B_1} = 0.767$ mA

and $$I_{BT} = 3.835\ mA$$

To calculate noise margin let us first find out the output voltages at two states.

When output is in low state $V_o = V_{CE_{sat}} = 0.2$ V. When this output is applied to load transistor, it will go into cut off. If noise causes it to become 0.5V ($V_\upsilon$ of transistor) then load transistors will conduct and circuit malfunctions. Thus low state noise margin.

$$\Delta 0 = V_\upsilon - V_{CE_{sat}} = 0.5 - 0.2 = 0.3\ V$$

*i.e.,* $$\Delta 0 = 0.3V$$

when the output of driver goes high all the load transistors goes to saturation and a current $I_{BT}$ flows. Thus the output voltage will be

$$V_o = V_{RBT} + V_{BEsat} \quad \text{(see Fig. 10.38(d))}$$

$$V_{RBT} = I_{BT}.R_{BT} = 3.835 \times 10^{-3} \times 90 \quad \text{for N = 5}$$

so $$V_{RBT} = 0.345 \text{ V} \quad \text{when N = 5}$$

thus $$V_o = V_{RBT} + V_{BEsat} = 0.345 + 0.8$$

$$V_o = 1.145 \text{ V} \quad \text{when N = 5}$$

So if this voltage is applied from driver to load, all the load transistors will enter into saturation. Since N = 5 was calculated for $h_{fe}I_B = I_{Csat}$, that means any voltage less than 1.145 V may not be able to drive the load transistors into saturation. So we may say that if it is reduced to 1.045 V load transistor may not be in saturation. So high state noise margin $\Delta 1 \cong 0.1$ V. In fact the high state noise margin depends upon the number of gates being driven. If lesser number of load gates are connected the noise margin would be improved.

The *Propagation Delay* is also affected by number of load gates. When output of driver is LOW all the load transistors are in cutoff and their base to emitter junction appears as capacitor. Since N load transistors are there, N such capacitor appears in parallel. If capacitance offered by one load transistor is $C_i$, then total capacitance would be

$$C_{TOTAL} = C_i + C_i + ...$$

$$C_{TOTAL} = NC_i \text{ when driver output is LOW}$$

when driver output goes to high from low this capacitor ($C_{TOTAL}$) must be charged to HIGH voltage by a time constant.

$$\tau = R_{eq}.C_{TOTAL}$$

where $$R_{eq} = 640 + \frac{450}{N} \quad \text{(see Fig. 10.38}(d))$$

so $$\tau = \left(640 + \frac{450}{N}\right).NC_i$$

$$\text{finally } \tau = (640 \text{ N} + 450)\ C_i \qquad ...(10.16)$$

We know that smaller the $\tau$ faster is the charging of capacitor and hence smaller is the propagation delay.

By equation (10.16), it is clear that larger the value of N larger the value of $\tau$ and hence propagation delay is large.

The collector resistor $R_C$ is called pull up resistor because it pulls the output of gate from low to high state. It is because when transistor is in LOW state the output capacitance $C_{TOTAL}$ is discharged and for LOW to HIGH transition the output capacitance $C_{TOTAL}$ must be charged to the Logic 1 voltage, the resistor $R_C$ provides the charging current path. Thus the name pull up resistor. Since $R_C$ is passive element, this is called **passive pull up.**

Also note that in Fig. 10.38(*a*) when driver output is HIGH a current $I_{BT}$ is supplied from driver side to the load side. Thus the logic is called as the **current source logic,** because the driver is sourcing the current to load.

### 10.3.3 Direct Coupled Transistor Logic (DCTL)

The Basic DCTL gate is a NOR gate shown in Figure 10.39. Comparing the Fig. 10.39 with Fig. 10.38(*a*) reveals the fact that DCTL is a RTL gate with no base resistor. In fact output of driver is directly connected to load and hence the name DCTL. Naturally in this case LOW output voltage is $V_{CE_{sat}} = 0.2$ V and the HIGH output voltage is $V_{BE_{sat}} = 0.8$ V. But the output logic swing is very small (0.8 – 0.2 = 0.6 V). Thus the noise margin is poor.

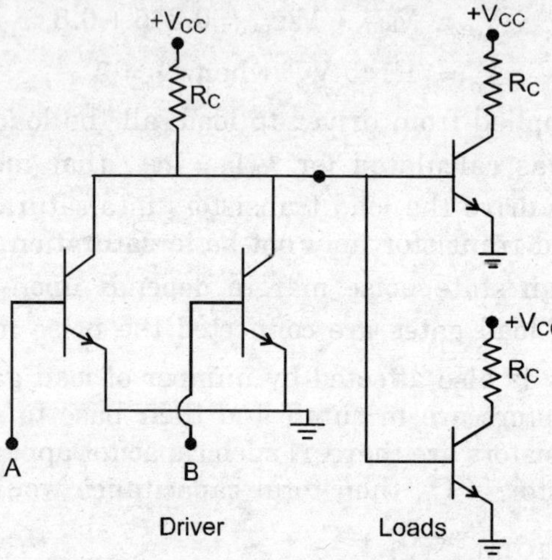


**Fig. 10.39** Basic DCTL NOR gate

The DCTL gates are simpler than RTL but suffers from a problem called *current hogging*. It occurs when driver output is logic 1. The input characteristic of all the transistors are assumed to be same in theory. But in practice it is not true. The input characteristics of transistor of same batch differ from each other causing variation in $V_{BE_{sat}}$. Thus if $V_{BE_{sat}}$ = 0.8 V for one transistor another may have 0.798 V, some other may have 0.796 V. When Driver's output is logic 1, the transistor having lowest value of $V_{BE_{sat}}$ (on the load side) will enter first into saturation and will take all the current supplied by the driver side. Thus the other transistors may not get sufficient amount of current to enter into saturation. This is called **current hogging.**

### 10.3.4 Diode Transistor Logic

The basic DTL gate is a NAND gate shown in Fig. 10.40. The two inputs of the gate are applied through the diodes $D_A$ and $D_B$ which are transmitted to the base of transistor $Q_D$ through diodes $D_1$ and $D_2$. Output of the gate is measured at the collector of $Q_D$.

A close inspection of the circuit reveals that the input diodes along with resistor R forms a diode AND gate whose output is available at point P. The transistor acts as inverter, thus the output of diode AND gate is inverted to give output of DTL gate as NAND gate.

#### *Circuit Operation*

Before describing the operation we first define value of V(0) and V(1). The output of gate is said to be HIGH when $Q_D$ is OFF and $V_O = V_{CC}$ = +5V. Thus V(1) = +5V. The output of gate is LOW when $Q_D$ is in saturation so $V_O = V_{CE_{sat}}$ = 0.2 V. Thus $V_{(O)}$ = 0.2V. From the figure it is evident that voltage at point P, $V_P$ is responsible to drive the transistor in cut off or in saturation. Let us calculate the voltage at point P, required to turn ON the transistor,

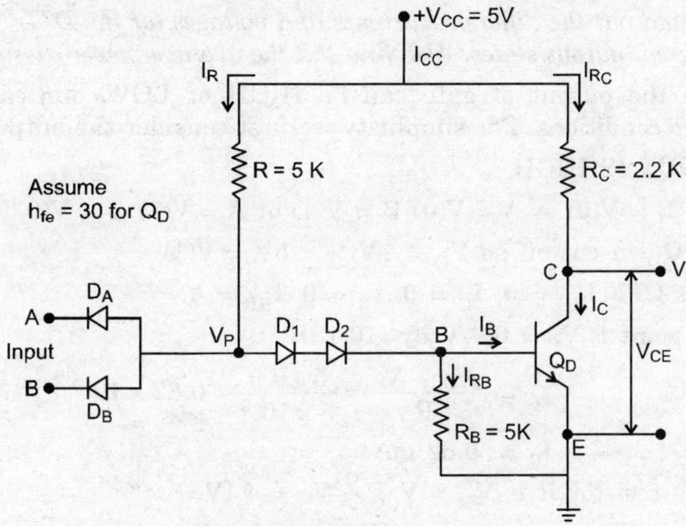


**Fig. 10.40** DTL NAND gate.

$$V_P(ON) = (V_\upsilon)_{D_1} + (V_\upsilon)_{D_2} + (V_\upsilon)_{Q_D}$$

but $\quad V_\upsilon = 0.6$ V for Diodes

and $\quad V_\upsilon = 0.5$ V for BJTs

so $\quad V_P(ON) = 0.6 + 0.6 + 0.5$

so $\quad V_P(ON) = 1.7$ V ...(10.17)

**when A = V(0) B = V(1),** the diode $D_A$ is conducting and $D_B$ is cut off. So voltage at point P is one diode drop above the V(0). So in this case

$$V_P = V(0) + V_{D_A} \text{ and } V_{D_A} = \text{drop across conducting diode } D_A = 0.7$$

thus $\quad V_P = 0.2 + 0.7 \quad V(0) = 0.2$V as defined earlier

$\quad V_P = 0.9$V ...(10.18)

Since $V_P < V_P(ON)$, transistor $Q_D$ is in OFF state and the output at the gate is $+V_{CC}$, *i.e.,* V(1).

Same will be the output when A = V(1) and B = V(0) and when A = B = V(0).

**when A = B = V(1),** the diodes $D_A$ and $D_B$ will be in OFF state and current $I_R$ flows through diodes $D_1$ and $D_2$, through base of $Q_D$. Consequently the transistor enters in saturation and the output becomes $V_0 = V_{CEsat} = 0.2$ V = V(0). Let us find out the voltage at point P in this case

$$V_P = V_{D_1} + V_{D_2} + V_{BEsat}$$

where $V_{D_1}$ and $V_{D_2} = 0.7$ V drop across conducting diodes $D_1$ and $D_2$ and $V_{BEsat} = 0.8$ V

thus $\quad V_P = 0.7 + 0.7 + 0.8$

so $\quad V_P = 2.2$ V ...(10.19)

since $V_P > V_P$ (ON), $Q_D$ is in ON condition and the output is low.

From the above discussion it is clear that output of gate is LOW only when both A = B = V(1), otherwise the output is HIGH. Thus the circuit behaves as NAND gates.

**Example 10.5.** *Find out the different currents and voltages for the DTL NAND gate shown in figure 10.40 in different output states. Also find out the average power dissipation in the gate.*

**Solution.** Since the output of gate can be HIGH or LOW, our calculation will be different for these two conditions. For simplicity we first consider the output in HIGH state.

1. WHEN OUTPUT IS HIGH

(*a*) Inputs A = B = V(0) or A = V(0) B = V(1) or A = V(1) B = V(0)

(*b*) Transistor $Q_D$ in cut off so $V_O = +V_{CC} = 5V = V(1)$

(*c*) Since $Q_D$ is OFF $I_{RC} = 0$, $I_C = 0$, $I_B = 0$, $I_{RB} = 0$.

(*d*) Voltage at point P $V_P = 0.9$ V by (10.18)

(*e*) Current $$I_R = \frac{V_{CC} - V_P}{R} = \frac{5-0.9}{5 \times 10^{-3}} = 0.82 \times 10^{-3}$$

*i.e.*, $$I_R = 0.82 \text{ mA} \qquad \text{...(10.20)}$$

(*f*) Drop across resistor R is $V_R = V_{CC} - V_P = 4.1V$

(*g*) Current drawn from supply in HIGH state $I_{CC}(1)$

$$I_{CC}(1) = I_R + I_{RC} = 0.82 \times 10^{-3} + 0$$

$$\text{So } I_{CC}(1) = 0.82 \text{ mA} \qquad \text{...(10.21)}$$

(*h*) HIGH state power dissipation $P(1) = V_{CC} . I_{CC}(1)$

$$P(1) = 4.1 \text{ mW} \qquad \text{...(10.22)}$$

2. WHEN OUTPUT IS LOW

(*a*) Inputs A = B = V(1) = +5V

(*b*) Transistor $Q_D$ in ON state so $V_0 = V_{CEsat} = 0.2$ V

(*c*) Voltage at point P $V_P = 2.2$ V by 10.19

(*d*) Drop across register R, $V_R = V_{CC} - VP = 5 - 2.2$

So $V_R = 2.8$ V

(*e*) The collector current in saturation $I_{Csat}$

$$I_{Csat} = I_{RC} = \frac{V_{CC} - V_{CEsat}}{R_C} = \frac{5-0.2}{2.2 \times 10^3}$$

so $$I_{RC} = I_{Csat} = 2.18 \text{ mA} \qquad \text{...(10.23)}$$

(*f*) Current through register R, $$I_R = \frac{V_{CC} - V_P}{R} = \frac{V_R}{R} = \frac{2.8}{5 \times 10^3}$$

so $$I_R = 0.56 \text{ mA} \qquad \text{...(10.24)}$$

(*g*) Current through resistor $R_B$, $I_{RB} = \frac{V_{RB}}{R_B}$

but the drop across $R_B$ is same as $V_{BEsat}$.

so $V_{RB} = V_{BEsat} = 0.8$ V

= drop across base to emitter junction in saturation.

thus $\quad I_{RB} = \dfrac{0.8\text{ V}}{5 \times 10^3}$

so $\quad I_{RB} = 0.16\text{ mA}$

(*h*) The current $\quad I_B = I_R - I_{RB}$ by KCL at point B

so $\quad I_B = 0.56 - 0.16$

or $\quad I_B = 0.4\text{ mA}$

(*i*) Check for transistor in saturation. For transistor to be in saturation it must follow

$$h_{FE}I_B \geq I_{C_{sat}}$$

given $\quad h_{FE} = 30$ for $Q_D$

so $\quad h_{FE}I_B = 30 \times 0.4 \times 10^{-3}$

or $\quad h_{FE}I_B = 12\text{ mA} \qquad \text{...(10.25)}$

Since this is greater than $I_{C_{sat}}$ = 2.18 mA, the transistor is in saturation.

(*j*) LOW state supply current $\quad I_{CC}(0) = I_R + I_{RC}$

$= 0.56\text{ mA} + 2.18\text{ mA}$

so $\quad I_{CC}(0) = 2.74\text{ mA} \qquad \text{...(10.26)}$

(*k*) LOW state power dissipation $\quad P(0) = V_{CC}.I_{CC}(0)$

$= 5 \times 2.74 \times 10^{-3}$

so $\quad P(0) = 13.7\text{ mW} \qquad \text{...(10.27)}$

To find out average power dissipation we assume 50% duty cycle at the output *i.e.*, occurrence of LOW and HIGH state is same then, the average power dissipation

$$P_{avg} = \frac{P(1) + P(0)}{2} = \frac{4.1\text{ mW} + 13.7\text{ mW}}{2}$$

so $\quad P_{avg} = 8.9\text{ mW} \qquad \text{...(10.28)}$

### *Loading of DTL Gate*

In the loading of DTL gate, we are concerned with finding out FANOUT and noise margin for the DTL NAND gate. We assume that all the load gates are identical and input B of load gates are connected to logic 1, for simplicity. The logic diagram is shown in Fig. 10.41.

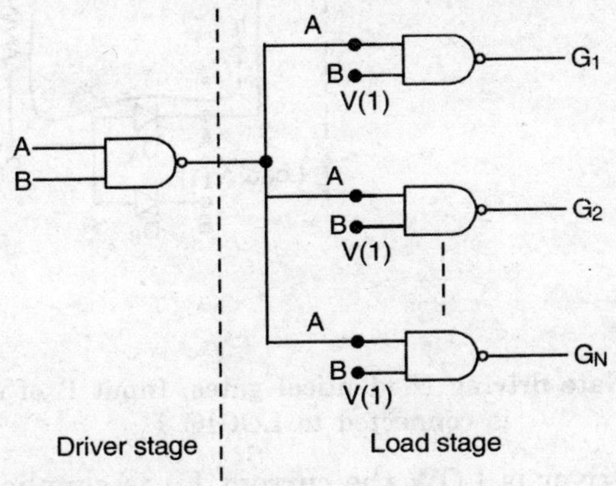


**Fig. 10.41** ADTL NAND gate driving N similar gate

The equivalent circuit diagram for loading of DTL gate is shown in figure 10.42. As evident from Figure 10.42 when the output $V_0$ of driver is HIGH then all the $D_A$ diodes of load gates are reverse biased so no current flows either from Driver to Load or from Load to Driver.

When output of Driver is low then $D_A$ diodes of load are forward biased and a current $I_L$ flows from each load gate towards driver gate. Since all load gates identical so they will draw same $I_L$ (which is $I_R$ as shown in Fig. 10.42) and hence total load current from load stage to driver state is

$$I_{LT} = N.I_L \qquad ...(10.29)$$

Also note that when diode $D_A$ of load gates conduct the output of all load gates are HIGH. In this situation

$$I_L = I_R = 0.82 \text{ mA see equation (10.20)}$$

thus total load current $I_{LT}$ = N.082 mA ...(10.30)

The current $I_L$ supplied by individual load gate is called *standard load*.

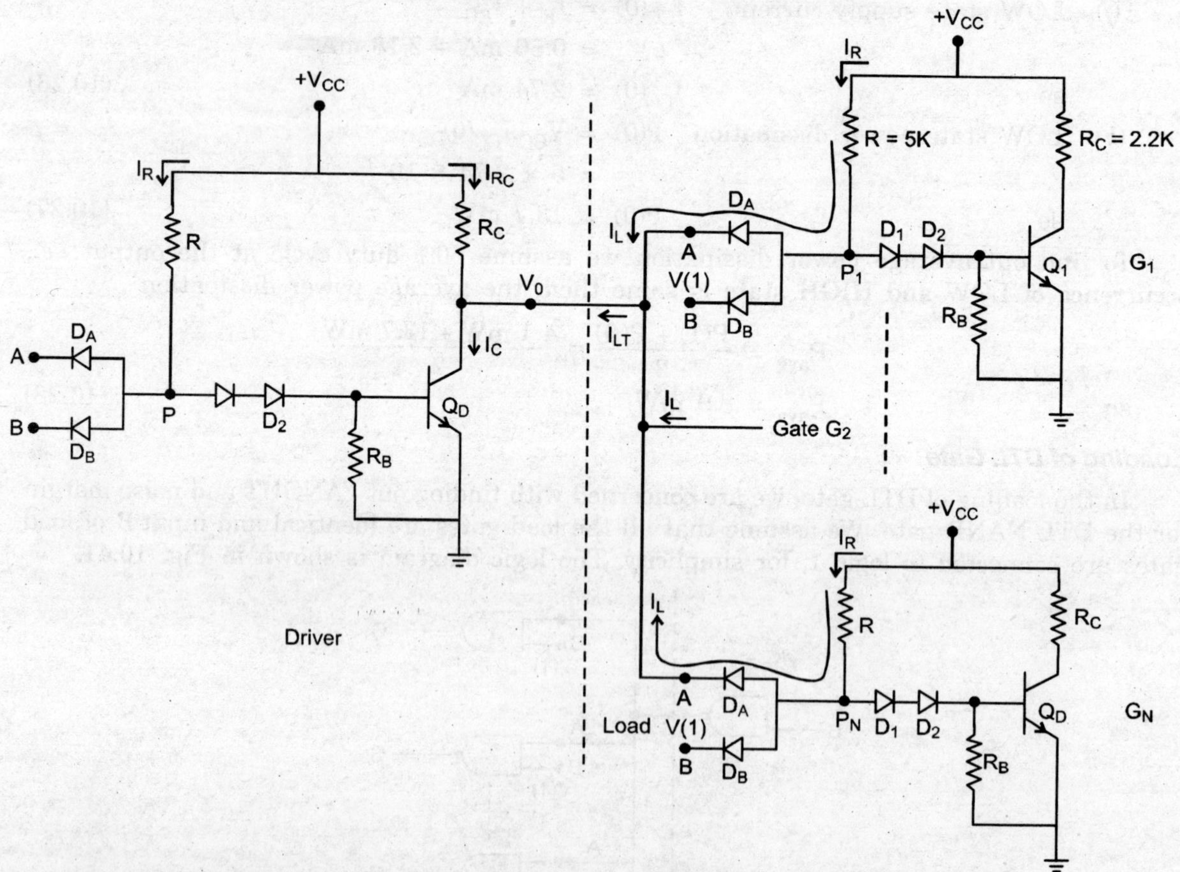


**Fig. 10.42** DTL Gate driving N identical gates. Input B of each load gate is connected to LOGIC 1

Thus when output of Driver is LOW the current $I_{LT}$ is supplied by load stage to $Q_D$ in addition to the current $I_{RC}$. Thus under loading

$$I_C = I_{RC} + I_{LT}$$

so $I_C = 2.18 \text{ mA} + 0.82 \text{ NmA}$ by equations (10.23) and (10.29) ...(10.31)

But the current $I_C$ given by equation 10.31 must satisfy $h_{FE}I_B \geq I_{C_{sat}}$ so that $Q_D$ remains in saturation and output of driver remains low. Thus we use this fact to determine FAN OUT. So

$$I_{C_{sat}} \leq h_{FE}\ I_B$$

but $h_{FE}I_B = 12$ mA when $Q_D$ is ON, by equation (10.25) then equation (10.31)

$$2.18 + 0.82\ N \leq 12$$

Calculating for worst case $2.18 + 0.82\ N = 12$

or $N \cong 12$

but for $I_{C_{sat}} < h_{FE}I_B$ we must have $N < 12$.

so let us select $N = 10$ ...(10.32)

***Noise, Margin***

When output of $Q_D$ is in HIGH state the Diode $D_A$ of load gates are reverse biased as shown in Fig. 10.43 since $V_P = 2.2$ V when input diodes are reverse biased, the amount by which $D_A$ is reverse biased $= V(1) - V_P = 5 - 2.2$

$= 2.8$ V

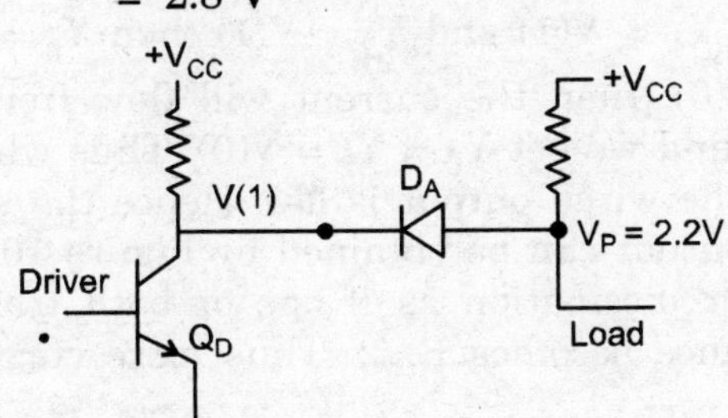


**Fig. 10.43** Circuit situation when driver output is high

Since $V_\upsilon = 0.6$V a negative spike of at least $2.8 + 0.6 = 3.4$ V present at the input of load gate will cause malfunction. Thus $\Delta 0 = 3.4$ V. It is called low state noise margin because HIGH output of driver causes a LOW output of load.

When output of $Q_D$ is LOW diode $D_A$ of load is forward biased and voltage $V_P$ on load side will 0.9 V, by equation 10.18. And High state noise margin is given as

$$\Delta 1 = V_P(\text{ON}) - V_P = 1.7\text{ V} - 0.9 = 0.8\text{ V}$$

Thus $\Delta 1 = 0.8$ V. Thus a positive noise spike of at least 0.8 V will cause circuit malfunction.

**Propagation Delay** is approximated by the capacitance present at the output of $Q_D$ due to load gates. When $Q_D$ turns ON these output capacitance discharge quickly through $Q_D$, thus giving low turn ON delays. But when $Q_D$ goes OFF the output capacitance has to charge through the register $R_C$ which takes large time. Thus giving large turn OFF delay. Again register $R_C$ is **pullup resistor** and this type of pull up is called **passive pullup** as $R_C$ is passive element.

**Current sink logic** DTL is called current sink-logic because when $Q_D$ is in ON state there flows a current from load stage to driver stage, and the $Q_D$ acts as current sink for these load currents. When $Q_D$ is in OFF state output is HIGH and input diodes of load gates are reverse biased. Practically there flows a very small amount of current from driver to load side. This current is equal to reverse saturation current of diodes. The driver is said to be sourcing this small current to load. Since sourcing of current is very-very small compared to sinking the overall logic is called current sink logic.

**Wired Logic** when outputs of gates are tied together through a wire, as shown in Fig. 10.44 additional logics performed. These are called wire-logic or implied logic consider Fig. 10.44(*a*) to find the wired logic.

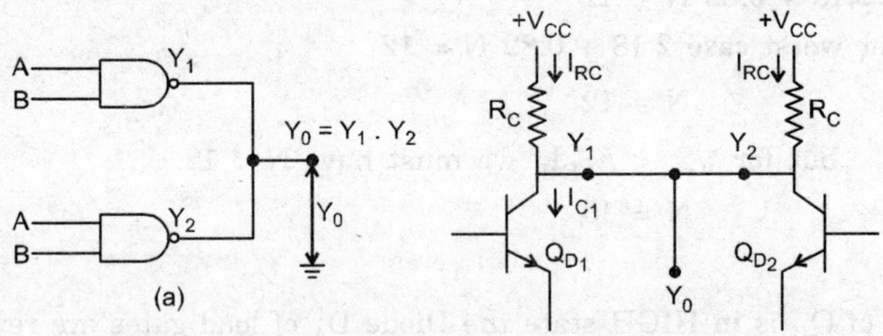


**Fig. 10.44** Wired-ANDing of DTL NAND gate

when $Y_1 = V(0)$ and $Y_2 = V(0)$ then $Y_0 = V(0)$

$Y_1 = V(1)$ and $Y_2 = V(1)$ then $Y_0 = V(1)$

when $Y_1 = V(1)$ and $Y_2 = V(0)$, then the current will flow from $Y_1$ to $Y_2$. Thus if $Y_0$ is measured with respect to ground we get $Y_0 = Y_2 = V(0)$. Thus when one or both of the gate output ($Y_1$ or $Y_2$) goes low, the wired output is low. Hence the above wired logic is wired-AND logic. The same wired output can be obtained by Figure 10.44(b). But the wired logic increases the low state power dissipation as if one or both transistors of figure 10.44(b) conduct then collector resistance becomes $R_C/2$. Thus more current is drawn.

Also the wired logic in DTL decreases to FAN OUT. If only $Q_{D_1}$ (in Fig. 10.44(b)) conducts then the collector current $I_{C_1}$ through $Q_{D_1}$ is $I_{C_1} = I_{RC} + I_{RC} = 2I_{RC}$. Thus the collector current is doubled than that of normal case. Since $h_{FE}I_B$ remains constant and collector current is increased, the effective FAN OUT is reduced.

### *Modified DTL Nand Gate*

In the analysis of DTL NAND gate we have calculated the FAN OUT by using the equation $h_{FE}I_B \geq I_{Csat}$. If somehow $I_B$ is increased the value of $h_{FE}I_B$ increases and the equation $h_{FE}I_B \geq I_{Csat}$ can be satisfied for larger no. of load gates. Thus the FAN OUT can be improved. The base current $I_B$ can be increased if the diode $D_1$ of Figure 10.40 is replaced by a transistor $Q_1$ as shown in figure 10.45. The register R is splitted to provide biasing of transistor $Q_1$. When $Q_1$ is conducting the base current $I_B$ of transistor $Q_D$ increases and thus value of $h_{FE}I_B$ increases significantly. As a consequence the FAN OUT of circuit shown in Fig. 10.45 increases significantly as compared to the circuit shown in Fig. 10.40.

In the last, we advise the readers to go through the DTL gate once again from beginning as these understandings would be needed when we will discuss the TTL. This is the reason why we have presented DTL exhaustively.

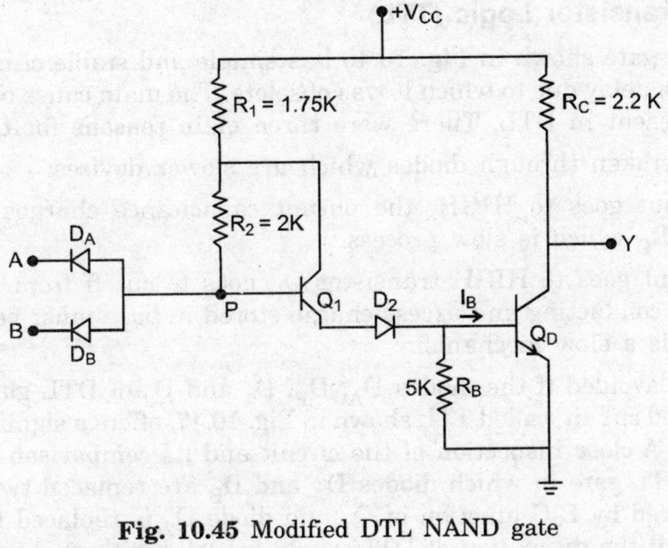


**Fig. 10.45** Modified DTL NAND gate

### 10.3.5 High Threshold Logic (HTL)

In the industrial environments, the noise levels are high. These are mainly due to high rating relays, various motors and variety of ON/OFF controls. In general the logic families like RTL, DTL do not offer such a noise margin so that higher noise levels can be tolerated. In fact due to lower noise margin the circuit will malfunction most of the time.

To suit the industrial application, modified DTL gate, shown in Fig. 10.45, is redesigned with higher $+V_{CC}$ supply and increased value of resistance and diode $D_2$ is replaced by a zener diode, as shown in Figure 10.46. The overall circuit provides same current level as that of DTL NAND gate. As evident from the circuit, the noise margins are dramatically improved. But presence of larger resistances severely affects the switching speed, causing the propagation delay in hundreds of nano seconds.

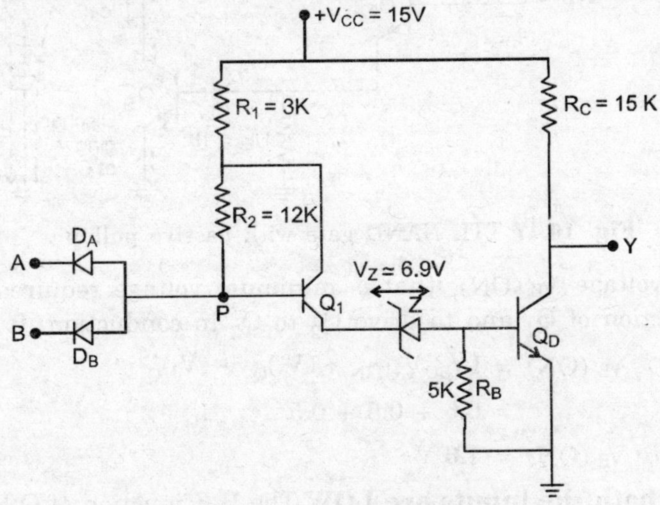


**Fig. 10.46** Basic HTL NAND gate

### 10.3.6 Transistor Transistor Logic (TTL)

The DTL NAND gate shown in Fig. 10.40 has simple and stable circuit design but has the larger propagation delay due to which it was obselete. The main cause of large propagation delays are diodes present in DTL. There were three main reasons for their slower speed.

1. Inputs are taken through diodes which are slower devices.
2. When output goes to HIGH, the output capacitance charges through collector resistance $R_C$ which is slow process.
3. When output goes to HIGH transistor $Q_D$ goes to cutoff from saturation $D_1$ and $D_2$ are non conducting and excess charge stored in base must be removed through $R_B$, which is a slow mechanism.

All these can be avoided if the diodes $D_A$, $D_B$, $D_1$ and $D_2$ of DTL gate are replaced by transistor. The modified circuit, called TTL shown in Fig. 10.47, offers a significant improvement in propagation delay. A close inspection of the circuit and its comparison with Figure 10.40 reveals that it is a DTL gate in which diodes $D_A$ and $D_B$ are replaced two E-B junctions of $Q_1$, diode $D_1$ is replaced by B-C junction of $Q_1$ and diode $D_2$ is replaced by B-E junction of transistor $Q_2$. Thus all the discussion of DTL would be valid with slight modifications. The capacitor $C_O$ is output capacitance that must be charged to the logic value of output. Before proceeding further let us assume that V(0) = 0.2V ($V_{CEsat}$) and V(1) = 5V ($+V_{CC}$).

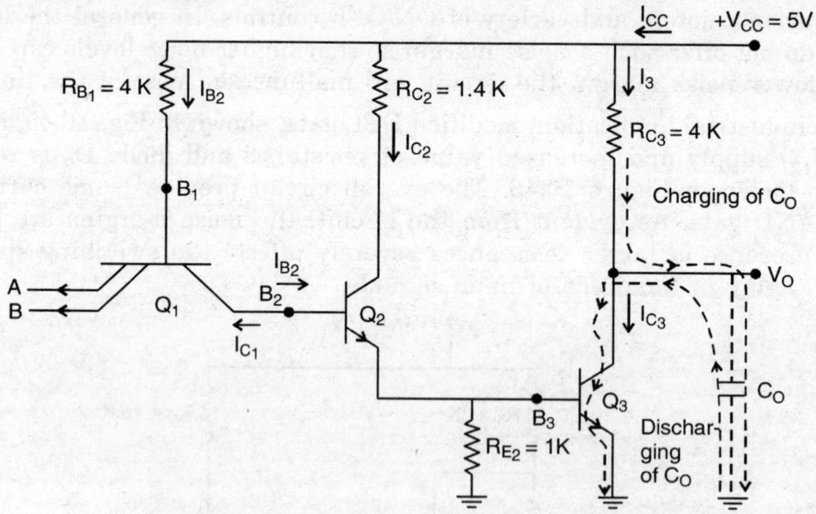


**Fig. 10.47** TTL NAND gate with passive pullup

Let us define a voltage $V_{B_1}(ON)$, that is minimum voltage required at Base of $Q_1$ to forward bias B-C junction of $Q_1$ and to drive $Q_2$ to $Q_3$ in conduction. It is given as

$$V_{B_1}(ON) = (V_{BC})_{CUTIN} + (V_\upsilon)_{Q_2} + (V_\upsilon)_{Q_3}$$

$$= 0.6 + 0.5 + 0.5$$

so $$V_{B_1}(ON) = 1.6 \text{ V} \qquad \text{...(10.33)}$$

**When either or both the inputs are LOW** The B-E junction of $Q_1$ conducts, thus the voltage at base $B_1$ is

$$V_{B_1} = V(0) + V_{BE_{ACTIVE}} = 0.2 + 0.7$$

so $$V_{B_1} = 0.9 \text{ V} \qquad ...(10.34)$$

Since $V_{B_1} < V_{B_1}(ON)$, transistor $Q_3$ is OFF and the output voltage $V_o = +V_{CC} = V(1)$.

**When both the inputs are HIGH** The B-E junction of $Q_1$ is reverse biased. If we assume that $Q_2$ and $Q_3$ are working then the voltage at base $B_2$ is given as

$$V_{B_2} = (V_{BE_{sat}})_{Q_2} + (V_{BE_{sat}})_{Q_3} = 0.8 + 0.8$$

or $$V_{B_2} = 1.6 \text{ V} \qquad ...(10.35)$$

Since base $B_1$ is connected to $+V_{CC}$ through resistor R, the C-B junction will be forward biased and transistor $Q_1$ is said to be working in inverse active mode. This causes current $I_{C_1}$ to flow in reverse direction and thus driving $Q_2$ and $Q_3$ in saturation. Thus the output voltage $V_o = V_{CE_{sat}} = 0.2 \text{ V} = V(0)$.

To understand improvement in propagation delay let us consider that both the inputs are HIGH and output of gate is LOW. Thus by equation (10.35), $V_{B_2} = 1.6$ V. If suddenly any one of the input goes LOW then corresponding drop at base $B_1$ is $V_{B_1} = 0.9$V. The $Q_2$ and $Q_3$ cannot turn OFF immediately as excess charge is stored at their base. So at this instant $V_{B_2} = 1.6$. This causes reverse biasing of B-C junction of $Q_1$, whereas B-E junction of $Q_1$ is already forward biased by LOW input. Thus $Q_1$ works in ACTIVE region. This is why we have taken $V_{BE_{ACTIVE}}$ while calculating equation (10.34). While $Q_1$ is in active region it conducts a large collector current $I_{C_1}$ in a direction opposite to $I_{B_2}$. This causes very fast removal of excess charge carriers from base of $Q_2$ and $Q_3$. Thus the propagation delay is reduced.

**PASSIVE PULLUP** As evident from figure register $R_{C_3}$ is **pull up resistor** for the reasons stated earlier. Since $R_C$ is passive element the circuit is called **passive pull up** circuit. In contrast to this, the resistor $R_E$ is called **pull down resistor,** as drop across RE turns ON the $Q_3$ and consequently output goes LOW from HIGH state.

NOTE that if in Fig. 10.47, we use single emitter transistor, then the circuit becomes **TTL Inverter or TTL** NOT gate.

### *Propagation Delay*

Propagation delay is determined by charging and discharging of output capacitance $C_O$ (Fig. 10.47) and removal of excess charge carriers from base of $Q_3$. $C_O$ is the capacitance that appears when looking from the output of logic gate. When the output is HIGH, $C_O$ is charged to $+V_{CC}$. When output makes HIGH to LOW transition the $Q_3$ goes to saturation. Thus $C_O$ can discharge through ON transistor $Q_3$. Since the resistance offered by the transistor $Q_3$ in saturation very small, $C_O$ can discharge quickly to V(0), through the path shown in Figure 10.47. When output makes LOW to HIGH transition, the excess charge of base of $Q_3$ removed by active mode working of $Q_1$ and $C_O$ charges to V(1) (or $+V_{CC}$) through resistor $R_{C_3}$ as shown in Fig. 10.47. Thus the charging time constant $\tau = R_{C_3} \cdot C_O$ is a bit large, thus charging of $C_O$ to V(1) is slower. This limits the switching time of gate. One way to improve is reducing $R_{C_3}$ but it will increase the collector current. This will increase the power dissipation and reduce the FAN OUT. Another way is to use active pull up arrangement, which is discussed is subsection 10.3.62.

**Clamping (or Protective) Diodes** are used to protect the circuit from damages that can occur due to excess current because of presence negative voltage at input. The input to TTL gates are always positive. Arrangement of clamping diodes is shown in Fig. 10.48. These diodes can clamp up the negative undershoot of approximately up to –0.7 V.

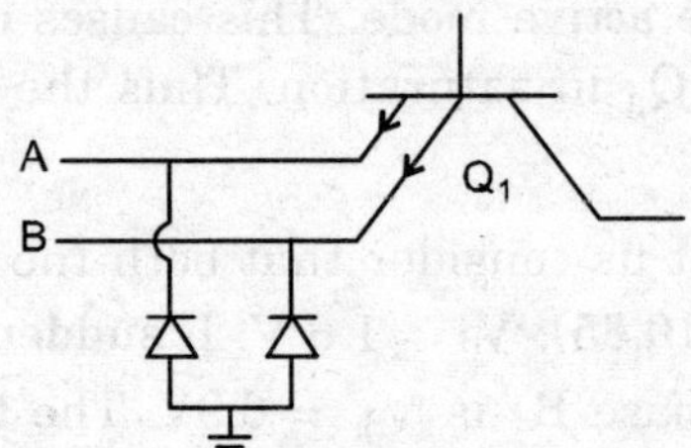


**Fig. 10.48** Clamping diodes at input

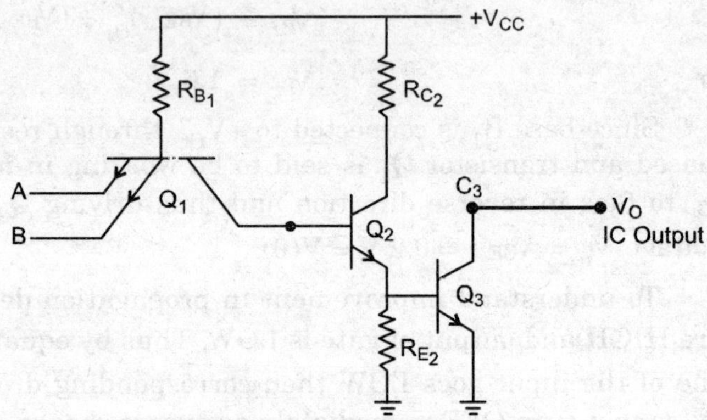


**Fig. 10.49** Open collector output of TTL

**Open collector output:** When the collector resistance $R_{C3}$ of figure 10.47 is removed and collector of output transistor $Q_3$ is made available directly as IC pin, the output is called open collector output. However, these outputs must be connected to $+V_{CC}$ through an external resistor, before taking the output.

**WIRED ANDING:** If the output of two TTL gates are wired together then the logic performed is AND. The explanation is same as DTL. For reasons stated for DTL, wiring of TTL gates reduce the FAN OUT. To improve the FAN OUT open collector output can be used under wired logic condition.

For this purpose, first of all the open collectors are tied together and then a single collector resistance is connected to $+V_{CC}$ from this joint. This ensures that collector resistance for all the gates remains same (which became $R_C/2$ in DTL and Passive Pullup TTL) and hence the collector current does not increase through output transistor $Q_3$ of all gates. Thus the FAN OUT can be improved than the FAN OUT obtained by wiring of passive pullup TTL.

**FLOATING INPUTS** of TTL are treated as logic 1 by the circuit. It is because when an input is HIGH the corresponding B-E junction is reverse biased and no current flow through it. Similarly when a input is unconnected *i.e.,* floating, no current flows through it. Thus the floating inputs are treated as logic 1. But floating TTL inputs can easily pickup the noise and circuit can malfunction. Thus it is highly recommended that unused TTL inputs should be tied to $+V_{CC}$.

#### *10.3.6.1 Specifications of Standard TTL*

The various current and voltage parameters, propagation delays are summarized in Fig. 10.50 and Table 10.5. These parameters are defined in subsection 10.2.2.

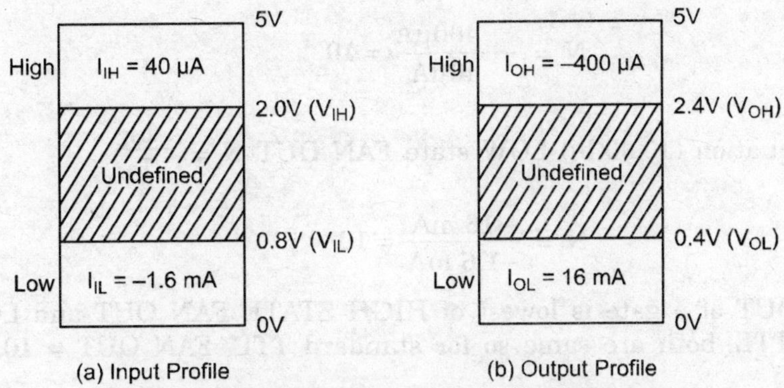


**Fig. 10.50** Input/Output profile of standard TTL

**Table 10.5 Parameters of standard TTL**

| *Parameter* | *Typical Value* |
|---|---|
| $t_{PHL}$ | 15 n sec |
| $t_{PLH}$ | 20 n sec |
| $I_{CC}(1)$ | 8 mA |
| $I_{CC}(0)$ | 22 mA |
| NOISE MARGIN | 0.4 V |
| FAN OUT | 10 |

**Example 10.6.** *Find out the FAN OUT, figure of merit, noise margin average power dissipation for a TTL gate with the help of datas given in Figure 10.50 and Table 10.5.*

**Solution.** To calculate FAN OUT consider the Figure 10.51 from figure it is clear that

$$I_{OH} = -NI_{IH} \quad \text{...(10.36(}a\text{))}$$

and

$$I_{OL} = -NI_{IL} \quad \text{...(10.36(}b\text{))}$$

by using the datas of figure 10.50, we have

$$I_{OH} = -400 \text{ μA} \quad \text{and} \quad I_{IH} = 40 \text{ μA}$$

$$I_{OL} = 16 \text{ mA} \quad \text{and} \quad I_{IL} = -1.6 \text{ mA}$$

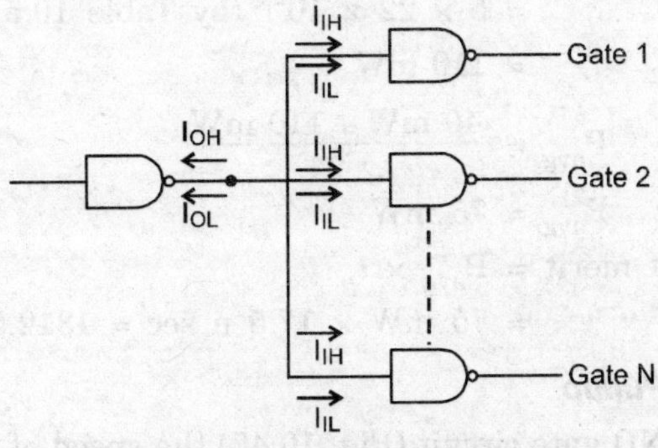


**Fig. 10.51** Loading of TTL

by using equation (10.36(a)) HIGH STATE FAN OUT $N = -\dfrac{I_{OH}}{I_{IH}}$

so $$N = -\frac{-400\mu A}{40\mu A} = 10$$

by using equation (10.36(b)) LOW state FAN OUT $N = -\frac{I_{OL}}{I_{IL}}$

so $$N = \frac{-16 \text{ mA}}{-1.6 \text{ mA}} = 10$$

The FAN OUT of a gate is lowest of HIGH STATE FAN OUT and LOW STATE FAN OUT. Since in TTL, both are same so for standard TTL, FAN OUT = 10.

$$\text{the propagation delay } t_p = \frac{t_{PHL} + t_{PLH}}{2}$$

$$= \frac{15 \text{ n sec} + 20 \text{ n sec}}{2} \quad \text{(by Table 10.5)}$$

so $$t_p = 17.5 \text{ n sec}$$

$$\text{High state noise margin } \Delta 1 = V_{OH} - V_{IH}$$

$$= 2.4 - 2.0 \quad \text{(by Fig. 10.50)}$$

$$= 0.4 \text{ V}$$

$$\text{Low state noise margin } \Delta V = V_{IL} - V_{OL}$$

$$= 0.8 - 0.4 \quad \text{(by Fig. 10.50)}$$

$$= 0.4 \text{ V}$$

$$\text{The average power dissipation } P_{avg} = \frac{P(1) + P(0)}{2}$$

$$P(1) = V_{CC} \cdot I_{CC}(1)$$

$$= 5 \times 8 \times 10^{-3} \quad \text{(by Table 10.5)}$$

so $$P(1) = 40 \text{ mW}$$

$$P(0) = V_{CC} \cdot I_{CC}(0)$$

$$= 5 \times 22 \times 10^{-3} \quad \text{(by Table 10.5)}$$

$$= 110 \text{ mW}$$

so $$P_{avg} = \frac{40 \text{ mW} + 110 \text{ mW}}{2}$$

so $$P_{avg} = 75 \text{ mW}$$

$$\text{figure of merit} = P_{avg} \times t_p$$

$$= 75 \text{ mW} \times 17.5 \text{ n sec} = 1312.5 \text{ pJ}$$

#### *10.3.6.2 TTL With Active Pullup*

In the basic TTL NAND gate circuit (Fig. 10.47) the speed of operation is limited mainly due to the charging of output capacitance $C_O$. Since $C_O$ charges through $R_{C3}$ process is time consuming. If the resistance $R_{C3}$ is replaced by a transistor $Q_4$ and a diode D, as shown in Fig. 10.52, then the delays can be reduced. Since the transistor $Q_4$ (which is an active device) provides the charging current to output capacitance $C_O$, the circuit shown in Fig. 10.52 is called as active pullup circuit, and the output is called **active pullup output.** Also note that transistors $Q_4$ and $Q_3$ forms a totem-pole pair, and hence the output is also called as **totem pole output.** Transistor $Q_2$ acts as phase splitter for totem pole transistor pair. Advantage of active pullup is increased speed without increasing power dissipation. The purpose of using diode D is to keep transistor $Q_4$ in cut off when output of gate is LOGIC O.

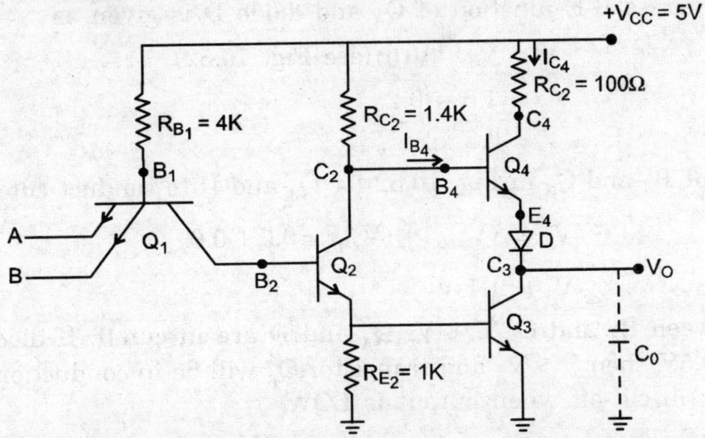


**Fig. 10.52** TTL NAND gate with active pullup

**When both the inputs are HIGH** transistor $Q_3$ conducts and the output of gate is LOW *i.e.,* $V(0) = V_{CEsat} = 0.2$ V.

**When any of input goes LOW** then transistor $Q_4$ conducts and enter into saturation. This causes charging of output capacitance $C_O$ through $Q_4$ and diode D. As the $C_O$ starts charging towards V(1) *i.e.,* HIGH, the current through $Q_4$ decreases. The transistor $Q_4$ goes to cut off as soon as $C_O$ charges to V(1). In fact under steady state $Q_4$ just comes out of conduction. Hence, the output voltage when output is HIGH can be given as

$$V(1) = V_{CC} - (V_v)_{Q_3} - (V_v)_D$$

$$V(1) = 5 - 0.5 - 0.6$$

so $$V(1) = 3.9 \text{ V} \qquad \text{...(10.37)}$$

***Effect of Q4***

Let us see the effect of $Q_4$ in the circuit. Due to $Q_4$ the value of V(1) is reduced to 3.9 V as calculated in equation 10.37. Secondly, the transistor $Q_4$ causes a large current spike to appear in the circuit when output makes a transition from LOW to HIGH. Thus if frequency of input is high then $Q_4$ turn ON for larger number of times per second. Hence the average power dissipation is increased if the gate is operated at high frequency.

**Example 10.7.** *Explain how diode D of Figure 10.52 keeps the pullup transistor of TTL gate in cutoff when output in LOW state.*

**Solution.** When the output of gate is in LOW state $V_0 = V(0) = 0.2$ V. At this time transistor $Q_2$ and $Q_3$ are in saturation. Thus voltage at collector of $Q_2$ is given as

$$V_{C_2} = (V_{BE_{sat}})_{Q_3} + (V_{CE_{sat}})_{Q_2} = 0.8 + 0.2$$

so $$V_{C_2} = 1.0 \text{ V}$$

Since base of $Q_4$ and collector of $Q_2$ are connected together so

$$V_{B_4} = V_{C_2} = 1.0 \quad \text{...(10.38)}$$

Thus the drop across B-E junction of $Q_4$ and diode D is given as

$$V = V_{B_4} - V(0) \text{ (see Fig. 10.52)}$$

$$= 1.0 - 0.2$$

*i.e.,* $$V = 0.8 \quad \text{...(10.39)}$$

is drop between point $B_4$ and $C_3$ in Fig. 10.52 for $Q_4$ and D to conduct cutoff value required

$$V_\upsilon = (V_\upsilon)_{Q_4} + (V_\upsilon)_D = 0.5 + 0.6$$

$$V_\upsilon = 1.1 \text{ V}$$

Since drop between $B_4$ and $C_3$ $V < V_\upsilon$ $Q_4$ and D are in cutoff. If diode is not present then $V_\upsilon = (V_\upsilon)_{Q_4} = 0.5$V, then $V > V_\upsilon$ and transistor $Q_4$ will be in conduction. Thus, presence of diode D keeps $Q_4$ in cut-off when output is LOW.

**Example 10.8.** *Explain how transistor $Q_4$ turns ON during LOW to HIGH transition of output. Calculate the current spike magnitude due to this transition.*

**Solution.** Let the output is in steady state LOW. At this moment the transistor $Q_3$ is in saturation and $Q_4$ is in cutoff, because all inputs are HIGH. If suddenly any of the input goes LOW then the corresponding B-E junction of $Q_1$ conducts. As a consequence the transistor $Q_2$ and $Q_3$ goes to cutoff. Since $Q_2$ is going to cutoff its collector voltage rises. Consequently the voltage at base $B_4$ rises. This causes $Q_4$ to enter into saturation. But the output cannot change instantaneously, as output capacitance $C_O$ cannot change its state instantaneously. So the voltage at base $B_4$ at this instant.

$$V_{B_4} = (V_{BE_{sat}})_{Q_4} + V_D + V(0)$$

$$= 0.8 + 0.7 + 0.2$$

so $$V_{B_4} = 1.7 \text{ V} \quad \text{...(10.40)}$$

Thus $$I_{B_4} = \frac{V_{CC} - V_{B_4}}{R_{C_2}} \quad \text{no } I_{C_2} \text{ flows as } Q_2 \text{ is in OFF state.}$$

$$= \frac{5 - 1.7}{1.4 \times 10^3}$$

so $$I_{B_4} = 2.36 \text{ mA} \quad \text{...(10.41)}$$

the current $$I_{C_4} = \frac{V_{CC} - (V_{CE_{sat}})_{Q_4} - V_D - V_O}{R_{C_4}}$$

$$= \frac{5 - 0.2 - 0.7 - 0.2}{100}$$

so $I_{C4} = 39$ mA.

Thus the current drawn from supply during the transition $I = I_{C4} + I_{B4} = 39$ mA + 2.36 mA

So $$I = 41.36 \text{ mA} \quad ...(10.42)$$

Thus high current spike is generated during LOW to HIGH transition of output. This current supply increases the power dissipation and generates noise in power supply distribution by drawing a current spike for short duration.

WIRED LOGIC is not recommended in TTL with active pullup. We have seen in example 10.8, during the LOW the HIGH transition of output high current spike is generated. Performing wired logic with active pullup will increase this spike. This excessive current can damage the whole circuit.

#### *10.3.6.3 Schottky TTL*

We have seen that the switching speed of TTL gates are limited mainly due to the storage time delay required by a transistor to go to CUT OFF from saturation. Although the transistor $Q_1$ of basic TTL gage helps fast removal of excess charges but the fact that transistor $Q_3$ will be driven into saturation makes the device slower. If the schottky transistors are used to create the TTL NAND gate circuit, speed will be high. It is because, as discussed in subsection 10.1.34, the schottky transistor are never driven hard into saturation, rather they are on the verge of saturation. Hence transistors operate in active region. This means there is no excess charge carriers accumulated because transistors are not saturated. Hence speed of operation is improved. The TTL gates employing schottky transistors have propagation delay as low as 2 n sec. Since transistors in this family are not driven in saturation, schottky family is called NON SATURATED LOGIC FAMILY.

#### *10.3.6.4 TTL Series*

As discussed we have different form of TTL circuits, suited for different applications and requirements. This evolved different series of TTL circuits available in ICs. Some of them are obselete and some of them are still in use. In particular the 74 XX and 54XX series are popular. The 74XX series is used for general purpose, and consumer applications whereas 54XX series is used for military applications. Obviously, the temperature range of two types differs. The 74XX has supply range 5 V ± 5% whereas 54XX has supply range 5 V ± 10%. For most practicle purposes 74XX series are used. The 74XX series is further divided into five categories summarised in Table 10.6.

**Table 10.6** Categories of TTL

| *TTL Series* | *Letter Prefix* | *Examples* |
|---|---|---|
| Standard TTL | 74XX | 7402, 7404 |
| HIGH Power TTL | 74HXX | 74H02 |
| LOW Power TTL | 74LXX | 74L02 |
| Schottky TTL | 74SXX | 74SO2 |
| Low Power Schottky TTL | 74LSXX | 74LSO2 |

Out of the five categories 74LSXX series is most popular. We next present summary of various specifications of TTL ICs in Table 10.7.

**Table 10.7 Specifications of various TTL families**

| *Parameters* | *Series* | | | | |
|---|---|---|---|---|---|
| | *7400* | *74H00* | *74LOO* | *74SOO* | *74LSOO* |
| $V_{OH}$ | 2.4 V | 2.4 V | 2.4 V | 2.7 V | 2.7V |
| $V_{OL}$ | 0.4 V | 0.4 V | 0.4 V | 0.5 V | 0.5 V |
| $V_{IH}$ | 2.0 V | 2.0 V | 2.0 V | 2.0 V | 2.0 V |
| $V_{IL}$ | 0.80 V | 0.8 V | 0.7 V | 0.8 V | 0.8 V |
| $I_{OH}$ | –400μA | –500 μA | –200 μA | –1000 μA | –400 μA |
| $I_{OL}$ | 16 mA | 20 mA | 3.6 mA | 20 mA | 8 mA |
| $I_{IH}$ | 40 μA | 50 μA | 10 μA | 50 μA | 20 μA |
| $I_{IL}$ | –1.6 mA | –2.0 mA | –0.18 mA | –2.0 mA | –0.36 mA |
| $t_{PHL}$ | 15 n sec | 10 n sec | 60 n sec | 5 n sec | 15 n sec |
| $t_{PLH}$ | 22 n sec | 10 n sec | 60 n sec | 4.5 n sec | 15 n sec |
| $I_{CC}$ (1) | 8 mA | 16.8 mA | 0.8 mA | 16 mA | 1.6 mA |
| $I_{CC}$ (0) | 22 mA | 40 mA | 2.04 mA | 36 mA | 4.4 mA |
| FAN OUT | 10 | 10 | 20 | 10 | 20 |

Note that specifications of standard TTL were already presented in subsection 10.3.61, but are summarized in Table 10.7 for comparison. Although the data presented in table 10.7 are typical for TTL families, we highly recommend to refer to manufacturers data sheet for exact ratings. Note that from table 10.7 it is very much evident that lower propagation delay comes at the cost of increased power dissipation.

### 10.3.7 Emitter Coupled Logic (ECL)

ECL is another NON Saturated LOGIC FAMILY in which transistors are driven into cutoff and active region. The ECL family offers improved noise performance and is fastest of all logic families. In fact propagation delays as low as 1 n sec are possible with ECL. Basic ECL gate is described in subsection 10.3.7.

In fact the basic TTL, DTL, RTL etc. all have limits on their speed because they are based saturation region operation of transistors. If transistors are driven in active region, then the speed can be dramatically improved. But active region spans to a small voltage width and small temperature variations, component drift can shift the transistors to saturation. Thus stable operation in active region is difficult. A high emitter resistance can solve this problem, but poses another problem. It makes difficult to turn the transistor in active region from cut off region with small voltage change at input. The problem can be solved if current drawn by the transistors from supply is not switched OFF and ON. The difference amplifier is a circuit in which current drawn from supply is never switched OFF, rather it is shifted from one transistor to another. Also note that using difference amplifier offers high CMRR, means there is effective rejection of noise.

The basic ECL gate is formed around a difference amplifier only. The logic operations are performed by difference amplifier and its outcome is given to output stage. For this reason, we first present simplified description of difference amplifier and then move to the basic ECL gate circuit.

### *10.3.7.1 Difference Amplifier*

Basic configuration of a difference amplifier is shown in Fig. 10.53. Voltage at the base of transistor $Q_2$ is kept constant by supplying a voltage $V_R$. The values of resistor $R_{E_1}$, $R_{C_2}$ and $V_R$ are choosen such that $Q_2$ operates in active region. Whenever an input $V_{i_1} > V_R$ is applied to the base of $Q_1$, the transistor $Q_1$ conducts in active region and $Q_2$ goes to cutoff. The situation is reversed when $V_{i_1}$ is well below the $V_R$. Let us see how it is happening.

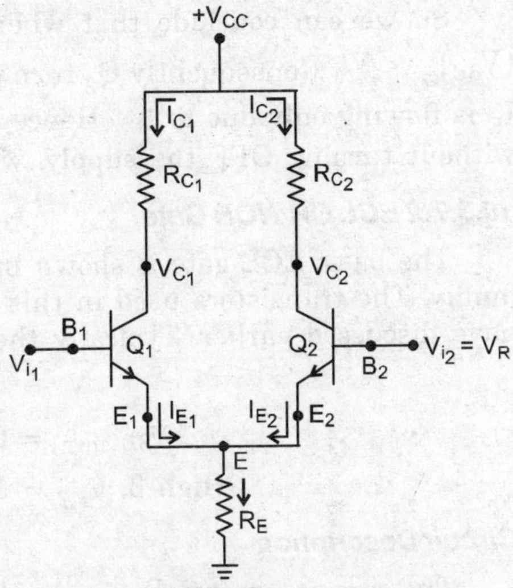


**Fig. 10.53** Difference amplifier

**When $V_{i_1}$ << $V_R$** *i.e.,* when $V_{i_1} < (V_v)Q_1$. At this time $Q_2$ start conduction causing a current to flow through the emitter resistance $R_E$. The current through emitter resistor $R_E$ is

$$I_E = I_{E_1} + I_{E_2}$$

$$= I_{E_2} \text{ as } I_{E_1} = 0$$

Thus the drop across the emitter resistance $R_E$ is

$$V_{RE} = V_E = I_{E_2}R_E \qquad ...(10.43)$$

Since $Q_2$ is conducting the drop $V_E$ is such that $(V_{BE})_{Q_2} > V_v$.

**When $V_{i_1}$ = $V_R$** As soon as $V_{i_1}$ exceeds $V_v$ for $Q_1$, it starts conduction and when $V_i = V_R$ both the transistors conduct same current, through them. This reduces the forward biasing of $Q_2$. Because,

$$(V_{BE})_{Q_2} = V_{B_2} - V_{E_2}$$

$$= V_R - V_{E_2}$$

$$(V_{BE})_{Q_2} = V_R - V_E \qquad ...(10.44)$$

and
$$V_E = (I_{E_1} + I_{E_2})\, R_E \qquad ...(10.45)$$

**When $V_{i_1}$ > $V_R$** $Q_1$ conducts more heavily and $Q_2$ conducts less because $V_E$ increases further when $V_{i_1} > V_R$. It is because

$$(V_{BE})_{Q_1} = V_{B_1} - V_E$$

but
$$V_{B_1} = V_{i_1} \text{ applied input}$$

so
$$V_E = V_{i_1} - (V_{BE})_{Q_1}$$

$$V_E = V_{i_1} - 0.7 \qquad ...(10.46)$$

Thus if $V_i \uparrow$ it causes $V_E \uparrow$.

By equation (10.44) $(V_{BE})_{Q_2} = V_R - V_E$

So if $V_E \uparrow$ is causes $(V_{BE})_{Q_2} \downarrow$

So we can conclude that when $V_{i_1} \uparrow$ we get $(V_{BE})_{Q_2} \downarrow$ and if $V_{i_1}$ is sufficiently high $(V_{BE})_{Q_2} < V_v$. Consequently $Q_2$ turn off and only $Q_1$ remains in conduction. Thus, the current $I_E$ is flowing only due to $I_{E_1}$. Hence applying $V_{i_1} > V_R$ the current $I_E$ is shifted from $Q_2$ to $Q_1$ without turning OFF the supply, which is the requirement.

### 10.3.7.2 ECL OR/NOR Gate

The basic ECL gate is shown in Fig. 10.54. As earlier stated it is a non-saturated logic family. The transistors used in this family needs slightly high specifications than those we have discussed earlier. Typically they require

$$V_v = 0.7\text{V}$$

$$V_{BE_{ACTIVE}} = 0.75 \text{ V}$$

$$\text{High } \beta,\ h_{FE} = 50 \text{ to } 150$$

### Circuit Description

The circuit essentially is divided into three parts. They are input stage, difference amplifier and emitter followers or level translators. Note that the $V_{CC} = 0$, *i.e.*, grounded and a negative supply is used. Thus the directions of current is conventional. Use of negative voltage offers better noise performance and protects the circuit from accidental grounding.

The input transistors are used to take logic inputs A and B. The two transistors are replaced for transistor $Q_1$ of Fig. 10.53.

Second stage is difference amplifier, which is heart of the circuit. All the logic operations are performed by this stage only. Also note that emitters of transistors in this stage are connected together and thus the name emitter coupled logic.

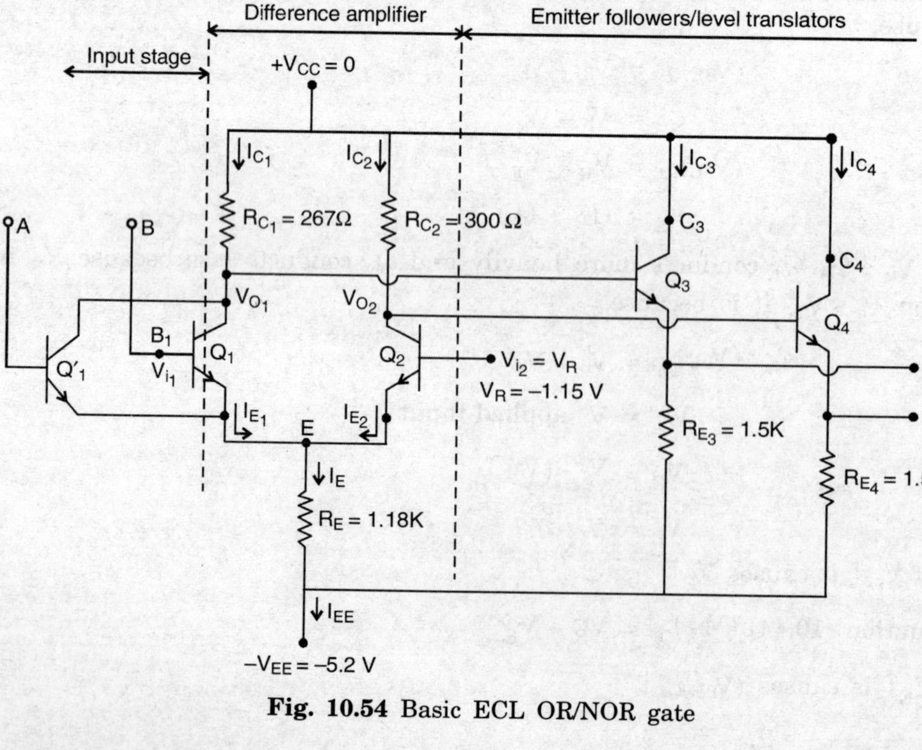


**Fig. 10.54** Basic ECL OR/NOR gate

The use of emitter followers increases the resistance that appears at emitter of difference amplifier, which is desired. It is also use to shift the output voltage such that output level and input voltage levels corresponding to V(0) and V(1) are same.

### Circuit Operation

**When all the inputs are LOW** transistors $Q_1$ and $Q'_1$ are OFF and $Q_2$ is ON. This causes a current $I_{C_2}$ to flow through the resistor $R_{C_3}$, and consequently collector of $Q_2$ goes LOW. This is provided at the output through $Q_4$ at $Y_{OR}$ output. Since current through $R_E$ only due to $Q_2$, voltage at common collector of input $V_{O_1}$ goes HIGH and this is provided at output $Y_{NOR}$ through transistor $Q_3$. Thus when all inputs are LOW *i.e.,*

$$A = B = \text{LOW}\, Y_{OR} = \text{LOW} \quad \text{and} \quad Y_{NOR} = \text{HIGH}.$$

**When either or both inputs are HIGH** the transistor $Q_2$ goes to cut off and input transistor(s) conduct causing a current $I_{C_1}$ to flow through resistor $R_{C_1}$. This causes the voltage $V_{O_1}$ to go LOW and this is provided at the output $Y_{NOR}$ through transistor $Q_3$. Since $Q_2$ is in cut off voltage $V_{O2}$ at its collector goes HIGH, which is provided at output $Y_{OR}$ through transistor $Q_4$. Thus

when $\quad A = B = \text{HIGH}$

or $\quad A = \text{HIGH and } B = \text{LOW or } A = \text{LOW and } B = \text{HIGH}$

then $\quad Y_{OR} = \text{HIGH and } Y_{NOR} = \text{LOW}$

The above discussion adequately concludes that the output available at $Y_{OR} = A + B$ and $Y_{NOR} = \overline{A+B}$. Unlike other gates, the ECL gate provides complementry outputs, which is helpful in many of the design problems. The symbol of ECL OR/NOR gate is shown in Fig. 10.55.

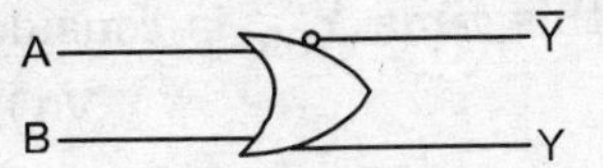


**Fig. 10.55** Symbol of ECL OR/NOR Gate

**OPEN EMITTER OUTPUT:** In high speed digital application the resistors $R_{E_3}$ and $R_{E_4}$ are not connected and the emitters of $Q_3$ to $Q_4$ are available directly as the output pin of IC, as shown in Figure 10.56. In fact in such applications the IC output is used to drive the load line directly. The load line at the other end is terminated by the characteristics impedance of load line.

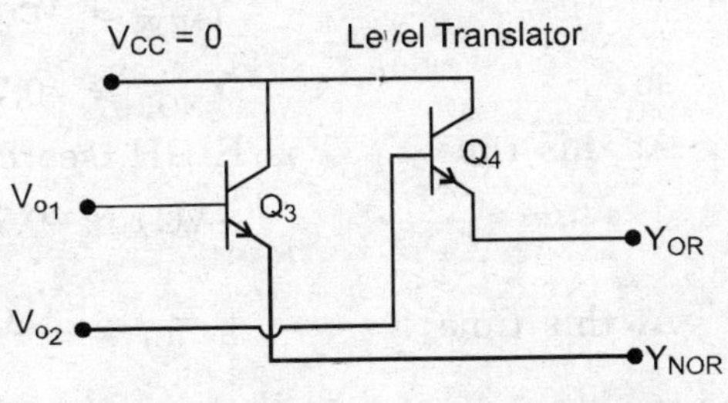


**Fig. 10.56** Open emitter output

### 10.3.7.3 Circuit Analysis

In this subsection, we are concerned with the calculate of various parameter. The main reason to separate this analysis from previous subsection is to simplify the discussion.

**Let us first consider that all inputs are Low**

In this situation, all input transistors are cut off, only $Q_2$ will conduct. Thus

$$I_{E_1} = 0$$

$$\text{Voltage at point E, } V_E = V_R - (V_{BE})_{Q_2}$$

$$= -1.15 - 0.75$$

$$V_E = -1.9 \text{ V} \quad \quad ...(10.47)$$

thus current $$I_E = \frac{V_E - V_{EE}}{R_E} = \frac{-1.9-(-5.2)}{1.18 \times 10^3} = 2.7966 \text{ mA}$$

So $$I_E \cong 2.8 \text{ mA} \qquad \text{...(10.48)}$$

Since $Q_2$ in active region $I_{B_2} << I_{C_2}$ so $I_{C_2} \cong I_{E_2} = I_E$

thus $$I_{C_2} \cong 2.8 \text{ mA}$$

So voltage across collector resistance $R_{C_2}$ is given as

$$V_{RC_2} = I_{C_2}.R_{C_2} = 2.8 \times 10^{-3} \times 300$$

$$V_{RC_2} = 0.84 \text{ V}$$

So voltage at collector of $Q_2$, is given as

$$V_{O_2} = V_{CC} - V_{RC_2} = 0 - 0.84$$

So $$V_{O_2} = -0.84 \text{ V} \qquad \text{...(10.49)}$$

At this time $Q_4$ is conducting, so

$$Y_{OR} = V_{O_2} - (V_{BE})_{Q_4} = -0.84 - 0.75$$

So $$Y_{OR} = -1.59 \text{ V} \qquad \text{...(10.50)}$$

At this time $Y_{OR}$ is considered LOW, see circuit operation, so

$$V(0) = -1.59 \text{ V} \qquad \text{...(10.51)}$$

since $Q_1$ and $Q_1'$ are in cut off $V_{O_1}$ = OV, thus $V_{C_3} = V_{B_3}$ = OV. Thus B-E-junction of $Q_3$ acts as diode. Thus

$$Y_{NOR} = V_{CC} - (V_{BE})_{Q_3} = 0 - 0.75$$

so $$Y_{NOR} = -0.75 \text{ V} \qquad \text{...(10.52)}$$

At this time $Y_{NOR}$ is HIGH, see circuit operation, so

$$V(1) = -0.75 \text{ V} \qquad \text{...(10.53)}$$

At this time $$I_{E_3} = \frac{Y_{NOR} - V_{EE}}{R_{E_3}} = \frac{-0.75-(-5.2)}{1.5 \times 10^3} = 2.966 \text{ mA}$$

So $$I_{E_3} \cong 3 \text{ mA} \qquad \text{...(10.54)}$$

**Let input A = HIGH,** in this case $Q_1$ will be conducting and $Q_2$ will be in cut off. So

$$V_E = V_{i1} - (V_{BE})_{Q_1} = V(1) - 0.75 = -0.75 - 0.75$$

So $$V_E = -1.5\text{V} \qquad \text{...(10.55)}$$

since $$V(1) = -0.75 \text{ V}$$

In this case emitter current $I_E$ is due to $Q_1$ only.

So $$I_{E_1} = I_E = \frac{V_E - V_{EE}}{R_E} = \frac{-1.5-(-5.2)}{1.18 \times 10^3} = 3.13559 \times 10^{-3}$$

So $$I_{E_1} = I_E \cong 3.14 \text{ mA} \qquad \text{...(10.56)}$$

$$V_{O_1} = V_{CC} - V_{RC_1} = 0 - 3.14 \times 10^{-3} \times 267 \text{ as } I_{C_1} \cong I_{E_1}$$

So $$V_{O_1} \cong -0.84 \text{ V} \qquad \text{...(10.57)}$$

and $$Y_{NOR} = V_{O_1} - (V_{BE})_{Q_3} = -0.84 - 0.75$$

So $$Y_{NOR} = -1.59 \text{ V} = V(O) \qquad \text{...(10.58)}$$

**So same voltage corresponding to LOW output is obtained, which justifies the use of level translators. In the similar way**

$$Y_{OR} = -0.75 \text{ V} = V(1)$$

**Example 10.9.** *Find out the noise margin and average power dissipation by the ECL gate.*

**Solution.** To find out noise margin we must find out the base to emitter drop of transistors when they are in cut off.

When $Y_{OR}$ = LOW $Q_1$ and $Q_1'$ are in cut off as A = B = V(0)

$$(V_{BE})_{Q_1} = V_B - V_E = V(0) - V_E$$

then by equation 10.47 and 10.51

$$(V_{BE})_{Q_1} = -1.59 - (-1.9)$$

$$= 0.31\text{V}$$

So $$(V_{BE})_{Q_1} \cong 0.3 \text{ V}$$

but for ECL transistors are choosen with $V_v$ = 0.7 V.

So a positive noise of 0.4 V will make $Q_1$ in conduction. Thus

$$\Delta 0 = 0.4 \text{ V} \qquad \text{...(10.59)}$$

Similar situation occurs when $Y_{OR}$ = HIGH and $Q_2$ is in cut off. At this time also

$$(V_{BE})_{Q_2} \cong 0.3 \text{ V}$$

and hence $$\Delta 1 = 0.4 \text{ V} \qquad \text{...(10.60)}$$

Note that, if we take transistors with cutin voltage of 0.5 V we will get nose margin of 0.2V. Thus using transistors of high cutin voltages are advantageous.

To find out average power dissipation we must find out the HIGH state and LOW state supply current.

**when $Y_{OR}$ = LOW,** then by equations (10.48) and (10.54), we get

$$I_E = 2.8 \text{ mA and } I_{E_3} = 3 \text{ mA}$$

and $$I_{EE}(O) = I_E + I_{E_3} + I_{E_4}$$

we've $$I_{E_4} = \frac{Y_{OR} - V_{EE}}{R_{E_4}} = \frac{-1.59 - (-5.2)}{1.5 \times 10^3} = 2.4066 \text{ mA}$$

So $$I_{E_4} \cong 2.41 \text{ mA} \qquad \text{...(10.61)}$$

thus $$I_{EE}(O) = 2.8 \text{ mA} + 3 \text{ mA} + 2.41 \text{ mA}$$

or $$I_{EE}(O) = 8.21 \text{ mA} \qquad \text{...(10.62)}$$

when $Y_{OR}$ = HIGH then by equation (10.56)

$$I_E = 3.14 \text{ mA}$$

at this time $I_{E_4}$ = 3 mA and $I_{E_3}$ = 2.41 mA, as situation for transistors $Q_3$ and $Q_4$ are just reversed.

$$\text{so} \quad I_{EE}(1) = 3.14 \text{ mA} + 3 \text{ mA} + 2.41 \text{ mA}$$

$$\text{or} \quad I_{EE}(1) = 8.55 \text{ mA} \quad \text{...(10.63)}$$

$$\text{we've} \quad P_{avg} = \frac{P(O) + P(1)}{2} = \frac{I_{EE}(0) + I_{EE}(1)}{2} . V_{EE}$$

$$= \frac{8.21 \text{ mA} + 8.55 \text{ mA}}{2} .5.2 \text{ V} = 43.576 \text{ mW}$$

$$\text{or} \quad P_{avg} \cong 43.6 \text{ mW} \quad \text{...(10.64)}$$

**FAN OUT** of ECL gates are higher. It is because they offers low output impedance and high input impedance. When all inputs are LOW input transistors offers high input impedance. When any input is HIGH then input impedance of emitter followers appears at input stage, which is already high. Thus input impedance of ECL gate is always High. At the output side $Q_3$ and $Q_4$ are always conducting either as diode or transistors. So output impedance is always low. Hence FAN OUT is HIGH.

**Wired Logic** performed by the ECL gates are OR. Hence if we simply wire the output of ECL gates we can obtain variety of functions. This is illustrated in Fig. 10.57.

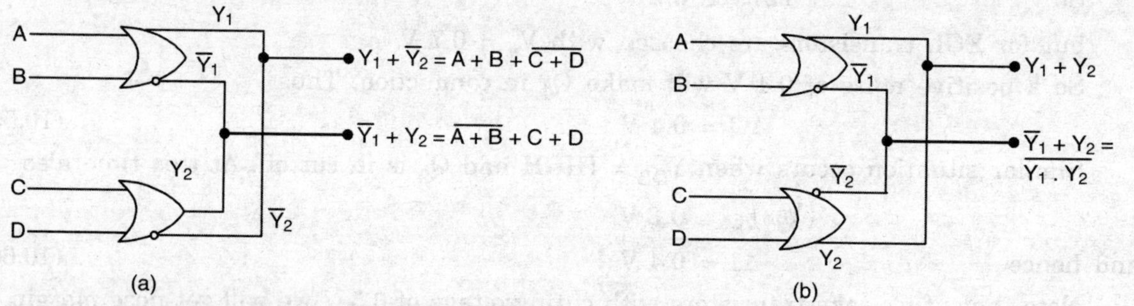


**Fig. 10.57** Illustration of wired logic for ECL gate.

Let us see how wired logic comes. Consider the wiring of only $Y_{OR}$ output as shown in Fig. 10.58(*a*). Before proceeding further we reinsert that all the voltages are measured with respect to ground.

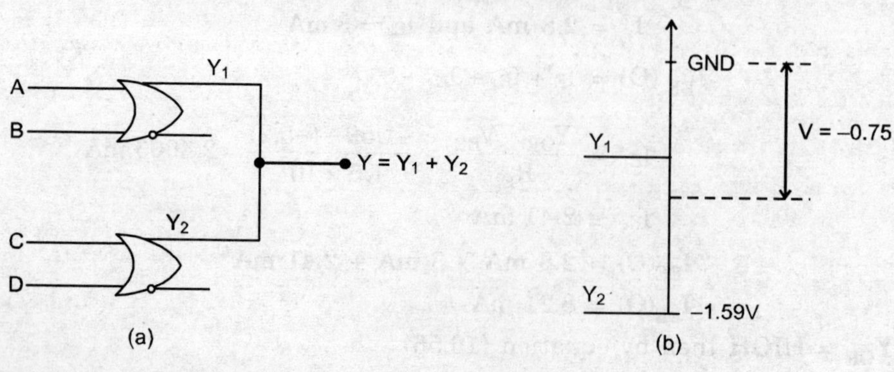


**Fig. 10.58** Illustration of wired-or ing in ECL

When both are LOW *i.e.,* $Y_1 = V(0) = -1.59$ V $= Y_2$ then Y = –1.59 V as $Y_1$ and $Y_2$ forms two equipotential points. Hence Y = V(0) = LOW.

When both $Y_1$ and $Y_2$ are HIGH *i.e.,* $Y_1 = Y_2 = V(1) = -0.75$ then Y = –0.75. So

$$Y = V(1) = \text{HIGH}.$$

When $Y_1 = V(1) = -0.75$ and $Y_2 = V(0) = -1.55$ V then when we measure Y with respect to ground we get Y = –0.75 $V_1$ as shown in Fig. 10.58(*b*). Thus Y = V(1) = HIGH.

This concludes that wiring two outputs of ECL gates perform wired-OR.

## 10.3.8 MOS Logic

MOS Logic has become popular logic because of their high packing density. As indicated in the beginning the MOS devices, however have larger propagation delays and thus have slower speed than the Bipolar logic families. But in present days due to advancements in VLSI technologies, MOS devices can be fabricated even in much smaller areas, which implies that propagation delays will be low. If the present trend continue, MOS families may match the speed of the Bipolar families. Another advantage of MOS is, we can use only MOS devices without using any resistor. A MOS device itself can be configured as resistance as shown in figure 10.59. When configured as load the MOS devices offers approximately 100 KΩ resistance. Even though either enhance mode or depletion mode devices can be as load, preferred are depletion mode load. It is because the depletion mode MOS have maximum current when gate voltage is O. It is good to use MOS as load resistance because a normal resistor takes area 20 times of area taken by a MOS device.

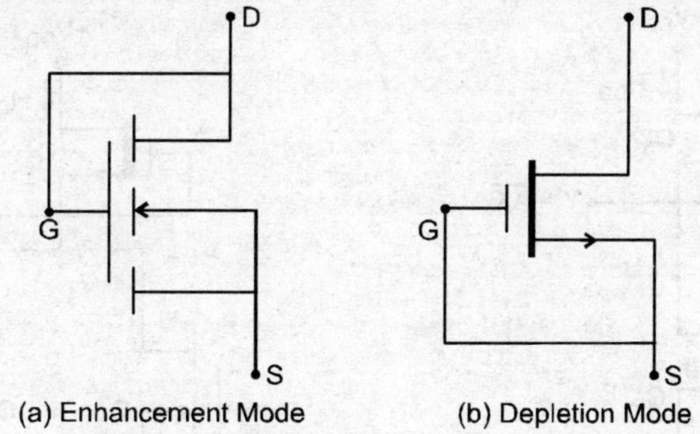


**Fig. 10.59** NMOS as load or resistor

### *10.3.8.1 NMOS Gates*

The various gates are shown below.

**NOT GATE** Basic NMOS NOT gate is shown in Fig. 10.60. Transistor $Q_2$ is a depletion mode transistor acting as load. Transistor $Q_1$ is driver transistor which performs logic operation.

**When $V_{in}$ = V(0) = 0,** transistor $Q_1$ does not conduct and acts as open circuit as shown in Fig. 10.60(*b*). Thus $+V_{DD}$ appears at the output, which is a HIGH voltage. So we get when $V_{in}$ = V(0) = LOW, $V_0 \cong +V_{DD}$ = V(1) *i.e.,* Y = HIGH.

**When $V_{in}$ = V(1) = $+V_{DD}$** transistor $Q_1$ start conduction and a current flows through the circuit. In this case transistors $Q_1$ acts as switch is closed, Condition, as shown in Fig. 10.60 (*c*). Thus ground voltage or OV appears at the output which is LOW state. Thus when $V_{in}$ = (1), $V_O$ = OV = V(0) *i.e.,* Y = LOW.

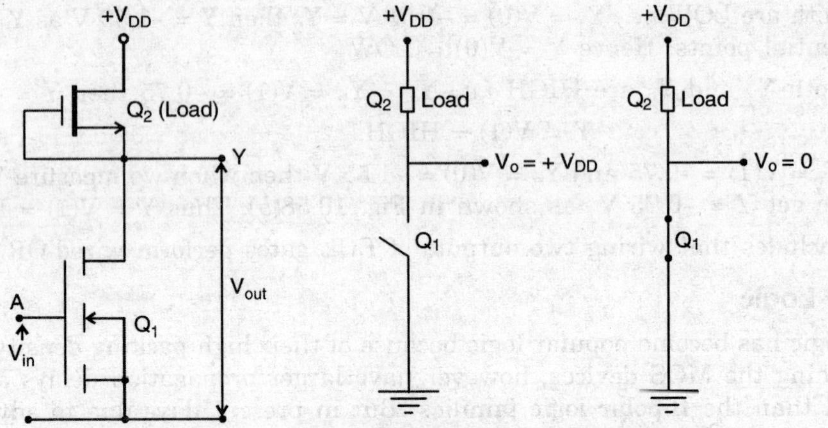


(a) Circuit diagram (b) Gate when $V_{in} = 0$ (c) Gate when $V_{in} = 1$

**Fig. 10.60** NMOS inverter with depletion load

From the above discussion it is also clear that the circuit shown in Fig. 10.60(*c*) is a NOT gate with the voltage levels V(0) = 0 V and V(1) = $+V_{DD}$.

**NAND GATE:** The NMOS NAND gate is shown in figure 10.61. As usual transistor $Q_3$ is load transistor and $Q_1$ and $Q_2$ are driver transistor which performs logic operation. From the circuit we observe that when A = B = HIGH = V(1), then $Q_1$ and $Q_2$ conducts and current $I_{DD}$ can flow in the circuit. In this situation $Q_1$ and $Q_2$ acts as switch in closed condition.

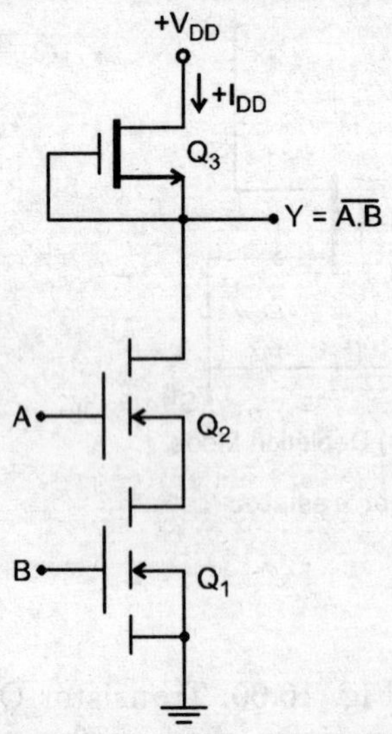


**Fig. 10.61** NMOS Nand gate with depletion load

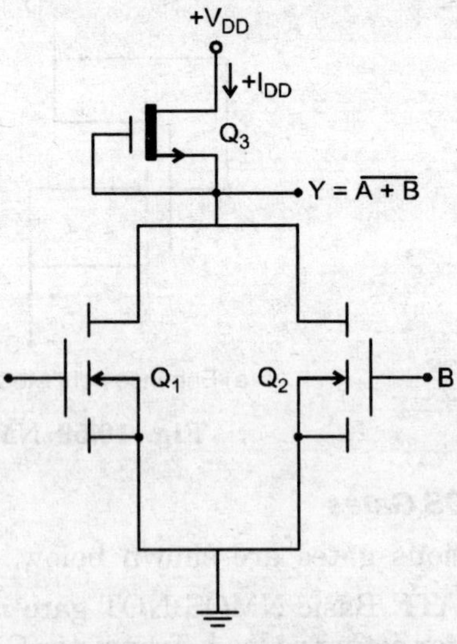


**Fig. 10.62** NMOS Nor gate with depletion load

Thus Y = V(0) = OV when A = B = V(1). If A = V(0) and B = V(1), then $Q_2$ acts as switch in open condition. Consequently $I_{DD}$ cannot flow in the circuit and Y = $+V_{DD}$ = V(1). Similar situation occurs when B is LOW and when both A and B are LOW. Thus the circuit gives Y = LOW when both A and B are HIGH otherwise = Y = HIGH. This clearly indicates that the circuit in Fig. 10.61 acts as NAND gate. Also note that the power dissipation will be low in this gate as current is drawn from $+V_{DD}$ only when both the inputs are HIGH. In all other situations no current is drawn.

**NOR GATE:** The NMOS NOR gate is shown in figure 10.62. Transistor $Q_3$ is load transistor and $Q_1$ and $Q_2$ are drivers which perform logic operation. It is evident from circuit that when both A = B = V(0), $Q_2$ and $Q_3$ does not conduct and current $I_{DD}$ does not flow. Thus Y = +$V_{DD}$ = V(1) = HIGH. If any of the inputs goes HIGH current $I_{DD}$-flows and consequently Y = OV = V(O) = LOW. Thus the output is HIGH only when all inputs are LOW otherwise output is LOW, which is clearly a NOR gate. Note that power dissipation in NOR gate is higher than NAND gate. It is because the current $I_{DD}$ does not flows only when both inputs are LOW. In all other input conditions current will flow in the circuit, and hence power dissipation is higher than NMOS NAND gate.

### *10.3.8.2 CMOS Gates*

A logic circuit that combines p-channel and n-channel MOS transistors on the same chip is known as complementary MOS or CMOS circuit. Major advantage of CMOS is very low power dissipation. Since, technology has improved such that a very small chip area is required to fabricated MOS devices the CMOS can now operate on faster speed. Indeed the CMOS circuits have already replaced TTL in many practical applications. CMOS can operate over a supply range of 3.3 V to 15 V. Low power CMOS circuits have emerged with supply of 3.3 V (as power dissipation is proportional to $V_{DD}^2$), but lower power supply reduces the noise immunity.

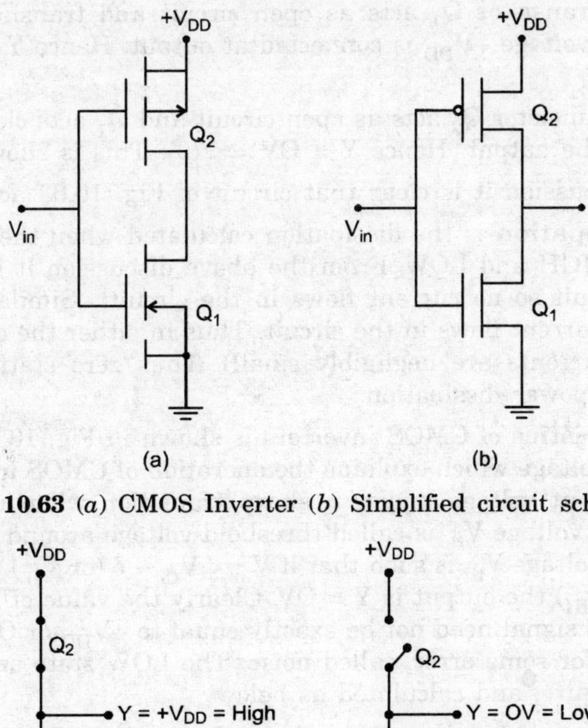


**Fig. 10.63** (*a*) CMOS Inverter (*b*) Simplified circuit schematic

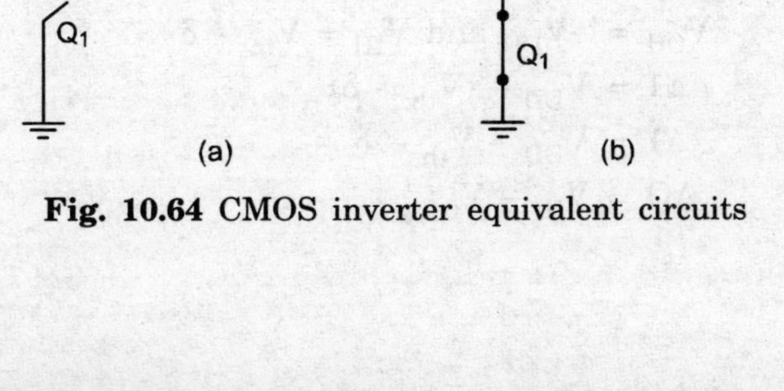


**Fig. 10.64** CMOS inverter equivalent circuits

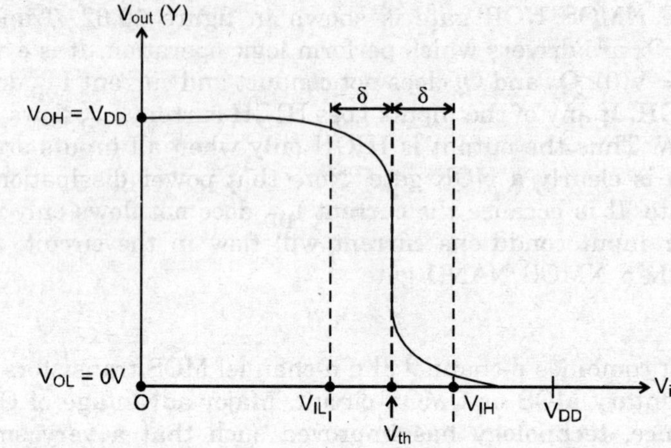


**Fig. 10.65** Voltage transfer characteristics of CMOS Inverter.

**CMOS INVERTER:** The basic CMOS gate is a NOT gate, called CMOS inverter shown in Fig. 10.63. Transistor $Q_1$ is an enhancement mode NMOS transistor and transistor $Q_2$ is enhancement mode PMOS transistor. The circuit operation is simple.

**When $V_{in}$ = V(0)** transistor $Q_1$ acts as open circuit and transistor $Q_2$ acts as close switch. Thus the supply voltage $+V_{DD}$ is connected at output. Hence Y = $+V_{DD}$ = V(1). This is shown in Fig. 10.64(*a*).

**When $V_{in}$ = V(1)** transistor $Q_2$ acts as open circuit and $Q_1$ acts close switch. Thus, the ground is connected at the output. Hence Y = OV = V(0). This is shown in Fig. 10.64(*b*).

From the above discussion it is clear that circuit of Fig. 10.63 acts as inverter.

**Static Power Dissipation** is the dissipation calculated when the output is static *i.e.,* output is steady state HIGH and LOW. From the above discussion it is clear that when Y = HIGH, $Q_1$ is open circuit so no current flows in the circuit. Similarly when Y = LOW, $Q_2$ is open circuit so no current flows in the circuit. Thus in either the case no current flows in circuit (as leakage currents are negligibly small). Thus zero static current flows and consequently zero static power dissipation.

**Transfer characteristics** of CMOS inverters is shown in Fig. 10.65. It is the curve of input voltage vs output voltage which explains the operation of CMOS inverter in detail. The curve indicates that output voltage makes a sharp transition when input voltage passes through a value $V_{th}$. The voltage $V_{th}$ is called threshold voltage around which the change in output takes place. The voltage $V_{th}$ is such that if $V_{in} < V_{th} - \delta$ (or $V_{IL}$) the output Y = $+V_{DD}$ and if $V_{in} > V_{th} + \delta$ (or $V_{IH}$) the output is Y = OV. Clearly the value of δ is very small. This does mean that the input signal need not be exactly equal to $+V_{DD}$ or OV to produce correct output. There is a room for some error, called noise. The LOW state and HIGH state noise margins are shown in figure, and calculated as below

$$\Delta 1 = V_{OH} - V_{IH} \qquad \text{...(10.65)}$$

For figure $\quad V_{OH} = +V_{DD}$ and $V_{IH} = V_{th} + \delta$

So $\quad \Delta 1 = V_{DD} - (V_{th} + \delta)$

or

$$\Delta 1 = V_{DD} - V_{th} - \delta \qquad \text{...(10.66)}$$

Similarly $\quad \Delta O = V_{IL} - V_{OL}$

$$= V_{th} - \delta - 0 \qquad \text{from figure}$$

or $$\Delta O = Vth - \delta \qquad ...(10.67)$$

This clearly indicates high noise immunity of logic gates.

**Dynamic Power Dissipation** is the dissipation that occurs when the gate is changing its output state *i.e.,* when output is going HIGH to LOW or LOW to HIGH. As indicated by transfer characteristics, around the $V_{th}$ there is situation when both $Q_1$ and $Q_2$ are conducting for a short while. It is because the devices cannot change its state instantaneously. This produces a short current pulse in the circuit with every change of state of output. Consequently there is power dissipation, called **dynamic power dissipation.** Thus in a CMOS circuit power dissipation depends upon the frequency of operation and increase linearly if frequency is increased. If $f$ is the frequency of switching and CMOS gate is driving a load capacitance C then the dynamic power dissipation is given as

$$P_D = f.C.V^2_{DD} \qquad ...(10.68)$$

where $V_{DD}$ is supply voltage.

**Propagation Delay** is mainly due to the high capacitance present at the input and output. When CMOS gate is driving N loads, the input capacitances of all N gates appears in parallel at the output of driver gate. Thus net output capacitance at drivers output is $C_{OUT} = C = C_O + NC_i$ where $C_O$ is capacitance of driver when looking back from output and $C_i$ is the input capacitance of load gates. Thus a large output capacitance is present whose charging and discharging is slower and hence the lower speed of operation. One way to improve it is to increase supply voltage, but this will increase the dynamic power dissipation and hence the average dissipation.

**Pull up and Pull down:** In the circuit shown in Fig. 10.63, we note that Y = HIGH when $Q_2$ conducts and $Q_1$ open circuit. Hence $Q_2$ can be regarded as pull up transistor. When Y = LOW, $Q_1$ conducts and can be regarded as pulldown transistor. Thus the circuit shown in fig. 10.63 can be redrawn as fig. 10.66. In fact Fig. 10.66 shows basic structure of any CMOS gate. Usually NMOS are used to form pull down network and PMOS are used to form pull up network. Connecting the two networks in a fashion shown in Fig. 10.66 can give variety of logic circuits. We use same methodology to draw NAND gates and NOR gates using CMOS.

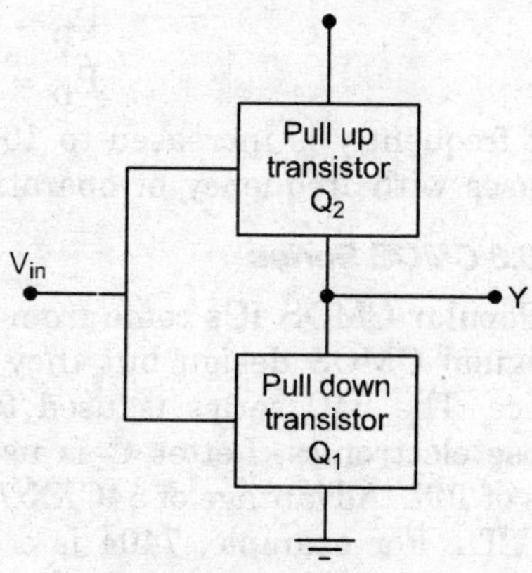


**Fig. 10.66** Structure of CMOS inverter

**NAND and NOR GATE:** Basic CMOS NAND gate and NOR gate circuits are shown in Figure 10.67 and 10.68. In both the cases $Q_1$ and $Q_2$ forms pull down network and $Q_3$ and $Q_4$ forms pull down network.

In NAND gate Y = OV = LOW only when both $Q_1$ and $Q_2$ conducts *i.e.,* when both A = B = V(1). In all other cases of input either or both the $Q_1$ and $Q_2$ are open so Y = $+V_{DD}$ = HIGH.

In NOR gate Y = $+V_{DD}$ = V(1) only when both $Q_3$ and $Q_4$ conduct and both $Q_1$ and $Q_2$ are open *i.e.,* at A = B = V(0) = OV. In all other cases either or both the $Q_1$ and $Q_2$ conducts so Y = OV = V(0) = LOW.

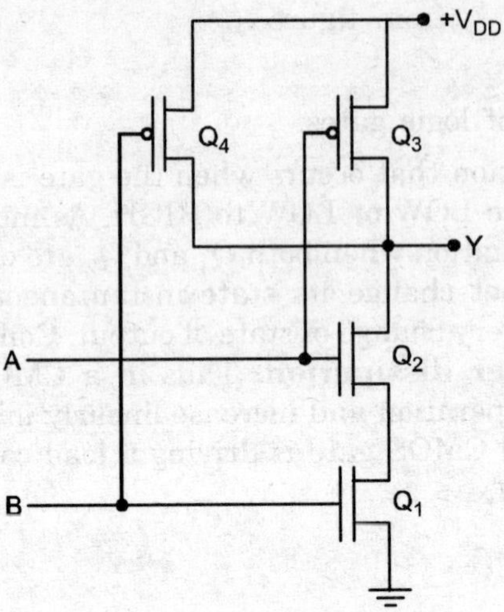


**Fig. 10.67** CMOS NAND gate

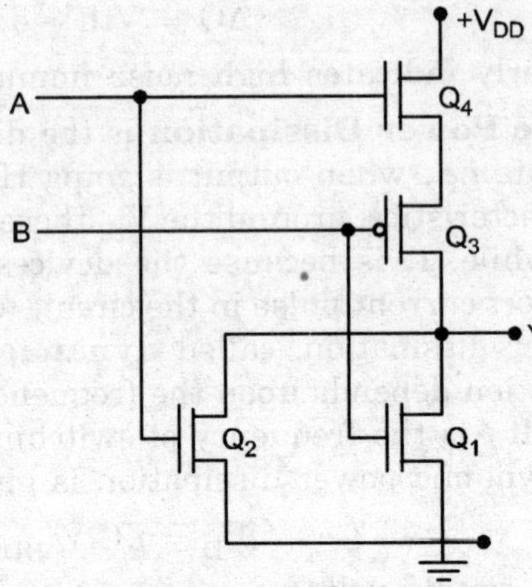


**Fig. 10.68** CMOS NOR gate

**Example 10.10.** *A CMOS inverter is driving an identical inverter at a supply of 5 V with the input feeded with square wave of 1MHz. If the input and output capacitances are 40 fF and 20 fF respectively then find out the dynamic power dissipation in the gate.*

**Solution.** We've $C_i = 40fF$ and $C_O = 20\ fF_1$ then at the output of Driver $C = C_i + C_O = 40\ fF + 20\ fF = 60\ fF$

Thus driver is said to be driving a capacitance of 60 *f*F. By equation 10.68 the dynamic power dissipation.

$$P_D = fCV^2{}_{DD} = 1 \times 10^6 \times 60 \times 10^{-15} \times (5)^2$$

$$P_D = 1.5\mu W, \text{ a considerably low dissipation.}$$

but if frequently is increased to 100 MHz, PD = 150 μW. Hence average power dissipation increases with frequency of operation.

#### *10.3.8.3 CMOS Series*

Popular CMOS ICs come from 40XX, 54CXX and 74CXX series. The 40XX series refers to original CMOS design but they lack compatibility with TTL, which is badly needed in practice. The 54C series is used for military purpose and 74C series is used for general purpose electronics. Letter C is used to discriminate the two series from 74XX and 54XX series of TTL. Advantage of 54CXX/74CXX is their pin to pin, function to function compatibility with TTL. For example, 7404 is a TTL inverter and 74C04 is a CMOS hex inverter. Both the ICs have inputs, outputs and supply at same pin number. Also a 54CXX series device can replace a 74CXX device, but it is rarely done due to higher cost of 54CXX devices. Table 10.8 summaries the different CMOS series and their compatibility with TTL.

**Table 10.8 Different CMOS series**

| *CMOS Series* | *Series Prefix* | *Example* | *Compatibility With TTL* |
|---|---|---|---|
| Standard CMOS series | 40XX | 4000<br>4009 | No compatibility |
| Compatible CMOS series | 74CXX | 74C00<br>74C04 | Pin to Pin and Function to function |

Contd...

| High speed Compatible CMOS series | 74HCXX | 74HC00<br>74HC04 | Pin to Pin and Function to function |
|---|---|---|---|
| High speed electrically compatible CMOS series | 74HCTXX | 74HCT04 | Pin to Pin<br>Function to Function<br>Electrically compatible |

Note that 74HCTXX series is electrically compatible means the current and voltage parameters are matched with TTL and at the same time pin to pin compatibility is available with TTL ICs. Various parameters for 74CXXCMOS series are summarized in figure 10.69 and Table 10.9, assuming supply voltage of 5 V.

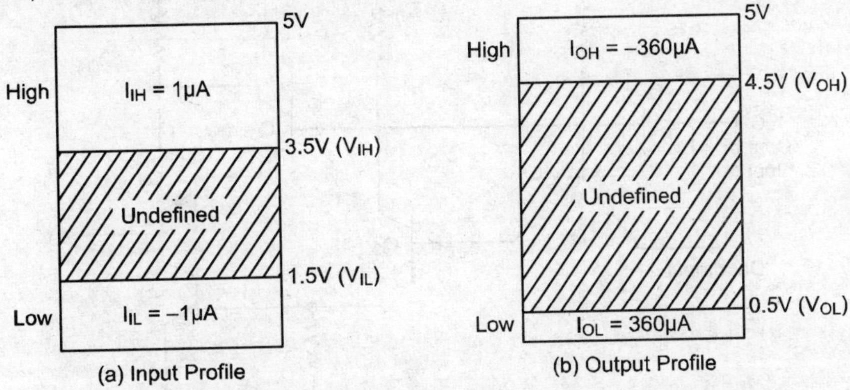


**Fig. 10.69** Input/output profile of 74CXX series with supply 5V

**Table 10.9 Parameters of 74CXX series with supply 5V**

| *Parameters* | *Values* |
|---|---|
| $t_{PHL}$ | 60 n sec |
| $t_{PLH}$ | 45 n sec |
| Static Power Dissipation | 10 nW |

## 10.3.9 Three State Logic (TSL)

In a logic circuit we have two output states LOW and HIGH. Logic circuits have been designed in which output can assume another state called high impedance state or High-z in short. Logics with three states of output are called tristate logic (TSL) or three state logic. When the output is in third state, the output is said to be disabled *i.e.,* neither HIGH nor LOW. In a microprocessor based system outputs of many logic devices has to be connected to a common **bus** which in turns may be driving number of other logic devices. Such connections cause a number of problem–

1. If the output is not in HIGH state it does not necessarily mean LOW state output.
2. Accidentally more than one logic device may drive the bus and can cause **bus contention,** which may damage the bus.
3. Active pull up outputs cannot be directly connected, because it introduces very high current spike. This causes overheating of IC and consequently IC may be damaged.

4. Connecting open collector output through a common external resistor causes problem of loading and speed.

To overcome such problems TSL are used, in which outputs are in High-Z, and they deliver a HIGH or LOW to bus only when they are made to come out of 3rd state through a control input.

The basic TSL circuit is a inverter called TSL inverter, and shown in Fig. 10.70. A close inspection of circuit reveals that it is a TTL NAND gate with some modification. Readers are advised to glance over the operation of TTL NAND gate.

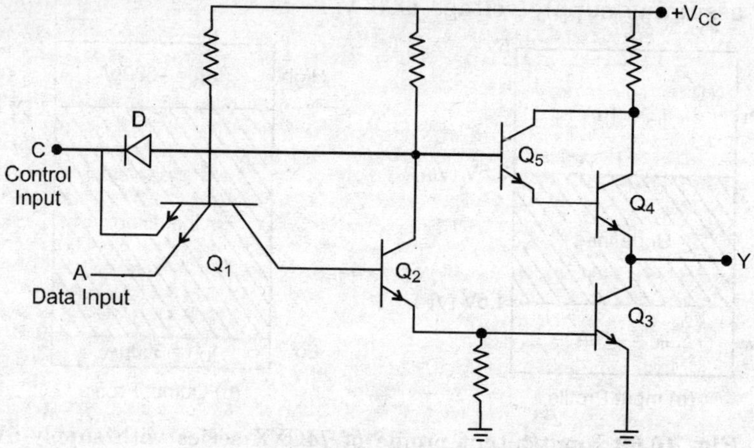


**Fig. 10.70** TSL inverter

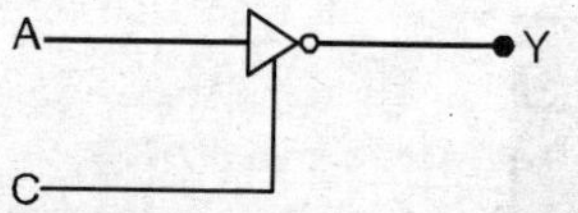


**Fig. 10.71** Logic symbol of TSL inverter

**Table 10.10 Truth table of TSL inverter**

| C | A | y |
|---|---|---|
| 0 | X | HIGH-Z |
| 1 | A | $\overline{A}$ |

**When C = V(0) = OV** diode D and corresponding B-E junction of $Q_1$ conducts. Recall that if any of B-E junction of $Q_1$ conducts, transistors $Q_2$ and $Q_3$ does not conduct and acts as open circuit. When diode D is conducting, the diode drop $V_D$ = 0.7 V appears at the base of $Q_5$ which is not sufficient to turn ON both $Q_4$ and $Q_5$, thus they act as open circuit. The result is very high impedance appeared at output. Thus, the output is in high impedance or 3rd state.

**When C = V(1) = +$V_{CC}$** The diode is open circuit and corresponding B-E junction of $Q_1$ is open circuit. The result is that the circuit behaves as 2-input TTL NAND gate whose one of the input is HIGH. Thus the gate acts as inverter.

The logic symbol of a TSL inverter and its truth table is shown in Fig. 10.71 and Table 10.10, respectively.

Another useful TSL circuit is **three state buffer** in which output is same as input. Such buffers are commonly used to enhance the driving capability of a logic device. The logic symbol and truth table of a three state buffer is shown in Fig. 10.72 and Table 10.11, respectively.

If we see datas for 74XX in table 10.7 we find that $I_{IL} = -1.6$ mA too much current for CMOS to sink. Thus, the output of CMOS cannot be connected directly to standard TTL. To overcome this problem CMOS buffers are used, as shown in Fig. 10.77. One such IC is 74C902 which is a hex buffer. Each of these buffers have

$$I_{OL} = 3.6 \text{ mA and } I_{OH} = 800 \text{ μA}$$

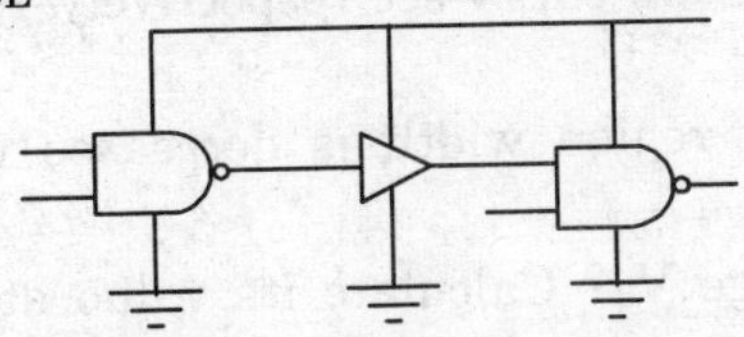


**Fig. 10.77** CMOS driving standard TTL

Thus if only one buffer of 74C902 is used then with $I_{IL} = -1.6$ mA of standard TTL and $I_{OL} = 3.6$ mA, we can obtain a FAN OUT of 2 gates. Use of remaining five buffers can increase the FAN OUT further.

## 10.5 COMPARISON OF LOGIC FAMILIES

A comparison of logic families is presented in table 10.12.

**Table 10.12 Comparison of logic gates**

| *Parameter* | *RTL* | *DTL* | *TTL* | | | | | *ECL* | *CMOS* |
|---|---|---|---|---|---|---|---|---|---|
| | | | *Standard 74XX* | *High Power 74HXX* | *Low Power 74LXX* | *Schottky 74SXX* | *Low Power Schottky 74LSXX* | | |
| Noise immunity | Average | good | very good | very good | very good | very good | very good | average | very good |
| Power Dissipation Per gate (mW) | 12 | 8-12 | 10 | 22 | 1 | 19 | 2 | 40-55 | 0.01 static 1 mW at 1 MHz |
| Propagation Delay Per gate (n sec) | 14 | 30 | 10 | 6 | 33 | 3 | 10 | 2 | 70 |
| Figure of Merit (PJ) | 168 | 300 | 100 | 132 | 33 | 57 | 20 | 95 | 0.7 |
| FAN OUT | 5 | 8 | 10 | 10 | 20 | 10 | 20 | 25 | Above 50 |
| Clocking Rate (MHz) | 8 | 72 | 35 | 50 | 3 | 125 | 45 | Above 60 | 10 |

## 10.6 EXERCISE

**1.** Define the terms 'Digital Circuits' and 'Logic Family'.

**2.** Why semiconductor devices are used in digital circuits instead of relays?

**3.** What is meant by integrated circuit (IC) and 'chip'?

**4.** (*a*) What is meant by intrinsic and extrinsic semiconductors?

(*b*) What type of impurities must be added to a pure semiconductor to obtain a p-type and n-type semiconductor?

5. Calculate the intrinsic carrier concentration in a standard silicon crystal at $t$ = 40°C.
6. Define the diffusion current and drift current.
7. Calculate the drift velocity of electrons and holes if mobility of electrons and holes are 1350 $cm^2/V$-sec and 450 $cm^2/V$-sec respectively. Assume applied electric field is 1 V/cm.
8. Explain how depletion region width is decreases when a PN junction diode is forward biased.
9. What is thermal voltage $V_T$? Calculate its value at room temperature.
10. Define the terms storage time and transition time for PN junction diode.
11. How schottky diode improves the speed of operation?
12. Why npn transistors are preferred over *pnp*?
13. Briefly explain how an emitter resistance can result in active mode operation of a transistor.
14. Explain the switching characteristics of a BJT with the help of diagrams.
15. Why switching speed of a BJT is limited? How a schottky transistor can improve it?
16. Explain the principle of operation of MOS devices.
17. Why MOS devices are called unipolar?
18. Define the threshold voltage of a MOS device.
19. Draw and explain $I_D$ Vs $V_{DS}$ curve of MOS devices.
20. Why packing density of NMOS is higher than PMOS?
21. What is CMOS? Why its use in digital circuit is advantageous?
22. Why switch ON to switch OFF time of a BJT switch is larger?
23. Define the terms MSI, VLSI and ULSI.
24. Classify the logic families on the basis of polarity of charge carriers used for current conduction.
25. Define the delays $t_{PHL}$ and $t_{PLH}$.
26. (*a*) What is meant by figure of merit of a logic gate?

    (*b*) For a gate value of figure of merit should be high or low. Why?
27. Explain the AC noise margin and DC noise margin. How it helps the designer?
28. Define FAN IN and FAN OUT of a logic gate.
29. What is meant by passive pull up and active pull up? Why they are called so?
30. What is meant by pull down?
31. What is meant by open collector output and open emitter output ? Where they are used?
32. What is the output logic performed by a RTL gates, when their output is wired?
33. Calculate the FAN OUT and NOISE Margin of RTL gates.
34. Why propagation delay of a RTL gate increases when number of load gates are increased?

**35.** What is current hogging in DCTL?

**36.** Why switching speed of HTL gate is severely affected?

**37.** Why average power dissipation increases when wired logic is performed?

**38.** What are the reasons behind limited switching speed of DTL gates? How it can be improved?

**39.** What is the purpose of transistor $Q_1$ in modified DTL gate shown in Fig. 10.45?

**40.** Why the speed of operation of passive pull up TTL is limited?

**41.** (*a*) What happens if an input of TTL is left floating?

(*b*) What will be the output of TTL gates shown below?

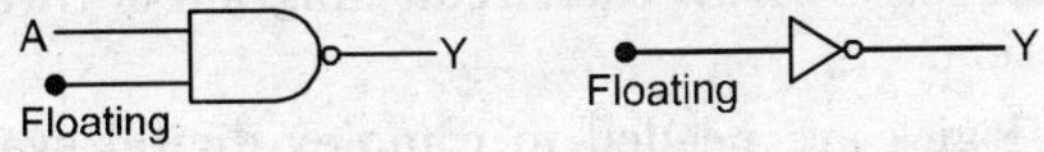


(i) (ii)

**42.** Calculate the FAN OUT of DTL NAND gate of Fig. 10.40 if transistor has

(*i*) $h_{FE} = 20$

(*ii*) $h_{FE} = 40$

**43.** When outputs of gates are wired, explain

(*a*) How the speed of operation is improved?

(*b*) Why the FAN OUT is reduced?

**44.** How FAN OUT of TTL in wired logic can be improved?

**45.** (*a*) Explain the operation of pull up transistor and phase splitter in active pull up TTL.

(*b*) What is the purpose of using diode in output circuit of active pull up TTL? Comment an its PIV rating.

**46.** Why wired logic is not recommended for TTL with active pull up?

**47.** With the help of data given in Table 10.7, calculate the FAN OUT and figure of merit of 7400, 74S00 and 74LS00.

**48.** Why schottky TTL is faster than standard TTL?

**49.** Which is the fastest logic family? Why?

**50.** Why propagation delay is lower in ECL?

**51.** Why FAN OUT of ECL is higher?

**52.** What are the advantages of using difference amplifier in ECL?

**53.** Explain the wired logic performed by ECL gates.

**54.** Why transistors of high $\beta$ and high cut in voltages are used in ECL?

**55.** Realize the boolean function $y = (A + B) + (C + D) + \overline{(A + B)(C + D)}$ by using minimum number of 2 input ECL gates only and 2 input TTL gates only. Comment on the result.

**56.** In MOS logic, why a MOS transistor is used as load instead of a resistor?

**57.** Why depletion mode load is preferred over enhancement mode load in MOS logic?

**58.** Draw the circuit diagram of NMOS NOR gate and explain its operation. Also draw the truth table in which voltage levels corresponding to logic states are shown.

**59.** Why power dissipation in an NMOS NAND gate is lower than that of NMOS NOR gate?

**60.** With the help of circuit diagram explain CMOS inverter.

**61.** What is meant by static and dynamic power dissipation?

**62.** Draw and explain transfer characteristics of CMOS inverters.

**63.** Why average power dissipation of a CMOS gate increases with frequency of operation?

**64.** What is three state logic? Draw the circuit diagram of three state NAND gate and explain its operation.

**65.** Why three state logics are needed in complex digital system?

**66.** What are the requirements of interfacing two logic gates?

**67.** With the help of data sheet, obtain interfacing of CMOS to 74LSXX TTL.

**68.** Compare CMOS and TTL.

# APPENDICES

## APPENDIX A

### INTEGRATED CIRCUITS

In 1948, Schokley, Baardeen and Brattain, invented the transistor device. This device was not only cheap, more reliable, less power consuming, but side by side very small in size as compared to the vacuum tubes prevailed in those days. As the size of the active component (*i.e.*, those components, which produces gain, viz., vacuum-tube amplifier etc) decreases, so the passive components (viz., resistors, capacitors, coils etc.) also got very much reduced in size, making the complete electronic circuitry very small. The development of "Printed Circuit Boards" (PCBs), further reduced size of electronic equipments as a whole, by eliminating bulky wiring and tie-points.

In early 1960s, a new field called as **Microelectronics** was developed, to meet the requirements of Military, which wanted to reduce the size of its electronics equipments, to about 1/10th of its existing one. This led to the development of microelectronic circuits, later called **integrated Circuits** (ICs), which were so small that the fabrication was done under microscopes.

An IC can be described as a complete microelectroniccircuit in which both the active and passive components are fabricated on a extremely thin chip of silicon (called as substrate), in general.

ICs are produced by the same processes, as are used for making individual diodes, transistors etc. In such circuits, different components are isolated from one another by isolation diffusion, within the crystal-chip, and are interconnected by an aluminum layer, that serves as wires. J.K. Kilby was the first to develop (in 1958) such an IC—a single monolithic silicon chip, with both the active and passive components. He was soon followed by Robert Noyce, whose IC included the interconnection, on the chip itself. It had about 10 individual components, the chip was 3 mm (0.12 inch) square. The development of Large-Scale Integration (LSI) during the early 1970s made it possible to pack thousands of transistors and other components on a chip of roughly the same size. This technology gave rise to the **Microprocessor** on IC, that contained all the arithmetic logic and control circuitry needed to carry out the functions of a digital computer's Central Processing Unit (CPU). Very Large Scale Integration (VLSI), developed during the 1980 has vastly increased the circuit-density of microprocessors, as well as of "memory" and support chips. This technology has yield, 30,00,000 transistors on a chip of less than 4 cm chip.

ICs are of several types: Monolithic ICs, also called semiconductor or silicon integrated circuits. These are formed by the superposition of layers of materials, in various patterns, to form a single, three-dimensional block of circuitry. The circuit elements are formed by the particular patterns and topology of conducting, semiconducting, and insulating layers, which have been used in building up the structure, The silicon "chip" is also called as **Wafer** (or Substrate). Thus, all the components are automatically part of the same chip. Active components like diodes, transistors, as well as passive ones like resistors, capacitors etc., are all fabricated at appropriate spots in the wafer, using epitaxial diffusion-technology. These types of ICs are in wide use because for mass-production, this (monolithic) process has proved to be more economical.

The other type of ICs is called as "Thick and Thin Film IC." These IC's are not formed within a silicon wafer, but on the surface of insulating substrate, such as glass ceramic material. Only passive components (resistors, capacitors) are formed through thick or thin film techniques, on the insulating surface. The active components (transistors, diodes) are added externally as discrete elements, to complete a functional circuit. These discrete active components, in their turn, are generally produced by using the monolithic process. To produce resistors and conductors using materials of different resistivity, the width and the thickness of the film is varied on the insulating surface. Capacitors are produced by switching an insulating oxide film between two conducting films. This deposition is done through a mask. Small inductors can be made by depositing a spiral formation of the film. Another method is called "Cathode Sputtering", in which atoms from a cathode made of the desired film material, are deposited on the substrate, which is located between the cathode and anode. However, both these (i.e., vacuum evaporation and cathode sputtering), methods come under thin film technology. In thick-film ICs, silk-screen printing technique is used. These screens are made of fine stainless steel wire meshes and the "Inks" are pastes (of pulverized glass and aluminium) which have conductive, resistive or dielectric properties. After printing, the circuits, are high-temperature fired in a furnace, to fuse the films to the insulating substrate (glass or ceramic). Here also, active components are added externally, as discrete components.

The third type of ICs is called Hybrid or Multi-Chip ICs. Here a number of chips are interconnected by a combination of film and monolithic IC techniques. In such ICs, active components are first formed within a silicon wafer (using monolithic technique), which is later covered with an insulating layer (such as $SiO_2$). Then they use the film technology to form the passive components on the $SiO_2$ surface. Connections are then made for the film to the monolithic structure through **Windows** cut to the $SiO_2$ layer.

Of these three types of ICs, monolithic types are most common with the advantage of lowest cost and highest reliability. But in these ICs (*i*) isolation in between the components is poorers, (*ii*) inductors cannot be fabricated alone, (*iii*) their range and a flexibility in design is very limited, because film ICs are made on an insulating surface, inter-components isolation is better. Further, because discrete active components are connected externally, it gives more flexibility in circuit design. The multi-chip ICs are the costliest and least reliable of the three types.

ICs may also be classified on the basis of their function. The two most important types are (*i*) Linear and (*ii*) Digital. Linear ICs are also called **Analog ICs** because their inputs and outputs can take on a continuous range of values, and the outputs are generally proportional to inputs (linearly). Linear ICs are quickly replacing their discrete circuit components in many applications, making the new unit more reliable, because so many external connections (major source of circuit failure) are eliminated. The LICs (Linear Integrated Circuits) are now being used as (1) Operational Amplifiers, (2) Small-signal Amplifiers, (3) Power Amplifiers, (4) R/F, I/F Amplifiers, (5) Microwave Amplifiers, (6) Multipliers, (7) Voltage Comparators, (8) Voltage Regulators etc.

However, about 80% of the IC market has been captured by Digital type of ICs (mostly the Computer Industry). These are mostly monolithic in construction. Such ICs use input and output voltages, limited to only two possible levels-low or high, as digitals, signals are usually binary. Sometimes, these are also called as Switching Circuits. Such ICs include (1) Logic Gates, (2) Flip-Flops, (3) Counter, (4) Clock-chips, (5) Calculator chips, (6) Memory chips, (7) Micro processors etc. In addition to the various ICs described above, we have monolithic ICs based on MOSFET structure. These are also processed in the same way as Bipolar ICs, however, their fabrication is much easier as in a single diffusion step, both the drain and source regions can be formed (compared to 2-4 steps needed in case of BJTs-ICs). Likewise, there is no need for isolation, technique for the Enhancement MOSFET devices. Since in their case, the drain and source regions are isolated from each other by a P-N Junction formed with the N-type substrate. Besides, packing-density of MOS ICs is at least 10 times maximum than that for Bipolar ICs. The MOS resistor occupies less than 1% of the area, as compared to the one by a conventially diffused resistor. This high packing density makes MOS ICs especially suited for LSI and VLSI mass productions. Their main disadvantage is slower operating speed, as compared to Bipolar ICs.

## IC FABRICATION TECHNIQUE (STEPS)

The actual process of IC fabrication consists of a number of steps. Which are described briefly as:

1. WAFER PREPARATION: A **Wafer** is a thin slice of a semiconductor material die 15-50 mm (mostly silicon) either circular or Wafer dimension rectangular in shape. These wafers are prepared on formed by cutting a P-type silicon bar into very thin slices (see Fig. A.1). These wafers, after being lapped and polished to micro-finish, same as the base (or substrate) for hundreds of ICs.

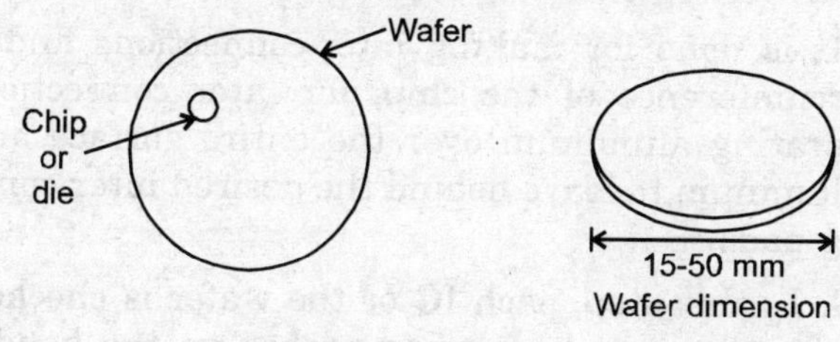


**Fig. A.1** Wafer preparation

2. EPITAXIAL GROWTH: An N-type of silicon layer (about 15 μm thick) is grown on the P-type substrate, by placing the wafer in a furnace at 1200°C and introducing a gas containing phosphorus (donor impurity). It is in the epitaxial layer, that all active and passive components of IC are formed. This layer ultimately becomes the collector for transistors, or on element for a diode or a capacitor.
3. OXIDISATION: A thin layer of silicon dioxide ($SiO_2$) is grown on the N-type layer by exposing the wafer to an oxygen atmosphere at about 1000°C (Fig. A.2).

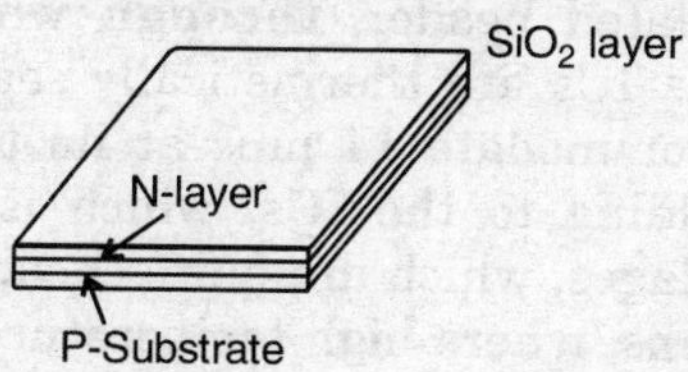


**Fig. A.2** Epitaxial growth and oxidation

4. PHOTO-LITHOGRAPHIC PROCESS: Here selective etching of $SiO_2$ layer is carried out with the help of a photographic mask, photoresist and etching solution. Thus, selective areas of the N-layer became subjected to diffusion.
5. ISOLATION DIFFUSION PROCESS: Which divides the layer into N-type Islands on which active components may be fabricated.
6. BASE AND EMITTER DIFFUSION: After getting the islands formed on the N-type layer, the P-type base of transistor is now diffused into the N-type layer, which itself acts as a collector. The sequence of steps is the same as 4 and 5 *i.e.*, by the use of photoresists and mask, which creates windows in the $SiO_2$ layer. This is carried out in a phosphorus (donor impurity) atmosphere. Next, N-type emitter is diffused into the base, after another photoresist and mask process. No further N-type diffusion is needed for the resistor, which uses the resistivity of the P-type metal itself for this purpose. Thus, one N-P-N transistor and one resistor fabricated simultaneously. (Fig. A.3).

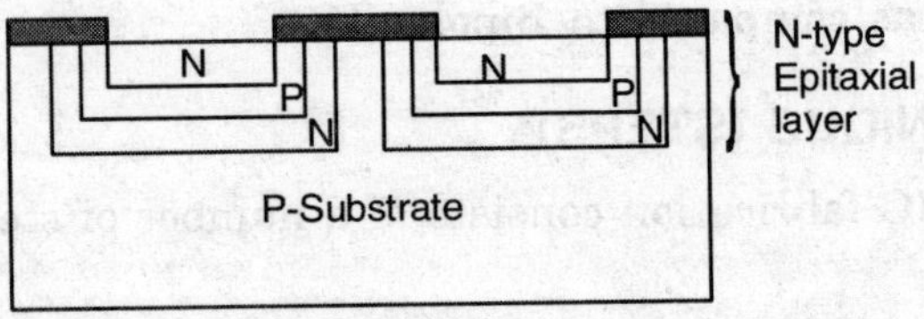


**Fig. A.3** Fabrication of transistor and resistor

7. PRE-OHMIC ETCH: N+ regions are diffused into the structure to ensure good metal-ohmic contact. This is done once again by the $SiO_2$ layer, photoresist and masking process.
8. METALLIZATION: It is done for making inter-connections and provide bonding pads around the circumference of the chip, for later connection of wires. It is carried out by evaporating aluminum over the entire surface and then selecting etching among the aluminum to leave behind the desired inter-connecting condition pattern, and bonding pads.
9. CIRCUIT PROBING: In this step, each IC or the wafer is checked electrically for *its* proper working. This is done by placing probes on the bonding pads. Faulty chips are marked, isolated and discarded, after the wafer has 'scribed' and broken down into individual chips.
10. SCRIBING and SEPARATING: After metallisation and test probing, the wafer is broken down into individual chips, containing the ICs. For this the wafers are first scribed with a diamond tipped tool and then separated into single chips.
11. MOUNTING and PACKING: As the individual chip is very small, it is cemented or soldered to a gold-plated header, **through** which leads **have already** been connected. After this the ICs are thermetically sealed. These can be (a) Top Hat package, which can accommodate 14 pins at its top. If the cover is of metal, it provides magnetic shielding to the ICs, which is not possible with ceramic or plastic top, (b) Flat packages, which are quite cheap and widely used for industrial and consumer applications, where high temperatures are not met. Ceramic is used

in those cases. Dual-in line (DIL) flat packages are more convenient for circuit break use then top hat ones, because being flatter, they allow high circuit densities.

12. ENCAPSULATION: After placing a cap over the circuit, sealing is done in an inert atmosphere. A few of the fabrications and their symbols are given in Fig. A.4. In (*a*) we have the resistor, in (*b*) a capacitor and in (*c*) a diode and in (*d*) a transistor.

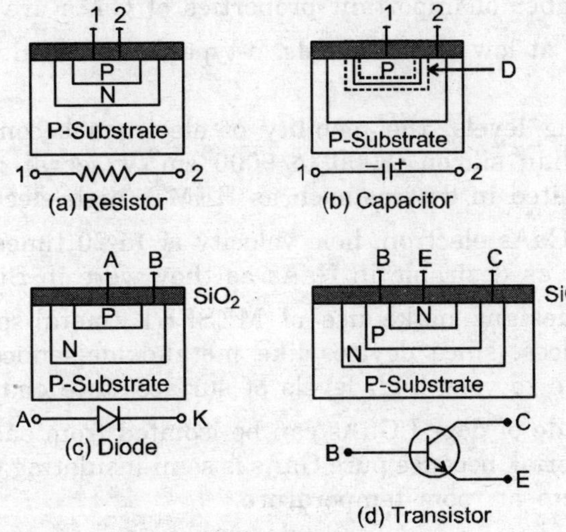


**Fig. A.4**

## ADVANTAGES OF ICs

The ICs are very popular, and being used in various electronic circuits. The astounding progress in Microelectronics, has been because ICs have the following plus points:

(1) Extremely small size

(2) Too little weight

Weight and size are of great importance in military and space applications:

(3) Very much low cost

(4) Extremely high reliability

Because of the absence of soldered connections. IC logic gate has been found to be ten times more reliable than a vacuum-tube logic gate, and two times more reliable than the BJT logic gate. High reliability indirectly means that ICs work for longer periods without any trouble-something very desirable, both for military and consumer application.

(5) Low power consumption

(6) Easy replacement

ICs are hardly repaired, because in case of failure. It is more economical to replace them than to repair.

(7) ICs are ideally suited for small-signal operation, as the various components of a IC are located very close to each other. In or On as silicon wafer, then chance of electrical pick up is preferably nil.

# APPENDIX B

## GaAs BASED CIRCUIT DESIGN

The GaAs based devices are used when faster switching speeds are required, where silicon-based designs becomes uneffective. The GaAs has electronic properties superior to those of silicon. The number of important properties of GaAs are

I. When operated at low electric fields, n-type GaAs circuits can be twice as fast as silicon circuits.

II. For light doping levels, the mobility of electrons becomes approximately 10-20 times higher than silicon (8000 to 9000 $cm^2/V$ sec at room temperature). This feature is exploited in devices such as HEMT (high electron mobility transition).

III. In compare to GaAs electron, hole velocity is 15-20 times lower. Therefore *p*-type devices are not as desirable in GaAs as they were in Si.

IV. Mostly GaAs designs make use of MESFET (metal-semiconductor field-effect transistor) devices, since devices like metal-oxide-semiconductor transistors are not possible due to very high levels of surface-state charge.

V. The devices made of doped GaAs can be isolated from each other by the insertion of undoped material, because pure GaAs is semi-insulating with a resistivity between $10^7$ and $10^9$ $\Omega$cm at room temperature.

VI. GaAs designs are more immune to radiation effect due to a larger band-gap and the semi-insulting substrate.

VII. GaAs is an extremely brittle and fragile material due to this limitation, it is difficult to achieve defect-free devices on GaAs.

There are two different GaAs devices – MESFET device and HEMT device are common with GaAs design.

### The MESFET Device

A cross-section of a GaAs MESFET is shown in figure B.1. It consists of a conductive n-type surface channel with a thickness T, located between two $n^+$ ohmic contacts that act as source and drain. Semi-insulating (undoped) GaAs is used as the substrate material. The device control terminal (the gate) is implemented by depositing a metal (typically Ti/Pd/Au) on a section of the channel, so that a schottky barrier diode is created. The resulting diode relies on single-carrier conduction, what results in fast switching times.

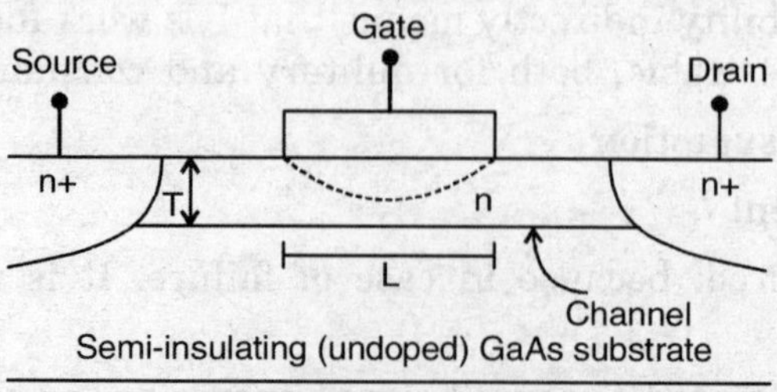


**Fig. B.1** Cross-section of a GaAs MESFET

The principles of operation and the basic relationships governing the device are similar to those of the silicon-junction FETs (JFET) and MOSFETs. The MESFET is a unipolar transistor, which means that conduction is due to one type of carrier, in this particular case the electron. Its operation can be understood from the following analysis.

- Under zero-bias conditions ($V_{GS=0}$), a depletion region is created under the gate due to the built in voltage of the metal-semiconductor junction as shown in figure B.1. This reduces the number of mobile carriers present in the channel. Typically, the thickness of the depletion layer is smaller than T, which means the channel is still conducting. The nominal MESFET transistor is therefore a **depletion device.**
- Applying a positive voltage to the gate reduces the width of the depletion layer. This increases the conductivity of the channel. However, once the gate-channel voltage is sufficiently high, the schottky diode becomes forward-biased and the current starts flowing into the gate. As no further increase in conductivity occurs from that point on, this condition is to be avoided in general. The voltage at which forward conduction of the gate occurs depends upon the gate metal and ranges around 0.5 – 0.7 V.
- When the gate voltage is reduced, the depletion region extends, and the channel conductivity drops owing to the smaller cross-sectional area of the conducting channel. This trend continues until the depletion region extends through the conductive layer (or $W_{depl.} > T$) and pinches off the channel. At that point, the transister is turned off as the channel conductivity drops to 0. The gate source voltage needed to make this happen is called the pinch-off voltage Vp. The pinch-off voltage is analogous to the threshold voltage in a MOS transistor and is a function of the thickness of the channel, the doping level, and the built in voltage of the schottky diode. Typical values of $V_P$ for the depletion devices ranges from –0.7 V to –2.5 V.

The depletion device is the generic MESFET GaAs transistor. An enhancement device can be realized by either reducing the channel thickness or by ion implantation, ensuring that channel pinch-off is achieved under zero-bias conditions. The logic swing for an enhancement-based logic gate is limited to the difference between the pinch-off voltage, which normally ranges between 0 to 0.2 V, and the voltage at which the Schottky-barrier diode begins to conduct (around 0.7 V).

There are several analytical models available for describing the operatin of MESFETs. The two device model for GaAs MESFET are curtice model and Raytheon model, for detail of these devices refer digital integrated circuits. A design perspective by JAN. M. RABAEY Section 5.4.

## The HEMT Device

While the MESFET is used in the majority of the GaAs digital designs, the HEMT (High Electron Mobility Transistor) is the device of choice when extreme performance is required. The cross-section of such a device is shown in Fig. B.2.

Its operation relies on the fact that mobility of the carriers is much higher in an undoped region than in a doped material. The HEMT structure seperates the donor regions ($n^+$ AlGaAs) that produces the electrons, but impede high mobilities, from the conducting channel (undoped GaAs) with its very high mobility. AlGaAs is selected as donor material because it has a wider band-gap (1.8 eV) than GaAs (1.4 eV). This causes free electrons from the ionized donors to diffuse to the undoped material due to the electron's inherent affinity to move to the lower band-gap region.

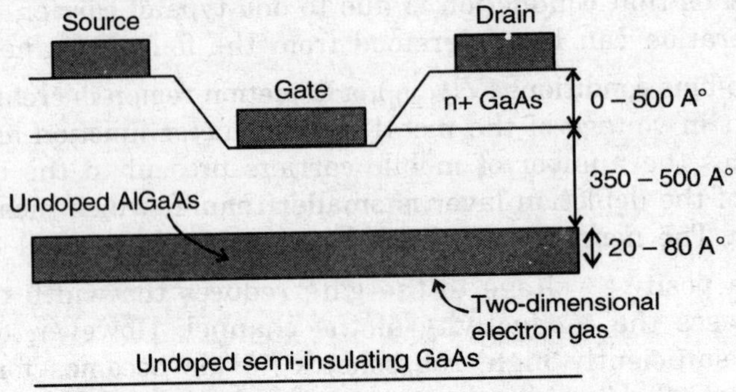


**Fig. B.2 :** Cross-section of AlGaAs/GaAs high electron mobility transistor

Electron mobilities of 8500 $cm^2/Vsec$ can be achieved in HEMT transistors, compared to the channel mobilities of 4500 $cm^2/Vsec$ in GaAs MESFETs (at 300 K).

From an operation point of view, the device of figure B.2 belongs to the class of the MESFETs with the gate Schottky diode formed by the junction of the gate metal and the $n^+$ AlGaAs layer.

## GaAs MESFET Logic Circuits

Gallium arsenide MESFETs have current voltage characteristics similar to those of silicon NMOS devices, with the difference that gate current exists in MESFETs if the gate junction voltage exceeds the Schottky barrier voltage. Some commonly used GaAs MESFET logic circuits are

I. Buffered FET logic
II. Direct-Coupled FET logic
III. Source-Coupled FET logic

# APPENDIX C

## BiCMOS LOGIC CIRCUITS

The dynamic response of MOSFET logic circuits deterorates at large capacitive loads. In particular, the increase in delay time precludes the use of low power, high-density MOSFET circuits for driving high current loads. Consequently, large-sized drivers are needed to interface MOS logic outputs to buses and commonly used Bipolar logic families.

The BiCMOS digital technology combines the speed and driving capability of Bipolar junction transistors with the density and low power dissipation of CMOS devices. It has been used to develop VLSI circuits and ASICs (application-specific integrated circuits).

### Basic BiCMOS Gates

Basic BiCMOS logic circuits use CMOS logic formation and incorporate Bipolar device techniques for charging and discharging of junction capacitances of the output devices.

The Fig. C.1 shows the basic BiCMOS inverter. The complementary pair of MOS transistors (NMOS and PMOS) $M_N$ and $M_P$ forms the inverter, and the pair of NPN transistor $Q_1$ and $Q_2$ forms the active pull-up/pull-down driver stage.

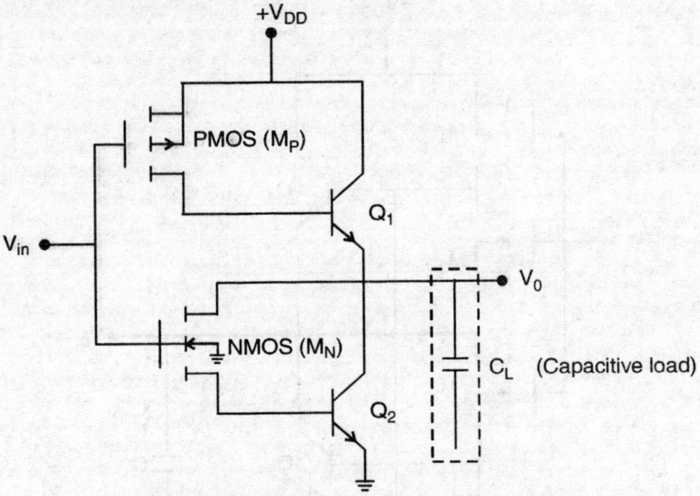


**Fig. C.1** Basic BiCMOS inverter

The analysis of the circuit operation for a capacitive load is as follows:

When the logic input ($V_i$) is LOW, the PMOS ($M_P$) is turned ON (in saturation) and the NMOS ($M_N$) is in cut-off. As no channel is formed in $M_N$, the base current for $Q_2$ is zero and therefore $Q_2$ is off. At the same time, a low-resistance conducting channel is formed in $M_P$ which provides the base current for $Q_1$. Therefore the load capacitor is charge through ($\beta$ + 1) times the base current at the emitter when $Q_1$ operates in the active mode. Hence, the output voltage is less than the supply voltage $V_{DD}$ by the base emitter junction voltage $V_{BE}$ of $Q_1$. Therefore $V_{OH} = V_{DD} - V_{BE}$. Thus for a low input, the output $V_0$ is in high state.

When the logic input is high, $M_N$ is turned ON while $M_P$ is turned off. Therefore, a low-resistance conducting channel is formed in $M_N$ that supplies base current to switch ON the transistor $Q_2$. $Q_2$ causes a large discharge current from the capacitor. Thus, the high-to-low transition occurs rapidly. When the output voltage reaches the base-emitter cut-in voltage of $Q_2$, no further discharge take place *i.e.*, $V_{OL} \approx V_{BE}$. Thus, for a HIGH input, the output $V_{out}$ is in LOW state and acts as an inverter. The logic swing in a basic BiCMOS inverter is therefore $V_{DD} - 2V_{BE}$.

The transfer characteristics and switching speed of the basic inverter can be improved by providing paths for discharging the excess carriers from the bases of $Q_1$ and $Q_2$ with additional NMOS devices, resulting in each BJT OFF while the other is ON.

The conventional BiCMOS inverter commonly used is shown in Fig. C.2 with additional NMOS devices. The operation of $M_1$ and $M_3$ in conventional inverter is the same as the NMOS devices in the basic inverter. $M_2$ and $M_4$ are turned on complement to $M_1$ and $M_3$, to discharge the base-emitter capacitances of $Q_1$ and $Q_2$. For example, when the logic input is LOW, $M_1$ is turned ON and the voltage at the base of $Q_1$ is $V_{DD}$. Therefore, the gate of $M_4$ is at $V_{DD} > V_T$. This turns $M_4$ ON, and the stored charge in the base of $Q_2$ is discharge to ground. Similarly, $M_2$ helps discharge the base of $Q_1$ during low-to-high transition at the input.

BiCMOS NAND and NOR gates are implemented by modifying the inverter shown in figure C.2. Two-input NAND and NOR gates are shown in figure C.4. The interested reader can reference article 7.4 of "Introduction to digital microelectronic circuits" by GOPALAN.

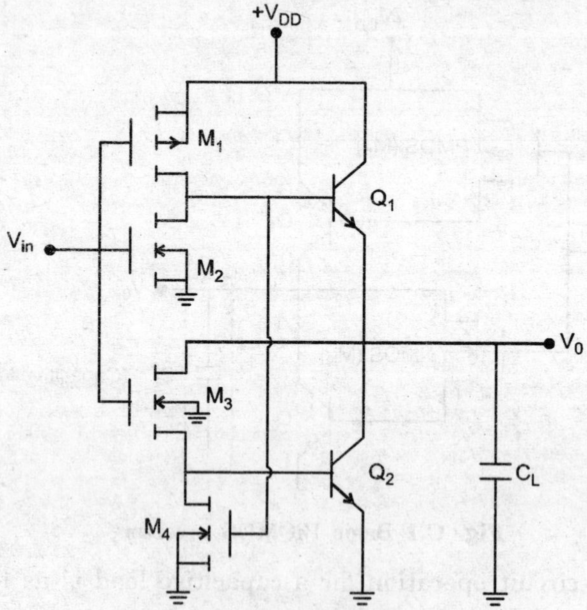


**Fig. C.2** Conventional BiCMOS inverter